South-East Asian Social Science Monographs

The Oil Boom and After

The Oil Boom and After

Indonesian Economic Policy and Performance in the Soeharto Era

Edited by
Anne Booth

SINGAPORE
OXFORD UNIVERSITY PRESS
OXFORD NEW YORK
1992

Oxford University Press

Oxford New York Toronto
Delhi Bombay Calcutta Madras Karachi
Petaling Jaya Singapore Hong Kong Tokyo
Nairobi Dar es Salaam Cape Town
Melbourne Auckland
and associated companies in
Berlin Ibadan

Oxford is a trade mark of Oxford University Press

© Oxford University Press Pte. Ltd. 1992

Published in the United States by
Oxford University Press, Inc., New York

ISBN 0 19 588969 X

British Library Cataloguing in Publication Data

The oil boom and after: Indonesian economic policy
and performance in the Soeharto era.—(South-east
Asian social science monographs)
I. Booth, Anne II. Series
330. 9598036

ISBN 0-19-588969-X

Library of Congress Cataloging-in-Publication Data

The Oil boom and after: Indonesian economic policy and performance in
the Soeharto era/edited by Anne Booth.
p.   cm. —(South-East Asian social science monographs)
Includes bibliographical references and index.
ISBN 0-19-588969-X:
1. Indonesia—Economic policy. 2. Indonesia—Economic
conditions—1945–   3. Petroleum industry and trade—Indonesia.
I. Booth, Anne, 1946–   . II. Series.
HC447.O45 1992
338.9598'009047—dc20
91–23712
CIP

Printed in Malaysia by Peter Chong Printers Sdn. Bhd.
Published by Oxford University Press Pte. Ltd.,
Unit 221, Ubi Avenue 4, Singapore 1440

In Memoriam
Kustiah Kristanto

Preface

ALMOST a decade ago, Peter McCawley and I edited a collection of papers on aspects of Indonesian economic development since the accession to power of President Soeharto. At that time the flow of published material on the Indonesian economy was still relatively meagre, although both the *Bulletin of Indonesian Economic Studies* and *Ekonomi dan Keuangan Indonesia* were appearing regularly and of course much applied economic research was being conducted by the World Bank and other international organizations, some of which was eventually published. The book entitled *The Indonesian Economy during the Soeharto Era* rapidly sold out, and over the years many people suggested that a new edition should be prepared. In the event what has emerged is a completely new book with only three of the original contributors still participating. Although the titles of the various chapters have not greatly changed, all have been completely rewritten to focus particularly on developments over the decade of the 1980s.

This decade has seen great changes not only in the pace and direction of Indonesian economic development but also in the state of the literature. Work on many aspects of economic and social development in Indonesia has been undertaken by professional economists and other social scientists from many countries, and increasingly this work finds its way into the mainstream academic journals and into books which compare and contrast economic policy-making across a range of developing countries. This work has been greatly facilitated by the steady flow of statistical material from the Biro Pusat Statistik (BPS); indeed the very high professional standards of the BPS and the willingness of its officers to make data available to both local and foreign scholars have been major reasons for the increased interest shown in Indonesia by the international scholarly community in recent years. No longer the 'chronic dropout', to use the phrase of Professor Benjamin Higgins, Indonesia is now recognized as a major developing country whose experience over the past four decades offers important lessons for policy-makers in many parts of the world.

Thus the essays in the present volume are intended to have two functions. On the one hand they survey and synthesize the growing scholarly literature on many aspects of Indonesian economic development. On the other hand they analyse events over the past decade, and in some cases over a rather longer time span, in order to clarify the Indonesian experience for scholars who are interested in Indonesia as a case-study, but who do not have the time or the opportunity to study the primary statistical sources. Thus the volume should be helpful to scholars and students not just of the Indonesian economy, but also of economic development in South-East Asia, and indeed in the broader international context.

Many of the authors in this volume are currently, or have been, associated with the Australian National University and especially with its Research School of Pacific Studies, without whose generous assistance this book would not have been possible. Over the years, the ANU has devoted considerable resources to the study of Australia's enormous northern neighbour. While some in Indonesia may be inclined to view that allocation of academic resources with suspicion, and even with hostility, there are many more within the Indonesian intellectual community who have always welcomed it and who feel that in the longer run Indonesia can only gain from the informed views of outsiders, many of whom have devoted a substantial part of their careers to the study of their endlessly fascinating country. In many respects Indonesia is the least xenophobic and most hospitable of countries for a foreign scholar to work in, which is doubtlessly why so many of those who have carried out research there continue to return and to broaden their knowledge and understanding. Certainly it is the hope of the editor and her colleagues that the various essays in this volume will be of some use to Indonesian academics, students, and policy-makers in their continuing pursuit of the goal of national economic development, and the attainment of a just and equitable society.

Canberra   ANNE BOOTH
December 1990

Contents

Preface   *vii*
Tables   *xiii*
Figures   *xviii*
Abbreviations and Glossary   *xx*
Notes on Contributors   *xxv*

1 Introduction   *1*
Anne Booth

Growth and Structural Transformation in the New Order   *1*
Aspects of Economic Liberalization   *24*
Problems for the Future   *28*

PART I MACROECONOMIC POLICY-
          MAKING   *39*

2 Fiscal Policy   *41*
Mukul G. Asher and Anne Booth

Introduction   *41*
Tax Reform Policies   *42*
The Tax Reform Programme: A Brief Description   *44*
Performance of the Reformed Tax System   *47*
Changing Expenditure Patterns   *57*
The Impact of the Budget   *60*
The Foreign Debt   *64*
Regional Finance   *68*

3 Financial Development in Indonesia   *77*
David C. Cole and Betty F. Slade

Introduction   *77*
Financial Growth and Structural Change in Indonesia   *79*
The Sequence of Financial Reforms   *84*
Capital Markets   *94*
Summing Up   *96*
Appendix: Financial Deregulation Packages: October
    1980–March 1989   *98*

4 Implementing Monetary Policy   *102*
Binhadi and Paul Meek

Introduction   *102*
Monetary Policies and the Financial Environment Prior to
    the Reforms   *102*
The Reforms and the Organization of Monetary Policy   *105*
Developing a New Monetary Control System after the
    1983 Financial Reform   *107*
The October 1988 Policy Package   *119*
The Present Monetary Control System   *120*
Conclusions   *128*

**5 Exchange Rate Policy, Petroleum Prices, and the
    Balance of Payments**   *132*
Peter G. Warr

Introduction   *132*
Indonesia's External Environment and Macroeconomic
    Performance   *133*
Adjustment to External Shocks: Theory and Practice   *137*
Exchange Rate Policy and Relative Prices   *148*
Conclusions   *156*

PART II SECTORAL GROWTH   *159*

6 Agriculture in Transition   *161*
Steven R. Tabor

Introduction   *161*
The Role of Agriculture in the Economy   *162*
The Role of the External Environment on Agriculture   *169*
The Food Subsector   *172*
High-cost Subsidies: A Negative Externality Resulting from
    the Rice Success   *177*
Agricultural Diversification   *186*
Policy Challenges for the 1990s   *196*

7 Manufacturing Industry   *204*
Hal Hill

Introduction   *204*
Industrial Structure and Trends   *207*
Issues in Indonesia's Industrialization   *223*
Spatial Patterns of Industrialization   *238*
Conclusion   *249*

8 **Transport and Communications: A Quiet Revolution**   258
Howard Dick and Dean Forbes

Introduction   258
The New Order Inheritance   260
Transport Improvements under the New Order   264
Transport Policies and Future Plans   274
Conclusion   279

9 **The Service Sector**   283
Jennifer Alexander and Anne Booth

Introduction   283
Private and Public Service Sector Development in
    Indonesia   290
Employment and Productivity in the Trade Sector   296
International Demand for Service Sector Output   311
Future Service Sector Developments   313

PART III HUMAN RESOURCE
          DEVELOPMENT   321

10 **Income Distribution and Poverty**   323
Anne Booth

Introduction   323
The Impact of Commodity Booms and Post-boom
    Reconstruction on Income Distribution   324
Trends in Indicators of Income Distribution   328
Have Rural Disparities in Income and Wealth Narrowed?   340
Trends in Indicators of Poverty: 1969–1987   342
Trends in Affluence   350
Trends in Inequality and Poverty: A Summing Up   353
Appendix: Poverty and Affluence Lines Used in
    Table 10.16   359

11 **Labour Force and Employment during the 1980s**   363
Gavin W. Jones and Chris Manning

Introduction   363
The Demographic Underpinnings of Labour Force
    Growth   364
An Overview of Employment and Wage Trends by Sector   372
Rural and Agricultural Employment   383
Manufacturing Employment   388
Trade and Services Employment   393

Unemployment and Underemployment   396
Educational Developments and Occupational Change   398
The 1990s and Beyond   400
Appendix: Data Sources and Problems of Estimating
    Recent Labour Force and Employment Growth in
    Indonesia   404

12 **Population and Health Policies**   411
Terence H. Hull and Valerie J. Hull

Introduction   411
The Place of Population in National Planning and Policies 412
Shaping Population Growth to the National Purpose:
    Fertility Control   413
Towards a Healthy Population: Policy Approaches and
    Health Indicators   423
Population Projections to the Year 2125   433

Author Index   437
Subject Index   441

Tables

1.1	Sectoral Growth Rates, 1960–1988	*2*
1.2	Annual Average Real Foreign Exchange Inflows to Indonesia, 1968–1989	*7*
1.3	Trends in GDY, 1960–1988	*8*
1.4	Composition of Growth of Imports	*12*
1.5	Sectoral Breakdown of Increment in Real GDP, 1967–1988	*14*
1.6	The Export Surplus in Three Resource-abundant Provinces as a Percentage of Regional GDP	*29*
2.1	Government Revenues and Expenditures as a Percentage of GDP, 1983–1989	*48*
2.2	Indicators of Revenue Reliance, 1969–1990	*49*
2.3	Composition of Income Tax Receipts and Numbers of Taxpayers in *Repelita IV*	*51*
2.4	Composition of Non-oil Tax Revenues, FY 1978– FY 1989	*52*
2.5	Trends in Major Components of Central Government Expenditures, 1969–1990	*58*
2.6	Components of Central Government Expenditures as a Percentage of GDP, 1969–1989	*59*
2.7	Changes in the Sectoral Allocation of the Development Budget in *Repelita IV*	*60*
2.8	Estimates of the Budget Deficit as a Percentage of GDP, 1980–1989	*62*
2.9	Indicators of External Debt: Indonesia and Selected Comparisons	*65*
2.10	Growth in Indonesia's External Debt, 1980–1988	*66*
2.11	Growth in Development Grants (Inpres) to Regions, 1983/4–1990/1	*68*
2.12	Projects Implemented by Inpres *Kabupaten*	*69*
3.1	Monetary Ratios, 1968–1988	*80*
3.2	Inflation and Interest Rates	*85*
3.3	Total Consolidated Bank Assets by Type of Bank	*89*
3.4	Interest Rates on the Jakarta Interbank Call Money Market	*92*

3.5   Funds Raised Annually through New Issues of Bonds
      and Equity Shares in the Capital Market   95
3.6   Indicators of Stock Market Growth   96
4.1   Changes in Factors Affecting Reserves and Money and
      Credit Growth   121
4.2   Monetary Programme   123
5.1   Comparative Macroeconomic Indicators of Large
      Petroleum-exporting Countries: Indonesia, Egypt,
      Mexico, and Nigeria   136
5.2   Indonesia: Macroeconomic Summary, 1968–1988   138
5.3   Indonesia: Absorption of Increased Petroleum Rev-
      enues   146
6.1   Agricultural GDP by Subsectoral Origin, 1978–1988   163
6.2   Landholdings by Agricultural Households According to
      the Agricultural Census, 1963–1983   166
6.3   Farm Households in 1983 by Operated Holding Size   167
6.4   Average Landholding Size by Island, 1973 and 1983   168
6.5   Production and Trade in Rice and Wheat   173
6.6   Agricultural Infrastructure Growth in Indonesia,
      1969–1985   174
6.7   Implicit Tariffs for Rice and Sugar   175
6.8   Production and Trade of Soy Beans and Soy Bean
      Meal   176
6.9   Government Financing of Irrigation O and M   179
6.10 Fertilizer Production: Imports and Exports, 1978–1987   181
6.11 Fertilizer and Pesticide Subsidies Compared to the
      Agricultural Sector Development Budget   182
6.12 Bulog Rice Operations   184
6.13 Physical Area Completed by Type of Irrigation
      Development, Repelita I to Repelita IV   186
6.14 Production and Trade of Corn and Cassava   188
6.15 Trends in World Market Prices for Estate Crop
      Exports   190
6.16 Public Sector Tree-crop Investments, 1979–1987   191
6.17 Tree-crop Smallholder Households, 1986   193
7.1   The Structure of Industrial Output and Employment,
      1975 and 1988   213
7.2   Output of Selected Industrial Products, 1969–1989   215
7.3   Major Manufactured Exports of Indonesia, 1980–1989   220
7.4   RCA Indices for Indonesian Manufactured Exports,
      1970–1988   222
7.5   Indonesian Industrialization in Comparative Perspective 224
7.6   Estimates of Effective Protection, 1989   228
7.7   Ownership by Major Industry Group, 1985   232
7.8   Major Foreign Investors in Manufacturing, 1967–1989   236
7.9   Spatial Patterns of Industrialization, 1985   240
7.10 Size Distribution of Industry, 1986   245

7.11 Estimates of Manufacturing Employment by Size Group, 1975 and 1986   246
8.1   Inter-*kabupaten* Passenger and Cargo Traffic, 1982   259
8.2   Condition of Roads, 1967   261
8.3   Railway Passengers and Cargo: Java and Sumatra   261
8.4   Domestic Airline Passengers   263
8.5   Transport Component of GDP and Labour Force   264
8.6   Number of Registered Motor Vehicles, 1968 and 1986   266
8.7   Regional Distribution of Registered Motor Vehicles, 1968 and 1986   266
8.8   Growth in Length of Roads by Level of Government   267
8.9   Length of Roads by Surface, 1970 and 1985   267
8.10 Length of Roads by Surface Condition and Level of Government, 1985   268
8.11 Condition of *Kabupaten* Roads by Island, 1985   268
9.1   Long-term Trends in Relative Product per Worker   286
9.2   Distribution of the Labour Force by Sector, 1971 and 1985   291
9.3   Percentage Breakdown of the Service Sector Labour Force by Job Status, 1985   292
9.4   Changes in the Composition of the Indonesian Civil Service by Class and Educational Attainment   294
9.5   Growth in Numbers of Government Employees   295
9.6   Relative Labour Productivities: Indonesia, the Philippines, Taiwan, and Thailand, 1985   296
9.7   Percentage Breakdown of Establishments and Labour Force in Unincorporated Enterprises in the Trade Sector, 1986   297
9.8   Percentage Breakdown of Unincorporated Trading Enterprises without Fixed Premises by Location and Nature of Business   298
9.9   Percentage Breakdown of Trading Enterprises by Days Worked per Month   298
9.10 Average Monthly Income of Households Engaged in Trading Activities, 1986   299
9.11 Household Incomes of Rural Trading Households without Fixed Premises and Agricultural Households, 1986   300
9.12 Breakdown of Households Operating Trading Enterprises without Fixed Premises by Income Sources   301
9.13 Percentage of Trading Enterprises without Fixed Premises, without Access to Credit, and Using Own Capital in Urban and Rural Areas   308
10.1 Urban Per Capita Expenditures in Indonesia as a Percentage of Rural Expenditures, 1969–1987   329
10.2 Average Annual Growth in Real Per Capita Monthly Expenditures   330

10.3   Percentage Average Annual Growth in Real Per Capita
       Consumption Expenditures: Java and Indonesia,
       1980–1987   *331*
10.4   Population Weighted Coefficients of Variation of Per
       Capita RGDP   *332*
10.5   Population Weighted Coefficients of Variation of Per
       Capita Consumption Expenditures   *333*
10.6   Average Annual Growth in Nominal Per Capita
       Expenditures in Jakarta Prices, 1980–1987   *334*
10.7   Trends in the Gini Coefficient in Indonesia   *335*
10.8   Trends in Gini Coefficient of Per Capita Expenditure in
       Urban Areas   *336*
10.9   Gini Coefficients of Household Income by City   *337*
10.10 Ratio of Family Income Where Family Head Is in
       Government Service to Average Household Income   *338*
10.11 Growth in Monthly Household Income by Status of
       Household Head, 1976–1982   *339*
10.12 Average Monthly Earnings of Employees by
       Educational Attainment, 1976–1986   *339*
10.13 Relationship between Average Household Income from
       Farming and the Percentage Increment Derived from
       Non-farm Activities by Province, 1983–1984   *341*
10.14 Decline in Percentage of Population under the Poverty
       Line According to Three Measures   *343*
10.15 Percentage of the Poor Population Living in Urban
       Areas According to Different Poverty Measures   *343*
10.16 Incidence of Poverty and Affluence in Java and the
       Outer Islands   *346*
10.17 Numbers in Poverty and Distribution of Poor and
       Total Populations, 1969/70–1987   *347*
10.18 Proportion of Urban and Rural Population below the
       Poverty Line by Province, 1980 and 1987   *348*
10.19 Regression of Provincial Poverty Incidence on Per
       Capita Expenditures   *349*
10.20 Distribution of the Affluent Population, 1969/70–1987   *351*
10.21 Probabilities of Inter-class Movement   *351*
10.22 Growth in Average Expenditures in Real Terms by
       Class of Population   *352*
11.1   Changing Regional Distribution of the Workforce   *364*
11.2   Indonesia: Population Aged 15 Years and Over, by
       Educational Attainment, 1961–1985   *365*
11.3   Shift in Employment Share by Major Industry Sectors
       in Indonesia, the Philippines, India, Republic of Korea,
       Peninsular Malaysia, and Taiwan, over Several Periods   *374*
11.4   Growth of Male Employment in Indonesia, 1971–1987   *376*
11.5   Growth of Male Employment in Java and the Outer
       Islands, 1971–1985   *377*

11.6   Recorded and Estimated Female Employment in
       Indonesia and Java, 1971–1985   *378*
11.7   Real Wage Trends in Various Sectors: Java and
       Indonesia, 1966–1988   *380*
11.8   Percentage Distribution of Rural Employment by
       Industry: Indonesia and Java, 1971–1985   *384*
11.9   Percentage of Workforce Employed Less than 35 Hours
       a Week in Main Job by Sector of Activity: West and
       Central Java, 1980–1985   *387*
11.10 Indonesia: Employment in Manufacturing Industry,
       1971, 1980, 1985, and 1987   *390*
11.11 Distribution of Employment in Large and Medium
       Manufacturing by Location: Java, 1980   *392*
11.12 Some Characteristics of Workers in Trade and Services,
       1971, 1980, 1985, and 1987   *394*
11.13 Unemployment Rates by Age and Education: Urban
       Indonesia, 1976, 1982, and 1986   *397*
11.A1 Female Labour Force, Unpaid Family Workers, and
       Agricultural Employment: Indonesia, 1971–1987   *405*
11.A2 Reported Employment Growth Rates by Work Status
       Groups: Indonesia, 1971–1985   *406*
11.A3 Recorded Growth Rates in Male Employment by
       Sector: Java, 1971–1985 and 1977–1987   *407*
12.1   Trends in the Marital Status Indexes of Women in
       Indonesia, 1971–1987   *414*
12.2   Trends in the Reported Demand for Children,
       1973–1987   *422*
12.3   Health Expenditure in ASEAN Countries, *c.*1985   *425*
12.4   Total Public Health Facilities, 1979/80–1989/90   *427*
12.5   Infant Mortality Rates by Province, 1971, 1980, and
       1985   *429*
12.6   Percentage of Adequately Nourished Children under
       5 Years by Age Group and Sex, Rural and Urban
       Areas of Indonesia, 1987   *430*
12.7   Selected Objectives in Health by the End of Repelita V
       and the Year 2000   *431*
12.8   Population Projections   *434*

Figures

1.1	Annual Percentage Change in GDP and GDY	3
1.2	Trends in the Commodity and Income Terms of Trade, 1960–1988	5
1.3	Trends in the ICOR, 1968–1988	11
3.1	Financial Assets as a Percentage of GDP, 1969–1988	82
3.2	Assets of Financial Institutions as a Percentage of GDP, 1969–1988	83
3.3	Monthly Trends in the Jakarta Interbank Rate, 1983–1989	91
4.1	Trends in Interest Rates: Jakarta and the US, 1983–1987	114
4.2	Weekly Fluctuations in Jakarta Interest Rates, July 1987–July 1988	117
4.3	Weekly Trends in SBIs Outstanding, July 1987–July 1988	118
4.4	Average SBI Auction Rates, January–September 1989	127
5.1	Indonesia: Terms of Trade and International Oil Prices, 1967–1988	134
5.2	Indonesia: Petroleum's Importance in Exports and Government Revenue, 1968–1986	135
5.3	A Model of Savings, Investment, and the Balance of Payments	140
5.4	Indonesia's Savings and Investment, 1967–1988	143
5.5	Tradables, Non-tradables, and the Balance of Payments	149
5.6	Indonesia: Three Indices of Tradable/Non-tradable Price Ratios, 1977–1989	152
5.7	Indonesia: The Tradable/Non-tradable Price Ratio and 'Competitiveness', 1971–1989	153
7.1	Indonesian Manufacturing Growth and GDP Shares, 1971–1989	208
7.2	Changing Composition of Industrial Output, Including and Excluding Oil, 1975–1988	210
9.1	Trends in the Agricultural Share of the Labour Force and the Service Share of the Non-agricultural Labour Force in Selected Countries, 1800–1985	284

11.1 Working Population by Age and Educational Attainment, 1987   *367*

11.2 Female Activity Rates by Age and Rural–Urban Residence, 1977–1987   *368*

11.3 Female Activity Rates by Age and Educational Attainment, 1977 and 1987   *370*

11.4 Female Activity Rates by Age for Each Educational Attainment Level, 1977 and 1987   *371*

11.5 Agricultural Employment as a Share of Total Employment in Java, 1977–1987   *385*

11.6 Indicators of Educational Progress, 1971–1985   *399*

12.1 Trends in the Total Fertility Rate at the National Level, 1968–1985   *419*

12.2 Provincial Variations in the Total Fertility Rate, 1967–70 and 1985   *420*

12.3 Trends in Projected and Actual Population, 1960–2000   *421*

12.4 Trends in Real Expenditures by the Central Government on Health, 1979/80–1987/8   *426*

Abbreviations and Glossary

arisan	circulating credit association
ASEAN	Association of South-East Asian Nations
bajaj	three-wheeled passenger vehicle of Indian origin
bakul	small trader, usually female
bapak angkat	foster parent; term used to denote firm which sub-contracts work to smaller firms
Bapepam	(Badan Pengembangan Pasar Modal) Capital Market Development Board
Bapindo	(Bank Pembangunan Indonesia) Indonesian Development Bank
Bappenas	(Badan Perencanaan Pembangunan Nasional) National Development Planning Board
becak	pedicab
bemo	small truck converted to passenger vehicle
Bimas	(Bimbingan Massal) Mass Guidance Programme for rice intensification
BKKBN	(Badan Koordinasi Keluarga Berencana Nasional) National Family Planning Co-ordinating Board
BKPM	(Badan Koordinasi Penanaman Modal) Capital Investment Co-ordinating Board
BPS	(Biro Pusat Statistik) Central Bureau of Statistics
BTN	(Bank Tabungan Negara) State Savings Bank
Buletin Ringkas	(Brief Bulletin) monthly statistical digest published by the Central Bureau of Statistics
Bulog	(Badan Urusan Logistik) State Logistics Board with special responsibility for food procurement
bupati	administrative head of a *kabupaten*
CBS	Central Bureau of Statistics (Biro Pusat Statistik)
CPO	crude palm oil
CV	(*commanditaire vennootschap*) partnership
Danareksa	literally 'to guard the funds'; a state-owned financial enterprise established in 1977
DMB	deposit money banks
DPR	(Dewan Perwakilan Rakyat) House of People's Representatives

DSP	(*Daftar Skala Prioritas*) Investment Priority List
EPI	Expanded Programme of Immunization
ESCAP	United Nations Economic and Social Commission for Asia and the Pacific
Ficorinvest	a non-bank financial intermediary 95 per cent owned by Bank Indonesia
FY	Fiscal year (In Indonesia the fiscal year runs from 1 April to 31 March.)
gabah	paddy rice which has been dried and threshed but not milled
GBHN	(*Garis-garis Besar Haluan Negara*) Broad Guidelines for State Policy
golongan ekonomi lemah	weaker economic groups
HGU	(*hak guna usaha*) land use rights
HPH	(*hak pengusahaan hutan*) forest exploitation rights
HYV	high-yielding variety
ILO	International Labour Organization
IMF	International Monetary Fund
Indikator Ekonomi	(Economic Indicators) monthly statistical bulletin published by the Central Bureau of Statistics
Inpres	(Instruksi Presiden) Presidential Instruction
Inpres Programme	central government subsidies to regional governments (province, *kabupaten*, and villages) for various kinds of infrastructure development and for the construction of primary schools and health clinics
Ipeda	(Iuran Pembangunan Daerah) regional development contribution; a land tax
JSE	Jakarta Stock Exchange
juragan	larger trader who usually operates from a market (*pasar*) and who is supplied by *bakul* (small traders)
kabupaten	level of administration below province
kantor wilayah	(*kanwil*) regional office
kapal perintis	pioneer ships calling at remote ports on a regular basis
Keppres	(Keputusan Presiden) Presidential Decision
KFM	(*Kebutuhan Fisik Minimum*) index of the value of minimum physical needs computed by the Department of Labour and the Biro Pusat Statistik for each province
KIK	(*kredit investasi kecil*) small investment credits
KLM	(Koninklijke Luchtvaart Mij) Royal Aviation Company
KMKP	(*kredit modal kerja permanen*) permanent working capital credit

Kosipa   (*koperasi simpang pinjam*) savings co-operatives
KPM   (Koninklijke Paketvaart Mij) Royal Packetboat
                     Company
kretek   Indonesian clove cigarettes
KUD   (*koperasi unit desa*) village co-operatives
Lampiran Pidato   Appendix to the State Speech delivered by the
   Kenegaraan   President annually just before Independence
                     Day
Laporan   (Weekly Report) weekly statistical bulletin pub-
   Mingguan   lished by Bank Indonesia
LDC   less developed country
Lebaran   the Idul Fitri holiday which concludes the Muslim
                     fasting month
LIBOR   London interbank offer rate
LIK   (*lingkungan industri kecil*) small industry centres
LNG   liquefied natural gas
malari   riots which followed the visit to Indonesia of the
                     Japanese prime minister in January 1974
MPR   (Majelis Perwakilan Rakyat) Council of People's
                     Representatives
MT   metric ton
NBFI   non-bank financial institution
NES/PIR   Nucleus Estate Scheme/Perkebunan Inti Rakyat
NIE   newly industrializing economy
Nota Keuangan
   dan Rancangan
   Anggaran
   Pendapatan
   dan Belanja   draft budgetary document presented to the DPR by
   Nasional   the President each January
NOTR   non-oil tax revenues
NTB   non-tariff barrier
NUDS   National Urban Development Strategy
OECD   Organization for Economic Co-operation and
                     Development
ojek   motor cycle or bicycle used for public transport
OPEC   Organization of Petroleum Exporting Countries
Pakdes I   package of policy measures released in December
                     1987
Pakdes II   package of policy measures released in December
                     1988
Pakem   package of policy measures released in May 1986
Pakmar   package of policy measures released in March 1989
Paknov   package of policy measures released in November
                     1988 deregulating inter-island shipping
Pakto   package of policy measures released in October
                     1988 which dealt mainly with financial deregula-
                     tion

palawija	non-rice food crops
PBB	(Pajak Bumi dan Bangunan) land and building tax which has replaced the old land tax (Ipeda)
pegawai negeri sipil	civilian state servant
Pelni	(Pelayaran Nasional Indonesia) Indonesian National Shipping Company
PKBI	(Perkumpulan Keluarga Berencana Indonesia) Indonesian Family Planning Association
PKK	(Pembinaan Kesejahteraan Keluarga) Family Welfare Education Movement
posyandu	(*pos pelayanan terpadu*) integrated health service post
PPD	(Perusahaan Pengangkutan Djakarta) Jakarta Transport Corporation
PPH	(Pajak Penghasilan) income tax
PPKBD	(*pos pelayanan keluarga berencana desa*) village family planning service post
PPN	(Pajak Pertambahan Nilai) value added tax
pribumi	indigenous Indonesian
puskesmas	(*pusat kesehatan masyarakat*) community health centre
PMA	(*penanaman modal asing*) foreign capital investment
PMU	Project Management Unit
PQLI	Physical Quality of Life Index (computed by the Biro Pusat Statistik)
PT	(*perseroan terbatas*) limited liability company
PTP	(*perseroan terbatas perkebunan*) limited liability estate company
PUAP	(Perusahaan Umum Angkasa Pura) State Air Enterprise
PUKA	(Perusahaan Umum Kereta Api) State Rail Enterprise
Repelita	(*Rencana Pembangunan Lima Tahun*) Five-Year Development Plan)
Repelita I	First Five-Year Development Plan, 1969/70–1973/4
Repelita II	Second Five-Year Development Plan, 1974/5–1978/9
Repelita III	Third Five-Year Development Plan, 1979/80–1983/4
Repelita IV	Fourth Five-Year Development Plan, 1984/5–1988/9
Repelita V	Fifth Five-Year Development Plan, 1989/90–1993/4
Sakernas	(*Survei Angkatan Kerja Nasional*) National Labour Force Survey carried out by the Biro Pusat Statistik in 1976, 1977, and 1978 and in 1986, 1987, and 1988

SBI	(Sertifikat Bank Indonesia) Bank Indonesia certificates which can be traded on the money market
SBPU	(Surat Berharga Pasar Uang) a promissary note or draft traded on the money market which was introduced in 1985
Sensus Ekonomi 1986	Economic Census carried out in 1986 by the Biro Pusat Statistik which gathered information on all non-agricultural productive enterprises
SGS	(Société Générale de Surveillance) a Swiss survey company which since 1985 has taken over many of the functions of the Directorate-General of Customs and Excise
SITC	Standard International Trade Classification
SKN	(Sistem Kesehatan Nasional) National Health System
Supas	(*Survei Penduduk antar Sensus*) Intercensal Population Survey carried out by the Biro Pusat Statistik in 1976 and 1985
Susenas	(*Survei Sosial Ekonomi Nasional*) National Socio-economic Survey carried out by the Biro Pusat Statistik at regular intervals since 1963, and covering household expenditure, labour force participation, educational attainment, etc.
SMAM	singulate mean age at marriage
tebasan	a system of using contractors to harvest a field the crop from which has already been purchased at a price agreed prior to the harvest
TRI	(Tebu Rakyat Intensifikasi) Smallholder Sugar Intensification Project
TSP	triple superphosphate
UNDP	United Nations Development Programme
UNICEF	United Nations (International) Children's (Emergency) Fund
USAID	United States Agency for International Development
VAT	value added tax
WHO	World Health Organization

Notes on Contributors

JENNIFER ALEXANDER is a Research Fellow in the Department of Anthropology, Research School of Pacific Studies, Australian National University.

MUKUL G. ASHER is Associate Professor, Department of Economics and Statistics, National University of Singapore.

BINHADI is Managing Director, Bank Indonesia, Jakarta.

ANNE BOOTH is Professor (Economics of Asia), School of Oriental and African Studies, University of London.

DAVID C. COLE is associated with the Harvard Institute for International Development, Harvard University. He is currently working with the Program for Financial Policy Studies and Training, Department of Finance, Jakarta.

HOWARD DICK is Senior Lecturer, Department of Economics, University of Newcastle.

DEAN FORBES is Senior Research Fellow, Department of Human Geography, Research School of Pacific Studies, Australian National University.

HAL HILL is Senior Fellow, Department of Economics, Research School of Pacific Studies, Australian National University.

TERENCE H. HULL is Senior Research Fellow, Department of Political and Social Change, Research School of Pacific Studies, Australian National University.

VALERIE J. HULL is Departmental Visitor, Department of Demography, Research School of Social Sciences, Australian National University.

GAVIN W. JONES is Professor of Demography, Research School of Social Sciences, Australian National University.

CHRIS MANNING is Senior Research Fellow, Department of Economics, Research School of Pacific Studies, Australian National University.

PAUL MEEK is retired Vice-President and Monetary Adviser, Federal Reserve Bank of New York.

BETTY F. SLADE is associated with the Harvard Institute for International Development, Harvard University. She is currently working with the Program for Financial Policy Studies and Training, Department of Finance, Jakarta.

STEVEN R. TABOR is an economist with the World Bank, Washington, DC. He previously worked with the Department of Agriculture in Indonesia.

PETER G. WARR is John Crawford Professor of Agricultural Economics, Research School of Pacific Studies, Australian National University.

1
Introduction

Anne Booth

Growth and Structural Transformation in the New Order

Phases of Growth since 1968

In retrospect, it is clear that the years from 1968 to 1981 were remark-able ones in the economic history of modern Indonesia. The average annual rate of growth accelerated to over 7 per cent per annum; this growth rate was quite stable and only dropped below 6 per cent in one year out of the fourteen (Figure 1.1). This was an impressive record compared to what had been achieved in the first two decades of inde-pendence, when growth had been on average much slower, and far more erratic. It was also an impressive record compared with many other developing countries. In the late 1960s, per capita GDP in Indonesia was still among the lowest in the world, but by 1981, the country had moved into the ranks of what the World Bank terms 'lower middle-income countries'. World Bank sources indicated that the Indonesian growth rate in the 1970s was not only better than that of most other Asian countries at similar levels of development, but also better than that of other 'populated petroleum economies' such as Nigeria and Venezuela (World Bank, 1983: 150).

Indonesian economic performance in the decade of the 1980s by con-trast was considerably less robust. Between 1981 and 1988, the average annual rate of growth of GDP slowed to 4.3 per cent per annum (Table 1.1). This was a slower rate of growth than that of the other ASEAN countries except for the Philippines, although faster than in many other parts of the developing world, and certainly faster than most other OPEC economies. Nigeria, for example, experienced negative growth between 1980 and 1988, and the middle-income economies on average grew at only 2.9 per cent per annum over these years (World Bank, 1990: 180). The slower growth of GDP, combined with two very substantial dollar devaluations meant that by 1988 per capita income in dollar terms had fallen to $480, compared with $530 dollars in 1980. In 1989 the World Bank reclassified Indonesia as a 'low-income' country

TABLE 1.1
Sectoral Growth Rates, 1960–1988 (percentage)

Sector	Share of GDP[a]			Annual Growth Rates[b]			
	1960	1973	1988	1960–7	1967–73	1973–81	1981–8
Agriculture	53.9	40.1	24.1	1.6	4.1	3.5	3.0
Mining	3.7	12.3	11.6	1.8	18.1	3.6	− 1.3
Manufacturing	8.4	9.6	18.5	1.0	9.6	14.2	11.1
Utilities	0.3	0.5	0.6	9.4	10.9	14.1	13.9
Construction	2.0	3.9	5.0	− 2.3	24.2	13.0	1.9
Trade	14.3	16.6	17.3	2.2	11.7	7.4	5.5
Transport	3.7	3.8	5.8	0.9	10.8	13.8	6.0
Finance	1.0	1.2	3.8	− 2.7	28.5	14.6	8.1
Dwellings	2.0	2.1	2.7	1.7	7.2	12.1	3.3
Public administration	4.5	6.0	6.8	4.6	4.9	12.8	7.4
Other services	6.2	3.9	3.8	2.4	2.3	2.4	3.6
Total	100	100	100	1.7	7.9	7.5	4.3

Sources: BPS, Pendapatan Nasional Indonesia [National Income of Indonesia], Main
   Tables, various issues, and unpublished data (1989); Sundrum (1986: Table 13).
[a]Current price data.
[b]1960–7: 1960 prices.
   1967–81: 1973 prices.
   1981–8: 1983 prices.

(World Bank, 1989: 164), a move which inevitably created the impression that many of the economic gains of the 1970s had been eroded in the 1980s.

But such an impression is misleading. One positive consequence of the slower growth in the Indonesian economy in the 1980s has been a lively debate about the country's economic performance, which in turn has led to the adoption and implementation of a series of measures designed to increase the efficiency of resource use in the domestic economy, remove disincentives to production for export, and improve resource mobilization for investment in both the public and the private sectors. Indeed, senior Indonesian officials have been quoted as saying that the end of the oil boom was a 'blessing in disguise' for the Indonesian economy in that it created the political climate which allowed them to implement broad-ranging economic reforms which would have been impossible in the 1970s. By the late 1980s, the fruits of five years of economic restructuring were already evident in accelerating rates of GDP growth, and in far more optimistic forecasts of economic performance in the 1990s than would have seemed possible in the years from 1982 to 1987.

Indonesia in the 1980s can thus be seen as an important case-study of economic restructuring in the wake of a collapsed commodity boom.

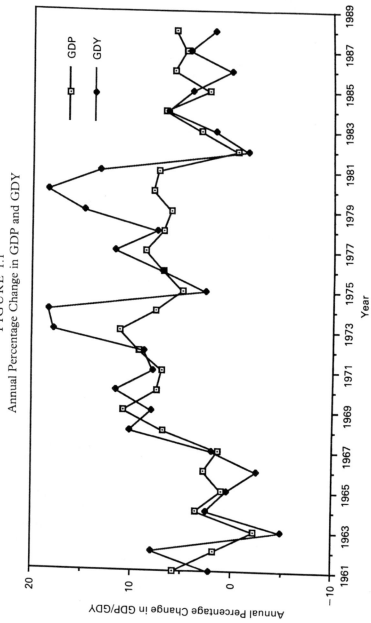

FIGURE 1.1
Annual Percentage Change in GDP and GDY

However, viewed in the longer-term context, the experience of the 1980s was hardly unique. Indeed there is a sense in which Indonesian economic history, at least since the 1870s, can be seen as a series of policy responses to fluctuations in the country's terms of trade, and to sudden and dramatic changes in world market conditions for key commodities. Thus the Indonesian experience of economic reform in the 1980s should be viewed not just in the contemporary international context, but also in the light of Indonesia's own economic past. In what way are the policy reforms of the 1980s different from those implemented in previous episodes of sudden deterioration in the terms of trade? Is the Indonesian economy now poised on the threshold of a period of economic growth and structural change, which will propel it into the ranks of the upper middle-income countries by 2025? Or are the foundations still inadequate for sustained transformation of the economy?

A major aim of this book is to look at these questions in the context of the main areas of macroeconomic policy (financial policy, fiscal policy, and exchange rate policy) as well as in the context of the important productive sectors (agriculture, industry, transport, and services). This introductory chapter examines the sources of economic growth in Indonesia since the late 1960s, and the structural changes which have taken place in the economy. It looks at the legacies of the oil boom, both positive and negative, and the nature and content of the restructuring process. Finally it reviews some of the most important economic problems which have emerged in the 1980s and which policy-makers will have to tackle in the 1990s and beyond.

Sources of Rapid Growth 1968–1981

Why did the Indonesian economy grow so fast between 1968 and 1981? The simple explanation that the growth was 'due to the oil boom' is clearly unsatisfactory. Having an exportable surplus of oil was neither a necessary nor a sufficient condition for rapid growth of GDP in the 1970s; some of the fastest growing economies such as South Korea and Taiwan were oil importers, and some of the large oil exporters grew very slowly. Furthermore the period of accelerated growth began well before the dramatic increase in world oil prices in late 1973. But it is clear that rapid growth in Indonesia was associated with a sustained improvement in the country's terms of trade. The net barter terms of trade, as calculated from the national income statistics, more than doubled between 1967 and 1973, and trebled again between 1973 and 1981. Export volume growth was also rapid in the years from 1967 to 1973, and the income terms of trade grew at the remarkable rate of more than 30 per cent per annum (Figure 1.2). After 1973, export volume growth was much more modest, but the income terms of trade continued to grow at over 20 per cent per annum. As much of the improvement in the terms of trade accrued directly to the government in the form of the oil company tax, and to a lesser extent other export taxes, these years also saw a dramatic growth in real government income and expenditures.

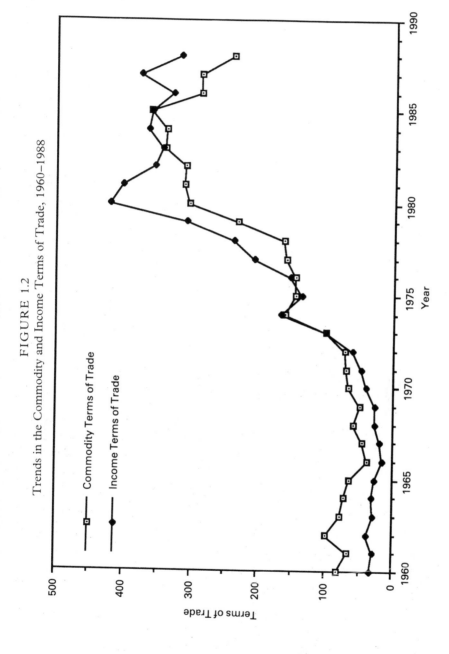

FIGURE 1.2

Trends in the Commodity and Income Terms of Trade, 1960–1988

Indonesia's experience of rapid growth in this period may thus seem to support the view that foreign exchange and government revenues were the two important constraints on economic growth in Indonesia in the first fifteen years of independence, and that a relaxation of these constraints, combined with 'sound economic management', have been the main causes of accelerated growth after 1968. But in order to understand the mechanisms through which the relaxation of these constraints led to more rapid growth, one has to look at the processes involved in more detail. In particular one must try to clarify the central role of foreign exchange earnings, especially those accruing from the export of oil. It has been stressed that the 1968–81 growth cannot just be attributed to the rapid growth in oil earnings which occurred as a result of the OPEC-induced price rises of 1973/4, as the acceleration in growth had started well before then. But after 1981, when oil revenues began to decline, growth did slow down. This raises important questions. To what extent could the growth rates of the years 1967–81, and especially in the period after 1973, have been achieved with much less foreign exchange? Was the rapid growth simply a phenomenon connected with the post-Sukarno economic stabilization and rehabilitation and the foreign exchange bonanza of the 1970s? Or could Indonesia have emulated the growth performance of the more successful oil-importing Asian countries such as Korea, Taiwan, or Thailand?

In seeking answers to these questions, one must consider the various ways in which the foreign exchange position of a country such as Indonesia might improve, and their potential impact on the rate of growth of GDP. Such an improvement could occur as the result of an increase in the quantity of exports, or through a rise in export prices. In addition the government may borrow abroad, or receive foreign aid. There may also be substantial inflows on private account, either in the form of equity investment in business ventures, or in the form of loans to private individuals and corporations. The available data on each of these categories are summarized in Table 1.2. Although revenues from the export of oil and gas have been important from 1967 through to the late 1980s, they were most prominent in the years from 1973 to 1981. The rapid increase in oil revenues after 1973/4 was of course largely due to the OPEC-induced price rises, although there was some increase in export volume up to 1979, and a decline thereafter. Prior to 1973, much more of the growth in commodity export earnings was due to growth in volume, both of oil and of other staples such as rubber and timber. But even between 1968 and 1973 there had been a considerable improvement in the country's commodity terms of trade; in fact it was faster than that which occurred after the first oil price shock, although not as rapid as the improvement between 1978 and 1981 as a result of the second oil shock (Figure 1.2).

An increase in the quantum of exports is reflected in the growth of real GDP, but an improvement in the terms of trade is not. The oil price increases in the OPEC countries were essentially an unrequited transfer

TABLE 1.2
Annual Average Real Foreign Exchange Inflows to Indonesia, 1968–1989[a]
(million dollars: 1975 prices)

	1968–72[b]	1973–81[b]	1982–9[b]
Exports			
Oil	930 (30)	8,000 (64)	6,700 (51)
Other	1,315 (43)	2,954 (24)	4,136 (31)
Net government aid and			
borrowing	539 (17)	1,321 (11)	1,777 (13)
Direct investment and other			
net private inflows[c]	297 (10)	163 (1)	581 (4)
Total	3,081 (100)	12,438 (100)	13,194 (100)
Index	100	404	428

Sources: Department of Information; *Lampiran Pidato Kenegaraan*, various years; International Monetary Fund, *International Financial Statistics*, various issues.
[a]Data refer to US$ values deflated by the US Export Unit Price Index.
[b]Figures in brackets are percentages of the total.
[c]Includes state enterprises.

payment, or as one writer has put it, 'cash made available to the country in return for nothing in the way of production by the economy in general' (Bruton, 1984: 131). In Indonesia, this cash accrued in large part to the government in the form of dollars, and the impact of these dollars on the growth of domestic production of goods and services depended on how they were spent. But before addressing this question, it is necessary to estimate the magnitude of the increase in resources made available to the domestic economy through the improvement in the terms of trade. The National Accounts Statistics (NAS) provide data on the improvement in Indonesia's foreign exchange position in the form of the excess of exports over imports in constant prices. Part of this increase was accumulated abroad in the form of foreign reserves, and the rest was absorbed domestically. There are several ways of decomposing the difference between exports and imports into reserve accumulation on the one hand and domestic absorption on the other (Sundrum, 1986: 45–7). The method used here is that adopted by several Indonesian agencies, including Bank Indonesia and the Biro Pusat Statistik (BPS), which involves breaking down the difference between the real value of exports and imports according to the following equation:

$$\frac{X}{P_x} - \frac{M}{P_m} = \frac{X-M}{P_m} - X\left(\frac{1}{P_m} - \frac{1}{P_x}\right)$$

The terms of trade effect is given by the second term on the right hand side of the equation. The concept of the Gross Domestic Income

(GDY) can then be defined as the GDP plus the terms of trade effect, as follows:

$$GDP + TOT = GDY$$

As expected, GDY grew more rapidly than GDP in the years from 1967 to 1981; between 1974 and 1981, the terms of trade improvement contributed over 3 percentage points to the growth in GDY (Table 1.3). But as has been seen, the growth in GDP was itself quite high in comparison with most other developing countries and with Indonesia's own previous performance. It is this rapid growth which has to be explained in terms of the growth of resources absorbed into the domestic economy through the terms of trade improvement.

To see how the resources absorbed into the domestic economy were used, one must consider the three categories of expenditure distinguished in the National Accounts Statistics, namely private consumption expenditure (PCE), government consumption expenditure (GCE), and gross domestic capital formation, or investment (INV). The impact on the domestic economy of an improvement in the terms of trade depends crucially on how it affects each of these variables. When the extra foreign resources accruing from an improvement in the terms of trade are used for importing goods and services for private consumption, there is an improvement in living standards of the population but this will not be shown in the GDP figures, as the increase in PCE will be offset by an

TABLE 1.3
Trends in GDY, 1960–1988

	Percentage of Increment in GDY Spent on				
	PCE	GCE	INV	TOT	Total
1960–6[a]	176.9	−21.6	44.9	−100.2	100
1967–73[b]	48.8	12.4	29.6	9.2	100
1974–81[b]	65.5	13.4	23.8	−2.7	100
1982–8[c]	62.4	10.7	25.5	−1.4	100

	Annual Average Percentage Growth Rates[d]				
	PCE	GCE	INV	GDP	GDY
1960–6[a]	1.6	−3.2	1.1	1.7	0.9
1967–73[b]	5.1	10.4	24.2	7.6	8.7
1974–81[b]	9.5	13.7	12.1	7.6	10.8
1982–8[c]	3.1	3.4	3.7	4.8	3.3

Sources: As for Table 1.1.
[a] 1960 constant price data.
[b] 1973 constant price data.
[c] 1983 constant price data.
[d] Calculated by fitting an exponential function to the data.

increase in imports. Of course the increase in imports will have some impact on domestic value added in the transport and wholesale and retail trade sectors but this is likely to be quite modest. It is also possible that higher levels of private consumption will lead to more labour effort and greater efficiency, but it is only in this indirect way that increased consumption goods will lead to growth in GDP in the longer run, and such indirect effects are very difficult to measure. In any case, it is unlikely that they could have played a major part in explaining the acceleration in GDP growth in Indonesia after 1967. To the extent that the increase in the terms of trade led to increased consumer imports, this is the clearest example of the case where an improvement in the terms of trade does not promote growth in real terms either in the current period or in the future. Indeed it may even damage the economy's productive capacity in the future if the imported consumer goods retard or destroy domestic industries. If by contrast the additional resources available from the terms of trade improvement are spent domestically on non-traded consumer goods and services in elastic supply, there will be an increase in current real GDP.

Exactly the same argument holds for the investment expenditure, with the important difference that investment expenditure enhances the future productive capacity of the economy. But an investment project consisting solely of imported capital goods will not lead directly to an increase in GDP, as the increase in investment expenditure will be offset by the increase in imports. But if investment also involves the use of non-tradable goods and services in elastic supply, then it will lead to some growth in GDP in the current period. Depending on how productive the investment is, investment expenditure will also lead to faster GDP growth in future.

The third category of expenditure distinguished in the NAS, government consumption expenditure, is important in the Indonesian context because the benefits of the improved terms of trade accrued primarily to the government. The government in turn used its improved financial position to increase its consumption expenditure, by expanding the civil service and by improving its remuneration. Even if the expansion in the public services did not make any difference to the level of production in the rest of the economy, GDP would grow simply because the contribution to GDP of the public administration sector is valued at its cost to the government rather than in terms of the value of its output. Here then is another case where an improvement in the terms of trade leads directly to growth of GDP in real terms during the period when the terms of trade improvement occurs. Will this growth be sustained in future periods? In practice it is likely that, if for example an increase in public sector remuneration increases bureaucratic efficiency, the longer-run productive capacity of the economy will also be enhanced. It is also likely that salary increases for teachers and health workers would improve the quality of public education and public health, which in turn should improve productive capacity in the longer run.

The effect of these various ways of absorbing a terms of trade improvement on the expenditure components given in the national accounts statistics is summarized in Table 1.3. In the years from 1967 to 1973 the rate of growth of investment was very high, partly as a result of the rapid growth in the government development budget, and partly as a result of growth in investment in the private sector, which in turn was influenced by the growth in direct foreign investment. But after 1973 the rate of investment growth fell while that of private consumption accelerated. There was also a slight acceleration in the rate of growth of government consumption. Another way of bringing out the change that occurred after 1973 is to examine the growth in these various categories of expenditure as a proportion of GDY. In 1967–73 private consumption expenditure accounted for just under half of the growth in GDY, while between 1973 and 1981 its share increased to two-thirds. Another important difference between the two periods was that between 1967 and 1973 almost 10 per cent of the growth in GDY was used to increase assets held abroad, while in the later period, foreign assets were in fact drawn down to a small extent. This suggests that much of the improvement in the terms of trade after 1973 was spent on consumption of both imports and locally produced goods and services, which in turn might have had a high import content.

Investment grew more rapidly than GDP throughout the period from 1967 to 1981, resulting in a steady rise in the investment ratio. To what extent did this increase in investment in turn lead to further growth? The usual way of answering this question is to estimate the incremental capital–output ratio (ICOR), i.e. the investment undertaken in one year as a ratio of the increase in GDP in the next period. The ICOR in Indonesia increased from a very low value of around 1.5 before 1973 to around 3 thereafter (Figure 1.3). It has frequently been argued that the low ICOR in the years up to 1973 was due to the emphasis placed on infrastructure rehabilitation projects in the First Five-Year Plan. While this is certainly one reason for the high returns to investment during these years, a more disaggregated sectoral approach is required if accurate estimates are to be obtained of the relationship between investment and growth, especially during a period when there was a marked change in the structure of production. Unfortunately data are not available from the national accounts on the sectoral allocation of investment, so there is little that can be said about sectoral differences in the productivity of capital.

Rather more can be said about the effect of the very rapid growth in import volume over this period on investment as import data, broken down into consumption goods, intermediate goods, and capital goods, are available. According to the old import classification, between 1967 and 1981, consumption goods made up 20 per cent of real imports on average, while raw materials and capital goods each accounted for about 40 per cent (Table 1.4). Consumer goods imports grew more slowly than those in other categories, so that the marginal share of the consumer goods was quite small at 5 per cent, and the marginal shares of the other categories were 50 per cent and 45 per cent respectively. The

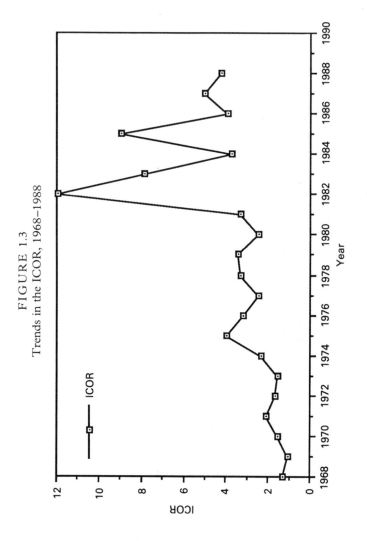

FIGURE 1.3
Trends in the ICOR, 1968–1988

TABLE 1.4
Composition of Growth of Imports

	Average Percentage Share				Annual Rate of Growth[a]			
	Consumer Goods	*Raw Materials*	*Capital Goods*	*Total*	*Consumer Goods*	*Raw Materials*	*Capital Goods*	*Total*
(i) Old Definition								
1967–81	20.7	39.7	39.6	100.0	10.1	19.3	21.4	17.9
1967–74	25.5	38.2	36.3	100.0	9.8	22.8	31.3	22.0
1975–81	15.3	41.4	43.3	100.0	10.1	18.0	13.7	15.0
(ii) New Definition								
1975–81	14.2	68.1	17.7	100.0	4.5	19.0	6.5	15.0
1982–88	5.8	75.8	18.3	100.0	–17.3	–1.6	–1.2	–2.5

Sources: Sundrum (1986: Table 9); BPS, *Indikator Ekonomi*, various issues.
[a]To calculate growth rates, US$ values were converted into rupiah at the prevailing exchange rate and deflated by the implicit import price index from the National Income Accounts.

fairly large share of capital goods in total imports shown by these data suggests that Indonesia's increased import capacity was used to a considerable extent to promote investment, which in turn enhanced the long-term growth capacity of the economy. But to the extent that the increase in imports consisted of raw materials, it promoted current growth in sectors where these raw materials were inputs, but not the longer-term growth capacity of the economy. In other words, any fall in import capacity would have an immediate adverse effect on production. This is indeed what happened in the 1960s, when acute shortage of foreign exchange meant that many factories were unable to obtain raw materials and spare parts and were thus forced to operate at levels far below capacity.

In the early 1980s, the Biro Pusat Statistik (BPS) revised its classification of imports according to the second revision of the international SITC (Standard International Trade Classification) code. Following this revision, intermediate imports were defined very broadly to include all food and beverages intended mainly for industry (such as wheat for the domestic flour-milling industry), all fuels and lubricants except those intended for direct household consumption, and all industrial supplies and parts and accessories for capital goods. Thus imports of raw materials grew very rapidly; they constituted over two-thirds of all imports on the average, and over 85 per cent of the increase in imports. On the other hand, according to the new definition, imports of both consumption and capital goods grew much more slowly from 1975 to 1981 (Table 1.4).

This suggests that most of the foreign exchange (almost 70 per cent) accruing to Indonesia between 1975 and 1981 was used for importing raw materials for industry, fuels and lubricants, and components and spare parts for the production of both consumer and capital goods. To the extent that without them growth in output would rapidly have run into bottlenecks, these imports can be said to have promoted current growth. But their role in enhancing the longer-run productive capacity of the economy is less obvious. They would do this only to the extent that they have led to domestic capital formation, but not if they have only constituted consumption at one remove.

If sectoral growth rates for the period 1967–81 are compared with those of 1960–7, one finds that there was an acceleration in growth rates in all sectors except miscellaneous services, but the fastest acceleration occurred in the non-agricultural sectors (Table 1.1). In the manufacturing sector, the rate of growth increased 14-fold, and there were also very large increases in the growth rates in construction, transport and communications, banking, residential accommodation, and public administration. When the years 1967–81 are divided into the pre- and post-oil boom periods, it is seen that although the overall growth remained quite steady, there were some significant changes in the growth of individual sectors. For much of the period, agricultural growth rates remained above 4 per cent, except for a slackening in 1973–7. The growth rate of mining and quarrying, by contrast, declined steadily, and in 1977–81 it was actually negative. There was a similar deceleration of growth in the construction and finance sectors. By contrast, there was a steady acceleration in manufacturing and public utilities.

But this analysis in terms of sectoral growth rates is not particularly helpful in explaining the overall growth of the economy. A sector's contribution to overall growth depends not only on its growth rate, but also on its relative size. Thus even a fast-growing sector may not contribute much to overall growth if it is small. Table 1.5 presents the growth in GDP by sector in terms of each sector's percentage contribution to the total growth which occurred. Once the sectoral growth pattern is analysed in this way, it is seen that between 1967 and 1973, the agricultural sector in fact contributed most to overall growth, followed by the trade sector. These two sectors accounted for over half the total growth in these years. Between 1973 and 1981, the shares of both agriculture and trade fell, while those of manufacturing and the public sector grew. Other sectors whose share increased in 1973–81 were construction, transport, and ownership of dwellings. All these sectors except for manufacturing were producing non-tradable goods and services. In the case of manufacturing, part of the growth occurred in the oil and gas processing sector itself, while much of the rest took place as a result of quantitative import controls so severe that domestic prices were largely insulated from world prices. Thus the evidence on sectoral growth rates after 1973 may be taken as lending some support to the neo-classical analysis of resource booms, or the so-called 'Dutch Disease', which predicts a movement of resources out of sectors producing traded goods and into those producing non-traded goods and services as a result of

TABLE 1.5

Sectoral Breakdown of Increment in Real GDP, 1967–1988

Sector	Percentage of Increment in Real GDP		
	1967–73	*1974–81*	*1982–8*
Agriculture	27.4	16.4	14.9
Mining	12.9	4.4	−0.3
Manufacturing	9.8	23.5	35.8
Utilities	0.7	1.1	1.2
Construction	7.6	8.4	2.9
Trade	25.9	17.1	17.9
Transport	4.4	8.1	6.5
Finance	4.4	3.0	5.1
Housing	1.6	3.9	2.1
Public administration	3.6	13.2	10.9
Services n.e.i.	1.6	1.0	2.9
Total	100.0	100.0	100.0

Sources: As for Table 1.1.

the real appreciation effect consequent upon the resource boom (Corden and Warr, 1981).[1]

In much of the literature, the sources of economic growth are divided into two types, increases in various inputs, especially labour and capital, on the one hand, and increases in the productivity of these inputs, on the other hand. This latter is usually described as technical progress. However, in explaining the growth which occurred in Indonesia between 1967 and 1981, it is necessary to examine each of these components in more detail. To begin with, the role of investment is considered. In so far as the investment is made in new infrastructure, plant, and equipment, it increases output by increasing the stock of capital in the economy. The extent to which output grows as a result of the increment in capital stock is usually analysed in terms of a particular production function, or, more roughly, in terms of an assumed incremental capital–output ratio. In the years from 1967 to 1973 the investment which was carried out was exceptionally productive (Figure 1.3). There are two obvious explanations for this; on the one hand, there was substantial rehabilitation of infrastructure which had fallen into disrepair, while on the other hand, the greater availability of raw materials and spare parts allowed the existing plant and equipment to be more fully utilized. Thus, even a modest amount of rehabilitation investment made a considerable contribution to growth, as indeed was the case in the early 1950s.[2] But the process of rehabilitation in both periods was a finite one. Just as the potential for rapid growth through rehabilitation of war-damaged plant and infrastructure was largely exhausted by the mid-1950s, so it was exhausted again by the early 1970s, and further growth entailed considerably more investment per unit of incremental output. It is therefore useful in the Indonesian case to make a clear distinction between rehabilitation and other types of investment in analysing sources of growth in different periods.

The other important input in elastic supply in Indonesia is labour. The availability of labour can grow for several reasons, of which the most obvious is growth in population. In addition labour force participation rates can increase, particularly for women, as a result of economic growth and changing social attitudes about female employment. In Indonesia the available evidence, discussed in detail in Chapter 11, suggests that the labour force has been growing at slightly under 3 per cent per annum since the early 1970s. But there are good reasons for assuming that the effective growth in labour availability has been much higher than the census and survey figures on the labour force would suggest. There can be little doubt that in the 1960s many employed workers in Indonesia were devoting most of their time to occupations characterized by very low productivity, and that this was the basic reason for the very high proportion of the population living below the poverty line at that time. During the 1970s many workers shifted out of these occupations and into much more productive employment, in terms of remuneration per hour of work, in response to the rapid growth in demand for labour in sectors such as construction, transport, and trade.

This growth in demand for labour was in turn the result of several factors. The decision of the government to spend a considerable part of the oil revenues domestically led to a rapid growth in the domestic deficit (the difference between domestic or non-oil revenues and domestic expenditures), which in turn led to rapid growth in aggregate purchasing power and thus to an increase in demand for both labour and physical capital.[3] The capital could be acquired from abroad, with relatively abundant supplies of foreign exchange. It might be expected that a rapid growth in real levels of remuneration of the labour force might have led to inflation, if supplies of wage goods, such as food and clothing, were not growing fast enough to keep up. But in fact the wage goods too could be imported from abroad, and the 1970s saw a rapid growth in imports of foodstuffs, textiles, and other consumer products. By the early 1980s, technical change in food-crop agriculture had brought about such an increase in domestic food supply that imports could be scaled down. Thus it can be argued that, quite apart from the growth in the labour force which occurred in the 1970s, the fuller utilization of underutilized labour resources was an important factor in the growth which occurred. There is a parallel here with the argument regarding rehabilitation investment, in that the growth which occurs as a result of more intensive utilization of the existing labour force must at some point cease, because the underutilized pool of labour is exhausted. But given the experience of the now-developed countries, this is unlikely to happen in Indonesia for several more decades.[4]

With regard to technical progress, it is often not possible to separate it sharply from investment in practice, and the 'learning by doing' literature usually considers the two in combination, with investment being the vehicle of technology transfer. But it is still desirable in principle to distinguish between these two sources of growth, because investment in physical capital depends heavily on the ability to import the required capital goods from abroad, while technical progress depends much more on improving the skills of the domestic labour force. Especially important in this regard are such government activities as extension services and education. To the extent that these are provided, the 'learning process' among producers can be greatly speeded up, and the benefits from new technologies can accrue much more rapidly. There can be little doubt that the revenues which the oil boom made available to the government in the 1970s permitted the rapid expansion both of general education and of extension services which facilitated the dissemination of new technologies, especially in agriculture. In addition the government used budgetary revenues to subsidize fertilizer and improve irrigation infrastructure which permitted the rapid adoption of the IRRI seed fertilizer technologies in the agricultural sector, while in the transport sector the adoption of new technologies was encouraged by increased government spending on roads and bridges.

One final factor must also be included in this catalogue of the sources of growth. This is the extent to which the growth of GDP was just a direct reflection of the growth of income due to the terms of trade effect.

It has been seen that, where this additional income was spent on imports, there would be no effect on current GDP growth, but where it was used to expand public administration, there was an increase in current GDP because of the accounting convention which puts all such expansion down to productivity increases. Given the importance of the public administration sector in overall growth, especially after 1973, this phenomenon should be treated as a separate source of growth.

The various sources of growth distinguished here vary greatly in the extent to which they depend on foreign exchange accruing through the terms of trade effect. They also have different implications for the enhancement of the economy's longer-run productive capacity, and thus for the sustainability of growth once the terms of trade stop improving, or start declining. Although their role cannot be quantified precisely, some rough estimates can be made of their contribution to the growth process in each sector. In the case of agriculture, which, as has been seen, accounted for a substantial share of total growth, particularly before 1973 (Table 1.5), Sundrum (1986: Table 17) has suggested that up to 40 per cent of the growth between 1973 and 1981 was due to growth in employment. The remainder was due to investment and technical progress, in the sense of farmers making more efficient use of the factors of production, land, labour, and capital.

Much of the growth was in the food-crop sector; here an important contribution to growth was the rehabilitation of irrigation and other agricultural infrastructure, which was given high priority in the First Five-Year Plan of the New Order (*Repelita I*). In addition there was considerable new investment in rural infrastructure, particularly outside Java, and this in turn led to the opening up of new land for food-crop agriculture. Also fertilizer consumption began to rise rapidly, and this, together with the improvement in irrigation, led to increases in rice yields, especially in Java. This was particularly important after 1973; between 1973 and 1981 rice yields in Java increased by 40 per cent, and accounted for a high proportion of the growth which took place in rice production (Booth, 1988a: 39). The growth in yields can thus be ascribed partly to investment in inputs such as improved seed and fertilizer, and partly to farmers becoming more skilled in the use of these new inputs. In the smallholder cash-crop sector, yields growth has been extremely slow and much more of the growth which has occurred has been due to growth in land area. Area expansion and associated planting of the land represents substantial new investment on the part of the smallholders, but given the stagnation in yields, little of the growth in this sector can be said to have been due to technical change. In the large-estates sector by contrast, there has been some area expansion, but more of the growth has been due to both rehabilitation and new investment in higher-yielding varieties, fertilizers, and other yield-raising technologies.

The mining and quarrying sector made an important contribution to overall growth between 1967 and 1973, although it was much less important after that (Table 1.5). Part of the growth which occurred in the years after 1967 may have been due to rehabilitation, although most was the result of new investment by foreign companies. Growth in the manufacturing sector by contrast, which was particularly important in the years after 1973, was about 50 per cent due to growth in employment (Sundrum, 1986: Table 17). Most of these new workers were drawn from less productive jobs in other parts of the economy. The rest of the growth of manufacturing was due to several factors, including rehabilitation of existing plant and equipment after 1967 and new investment. This in turn was in part due to inflows of foreign direct investment in manufacturing, which were particularly large in the years from 1973 to 1981. Technical progress, in the sense of using the available factors more efficiently, was probably less important as a source of growth in manufacturing than in the food-crop sector.

The construction sector made a significant contribution to GDP growth over the entire period 1967–81. It also experienced very rapid growth in employment, and much of its output growth appears to have been due to this. Much the same is true of the trade sector (comprising wholesale and retail trade, hotels and restaurants). Although employment growth in this sector was slower than in construction, it was already a large employer of labour in the 1960s, and it accounted for the largest share of the growth in employment between 1971 and 1980 of any sector except agriculture. In the transport sector, by contrast, more of the growth was due to new investment; the scale of this investment can be appreciated from the figures on growth in numbers of registered vehicles. In the four years from 1977 to 1981 numbers of buses and trucks more than doubled; in addition there was an enormous growth in the numbers of small vehicles serving both the passenger and freight markets in even the most remote parts of the country. (See Chapter 8 for further discussion.)

The public administration sector also made an important contribution to overall growth, especially after 1973. Sundrum (1986: 62) estimates that over half the growth which occurred was due to labour productivity increases, but points out that 'it is likely that this represents the payment of higher salaries rather than growth in productivity'. While most observers would agree that there was a marked improvement in the competence and professionalism of the Indonesian civil service in the 1970s, there seems to be little doubt that at least part of the apparent growth of GDP accruing from the public services simply reflected the growth in GDY through the improvement in the terms of trade.

To sum up, there can be little doubt that much of the growth which occurred in Indonesia in the years from 1967 to 1981 was due to growth in labour supply on the one hand and investment on the other. The growth in labour supply was in turn due not just to population growth, but also to a considerable movement of employed workers from tasks characterized by very low productivity to new jobs where productivity was higher. Part of this growth in employment was due to growth in investment, but especially in the years from 1967 to 1973 a considerable part appears to have been due to technological progress in the sense of an increase in the incremental output–capital ratio in per capita terms.

This reflected the fact that there was in these years considerable rehabilitation of run-down infrastructure and growth in capacity utilization in industry. After 1973, more investment was required to maintain the growth momentum, and imports of intermediate goods and capital goods continued to grow rapidly.

Compared with many other OPEC (Organization of Petroleum Exporting Countries) economies, Indonesia spent relatively little of the foreign exchange bonanza of the 1970s on imports of consumption goods, and for this reason experienced higher growth rates. But there were several reasons for suspecting that some part of the growth which occurred was a direct consequence of the terms of trade improvement and could not be sustained if the terms of trade began to deteriorate. Especially after 1973, part of the higher growth rate reflected growth in spending on public administration, which was only partially an indication of improved productivity in this sector. Within the context of a balanced budget policy, continued increases in such expenditure in the face of falling government revenues could only be maintained through severe cut-backs in other components of government expenditure, including expenditures on development projects. Further, although very little foreign exchange was used to import consumer goods, much was used to import raw materials and intermediate products. To the extent that the growth of the manufacturing sector was mainly devoted to the final stages of production of imported raw materials and components to be sold on the domestic market, it could not be sustained when the capacity to import declined. It would be necessary to reorient production to goods which could be sold on the international market.

The Slow-down in Growth after 1981

Between 1981 and 1988, the average rate of GDP growth dropped considerably, and became more erratic (Figure 1.1). Only in one year (1984) did the growth rate exceed 6 per cent per annum. This performance was still better than that which was achieved in the very disturbed years of the early 1960s, but disappointing in comparison with the rapid growth of the years from 1968 to 1981. The most obvious explanation for the decline in growth rates was the decline in the world price of oil which led to a decline in the income terms of trade (thus reducing import capacity), and in government revenues. A second reason for the decline in growth was the imposition of OPEC quotas, to which Indonesia adhered with a greater degree of fidelity than many of its OPEC colleagues. These quotas had the effect of reducing the volume of oil output, and of value added in mining sector GDP (Table 1.1). A third reason for the decline was the generally more depressed state of the world economy in the 1980s, which has affected both the prices of, and markets for, Indonesia's non-oil export staples, and also inflows of private foreign investment. A fourth reason for the growth slow-down can be framed in terms of government policy responses to the changing economic climate of the 1980s. The government reacted to falling oil revenues, declining income terms of trade, and rising foreign debt service obligations by cutting both salaries and wages of government employees and development expenditures. These policies affected the construction and public administration sectors of GDP, whose growth slowed considerably after 1981 (Table 1.1).

On the face of it, these may seem plausible enough explanations for the fall in growth rate after 1981. Certainly most of the other OPEC countries, as well as Indonesia's ASEAN partners, experienced a fall in growth rates in the early part of the 1980s. But on closer examination, some difficulties are encountered with the first and third explanations in particular. The commodity terms of trade actually improved between 1980 and 1985, although there was a severe deterioration between 1985 and 1988. The income terms of trade (the purchasing power of export earnings in terms of imports) certainly fell from their 1980 peak (Figure 1.2), although the magnitude of the fall was cushioned by the very rapid growth in non-oil exports, which by 1988 accounted for 60 per cent of commodity export earnings (Pangestu and Habir, 1990: Table 7). Neither does it seem correct to argue that the years since 1981 witnessed a catastrophic decline in real foreign exchange receipts from all sources, including net government borrowing. In fact the annual average inflow of foreign exchange in real US dollar terms from all sources was $13.2 billion in 1982–9 compared with $12.4 billion in 1973–81 (Table 1.2). Certainly there was a fall in oil receipts, but this decline has been offset by increases in receipts from non-oil exports, from aid and borrowing on government account, and from other net private inflows. Thus it would seem that the decline in growth since 1981 is not a direct consequence of declining foreign resources available to the economy, but rather due to the cost of these resources (in particular government borrowing) and the way they were spent.

The first year in which the growth rate fell drastically was 1982. If one examines the sectoral contributions to growth, it is clear that the poor performance was due to a sharp contraction in output in the mining sector on the one hand and poor performance in agriculture and manufacturing on the other (Sundrum, 1988: Table 4). The fall in mining output was mainly due to the impact of the OPEC quotas, while the poor agricultural performance was due at least in part to drought. The fall in mining output together with lower world prices for most non-oil exports led to a fall in nominal export receipts, while nominal imports continued to rise. The result was a rapid increase in the deficit on the current account of the balance of payments, which was funded partly by drawing down reserves, but mainly by foreign borrowing. This borrowing allowed private consumption expenditure, government consumption expenditure, and investment to continue to rise, in spite of the fact that GDP actually contracted in 1982, but clearly such a policy had its dangers. The drawing down of foreign assets had a contractionary impact on domestic money supply, which was barely offset by lending to government and the private sector, so that in real terms narrow money hardly grew at all in 1982, after fifteen years of continuous expansion. The resulting slow-down in growth of purchasing power in turn affected demand for a wide range of domestically produced goods and services, and led to the slow-down in output in sectors such as manufacturing, construction, trade, and transport.

These trends continued in 1983, although there was some improvement in economic growth, due partly to the improved performance of the agricultural sector, and partly to the public administration sector, whose growth in fact accounted for almost 30 per cent of total GDP growth. Although there was some growth in export volume, imports continued to grow more rapidly; at current prices imports accounted for over 25 per cent of GDP. The continuing high levels of imports led to another large balance of payments deficit in 1983, which was funded mainly by government borrowing. Almost 30 per cent of the increase in imports in the years from 1981 to 1983 was accounted for by consumption imports, especially petroleum products. For the first time since the mid-1960s, real money supply contracted (Sundrum, 1988: Table 17).

In 1984, GDP grew by almost 7 per cent, and it seemed that a return to sustained growth rates similar to those achieved in the 1970s was again possible. Much of the improvement was due to the performance of agriculture, mining, and manufacturing. But on closer inspection, there were several special features about the growth in 1984 which suggested that it might not be sustainable. Over 40 per cent of the growth was due to the manufacturing sector, and much of this was due in turn to a 49 per cent increase in value added in the processing of LNG (liquefied natural gas), primarily for export. This was essentially a once-over effect, as new trains which had been under construction for several years were brought on stream. The growth in agriculture was almost entirely in the food-crop and livestock sectors, and there was concern also about its sustainability. Domestic rice production (which increased by 8 per cent in 1984), was growing much faster than domestic demand, and Bulog (Badan Urusan Logistik), the State Logistics Board responsible for food procurement, was having to purchase and warehouse large stocks to maintain domestic prices. The very low world price of rice meant that Indonesia could not export its rice surplus profitably. Under these circumstances, the policy options were to expand demand for rice through some form of fiscal stimulus, or to cut back on production through manipulating the rice farmers' terms of trade.

In 1985, the government chose the second of these policy options; the terms of trade for rice farmers fell sharply in the major producing areas in Java, and total domestic production increased by only 2.4 per cent (Hobohm, 1987: Tables 8 and 9). There was some further growth in the manufacturing sector, again largely due to the increase in LNG processing. But agricultural growth was less than half what it had been in the previous year, and most other sectors of the economy registered very little growth at all. The mining sector actually contracted, as a further round of OPEC quota restrictions meant that petroleum output fell back to 1982 levels. This in turn was a major reason for the decline in export volume of 8 per cent. Overall GDP rose by only 2.5 per cent in 1985 (Figure 1.1).

In the 1986/7 Budget Speech, the President announced the first nominal decline in budgetary expenditures in the history of the New Order, and this led commentators to predict a slow-down in the rate of economic growth (Glassburner, 1986: 18). In the event, budget policy in the years 1986/7 and 1987/8 was less contractionary than it appeared for reasons explained in detail in Chapter 2. Oil and gas production increased in 1986 after the production decline of 1985, and the agricultural and manufacturing sectors also performed well, so that total GDP rose by almost 6 per cent. The substantial devaluation of the rupiah in September 1986, and a further austerity budget announced in January 1987 again provoked fears of a growth slow-down but the manufacturing sector continued to perform well in 1987 and 1988 with an increasing proportion of the increment in output oriented to export. Slower agricultural growth and stagnant mining sector output meant that GDP growth fell to under 5 per cent in 1987, but there was a marked recovery in 1988 and optimistic forecasts for 1989 of around 7 per cent. The sectoral breakdown of the growth in GDP which took place between 1982 and 1988 allows us to see how important the manufacturing sector has been, contributing almost 36 per cent of total growth (Table 1.4). No other sector contributed more than half this amount. Between 1967–73 and 1982–8, the contribution of the manufacturing sector to total growth has almost quadrupled, while that of the agricultural sector has almost halved.

The sharp deterioration in the terms of trade which occurred after 1985 is reflected in the much slower growth of GDY compared with GDP over the period 1982–8 (Table 1.3). GDY grew at only one-third the rate at which it grew between 1974 and 1981, and this was reflected in the marked slow-down in growth of both private and government consumption as well as investment. But in spite of the much slower growth in investment after 1982, there was a considerable jump in the ICOR (Figure 1.3). The national income accounts do not present any data on investment broken down by sector, so one cannot determine to what extent the rise in the ICOR has been due to a reallocation of investment away from sectors such as agriculture and towards sectors such as industry, infrastructure, and real estate, and to what extent it has been due to a rise in intrasectoral ICORs. If the latter has been an important cause of the aggregate ICOR increase, it would appear to indicate a decline in the efficiency of investment, both public and private, rather than simply the gradual exhaustion of the quick-yielding rehabilitation investments which were so abundant in the 1970s.

A sharp rise in the ICOR within a sector such as manufacturing could be attributed to heavy investment in enterprises either protected by tariffs and quotas or assisted through subsidized credit. However, if such investment had been increasing through the 1980s it would presumably be reflected in growth of imports of capital goods and raw materials. In fact imports have declined in real terms through the 1980s although the trend has been somewhat erratic (Table 1.4). This lends some support to the argument that the rise in the ICOR which has occurred in the

1980s has been due more to a reallocation of investment towards sectors such as manufacturing and construction where production processes are more capital-intensive than in agriculture but not necessarily highly import-intensive. But whatever the reason for the decline in investment productivity in the 1980s, it must be seen as one cause of the slower growth rate.

It has been argued that the slow growth of investment expenditures after 1981 also affected the economy on the demand side (Sundrum, 1988: 49). Investment expenditures have an important direct employment impact especially in sectors such as construction, and this employment in turn generates demand for a range of domestically produced goods and services in elastic supply. The high investment expenditures of the 1970s pulled labour out of low-productivity rural employment into more productive employment and this was an important factor in the rapid growth of that decade. The slow-down in investment expenditures after 1981, due in part to the cut-backs in the government development budget certainly played a part in the reduction of the growth rate. In addition, of course, the cut-back in expenditures on salaries and wages of the military and civilian bureaucracies had both a direct impact on growth of the public administration component of GDP, and an indirect impact on the economy as a whole through the reduction in demand.

Towards Sustained Growth in the 1990s

The evidence of a recovery in growth in 1987 and 1988 contained in the revised national income statistics issued in late 1989, and optimistic forecasts for 1989 and 1990 dramatically changed the climate of opinion concerning Indonesia's medium-term growth prospects.[5] Of particular note was the rapid growth in the manufacturing sector, which was seen to be in large part due to growth in production for export. The improved growth performance was interpreted as a vindication of the adjustment policies of the 1980s and by early 1990 there was considerable optimism that growth rates of at least 7 per cent per annum could be sustained into the 1990s. This was in turn based on the evidence of continuing strong investment in export-related activities particularly in manufacturing but also in forestry, non-oil mining, and the tourism sector.

There can be little doubt that the role of the secondary, and especially the manufacturing, sector will be crucial as the engine of growth over the next few decades. Given that the secondary sector (manufacturing, utilities, and construction) already accounted for 24 per cent of GDP in 1988, and the primary sector (agriculture and mining) 36 per cent, it is clear that if the growth of secondary sector value added can be sustained at 12 per cent per annum, and if the tertiary sector can grow at around 8 per cent, then aggregate GDP growth could exceed 7 per cent per annum, even if primary sector growth is only in the range of 3 per cent per annum. Growth rates of 12 per cent or more in the secondary sector have been the driving force behind rapid rates of GDP growth in economies such as South Korea in recent decades, and it should not be impossible for Indonesia to achieve this target.[6]

Aspects of Economic Liberalization

The Legacy of the Oil Boom

Before considering the nature of the restructuring process embarked upon after 1982, it is useful to recall the economic changes that the oil boom years brought in their wake. The most obvious concerned the role of revenues from oil and gas in the government budget and in the balance of payments. In 1969, 80 per cent of government tax revenues were derived from non-oil sources. By 1974 this had fallen to 42 per cent and by 1981 to 27 per cent (see Chapter 2, Table 2.2). Even more extreme was the dominance of oil and gas earnings in commodity export earnings. In the late 1960s these exports already accounted for 35 per cent of total commodity exports; by 1974–6 this had jumped to 72 per cent, and by 1981 to 82 per cent (Rosendale, 1981: Table 6.4; BPS, *Indikator Ekonomi*, September 1989: Table 6.7).

This extreme reliance of both government revenues and export earnings on a very small number of closely related commodities was in fact something quite new in Indonesian economic history. In the nineteenth century, the Netherlands Indies were characterized by very low export concentration in comparison with most other Asian and Latin American economies (Hanson, 1980: 40). In the twentieth century, exports became even more diversified as new commodities such as rubber, petroleum, and palm oil were added to traditional export staples such as coffee and sugar. During the years from 1950 to 1966, export volume growth in Indonesia was extremely slow but the composition of exports was still quite diverse although restricted entirely to primary products (Rosendale, 1975: 73; Rosendale, 1981: Table 6.4). Similarly in late colonial times government revenues were diversified between income taxes, excises, and foreign trade taxes with no one revenue source accounting for more than 30 per cent of revenues (Booth, 1990: Table 10.4). After independence, reliance on foreign trade taxes increased, while the share of income taxes and domestic indirect taxes fell, but at no time after the Korean War boom did trade taxes account for more than half of total government revenues.

A further legacy of the oil boom concerned its effects on the allocation of resources in the domestic economy. The 'Dutch Disease' literature predicted that there would be a substantial real appreciation of the Indonesian rupiah as a result of the oil boom, and that this would encourage resources to flow from sectors producing traded goods (other than oil) to those producing non-traded goods and services. That such a real appreciation occurred is beyond dispute, and it is argued that the evidence on sectoral growth rates after 1973 indicates that the flow of resources predicted by the 'Dutch Disease' literature did in fact take place.[7] However, the government came under increasing pressure during the decade to protect certain sectors and industries producing traded goods. The protection took several forms. The politically sensitive rice sector was assisted through substantial government input subsidies for irrigation, fertilizers, and pesticides. In addition Bulog was given an import monopoly for both rice and other key foodstuffs, which enabled it to insulate domestic markets from world price movements. Non-food agriculture received far less direct government assistance, although world prices of some commodities such as rubber and coffee increased in the latter part of the 1970s and cushioned producers from at least part of the real appreciation. In the manufacturing sector a combination of high tariffs and quantitative restrictions on a range of consumer durables, motor cycles, and automobiles effectively insulated domestic producers from foreign competition. The 1978 devaluation was intended to give all producers of traded goods protection against the real appreciation of the rupiah, but in fact the impact of the devaluation on relative prices of traded and non-traded goods was quickly eroded, and by the time of the March 1983 devaluation only one-quarter of the initial relative price effect remained (Warr, 1984: 74 and Figure 5.5 in this volume).

Throughout the 1970s the Indonesian trade regime was characterized by high and variable effective rates of protection for importables and low or negative rates for exportables. This in fact had already been the case in 1971, and the 1970s almost certainly witnessed an increase in the bias of the trade regime against exportables (Pitt, 1981; Pangestu and Boediono, 1986). Such a regime could possibly have been tolerated as long as high world prices for oil continued. But with the decline in oil prices and the dramatic widening in the balance of payments deficit in 1982/3 the government was faced with a stark choice. It could either retreat from even the partial liberalization of commodity trade which had occurred after 1968 and return to the regime of quantitative controls which had prevailed prior to 1965 in the hope of restricting imports, or remove the disincentives to export production in the existing trade regime in the hope of encouraging a dramatic acceleration in non-oil exports.

In the years from 1982 to 1985 it appeared that the government was adopting the former course, i.e. resorting to further quantitative controls on imports while at the same time adopting other measures (including the appointment of a Minister for the Promotion of Use of Domestic Products) which appeared to reinforce the emphasis on import substitution rather than export promotion. In November 1982, the government introduced the 'approved importers' system which added several new import licences to the two then in use, the general import licence and the import licence for producers to import inputs. The net effect of the new arrangements was to restrict the type and amount of goods imported by limiting both the number of importers and the type of goods they could import. In the most restrictive cases, imports of some key raw materials, intermediate goods, and agricultural products were limited to a few, or even one importer, frequently a state trading enterprise. Examples included iron and steel products, plastics, cotton, wheat flour, milk and milk products, and some agricultural products such as soy beans, cloves, and sugar. Licences were also granted to producer–importers, which gave domestic producers a monopoly over competing imports. The official reason for the introduction of this restrictive regime was to stabilize the supply and price of 'strategic' commodities and increase bargaining power with overseas suppliers (Pangestu, 1987: 28).[8]

Towards Economic Liberalization

The process of post-oil boom economic restructuring began in 1982/3 with several new initiatives in monetary, fiscal, and exchange rate policies. Several large public sector industrial projects were rescheduled in order to ease the burden on the budget, the rupiah was devalued in March 1983, and a number of new deregulation initiatives were announced in the financial sector (Arndt, 1983). In December 1983, the Indonesian parliament approved three tax reform laws which were implemented over the following eighteen months. But at the same time as some degree of financial liberalization was taking place, quantitative restrictions on imports were increasing. By early 1985 a lively debate had emerged within the economics profession and in the media over the causes of the 'high cost economy' and the need for liberalization of the 'real' economy. The essence of the economists' case was that a major cause of the high-cost economy was excessive protection from both tariff and non-tariff barriers.

This protection became a burden upon consumers and, in the case of domestic manufacture of inputs, upon downstream industries. If protection were to be given to new industries, it should be for some finite period and with regard to the potential for those industries to become internationally competitive in terms of the country's evolving comparative advantage (Dick, 1985: 19).

The first intimation that the government was heeding these calls for a more export-oriented trade regime came in March and April 1985. In March, the tariff system was rationalized through a reduction in the maximum *ad valorem* rate from 225 per cent to 60 per cent and a reduction in the number of rates. More dramatically, in April the notorious Directorate-General of Customs was relieved of all responsibility for the export and import of goods. Customs surveillance was handed over to a Swiss company with long experience in many parts of the developing world, clearance procedures were greatly simplified (the number of signatures required was reported to have declined from around 20 to just one), and the time taken to complete formalities was greatly reduced. Inter-island trade also benefited from the long overdue elimination of customs controls and the introduction of more efficient transhipment procedures (Dick, 1985: 11).

Such measures certainly served to startle the outside world into acceptance of the seriousness of the Indonesian government's deregulation drive. But they were insufficient in themselves to greatly affect the high-cost structure faced by many firms in manufacturing, trade, and transport which prevented them from becoming competitive international producers of goods and services. In spite of the sharp decline in the world oil price in early 1986 it appeared that the government was determined to continue with the policy of import restrictions through more systematic and comprehensive licensing, rather than move to a policy of active non-oil export promotion. The turning point came in May when a wide-ranging package was announced whose aim was to facilitate the purchase of imported inputs at world prices by firms producing in whole or part for export. Exporters were in fact allowed to import their raw materials directly, thus bypassing licensed importers entirely. The scheme was operated not by the Department of Trade but by the Department of Finance which was seen as a major victory for the deregulators in that ministry (Muir, 1986: 23).

The substantial devaluation of the rupiah in September 1986 was primarily intended to improve the competitiveness of Indonesian exports, and encourage domestic producers to begin selling in international markets.[9] Its initial impact, however, was on business confidence which was badly shaken. Even the announcement in October 1986 and January 1987 of substantial relaxations of quantitative restrictions on imports did not entirely restore confidence in the credibility of government policy-making. Assessments of the country's economic outlook through 1987 and into 1988 remained rather pessimistic. But the deregulation drive did not lose momentum. In July 1987 the system of textile and garment quota allocations to exporters was rationalized and in December a package of reforms was announced which were intended to further reduce quantitative import barriers, remove export licences and other barriers to export production, improve incentives for foreign investors, and revive the moribund domestic share market (Booth, 1988b). Various incentives were also given to the tourism industry. In October 1988 a long-awaited banking reform package was announced whose scope and consequences are discussed in detail in Chapter 3. In November further deregulation of inter-island shipping was announced and in 1989–90 further financial sector reforms were implemented. A start was also made on the complex issue of establishing performance criteria for state enterprises, with the aim of deciding what form ownership and control of such enterprises should ultimately take (Mackie and Sjahrir, 1989: 26–30).

Looking back on the achievements of the period from 1983 to 1990, it is obvious that much progress has been made towards the goal of making the Indonesian economy more internationally competitive. Certainly the government has been extremely successful in controlling domestic inflation after two large devaluations, thus bringing about a large and sustained fall in the real effective exchange rate.[10] This in turn has been an important factor in the growth of non-oil exports. But perhaps the most considerable achievement has been in changing the mental attitudes of both government officials and the business community. Although many officials are still hostile to the deregulation drive, especially when it threatens their jobs, status, and monetary remuneration, there can be little doubt that a sizeable constituency for liberalization has been built up within the government apparatus. This in turn has helped the confidence of both the foreign and domestic business community in exploiting the full potential of existing investments and in committing new investment funds.

There is no shortage of observers both in Indonesia and abroad who complain of the slow pace of reform, the 'zig-zag' character of the policy-making process and the 'mixed signals' which the government has been giving to the private sector.[11] They point to the continuing high, and varying, levels of tariff protection as evidence of the failure to liberalize the real economy as rapidly as the monetary sector, to the use of export bans to foster particular industries such as wood processing and rattan furniture, and to the persistent tendency to accord some state enterprises special privileges, especially those under the control of the Minister of Research and Technology.[12] Concern has also been expressed at the directives issued by the President to boost the role of co-operatives in the economy by, among other policies, facilitating their purchase of shares. Given the widespread evidence from unimpeachable sources that the vast majority of small enterprises in Indonesia in agriculture, manufacturing, trade, and transport make no use at all of the services of co-operatives, many question why they should become the principal vehicle of government redistributive policies.[13] There can be little doubt that, in issuing such directives, the government is reacting to perceived problems in society, some of which are deeply rooted and some of which have arisen as a direct result of the restructuring policies of the 1980s. It is thus appropriate to examine the nature of these problems, and what challenges they will pose for policy-making in the 1990s and beyond.

Problems for the Future

Java versus the Rest

The first and possibly the most serious of the problems facing Indonesia over the next decade concerns the issue of regional development. During the last decades of the colonial era there was widespread concern about declining living standards in Java, and this continued into the post-colonial period. That the poverty problem in Indonesia was predominantly a Javanese problem was true as late as 1976, when World Bank calculations indicated that 70 per cent of the urban poor and 74 per cent of the rural poor were located in Java (World Bank, 1980: 84). The regional distribution of the poor has been changing rapidly through the 1980s, in ways which are discussed in detail in Chapter 10. Real per capita consumption expenditure has been increasing more rapidly in urban Java than elsewhere, and by 1987 Java's share of the total poor population had fallen below 50 per cent. In 1987 eleven provinces outside Java had a higher proportion of their rural populations in poverty than any province in Java. These provinces include not just the traditionally backward provinces of West and East Nusa Tenggara but also resource-rich provinces such as East and Central Kalimantan, and agriculturally developed areas such as Bali, and South and Central Sulawesi.

Poverty levels in these and other provinces outside Java have not fallen as fast as in Java over the past decade because real per capita expenditures have not been growing as rapidly. It may seem surprising that in a province such as East Kalimantan, where accelerated exploitation of both petroleum and timber resources had led to the highest per capita GDP in the entire country by 1986, rural poverty levels were apparently higher than anywhere in Java (Table 10.18). In large part this paradox can be explained by the fact that only a small proportion of total gross regional domestic product was in fact retained in the province for either consumption or investment purposes (Table 1.6). In 1983–7 the export surplus (the difference between exports and imports of goods and non-factor services) in East Kalimantan amounted to, on average, over 60 per cent of regional GDP, while in Aceh it was over 70 per cent and in Irian Jaya just under 60 per cent.

The issue of unrequited export surpluses (or the 'drain') was a highly emotional one in the colonial period, both at the national and the regional level. Thee (1977: 59–60), has shown that the export surplus from the East Coast of Sumatra in the interwar period was much larger than for Indonesia as a whole, while Lindblad (1988: 213) has argued that South-east Kalimantan in the latter part of the colonial period earned 'a great deal from its export sales but precious little of the returns found their way back to the region, either as expenditures by recipients of wages or as a strengthened financial foundation of regional public policy'. In colonial times, the large national export surplus reflected substantial repatriation of expatriate salaries and profits abroad; in the immediate post-independence period the national surplus declined somewhat, but that from Sumatra, Kalimantan, and Sulawesi did not. This gave rise to the conviction that the export-producing Outer Islands

TABLE 1.6

The Export Surplus in Three Resource-abundant Provinces as a Percentage of Regional GDP[a]

Year	Aceh	East Kalimantan	Irian Jaya
1983	66.4	74.0	62.3
1984	74.3	67.8	66.7
1985	73.3	61.6	60.3
1986	73.0	56.6	55.0
1987	73.7	49.3	55.0

Source: BPS, Pendapatan Regional Provinsi-provinsi di Indonesia menurut Penggunaan, Jakarta, 1989, Tables 33–37.

[a] Calculated from data in constant 1983 prices. The export surplus is defined as the difference between exports and imports of goods and non-factor services.

were subsidizing the development of Java, and the resulting resentments
in turn fuelled the regional rebellions of the late 1950s and early
1960s.

In retrospect it is surprising that the oil boom period brought with it
no resurgence of regional nationalism in Indonesia, nor any demand for
a larger share of the profits to remain in the producing provinces. There
would seem to be two distinct reasons for this. On the one hand, most of
the oil came from Riau and East Kalimantan, two small and isolated
provinces conspicuously lacking in strong regional identities, or in much
tradition of regional nationalism. On the other hand, as numerous
authors have pointed out, the central government was astute in its recycling of the oil revenues, and through both the Inpres (Instruksi
Presiden) grants and foreign aid programmes, many of the more backward, resource-scarce provinces in both Java and the Outer Islands
received a considerable increase in development assistance in the 1970s.
But as is described more fully in Chapter 2, there was a steady decline in
the Inpres grants as a percentage of budgetary expenditures through the
1980s which was only partially made up in the more expansionary
1990/1 budget. In addition, the growing evidence that consumption
standards were increasing more rapidly in Java (especially urban Java)
than elsewhere, combined with Java's superior endowment of economic
and social infrastructure, have led to a widespread impression that the
national development process is favouring Java at the expense of the rest
of the country. This impression is reinforced both by the statistical evidence of the 'drain' from the resource-rich provinces, and by policies
such as the banning of exports of *rotan* (cane) which in effect is a tax on
smallholder producers outside Java, and a subsidy to the Java-based processing industry.

Solving these problems will not be easy or painless. One element in
the solution must be a more rational system of regional finance which
gives the provinces and subprovincial levels of government more taxing
powers and more expenditure responsibilities. It is suggested in Chapter 2 that such a system will probably involve greater provincial autonomy and greater control on the part of the regional governments over
the resources within their borders. At the same time, the central government will probably have to do more to even up the quality of central
government-provided services such as health and education between
provinces.

Matching Employment Opportunities with Educational Qualifications

One of the most significant achievements of the New Order government
has been a dramatic expansion in educational enrolments at all levels.
The share of plan resources committed to education has risen steadily
since *Repelita II* and the results of this are clearly obvious in the primary
and lower secondary enrolment ratios, which are now above the average
for low-income countries (World Bank, 1990: 234). Indeed from being
one of the least-educated of Asian countries, Indonesia has moved to a
position where primary education is almost universal, and where over

50 per cent of children in the 13–15 age group are enrolled in lower secondary schools. The *Repelita V* document contains further ambitious growth projections for enrolments at the lower and upper secondary levels, and in tertiary institutions (Booth, 1989: Table 11). Even if these targets are not fully met, there can be little doubt that the numbers of young people graduating from secondary and tertiary institutions and looking for employment will be at least a third higher in the mid-1990s than in 1988.

It appears that the government is determined to maintain the momentum of secondary and tertiary educational expansion, despite the evidence that graduates from these levels are already having considerable difficulty in finding the kinds of jobs that they and their parents might have expected, and that disparities in remuneration by educational level are diminishing (see Tables 10.12 and 11.13). The evidence from the 1986 *Sakernas* (National Labour Force Survey) indicates that senior secondary and tertiary graduates accounted for about half the unemployed, compared with only 17 per cent a decade earlier. Furthermore the great majority of these educated unemployed were under 30, and close to 70 per cent were in urban Java. There is in fact growing evidence that high school and tertiary graduates from the Outer Islands move to Java in the expectation that they will be able to find employment appropriate to their qualifications.

The government is clearly disturbed at the prospect of large numbers of educated young people congregating in urban Java in the hope that they will be able to find well-remunerated, white collar jobs in either the public or the private sector. The *Repelita V* document frankly acknowledges that many young people with tertiary qualifications are going to have to accept work that would not have been considered appropriate to their qualifications a few years ago. This will be even more true of the far more numerous graduates from the high school system. As Keyfitz (1989) has argued, such a 'levelling down' of employment expectations should not be considered a disaster but rather an inevitable part of the development process. In this sense the problem of the educated unemployed is more political and social than economic. But at the same time, there will have to be greater provision of training at the post-secondary level which is geared more closely to the needs of the labour market. The private sector is responding rapidly to this challenge, as the proliferation of 'academies' offering secretarial, bookkeeping, English, and computer courses makes clear. But access to these private institutions is very much determined by income. The limited state funds available for subsidizing post-secondary education in Indonesia over the next five years (beyond what is allocated to the universities and the polytechnics) must be reserved for programmes with substantial benefits to society as a whole, which the private sector is neglecting or under-investing in, and which benefit young people from the lower income groups. Such programmes might include certification courses for skilled tradespeople, and training for small entrepreneurs with proven 'survival capacity' who require new skills in order to expand their businesses.

Conglomerates, the Chinese Minority, and the Distribution of Wealth

In July 1989 a prominent Jakarta business magazine featured a table listing the 40 largest private business groups in Indonesia together with an estimate of their annual sales and assets.[14] Total annual sales of the 40 groups in 1988 were estimated to be Rp 37 trillion. Of this, the top 10 groups accounted for almost 57 per cent; all were controlled by Indonesians of Chinese extraction. The three largest *pribumi* businesses were controlled (in order of sales) by Julius Tahija, an Ambonese who was formerly General Manager of Caltex Pacific Indonesia, Bambang Trihatmodjo, the middle son of President Soeharto, and Soedarpo Sastrosatomo, who had established himself in shipping in the 1950s and had subsequently diversified into banking and pharmaceuticals.[15] In total, 12 of the 40 groups listed were controlled by *pribumi* interests, 4 of which were closely connected with the President's family. Other prominent indigenous businessmen included Aburizal Bakrie, the son of Achmad Bakrie who founded a successful commodity trading enterprise in the 1930s, Ibnu Sutowo, the former head of Pertamina, the state oil corporation, and Sumitro Djojohadikusumo, a former cabinet minister and university professor. The 12 *pribumi* firms together accounted for 17.9 per cent of total sales.

The list served to highlight the degree to which the Indonesian economy is dominated by a relatively small number of business groups, most of which are owned by Indonesians of Chinese descent. Indonesia is of course by no means unique in possessing a highly concentrated industrial structure; writers such as Leff (1978, 1979) have emphasized the extent to which product markets in the less developed countries (LDCs) are characterized by a high degree of concentration in industrial activities: 'In reality, however, the degree of market power is much greater than might appear from a consideration of concentration ratios in individual industries. This is because of a special feature of industrial organisation in the developing countries, the "large industrial house" or "Group".' (Leff, 1979: 722.) Leff goes on to argue that the oligopsonistic (imperfectly competitive) features of the large vertically integrated industrial groups impose considerable costs on the domestic economies of developing countries. These costs include not just static allocational inefficiencies, but also broader adverse economic effects, including distorted relative prices *vis-à-vis* the rest of the economy, a bias against labour absorption, and a downward rigidity in the prices of important industrial products which aggravates inflationary tendencies and frustrates attempts to alter domestic relative prices through, for example, exchange rate adjustments. 'In these conditions, private capitalism is often viewed unfavourably in the less-developed countries.' (Leff, 1979: 728.) This is especially likely to be the case when the profits from oligopolistic capitalism are seen to accrue to a closed circle of powerful entrepreneurs and their political patrons, from which the great majority of the population is excluded.

Whether the degree of industrial concentration and monopoly power in Indonesia is greater than in other developing countries is a difficult point to establish, although the evidence reviewed in Chapter 7 certainly suggests that many parts of the Indonesian manufacturing sector are characterized by a very high degree of market concentration.[16] But what makes the Indonesian situation unusual in comparison with other countries characterized by a high degree of industrial concentration (such as Pakistan, Mexico, or Brazil) is the fact that so many of the largest groups are either controlled by members of a numerically small ethnic minority (the Chinese), or by the family and close associates of the President. Inevitably this must give rise to a feeling among indigenous Indonesian entrepreneurs that the playing field is far from level, and that free and fair competition is being stifled in the interests of large profits for the few. What then can the government do to promote a more open and competitive entrepreneurial culture in Indonesia in the coming decade?

Equity and the Growth of an Entrepreneurial Culture

It can be plausibly argued that Indonesia is now a less regulated, more open, and competitive economy than at any time since the onset of the Great Depression in 1929. But the pre-war economy was still colonial in structure, with a large expatriate presence in both the government and the private sector, the Chinese minority dominating those parts of the urban economy such as retail trade which foreign enterprise was not interested in controlling, and the indigenous majority confined largely to peasant agriculture and denied access to modern education. This situation still prevailed in the early 1950s, after power was transferred to an independent government. In the late 1950s the government moved to expel Dutch-owned commercial enterprises and to curtail the role of the Chinese in the economy. Under other circumstances, these policies could have assisted the growth of an indigenous entrepreneurial class, but the economic and political climate of the 1960s was hardly conducive to such a development. The official rhetoric favoured state rather than private enterprise; indeed, as Castles (1965: 13) argued, 'rejection of capitalism and espousal of socialism as the preferred pattern of economic organization has been an almost universal element in Indonesian political ideology since independence'. Although there was little consensus about what sort of 'socialist' policies Indonesia should or could adopt, it was clear that the government did not wish to encourage the emergence of a vigorous, independent, and competitive class of private entrepreneurs, especially when they came from ethnic groups which tended to ally themselves with regional and religious opposition groups. The dominant Javanese military and bureaucratic élite preferred to deal on a patron–client basis with foreign or ethnic Chinese businesses over whom they could exert more control, and from whom they could extract more rents.

There is much evidence that these attitudes have continued into the New Order era, in spite of changing economic and social conditions and the progress towards economic liberalization which has characterized the 1980s. Certainly a wide range of credit and extension policies have been implemented which seek to encourage small entrepreneurs in all sectors of the economy, and the greatly increased access to secondary and tertiary education has expanded the pool of potential entrepreneurs enormously compared with the colonial and Old Order periods. But in spite of such obvious progress, the attitude of the government to the development of independent private enterprise remains at best ambivalent, and indeed some policy measures adopted by the government such as the removal of small traders from the precincts of new shopping centres have been seen as overtly discriminating against small entrepreneurs. By the late 1980s important segments of public opinion in Indonesia in the media, academe, and Parliament were increasingly ready to argue that, whatever the official rhetoric about supporting small entrepreneurs, the deregulation drive was benefiting only the large business groups and that the great majority of the population was gaining little from it.

That the government is concerned about such criticism is obvious, but its reaction has been somewhat ambivalent. On the one hand, it was announced in early 1990 that the 'soundness rating' accorded commercial banks by Bank Indonesia would in part be based on whether at least 20 per cent of their loan portfolio consisted of loans to 'small businesses' (Pangestu and Habir, 1990: 30), a measure clearly intended to push both state and private bank lending more in the direction of new entrepreneurs. On the other hand, the President reiterated that co-operatives must play a more important part in redistributing wealth, and made a highly publicized plea to the large private companies to sell 25 per cent of their shares to co-operatives in order to distribute profits more 'equitably'. Given the poor financial performance of many existing co-operatives, it is expected that most companies would probably meet this demand by establishing their own employee co-operatives, to which shares could then be sold, probably at a concessional rate.[17] While this might be desirable as a way of increasing employee participation in the particular enterprise, it is most unlikely to have much impact on the distribution of wealth in the economy at large. Neither is it likely to have any effect on the present high concentration of ownership in the non-agricultural sectors of the economy.

Indeed it is not even obvious that the government perceives this high concentration as a problem. Many senior officials, probably influenced by their interpretation of the 'Japanese' or the 'Korean' model, seem convinced that large conglomerates (and large state enterprises) are essential if Indonesia is to 'catch up' with modern technology, and compete internationally. This equation of 'bigness' with efficiency persists in spite of evidence that the industries which have been particularly successful in boosting exports, such as garments and footwear, are not dominated by large conglomerates but rather consist of quite a large number of enterprises which concentrate on one product, or on a small range of products. It can in fact be argued that the continued success of the non-oil export drive will depend upon a growing number of new entrepreneurs entering a range of manufacturing industries and tourist-related services, rather than upon the existing conglomerates becoming even larger.

The issue then becomes how government can best facilitate the emergence of new entrepreneurs. It is not obvious that the imposition of arbitrary quantitative targets on lending institutions is desirable; they may result in a large number of non-performing assets which in the longer run will raise the price of credit to efficient enterprises. Neither are continued attempts to promote co-operatives likely to foster the growth of an entrepreneurial culture. What is crucial is the continued ability of Indonesia's economic managers to create and maintain an open and competitive domestic trading environment, reduce barriers to entry in all sectors of the economy, and provide access to credit and other support services at market-determined prices. While it is true that key economic policy-makers in the Ministry of Finance, Bank Indonesia, and the National Development Planning Board (Bappenas, Badan Perencanaan Pembangunan Nasional) have been able to operate with relative freedom over the past decade, avoiding 'capture' by special interest groups, it cannot be taken for granted that this will continue. Powerful individuals and corporations can easily exploit the genuine concern in many quarters over the distribution of income and wealth in order to persuade the government to implement policies which will benefit narrow sectional interests at the expense of longer-run growth and greater equity. Whether the government will be sufficiently strong and far-sighted to avoid these pressures, and continue to support the process of economic restructuring into the 1990s and beyond remains to be seen.

1. Under a regime of flexible exchange rates, the real appreciation effect would have been reflected in an actual appreciation of the exchange rate; in Indonesia where the rate against the US dollar was fixed for seven years, the appreciation occurred through the faster rate of domestic inflation relative to major trading partners. See in particular the discussion in McCawley (1980) and Corden and Warr (1981).

2. For an estimate of ICORs in the main Asian economies in the early 1950s, see *Economic Survey of Asia and the Far East, 1961* by the United Nations Economic Commission for Asia and the Far East (1962: 24).

3. See Chapter 2 and the literature cited there for a more detailed discussion of this point.

4. See in particular Cornwall (1977: Chapter 5) for an illuminating discussion of the OECD experience.

5. Preliminary figures released by the BPS in August 1990 estimated that GDP grew in 1989 by 7.4 per cent, and non-oil GDP grew by 8.2 per cent.

6. In fact manufacturing sector growth rates averaged 11.7 per cent per annum between 1983 and 1989, according to the most recent BPS data.

7. See Warr (1986) and Chapter 5 for an extended discussion of this issue.

8. In a more recent paper, Pangestu (1989) has asserted that 'it was not the idea of the originators of the system that quantitative restrictions should develop'. Rather the idea was to encourage the professional development of importers, and to assist them in bargaining with international suppliers.

9. Assertions by some commentators that the 1986 devaluation was mainly intended to increase government revenues through the impact on the rupiah value of oil revenues were clearly wrong. By 1986 the foreign surplus on the budget (i.e. the difference between foreign revenues and foreign expenditures) was very small because of the rapid rise in foreign debt servicing obligations. There can be little doubt that the devaluation was carried out mainly for balance of payments reasons.

10. For comparative data on real effective exchange rates in Asia, see Asian Development Bank (1990: 246–7). Indonesia has effected the largest decline in the real effective exchange rate since 1980 of any country in the region. However, as is pointed out in Chapter 5, the very sharp decline in the real effective exchange rate may not be a reliable indicator of the trend in relative prices of traded and non-traded goods within the domestic economy, especially in the aftermath of a large devaluation.

11. In an illuminating discussion of the 'political economy' of deregulation in Indonesia, Soesastro (1989) has pointed out that key technocrats, such as the former Co-ordinating Minister of Economic Affairs, have not been concerned about the slow pace of reform, as a policy of gradualism made it easier for them to enlarge the constituency for further reform.

12. See Mackie and Sjahrir (1989: 30) for further details.

13. For a discussion of the evidence on the use of the rural KUDs by rice farmers, see in particular Booth (1988a: 153). Chapter 9 in this volume discusses the evidence on the use of co-operatives by small traders.

14. *Warta Ekonomi*, 31 July 1989.

15. See Yoshihara (1988: 173–83) for further details of these and other *pribumi* businessmen in Indonesia.

16. A comparison with data on the Korean conglomerates or *chaebol* is instructive. According to one estimate, in 1974, the sales of the top ten *chaebol* equalled 15.1 per cent of Korean GDP. In 1984 this had risen to 67.4 per cent (Amsden, 1989: 116). By way of comparison, sales of the top ten companies listed in *Warta Ekonomi* accounted for 14.8 per cent of GDP in 1988.

17. One model which attracted attention in early 1990 was the sale of shares in a tea estate whose issued capital was largely owned by foundations closely connected to the Soeharto family. The shares were sold at par, funded by interest-free loans to be repaid from dividend earnings. The recipients were KUD in the area, and employee and smallholder co-operatives. Other high-profile entrepreneurs such as Mr Bob Hasan were reported to be following suit. See Conroy and Drake (1990).

REFERENCES

Amsden, Alice H. (1989), *Asia's Next Giant: South Korea and Late Industrialisation*, New York: Oxford University Press.

Arndt, H. W. (1983), 'Survey of Recent Developments', *Bulletin of Indonesian Economic Studies*, 19(2): 1–26.

Asian Development Bank (1990), *Asian Development Outlook 1990*, Manila: Asian Development Bank.

Biro Pusat Statistik (BPS) (monthly), *Indikator Ekonomi* [Economic Indicators], Jakarta.

Booth, Anne (1988a), *Agricultural Development in Indonesia*, Sydney: Allen & Unwin for the Asian Studies Association of Australia.

_____ (1988b), 'Survey of Recent Developments', *Bulletin of Indonesian Economic Studies*, 24(1): 3–36.

_____ (1989), 'Repelita V and Indonesia's Medium Term Economic Strategy', *Bulletin of Indonesian Economic Studies*, 25(2): 3–30.

_____ (1990), 'The Evolution of Fiscal Policy and the Role of Government in the Colonial Economy', in Anne Booth, W. J. O'Malley, and Anna Weidemann (eds.), *Indonesian Economic History in the Dutch Colonial Era*, New Haven: Yale University, Southeast Asia Studies.

Bruton, Henry (1984), 'Economic Development with Unlimited Supplies of Foreign Exchange', in G. Ranis, R. West, M. Leiserson, and C. T. Morris (eds.), *Comparative Development Perspectives: Essays in Honour of L. G. Reynolds*, Boulder: Westview Press.

Castles, Lance (1965), 'Socialism and Private Business: The Latest Phase', *Bulletin of Indonesian Economic Studies*, No. 1: 13–39.

Conroy, J. D. and Drake, P. J. (1990), 'Survey of Recent Developments', *Bulletin of Indonesian Economic Studies*, 26(2): 5–41.

Corden, W. M. and Warr, P. G. (1981), 'The Petroleum Boom and Exchange Rate Policy in Indonesia', *Ekonomi dan Keuangan Indonesia*, 29: 335–59.

Cornwall, John (1977), *Modern Capitalism: Its Growth and Transformation*, Oxford: Martin Robertson.

Dick, H. W. (1985), 'Survey of Recent Developments', *Bulletin of Indonesian Economic Studies*, 21(3): 1–29.

Glassburner, Bruce (1986), 'Survey of Recent Developments', *Bulletin of Indonesian Economic Studies*, 22(1): 1–33.

Hanson, John R. (1980), *Trade in Transition: Exports from the Third World, 1840–1900*, New York: Academic Press.

Hobohm, Sarwar O. H. (1987), 'Survey of Recent Developments', *Bulletin of Indonesian Economic Studies*, 23(2): 1–37.

Keyfitz, Nathan (1989), 'Putting Trained Labour Power to Work: The Dilemma of Education and Employment', *Bulletin of Indonesian Economic Studies*, 25(3): 35–56.

Leff, Nathaniel H. (1978), 'Industrial Organisation and Entrepreneurship in the Developing Countries: The Economic Groups', *Economic Development and Cultural Change*, 26(4): 661–75.

____ (1979), '"Monopoly Capitalism" and Public Policy in Developing Countries', *Kyklos*, 32(4): 718–38.

Lindblad, J. Thomas (1988), *Between Dyak and Dutch: The Economic History of Southeast Kalimantan, 1880–1942*, Dordrecht: Foris Publications for KITLV.

McCawley, P. T. (1980), 'Indonesia's New Balance of Payments Problem: A Surplus to Get Rid Of', *Ekonomi dan Keuangan Indonesia*, 28(1): 39–58.

Mackie, Jamie and Sjahrir (1989), 'Survey of Recent Developments', *Bulletin of Indonesian Economic Studies*, 25(3): 3–35.

Muir, Ross (1986), 'Survey of Recent Developments', *Bulletin of Indonesian Economic Studies*, 22(2): 1–27.

Pangestu, Mari (1987), 'Survey of Recent Developments', *Bulletin of Indonesian Economic Studies*, 23(1): 1–39.

____ (1989), 'Indonesian Trade Policy: A Perspective', Paper presented at the Conference on Indonesia's New Order, Australian National University, Canberra, 4 – 9 December.

Pangestu, Mari and Boediono (1986), 'Indonesia: The Structure and Causes of Manufacturing Sector Protection', in Christopher Findlay and Ross Garnaut (eds.), *The Political Economy of Manufacturing Protection: Experiences of ASEAN and Australia*, Sydney: Allen & Unwin, pp. 1–47.

Pangestu, Mari and Habir, Manggi (1990), 'Survey of Recent Developments', *Bulletin of Indonesian Economic Studies*, 26(1): 3–36.

Pitt, Mark (1981), 'Alternative Trade Strategies and Employment in Indonesia', in Anne O. Krueger et al. (eds.), *Trade and Employment in Developing Countries, Vol. 1*, Chicago: University of Chicago Press for the NBER, pp. 181–236.

Rosendale, Phyllis (1975), 'The Indonesian Terms of Trade: 1950–73', *Bulletin of Indonesian Economic Studies*, 11(3): 50–80.

_____ (1981), 'The Balance of Payments', in Anne Booth and Peter McCawley (eds.), *The Indonesian Economy during the Soeharto Era*, Kuala Lumpur: Oxford University Press, pp. 162–80.

Soesastro, M. Hadi (1989), 'The Political Economy of Deregulation in Indonesia', *Asian Survey*, 29(9): 853–69.

Sundrum, R. M. (1986), 'Indonesia's Rapid Economic Growth: 1968–81', *Bulletin of Indonesian Economic Studies*, 22(3): 40–69.

_____ (1988), 'Indonesia's Slow Economic Growth: 1981–86', *Bulletin of Indonesian Economic Studies*, 24(1): 37–72.

Thee Kian Wie (1977), *Plantation Agriculture and Export Growth: An Economic History of East Sumatra, 1863–1942*, Jakarta: National Institute of Economic and Social Research.

United Nations Economic Commission for Asia and the Far East (1962), *Economic Survey of Asia and the Far East, 1961*, Bangkok: United Nations.

Warr, Peter G. (1984), 'Exchange Rate Protection in Indonesia', *Bulletin of Indonesian Economic Studies*, 20(2): 53–89.

_____ (1986), 'Indonesia's Other Dutch Disease: Economic Effects of the Petroleum Boom', in J. Peter Neary and Sweder van Wijnbergen (eds.), *Natural Resources and the Macroeconomy*, Oxford: Basil Blackwell, pp. 288–323.

World Bank (1980), *Employment and Income Distribution in Indonesia: A World Bank Country Study*, Washington, DC.

_____ (1983), *World Development Report*, Washington, DC.

_____ (1989), *World Development Report*, Washington, DC.

_____ (1990), *World Development Report*, Washington, DC.

Yoshihara, Kunio (1988), *The Rise of Ersatz Capitalism in South-East Asia*, Singapore: Oxford University Press.

PART I
MACROECONOMIC
POLICY-MAKING

2
Fiscal Policy
Mukul G. Asher and Anne Booth

Introduction

FROM its inception, the New Order government viewed the failure of fiscal control as a major reason for the economic disintegration of the early 1960s, and set itself a number of ambitious targets in this area of policy. The revenue base was to be diversified away from reliance on foreign trade taxes, and the budget was to be strictly balanced in the sense that total expenditures would not exceed receipts from all sources, including foreign aid and borrowing. Furthermore government savings (defined as total government revenues minus foreign aid and borrowing minus routine expenditures) were to increase over time to allow the gradual elimination of foreign aid and borrowing as a means of financing the development budget. This would be done by curbing routine expenditures on the one hand and intensifying the collection of domestic revenues on the other.

During the 1970s the realization of these goals was both aided and impeded by the oil boom. On the one hand the oil revenues greatly increased domestic (i.e. non-aid) revenues and thus enabled a growing proportion of development expenditures to be funded from these revenues, albeit at the cost of growing inflationary pressures. But the very rapid growth in oil revenues meant there was little incentive to intensify collections of non-oil domestic revenues such as the income and the sales tax. By 1980 non-oil tax revenues accounted for less than 30 per cent of total tax revenues and only 25 per cent of total budgetary expenditures.

The major aim of the tax reforms of the 1980s was to intensify collection of non-oil taxes, and by 1990 it was clear that considerable success had been achieved in this area of policy reform. But the process of fiscal readjustment imposed on the government by the oil price decline brought other problems in its wake. In the early 1980s both the government and the state enterprises borrowed heavily abroad (much of it in non-dollar currencies) to fund development programmes. Two large devaluations of the rupiah together with the dollar realignment of 1985–6 meant that the rupiah burden of financing the resulting debt

service obligations grew steadily as a proportion of government expenditures through the 1980s. As a result of the rapid growth in debt service
expenditures, both non-debt routine expenditures (mainly salaries and
wages) and non-aid funded development expenditures have fallen
sharply relative to total government expenditures and relative to GDP.
By the late 1980s the proportion of the development budget funded by
foreign aid and borrowing was even higher than in 1969.

The *Repelita V* document forecasts a rapid decline in aid reliance in
the first four years of the 1990s. To achieve this target it will be essential
to improve non-oil tax performance further over the level achieved in
the late 1980s; it will also be essential to curb routine expenditures, and
especially debt service obligations, relative to development expenditures.
The prospects for such changes are assessed in the following sections. A
further legacy of the oil boom, the highly centralized nature of the fiscal
system, and ways in which this could be reformed in the 1990s are also
examined.

Tax Reform Policies

As a broad generalization, it can be claimed that from 1950 to the beginning of the 1980s, tax policy changes in Indonesia were confined to
piecemeal changes, involving only certain aspects of a particular tax or a
small set of taxes, leaving the overall tax structure and procedures
broadly unchanged.[1] Since the initiation of the tax reform process in
January 1981, Indonesia has implemented far-reaching systemic changes
in tax policy and administration. The Harvard Institute of International
Development (HIID) was chosen as the external institution for carrying
out a variety of technical studies, and for drafting a tax reform package
and the necessary legislation. Three years elapsed between the initiation
of the tax reform process and the passage of tax laws by Parliament in
December 1983 which embodied the initial tax reform programme. The
process of drafting the reform programme was secretive and authoritar-
ian rather than open and participative, and because the technical studies
which presumably formed the basis for the proposals have not been
published, it is difficult to make an independent evaluation of their
quality.[2] But six years after the passage of the tax laws it is possible to
make a preliminary evaluation of their impact.

In December 1983, the Indonesian Parliament in fact approved three
laws: General Tax Provisions and Procedures (Law Number 6, 1983);
Income Tax Law (Law Number 7, 1983); and Value Added Tax on
Goods and Services and Sales Tax on Luxury Goods (Law Number 8,
1983). The law concerning the Land and Buildings Tax (Law Number
12, 1985) and the Stamp Duty Law (Law Number 13, 1985) were
passed in 1985. President Soeharto called the 1983 Laws 'national
monuments'. This designation ensured almost no opposition to them,
and parliamentary approval was swift, with almost no changes. The new
income tax was implemented in January 1984; while the value added tax

and the luxury sales tax (henceforth the VAT package) were implemented in April 1985. The land and buildings tax and the new stamp duty
were initiated in January 1986. Several modifications, particularly in the
VAT package, have been introduced since then. There have also been
changes in the taxes not covered under the tax reform programme, such
as foreign trade taxes.

In analysing the impact of this bold programme of reform, two major
constraints should be kept in mind. The first is the relatively short time
period which has elapsed since the introduction of the tax reform programme; some significant modifications were introduced only in April
1989, and their impact can only be guessed at. Second, fiscal and other
relevant information in Indonesia is not yet regarded as a public good
and even such basic information as the number of taxpayers and the
sectoral or other breakdowns of tax revenue is not available from regularly published sources. As a result, the discussion here, by necessity, is
largely qualitative and deductive.

Objectives of the Tax Reform

Among the major deficiencies of the pre-reform tax system were its
inadequate revenue productivity as reflected in the low and declining
non-oil tax revenue (NOTR) to GDP ratio (Table 2.1); uneven
enforcement and compliance, in part due to complexities and ambigu-
ities in the tax laws, regulations, and procedures; and the unintended
wide dispersion in effective rates among activities, sectors, and products
leading to both inefficiency in allocation of resources and horizontal and
vertical inequities among individual taxpayers. Moreover, the fiscal system was highly centralized (Booth, 1986: 79), an issue which is
addressed in more detail below. In general, the objectives of the tax
reform were designed to overcome these deficiencies. The first objective
was to increase the NOTR/GDP ratio.[3] While no specific target was
provided, it appears that *Repelita IV*'s target of a NOTR/GDP ratio of
10 per cent by 1988/9 was taken as a working goal. According to the
Repelita V document, NOTR is projected to equal 12.8 per cent of
GDP over the *Repelita V* period; non-oil domestic revenues, including
non-tax revenues, will average 14.4 per cent of GDP (Booth, 1989a:
13).

The second objective was to streamline the tax laws and improve the
efficiency of the administrative system charged with the transfer of
resources to the public sector. The third objective was to reduce tax-
induced distortions in the allocation of resources. The fourth objective
was to ensure that the poor would not be made worse off as a result of
the reform, although the programme was not designed to improve
income distribution.

From the beginning it was clear that the main instrument for achieving the first objective of increasing the NOTR/GDP ratio was the VAT
package. The expectation was that the income tax, the land and buildings tax, and improved administration would together make a significant

contribution to improving the NOTR/GDP ratio only in the medium term. To achieve the second objective, the new tax laws have been designed to be substantially free of ambiguity. Extensive definitions of taxable objects and subjects with quantified criteria are included in the laws themselves and the statutory bases have been clearly identified. The legal base for the various taxes is defined quite broadly, and exemptions and exclusions are minimized. Instead of the old official assessment system, the reform programme adopts self-assessment, thus transferring to the taxpayer primary responsibility for filing a return, for determining tax liability, and for paying taxes. Failure to meet these responsibilities on the part of the taxpayer is, under the law, subject to automatic fines and penalties. These tax procedures are designed to enhance 'deperson-alisation' of tax administration. This implies a considerable reduction in the contacts between tax administration personnel and taxpayers, and a substantial reduction in opportunities for bargaining over tax liability. The enforcement is to be undertaken primarily through selective audit-ing and internal checking. Modern management techniques, including computerization of tax administration and extensive training schemes, have also been adopted.

The third objective of reducing tax-induced distortions was to be achieved by defining the income tax base broadly, and by eliminating all income tax based fiscal incentives. Nominal tax rates were reduced sub-stantially, particularly at the upper end of the income scale, and a com-mon rate structure for the income tax on both individuals and companies has been established. Introduction of the VAT was expected to reduce input taxation which was regarded as an important source of distortion in commodity taxation. Greater uniformity and consistency in tax administration was also expected to lead to a reduction in tax-induced distortions. It should be stressed that the tax reform programme sought neutrality in taxation, i.e. uniform tax rates across sectors, activ-ities, and commodities, as a practical means of reducing distortions in allocation of resources.

The fourth objective of not making the poor worse off was to be achieved by keeping the nominal rates low; by eliminating exemptions enjoyed by high-income groups; and by using exemption levels, particu-larly for the income tax and the land and buildings tax, to keep the poor outside the tax net.

The Tax Reform Programme: A Brief Description

The Income Tax

As a result of the tax reform, there is now a single income tax called Pajak Penghasilan (PPH), thus ending the previous practice of applying separate laws to individuals and to businesses. The new law represents a fundamental departure from the old income tax law in several ways. It adopts the principle of broad-base low nominal rates; adopts an identical rate structure for the personal and company income tax;[4] uses a 'self-assessment' system instead of the 'official assessment' used earlier; and structures the income tax in such a manner as to reduce as much as possible the discretionary powers of the tax administrator. Each taxpayer is required to register and acquire a unique taxpayer identification number.[5] The new income tax law does not contain any income tax based fiscal incentives for attracting investment, though those based on indirect taxes such as import duties are retained. Extensive use of withholding provisions to collect income (and other taxes) is also envisaged.[6]

Under the old personal income tax system, there were seventeen rates (from 5 per cent to 50 per cent). For corporations, rates of 20, 30, and 45 per cent were applied. The new income tax is levied at rates of 15, 25, and 35 per cent; this applies to both individuals and companies. However, foreign firms which remit dividends abroad are subject to a 20 per cent tax on the amount remitted, so that the effective tax rate for repatriated income is 48 per cent (Gillis, 1989: 103). The 20 per cent rate, however, can be lowered by a tax treaty.

Only individuals are allowed personal deductions. A principal earner, with a non-working wife and three dependants, is subject to income tax only if his income exceeds Rp 2.9 million per year or about four times per capita income in 1988. This is expected to increase to Rp 4.3 million in 1990 or slightly less than six times 1988 per capita income. Before the tax reforms, the exemption level was around two and a half times the 1983 per capita income for a principal earner with three children. An additional Rp 960,000 (Rp 1.4 million from 1990) is allowed as a deduction for a wife who has income from business or professional work not related to that of her husband or another family member.

The tax base is defined quite broadly, and includes most fringe benefits. Capital gains are also taxed in principle, but this has not yet been implemented. From 1990, however, a capital gains tax on share transactions will be introduced. Since late 1988, income from interest on time and savings deposits has also been subjected to tax. From 1990, however, interest on deposits of up to Rp 5 million will be exempted from the income tax. Contributions to approved pension funds are fully deductible, while pension benefits are taxed when received. The exit tax of Rp 250,000 is considered to be an advance payment on the personal income tax and can be deducted fully from the final personal income tax liability in any given year.

The new income tax law also incorporates a simplified depreciation scheme, which generally results in more rapid depreciation than was previously permitted. Vintage accounting using historical costs is now replaced by the declining balance method using the written down value as the basis for depreciation (an exception is made when a 5 per cent depreciation rate is applied). Four different depreciation rates apply compared with ten previously. Firms with an annual turnover of less than Rp 120 million may apply for special calculation norms for the determination of taxable income. Overseas income earned by a domestic taxpayer is taxable in Indonesia. However, a foreign tax credit is allowed. Thus, in principle, tax liability is determined on global income.

The VAT Package

Under the VAT package implemented in April 1985, the VAT is levied on domestically produced goods and on imports. Exports and capital goods are zero-rated. Exemptions from the VAT are confined to unprocessed foods and a few other items. The difference between the zero rate and exemption is that input taxes on the former are refundable, while this is not the case for exempted goods. Analytically, the main distinction between the old and new sales tax is that all input taxes can now be credited against the output tax. Small firms, defined as those having an annual turnover of Rp 60 million or less (Rp 30 million for service firms) are exempt from the VAT. This means that while they do not pay output tax, input taxes paid by such firms are not refundable. In the original VAT package, contractors' services were also subject to the VAT. The VAT package also included a luxury tax. This tax is in addition to the VAT, and cannot be credited against an output tax.

At the time of the introduction of the VAT package, the VAT rates were zero for exempt goods and services, 10 per cent for taxed goods and services, and 10 and 20 per cent for the luxury sales tax. Effective from 15 January 1989, a 30 per cent category for luxury goods has been added and the number of such items expanded. From 1 April 1989, the VAT has been extended to wholesalers and to 21 services. VAT on domestic air transportation and telecommunications services became effective from 15 January 1989. In both these cases, VAT is based on turnover and cannot be credited against the output tax.

The Land and Building Tax (Pajak Bumi dan Bangunan or PBB)

This tax replaces taxes relating to property levied under seven ordinances (Soemitro, 1986). The rate is 0.5 per cent. The base is the sales value of land and buildings instead of the annual rental value used previously. Since 20 per cent of the sales value is used as the base, the effective rate is 0.1 per cent (0.20 x 0.5) of the sales value. The official market values for land range from Rp 100 to Rp 3.1 million per square metre, and for buildings from Rp 50,000 to Rp 1.2 million per square metre. Buildings with a sales value below Rp 3.5 million are not taxed; this value is considered high enough to exempt virtually all rural housing and a large share of low income urban housing. There are minimal formal exemptions from the PBB. In practice, exemptions for individuals who may have large assets but little cash flow have been given on a case by case basis. The PBB is administered centrally, though regional authorities have important collection responsibilities. The revenue from the PBB is shared among various levels of government as follows: central government, 19 per cent; provinces, 16.2 per cent; and municipalities and kabupaten, 64.8 per cent. However, from the viewpoint of initiation and control, the PBB is a central rather than local tax, as indeed was the old Ipeda (Iuran Pembangunan Daerah) which it replaces.

Stamp Duties

The complicated 1921 Stamp Duty Law, involving both specific and *ad valorem* rates, has been replaced by a new law which levies only two specific rates of Rp 500 and Rp 1,000 depending on the type of document and the amount mentioned in the document.

Other Taxes

During the 1980s, but particularly since 1986, Indonesia has tended to move away from non-tariff barriers and towards tariffs. In April 1985, the government completely reorganized the operations of the Directorate-General of Customs. The contract to undertake most of the inspection of imported goods and to collect taxes and duties was given to a Swiss firm, Société Générale de Surveillance (SGS). The indications are, however, that the Indonesian government will once again undertake the tasks currently performed by the SGS when the company's current contract expires in April 1991. Indonesia continues to levy export duties on selected commodities such as pepper and timber at specific or *ad valorem* rates depending on the type of commodity. However, export tax receipts have declined sharply since 1979/80, when a supplementary tax was imposed, and are now a very small revenue earner. There have been few significant changes in excises which are levied on cigarettes, beer, and a limited number of other items.

Performance of the Reformed Tax System

The analysis of the performance of the reformed tax system below is based on the extent to which the four tax reform objectives listed above have been realized.

The NOTR/GDP Ratio

During the first year of tax reform when only the new income tax law was implemented, the NOTR/GDP ratio fell from 5.7 per cent in 1983/4 to 5.3 per cent in 1984/5 (Table 2.1). The ratio, however, increased sharply in 1985/6 when the VAT package was implemented. It was fairly constant for the next two years and then increased sharply again in 1988/9 to 8.5 per cent of GDP (revised estimates). Between 1984/5 and 1985/6 the VAT accounted for about four-fifths of the total increase in NOTR, while the income tax accounted for just one-tenth. Between 1987/8 and 1988/9 the contribution of the income tax to the growth in NOTR was 41 per cent; this was higher than that of the VAT (35.6 per cent). The 1988/9 ratio, while still short of the *Repelita IV* target of 10 per cent, was much closer to the target than could have been

TABLE 2.1

Government Revenues and Expenditures as a Percentage of GDP,
1983–1989[a]

Year[b]	Total Revenues	NOTR[c]	Oil and Gas Revenues	Foreign Aid and Borrowing	Total Expenditures
1983	23.5	5.7 (7.3)	12.3	5.0	23.6
1984	21.6	5.3 (6.8)	11.6	3.9	21.6
1985	23.5	6.8 (8.3)	11.5	3.7	23.5
1986	21.3	8.4 (8.7)	6.1	5.6	21.3
1987	21.6	7.0 (8.4)	8.0	4.9	21.6
1988	23.2	8.4 (9.9)	9.5	7.0	23.2
1989	22.9	9.3 (10.7)	10.5	5.7	22.9

Sources: Bank Indonesia, Indonesian Financial Statistics, October 1989; GDP data as
   issued by BPS in September 1989.
[a]Revised GDP estimates as published in 1990.
[b]Fiscal year beginning in year shown. GDP data are calendar year figures.
[c]Figures in brackets refer to NOTR as a ratio of GDP excluding oil and gas.

predicted on the basis of the 1987/8 performance. (It was in fact almost
exactly 10 per cent of GDP, excluding the oil and gas sectors.)

The NOTR to GDP ratio is estimated to be 9.5 per cent for 1989/90
(Table 2.1). As noted earlier, significant extensions of the VAT, widening the income tax base to include interest on time and savings deposits,
and an increase in the tax base of the PBB all became fully effective only
in 1989/90. The share of the NOTR in total tax revenue is expected to
be almost two-thirds in 1989/90, compared to slightly less than one-
third in 1983/4 (Table 2.2).

The above discussion suggests that the role of NOTR in the revenue
structure has increased significantly. The increase in the NOTR/GDP
ratio from 5.7 per cent in 1983/4 to 8.5 per cent in 1988/9, while not
entirely in accord with the Repelita IV target, was a reasonable performance. It is worth noting, however, that, even assuming that the revenue
target for 1989/90 is realized, only two-fifths of total expenditure will be
financed from NOTR (Table 2.2). While this represents a substantial
improvement on the Repelita III performance, the role of development
receipts, i.e. programme and project aid and foreign borrowing, in
financing development expenditure has increased sharply during the
1980s, from only 25 per cent in 1981/2 to 86 per cent in 1989/90,
although this percentage should decline somewhat in 1990/1. Thus,
Indonesia's reliance on external financing of government expenditure
has increased substantially in spite of the Repelita IV NOTR/GDP target
being largely met.

Revenue targets for the Repelita V period are more ambitious than
those for the previous plan. NOTR is projected to account for
68.4 per cent of total domestic revenues in 1993/4, compared with

TABLE 2.2
Indicators of Revenue Reliance, 1969–1990

Fiscal Year Beginning	NOTR as a Percentage of Total Tax Revenue	NOTR as a Percentage of Total Expenditure	Foreign Aid and Borrowing as a Percentage of Development Expenditure
1969	80.1	57.6	77.1
1974	42.3	36.1	24.1
1979	34.6	27.9	34.4
1980	29.2	24.7	25.3
1981	27.4	23.3	24.6
1982	31.8	26.6	26.4
1983	31.6	24.0	39.2
1984	31.5	24.7	34.9
1985	37.3	29.0	32.9
1986	57.7	39.5	69.0
1987	46.6	32.6	65.0
1988	55.6	36.1	81.6
1989	57.8	40.4	68.2
1990[a]	62.8	42.5	69.6

Source: Bank Indonesia, *Indonesian Financial Statistics*, various years.
[a]Budget estimates.

58.6 per cent in 1988/9, while the proportion of the development budget funded by foreign aid and borrowing is expected to decline to 40.1 per cent (Booth, 1989a: 11). Further scope for extension of the base of major taxes, increases in tax rates, and rapid economic growth are likely to be of relatively minor importance in achieving these targets. The main instrument will have to be improvements in administrative efficiency and capability, and continued political determination to increase the compliance levels. The need for continued political will arises because achieving the revenue targets will clearly require much larger tax payments from both Chinese and *pribumi* professionals and businessmen, as well as from foreign investors. These groups have benefited significantly from the economic policies pursued under President Soeharto and are important supporters of the present regime. Bringing them more firmly into the tax net will be a major challenge for tax administrators over the next five years.

What have been the effects of the tax reform programme on the tax mix? To answer this question, a brief discussion of the contribution of various taxes to changes in NOTR during the post-tax reform period is necessary, beginning with income tax. Before 1988/9, the revenue performance of income tax was disappointing. Indeed, in 1987/8 the income tax revenue to GDP ratio was lower than the pre-reform ratio. Throughout the *Repelita IV* period, it has been corporate rather than personal income which has provided the bulk of income tax revenue (Table 2.3). State enterprises provided a significant proportion of corporate income tax revenue although their share has been declining relative to that of private companies. Extensive withholding provisions must have meant significant increases in contributions from wage and salary income, so it is the failure to tax income of the self-employed and income from capital effectively which is the main reason for the disappointing performance.[7]

The income tax revenue to GDP ratio increased to 2.8 per cent of GDP in 1988/9, and is projected to reach 3.2 per cent of GDP in 1989/90 (Table 2.4). This is substantially higher than the ratio before the reform. Both personal and corporate income tax revenues are expected to rise significantly in 1989/90 and 1990/1; some analysts estimate that the tax on time and saving deposits interest, which was implemented in November 1988, will alone contribute about 10 per cent of income tax revenues. As disaggregated data are not available, it is not possible to ascertain in which sectors and activities the sudden increases in income tax revenues occurred in 1988/9 or where the large projected increases are expected to come from. Was the increase in 1988/9 the result of increased technical capability on the part of the tax administration, achieved through investment in training and hardware, and matched by heightened political will to enforce the law? If the answer is yes, then the increase could signal a qualitative change in tax administration in Indonesia. It is also possible that certain technical changes, such as classifying a proportion of royalties from oil or dividends from public enterprises as income tax revenue contributed significantly to the 1988/9 increase in income tax revenue. In the absence of any official explanation, it is difficult to be specific.

In contrast to the income tax, revenues from the VAT package began to increase immediately after the new laws were implemented. The VAT revenue to GDP ratio in 1988/9 was about three times the corresponding ratio in 1983/4 (Table 2.4). Even considering that the VAT package included petroleum products which were untaxed earlier, that cigarettes and alcoholic products were for the first time subjected to both the VAT and the excise, and that the VAT paid by government departments is included in the revenue figures, the growth in revenues still remains impressive. While the VAT is not self-enforcing, and the cross-checking potential of the VAT has not been much utilized in Indonesia so far, it does appear that the VAT is more difficult to evade than the single stage manufacturer–importer sales tax it replaced.

Because of the extension of the VAT to wholesalers and to a large number of services, and because of increases in rates for the luxury sales tax, the revenue from the VAT is expected to increase significantly in 1989/90 and in 1990/1. The importance of the VAT for revenue generation is evident from a comparison of shares of the income tax and the VAT in NOTR before and after tax reform. In 1983/4, the income tax accounted for 40.6 per cent of the NOTR, while the sales tax accounted for 18.9 per cent. By 1988/9, the shares were 33.2 per cent and

TABLE 2.3

Composition of Income Tax Receipts and Numbers of Taxpayers in *Repelia IV*

Fiscal Year	As a Percentage of Revenue			Number[a] of Taxpayers ('000)		
	State Corporations	Private Corporations	Individuals	Employees	Corporate Bodies	Self-employed
1984/5	33.9	24.4	41.7	–	330	344
1985/6	29.0	19.9	51.1	–	441	554
1986/7	36.5	26.0	37.5	197	563	643
1987/8	30.0	33.1	36.9	–	632	675
1988/9	26.8	35.4	37.8	977[b]	653	687

Sources: Directorate-General of Taxation as reported in *Kompas* (4 November 1988) and *Warta Ekonomi* (14 August 1989).
[a] Data refer to numbers of registered taxpayers on 1 January of year shown, except 1988/9 where data refer to 1 May. It should be noted that not all registered taxpayers submitting a return would actually be liable for tax.
[b] Includes public and private enterprises.

TABLE 2.4
Composition of Non-oil Tax Revenues, FY 1978–FY 1989

Tax Category	Pre-Tax Reform Period (Fiscal Year Beginning)						Post-Tax Reform Period (Fiscal Year Beginning)					
	1978	1979	1980	1981	1982	1983	1984	1985	1986	1987	1988	1989
Income Tax[a]												
Amount[b]	581.0	736.0	1045.0	1279.0	1606.0	1785.0	2121.0	2313.0	2271.0	2663.4	3949.0	5488.0
Percentage of Total Tax Revenue	14.2	11.3	10.5	10.8	13.4	12.8	13.9	13.0	16.2	14.1	18.4	20.6
Percentage of NOTR[c]	32.9	32.7	36.1	39.4	42.1	40.6	44.3	35.0	29.7	30.3	33.2	35.6
Percentage of GDP	2.4	2.1	2.1	2.2	2.6	2.3	2.4	2.4	2.2	2.1	2.8	3.3
Sales Tax[d]												
Amount[b]	347.0	329.0	461.0	534.0	708.0	830.6	878.0	2326.7	2900.0	3390.4	4505.0	5837.0
Percentage of Total Tax Revenue	8.5	5.1	4.7	4.5	5.9	6.0	5.8	13.1	20.7	18.0	21.0	21.9
Percentage of NOTR[c]	19.7	14.6	15.9	16.4	18.6	18.9	18.3	35.2	37.9	38.6	37.8	37.8
Percentage of GDP	1.4	1.0	0.9	0.9	1.1	1.1	1.0	2.4	2.8	2.7	3.2	3.5
Land and Building Tax[e]												
Amount[b]	63.0	72.0	87.0	94.0	105.0	132.0	157.0	167.0	190.0	275.1	424.0	590.0
Percentage of Total Tax Revenue	1.5	1.1	0.9	0.8	0.9	1.0	1.0	0.9	1.4	1.5	2.0	2.2
Percentage of NOTR[c]	3.6	3.2	3.0	2.9	2.8	3.3	3.3	2.5	2.5	3.1	3.6	3.8
Percentage of GDP	0.3	0.2	0.2	0.2	0.2	0.2	0.2	0.2	0.2	0.2	0.3	0.4

Excise Taxes

Amount[b]	253.0	326.0	438.0	544.0	620.0	773.2	873.0	943.7	1056.0	1105.7	1390.0	1477.0
Percentage of Total Tax Revenue	6.2	5.0	4.4	4.6	5.2	5.6	5.7	5.3	7.6	5.9	6.5	5.5
Percentage of NOTR[c]	14.3	14.5	15.2	16.7	16.3	17.6	18.2	14.3	13.8	12.6	11.7	9.6
Percentage of GDP	1.1	1.0	0.9	0.9	1.0	1.0	1.0	1.0	1.0	0.9	1.0	0.9

Import Duties

Amount[b]	295.0	317.0	448.0	536.0	522.0	557.0	530.0	607.3	960.0	938.4	1192.0	1587.0
Percentage of Total Tax Revenue	7.2	4.9	4.5	4.5	4.4	4.0	3.5	3.4	6.9	5.0	5.6	5.9
Percentage of NOTR[c]	16.7	14.1	15.5	16.5	13.7	12.7	11.1	9.2	12.6	10.7	10.0	10.3
Percentage of GDP	1.2	0.9	0.9	0.9	0.8	0.7	0.6	0.6	0.9	0.8	0.9	1.0

Sources: As for Table 2.1.

[a] Excludes income tax on oil and gas. Includes personal and corporate income tax and withholding tax.

[b] Amount is in Rp billion.

[c] NOTR refers to non-oil tax revenue. It excludes only the corporate income tax derived from oil and gas sector.

[d] Data are for VAT, including the luxury sales tax beginning with the fiscal year 1985. For the earlier years, the data are for sales tax existing at the time.

[e] Before 1986, this tax was classified as a land tax (Ipeda).

[f] This is defined as a residual and includes the export tax, stamp duties, and minor direct taxes.

37.8 per cent respectively (Table 2.4). Thus, the relative importance of the VAT has increased considerably since the tax reform programme was implemented, although the 1989/90 and 1990/1 budgets indicate that the VAT share will probably be quite stable over the next few years.

Between 1983/4 and 1987/8, revenue from the land and building tax or PBB as a proportion of GDP remained nearly constant. However, since then, its revenue importance has increased sharply, though as a proportion of NOTR, revenue from this tax still remains relatively small (Table 2.4). According to unpublished data supplied by the PBB Directorate, between 1986/7 and 1988/9, only two components of the PBB, mining and forestry, grew relative to the total while the rural, urban, and plantation shares declined. A similar breakdown for 1989/90 is not yet available, but it appears unlikely that increases in total revenue can be achieved without reversing the declining share of the urban property component. There are indications, such as classification and valuation exercises for various types of land and buildings, that the authorities are planning to address the issue of undertaxation of urban property noted over the years by many analysts (Booth and McCawley, 1981; Lerche, 1980). Certainly the budget target for PBB was increased by 50 per cent in 1989/90 over the previous year's realized collection, which in turn had increased almost threefold since 1984/5. Whether increases of this magnitude can be sustained in the medium term remains to be seen.

Among the taxes not covered by the tax reform programme, the share of excises and import duties in the NOTR has declined. However, as a proportion of GDP, the share of excises has remained nearly constant, while that of import duties has increased as Indonesia has moved from non-tariff barriers to tariffs. But even with this change, import duties are expected to generate revenue equal to only 1 per cent of GDP in 1989/90. The corresponding percentages in 1987 are 2.4 for Malaysia, 3.1 for Thailand, and 3.2 for South Korea (IMF, 1989). Thus substantial scope would seem to exist for increasing revenue from import duties. But care will have to be taken to ensure that revenue-generating tariff reforms are consistent with recent liberalization of the trade regime.

To summarize, if the VAT (or the sales tax), excise taxes, and import duties are regarded as indirect taxes, then their share in the NOTR has increased from 48.5 per cent in 1983/4 to 58.6 per cent in 1989/90 (Table 2.4). The central shift, however, has been the emergence of the VAT as the single most important tax from the point of view of revenue generation. Thus the overall revenue objective of the tax reform has been achieved, and the expectation that while the VAT will generate revenue in the short term, the income tax and the PBB will be significant contributors to NOTR in the medium term seems to have been vindicated.

*Simplification of the Tax Laws and Improving the Efficiency
of Tax Administration*

There can be little doubt that the new tax laws, regulations, and procedures are simpler and clearer compared with those prevailing before
the reform. If this is to continue to be the case, *ad hoc* changes in tax
regulations and procedures must be minimized. The authorities have
taken several measures to increase the technical capabilities of the tax
administration. Technical assistance from the IMF, the Internal
Revenue Service of the USA, and the German Technical Assistance
Agency (GTZ) have been used for such tasks as training key personnel,
modernizing auditing and other procedures, and developing a new management reporting system. The tax appeal system is also reported to be
operating reasonably well. From 1 April 1989, the Directorate-General
of Taxation has been reorganized into six functional areas, compared
with sixteen departments previously. It is too early to tell whether the
reorganization and the new management reporting system will overcome
the criticism made by Gillis (1989: 107) that, even by 1987, there was
little evidence that administrative practices had improved significantly.
But the technical capability of the tax administration does appear to
have increased noticeably since then. While there is still room for further
improvement, particularly because the extension of VAT will raise
potential VAT payers from 80,000 to about 600,000, the key to
improved enforcement and compliance lies with administrative practices
which in turn are related to the political economy of fiscal policy and
administration.

Because of the low levels of NOTR relative to GDP before the tax
reform, the design of the VAT, and the availability of 'softer' target tax
payers such as wage earners, state enterprises, and foreign enterprises,[8]
there have been fewer non-technical problems in raising NOTR.
Further revenue increases will inevitably involve substantial increases in
the tax liabilities of high-income individuals and local businesses, both
Chinese and *pribumi*, thus raising the cost of tax reform for these
groups. Recent extensions of the VAT and changes in the PBB will also
increase the tax burden on middle-income and possibly lower-income
groups. As a result, to meet *Repelita V* targets, increasing the technical
capability of tax administration, though vital, will not be enough. To
translate this capability into higher enforcement and compliance will
require increased political will. The recent publicity given to those companies judged to be 'model' taxpayers is one way of pressuring others
into greater compliance, although for some, harsher measures may be
necessary.[9]

Efficiency in Resource Allocation

Various measures taken since 1985, such as the widening of the income
tax base, elimination of tax-based fiscal incentives, greater certainty of
tax laws and procedures, and a reduction in input taxation as a result of

the VAT, could all be expected to lead to a reduction in non-neutrality. On the other hand, retention of the classical system of income taxation, non-retail level VAT, the luxury sales tax, and other such design features suggest that some non-neutralities remain. In addition the new laws have produced several additional sources of non-neutrality.

First, to the extent that enforcement and compliance differ according to various types of income (capital versus labour), and activities (wage versus self-employment), by types of firms (local versus foreign, private versus public, large versus small, goods versus services providing firms), or by sectors (the filing ratios for the VAT vary considerably by sectors), effective tax rates will also differ significantly. Second, neutrality requires equal tax rates not before but after the shifting process has been completed. Since the shifting responses will differ, particularly in an economy where the structure of markets deviates considerably from the competitive norm, the effective rates are also bound to differ. Third, recent extensions of the VAT have reduced the availability of tax credit for inputs, and have increased the tax rates for many commodities. Both these are likely to result in greater non-neutrality among products and types of firms. A fourth point concerns the treatment of foreign investors. As the Indonesian income tax regime becomes less competitive because of more generous tax incentives offered by other countries competing for foreign investment, it may become necessary to reduce income tax rates or provide selective income tax based incentives.[10] The latter option would represent a deliberate departure from the neutrality objective.

The reform programme has made tax policies more compatible with the objective of making the Indonesian economy more competitive internationally. It has also facilitated continued conservative macroeconomic management. Thus, in a broader and more general sense, the tax reform programme has had positive effects on resource allocation and economic growth.

Protection of the Poor and Income Redistribution

Those in charge of designing the Indonesian tax reform argued that distributional concerns should be dealt with through the expenditure rather than the tax side of the budget. But they did try to ensure that the poor were not made worse off as a result of tax reform. Clearly the poor would have been adversely affected had the implementation of the VAT package led to even a once over increase in the cost of living. Gillis reports that '... the introduction of the VAT in Indonesia not only had no impact on inflation ..., but the implementation of the tax had no noticeable effects on the price level' (1989: 107). However, the basis for this conclusion is not entirely clear. Without a more disaggregated analysis of the price behaviour of the consumption basket of the poor, a firm conclusion that the poor were not affected cannot be drawn. Moreover, the consumer price index in Indonesia is entirely urban, and commodities such as rice and petroleum products whose prices are officially controlled have quite large weights. The rural nine commodity indexes for Java and the Outer Islands have in fact shown a rather faster rate of inflation over the past five years than the urban ones, although this probably has little to do with the impact of the VAT.

Did the tax reform programme as a whole result in an increased tax burden on the poor? A study using a conventional incidence analysis framework found that, for 1982, effective rates for the bottom four household groups were higher for both the income and the expenditure base under the reformed tax system, while the rates for the highest income and expenditure group were significantly lower (Mangkoesoebroto, 1986: Tables 12, 29, 30, 37, and 38). These estimates were based on the revenue neutral assumption. The reformed tax system, however, is not revenue-neutral. In particular, the relative importance of the VAT package has been substantially higher than under the pre-reform regime. Without more micro data on household purchases, it is difficult to indicate whether the departure from revenue neutrality would make the reformed system more or less regressive. The presumption, however, must be towards greater regressivity.[11] Further micro data are also necessary to analyse the extent to which those within the same income group bear differing tax burdens due to differing consumption patterns. This problem of horizontal equity needs to be studied in greater detail.

Changing Expenditure Patterns

Changing Patterns of Central Government Expenditures in the 1980s

Although the 1980s, and especially the *Repelita IV* years, are frequently spoken of as a period of fiscal 'austerity' in Indonesia, in fact the ratio of central government revenues and expenditures to GDP has shown little change (Table 2.1). There was a slight fall in 1986/7 and 1987/8 and some recovery since then, so that by 1989/90 the budgeted ratio is little different from that which prevailed at the end of *Repelita III*. But the change in the composition of central government expenditures through the 1980s has been dramatic. As a percentage of total expenditures, debt charges jumped from under 7 per cent in 1981/2 to over 33 per cent in 1989/90. The two components of the budget which have been squeezed to make room for the heavy burden of debt servicing have been non-debt routine expenditures (mainly salaries and wages and recurrent expenditures on items such as office supplies) and non-aid development expenditures which include capital expenditures by departments and other government agencies, grants to regions to carry out development projects (the so-called Inpres allocations), some subsidies including those on fertilizer and insecticides, and government equity participation in public enterprises. In 1989/90, these categories of expenditures were only 40 per cent of total expenditures compared with 80 per cent in 1980/1 (Table 2.5).

As a proportion of GDP, both non-debt routine expenditures and total development expenditures have fallen sharply in the 1980s (Table 2.6).

TABLE 2.5
Trends in Major Components of Central Government Expenditures,
1969–1990

			Percentage of Total Expenditure		
Fiscal Year Beginning	Non-debt Routine	Debt Servicing	Development Expenditures Excluding Project Aid	Development Expenditures Financed by Aid	Total Subsidies[a]
1969	60.6	4.2	27.8	7.5	0
1974	47.6	3.7	38.7	9.9	26.6
1979	41.8	8.5	33.4	16.3	15.5
1980	42.8	6.7	38.3	12.2	18.5
1981	43.4	6.7	37.9	12.0	19.6
1982	40.2	8.5	37.9	13.4	14.3
1983	34.5	11.5	32.9	21.1	12.5
1984	34.3	14.3	33.8	17.6	10.6
1985	37.8	14.6	32.3	15.3	7.4
1986	38.8	23.1	20.7	17.3	4.9
1987	34.4	30.4	15.0	20.1	6.4
1988	29.7	33.2	13.0	24.1	3.3
1989	32.5	31.3	14.2	22.1	3.1
1990[b]	31.4	30.3	18.2	19.6	3.0

Source: Bank Indonesia, *Indonesian Financial Statistics*, various issues.
[a] Includes subsidies in both the routine and development budgets. Subsidies for foodstuff and petroleum products are included in the routine budget and those for fertilizer and insecticides, and government equity participation are included in the development budget.
[b] Budget estimates.

By 1989/90 government debt-servicing charges had risen to almost 8 per cent of GDP. Some components of the development budget fell further relative to GDP than others; in 1989/90 departmental expend-itures as a proportion of GDP were only 32 per cent of the ratio in 1981. Regional development expenditures were halved. On the other hand, project aid expenditures more than doubled relative to GDP.

Impact of the Changing Spending Patterns

The macroeconomic impact of these changes is discussed in more detail in the next section. Here their immediate impact on the government apparatus and its functioning is noted. There can be little doubt that the sharp contraction in non-debt routine expenditures relative to total expenditures and to GDP has been mainly reflected in the salaries and perquisites of the military and civilian bureaucracies. Basic salaries remained frozen from 1985/6 to 1988/9 and were then increased by only 10 per cent. In addition, other forms of remuneration from both the routine and development budgets have also been cut. In real terms most

TABLE 2.6

Components of Central Government Expenditures as a Percentage
of GDP, 1969–1989

Fiscal Year Beginning	Non-debt Routine	Debt	Development Expenditure			
			Departmental Development	Regional Aid	Project Development	Total[a]
1969	7.5	0.5	2.9	0.2	0.9	4.3
1974	7.9	0.6	1.9	1.3	1.6	8.1
1979	9.7	2.0	4.2	1.6	3.8	11.5
1980	10.3	1.6	5.1	1.7	2.9	12.1
1981	10.4	1.6	4.7	2.0	2.9	11.9
1982	9.2	2.0	5.2	1.7	3.1	11.8
1983	8.1	2.7	4.1	1.9	5.0	12.7
1984	7.4	3.1	3.9	1.7	3.8	11.1
1985	8.9	3.4	4.6	1.6	3.6	11.2
1986	8.3	4.9	2.0	1.4	3.7	8.1
1987	7.4	6.6	1.1	1.1	4.4	7.6
1988	6.9	7.7	1.3	1.1	5.6	8.6
1989	7.5	7.2	1.5	1.0	5.1	8.3

Sources: As for Table 2.1.
[a] Individual percentages do not quite add up to the total because of the exclusion of the 'other' category of development expenditures.

civil servants have endured a steep decline in their incomes since 1984/5, both in absolute terms and relative to other sectors of the economy. An inevitable consequence has been an increase in moonlighting, and a decline in efficiency and dedication even during the time actually spent on the job.

As far as the development budget is concerned, the sharp decline which occurred relative to GDP after 1983/4 together with the much greater reliance on funding from foreign aid and borrowing has had a significant impact on the sectoral allocation of development funds. Between 1983/4 and 1988/9 (i.e. the *Repelita IV* period) total development expenditures increased by about 24 per cent in nominal terms; however, all this increase was due to growth in aid and borrowing which more than doubled in nominal terms. Well over half the increase in development funds from aid and borrowing were absorbed by just two sectors of the development budget: agriculture (including irrigation) and education. Other sectors which benefited from the growth in aid and borrowing in *Repelita IV* were transport (including roads), housing, defence, and science and technology. Four sectors suffered a decline in budgetary allocations over the period: industry, mining and energy, transmigration, and the environment. In the first two cases, the decline was in part due to a decline in aid funding while in the latter two sectors an increase in funding from aid and borrowing failed to compensate for a decline in funding from the rupiah budget (Table 2.7).

TABLE 2.7
Changes in the Sectoral Allocation of the Development Budget
in *Repelita IV*

Sector	Nominal Percentage Growth in Expenditures, 1983/4–1988/9	Percentage Breakdown of Growth, 1983/4–1988/9		
		Total	Aid	Domestic
Agriculture[a]	76.8	29.8	39.6	−9.8
Industry	−12.9	−2.8	−1.3	−1.5
Energy	−9.8	−9.6	−3.9	−5.8
Transport	31.6	20.5	22.8	−2.2
Trade	58.2	4.9	5.0	−0.1
Transmigration	−41.8	−8.1	2.2	−10.3
Regional	51.9	16.5	1.6	14.9
Education	55.6	24.4	51.4	−27.0
Health	21.7	2.6	2.7	−0.1
Housing	117.9	11.1	14.8	−3.8
Defence	5.5	1.2	15.3	−14.1
Science	138.2	17.8	16.5	1.3
Business support	57.5	5.6	7.1	−1.5
Environment	−25.2	−2.3	4.7	−6.9
Other[b]	−62.3	−11.6	−4.9	−6.7
Total	23.8	100.0	173.6	−73.6

Source: Department of Information, *Lampiran Pidato Kenegaraan 1989*, pp. IV/40–IV/44.
[a]Includes irrigation.
[b]Includes religion, law, information, and grants to government corporations.

The Impact of the Budget

Throughout the 1980s, the Indonesian government have continued to run a 'balanced' budget in the sense that total government receipts from all sources including foreign borrowing equal total expenditures. However, as has been emphasized before, this outcome is due to the fact that items which in most countries are classified as means of financing the budget deficit have been classified as receipts in Indonesia.[12] The goal of budgetary balance has been, of course, one of the cornerstones of New Order macroeconomic policy both in the boom years of the 1970s and in the much tighter fiscal climate of the 1980s. Especially in the latter period it has served as a means of imposing discipline and avoiding the experience of the early 1960s when the sharp decline in the terms of trade caused a decline in government revenues which was not matched by a corresponding decline in expenditures. The resulting deficit was in large part financed by borrowing from the domestic banking system and led to rapid inflation culminating in hyperinflation.

The decline in world oil prices in the 1980s has led to a sharp fall in revenues accruing to government through the oil company tax. But total revenues did not fall very markedly relative to GDP because of increased non-oil tax revenues and increased foreign aid and borrowing. The increased borrowing in turn affected the expenditure side of the budget through increased expenditures on debt repayments. These changes meant that although the budget remained 'balanced' according to the conventional presentation, its actual economic impact has changed considerably in the 1980s.

The Overall Budget Deficit

The most commonly used concept of the budget deficit is that which measures the total borrowing requirement of the government sector. This is the concept which is used by the International Monetary Fund (IMF) and by many national governments in their budgetary documents.[13] The Indonesian government has never presented budgetary data in a way which facilitates calculation of the overall deficit, possibly because the issue of borrowing, both domestic and foreign, is a sensitive one and the government is reluctant to acknowledge its extent. Some studies have attempted to equate the overall budget balance with the difference between total budgetary expenditure and what the budgetary document terms 'domestic' revenues, i.e. revenues net of aid and borrowing. But this exaggerates the size of the borrowing requirement as it includes expenditures financed by foreign grants and soft loans. The International Monetary Fund in its presentation of Indonesian budgetary accounts separates out concessional aid flows from commercial loans and thus presents a more accurate estimate of the overall deficit. This IMF deficit is presented as a ratio of GDP in Table 2.8. Since 1979 it has fluctuated at around 2 per cent of GDP. This is, as would be expected, a much lower ratio than that derived from the 'crude' deficit defined as total budgetary expenditures less revenues excluding all aid and borrowing.

However, what is of interest is not just the size of the borrowing requirement relative to GDP but the source of the borrowing. When the government borrows from abroad, or from domestic institutions and individuals through the sale of bonds, the immediate impact on the domestic economy should not be inflationary. But when it borrows from the banking system to finance the deficit (as it did in the early 1960s), the effect is usually highly inflationary. For the years up to 1982, the IMF data indicate that Indonesia has been funding its deficit by borrowing abroad. Domestic borrowing from any source was either very small or negative. This changed in 1983, when the central government began to fund a significant part of the deficit from domestic sources, mainly by borrowing from the monetary authorities. In 1987 over half the deficit of Rp 1.03 trillion was funded domestically. Most of this consisted of borrowing from the monetary authorities. In 1988 foreign borrowing funded over 80 per cent of the deficit of Rp 4.2 trillion, while the balance was borrowed from the monetary authorities.[14]

TABLE 2.8
Estimates of the Budget Deficit[a] as a Percentage of GDP,[b] 1980–1989

Fiscal Year Beginning	Overall Budget Deficit		Domestic[d] Deficit	Monetary Deficit[e]
	IMF	Budget[c]		
1969	n.a.	3.3	2.4	(0.4)
1974	1.4	1.9	5.6	(1.1)
1979	2.2	4.0	8.2	(2.4)
1980	2.3	3.0	10.1	(3.9)
1981	2.0	2.9	10.7	(1.0)
1982	1.9	3.1	8.8	0.7
1983	2.4	5.0	7.4	(1.5)
1984	(1.4)	3.9	6.6	(3.7)
1985	1.0	3.7	6.0	(0.2)
1986	3.5	5.6	1.8	0.5
1987	0.8	4.9	0.9	1.2
1988	2.9	7.0	(0.5)	0.2
1989	2.0	5.7	(0.8)	(0.7)

Sources: Bank Indonesia, Indonesian Financial Statistics, various issues; IMF (1989: 511; 1990: 340).
[a]Figures in brackets refer to a surplus.
[b]GDP data refer to calendar years.
[c]Expenditures less all revenues excluding aid and borrowing.
[d]See footnote 13 for details of calculation.
[e]Data refer to calendar years.
n.a. = Not available.

Domestic Deficit

It has frequently been argued in Indonesia since the early 1970s that the overall deficit concept is of limited use in an economy where a substantial part of both government revenues and government expenditures were received from, and spent, abroad. In the early years of the New Order a large part of the development budget was funded by concessional aid; but as there was generally a fairly tight link between aid receipts and foreign expenditures, aid was not seen as boosting domestic purchasing power. After 1973 when oil revenues began to climb rapidly and account for an ever-growing share of total budget revenues, the concept of the domestic deficit, or the difference between domestic revenues and domestic expenditures, attracted more attention, as a more accurate measure of the impact of the budget on aggregate demand.

As the Indonesian government, like most others, does not publish separate accounts of domestic and foreign transactions, calculations of the domestic deficit have to be made on the basis of some rough assumptions about the foreign content of both revenues and expenditures. Typically revenues from the oil and gas sectors are classified as 'foreign' because they do not affect domestic purchasing power. All other revenues classified as 'domestic' in the budgetary documents are assumed to reduce domestic purchasing power and are thus classified as domestic revenues for the purposes of calculating the deficit. Estimating domestic expenditures is more difficult as rather rough assumptions have to be made about the domestic impact of each category of routine and development expenditure and how this is likely to change over time.[15]

There can be little doubt that, for any plausible set of assumptions about the foreign and domestic content of budgetary expenditures, the domestic deficit increased rapidly relative to GDP during the 1970s and has declined steadily in the 1980s. This indeed is what would be expected given the falling importance of oil revenues after 1981 and the rapid increase in expenditure on foreign debt servicing. Indeed in 1988/9 and 1989/90 the domestic deficit has turned into a domestic surplus; in the latter year it is estimated to be around 0.8 per cent of GDP (Table 2.8). To the extent that these calculations accurately reflect the impact of the budget on domestic purchasing power in Indonesia, they indicate that this impact has changed from being very expansionary in the 1970s to being quite contractionary in the late 1980s.

Monetary Deficit

A further measure of the impact of the central government on the economy which has been used in Indonesia is derived from the data published by Bank Indonesia on factors affecting the money supply. These data show how much of the increase in the money supply over a given period can be attributed to the central government; in effect what is measured is the government's net position with the banking system. Given that, according to the budgetary accounts, the difference between total expenditures and domestic revenues in New Order Indonesia has always been covered by foreign aid and borrowing one would expect the central government's position with the domestic banking system to have changed very little. But in fact it has done so in ways which have tended to compensate for the domestic deficit. During the oil boom years the central government usually ran a surplus with the monetary system; indeed this trend was maintained until the mid-1980s (Table 2.8). Only since 1986/7 has the monetary balance in fact been negative, indicating that in these years the central government has been borrowing from the banking system.

Several commentators have pointed out the difficulties inherent in trying to reconcile the monetary figures with the other concepts of the budget deficit in common use in Indonesia.[16] Certainly in the oil boom period there can be little doubt that the government understated oil tax revenues in the budget and held the balance between actual and reported revenues with Bank Indonesia. They could also, at various times, have understated foreign borrowings or overstated expenditures in the budget. In the more recent period it is probable that monetary balances held with the central bank have been drawn down to provide rupiah counterpart funding for development projects; this indeed is confirmed by the IMF figures referred to above.

The Impact of Fiscal Policy in the 1980s

By the mid-1980s, the effect on the domestic economy of severe cuts in budgetary expenditures, and especially development expenditures, was causing concern to many observers. As Glassburner (1986: 22) pointed out, 'the costs of hyperconservative policy may well turn out to be very high in terms of output growth forgone and increased unemployment'. Glassburner and others argued that some measure of monetary expansion on the part of government need not be inflationary nor need it have an unduly adverse effect on the balance of payments. In fact, since 1986, the Indonesian government seems to have been following this advice, although for political reasons the expansion has not shown up in the budget documents. The modest degree of monetary stimulation given by the government probably served to lessen the impact of the severe decline in the terms of trade on the domestic economy and facilitate the recovery after 1987.

Could the government have done more to stimulate the economy after 1982 without placing intolerable strain on the balance of payments? Before answering this question, one needs to examine in greater detail the issue of foreign debt which had come to dominate most aspects of macroeconomic policy-making in Indonesia by the latter part of the 1980s.

The Foreign Debt

The Size of the Debt

In 1980, few observers were concerned with the level of Indonesia's foreign indebtedness. The total stock of external debt as a ratio of exports of goods and services was only slightly higher than the average for all East Asian countries and rather lower than the average for oil exporters (Table 2.9). Of the ASEAN countries, most attention was directed to levels of foreign debt in the Philippines, while Brazil and Mexico were already causing concern in Latin America. Most of the Indonesian external debt of $20.9 billion in 1980 was long-term and about 75 per cent was public or publicly guaranteed. Indeed almost half the debt was to official multilateral and bilateral creditors.[17]

By 1987 the ratio of external debt to exports in Indonesia had almost trebled, as had the ratio of debt to GNP. The debt to export ratio was much higher than the East Asian average although still rather lower than the average for all oil exporters (Table 2.9). Total foreign debt service payments accounted for a third of exports of goods and services and almost 10 per cent of GNP. In 1988 the World Bank estimated total debt stock outstanding to be $52.8 billion of which $41.3 billion was public or publicly guaranteed, and $26.6 billion was debt to official

TABLE 2.9

Indicators of External Debt: Indonesia and Selected Comparisons
(ratios expressed as percentages)

Country	EDT/XGS		EDT/GNP		1987	
	1980	1987	1980	1987	TDS/XGS	TDS/GNP
Indonesia	94.1	270.2	27.9	79.7	33.3	9.8
Nigeria	32.0	382.4	8.9	129.5	11.7	3.9
Thailand	96.3	125.5	25.9	43.8	20.6	6.3
India	128.2	238.3	11.1	18.8	21.6	1.7
Venezuela	132.6	284.7	49.6	94.5	32.0	10.6
Pakistan	208.7	243.1	42.4	47.1	17.8	3.5
Philippines	212.0	317.8	49.4	86.5	25.2	6.9
Mexico	233.3	364.7	30.4	58.0	38.4	8.2
Brazil	303.1	432.2	30.4	39.4	33.2	3.0
East Asia	73.1	103.2	17.2	33.8	5.9	1.8
Oil exporters	120.8	314.7	32.1	75.0	31.8	7.6

Source: World Bank, *World Debt Tables 1988/89*.
EDT = Total Debt Stock.
XGS = Exports (Goods and Services).
TDS = Total Debt Service Payments.

creditors. Thus the growth in Indonesia's foreign indebtedness through
the 1980s was largely due to the public sector. Between 1980 and 1988
the private non-guaranteed component of long-term debt rose by only
$1.3 billion, or less than 5 per cent of the total. Up to 1985, a consider-
able part of the foreign borrowing undertaken by government agencies
was denominated in non-dollar currencies, especially yen and marks.
Thus after the currency realignments of 1985/6, the dollar value of the
accumulated debt stock jumped considerably.

The Causes and Consequences of Foreign Borrowing

In a survey of the world debt problem published in 1985, Dornbusch
and Fischer made the following comments about the origins of the crisis.

The reasons for debt accumulation vary. In some countries the debt was associated primarily with investment booms, while in others the debt represented lack
of adjustment to external interest rates or terms of trade, or denoted significant
capital flight. The experience of several Latin American countries illustrates the
interaction of domestic policy mistakes and world macro-economic developments. Domestic expansionary policies financed by external debt accumulation
were pursued on a very large scale, a course that became extraordinarily difficult
and costly to correct when interest rates escalated and commodity prices plum-
meted. (Dornbusch and Fischer, 1985: 70.)

In the Indonesian case, the government, state enterprises, and the private sector all tried to maintain previous levels of expenditure as oil

prices began to decline after 1981. This resulted in an enormous increase in the balance of payments deficit on current account, which reached $7.04 billion in 1982/3. The 1983 devaluation did curb the balance of payments deficit which fell to $2 billion by 1984/5 (Table 2.10). But the government was loath to cut back development expenditures too drastically, and so reliance on aid and foreign borrowing as a source of development finance escalated. This permitted development expenditures in such crucial areas as agriculture, irrigation, transport, and education to grow far more rapidly in *Repelita IV* than would have been possible if only domestic sources of funds had been available (Table 2.7). But it also added to the stock of debt, and thus to the government's debt-servicing obligations. In addition, state enterprises continued to borrow, sometimes for projects which were probably more difficult to justify in economic terms than those included in the development budget. This continuing reliance by the public sector on foreign sources of funds together with the currency realignments of 1985/6 led to a rapid growth in the dollar value of the external debt.

The real crisis hit in 1986. Although the 1983 devaluation did give some stimulus to non-oil exports (total export earnings in nominal dollar terms grew between 1983 and 1984), the real impact of this devaluation had begun to taper off by 1985. The sharp drop in oil prices in early 1986 led to a decline in nominal export receipts in that year of 21 per cent. The ratio of debt service charges to export earnings was already 36 per cent and the rapidly deteriorating balance of payments and budgetary situations would inevitably have led to more foreign

TABLE 2.10
Growth in Indonesia's External Debt, 1980–1988 (US$ billion)

	EDT	Nominal Interest Rate (per cent)	Current Account Deficit[a]	XGS	Annual Growth in XGS (per cent)
1980	20.937	8.1	(2.131)	22.208	
1981	22.755	8.7	2.790	24.878	12.0
1982	26.508	9.0	7.039	21.274	−14.5
1983	30.092	8.7	4.151	19.876	−6.6
1984	31.871	9.0	1.968	22.205	11.7
1985	35.981	7.3	1.832	20.200	−9.0
1986	43.116	7.2	4.051	16.043	−20.6
1987	52.727	6.1	1.707	18.902	17.8
1988	52.825	5.2	1.859	21.515	13.8

Sources: World Bank, *World Debt Tables, 1988/89* (Second Supplement): 46−9; Department of Information, *Lampiran Pidato Kenegaraan*, various issues.
[a]Figure in brackets refers to a surplus. These data refer to financial years.
EDT = Total Debt Stock.
XGS = Exports of Goods and Services.

borrowing. The only option was to adopt policies which would accelerate non-oil export earnings while at the same time curbing future public sector borrowing requirements.

This was what the 1986 devaluation and the subsequent deregulation packages were designed to achieve. In addition the 'austerity' budgets of 1986/7, 1987/8, and 1988/9 squeezed non-debt routine expenditures and development expenditures so hard that the domestic deficit rapidly became a surplus (Table 2.8). These actions together led to the dramatic growth in export earnings in 1987, 1988, and 1989. They also served to strengthen the confidence of the private sector so that capital flight, which had proven to be such a problem in the Latin American stabilization programmes, had largely abated in Indonesia by late 1987. In 1988, for the first time in the decade, there was no net addition to the stock of foreign debt (Table 2.10).

The Next Five Years

The sharp growth in debt servicing as a share of exports and government expenditures during the *Repelita IV* period has caused considerable unease among many sectors of Indonesian public opinion. The government responded to this by announcing that a major goal of *Repelita V* would be a reduction in the debt service ratio to 25 per cent by 1994. The achievement of this target will depend on three factors:
(1) the rate of growth of non-oil exports;
(2) the size of the non-interest current account deficit; and
(3) trends in world interest rates.

Domestic policies can have a major impact on (1) and (2), but only a minor effect on (3). The *Repelita V* document forecasts that non-oil exports will continue to grow at the rate achieved in *Repelita IV*, while oil and gas exports will grow more slowly, so that total export receipts will grow from $21.8 billion in 1989/90 to $34.7 billion in 1993/4.[18] If we accept the World Bank projections of debt service obligations on the existing pipeline, then the debt service ratio (only taking into account existing debt) will fall to 18.5 per cent by 1993.[19] Obviously some new borrowings will be undertaken; their extent will depend on the size of the balance of payments deficit which in turn depends on how rapidly imports will grow relative to exports. If prudent public investment and domestic demand management policies are pursued, there is every reason to expect that the *Repelita V* target will be met and even exceeded which implies that the current account could well be in balance by 1993/4.[20]

It is of course possible that world economic performance could deteriorate over the next few years leading to higher interest rates and slower growth. This would obviously damage Indonesia's prospects for exporting its way out of the current debt situation, as it would the prospects of many other indebted countries. But barring an unexpected and major slow-down in world economic activity in the early 1990s, the burden of the external debt on the Indonesian budget and balance of payments should steadily decline.

Regional Finance

Trends in Central Government Funding of
Regional Finance in the 1980s

The first fifteen years of the New Order era witnessed a rapid growth in central government subsidies to the regions for both routine and development purposes. In particular, the system of allocating a share of the development budget to the regions for infrastructure development (the so-called Inpres allocations) expanded rapidly with the growth of oil revenues, so that by 1981 regional development expenditures accounted for 16 per cent of the development budget and 2 per cent of GDP (Table 2.6). But after 1983 the regional development component of the development budget began to decline relative to GDP and by 1989/90 it was only 1 per cent of GDP compared with 2 per cent at the beginning of the decade. Although this decline was not as drastic as that of departmental development expenditures, there was a widespread feeling that the Inpres funds financed projects which were more labour-intensive and of greater benefit to rural communities and that their decline would have a more immediate and severe impact on rural welfare.

TABLE 2.11
Growth in Development Grants (Inpres) to Regions, 1983/4–1990/1
(Rp billion)

Inpres Expenditures	1983/4	1988/9	1989/90	1990/1
Grants to Regions				
Village	92	112	112	181
Kabupaten	194	267	270	392
Province	253	334	324	486
East Timor	5	6	–	–
Sectoral Grants				
Primary Schools	549	130	100	370
Health Clinics	87	99	122	189
Markets	11	3	3	3
Reafforestation	59	16	16	33
Road Development	65	180	295[a]	679[a]
Total	1,315	1,147	1,242	2,332
As Percentage of				
Budget Expenditures				
Development	13.3	9.4	9.5	14.4
Total	7.2	3.5	3.4	5.4

Source: Department of Finance, *Nota Keuangan dan Rancangan Anggaran Pendapatan dan Belanja Negara*, various issues.
[a]In 1989/90, 76 per cent of these funds was spent at the *kabupaten* level and the balance at the province; in 1990/1 70 per cent was spent at the *kabupaten*. Data for 1990/1 are budget estimates.

In fact the decline in Inpres expenditures during the *Repelita IV* period was entirely due to the sharp reduction in the primary school building programme (Table 2.11). Although budget stringency was part of the reason for this decline, primary school enrolments had risen to over 90 per cent of the 7–12 age group in most parts of the country by 1985, reducing the demand for further construction of new schools. Allocations to the reafforestation and market programmes were cut back, but this reflected the perceived failure of these programmes to achieve their aims rather than fiscal austerity *per se*. Other sectoral grants, most notably those for road development, showed a rapid increase through *Repelita IV*. Grants to provinces and *kabupaten* also increased (although they barely kept up with inflation) but those to villages grew much less rapidly.

In 1990/1 improved prospects for both growth and the balance of payments encouraged the government to formulate a more expansionary budget, with non-aid development expenditures almost doubling as a proportion of total budgetary expenditure (Table 2.5). Development expenditures channelled through the Inpres programme, however, were projected to grow rather less rapidly than non-aid financed development expenditures as a whole. Some components of the Inpres programme such as village grants, maintenance of school buildings, and road development were allocated substantial funding increases but overall Inpres

TABLE 2.12
Projects Implemented by Inpres *Kabupaten*

| Year | Total Projects | Volume | | | Direct Employment Creation ('000 jobs[a]) |
		Roads (km)	Bridges (m)	Irrigation ('000 ha)	
1974/5	4,008	6 848	913	128.2	905
1975/6	4,295	6 089	853	158.9	1,005
1976/7	3,784	7 186	893	82.8	824
1977/8	3,174	7 314	520	112.0	771
1978/9	3;250	8 036	532	112.4	788
1979/80	3,427	10 322	510	72.7	564
1980/1	3,850	14 577	630	64.9	559
1981/2	4,407	15 951	689	91.7	589
1982/3	4,677	14 801	652	49.7	589
1983/4	4,325	17 579	563	44.3	469
1984/5	3,510	25 755	406	26.0	503
1985/6	3,270	33 321	446	23.7	491
1986/7	3,693	35 621	377	26.4	635
1987/8	3,448	41 234	342	76.7	520
1988/9	3,802	33 812	351	47.8	536

Source: Department of Information, *Lampiran Pidato Kenegaraan*, various issues.
[a] Each job estimated to last 100 days.

expenditures in 1990/1 still accounted for a lower percentage of total budgetary expenditures than in 1983/4 (Table 2.11).

One possible reason for government reluctance to continue to fund the Inpres programmes at the levels reached in the 1970s could be that their direct impact on employment creation has been rather modest. Although official figures are difficult to obtain for most of the Inpres schemes, they are published on an annual basis for the *kabupaten* programme. The data indicate that one million jobs, each of 100 days' duration, were created through the programme in 1975/6, but by 1981/2 this had fallen to under 600,000 (Table 2.12). The decline continued at a more modest rate through the 1980s, although there was a marked increase in jobs created in 1986/7. Both the decline through the latter part of the 1970s and the early 1980s and the subsequent increase appear to be associated with the number and size of irrigation projects undertaken. Hectarage of land irrigated under the Inpres *kabupaten* fell sharply after 1978/9 while the volume of road projects accelerated. The obvious conclusion appears to be that road projects create fewer jobs than irrigation projects. If true, this has important consequences for the future employment potential of the Inpres schemes, as the Inpres *jalan* or road programme has grown very rapidly over the last decade and is now the single largest Inpres scheme (Table 2.11).

Allocation Criteria of Central Grants to the Regions

The various Inpres programmes developed rapidly through the 1970s in response to increasing government revenues on the one hand and the obvious need for economic and social infrastructure everywhere in the country on the other. But by the early 1980s, several commentators were drawing attention to the rather arbitrary way in which not just the Inpres grants but other central government grants to the regions were being allocated. As far as the various Inpres allocations were concerned, there was a very marked tendency for the smaller less densely settled provinces outside Java to receive larger grants in per capita terms (Ravallion, 1988; Bawazier, 1989). This was partly due to the fact that the provincial Inpres grant had largely been converted to a lump sum grant by *Repelita IV*, so that the smaller provinces received more in per capita terms. But there was also evidence that the Inpres grants for primary health facilities and primary schools were larger in per capita terms in the smaller and more remote provinces (Booth, 1989b). There was also a significant negative correlation between total central grants to the regions (i.e. all routine and development grants plus sectoral spending) and population densities (Bawazier, 1989).[21]

Is there any evidence that the allocation of central government grants favours relatively poor provinces in terms of per capita incomes or per capita consumer expenditures? The evidence seems rather inconclusive. Ravallion (1988: 68) has argued that in 1985/6 the allocation of all Inpres grants revealed 'a mild aversion to regional inequality'. Inpres receipts as a proportion of regional income (as measured by consumption expenditure) decreased as income increased, holding other province-specific attributes constant. Bawazier (1989) found a negative relationship between per capita grants from the centre (including routine grants and sectoral development expenditures) and per capita GDP by province, although the relationship was not as significant as that with population. Together these results might suggest that the grant system was having a mitigating impact on regional inequalities although the effect was quite modest.

Incentives for Own Revenue Effort

An important consequence of the system of central government grants to the regions as it has evolved since the late 1960s is that the Indonesian fiscal system has become highly centralized in comparison with other developing countries of similar size. According to World Bank sources, the proportion of total government revenues raised by subnational governments in Indonesia was very low by international standards in the years 1974–86 (World Bank, 1988: 155). Indeed 'own source' revenue in Indonesia covered a lower proportion of total subnational expenditure than in any other developing country for which data were given. Furthermore, there is evidence that the situation has been deteriorating since the early 1970s. In 1973/4 central subsidies comprised just over 60 per cent of all revenues accruing to provincial governments; by 1988/9 they comprised almost 80 per cent. There appears to have been a similar decline in own revenue performance at the *kabupaten* level (Booth, 1989b: 206). The performance of individual provinces varies considerably, as would be expected. In East Java, the largest province in the country and one which has traditionally had a high standard of public administration, provincial own revenues in fact covered a smaller proportion of total expenditure than for the country as a whole.[22] In some of the smaller provinces outside Java, they cover a rather higher proportion of total expenditures, although only in Jakarta is the ratio above 50 per cent.

It has frequently been argued that the central grants system should be reformed so as to reward provinces and *kabupaten* for increasing their own revenue effort. In the mid-1980s there did appear to be a positive correlation between per capita transfer from the centre (routine and development) by province and per capita own revenues, although it is unlikely that this was the result of any conscious policy (Davey, 1989: 181). But per capita own revenues are not in themselves an indicator of revenue 'effort'; own revenues have to be evaluated in relation to some indicator of taxable capacity such as income. Most investigations have shown that own revenues at both provincial and *kabupaten* level are a very low ratio of regional GDP, and that their elasticity with respect to GDP is significantly above unity.[23] In other words the richer provinces tend to collect more revenues relative to income than the poorer. Thus any central grants system which only rewarded provinces for own revenue effort would tend to discriminate against the poorer provinces. Obviously both equity and incentive provisions would have to be built into any reformed system of centre–regional financial relations.[24]

A decade ago it seemed that pressure for the more rapid development of infrastructure everywhere in the archipelago, together with the continuing centralization of revenues from natural resource extraction, would tend to perpetuate the strong centralist tendencies which the Indonesian fiscal system has always exhibited (Booth and McCawley, 1981: 153). As the country faces the very different challenges of the 1990s, this seems less certain. The inefficiencies and inequities of the existing system of centre–regional financial relations seem more obvious now than in the oil boom era when government expenditures were growing rapidly everywhere in the country. Even after the tax reforms of 1983–5, the central government has kept a strong hold over all the lucrative tax handles and done very little to encourage regional governments to improve their own revenue performance. Although the major grants from the centre to the regions have been increased in the 1989/90 and 1990/1 budgets, allocation procedures have not greatly changed and there has been little attempt to orient grants more specifically to the particular needs of a given province, *kabupaten* or *desa* (village).

Paradoxically such an orientation may become easier over the next decade. In the past there has been an obvious contradiction between 'poverty-oriented' programmes and those directed more exclusively at improving infrastructure. This arose because the great concentrations of poverty were in Java while the greatest need for improved roads, irrigation, and electric power were in other parts of the archipelago. But, as will be discussed more thoroughly in Chapter 10, the most recent evidence indicates that over time a higher proportion of Indonesia's poor will be located outside Java in precisely those areas where both physical and social infrastructure is lacking, compared to the more densely settled parts of the country. Furthermore, the provinces where the incidence of poverty now appears to be the highest are not just the resource-poor provinces such as East Nusa Tenggara and East Timor but also provinces such as East Kalimantan, Central Kalimantan, and Irian Jaya which obviously have far greater economic potential. The challenge for the central government will be to permit a much greater proportion of the revenues from natural resource extraction to stay in the province of origin to be used for infrastructural and social development especially in rural areas.

In the more densely settled parts of the archipelago where future economic development will depend on the rapid growth of a modern industrial base, the challenge for the centre will be to give the provinces and *kabupaten* greater incentives to exploit their own tax potential. Given the fact that most provincial and *kabupaten* taxes have very low revenue potential, one possible way of encouraging greater tax effort at the sub-national level would be to allow provinces (or in some cases *kabupaten*) to impose surcharges on central taxes such as the income tax or the

VAT. Another possibility is to allow the provincial governments greater flexibility in setting the rates for the land and building tax (PBB), and to reward their efforts in collecting this tax by matching a part of the provincial and *kabupaten* Inpres allocations to PBB revenues.

A more radical approach to fiscal decentralization in Indonesia over the next two decades would involve much greater devolution of both taxing and project implementation powers to whatever level of government was deemed most suitable; for example, villages could be given responsibility for primary education and basic health care and the *kabupaten* could take over lower secondary education, minor roads, tertiary irrigation facilities, and agricultural extension. Provinces could run upper secondary schools, some tertiary institutions, hospitals and, together with the central government, maintain the main road network. In each case, regional governments would have to be given tax powers commensurate with their additional expenditure responsibilities. In Java where the administrative capacities of *kabupaten* and village governments are probably greater than elsewhere, more implementation responsibilities could be devolved to subprovincial levels especially in areas such as education and health care (Booth, 1986: 97–8).

It is only by devolving far greater financial responsibilities to lower-level governments that the 'apathetic attitude' which they tend to display towards central government policies can be effectively remedied.[25] How far such financial devolution can proceed without allowing a greater measure of political freedom at the local level is obviously a crucial question, although one which can hardly be addressed here. But there can be little doubt that reform of centre–regional financial relations remains the major challenge for fiscal reformers in Indonesia in the 1990s.

1. For details of the tax system prior to the reform in the 1980s, see Booth and McCawley (1981); Asher and Booth (1983); Mansury (1984); Conrad (1986); Gillis (1985) and (1989); Lerche (1980); Odano (1987).

2. See, however, two papers by the Director of the HIID team (Gillis, 1985 and 1989).

3. The initial plan was for revenue neutrality in the near term, rather than increased NOTR/GDP ratio. It was anticipated that base-broadening and lower nominal rates envisaged in the reform proposals would make the tax system capable of generating additional revenue quickly if the need arose. Before submission of the proposals to Parliament in late 1983, however, the need for increased revenue had become evident (Gillis, 1989: 87).

4. The individual and company income tax are, however, not integrated, i.e. double taxation of dividends is retained.

5. In April 1984 a tax amnesty was introduced primarily to identify potential income taxpayers. According to the data provided by the Directorate-General of Taxation, by the end of the amnesty period in June 1985, 195,305 individuals and 25,685 companies or organizations had applied for the tax amnesty. The total revenue generated from the tax amnesty was, however, only Rp 69.6 billion or 3.3 per cent of the total income tax revenue in 1984/5. Because tax rates under amnesty were much lower than the normal rates, it is not clear how many genuinely new taxpayers were identified.

6. For detailed withholding provisions, see Articles 21, 22, and 23 of the Income Tax Law. See also Morgan (1989).

7. The large number of employees (*karyawan*) which were reported as registered tax-payers in 1988 probably reflects the impact of Keppres 71/1985 which obliged all civil servants in Class IIIA and above (an estimated 382,000 people) to register as taxpayers, as well as the withholding provisions implemented in large private sector enterprises. The numbers of employees in Indonesia with incomes above the tax threshold should not, however, be exaggerated. The 1987 *Sakernas* found that there were only 1.4 million salary earners outside the agricultural sector with incomes above Rp 150,000 per month; although reported incomes in these surveys tend to be understated, it seems improbable that there are more than one million wage and salary earners in Indonesia with taxable incomes above the threshold.

8. The tax reform has not eliminated tax-planning possibilities and particularly the use of transfer pricing (Wakui and Van Hien, 1988).

9. See *Tempo*, 12 August 1989 and *Warta Ekonomi*, 14 August 1989.

10. It needs to be stressed that in spite of the removal of income tax based incentives, foreign investment has accelerated sharply since 1987, especially in export-oriented activities. Thus Indonesian experience suggests that the presence of fiscal incentives is not essential to attract investment, though some types of firms may be discouraged.

11. In a recent paper Shah and Whalley (1990) have argued that traditional incidence analysis does not take into account important developing country features, such as import quotas, price controls, and underground economic activity. They argue that these features could make the incidence of a broad-based sales tax such as VAT, and trade taxes progressive rather than regressive. However, they provide no empirical evidence for this proposition.

12. See in particular Booth and McCawley (1981: 143–50) for a discussion of various concepts of the budget deficit and their application to Indonesia in the 1970s.

13. See in particular the annual publication of the IMF (International Monetary Fund), *Government Finance Statistics Yearbook*.

14. See IMF, *Government Finance Statistics Yearbook*, 12(1988): 511 and 13(1989): 340.

15. For a discussion of the domestic content of various components of the government budget in the 1970s, see Booth and McCawley (1981: 157–8). In estimating the domestic deficit in Table 2.8, rather different assumptions were used reflecting the changed circumstances of the 1980s. Only 5 per cent of the routine budget was estimated to have been spent abroad, 20 per cent of the departmental development budget, and 10 per cent of the regional development component of the development budget. Forty per cent of the 'other' component of the development budget (fertilizer subsidies, government equity in state enterprises, and other unspecified expenditures) were considered to have been made abroad. All aid expenditures were considered as 'foreign' although this is probably an overestimate, given the fact that many important donors are now supplying some rupiah counterpart funds.

16. See Booth and McCawley (1981: 150).

17. These and subsequent figures are taken from World Bank, *World Debt Tables 1988/89* (Second Supplement): 46–9.

18. These figures are derived from Chapter 5 of the *Repelita V* document. They include projected exports of commodities and projected revenues from tourism.

19. The World Bank projections are contained in the source cited in footnote 17.

20. The most recent estimates of the 1989/90 and 1990/1 current account deficits, contained in the 1990/1 budget documents indicate that the size of the deficit is already well below *Repelita V* projections. In 1990/1 the latest estimate is a current account deficit of $1.3 billion compared with the plan target of $2.2 billion.

21. Bawazier (1989) produced the following OLS (Ordinary Least Squares) regression:

Dependent Variable	Constant	Per Capita Non-grant Revenues	Per Capita Income	Population Density	R^2
Per capita grants	0.8612 (4.151)	0.1921 (1.398)	−0.2883 (−1.566)	−0.1951 (−3.947)	0.68

(N = 25) (t ratios in brackets)

22. Bawazier (1989) found that, on average, provinces in 1988/9 were deriving 79.2 per cent of their total revenues from central grants. East Java derived 93 per cent from central sources. South Sulawesi by contrast received only 66 per cent from the centre.

23. In 1986/7 the elasticity of provincial own revenues with respect to RGDP was 1.57. This was calculated from data presented by Bawazier (1989).

24. For more detailed discussions of the problems facing Indonesia in reforming regional and local government finance, see in particular the papers in Devas (1989).

25. This expression was used by Bawazier (1989).

REFERENCES

Asher, Mukul G. and Booth, Anne (1983), *Indirect Taxation in ASEAN*, Singapore: Singapore University Press.

Bawazier, Fuad (1989), 'Keuangan Daerah', Paper presented to the Conference on Regional Economic Development: Processes and Policies, Jakarta, University of Indonesia.

Booth, Anne (1986), 'Efforts to Decentralize Fiscal Policy: Problems of Taxable Capacity, Tax Effort and Revenue Sharing', in Colin MacAndrews (ed.), *Central Government and Local Development in Indonesia*, Singapore: Oxford University Press, pp. 77–100.

———— (1989a), 'Repelita V and Indonesia's Medium Term Economic Strategy', *Bulletin of Indonesian Economic Studies*, 25(2): 3–30.

———— (1989b), 'Central Government Funding of Local Government Development Expenditures', in N. Devas (ed.) (1989), *Financing Local Government in Indonesia*, Ohio University Monographs in International Studies, Southeast Asia Series, No. 84, Athens: Ohio University Press, pp. 191–212.

Booth, Anne and McCawley, Peter (1981), 'Fiscal Policy', in Anne Booth and Peter McCawley (eds.), *The Indonesian Economy during the Soeharto Era*, Kuala Lumpur: Oxford University Press, pp. 126–61.

Conrad, Robert (1986), *Essays on the Indonesian Tax Reform*, CPD Discussion Paper No. 1986–3, Washington, DC: World Bank.

Davey, Kenneth (1989), 'Central–Local Financial Relations', in N. Devas (ed.) (1989), *Financing Local Government in Indonesia*, Ohio University Monographs in International Studies, Southeast Asia Series, No. 84, Athens: Ohio University Press, pp. 169–90.

Devas, N. (ed.) (1989), *Financing Local Government in Indonesia*, Ohio University Monographs in International Studies, Southeast Asia Series, No. 84, Athens: Ohio University Press.

Dornbusch, R. and Fischer, S. (1985), 'The World Debt Problem: Origins and Prospects', *Journal of Development Planning*, 16: 57–81.

Gillis, Malcolm (1985), 'Micro and Macroeconomics of Tax Reform' *Journal of Development Economics*, 19(3): 221–54.

———— (1989), 'Comprehensive Tax Reform: The Indonesian Experience, 1981–1988', in Malcolm Gillis (ed.), *Tax Reform in Developing Countries*, Durham: Duke University Press, pp. 79–114.

Glassburner, Bruce (1986), 'Survey of Recent Developments', *Bulletin of Indonesian Economic Studies*, 22(1): 1–33.

IMF (International Monetary Fund) (1989), *Government Finance Statistics Yearbook, 1988*, Washington, DC.

———— (1990), *Government Finance Statistics Yearbook, 1989*, Washington, DC.

Lane, Malcolm G. and Hutabarat, H. (1986), 'Computerization of the VAT in

Indonesia', Paper presented to the Conference on Value Added Taxation in Developing Countries, sponsored by the Public Economics Division, World Bank, Washington, DC, 21–23 April.

Lerche, D. (1980), 'Efficiency of Taxation in Indonesia', *Bulletin of Indonesian Economic Studies*, 16(1): 34–51.

Mangkoesoebroto, Guritno (1986), 'Tax Incidence in a Developing Country: The Case of Indonesia', Ph.D. thesis, University of Colorado.

Mansury, R. (1984), 'A Bird's Eye View of Indonesian Income Taxation History', *Asian Pacific Tax and Investment Bulletin*, 2(12): 503–9.

Morgan, Frank B. (1989), 'Withholding Taxes under Indonesia's Income Tax Law', in David O'Reilly (ed.), *Income Taxation in ASEAN Countries*, 2nd edn., Singapore: Asian Pacific Tax and Investment Research Centre, pp. 169–81.

Odano, Sumimaru (1987), 'Government Budget and Taxation in Indonesia', *Asian Economic Journal*, 1(2): 147–76.

Ravallion, Martin (1988), 'Inpres and Inequality: A Distributional Perspective on the Centre's Regional Disbursements', *Bulletin of Indonesian Economic Studies*, 24(3): 53–72.

Shah, Anwar and Whalley, John (1990), 'An Alternative View of Tax Incidence Analysis for Developing Countries', Paper presented to the World Bank Conference on Tax Policy in Developing Countries, Washington, DC, 28–30 March.

Soemitro, Rochmat (1986), *Pajak Bumi dan Bangunan*, Bandung: PT Eresco.

Wakui, Yoshiko and Van Hien, Leonard (1988), 'Japanese Investment in Indonesia', *Tax Planning International Review*, 15(12): 10–12.

World Bank (1988), *World Development Report*, Washington, DC.

____ (1989), *World Debt Tables, 1988/89* (Second Supplement), Washington, DC.

3
Financial Development in Indonesia
David C. Cole and Betty F. Slade

Introduction

INDONESIA in the 1980s provides an unusual, if not unique, example in modern times of both substantial deregulation and rapid development of a domestic financial system in the context of a very open international financial regime. Most developing countries have clung to some form of foreign exchange controls long after they freed up many aspects of their domestic financial system. Several Latin American countries, in the late 1970s and early 1980s, suddenly removed most domestic and foreign financial controls and, after an initial period of favourable response, subsequently experienced severe instability and inflation. This led to a new dogma among some financial development specialists to the effect that liberalization or deregulation of a financial system should follow a sequential path starting with relaxation of internal trade controls and maintenance of a 'realistic' exchange rate to get domestic prices of goods and services in line with world market prices. Then it would be appropriate to free up domestic financial controls over interest rates and credit allocation; and finally, when everything else was in order, to remove controls over foreign capital flows.[1] Only in this way, it was claimed, could excessive foreign capital inflow and, more critically, capital outflow, be avoided.

Indonesia, however, removed all foreign capital controls in 1971, when its foreign exchange position was still rather precarious. The main reason for taking such an action at that time was that the government could not exert effective control over foreign capital movements anyway. Singapore was a major financial and trading centre located very close to Indonesia, and commodities and finance flowed freely between the two countries in spite of controls. Attempts to enforce foreign exchange controls wasted scarce administrative resources and were seen as doing more harm than good to the domestic economy. Since 1971 avoidance of controls over foreign capital movements has been a cornerstone of Indonesian economic policy. Another, not unrelated, tenet of policy has been a balanced domestic government budget. Maintenance of these policy stances was made easier by the large inflow of oil earnings after 1973, but they have been continued through the 1980s despite the decline in oil revenues and other disturbances in international financial markets.

The inflow of oil earnings from 1973 to 1982 also removed any serious need for efforts to promote domestic financial development within Indonesia. Finance was abundant, either from domestic sources or from foreign institutions willing to lend to Indonesian enterprises on the basis of expected future earnings derived either directly or indirectly from oil. The main concerns of the monetary authorities during the oil-boom period were to control domestic credit expansion and to curb foreign borrowing. The domestic objective was addressed through the imposition of credit ceilings on each bank, which had the effect of limiting the growth of the domestic banking system. But, with the open foreign capital system, excess funds of banks, businesses, or individuals were easily invested abroad. The limit on foreign borrowing was enforced most effectively over the state-owned oil company, Pertamina, after its excessive appetite for foreign loans was curbed in 1976. Other enterprises were able to borrow abroad either on their own name or against compensating deposit balances at banks in Singapore and Hong Kong. Thus the monetary policies of the oil-boom era, combined with the open foreign capital system, shifted the locus of much financial activity, both lending and borrowing, offshore. Domestic activity of financial institutions hardly grew at all relative to GDP and became increasingly focused on state-owned banks serving state-owned enterprises, or carrying out government-sponsored credit programmes as so-called 'agents of development'.

Since 1983 the Indonesian government has been pursuing a policy of financial reform to stimulate growth and improve the efficiency of the domestic financial system, within the context of an open foreign exchange system. The first phase of this reform, initiated in June 1983, was focused on the banking system. It involved the removal of credit ceilings and interest rate controls on commercial banks and, as a consequence, forced the central bank to devise new indirect instruments of monetary policy. This reform resulted in rapid growth of the whole commercial banking system, and a significant gain in the share of the private domestic commercial banks, at the expense of both the government-owned banks and foreign banks. It also led to a period of experimentation with various techniques and instruments for influencing the supply of money, interest rates and foreign exchange movements. (This experience is described in Chapter 4 by Binhadi and Meek.) It moved the financial system some way towards market-based operation but, with many restrictions remaining on entry and initiation of new activity, the markets were only partially effective.

Subsequent to the 1983 reforms there have been several financial crises, usually manifested in a sudden, sharp loss of foreign exchange reserves by the central bank. These could have, and in many other countries probably would have, led to the imposition of some form of foreign exchange controls. But in Indonesia this solution, though sometimes speculated about in the press, was never seriously considered by the government. Instead, officials used other measures to stem the outflow of foreign exchange. Initially some of these measures were somewhat harsh, such as the 50 per cent devaluation in October 1986, and the withdrawal of practically all available legal reserves of the banking system in June 1987, but since that time the measures have become more finely tuned and subtle in their application. This has contributed to greater stability and confidence in the management of financial policy.

It also laid the foundation for another round of financial reform in 1988–90 that was directed towards promoting more fundamental structural and operational changes in the financial system. These reforms, which are still evolving, have consisted of changes in regulations that

1. opened up entry for new domestic and joint-venture banks, and encouraged greater geographical dispersion, and a wider range of activities;
2. stimulated the development of domestic money and capital markets and instruments; and
3. promoted a broad range of new types of financial institutions and services.

These reforms also focused attention on the need for strengthened supervisory capabilities to ensure that these services will be provided within the framework of a fair and competitive market environment.

In this chapter, time series data depicting the changing size and structure of the Indonesian financial system for the twenty-year period 1968–89 are first presented. This series covers both the period from the first financial reform in 1968, which preceded the adoption of the open capital account, and the second reform period beginning in 1983 and continuing up to the present day. Next the major reform measures are studied chronologically and their impact on the development of the financial system is analysed. Several financial crises and significant events are noted and government policy responses discussed. This discussion helps to convey an understanding of the impact of the open account on the domestic financial system. It also indicates how it has been possible to carry out domestic financial reforms under such an open regime. The 1987–9 reforms are then described in some detail and a preliminary evaluation is presented. Finally, comments are offered on some of the areas of financial development that are currently receiving attention by the Indonesian government and are likely to undergo further policy or institutional changes in the near future.

Financial Growth and Structural Change in Indonesia

The Indonesian financial system has experienced two growth spurts since recuperating from the destructive effects of hyperinflation in the mid-1960s. These longer-term trends are best indicated by the ratio of broad money (M2) to GDP (Table 3.1). The first growth spurt was from 1968 to 1972, when the M2/GDP ratio rose from 6 per cent to 13 per cent. During this period the monetary authorities set relatively high nominal interest rates on bank time deposits, and the Central Bank

TABLE 3.1
Monetary Ratios, 1968–1988

Year	Percentage of GDP[a]				
	Currency (CU/GDP) (1)	Demand Deposits (DD/GDP) (2)	Quasi- money (QM/GDP) (3)	Narrow Money (M1/GDP) (4)	Broad Money (M2/GDP) (5)
1968	3.58	1.86	0.57	5.44	6.01
1969	4.27	2.50	1.84	6.77	8.61
1970	4.79	2.96	2.47	7.75	10.22
1971	5.42	3.30	4.03	8.71	12.75
1972	5.96	4.45	4.82	10.41	15.23
1973	5.55	4.35	4.71	9.91	14.61
1974	4.61	4.14	4.81	8.75	13.56
1975	4.94	4.94	5.76	9.89	15.65
1976	5.05	5.31	6.65	10.36	17.01
1977	5.14	5.40	5.91	10.54	16.45
1978	5.45	5.49	5.81	10.94	16.75
1979	4.85	5.72	5.74	10.57	16.31
1980	4.74	6.25	5.93	10.99	16.92
1981	4.73	7.27	5.98	12.00	17.98
1982	4.92	7.02	6.63	11.94	18.57
1983	4.29	5.45	9.13	9.74	18.88
1984	4.14	5.43	10.42	9.56	19.99
1985	4.58	5.85	13.47	10.43	23.91
1986	5.21	6.18	15.59	11.39	26.97
1987	4.64	5.54	16.98	10.19	27.15
1988	4.40	5.74	19.44	10.13	29.57

Sources: Bank Indonesia, Indonesian Financial Statistics, various issues, and Laporan
  Mingguan [Weekly Report], various issues; BPS, Pendapatan Nasional Indonesia
  [National Income of Indonesia] Main Tables, various issues and unpublished revised
  estimates for years 1983–8.
[a]Revised GDP estimates used from 1972 onwards.

(Bank Indonesia) gave a partial subsidy on those interest rates. Over the
next decade, the M2/GDP ratio showed a mild upward trend reflecting
a rise of about 2 percentage points in both the M1 and the quasi-money
ratios.

The second important growth spurt started in 1983 and continued
through 1989. This latter period of rapid growth was manifested initially
by a drop in the M1/GDP ratio and a large increase in the quasi-money
ratio, resulting in only a moderate increase in the M2/GDP ratio.
Subsequently the M1 ratio has stabilized and the quasi-money ratio has
continued to rise rapidly. This second growth spurt resulted mainly
from the removal of credit and interest rate ceilings in June 1983, and
from the growing competition among banks to attract deposits, especially time deposits, since that time.

Over the period from 1968 to 1989, the ratio of narrow money (M1) to GDP has approximately doubled. Since narrow money is primarily a means of payment, this suggests that the monetization of the economy has roughly doubled over this period. On the other hand, the ratio of quasi-money, or time and savings deposits, to GDP has increased from practically 0 to 20 per cent in the two decades. It was the rise in this ratio that accounted for most of the growth in the two major spurts. Since quasi-money is mainly longer-term deposits, its growth is indicative of increases in financial savings that are held in the form of claims on the domestic banking system. Both of these measures are limited in that they do not include other means of payment and forms of financial saving. The most important of these, in the Indonesian context, are likely to be deposits and other claims held abroad. Undoubtedly part of the spurt in domestic time and savings deposits in the high growth periods reflects the repatriation of claims held abroad, but there is no reliable way of estimating the magnitudes involved.

It is noteworthy that the periods of high domestic financial growth are not closely correlated with periods of high real growth of the Indonesian economy. The initial period of financial growth occurred at a time when the economy was growing quite rapidly, but this growth was mainly due to recovery from a long period of mismanagement and deterioration. Then during the decade of high economic growth and high investment deriving from the oil boom, the domestic financial system languished. Finally, after the oil boom ended, and real growth slowed down, domestic financial growth accelerated. This is a first, crude indication that domestic financial growth was influenced more by financial policy measures than by the overall growth of the economy. It also suggests that, during the years of high economic growth and increases in real income, a substantial portion of the increases in savings that would be expected to be associated with those higher incomes was placed abroad.

A broader measure of financial development can be obtained by looking at the total assets of various types of financial institutions. These inevitably include some double counting because, for example, the assets of insurance companies include deposits at banks, which in turn are matched by bank assets. Of greater significance, a sizeable portion of the assets of Bank Indonesia (BI) consists of loans to deposit money banks (DMBs) which are then on-lent to their customers. Another distortion arises from the likely overstatement of the real, or market, value of many financial assets such as bad loans of the banks, and, on the other hand, the understatement of the market value of real assets. Despite all these limitations and the gaps in the data for earlier years, the data plotted in Figures 3.1 and 3.2 give an indication of the relative size and growth of various types of financial institutions in Indonesia over the past two decades. The best overall measure of financial size and growth is the ratio of financial assets to GDP, where financial assets are defined to exclude BI claims on the deposit money banks, because this ratio omits the double counting of Bank Indonesia loans to deposit money banks.

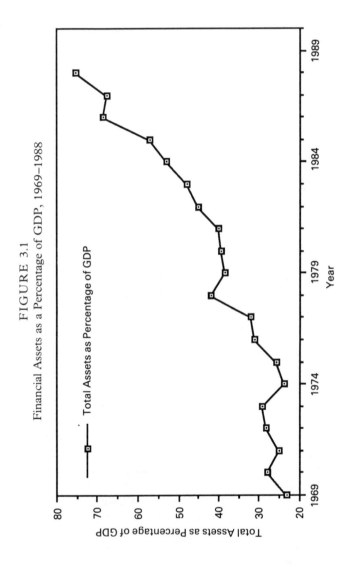

FIGURE 3.1

Financial Assets as a Percentage of GDP, 1969–1988

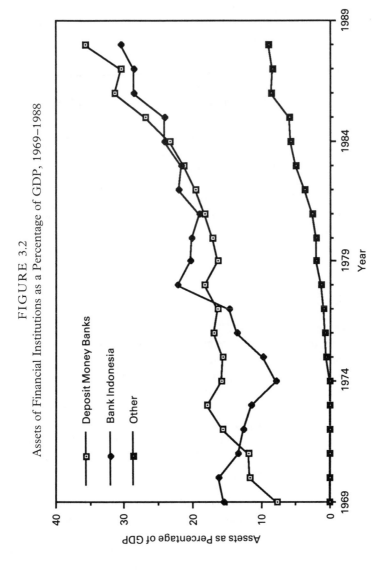

FIGURE 3.2

Assets of Financial Institutions as a Percentage of GDP, 1969–1988

This ratio has risen from about 23 per cent of GDP in 1969 to 75 per cent of GDP in 1988 (Figure 3.1).

During the initial growth spurt (1968–72), the deposit money banks raised their share of total financial assets relative to Bank Indonesia. This is seen most readily by comparing 'total assets of DMBs less loans from BI' with 'total assets of BI' in Figure 3.2. In 1969 the DMBs' net assets were equal to roughly half the total assets of BI, but by 1972 they were about 25 per cent greater than the total assets of BI. This change was largely due to the effective mobilization of deposits by the DMBs during this period. By 1982, however, 'total assets of DMBs less loans from BI' were roughly equal to the total assets of BI. After the second growth spurt (1983–8), they had again risen to 117 per cent of the total assets of BI. But it must be noted that there had also been substantial growth in the total assets of other financial institutions including insurance companies, leasing companies, pension funds, non-bank financial institutions (NBFIs), and the State Savings Bank (Bank Tabungan Negara, BTN). Although data for these other financial institutions are not available for the earlier period, they were probably of negligible importance. Their recorded growth in recent years has been very rapid and has accounted for an important part of the rise in the ratio of total financial assets to GDP.

The Sequence of Financial Reforms

The Early Years of the New Order

In September 1968, when inflation was decelerating but still running at a rate of about 50 per cent per annum, and the economy was just beginning to recover from the profligate Sukarno years, the first major move was made to revive and reform the financial system. This consisted of a large increase in bank time deposit interest rates from 30 per cent to 72 per cent per annum on 1-year time deposits and a rise in maximum bank lending rates to 60 per cent. The difference between the deposit and lending rates was covered in part by Central Bank subsidy payments. This measure led not only to the rapid increase in bank time deposits shown in Table 3.1 but also to a large inflow of foreign exchange and a 25 per cent appreciation of the floating exchange rate in a 6-month period. It also permitted more rapid expansion of Central Bank credit which, together with the growing deposit resources of the commercial banks, led to a substantial real increase in the availability of bank financing. As both domestic credit and foreign exchange became more available and less expensive in real terms, businesses were able to rehabilitate and, in some cases, expand their productive capabilities.

Over the next few years economic conditions improved steadily so that by 1971 the government was able to move to an unregulated foreign exchange system with a unified rate pegged to the US dollar. Nominal deposit and loan interest rates had been brought down to 24 per cent and 19 per cent respectively (Table 3.2). The direct subsidy

TABLE 3.2
Inflation and Interest Rates

| Year | Annual Inflation Rate | | Interest Rate | |
	CPI (1983=100)	CPI (annual percentage change)	Nominal	Real
1968	10.99	125.20	72.0	−24.0
1969	12.95	17.88	60.0	35.7
1970	14.56	12.36	24.0	10.4
1971	15.14	4.00	24.0	19.2
1972	16.16	6.73	18.0	10.6
1973	21.11	30.63	15.0	−12.0
1974	29.77	41.03	15.0	−18.4
1975	35.37	18.83	15.0	−3.2
1976	42.43	19.96	15.0	−4.2
1977	47.09	10.98	12.0	0.9
1978	50.95	8.19	9.0	0.7
1979	61.43	20.57	9.0	−9.6
1980	72.78	18.48	9.0	−8.0
1981	81.66	12.20	9.0	−2.9
1982	89.45	9.54	9.0	−0.5
1983	100.00	11.80	18.0	5.5
1984	106.42	6.42	18.3	11.1
1985	108.51	1.97	15.0	12.8
1986	124.09	14.36	15.0	0.6
1987	139.23	12.20	17.5	4.7
1988	150.48	8.08	18.5	9.6
1989	159.67	6.11	16.5	9.8

Source: BPS, Indikator Ekonomi, various issues.
[a]Rate on one-year time deposits of state banks. The real interest rate is the nominal rate deflated by the CPI.

on time deposit interest was reduced. Financial institutions continued to grow and provide a mixture of commercial and term financing, which was augmented by a large inflow of foreign financing for major development projects as well as for business investment.

At that point in time it was reasonable to conclude that the partial financial reform process of 1968, in the context of a broad macroeconomic policy reorientation and, after 1971, an open capital account, was moving ahead very successfully. There was still much room for improvement in the management and operation of financial institutions and a deepening of financial markets, but progress on all these fronts was readily apparent.

Financial Restriction and Displacement 1973–1983

The rise in world oil prices in late 1973 immediately affected Indonesia, generating balance of payments surpluses and budgetary revenues that soon boosted domestic spending and inflation. The Central Bank was unable to control the growth of reserve money and therefore shifted to credit ceilings on the commercial banks in an attempt to control growth of the money supply. Interest rate ceilings, which had been carried over from earlier years, were kept well below the inflation rate so that real deposit rates became negative (Table 3.2). As a consequence, bank deposits increased only moderately as a share of GNP. Much of the investment and working capital of business over the next decade was financed by the government budget or by loans from abroad. The large government budget was funded through a combination of oil revenues and continuing inflows of foreign assistance. The foreign borrowings of the business sector consisted of direct foreign loans and equity investments, and also of sizeable borrowings from banks in nearby financial centres such as Singapore and Hong Kong.

Because of the ceilings on domestic bank lending, and also the low interest rates on bank deposits, many Indonesian businesses found it expedient to hold substantial deposit balances abroad and to use those balances as collateral for loans from abroad. At the same time any domestic bank which had surplus funds beyond its domestic loan ceilings tended to place them abroad in foreign exchange in order to obtain higher interest rates. The open capital account system and the stability of the foreign exchange rate made such loans relatively risk-free operations. Thus, the ceilings on domestic credit did not become a significant constraint on the availability of financial services for most Indonesian businesses of medium to large scale. They simply shifted their financial activities offshore. Smaller businesses and households, especially in the rural areas, were not well served by the formal financial institutions, but there was ample liquidity within the country as a whole, and a large network of semi-formal and informal institutions in both urban and rural areas saw to it that financial services were available wherever they were profitable.[2] The abundance of financing and domestic spending raised the inflation rate to an annual average of 25 per cent from 1973 through to 1977 as measured by either the GDP deflator or the consumer price index. The ratio of deposit money bank total assets to GDP declined from 20.4 per cent to 19.7 per cent during the same period.

The tranquillity induced by this combination of domestic and foreign financing was shaken in 1978 when the government carried out an unexpected 50 per cent devaluation of the rupiah relative to the US dollar. The primary purpose of the devaluation was to correct for the disparity in inflation rates between Indonesia and the rest of the world in order to reduce disincentives to domestic producers of tradable goods. But the financial effect was to give those domestic banks and businesses which had large credit balances abroad a sudden windfall profit on their net foreign exchange assets, and to impose a corresponding cost on all those with net foreign indebtedness. Once the devaluation was implemented, expectations of further devaluation were reduced, so borrowers were again encouraged to make use of foreign financing. The expansionary effects of this were then reinforced by the second increase in world oil prices in 1979. Indonesia continued to have ample sources of financing despite negative real interest rates and repression of domestic banking institutions.

In the late 1970s the Indonesian government attempted to stimulate development of the capital market in Jakarta.[3] It set up a new agency, Badan Pengembangan Pasar Modal (Bapepam), to manage and regulate the stock exchange, and a government-owned corporation, Danareksa (literally, 'to guard the funds'), to underwrite new issues and offer investment fund units to the public. The main objectives of these early efforts were to increase Indonesian ownership of foreign joint ventures operating in Indonesia, and to broaden public participation in the capital markets. After an initial spurt of activity, the markets reverted to a relatively dormant state, and never did succeed in raising much capital.

The 1983 Reforms

The decline in oil prices beginning in 1982 signalled a sharp reversal in Indonesia's economic circumstances and brought on a second round of retrenchment and reorientation of macroeconomic measures in 1983, coinciding with the installation of a new cabinet following the re-election of President Soeharto. The first move was in the fiscal area as the government scaled back sharply budgetary commitments for large investment projects to keep expenditures within available revenues and maintain the balanced budget principle. This was followed by another large devaluation of the rupiah by 38 per cent at the end of March 1983. This devaluation was intended not only to encourage exports and restrain imports, but also to boost the rupiah value of budgetary revenues from oil exports.

The third major move was in the area of financial policy. The Central Bank announced removal of all bank credit ceilings, and also of interest rate ceilings on the government-owned banks. (Previously, private banks had not been subject to interest rate ceilings, but they were subject to credit ceilings, and this had limited their interest in mobilizing deposits.) The fourth move, announced in September 1983, was a broad tax reform, introducing a value added tax and shifting from a schedular to a global income tax. As has been discussed in Chapter 2, implementation of the tax reform was a gradual process over the next few years and proved crucial in sustaining government revenues in the face of further declines in the oil prices. The financial reform, on the other hand, was quicker to take effect and produced a substantial increase in bank deposits and loans within the first seven months of its enactment.

One of the great unknowns in Indonesia, with its totally open capital account system, is just how much of any change in domestic financial asset holdings is simply a shifting of activity from offshore to onshore or vice versa. There was a rise in the ratio of total bank assets to GDP between the end of 1982 and 1988 from 25.5 per cent to 45.4 per cent. Such a high growth of bank assets, occurring during a period when GNP per capita was growing at little more than 4 per cent per annum in real terms and when the terms of trade were moving against Indonesia, did not reflect a comparable real increase in national savings. It also did not reflect accurately the increase in financial saving. Instead, it was some combination of increased real saving, increased saving in the form of financial assets, and repatriation of past financial savings from overseas.

At the time of the financial reform in June 1983, one of the major concerns was that there might be a rapid inflow of past foreign asset accumulations which would cause a sudden increase in domestic reserve money, credit, and money supply, with possible inflationary consequences that could undermine the positive effects of the devaluation. Similar inflows of foreign capital in 1973–4 had led to the imposition of credit ceilings in the first place, and removal of those ceilings in 1983 left the monetary authorities with no effective instruments for controlling the growth of the money supply, except possibly through increases in reserve requirements. As pointed out in Chapter 4, there was some return flow of foreign exchange in response to both the devaluation and the rise in domestic interest rates, but no large increase in bank credit, domestic spending, or inflation.

A major reason for this was the sluggish response of the government-owned commercial banks to the removal of loan ceilings. The state banks, still operating in the bureaucratic control mode, were accustomed to making prospective borrowers wait for months for loan approvals, and they did not change their management style quickly despite the rapid build-up of their deposits in response to higher interest rates. Instead the state banks found it expedient to increase their foreign exchange holdings abroad or to lend excess funds through the newly active Jakarta interbank market to the private banks which were much more aggressive in expanding lending. Over the next several years, from March 1983 to March 1988, the private national banks increased their share of total bank assets from 11 to 22 per cent, reflecting their strong response to the removal of credit ceilings (Table 3.3).

This pattern of deposit mobilization by the state banks, which was then intermediated through the private banks to the ultimate borrowers, worked quite well without causing any serious pressures on interest or exchange rates, until September 1984, when the Indonesian financial system experienced not an excess of liquidity from foreign capital inflow, but instead a liquidity squeeze. This was due to the absence of any effective instrument for supplying liquidity or adjusting the available liquidity to changes in other factors affecting the supply of reserve money in the financial system. A sudden transfer of government deposits to the central bank reduced the supply of reserve money and, without any offsetting adjustment from the central bank, caused the liquidity squeeze.

Normally such a squeeze would have been met by a short-term inflow of funds from abroad under Indonesia's open foreign exchange system, but this liquidity squeeze was exacerbated by a concurrent accelerated depreciation in the exchange rate set by the Central Bank that made

TABLE 3.3

Total Consolidated Bank Assets by Type of Bank[a] (Rp billion)

Group of Banks	1980	1981	1982	1983	1984	1985	1986	1987	1988	1989	1990
State Banks[b]	6,073	8,305	10,857	14,298	16,544	21,184	25,129	29,544	34,657	72,256	96,620
Private National Banks	688	983	1,356	2,079	3,076	4,402	6,149	8,060	11,225	31,141	52,136
Regional Development Banks	266	402	488	589	769	1,004	1,174	1,252	1,558	2,794	4,016
Foreign Banks	661	720	936	1,603	1,729	2,258	2,418	2,585	2,894	4,674	6,331
Total	7,688	10,410	13,637	18,569	22,118	28,848	34,870	41,441	50,334	110,865	159,103
						Percentage of Total					
State Banks[b]	78.99	79.78	79.61	77.00	74.80	73.43	72.06	71.29	68.85	65.17	60.73
Private National Banks	8.95	9.44	9.94	11.20	13.91	15.26	17.63	19.45	22.30	28.09	32.77
Regional Development Banks	3.46	3.86	3.58	3.17	3.48	3.48	3.37	3.02	3.10	2.52	2.52
Foreign Banks	8.60	6.92	6.86	8.63	7.82	7.83	6.93	6.24	5.75	4.22	3.98
Total	100.00	100.00	100.00	100.00	100.00	100.00	100.00	100.00	100.00	100.00	100.00

Source: Bank Indonesia, *Annual Report*, various issues.

[a] At end of fiscal year—31 March.

[b] Includes Bapindo and excludes BTN (State Savings Bank).

the commercial banks very reluctant to sell foreign exchange, even for a few days, to cover their reserve requirements. As a consequence, the domestic interbank interest rate shot up to 90 per cent, which was the annualized rate of the daily depreciation of the exchange rate (Figure 3.3). Bank Indonesia responded to the liquidity crisis by pumping large amounts of 3- to 6-month liquidity credits into the banking system, bringing down the interbank interest rate to below 15 per cent in a few days. This experience demonstrated the many problems of implementing indirect monetary controls and the necessity of building up the institutional base for their use. Specifically, it high-lighted the need for the Central Bank to keep better track of the available supply of reserve money in the financial system, to develop further its instruments for controlling the supply of reserve money, and to avoid too predictable a depreciation of the currency.[4]

When the new monetary policy instruments, Sertifikat Bank Indonesia (SBI) and Surat Berharga Pasar Uang (SBPU), were first introduced, the plan was that their issue prices would fluctuate according to chang-ing market conditions, and that active secondary markets would develop. But, because BI in effect stood ready to supply to banks or buy from banks whatever amounts they desired, at 'cut-off' interest rates deter-mined by Bank Indonesia, the secondary markets did not emerge. This practice did succeed in stabilizing the interest rates on these instruments and accustomed the banks to buying and selling them, but it precluded the development of a real secondary market which could have facilitated BI's control over reserve money.

In addition to setting the short-term interest rate, the Central Bank also set the foreign exchange rate and the premium on foreign exchange swaps that it offered to those financial institutions and businesses with future foreign exchange commitments. (Initially the swap facility was offered in limited quantities, but the limits were removed in October 1986, following the devaluation.) Thus the Central Bank controlled the following key prices: the SBI and SBPU money market interest rates, the foreign exchange rate, and the swap rate on forward foreign exchange. It also stood ready to be the residual supplier of any excess demand or buyer of excess supply, within broad limits, in all these markets.

This pattern of price setting coupled with willingness to meet excess demand made the Central Bank particularly vulnerable to speculation about changes in the foreign exchange rate. Such speculation had been fostered by the three sudden and large devaluations in 1978, 1983, and 1986. Whenever rumours spread in the financial markets that there might be another devaluation, most financial institutions and businesses took advantage of the open capital markets and bought foreign exchange, or sold it to the Central Bank under a currency swap agree-ment. Very large movements in short-term interest rates would have been required to counteract such speculation, and the Central Bank was reluctant to permit such moves in the short-term rates that it controlled. As a consequence, the interbank borrowing rate, which the Central Bank did not control, became very volatile (Table 3.4).

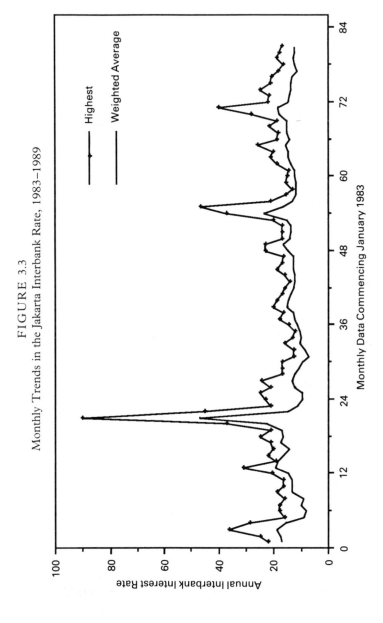

FIGURE 3.3

Monthly Trends in the Jakarta Interbank Rate, 1983–1989

TABLE 3.4
Interest Rates on the Jakarta Interbank Call Money Market
(per cent per annum)

Year	Lowest[a]	Highest[a]	Weighted Average
1983	3.5	28.8	12.9
1984	6.0	90.0	19.0
1985	4.5	25.0	10.0
1986	10.5	23.0	13.8
1987	9.0	46.5	14.5
1988	11.6	40.0	15.0
1989	7.0	25.0	12.4

Source: Bank Indonesia, Laporan Mingguan [Weekly Report]: Table 4d.
[a]Figures refer to the lowest and highest daily rates for the year shown.

In June 1987, there was a speculative run on the rupiah; the overnight interbank rate rose to 37 per cent. The authorities, having concluded that there was no underlying justification for another devaluation, took drastic measures to reduce the supply of reserve money and thus force a return flow of foreign exchange to cover bank reserve requirements. The reduction in reserve money was accomplished in two ways. First, commercial banks were required to repurchase their commercial bills (SBPUs) from the Central Bank—i.e. the ceilings on such rediscounts for each bank were suddenly reduced to zero. Second, the government instructed four state enterprises (which had large time deposit balances at the commercial banks) to use those deposits to buy SBIs. Both measures shifted large amounts of reserves from the commercial banks to the Central Bank. However, the forced redemption of the SBPUs dramatically reduced their use by banks for liquidity and thus eliminated that instrument of monetary policy until May 1989. The forced purchase by the state enterprises of SBIs with 6-month maturity at a set interest rate created a two-tier system of SBIs: longer maturities with fixed rates sold on a command basis, and short maturities (7-day) which were auctioned at more variable rates and amounts as a flexible tool of monetary policy.

The effect of these strong measures turned out to be positive in one sense: it was made clear that the government was prepared to defend the exchange rate and avoid any further large devaluations. This in turn had an important psychological influence on domestic interest rates. The cost was at least a temporary loss to the Central Bank of one of its market-based instruments for short-term liquidity management, the SBPU.

The 1988–1989 Reforms

In late 1988 the Indonesian authorities announced a broad set of financial reform measures. This time the focus was primarily on the structure of the financial system, and the main aims were:

1. to promote competition, particularly within the banking sector, by allowing new entry, expansion of activities, reduction in compartmentalization, and more bank autonomy in decision-making;
2. to promote public confidence in the banking system through stronger supervision by BI, prudential controls on foreign exchange positions, stronger capital positions, and lending limits;
3. to promote rationality, internationalization and confidence in the insurance sector;
4. to broaden the range of financial services by promoting the development of private sector activity in capital markets, leasing, venture capital, and other services;
5. to develop money markets, both primary and secondary, and to improve the use of monetary policy instruments; and
6. to shift from relatively fixed to more flexible interest and exchange rates.[5]

A significant outcome of these measures was that both exchange rate and money market interest rate management became more flexible. Gradual depreciation of the rupiah against the US dollar, through a kind of crawling peg, was designed to give more certainty, thus discouraging unfounded speculation about a major devaluation. At the same time the movement in the foreign exchange swap rate would be consistent with the prevailing spread between rupiah and dollar interest rates. Regular weekly auctions by the Central Bank of 1-week, 4-week, and 13-week SBIs became more accepting of, and consistent with, the prevailing interest rates in the secondary market.

The most significant aspects of the deregulation packages were those that provided new opportunities for engaging in practically all aspects of financial activity. The Indonesian government opened the doors to new licensing of domestic banks. It also permitted the foreign banks already operating in Indonesia to open branches in the major provincial cities, and licensed several new joint ventures between foreign and Indonesian banks. The way was also opened for joint ventures in the areas of insurance, securities companies, and other types of financial institutions.

The October 1988 reforms also gave a considerable stimulus to the development of the domestic short-term money markets. Restrictions on interbank borrowing were removed. Along with a reduction in the required reserve ratio to 2 per cent of all bank third-party liabilities, all commercial banks were initially required to buy specified amounts of 3- and 6-month SBIs to offset 80 per cent of the reduction in required bank reserves. After this initial forced sale at fixed interest rates, the banks were encouraged to begin using and trading these SBIs as instruments for managing their liquidity needs. Bank Indonesia appointed a group of fifteen banks and NBFIs as market makers, and two as brokers, in these money market instruments as a further encouragement to the development of a secondary market. Also, over time, Bank Indonesia improved the management of its daily and weekly auctions of 7- to 91-day SBIs so as to support the growth of the secondary market and let interest rates respond to changing liquidity conditions.

Another measure that has helped to shift money market activity from overseas foreign exchange markets to domestic rupiah money markets, was the imposition on 1 May 1989, of net foreign exchange open position limits on all banks equal to 25 per cent of their total capital. This measure, along with a shift from same-day settlement to two-day settlement of foreign exchange transactions with Bank Indonesia, and the more gradual adjustment of the exchange rate seems to have largely eliminated short-term movements in and out of foreign exchange as the main means of liquidity management by the banks. There has been a marked shift to domestic money markets where daily transactions averaged probably Rp 300 billion, or approximately US$150 million in November 1989. The outstanding volume of money market instruments was probably in the range of Rp 5–6 trillion, with SBIs averaging Rp 3 trillion. For purposes of comparison, narrow money supply (M1) was about Rp 15 trillion, the total reserves of the deposit money banks were about Rp 1.7 trillion and required reserves about Rp 0.7 trillion.

Capital Markets

Capital markets in Indonesia were very quiet in the first eight years of the 1980s. However, in December 1987 the government began to take steps to activate the moribund capital market with a package of measures known as Pakdes I (Paket Desember 1987). Foreign investors were, for the first time, allowed to buy and sell up to 49 per cent of issued capital. (However, only eight of the twenty-four stocks listed on the Exchange were not already majority-owned by foreign interests, so the opportunities proved limited.) The limits on price movements on the Exchange were also lifted, and licensing requirements for brokers and dealers and other capital market supporting professions, and clearer procedures for new issues, were set out. A Bursa Paralel, or over-the-counter market, was authorized.

Pakto 27 (Paket 27 October 1988) included several more measures which encouraged capital market development, and a withholding tax of 15 per cent was imposed on interest on time deposits, previously tax-free, thus improving the competitiveness of shares as assets. In addition, financial institutions were allowed to issue shares to the public, enhancing the potential supply of shares. In December 1988, in the set of reforms known as Pakdes II (Paket Desember 1988), important capital market provisions were included: private securities exchanges could be set up, the priority of Danareksa, the state-owned securities and investment fund company, to underwrite 50 per cent of all new issues was removed,[6] and joint-venture firms in newly authorized financial services (of most importance are securities companies) were authorized with up to 85 per cent foreign participation. In November 1989 securities companies were given the right to seek licences for underwriting.

These measures set the stage for rapid development in Indonesian capital markets. A privately owned and managed Securities Exchange was set up in Surabaya in June 1989,[7] new brokers and dealers' firms and new securities companies sprang up, and competition in the under-writing business was opened up (Table 3.6). The over-the-counter market, the Bursa Paralel, had its first listing in February 1989 (six listings as of the end of 1990). During 1989 the government, under the dynamic leadership of the chairman of the Capital Market's Executive Board, a state agency, made a determined effort to encourage new issues after years of total inactivity. The response was outstanding. Table 3.5 compares the capital market activity at the end of 1987 with that in March 1990. The number of companies listing shares and bonds increased from 24 (listing shares only) to 126. The Jakarta Stock Exchange (JSE) Composite Index moved from 82.5 to 418 (Table 3.6). The government also announced in 1989 that in 1990–1, 52 state firms would go public.[8]

The supply response has been significantly encouraged by the fact that a number of foreign-based investment funds designed for portfolio investment in Indonesia have been set up since late 1987.[9] The first 'foreign-based country fund' (actually for Indonesia and Malaysia) appeared on the Jakarta Stock Exchange in November 1988, initiating a surge of foreign interest, with domestic investors riding on their heels. In fact, acknowledging the potential benefits from growing demand by foreign investors, the government issued a decree in September 1989 which permitted foreign investors to buy 49 per cent of the shares in any new primary issues and of the already listed shares, in all sectors of the economy except private banking. This was a major policy change in that formerly, certain categories of firms were restricted by the Capital Investment Co-ordinating Board (Badan Koordinasi Penanaman Modal or BKPM) or the Ministry of Trade from selling their shares to foreigners. This new decree has ruled that so-called 'joint ventures'

TABLE 3.5

Funds Raised Annually through New Issues of Bonds and Equity Shares
in the Capital Market

Year	Issues (Rp million)		
	Shares[a]	Bonds	Total
1977–83	117,205	94,718	211,923
1984	13,951	60,000	73,951
1985	490	100,000	100,490
1986	769	150,000	150,769
1987	411	131,000	131,411
1988	57,481	320,000	377,481
1989	3,678,217	671,500	4,349,717
1990	11,805,117	385,000	12,190,117

Source: Capital Market Executive Agency, *Monthly Report*, December 1990.
[a]Include stock splits, bonuses, dividends, private placements, company listings, and rights issues.

TABLE 3.6
Indicators of Stock Market Growth

	End December 1987	End December 1990
Market Composite Index		
JSE	82	418
Number of brokers/dealers	39	211
Number of Security		
Companies	0	63
Number of firms listing		
Jakarta Exchange	24	126
Bursa Paralel	0	6
Number of bonds listed		
Jakarta Exchange	16	53
Bursa Paralel	0	3

Sources: Capital Market Executive Agency, *Monthly Report*, December 1990; *Bisnis Indonesia*; and unpublished data from the Department of Finance, Directorate of Financial Institutions and Accountancy.

(*penanaman modal asing* or PMA firms) are 'domestic' investors, and that they too may sell up to 49 per cent of listed shares to other foreign investors.

Summing Up

Financial development in Indonesia has been characterized by two periods of rapid growth in bank deposits and assets, from 1968 to 1972 and from 1983 through to 1990. The broad opening up of opportunities for new entry and new activities, which began in 1988 has already changed fundamentally the structure of the financial system. Financial development has been driven mainly by changes in government policies rather than changes in the rates of economic growth. One could say that the domestic financial system was also affected by the 'Dutch Disease' along with most other parts of the domestic economy from 1973 to 1982, but has largely recovered as a result of various policy changes since 1983.

The recorded growth of the domestic financial system has reflected partly real growth of holdings of financial assets and liabilities by Indonesian entities, and partly the repatriation of such holdings from abroad as well as new inflows of investments by foreigners. There is no way of precisely estimating the relative magnitudes of these factors. The open capital account since 1971 has permitted easy substitution of foreign and domestic assets. At times this has been destabilizing, but overall it has been a healthy influence. It has forced the government to avoid fiscal deficits, and it has necessitated that monetary and other financial policies be formulated in ways that would not precipitate capital flight. Foreigners were forbidden to invest in the portfolios of firms before the end of 1988 and were also restricted in direct investment. But the reforms initiated by Pakdes I have largely removed these constraints.

Three large devaluations—in 1978, 1983, and 1986—contributed to continuing expectations of further large devaluations. While the latter two devaluations helped to reverse capital flight for a time, these beneficial effects were soon overtaken by fears of further devaluations, which were readily manifested in volatile, uncontrolled interbank interest rates. The strong contractionary medicine, known as the 'Sumarlin Shock' administered in mid-1987, and the subsequent, more stable management of crawling-peg exchange rate adjustments, seem to have eliminated fears of further big devaluations for the time being and permitted further actions to promote financial development. The newly emerging money and capital markets have added substantially to the liquidity and attractiveness of domestic financial asset holdings. Greater confidence in exchange rate policies along with attractive rupiah interest rates and restrictions on banks' foreign exchange positions have all led to increased demand for rupiah denominated financial assets. As these markets broaden and deepen, they could become more stable. On the other hand, they could contribute to more speculation and instability.

Bank Indonesia, through the careful management of policies described in detail in Chapter 4, is actively trying to impart stability to the domestic money markets and the foreign exchange markets with, so far, considerable success. But there is still need to improve the regulatory structure of the capital markets and encourage institutions, such as private investment funds, all of which should provide greater continuity, stability, and growth in these new markets. The development of properly regulated pension funds and insurance companies will further contribute to healthy financial development.

Further measures that are intended to strengthen the legal and institutional base for financial development are underway in the arena of financial policy. These include new legislation dealing with banking, insurance, and pensions, and new regulations covering investment funds, securities companies, and other capital market activities. There is a need to clarify and strengthen regulations to try to prevent unfair practices and give adequate protection to investors.[10]

1. See World Bank (1989: 122–32) for further discussion of individual country experience of liberalization programmes.

2. See Patten and Rosengard (1989) and Alexander and Alexander (1986) for further discussion.

3. See Dickie (1981) for a lengthy discussion of the early stages of development of the Jakarta capital markets.

4. In Chapter 4, Binhadi and Meek present a detailed discussion of the process by which Bank Indonesia sought to develop an appropriate set of money market instruments. We will not duplicate that discussion here, but merely highlight some of the problems that have arisen while these instruments were being developed and trace their effects on the overall growth of the financial system.

5. For more details on the various packages, see the Appendix to this chapter.

6. Danareksa is a state-owned financial enterprise set up by Presidential Decree in 1977. It operates the only authorized open-end investment funds in Indonesia, has broker-age and dealing operations, and has been a dominant underwriter. Until December 1988 it had priority to buy (underwrite) 50 per cent of all new issues. Before early 1990, the only other underwriters in Indonesia were Bank Pembangunan Indonesia (Bapindo) and 12 NBFIs (joint ventures with both government and private ownership), which also have brokerage and dealing operations.

7. The Surabaya Stock Exchange enjoys cross-listing with the Jakarta Exchange and receives one-half the income of the Jakarta Exchange, even though its volume is relatively small.

8. For further discussion of these measures, see Mackie and Sjahrir (1989) and Pangestu and Habir (1990).

9. These funds are foreign-based and theoretically do not sell units to Indonesian investors. The government welcomes these funds and has made no effort to restrict them other than imposing a limitation on proportions of shares that foreigners can hold. At any rate the lack of any foreign exchange controls generally puts the operations of these funds beyond Indonesian supervisory authority. As of early 1990, there were over 16 such funds with substantial interest in Indonesian securities, besides the so-called regional funds.

10. By mid-1991 most of these measures had, in fact, been enacted.

APPENDIX

Financial Deregulation Packages:
October 1988–March 1989

I. Pakto 27 (October 1988)

A. Banks

1. NEW ENTRY PERMITTED

Capital Requirements
Banks wholly owned by Indonesian nationals
  General banks: Rp 10 billion.
  Rural banks: Rp 50 million.
Up to 85 per cent owned by foreign banks (joint ventures)
  General banks: Rp 50 billion.
Branches of foreign banks in Indonesia
  No new entry.
NBFIs
  No new entry.

Other Requirements
New joint ventures:
  Joint ownership by domestic banks and foreign banks (maximum of 85 per cent of shares by foreign partner). Domestic bank must be classified 'sound' 20 of last 24 months. Location restricted to seven major cities. Within 12 months, outstanding export credits must equal 50 per cent of total credits outstanding.
  Foreign bank partner must:
  (a) have a representative office in Indonesia;
  (b) be reputable in its country of origin;
  (c) be from a country with reciprocity agreement with Indonesia.

2. NEW BRANCHES

Banks wholly owned by Indonesian nationals
Must have 20 months' 'sound' classification in last 24 months.
Can open branches anywhere in Indonesia.
NBFIs
Must have 20 months' 'sound' classification in last 24 months.
Can open one branch only in each of seven major cities.
Existing foreign bank branches in Indonesia
Must be classified as sound.
Can open one sub-branch only in each of seven major cities.
Within 12 months, outstanding export credits must equal 50 per cent of total credits outstanding.
Rural banks
No restriction on branch office in same district as head office.
Must be located outside Jakarta, provincial capitals, and municipalities; otherwise must move or become a general bank (capital at Rp 10 billion).

3. FOREIGN EXCHANGE BANKS

Branches of existing foreign exchange banks automatically have right to deal in foreign exchange.
Domestic non-foreign exchange banks may deal in foreign exchange if:
classified 'sound' in 20 of last 24 months.
total assets greater than Rp 100 billion.

4. CERTIFICATES OF DEPOSIT

All banks, except rural banks, and NBFIs can issue certificates of deposit (Rp 1 million and 30-day minimum).

B. *Money-changers*

Licences issued for unlimited period; no specific restrictions on entry.

C. *Other Measures*

1. State enterprises may put 50 per cent of deposits with private national banks, development banks, and NBFIs: up to 20 per cent may be placed in one single bank.
2. Maximum legal lending limits were imposed on banks and NBFIs (as a percentage of lender's capital):
   20 per cent to a single borrower;
   50 per cent to a group of borrowers.
   Various restrictions on borrowing by the Board of Commissioners, shareholders, other affiliates, and staff.
3. Reserve requirements on banks lowered from a nominal 15 per cent to 2 per cent of liabilities to third parties. Lagged reserve accounting adopted; 3-month and 6-month Pakto SBIs issued.
4. Maximum limit on interbank borrowing eliminated.
5. SBI maturities extended from only 7 days up to six months. Auction process strengthened.
6. Final withholding tax of 15 per cent imposed on the interest of time deposits. Exemption allowed for certain 'savings' schemes. Anonymity preserved.

7. Banks and NBFIs can issue new shares on capital market.
8. Swap premium of BI made to reflect market conditions. Swap maturity lengthened.
9. Two-day settlement for foreign exchange transactions by BI.

II. Pakdes II (December 1988)

1. Allows for establishment of private securities exchanges. Securities can be traded on more than one securities exchange.
2. Priority of Danareksa to purchase 50 per cent of new issues is eliminated. Simple 'priority' is retained.
3. Permits licensing of wholly owned Indonesian firms and joint ventures in the financial service activities shown in (4) with up to 85 per cent foreign capital participation. Existing firms must adjust within two years.
4. Licensing of single- and multi-activity firms in:
   (a) Leasing companies
   (b) Venture capital
   (c) Securities trading
   (d) Factoring
   (e) Consumer finance
   (f) Credit card.
5. Banks permitted to set up subsidiaries for 4(a) and 4(b), and to engage in 4(d) through 4(f) without separate licence. Must obtain licence for 4(c).
6. Capital Requirements for Single Activity:
   Wholly owned by Indonesians:
   Factoring, Securities Trading, Credit Card, and Consumer Finance: Rp 2 billion.
   Leasing, Venture Capital: Rp 3 billion.
   Joint ventures:
   Factoring, Securities Trading, Credit Card, and Consumer Finance: Rp 8 billion.
   Leasing, Venture Capital: Rp 10 billion.
7. Capital Requirements for Multi-activity:
   Wholly owned by Indonesians: Rp 5 billion.
   Joint ventures: Rp 15 billion.
8. Regulations for Insurance:
   (a) Joint ventures allowed; up to 80 per cent foreign share.
   (b) Regulations set forth for solvency, admitted assets retention ratios.
   (c) Supervision strengthened.

III. Pakmar (March 1989)

1. Clarifies and interprets Pakto 27 concerning:
   (a) Licensing mergers of banks.
   (b) Definition of 'Capital' and 'Groups' used to calculate lending limits. 'Exempted credits' defined.
   (c) Definition of 'Export Credits' used in requirements for foreign and joint-venture bank operations.
   (d) Shares of foreign banks in joint ventures.
2. Eliminates ceiling on offshore loans by banks and NBFIs.
3. Banks and NBFIs are restricted to maximum net open position equal to 25 per cent of capital.

4. Announcement of schedule for removal of subsidy on interest rates for export credits within the year.
5. Exempts 'existing' rural banks from Pakto provisions.
6. Eliminates existing requirements that medium- and long-term bank loans must be approved by Bank Indonesia.
7. Allows Bapindo and NBFIs to hold all types of equity.
8. Allows general banks to hold equity in financial activities with certain limits; they can hold equity in other firms only with the approval of the Minister of Finance.
9. Reaffirms underwriting authority to NBFIs and Bapindo. Prohibits general banks from underwriting.

REFERENCES

Alexander, Jennifer and Alexander, Paul (1986), 'Finance and Credit in a Rural Javanese Market: An Anthropological Perspective', Paper presented at a conference on Financial Development in Indonesia, Jakarta, HIID, August.

Dickie, Robert B. (1981), 'Development of Third World Securities Markets: An Analysis of General Principles and a Case Study of the Indonesian Market', *Law and Policy in International Business*, 13.

Mackie, J. A. C. and Sjahrir (1989), 'Survey of Recent Developments', *Bulletin of Indonesian Economic Studies*, 25(3): 3–34.

Pangestu, Mari and Habir, Manggi (1990), 'Survey of Recent Developments', *Bulletin of Indonesian Economic Studies*, 26(1): 3–36.

Patten, Richard and Rosengard, Jay (1989), 'Progress with Profits: The Development of Rural Banking in Indonesia', Jakarta: Harvard Institute for International Development, mimeo.

World Bank (1989), *World Development Report*, Washington, DC.

4

Implementing Monetary Policy*

Binhadi and Paul Meek

Introduction

SINCE the financial deregulation measures of 1983, Bank Indonesia (the Central Bank) has been actively engaged in developing a market-oriented approach to monetary control. It has developed annual targets for growth of the monetary aggregates and of the monetary base as reference points for policy-making. As was discussed in Chapter 3, the actual conduct of policy has involved a continuing tension between domestic monetary objectives and the expected level of the rupiah exchange rate in an open economy with free capital movements. This chapter focuses primarily on the development of new money market instruments and Bank Indonesia's approach to domestic monetary control during the liberalization process.

Monetary Policies and the Financial Environment Prior to the Reforms

Responses to the Oil Shocks

As is well known, the rice crisis of 1972/3, followed by the first oil shock, led to a rapid growth in inflation, from the low level which had been achieved in the years from 1969 to 1971.[1] Bank Indonesia responded by introducing in 1974 a system of individual bank credit ceilings as a primary defence against excessive domestic money growth (Arndt, 1974: 9; Arndt, 1979: 113 ff.) There was also a complex system of rediscount credits to priority sectors (called liquidity credits) and regulation of the deposit and loan rates of the five state banks, which accounted for three-quarters of commercial bank deposits (Sundararajan and Balino, 1984: 11–14). The allowable credit expansion for each fiscal year was based on money supply estimates consistent with expected growth and inflation, and balance of payments targets. The openness of the financial system, with capital movements virtually free of controls,

*An earlier version of this chapter was prepared for a SEANZA course at the Reserve Bank in Sydney in 1988.

necessitated caution in the amount of credit expansion allowed. Credit quotas were allocated to banks on the basis of their historical deposit performance with adjustments made during the year. At the same time Bank Indonesia, in consultation with the Department of Finance, worked out a credit ceiling for each public enterprise.

The system of liquidity credits already in place expanded with the oil boom. The state banks provided investment and working capital credits at subsidized rates to favoured sectors, including agriculture and small enterprises, based on their ability to rediscount specified proportions of priority loans at Bank Indonesia on concessional terms. Credit extended by Bank Indonesia under this scheme grew very rapidly and accounted for 56 per cent of banking sector claims on the private sector by the end of the first quarter of 1983. Until June 1983 Bank Indonesia set ceilings on both the rates that the state banks could pay on deposits maturing in more than three months and the rates they could charge on their loans. All government enterprises were required to keep their deposits with the five state commercial banks and one state development bank, which together had 824 branches distributed throughout the country. Local governmental bodies were permitted to keep deposits in the regional development banks as well. Although constrained in their ability to open branches, the private banks, both national and foreign, were free to set rates on both deposits and loans. In December 1982 the weighted average deposit rate of the private banks was 18 per cent, compared with 12 per cent for the state banks, while the loan rates of the private banks averaged around 20 per cent compared with rates of about 11 per cent at the state banks. Although the state banks could pay somewhat lower interest rates because they were deemed less risky than the private banks, the large disparity in rates led to much faster growth in the deposits of the private banks. Over the years 1978 to 1982, time deposits at private banks rose at an annual rate of 55 per cent compared with only 14 per cent rate for the state banks.

Sundararajan and Balino (1984) found that the system of annual credit ceilings was reasonably effective in controlling credit expansion in most years. The growth of liquidity credits by Bank Indonesia was roughly offset by the build-up of government deposits at the bank. However, deposit growth at commercial banks often exceeded allowable credit growth, leaving a sizeable volume of excess reserves. As was noted in Chapter 3, banks moved considerable amounts of excess funds abroad to invest, and to hedge the foreign currency deposits maintained with them by their domestic customers.[2] The commercial banks' share of the banking system's net foreign assets rose from 8 per cent at the end of 1977 to 52 per cent in mid-1983. As the balance of payments deteriorated in 1982/3 and concerns about a devaluation increased, Bank Indonesia required the banks to hold special deposits with it, using repatriated funds. Bank Indonesia, which was already paying interest on excess rupiah reserves to restrain bank investment abroad, paid an interest rate on repatriated deposits that was tied to the London interbank offer rate (LIBOR).

Banks and Non-Bank Financial Institutions

The banking system in Indonesia, to which the 1983 reforms were applied, was and remains quite highly concentrated, at least in comparison with the USA.[3] Bank Indonesia itself accounted for 42 per cent of the assets of the financial system at the end of 1982, reflecting the large volume of currency outstanding as well as the high level of government deposits. The 113 deposit money banks (DMBs) accounted for a further 50 per cent. Non-bank financial institutions (NBFIs), insurance companies, savings banks, and leasing companies made up the balance. (The term NBFI is applied in Indonesia to finance companies that fund their lending activities by issuing promissory notes.)

As for Bank Indonesia, its foreign exchange holdings accounted for 27 per cent of assets, about the same as loans to the central government and state enterprises. Claims on the deposit money banks added another 27 per cent, largely reflecting liquidity credits to the banks. On the liability side, currency outstanding amounted to a quarter of total liabilities. Government deposits accounted for a slightly larger share, as did other liabilities. Bank reserves were only 5 per cent of the total. The five government-owned commercial banks dominated the commercial banking scene, accounting for about 75 per cent of DMB deposits at the end of 1982. This high degree of concentration had been fostered by the use of these banks to channel liquidity credits to favoured economic sectors, and the requirement that government institutions and state enterprises deposit funds only with these banks (Nasution, 1986). Life insurance companies were also obliged to hold their deposits with the state banks. Given their large number of branches, the state banks had substantial liquid funds at the time of the 1983 reforms, including funds held abroad.

The private national banks and foreign banks also became a significant force in the economy during the 1970s and accounted for about 19 per cent of commercial bank deposits at the end of 1982. The 10 national banks holding foreign exchange licences far outweighed in importance the 59 purely domestic commercial banks and the 28 regional development banks. Many of the major private banks were, and continue to be, affiliated with large business conglomerates (Mackie and Sjahrir, 1989: Table 7). The foreign banks were restricted to the greater Jakarta area until late 1988. The private and foreign banks grew rapidly in the years before the 1983 reform, in part because of the higher deposit rates they paid to attract deposits. However, the banks were often related through ownership to enterprises which did not have access to liquidity credits, and were thus excluded from this type of government subsidy. A number of private banks suffered from unsound lending practices, and Bank Indonesia found it necessary to sponsor consolidation of private banks in the 1970s to bolster public confidence in the system.

There were 12 non-bank financial institutions in Jakarta in the early 1980s, 9 investment finance companies, and 3 development finance companies (McLeod, 1984; Nasution, 1986: 6–7). Bank Indonesia and the state commercial banks are the majority stockholders in most of these. Most NBFIs have foreign partners as minority shareholders with the remaining capital provided by domestic investors. The investment companies issue short-term promissory notes to finance lending to business, usually for short periods that protect the lender from interest-rate risk.

The Money Market

At the time of the 1983 reform, the money market consisted of an inter-bank market, a small market for finance paper issued by the NBFIs, and the foreign exchange market. The interbank market consisted primarily of a deposit market, in which banks with surplus funds placed them with banks in need of funds (Sundararajan and Balino, 1984: 7–9). Generally speaking, such interbank deposits were for two weeks or less; most, in fact, ranged from overnight to one week in duration. The state banks were usually net lenders in the market, maintaining a sizeable liquidity position in this form, but they also borrowed occasionally to meet reserve drains. Interbank deposits served the state banks as a buffer for the movement of deposits placed with them by state enterprises, which often had large net receipts or disbursements. The national private banks and the foreign banks were usually net borrowers. Their loan demands tended to outstrip the resources mobilized through deposits. They also found the rates at which they could obtain short-term deposits from depository institutions with surplus funds attractive. Transactions in the market were generally negotiated directly between two institutions without the benefit of a broker.

The non-bank financial institutions, modest in size, funded their lending operations by selling their own short-term obligations to banks, businesses, and other investors. Exempt until late 1988 from reserve requirements on their liabilities, they were able to pay higher rates than the banks. They were viewed as creditworthy by virtue of their owner-ship and the participation of foreign partners in their management.

The Reforms and the Organization of Monetary Policy

The 1983 Reforms

The downturn in oil and other commodity prices in 1982, and the con-sequent decline in export earnings, posed a serious challenge to Indonesian economic policy-makers, to which they responded with a series of reforms which have been discussed in detail in other chapters. The most striking element of the monetary reforms was the abolition of the system of credit ceilings that had hitherto been used as a means of monetary control. Henceforth, Bank Indonesia had to develop money market instruments and its own procedures for pursuing annual mon-etary growth objectives without direct interference in the lending and deposit-taking activities of the commercial banks. To reduce the injection of reserves through liquidity credits, about 60 per cent of credits outstanding in March 1983 were made ineligible for renewal. The rediscount rate was set at 3 per cent for loans still eligible while the bank lending rate was set at 12 per cent. In addition, the state banks were freed from interest rate restrictions on deposits while most borrowers would no longer be eligible for an interest rate subsidy through liquidity credits. The withholding tax on foreign currency deposits was eliminated and banks were permitted to sell bearer certificates of deposits for the first time.

The Monetary Council

The present Central Bank law establishes the legal basis of the Monetary Council to assist the government in 'planning and establishing monetary policy'. Members of the Council include the Minister of Finance, who serves as Chair and is responsible for organizing the secretariat, the Governor of Bank Indonesia, and the Minister of Trade. The Co-ordinating Minister for Economic, Financial, and Industrial Affairs and the Minister/Chair of the National Development Planning Board (Badan Perencanaan Pembangunan Nasional or Bappenas) have been added to the group and other senior officials are frequently consulted during its deliberations on important policy questions. The formal task of the council is to manage and co-ordinate the implementation of monetary policy determined by the government. Decisions are to be taken by 'deliberate negotiation for agreement'. Should the Governor of Bank Indonesia be unable to agree with the result of the negotiations, he may present his views directly to the President.

Before mid-1987, the Monetary Council did not meet regularly to consider monetary policy issues in a formal way. The four principals of the council consulted frequently and informally, aided by the input of their respective staffs, and major decisions, such as the June 1983 reforms and changes in the reserve requirements, were taken after substantial prior discussion among the council members and their staffs. But since the foreign exchange crisis of 1987, the council has met much more frequently, with its own staff, and that of Bank Indonesia, preparing recommendations for institutional change together with supporting documents for consideration.

Bank Indonesia's Role as the Central Monetary Authority

The implementation of domestic monetary policy from the late 1960s to 1983 concentrated on establishing overall objectives for bank credit growth which were considered to be consistent with projected real economic growth, an acceptable rate of inflation, and the official balance of payments targets. Bank Indonesia translated the targeted credit growth into credit ceilings for the individual banks. It monitored the actual credit performance of each bank relative to its credit ceilings as well as the behaviour of aggregate credit. After the June 1983 reforms, Bank

Indonesia was given the task of pursuing aggregate monetary growth objectives through the use of traditional Central Bank instruments, including the discount rate and open market operations. The framework for establishing monetary objectives for narrow money (M1) and broad money (M2) for each fiscal year remained essentially the same as before. In November–December of each year Bappenas makes projections of the economy's real growth for the ensuing fiscal year, which begins in April. It relates that projection to the current Five-Year-Plan. Its presentation includes a forecast of the balance of payments after intra-governmental discussion of estimates made initially by Bank Indonesia. At the same time the Department of Finance completes work on the budget for inclusion in the plan document and for submission to Parliament at the beginning of the new calendar year.

Within this framework, Bank Indonesia's Research Department estimates the growth of broad and narrow money likely to be consistent with projected real growth and acceptable price inflation. It utilizes a money demand model which takes the interest rate on bank time deposits as one input in its calculation of the demand for currency and for demand, time, and savings deposits. Applying the appropriate reserve requirement ratios and adding an allowance for excess reserves, this procedure arrives at a projected growth in the monetary base, believed to be consistent with the nation's broader economic objectives. With an open foreign exchange system, Bank Indonesia necessarily has to pay close attention to the relation of domestic interest rates to those in offshore centres and to the flow of funds across the exchanges. Tracking actual developments in the base against its own guidelines alerts the bank to the need for short-term interest rate adjustment in order to speed up or restrain monetary growth, subject to the constraints of the balance of payments and its stock of foreign exchange reserves. Inevitably therefore, monetary policy since deregulation in 1983 has had to focus operationally on short-term domestic interest rates (Sundararajan and Molho, 1987: 5–9).

Developing a New Monetary Control System after the 1983 Financial Reform

The Challenge

With the end of quantitative controls on bank credit, Bank Indonesia turned naturally to the control of bank reserves as its primary concern (Meek, 1986). In its economic policy role, the Central Bank sought that rate of monetary growth which it believed was consistent with the desired performance of the economy. In managing bank liquidity, it undertook to cushion seasonal and irregular variations in the supply of reserves and in the banking system's demand for them. In the short run, after the 1983 reforms, this function was performed by providing, or absorbing, bank reserves through some combination of open market and discount window operations so that the rate in the overnight interbank market was stabilized within a reasonable range. Over the longer term, Bank Indonesia had to change the terms on which it accommodated the system's demand for reserves in order to promote broader economic policy objectives.

The Indonesian authorities faced a major problem in the openness of the financial system. Since 1970, Bank Indonesia has stood ready to buy or sell foreign exchange on demand at rates established each morning to satisfy the demands of the banks in the daily bourse settlement. Residents were free to move between the rupiah and foreign currencies and could hold deposits denominated in foreign currencies with any of the foreign exchange banks. Such deposits amounted to about 16 per cent of the deposit liabilities of the deposit money banks at the end of 1982. After the 1983 devaluation, which had been widely anticipated, banks and residents repatriated a sizeable volume of funds.[4] But a high degree of sensitivity to the possibility of devaluation remained. Thus the level of foreign exchange reserves was, and continues to be, a constant preoccupation of Bank Indonesia. As the bank developed its new approach to monetary control in late 1983, devaluation rumours led to an outflow of domestic deposits, draining reserves, and tightening up the banking system. The interbank rate rose as high as 28 per cent in January 1984 and averaged 19 per cent for the month, compared with about 13 per cent in October–November 1983. This, in turn, brought some repatriation of bank funds from abroad as talk of further devaluation subsided.

Before the financial reform, Bank Indonesia had made liquidity credits available to banks encountering temporary reserve shortages. In February 1984 as part of its new monetary control system, the bank introduced new discount window facilities to deal with reserve needs. The 'Facility I' discount window provided credit for liquidity purposes, initially for a period of two weeks, for amounts of up to 5 per cent of each bank's deposits. The initial discount rate was set at 17.5 per cent, a penalty rate, to discourage refinancing of maturing liquidity credits. The 'Facility II' window was opened to encourage banks to make term loans. It offered a two-month initial term to guard against inadequate deposit growth, and the possibility of renewal for an additional two months. Access was limited to 3 per cent of a bank's deposits. Renewal of borrowings, or credit in excess of the basic allotment, was made subject to marginal increases in rates above the basic rate. Banks borrowing at either window submitted their own promissory notes to Bank Indonesia as evidence of indebtedness.

Indonesia is one of the very few countries in the world with no domestic government securities outstanding. Given this complete absence of any sort of government paper, Bank Indonesia needed an instrument for mopping up the sizeable volume of excess reserves in the banking system. In February 1984 it therefore initiated the sale of new Central Bank certificates (Sertifikat Bank Indonesia or SBIs) to banks and NBFIs as a means of mopping up reserve excesses. Both money supply and reserve growth had been quite rapid in 1983 and inflation had risen to 11.5 per cent. Bank Indonesia posted initial interest rates of 14 per cent on 1-month SBIs and 15 per cent on 3-month SBIs. In early 1984 Bank Indonesia reduced the rate it was then paying on excess rupiah reserves from 13 per cent to 7 per cent and announced that it would cease paying any interest on these excess reserves after an additional 3 months. At the same time it announced it would immediately cease paying any interest on excess foreign exchange reserves deposited with Bank Indonesia.

Eliminating payments by Bank Indonesia on excess reserves increased the need for an active domestic money market (Binhadi, 1987: 5). Commercial banks had been accustomed to simply investing excess reserves with Bank Indonesia and drawing on them as the first line of defence in case of need. In fact, activity had already picked up significantly in the interbank market with the curtailment of liquidity credits. The role of this market was to become more crucial in 1984 and beyond.

The Development of Operational Procedures and Money Market Instruments

Initially, SBIs were sold on the basis of pre-announced rates. Subsequently, the banks and NBFIs eligible to bid were required to submit tenders. Those bidding below the Bank Indonesia's cut-off rate were awarded their allotments in full while those bidding at the cut-off rate were subject to pro rata allotment if bids exceeded the amount the bank wished to sell (Sundararajan and Molho, 1987: 14). Initially, the response of the banks and NBFIs eligible to bid was lukewarm, in view of the higher yields available in the interbank market. However, Bank Indonesia did not wish to offer higher rates on SBIs, being content with the higher interest rates generated by the outflow of capital and the strong demand for loans (Siregar, 1985: 12).

The banks proved very reluctant to borrow from Bank Indonesia through either of its discount windows. The Central Bank's circulars setting up the windows emphasized the 'lender of last resort' function, in part because of the bank's desire to distinguish the new facilities from the discounts made available as liquidity credits. A major purpose of the reform was to increase the reliance of the banks on deposits and reduce dependence on Bank Indonesia. As a result, bankers came to regard use of the windows as an indication that a bank was in trouble, or was poorly managed. Matters came to a head in September 1984 when capital outflows precipitated a serious situation in the money market. Through most of 1984, Bank Indonesia had been permitting the rupiah to decline gradually against the rising US dollar to avoid an appreciation of the real effective exchange rate that would impair the competitiveness of non-oil exports and encourage imports. But banks and domestic residents became alarmed in late August and early September when the rate of depreciation accelerated. The exodus of capital drained reserves from a system that had seen excess reserves shrink significantly in previous months (Meek, 1986: 10–12). The overnight interbank rate rose sharply, peaking at 90 per cent, with some state banks holding on to their reserves rather than lending in the market.

In these strained circumstances, Bank Indonesia intervened to steady the rupiah exchange rate and invited banks experiencing difficulties to use the windows. When it became apparent that the needs of some exceeded the 5 per cent limit on Facility I, the bank opened a temporary special window. The rate on the new facility was set at 26 per cent, a percentage point higher than the then prevailing basic discount rate but well below average interbank rates in September. Bank Indonesia also set a ceiling on interbank borrowing of 7.5 per cent of third-party liabilities (raised to 15 per cent in August 1985). To allow time for adjustment, banks were given six months to repay half their special loans and an additional six months for settling the remainder.

As a result of these measures, bank borrowings from Bank Indonesia rose from Rp 34 billion at the end of August to Rp 299 billion by the end of October. At the same time a reversal of capital flows prompted by the high domestic rates and the end of further depreciation added to bank reserves. The average interbank rate fell from 47 per cent in September to 14.7 per cent in October. The bank's discount rate was cut in stages by 3 percentage points to 22 per cent and the rate on temporary credit was also reduced. In this environment demand picked up sharply for the 30- and 90-day SBIs, whose rates had reached a peak of 18 and 18.5 per cent, respectively. Bank Indonesia issued SBIs daily to give banks greater flexibility in investing excess reserves. SBIs outstanding rose to Rp 212 billion at the end of the year.

The September 1984 episode underscored the need for a more flexible means of injecting reserves when the system experienced sudden reserve drains. The Governor announced in his January 1985 speech to the annual Bankers' Dinner that Bank Indonesia would soon introduce a new bank-endorsed instrument that it could purchase to supply reserves when necessary. In February 1985 the SBPU (Surat Berharga Pasar Uang), a debt obligation maturing in 30 to 90 days (later extended to 180 days), was introduced. The SBPU could be one of the following: (1) a promissory note issued by a customer to a bank or NBFI to finance a specific transaction and endorsed by the institution, (2) a promissory note issued by a bank or NBFI to borrow in the interbank market, (3) a draft (or trade bill) drawn by one business and accepted by a customer of a bank or NBFI, and (4) a draft, or banker's acceptance, drawn by a customer and accepted by a bank or NBFI.[5] The first bank or NBFI endorsing the paper was made fully responsible for paying the SBPU at maturity. Bank Indonesia instructed Ficor (or Ficorinvest, an NBFI which is 95 per cent owned by Bank Indonesia) to make a secondary market for the new instrument. Only bank-endorsed paper was made eligible for discounting at Bank Indonesia or at Ficor. Bank Indonesia stood ready to rediscount SBPUs bought by Ficor. It also established prudential limits on the amount of paper that Ficor could discount for each bank and NBFI.

The introduction of the SBPU coincided with a vigorous Central Bank effort to lower interest rates during 1985 to foster economic expansion (Meek, 1986: 16). Bank Indonesia wrestled through much of the year with the question of the bid-offer rate structure to be posted by Ficor on SBPUs and its relation to the cut-off rates posted by the Central Bank on SBIs. Ficor's bid-asked spread on one-month paper was cut from 2 percentage points in March to 25 basis points in November. The state banks showed considerable interest in buying the new instrument. Ficor's endorsement, which constituted an implicit Central Bank guarantee, gave the paper virtually the same credit quality as the SBI while the return was higher. The one-month maturity, for example, yielded half a percentage point more than a one-month SBI.

To encourage more interest in the SBI, Bank Indonesia decided in August 1985 to permit holders to discount SBIs before maturity with Ficor at the original issuing rate. Ficor, in turn, could discount them at the bank. This change led to a surge in sales of first 30-, and then 90-, day SBIs at the established cut-off rates of 14 and 15 per cent, respectively. Indeed, a number of state and other banks sold short-dated SBPUs to Ficor, either outright or under 1-week repurchase agreements which bore a lower rate than the 30-day SBI. They then invested in SBIs, increasingly confident of being able to meet any liquidity need by rediscounting the paper with Ficor. The volume of SBIs outstanding, and the volume of SBIs and SBPUs discounted at Ficor (and hence Bank Indonesia), rose sharply, in part because of this arbitrage operation.

Data on Ficor's credit ceilings for the different groups of banks shows that the state banks had quotas equal to about half of the Rp 1.4 trillion in mid-1986 (Nasution, 1986: 32–4). The national private banks, regional development banks, and NBFIs as a group were allocated about 40 per cent of the total and foreign banks accounted for 11 per cent. The state banks, which are the principal suppliers of funds to the money market, used Ficor's discount facilities rather sparingly until mid-1986, using only 20 per cent of their lines. Average use of their lines by the group of national private banks, regional development banks, and NBFIs was 48 per cent while the foreign banks were more active at 62 per cent.

In August 1986, Bank Indonesia modified its procedures with regard to SBIs (Binhadi, 1987: 10). It abandoned the daily sale of the 30- and 90-day instruments, reverting to a weekly auction with the 14 and 15 per cent cut-off rates which had prevailed since August 1985. Holders could discount SBIs maturing in 21 days or less with Ficor at market rates. Longer maturities could be discounted directly with Bank Indonesia, but only at a penalty rate of 15.5 per cent compared to the 14 and 15 per cent rates available on 30- and 90-day maturities, respectively. This change immediately led banks to switch from the 90-day maturity to the 30-day issue. As arbitrages unwound, the amount of SBIs outstanding dropped by Rp 842 billion in August to Rp 1,551 billion, while the amount being discounted at Ficor declined by Rp 756 million to Rp 524 million.

The New Facilities in Operation

Bank Indonesia's operations in SBIs and SBPUs through Ficor provided a mechanism that enabled the banking system to accommodate smoothly short-term variations in the supply of and demand for reserves. If individual banks found themselves short of reserves that could not be recouped easily in the interbank market, they could discount SBPUs at Ficor. Ficor would try to sell these to others, either outright or under short-dated repurchase agreements (repos). If it could not, it would discount them at Bank Indonesia at the mid-point of the bid-asked spread, thereby providing reserves to the banks. Individual banks that found themselves in surplus after the operation of the morning interbank market could buy SBPUs or SBIs from Ficor, again either outright or under a repurchase agreement. Bank Indonesia's weekly auctions of SBIs made available a new supply of 30- and 90-day issues to banks with excess reserves.

This mechanism enabled banks to reduce significantly their excess rupiah reserves, which fell from a monthly average of Rp 264 billion in 1984 to Rp 113 billion in 1986. It essentially provided reserves, or absorbed them, on the demand of the banks at the posted rates for SBPUs and SBIs. Bank Indonesia's open market operations provided a kind of two-way discount window. Facilities I and II remained practically unused because their penalty rate normally remained well above the interbank rate and Ficor's buying rates for SBPUs. The interbank market, too, functioned more efficiently, although the limit on bank borrowing to 15 per cent of third-party liabilities was at times a constraint. Bank Indonesia served as an intermediary between the banks that usually needed reserves and the state banks. The state banks were the principal buyers of SBIs by virtue of their need for a large liquidity cushion. Such purchases reduced the extent of their daily need to lend funds in the interbank market. At the same time the ability of the private national banks and foreign banks to discount SBPUs at Ficor at posted rates strengthened their bargaining position with the state banks in the interbank market.

Bank Indonesia found that the new instruments gave it added flexibility when it undertook in 1985 to lower domestic interest rates to stimulate domestic activity. The economy was experiencing slower growth and the rate of inflation was falling. The Central Bank used purchases of SBPUs through Ficor in February and March to offset the reserve effects of repayments of the special discount window credits extended in September–October 1984. The interbank rate fell from 11.2 per cent in the first quarter to 8.4 per cent in the third. This made possible a reduction of about 3 percentage points in the basic rate structures posted for both the SBI and SBPU. The basic discount rate on Facility I was also cut by 3 percentage points over the same interval.

From August 1985 to May 1987 Bank Indonesia continued to foster economic recovery, stabilizing the interest rates posted for SBIs and SBPUs at lower levels. Both bank time deposit and loan rates continued to move lower through September 1986 in response to the Central Bank's earlier moves and to the sluggishness affecting many sectors of the economy. The rate decline on 3-month bank time deposits from December 1984 amounted to 3 percentage points at the state banks and 6 to 7 percentage points at private national and foreign banks, bringing the level down to 14–15 per cent. Average loan rates on non-priority credits declined by somewhat less to between 19 and 25 per cent. (The widening of margins was understandable in view of problems of loan quality, especially with regard to loans to medium-scale enterprises.) Given that the annual increase in the consumer price index was 6.8 per cent in the year to September 1986, the level of real interest rates remained high.

Bank Indonesia's design of the SBI/SBPU mechanism provided a certain degree of automatic response in the interbank market whenever outflows of foreign exchange developed. In February and March 1986 the authorities decided to maintain the levels of posted rates, despite an exodus of funds spurred by devaluation fears. The state banks holding SBIs were able to offset reserve losses by stepped-up discounting of SBIs at Ficor. The sale of SBPUs to Ficor also increased but a number of private and foreign banks had limited leeway under Ficor's ceilings for increasing their discounts of SBPUs. They had to depend increasingly on the interbank market or on repatriating funds held abroad. Accordingly, the short-term interbank rate rose, helping stem the outflow of capital (Figure 4.1).

In September 1986, the authorities took advantage of the extended stability of the domestic money market to devalue the rupiah. The surprise move was intended to improve the competitive position of non-oil exports and thus to accelerate the economy's growth. At the same time Bank Indonesia liberalized access to the forward cover available to Indonesian companies borrowing abroad or to foreigners investing in Indonesia. The premium charged for such cover was increased to 9 per cent. The devaluation itself should have defused fears of further exchange rate depreciation in the immediate future. But in late 1986 and early 1987 the foreign exchange deposits of domestic residents rose. There being no basis for any further change in the exchange rate, Bank Indonesia chose to continue supporting domestic growth by maintaining the existing domestic rate structure. It relied on existing mechanisms to deal with the reserve effects of the outflow. This time there was heavy discounting of SBPUs at Ficor, sizeable discounting of SBIs at the penalty rate, and moderate use of the Facility I discount window at its penalty rate. Use of Bank Indonesia's credit facilities expanded by Rp 1.1 trillion in December while SBIs outstanding also dropped by Rp 550 billion. The interbank rate rose from 12.9 per cent in November to 16.5 per cent in January 1987 (Figure 4.1).

A still more serious challenge began to build up in April 1987. Bank Indonesia sought initially to maintain its low interest rate policy, but this

114

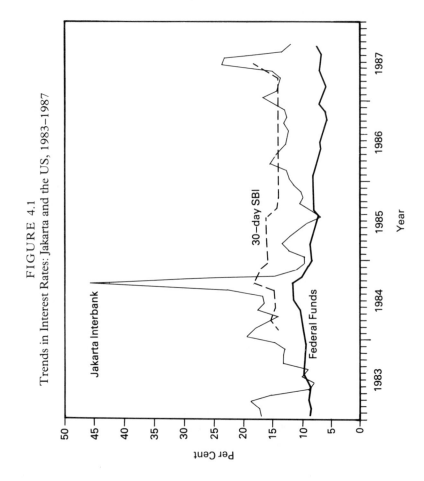

FIGURE 4.1
Trends in Interest Rates: Jakarta and the US, 1983–1987

proved impossible. In an effort to stem the outflow of foreign exchange, the bank in early May increased the 30-day SBI rate from 14 to 16 per cent and the 90-day rate from 15 to 17 per cent. Similar adjustments were made in the SBPU rate structure. When the outflow continued unabated, at the end of June the acting Minister of Finance, Dr Sumarlin, ordered four state enterprises to withdraw deposits from the state commercial banks and buy SBIs from the Central Bank. This action drained Rp 900 billion from bank reserves, leading to a scramble for funds domestically and internationally. On 28 June Bank Indonesia increased the rates once more on money market instruments, to a 17.75 per cent cut-off rate on the 30-day SBI and to a bid rate of 18.75 per cent on the 1-month SBPU. On 3 July, the Central Bank announced that it was cutting by 30 per cent the Rp 1.4 trillion ceiling maintained by Ficor on its committed credit lines for the purchase of SBPUs. This necessitated the repurchase by some of the banks of Ficor's holdings in excess of this amount.

These drastic steps in defence of the existing exchange rate produced the desired result. The interbank rate rose from 13.6 per cent in April to 23.5 per cent in June, reaching a peak rate of 39 per cent in early July. The commercial banks borrowed at the discount window and re-patriated funds from abroad. The high domestic rates also attracted, with a lag, the dollar deposits held offshore by Indonesian residents. The Central Bank's foreign exchange assets rose to US$6.25 billion at the end of July, compared with US$5 billion at the end of April.

A Major Change in Approach

The 1987 exchange crisis, and its successful resolution, led Bank Indonesia to rethink its approach to reserve management. It concluded that the existing institutional arrangements erred in providing committed credit lines to the commercial banks through Ficor's discounting of SBPUs. Also it decided that meeting the banking system's entire demand for SBIs at a fixed rate was unduly rigid. The Central Bank decided that henceforth it would purchase SBPUs, and sell SBIs, only on its own initiative, reserving to itself the decision on the scale of opera-tions and the rates at which it would deal.

During July 1987 Bank Indonesia gradually phased out Ficor's com-mitted lines for discounting SBPUs. It announced in late July that it would play a more active role in managing liquidity, selling and buying SBIs and SBPUs on an auction basis through Ficor, guided by its mon-etary targets (Binhadi, 1987: 16–19). Banks could no longer discount SBPUs at Ficor on their own initiative; the back-door discount window that had facilitated bank adjustment and money market efficiency was closed. The reserves drained by a currency outflow could no longer be replaced automatically by such discounting. Bank Indonesia would decide itself what volume of reserves to inject as the tightening effect of a reserve drain raised the interbank rate.

With the return flow of capital pumping up the monetary base, Bank

Indonesia's chief task became one of mopping up surplus reserves while allowing interest rates to decline from their crisis peaks in an orderly manner. The bank initiated a daily auction of 1-week maturity SBIs through Ficor in which commercial banks, development banks, and NBFIs could bid either for their own accounts or for the accounts of customers. Operations were directed at helping the market settle down after the strains of the recent past. When operations began, the interbank rate had already tumbled from a peak of 39 per cent to 19.5 per cent under the weight of the return flow from abroad. By mid-August, the bank's operations had facilitated a further decline to the level that had prevailed in April. The bank cut its basic discount rate on Facility I in six steps from 30 per cent in early July to 17 per cent in October. Use of the window dried up because of the large penalty this represented over the interbank rate.

Bank Indonesia expected that its new system would involve operations in both SBIs and SBPUs at flexible interest rates. In the first few weeks, it bought SBPUs on a few occasions, using the competitive auction technique employed for selling SBIs. Subsequently, until May 1988, the bank relied almost exclusively on daily sales of 7-day SBIs on a competitive basis. It chose to sell less than the banks wanted to buy at existing rates so that the cut-off rate fell progressively. Banks with remaining surpluses had to turn to the interbank market to dispose of them so that the daily average rate receded to a range of 10.5 to 12.25 per cent during October (Figure 4.2). The bank continued to depend on selling 7-day SBIs, almost daily, as its means for controlling the domestic interbank rate in the short run and influencing the behaviour of the monetary base and the money supply over the longer term. The auction technique enabled the bank to use the cut-off rate, the highest rate it would accept, as a means of signalling whether it wished short-term rates to move higher or lower. Through its daily auctions it nudged rates gradually higher in the first quarter of 1988 to resist speculative capital outflows at the beginning of a new presidential term with its attendant changes in cabinet. The bank introduced a refinement in February 1988 to reinforce the upward pressure on rates, making direct sales to banks after the daily auction had been completed. Its reliance on SBI sales was intended to emphasize its commitment to keeping the reserve situation on a tight leash to deter exchange rate speculation.

The experience with competitive rate setting marked a distinct improvement over the administered setting of rates prior to July 1987, introducing an element of flexibility into management that had been absent before. Still, the concentration on daily sales of such short maturities and the absence of operations in SBPUs led to a narrowing of the adjustment options available to commercial banks. Nearly all sales were to the state banks with the amount sold depending largely on their reading of their own reserve positions. The SBPU market dried up, depriving private national and foreign banks of a valuable means of adjusting positions and leaving them dependent on the state banks or external sources for meeting short-term reserve needs.

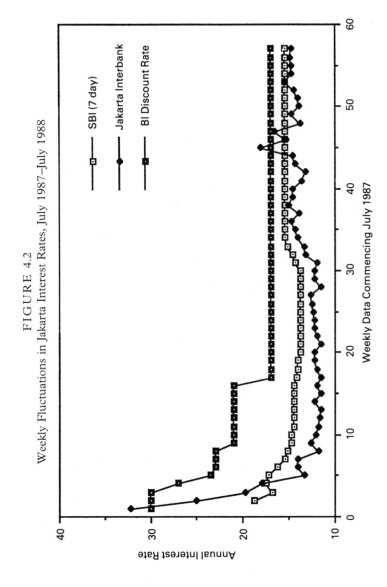

FIGURE 4.2
Weekly Fluctuations in Jakarta Interest Rates, July 1987–July 1988

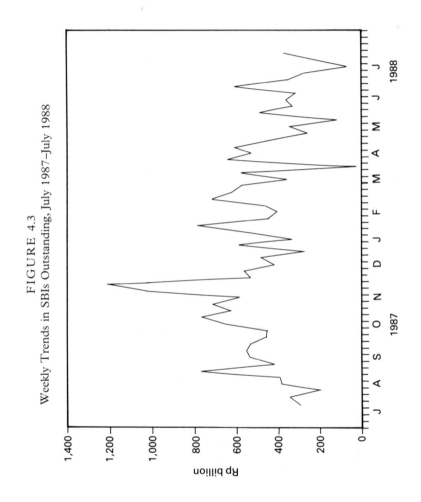

FIGURE 4.3

Weekly Trends in SBIs Outstanding, July 1987–July 1988

Since Bank Indonesia normally met most of the demands each day, the volume of SBIs outstanding rose and fell with the change in their reserve positions (Figure 4.3). The scale of daily SBI operations was usually much larger than the activity in the interbank money market itself because of the need to roll over the entire volume of SBIs weekly. The state banks were also able to obtain for their surplus funds a substantial, though diminishing, yield spread over the rate available in the interbank market. After the pressures associated with the cabinet change had passed, Bank Indonesia sought to conduct operations more flexibly. Operations again became two-sided. The bank resumed short-term operations in SBPUs to deal with several periods of reserve strain in May, June, and July 1988. It continued to make frequent sales of seven-day SBIs, but these were made only when market conditions suggested the need rather than daily.

Bank Indonesia's long absence from the SBPU market set back the development of this useful instrument for financing bank-lending and business activities. Banks still issued SBPUs in the course of their interbank lending activities, but the placement of paper outside the banks, always modest, declined as the liquidity previously provided by Ficor's discounting disappeared. While the state development bank, Bapindo, organized a revolving underwriting facility for Ficor, the cost of financing proved too high to permit Ficor to continue its market making for SBPUs on a significant scale.

The October 1988 Policy Package

The accession of a new cabinet in April 1988 and the appointment of a new Central Bank governor led to an intensive review of the financial system, including the tools available to Bank Indonesia for conducting monetary policy. In October 1988 the government announced a comprehensive series of measures intended to make the financial system more competitive and enhance Bank Indonesia's effectiveness. These steps were designed to enable the financial system to contribute to the attainment of broader economic goals, notably the further diversification of the economy and the expansion of non-oil exports.

Monetary Policy

As discussed in Chapter 3, the policy package announced in October 1988, and promptly dubbed Paket Oktober 1988 or Pakto 88, had profound consequences for the Indonesian banking industry. As far as the conduct of monetary policy was concerned, perhaps the most important Pakto provision was the one governing reserve requirements for financial institutions. For banks, these were reduced from 15 per cent to 2 per cent of their third-party liabilities (demand, time, and savings deposits). Bank Indonesia also imposed a 2 per cent reserve requirement for NBFI liabilities. The release of reserves served as a major offset to the cost to the banks of introducing a flat tax of 15 per cent on interest paid on time deposits and certificates of deposit. (Initially, banks were required to invest 80 per cent of the funds released in 3- and 6-month Pakto SBIs at fixed interest rates.) These changes represented a shift from relying on the indirect tax of reserve requirements, which accrued to Bank Indonesia, to direct taxation accruing to the government budget.

The policy package also authorized Bank Indonesia to develop further its operations in SBIs and SBPUs as a means of exercising more flexible monetary control. Accordingly, in January 1989, Bank Indonesia organized a syndicate of 15 private banks and NBFIs to act as dealers and agents for the issue of SBIs in a regular weekly auction and as market makers in the secondary market. Syndicate members are paid a small commission on their successful bids. Initially, the bank sold 1-month maturities of SBIs but a 13-week maturity was introduced in May 1989. It also took steps to make the issues easily transferrable so that the market makers could resell them to non-banks as well as banks, either outright or under repurchase agreement. Bank Indonesia continued to sell 7-day SBIs regularly in the course of managing reserves; it also began to purchase SBPUs periodically in the secondary market under repurchase agreements.

The Present Monetary Control System

Recent Developments

The general framework within which Bank Indonesia's monetary control is exerted is set forth in Table 4.1. The major autonomous forces beyond the bank's control include the government's net position with the Central Bank. Until 1987/8, the government's deposits usually rose more than credits to government instrumentalities; thereafter, as discussed in Chapter 2, Bank Indonesia's net lending to the government increased. Among other major forces affecting reserves are the balance of payments on both current and capital account and the liquidity credits extended by Bank Indonesia to what the government judges to be priority sectors of the economy, largely through the state banks. Net 'other items' includes capital transactions. Bank Indonesia's liquidity credits to the banks remained an important source of additions to bank reserves until the end of the decade, despite the effort made in the 1983 reform to reduce the scope and slow the growth of such credits. It was only in January 1990 that liquidity credits were finally abolished.[6] The rise in government deposits at Bank Indonesia until 1987/8 sharply reduced the impact these credits would otherwise have had on the monetary base. Subsequently the two factors have added to bank reserves.

Bank Indonesia's open market operations have enabled it to affect bank reserves on its own initiative, whatever the changes flowing from the dominant autonomous forces. On balance, these operations have been rather successful in providing stability in the money market most of the time and in enabling the authorities to nudge interest rates in the

TABLE 4.1

Changes in Factors Affecting Reserves and Money and Credit Growth
(Rp billion)

	Fiscal Years Ending in March				
	1984/5	1985/6	1986/7	1987/8	1988/9
Autonomous factors	318	1,708	−231	2,700	1,299
Net foreign assets	1,282	1,770	1,095	3,070	2,316
Net claims on government	−2,360	−434	−1,960	1,778	752
Liquidity credits to banks	1,085	936	1,264	2,666	2,899
Net other items	311	−564	−630	−4,814	−36
Policy factors	179	13	670	−1,585	−1,601
SBIs outstanding	−198	−1,151	1,233	−607	−1,601
SBIs rediscounted	0	904	−863	−41	0
SBPUs rediscounted	205	418	312	−935	0
Facilities I, II, and special credit	172	−158	−12	−2	0
Reserve money	497	1,721	439	1,115	−302
Currency outside banks	231	1,327	616	115	640
Bank reserves	228	446	−184	992	−1,010
Other deposits	38	−52	7	8	68
	Rates of Growth (per cent)				
Money and credit[a]					
Net domestic credit	9.5	50.9	8.0	50.3	39.5
Net government deposits	49.1	−30.3	75.9	−19.3	1.6
Private credit	28.7	24.5	26.5	32.6	34.4
M2	23.4	24.3	17.9	25.2	23.9
Reserve money	9.3	29.5	5.8	14.0	−3.3

Source: Bank Indonesia.

[a]Rates of change include the effect of the September 1986 devaluation on the rupiah value
of domestic and foreign assets and of liabilities denominated in foreign currencies. The
valuation adjustment on foreign currency deposits accounted for about 6 percentage
points of the increase shown for M2 in 1986/7.

direction desired. They also fostered, until mid-1987, a modest redirec-
tion of credit towards the private sector operating without liquidity
credits, which has probably contributed to greater allocative efficiency.
In the year ending in March 1986 the increase in SBIs and SBPUs discounted exceeded slightly the sales of SBIs. Sizeable increases in net
foreign assets and in liquidity credits provided a strong stimulus to
monetary expansion, more than offsetting the rise in government
balances and the increase in other liabilities. In the following year the fall
in SBIs outstanding and the increase in SBPUs discounted provided
some growth in the reserve base at a slower pace despite a net contraction arising from the autonomous factors.

The monetary expansion generated in 1985/6 and the substantial
devaluation of the rupiah in September 1986 stimulated the real growth

of the Indonesian economy. Non-oil exports increased rapidly in the wake of the devaluation, equalling exports of petroleum and gas in 1987. Inflation also accelerated to nearly 9 per cent in 1987 and 1988 as a result of the monetary stimulus and the devaluation. But the foreign assets of the banking system and Bank Indonesia rose in 1987 after falling in the previous year. In the two fiscal years ending in March 1989, Bank Indonesia managed to maintain growth in M2 at around 25 per cent annually. While both liquidity credits and the rise in lending to government swelled bank reserves, the sale of SBIs outstanding and a decline in foreign assets enabled the Central Bank to keep monetary growth from accelerating significantly.

The Role of Reserve Estimates in Domestic Policy Implementation

The Steering Committee of Bank Indonesia oversees the routine execution of open market operations. It has before it in its weekly meetings a spreadsheet of the autonomous and policy factors affecting reserves. A simplified version of this sheet is presented in Table 4.2. Before explaining this table, a word about reserve requirements is in order. Indonesian banks must meet their requirements contemporaneously; verification is after the fact. Reports are available in two weeks from the Jakarta clearing-house banks and in about one month from other banks. (These banks account for about 60 to 75 per cent of total bank liabilities.) There are four reserve maintenance periods per month, ending on the seventh, fifteenth, twenty-third, and the last day of the month. Sundays and holidays are not counted so that most reserve periods involve six business days. Up to October 1988, banks in Indonesia were required to maintain reserve requirements equal to 15 per cent of their demand deposits and other current liabilities. Included as current liabilities for the state and foreign banks were two-thirds of their time and savings deposits. For national private banks one-third of such deposits were reservable. In October 1988 reserve requirements were reduced to 2 per cent of third-party liabilities for all banks. (At the same time the banks were made liable for tax payments to the Department of Finance equal to 15 per cent of their interest payments on deposits.)

The data in Table 4.2 are presented to the Steering Committee at its weekly meeting. The table follows the format of Table 4.1 except that levels are presented rather than changes. The data presented to the Steering Committee involve estimates of the actual levels up to the day before the meeting. In addition, projections are made of the levels expected at the end of each of the two reserve periods ending after the meeting. These provide an input to the decisions taken between meetings on open-market operations, although these decisions are based mainly on conditions in the money market. The Steering Committee also uses the spreadsheet to track unfolding monetary and foreign exchange developments. The spreadsheet is organized with the autonomous factors affecting bank reserves shown at the top (A.I) followed by the display of the *ex post* record of the net position in SBIs,

TABLE 4.2

Monetary Programme (Rp billion at end of period shown)

	April 1989	23 May 1989	29 May 1989	Change (23–29 May 1989)
A. *The Monetary Base*				
I. Monetary base determinants				
I.1 Autonomous	11,038	10,898	11,154	+256
1. Net foreign assets	10,254	10,181	10,102	−79
2. Net claims on government	−5,839	−6,249	−6,259	+10
3. Liquidity credits to banks	12,127	12,372	12,377	+5
4. Net other items	−5,463	−5,406	−5,066	+340
I.2 Policy factors	−2,328	−2,852	−2,988	−136
5. SBIs outstanding				
(net of rediscounted)	−1,085	−2,806	−2,944	−138
6. Pakto SBIs	−1,453	−46	−44	+2
7. SBPUs rediscounted	210	0	0	0
8. Discount facilities	0	0	0	0
II. Monetary base	8,710	8,046	8,166	+120
1. Private deposits	133	142	134	−8
2. Currency outside banks	6,733	6,268	6,496	+228
3. Required reserves	623	614	611	−11
4. Excess reserves	1,221	1,022	925	−97

(continued)

TABLE 4.2 (continued)

	April 1989	23 May 1989	29 May 1989	Change (23–29 May 1989)
B. Short-run Targets				
1. Excess Reserves	938	921	916	
2. Deviation	−289	−101	−9	
C. Transactions				
1. Sales of SBI	1,793	1,395	401	
2. Maturities SBI	1,624	924	311	
3. Net	−169	−471	−90	
4. Pakto SBI transactions	0	+123	+1	
5. SBPU transactions	+210	−98	0	
6. Total	+41	−446	−89	
D. Monetary Base Tracking Path	8,423	8,507	8,535	+28

Source: Bank Indonesia.

SBPUs, and credit operations. The next segment (A.II) gives the total of the *ex post* monetary base, the sum of A.I.1 and A.I.2. Data on cash in vault held by the commercial banks and bank deposits at Bank Indonesia are estimated until firm figures are received at the head office from the branches with a lag of about ten days. Required reserves are estimated using the latest information from the members of the Jakarta clearing-house. (Data on nationwide deposits lag by about seven weeks.) Excess reserves (A.II.4) emerge as a residual. This estimate of excess reserves is compared with a projection of the average level expected (B.1). Since the cut in reserve requirements to 2 per cent announced in October 1988, the allowance for excess reserves has been increased to 3 per cent of reserve requirements. The net (B.2 = A.II.4 − B.1) was once taken as an indicator of the need to supply or absorb reserves, but it was then realized that this was only an *ex post* result. The table also show *ex post* data on actual open market operations (C) as a flow.

Actual operations (C) are unrelated to the discrepancy between past and projected excess reserves (B.2). As described below, they seek to offset the actual behaviour of the autonomous factors and of the banking system's variable demand for currency and excess reserves. The banks themselves, drawing on internal reporting systems on required reserves and their positions, undertake money market transactions, including those with Bank Indonesia. These enable them to do a fair job of maintaining reserves about in line with requirements despite the day-to-day variations in reserve availability. However, excess reserves have been higher since the cut in reserve requirements because of the banks' need for cash in vaults throughout their branch systems and for positive balances with Bank Indonesia in Jakarta.

The historical data which the spreadsheet provides to the Steering Committee on the relation between the actual behaviour of the monetary base (A.II) and the bank's longer-run objectives for the base (D) permit members to see how much the base is over, or under, the path believed consistent with the desired growth of the economy. The projected path is itself built up from the application of reserve requirements to the estimated demand for M1 and M2 on the basis of models that incorporate expected real economic growth and an acceptable rate of inflation. The committee in its discussions of the economy can factor in monetary behaviour and advise the Governor on the need to raise or lower short-term interest rates to affect monetary growth in the desired direction or to deal with exchange gains or losses.

The Conduct of Operations

Bank Indonesia, like most central banks that rely on indirect methods of monetary control, pursues its intermediate objectives by open-market operations affecting the quantity and cost of reserves in the banking system. Whether Bank Indonesia couches its intermediate objectives in terms of the exchange rate, interest rates, nominal GNP, or the growth of one or more monetary or credit aggregates, daily operations affecting excess reserves and the overnight rate are the basic tools for exerting leverage in the desired direction. Changes in the overnight interbank rate, set in motion by its operations in SBIs and SBPUs, affect rates on maturities of one week and longer in the interbank market and through them rates on customer time deposits. In this way the Central Bank can increase or decrease the attractiveness of bank time deposits to depositors and affect the terms on which banks lend to borrowers. This indirect influence on the cost and availability of bank credit affects, in turn, economic activity. Needless to say, the level of foreign exchange reserves and the availability of international credit facilities impose limits on the extent to which the Central Bank can reduce interest rates to promote domestic expansion or the restructuring of the economy.

Bank Indonesia has a well-formulated approach to daily reserve management in its transactions with the 15 market makers (dealers) with whom it deals. To maintain the overnight interbank rate within a desired range, it relies primarily on short-term transactions, either sales of SBIs maturing in one week or repurchase agreements on SBPUs or SBIs for one week to one month. The managing director governs the scale of his operations by his estimates of the factors affecting reserves over the next several days, taking into account the rates and volume of the competitive bids or offers submitted by the dealers. The highest rate at which he sells SBIs or the lowest rate at which he buys SBPUs under repurchase agreements can serve as a signal if he is trying to raise or lower the overnight interbank rate for monetary policy reasons. But most of the time Bank Indonesia is satisfied with the range of the overnight rate and the cut-off rate can move up or down without policy implications. Only a consistent pattern of change in one direction over a succession of days conveys an unmistakable signal of a policy change.

Bank Indonesia's introduction in January 1989 of a weekly auction of longer-dated SBIs, and the appointment of 15 market makers committed to bid in each weekly auction, marked the beginning of a serious effort to establish a viable secondary market for the instrument. So long as Bank Indonesia sold only 7-day SBIs, there was no opportunity for market trading to develop. The state banks could depend on the daily sales and maturities as a means of managing their reserve positions. The sale of a longer-dated SBI offers an opportunity to them and other investors to earn a higher rate of return and to meet their cash needs by the redemption of a ladder of SBI maturities or sales in the secondary market. It permits market makers to take down such issues for subsequent resale to the state banks and other investors between the weekly auctions and to make markets in the outstanding maturities of the longer SBIs.

The procedure used for auctioning 1-month and, later, 3-month SBIs differs from that used for Treasury bills and similar instruments in most developed money markets. In the developmental stage, the amount to be sold was not standardized nor announced in advance. This left Bank Indonesia free to determine the cut-off rate which seemed consistent with desired monetary conditions. The strong liquidity preference of the

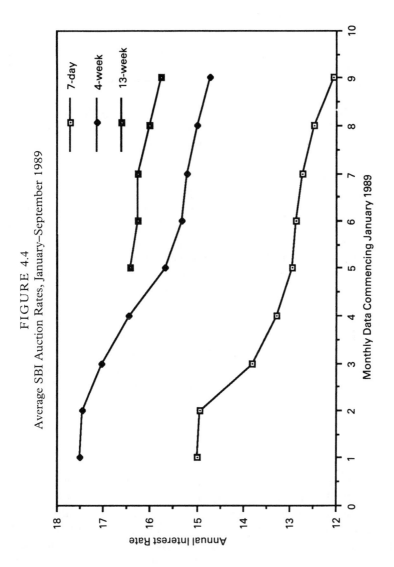

FIGURE 4.4
Average SBI Auction Rates, January–September 1989

banks themselves was evident in the shape of the yield curve. In early 1989 the overnight interbank rate was in the 13 to 14 per cent range while the 1-week SBI bore a 15 per cent rate and a rate of around 17.5 per cent was established in the auction of the 4-week SBI. This preference probably reflects past experience with large deposit swings between the Department of Finance and the banks as well as with large past shifts of funds abroad by bank customers. The wisdom of not pre-determining the amount was confirmed by the first four weekly auctions, in which awards ranged between Rp 75 billion and Rp 301 billion.

In February 1989 Bank Indonesia began lowering domestic interest rates. The managing director allowed excess reserves to accumulate in the banking system, bringing downward pressure on rates in the inter-bank market and lowering the cut-off rate in his daily sales of 7-day SBIs. By mid-1989 the overnight rate ranged between 11 and 12 per cent while the rate on 1-week SBIs was around 13 per cent. Given declining rates, Bank Indonesia was able to begin selling a 13-week SBI at the weekly auction. At the end of September 1989, outstanding 4-week SBIs amounted to Rp 587 billion, while 13-week maturites were Rp 1.1 trillion. Figure 4.4 traces the average discount rates established in the auctions of 7-day, 4-week, and 13-week SBIs.

Outright trading in the 4-week and longer maturities developed slowly. In the beginning, the dealers were very cautious in bidding on their own account in the auctions or in the market afterward. Most dealers bid principally as agents for the larger banks, collecting the Central Bank's commission without any underwriting risk. They did have some success in selling SBIs to smaller banks and other non-bank financial institutions but most of these transactions were sales under repurchase agreements. The dealers then began to buy on their own account, and sell in the secondary market. A major task ahead is to develop the non-bank demand for the longer-dated SBIs so that dealers will be able to shift interest-rate risk to customers who can better bear it.[7]

Conclusions

Bank Indonesia has made significant progress since the financial reform of June 1983 in the development of money market instruments and in increasing its own ability to affect monetary conditions through open-market operations. The process of developing domestic instruments and operational strategies has been arduous, involving repeated challenges in the form of speculative outflows of capital. But the foreign exchange crisis of mid-1987 brought a new flexibility in setting short-term rates that was a distinct advance over the administration of rates that had prevailed previously. The introduction of weekly auctions of longer-dated SBIs in January 1989 began the development of 1-month and 3-month SBIs as genuine market instruments, which can provide a benchmark for other short-term interest rates.

There remain a number of obstacles to the development of a good secondary market for these instruments. First, the state banks still dominate the financial scene to such an extent that they often seek to extract extra returns from their size, protecting the rate they earn even at the cost of accumulating unusable excess reserves. The state banks need a secondary market that can deal in larger amounts than the smaller banks and the non-bank financial institutions that constitute the 15 market makers. They depend unduly on adjusting bilaterally with Bank Indonesia through the daily SBI auctions and have been slow to reduce liquidity in return for the higher yields available on the longer-dated instruments. The structural obstacles to competitive markets may be alleviated over time if the private banks compete effectively for state enterprise deposits and the state banks in turn become more profit-oriented.

The development of an efficient secondary market for SBIs and SBPUs depends as well on Bank Indonesia's willingness to permit the market to perform its rate-setting function. This means a willingness to allow the cut-off rates set in daily operations and the auctions to vary sufficiently so that bidders will regularly enter tenders at a range of rates. Once the market develops further, the bank intends to pre-announce the amount to be sold in the weekly auctions, a move that should produce enough week-to-week variability in rates to promote more secondary market activity. There is also a need to find ways of encouraging the dealers to make markets, even of moderate size, to all comers so that they can develop non-bank investment interest. Dealers who show little interest in bidding in auctions or in making markets should be pressured to improve or to give way to new entrants. A well-defined Central Bank strategy of developing the SBPU market is also needed.

The improvement of Bank Indonesia's monetary control procedures can proceed hand-in-hand with the development of the money market. The experience since mid-1987 has already demonstrated that open-market operations can be used flexibly to ease or tighten money market conditions as domestic or external conditions require. Bank Indonesia still has much to do to improve the data flow on reserve positions. There remain long lags in the compilation of reserve figures that could be speeded up by sampling procedures. The managing director needs daily forecasts of the likely behaviour of factors affecting reserves in the weeks ahead to improve his ability to tailor operations to each reserve maintenance period. Co-operation with other government agencies is essential to improve the flow of information on factors affecting reserves. But the prospects are good for continuing development of the money market, given the proven ability of Bank Indonesia to manage the financial system in the interest of the country's economic development.

1. This section draws heavily on Sundararajan and Balino (1984) and Balino and Sundararajan (1985). Arndt (1979) and Dickie and Layman (1988: 28–73) also describe developments in the Indonesian financial sector in the 1970s.

2. See Arndt and Suwidjana (1982) for an account of the growth of the Jakarta dollar market in the 1970s.

3. Sundararajan and Balino (1984: 1–5). Data are drawn from the Bank Indonesia monthly publication, *Indonesian Financial Statistics*, various issues.

4. Sundararajan and Molho (1987: 34) estimate that inflows cumulated to about $2.5 billion in the three years after the 1983 devaluation, reversing the outflows of the two previous years.

5. Binhadi (1985: 4–6) and Bank Indonesia 'Circular' [English translation], 28 January 1985, pp. 1–2.

6. Certain credits to Bulog for the holding of food stocks, to development banks, farmers, and co-operatives remain, but they have had their interest rates raised to 16 per cent per annum which was in mid-1990 about equal to the prime rate the state banks charge their best customers. Other types of liquidity credit, most notably those to exporters, have been completely phased out. For further discussion, see Conroy and Drake (1990).

7. Interbank interest rates declined from September 1989 well into the first half of 1990. The volume of outstanding SBIs peaked at about Rp 3 billion at the end of 1989 and fell to around Rp 2 billion by mid-1990 as foreign exchange reserves fell. The decline in reserves led Bank Indonesia to increase interest rates significantly from the middle of 1990 onwards. See Conroy and Drake (1990: 31–5).

REFERENCES

Arndt, H. W. (1974), 'Survey of Recent Developments', *Bulletin of Indonesian Economic Studies*, 10(2): 1–34.

_____ (1979), 'Monetary Policy Instruments in Indonesia', *Bulletin of Indonesian Economic Studies*, 15(3): 107–22.

Arndt, H. W. and Suwidjana, Nyoman (1982), 'The Jakarta Dollar Market', *Bulletin of Indonesian Economic Studies*, 18(2): 35–64.

Balino, Tomas J. T. and Sundararajan, V. (1985), 'Financial Reform in Indonesia: Causes, Consequences and Prospects', in Cheng Hang-Sheng (ed.), *Financial Policy and Reform in Pacific Basin Countries*, Lexington and Toronto: D.C. Heath and Lexington Books.

Bank Indonesia (1985), 'Circular' [English translation], 28 January, Jakarta.

Binhadi (1985), 'The Operation of SBPUs in Practice', Jakarta: Bank Indonesia, mimeo.

_____ (1987), 'Banking Anticipation of Monetary Contractions and Expansions through SBI and SBPU' [English translation], Jakarta: Bank Indonesia.

Conroy, J. D. and Drake, P. J. (1990), 'Survey of Recent Developments', *Bulletin of Indonesian Economic Studies*, 26(2): 1–36.

Dickie, Robert B. and Layman, Thomas A. (1988), *Foreign Investment and Government Policy in the Third World*, New York: Macmillan Press.

International Monetary Fund (1988), *Indonesia: Financial Reform and Monetary Policy*, Washington, DC, 6 January.

Mackie, J. A. C. and Sjahrir (1989), 'Survey of Recent Developments', *Bulletin of Indonesian Economic Studies*, 25(3): 1–34.

McLeod, Ross (1984), 'Financial Institutions and Markets in Indonesia', in M. T. Skully (ed.), *Financial Institutions and Markets in Southeast Asia*, London: Macmillan.

Meek, Paul (1986), 'Recent Use of Monetary Instruments in Indonesia', *Indonesian Financial Policy Papers*, August.

Nasution, Anwar (1986), 'Instruments of Monetary Policy in Indonesia after the 1983 Banking Deregulation', *Indonesian Financial Policy Papers,* August.

Pangestu, Mari and Habir, Manggi (1990), 'Survey of Recent Developments', *Bulletin of Indonesian Economic Studies,* 26(1): 1–36.

Siregar, Arifin (1985), 'Annual Address at the Bankers' Dinner', Jakarta, 17 January.

Sundararajan, V. and Balino, Tomas (1984), *Instruments of Monetary Policy in Indonesia: Problems of Coordination and Monetary Control,* Washington, DC: International Monetary Fund.

Sundararajan, V. and Molho, Lazaros (1987), 'Financial Reform and Monetary Control in Indonesia', Paper presented at a conference sponsored by the Federal Reserve Bank of San Francisco, 23–25 September.

5
Exchange Rate Policy, Petroleum Prices, and the Balance of Payments

Peter G. Warr*

Introduction

INDONESIA'S impressive economic performance since 1965 owes much to the export revenues generated from its petroleum sector and to the way those revenues have been used within Indonesia. Not only Indonesia's foreign exchange earnings from exports, but also its government revenue receipts have depended heavily on the petroleum sector. Nevertheless, dependence on petroleum exports has brought with it two major problems. First, the instability of international petroleum prices has meant instability of both export earnings and government revenues, leading to significant problems of short-term macroeconomic adjustment. Second, while the export revenues from petroleum were clearly beneficial, their domestic absorption produced medium-term structural problems within the Indonesian economy.[1]

Through most of the 1970s, Indonesia's central adjustment problem was one of managing the effects of an economic boom induced by rising petroleum prices. Through most of the 1980s this problem was exactly reversed. As oil prices declined sharply, Indonesia had to find alternative ways of earning foreign exchange and raising public revenue. The extreme volatility of international petroleum prices since the early 1970s has produced severe economic problems for all countries which, like Indonesia, depend heavily on petroleum for their export revenues. For some, this period of instability has been disastrous. Uncontrolled inflation and severe recessions at home combined with heavy external indebtedness have produced not only economic hardship but political turmoil as well. Indonesia has been an exception in that the potential for severe economic instability has largely been avoided. This chapter looks at the role of macroeconomic management in achieving this outcome.

Indonesia's exchange rate policy is a major component of the policy

*This chapter has benefited from the excellent research assistance of Zita Albacea, Liu Jin, and Zhang Xiao Guang, and from helpful discussions with Anne Booth, Soonthorn Chaiyindeepum, Hal Hill, Will Martin, and Thee Kian Wie. The author is responsible for all views and defects.

adjustments to be studied here. Since 1969 Indonesia's currency has been freely convertible and since 1971 capital movements into and out of the country have been essentially free of government controls. Until 1978 the value of the rupiah was pegged to the US dollar. A substantial (50 per cent) devaluation occurred in November 1978. A tightly managed float was then maintained until March 1983, when the rate was devalued again (by 37 per cent) and a somewhat more flexible, but still closely managed float was introduced. The rate was devalued by a further 50 per cent in October 1986.

Within Indonesia exchange rate policy has been recognized to be not only an instrument for the management of external balance—attainment of an appropriate current account surplus or deficit—but also an instrument with important implications for the structure of the domestic economy. Analytically, the two are closely related. The attainment of external balance is directly connected to the balance between traded goods and non-traded goods production. What is interesting about the Indonesian experience is that this analytical relationship has been at the forefront of economic policy discussion about exchange rate management.

Indonesia's External Environment and Macroeconomic Performance

The instability of Indonesia's external trading environment through the 1970s and 1980s is illustrated in Figure 5.1. The figure shows Indonesia's commodity terms of trade—an index of the average international prices of its exports relative to those of its imports—from 1967 to 1988. The volatility of this series is obvious. The figure also shows an index of the international price of petroleum relative to an index of manufactured goods prices. To facilitate comparison of the two, the logarithm of each relative price in the figure is shown. The correlation between the two series illustrates the degree to which changes in Indonesia's external trading environment are dominated by changes in international petroleum prices.

Figure 5.2 shows the implications of these external events for Indonesia's export earnings from petroleum, as a proportion of total export earnings, and for the proportion of total government revenues derived from petroleum. In Figures 5.1 and 5.2, three periods stand out:

Shock I : the 1973–74 petroleum price increase;
Shock II : the 1979–80 petroleum price increase;
Shock III: the 1984–86 petroleum price decline.

Table 5.1 provides some international perspective on Indonesia's performance in managing the effects of external economic instability. It compares Indonesia with Egypt, Mexico, and Nigeria. For all four countries, petroleum accounts for a high proportion of export earnings but unlike many petroleum exporters of the Middle East, these countries all possess very substantial non-petroleum agricultural and manufacturing sectors as well.

134

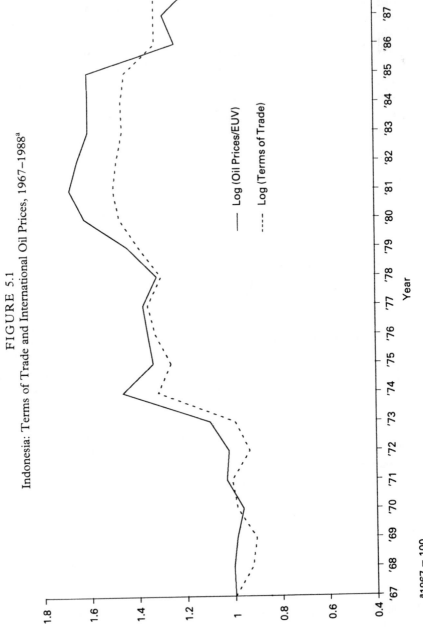

FIGURE 5.1
Indonesia: Terms of Trade and International Oil Prices, 1967–1988[a]

a1967 = 100.

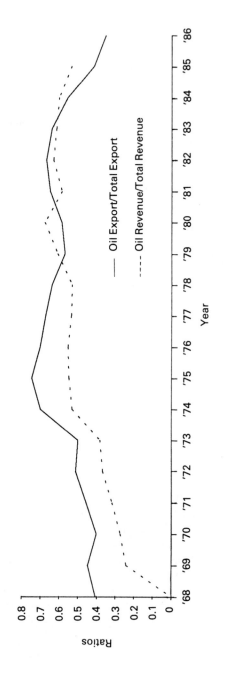

FIGURE 5.2

Indonesia: Petroleum's Importance in Exports and Government Revenue, 1968–1986

TABLE 5.1

Comparative Macroeconomic Indicators of Large Petroleum-exporting
Countries: Indonesia, Egypt, Mexico, and Nigeria

		Indonesia	Egypt	Mexico	Nigeria
Real GDP growth	1965–80	5.6	4.7	3.4	4.4
rate per capita (per cent)	1980–8	3.0	3.0	−1.7	−4.3
Inflation	1965–80	34.2	7.3	13.0	13.7
(per cent per annum)	1980–8	8.5	10.6	73.8	11.6
Petroleum exports/	1982	75.0	70.0	77.0	95.0
total exports (per cent)	1988	35.0	31.0	32.0	(95)[a]
Manufactured exports/	1982	16.0	27.0	52.0	n.a.
total non-oil exports					
(per cent)	1988	45.0	36.0	81.0	(40)[a]
External public	1973	33.5	23.0	10.2	7.0
debt/GDP (per cent)	1982	21.1	52.4	32.7	8.5
	1988	55.7	123.4	48.0	101.3
Total debt service/	1973	6.3	40.2	22.2	4.0
total exports (per cent)	1982	8.3	70.9	29.5	9.5
	1988	34.1	13.9	30.0	24.2
Gross international reserves	1982	3.0	1.9	0.6	1.1
(months of imports)	1988	3.3	1.8	2.1	1.3
Current account balance/	1982	−3.3	−7.7	−13.2	−37.6
merchandise exports					
(per cent)	1988	−6.0	−41.5	−14.1	−13.9

Sources: World Bank, *World Development Report*, various issues, and *World Debt Tables*,
various issues; International Monetary Fund, *International Financial Statistics*, various
issues.
[a] 1987 data, 1988 data not available.
n.a. = Not available.

All four countries prospered during the period of rising oil prices in
the 1970s. Real growth rates of GDP per capita were well in excess of
3 per cent. During the 1980s, all four countries were adversely affected
by falling oil prices; none of the four enjoyed real GDP growth per
capita higher than 3 per cent and Nigeria and Mexico experienced negative per capita growth. It is notable that for each of the above periods
Indonesia's performance was the best or equal best of the four countries
shown. Indonesia's average inflation rate over the 1965 to 1970 period
was strongly affected by the hyperinflation of the early and mid-1960s
but its inflation rate fell thereafter. From 1970 to 1980 Indonesia's average annual rate was 16 per cent. During the 1980s its average rate, at
under 9 per cent, was the lowest of the four countries shown.

Petroleum exports accounted for more than 70 per cent of total exports for all four countries through the 1970s and early 1980s, but for all except Nigeria this proportion subsequently declined to less than half this level. Nigerian trade data are notoriously poor and it is not clear whether such a transformation occurred in Nigeria or not. Within the non-oil export category, Indonesia's expansion of manufactured exports is important and has been discussed in Chapter 7 but it is notable that Egypt and Mexico also experienced a similar phenomenon.

The table shows three indicators of indebtedness: the ratio of external public debt to GDP; the ratio of total debt service to total exports; and the level of gross international reserves expressed as months of import coverage. Mexico is usually regarded as a highly indebted country, and the comparison with Indonesia is instructive. In 1982 Indonesia's external public debt to GDP ratio and total debt service to total exports ratio were both lower than Mexico's but by 1988 this comparison had been reversed in terms of both indicators. As a proportion of total exports, Indonesia's debt service obligations were the highest of the four. By all indicators except the level of international reserves, at the end of the 1980s Indonesia's debt position was obviously a cause for worry.

A more detailed overview of Indonesia's macroeconomic performance is provided in Table 5.2, covering the period 1968–88. The table shows that over this period not a single year of significantly negative real growth of GDP per capita occurred.[2] Considering the volatility of Indonesia's external economic environment, this is a remarkable record of internal stability. The record on price stability is somewhat less striking but still impressive, especially when compared with the hyper-inflation of the early and mid-1960s. Nevertheless, for most of the twenty-five years since 1965 Indonesia's inflation rate has remained above that of its major trading partners, placing persistent pressure on exchange rate management.

Adjustment to External Shocks: Theory and Practice

This section examines how the pattern of macroeconomic adjustment observed in Indonesia compares with the characteristics of an optimal adjustment policy. First, the question of what pattern of macroeconomic adjustment would be appropriate for a country faced with the kind of external instability shown in Figure 5.1 is studied. Then the Indonesian experience is examined within this perspective.

A Model of Saving, Investment, and the Balance of Payments[3]

A simple theoretical model of the adjustment of saving, investment, and the balance of payments to an external shock is presented in Figure 5.3. The axes show aggregate national consumption and production of a single commodity in each of two periods: period 0, the present, shown on the horizontal axis; and the future, period 1, shown on the vertical axis. The initial output in each of the two periods is shown by point A.

TABLE 5.2
Indonesia: Macroeconomic Summary, 1968–1988

	Units	1968	1969	1970	1971	1972	1973	1974	1975	1976	1977
1. GDP real growth rate	Per cent	10.9	6.8	7.6	6.7	9.4	11.3	7.6	5.0	6.9	8.8
2. Inflation (CPI growth rate)	Per cent	84.8	17.4	12.3	4.4	6.4	31.0	40.6	19.1	4.8	11.0
3. Terms of trade	Index (1980 = 100)	28.3	27.2	32.6	34.2	28.9	33.1	69.1	61.6	70.6	76.2
4. Exchange rate	Rp/US$	326	326	378	415	415	415	415	415	415	415
5. Total government revenue/GDP	Per cent	7.2	10.0	10.8	12.0	13.7	14.7	16.7	18.0	19.1	19.1
6. Oil tax revenue/GDP	Per cent	0	2.4	3.0	3.8	5.1	5.7	8.9	9.9	10.6	10.3
7. Total debt outstanding	US$ b.	2.7	3.0	2.9	4.3	5.1	6.7	9.2	11.8	14.6	16.2
8. Total debt service	US$ m.	49	56	76	94	126	211	289	587	761	1,262
9. International reserves	US$ m.	83	118	156	185	572	805	490	584	1,497	2,509
10. Exports—total	US$ m.	731	854	1,108	1,234	1,777	3,211	7,426	7,102	8,547	10,853
11. Exports—oil	US$ m.	298	383	446	565	913	1,609	5,211	5,311	6,004	7,298
12. Imports	US$ m.	716	781	1,002	1,103	1,562	2,729	3,842	4,770	5,673	6,230
13. Current account balance	US$ m.	−225	−336	−310	−372	−334	−475	598	−1,109	−908	−50

	Units	1978	1979	1980	1981	1982	1983	1984	1985	1986	1987	1988
1. GDP real growth rate	Per cent	6.9	5.8	8.5	7.2	0	0.3	6.7	2.5	5.9	4.8	5.7
2. Inflation (CPI growth rate)	Per cent	8.1	20.6	18.5	12.2	9.5	11.8	10.5	4.7	9.1	9.3	5.6
3. Terms of trade	Index (1980 = 100)	66.9	82.8	100	105.7	101.9	96.4	97.4	93.9	69.7	70.0	69.9
4. Exchange rate	Rp/US$	625	627	627	644	692	994	1074	1125	1641	1650	1731
5. Total government revenue/GDP	Per cent	19.1	21.9	22.9	24.4	20.8	21.1	20.0	21.6	20.2	21.3	20.2
6. Oil tax revenue/GDP	Per cent	10.2	13.3	15.4	14.2	13.1	12.9	12.0	11.3	6.6	9.1	7.4
7. Total debt outstanding	US$ b.	19.0	21.2	22.5	27.2	32.2	35.6	36.6	42.5	49.9	59.9	58.0
8. Total debt service	US$ m.	2,062	2,099	1,758	2,047	2,246	2,542	3,240	3,993	4,380	5,452	7,296
9. International reserves	US$ m.	2,626	4,062	5,592	5,014	3,144	3,718	4,773	4,974	4,051	5,592	5,048
10. Exports—total	US$ m.	11,643	15,591	21,909	22,260	22,293	21,152	21,902	18,590	16,075	17,135	19,219
11. Exports—oil	US$ m.	7,439	8,871	12,850	14,390	14,861	13,478	12,097	7,670	5,167	5,919	7,681
12. Imports	US$ m.	6,690	7,202	10,834	13,272	16,859	16,352	13,882	10,262	10,718	12,891	13,249
13. Current account balance	US$ m.	-1,436	946	2,804	-816	-5,458	-6,442	-1,970	-1,950	-4,099	-2,098	-1,189

Sources: BPS, *Indikator Ekonomi*, various issues; World Bank, *World Development Report*, various issues, and *World Debt Tables*, various issues; International Monetary Fund, *International Financial Statistics*, various issues.

FIGURE 5.3

A Model of Savings, Investment, and the Balance of Payments

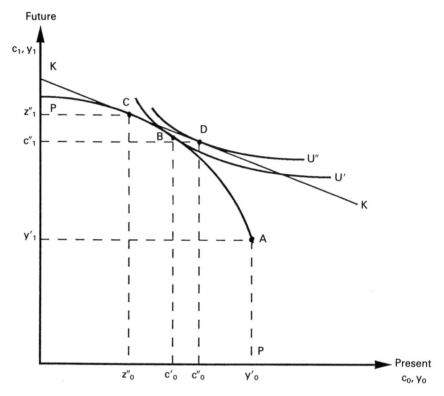

The initial output in period 0, y_0, may be consumed or invested. Investment allows output in period 1 to be increased. The schedule PP describes these investment possibilities.

In a closed economy, in which borrowing from or lending to other countries is not possible, consumption and production must both occur on the PP schedule. If social preferences have the form described by indifference curve U', then consumption and production will each occur at point B. Investment in period 0 is given by $y_0 - c_0$, which is also the level of saving. This enables future consumption (period 1) to exceed output (dissaving).

If an international capital market is introduced into this analysis, borrowing from or lending to other countries becomes possible. The line marked KK describes these possibilities. Its slope is $-(1 + r)$ where r is the international rate of interest, in real terms. The optimal production point is now point C and consumption ideally occurs at point D, allowing a level of social welfare U", higher than U', to be attained. There is now a difference between saving and investment in period 0. Saving is given by $y'_0 - c''_0$ and investment is higher at $y'_0 - z''_0$. The difference between investment and saving in period 0 corresponds to $c''_0 - z''_0$, that is, it is optimal for investment to be $y'_0 - z''_0$ and for this to be financed in part by domestic saving ($y'_0 - c''_0$) and in part by borrowing from abroad $(c''_o - z''_o)$. The amount borrowed from abroad is equivalent to a current account deficit and a capital account surplus. This deficit is given by the national accounting identity

$$D_t = M_t - X_t = I_t - S_t$$

where D_t is the deficit, in year t, and M_t, X_t, I_t, and S_t denote imports, exports, investment, and saving in year t, respectively.

Before using this diagram for the analysis of trade shocks, it is useful to note that a balance of payments deficit or surplus is not in itself necessarily either desirable or undesirable. In the case shown, optimal utilization of the opportunities provided by international capital markets and domestic investment opportunities requires that a current account deficit exist in period 0. There is nothing undesirable about this. Of course, the borrowings must be repaid in the future, but social welfare is raised in the process.

Obviously, the actual level of any current account deficit which might be observed in period 0 could in principle be either larger or smaller than this optimal amount. This point is important because it is common for observers of macroeconomic statistics to describe any increase of a current account deficit as a 'worsening' and any reduction as an 'improvement'. The analysis above shows that this level of thinking is inadequate. An increase or a reduction in a current account deficit from one year to the next could be either desirable or undesirable depending on whether it represented a move towards or away from an optimal intertemporal allocation of resources. Equivalently, the analysis in Figure 5.3 suggests that for a net borrower there is an optimal level of debt in the present period. A current account deficit in any year is a flow item which adds to the existing stock of debt (minus reserves). This is desirable if the present level of debt is suboptimal, and undesirable if present debt is excessive.

Optimal Adjustment to an External Shock

The foregoing apparatus can now be used to analyse the optimal adjustment to an external shock such as an improvement in the country's terms of trade. A distinction between temporary and permanent shocks is central to the analysis. A temporary shock is one that improves the value of production possibilities in period 0, leaving the value of period 1 potential output unchanged from before. A permanent shock will be one which raises production possibilities in both periods. The optimal response to these two types of shocks will be different.

A temporary positive shock may be represented in Figure 5.3 as a rightward movement of the endowment point, A, and the associated investment possibilities schedule, PP. Each point on the new PP schedule will have the same slope as one on the old PP schedule immediately to its left. A permanent, positive shock will correspond to a movement of point A outwards along a ray from the origin, and a corresponding proportional movement of each point on the PP schedule outwards from the origin. The resulting diagrams are detailed and it is sufficient here to summarize the characteristics of an optimal adjustment as they would be observed in period 0. The international real interest rate r is held constant throughout the analysis.

The effects of a temporary shock will be considered first. In response to a temporary and positive shock, the optimal level of investment would be unchanged. The intuitive reason for this outcome is that the optimal level of investment depends on the shape of the PP schedule and the international interest rate, neither of which is affected by a temporary shock. Only the position of the PP schedule changes. On the other hand, saving in period 0 rises. The intuitive reason is that present consumption is only an imperfect substitute for future consumption. Smoothing consumption over time is therefore desirable and saving a high proportion of the temporary windfall is a way of achieving this outcome. It follows from the above that the current account deficit, the difference between aggregate investment and saving, must decline.

A permanent shock will induce an increase in investment, because the change in the shape of the PP schedule implies improved productivity of investment. Savings will also rise, but not as much as in the case of a comparable temporary shock—i.e. one which has the same effect on output in period 0—because output possibilities in period 1 are also improved and the necessity for consumption smoothing is thus reduced. The current account deficit may rise or fall but any decline would be smaller than that observed under a comparable temporary shock.

In the foregoing discussion, adjustment to a positive trade shock is described. An example, in the case of a petroleum exporter like Indonesia, is an increase in petroleum prices. The optimal patterns of adjustment to a price reduction will be the reverse of those described. Indonesian data are examined below to see how they compare with the patterns of optimal adjustment.

Short-run Adjustment to Fluctuating Petroleum Revenues

Figure 5.4 shows the behaviour of aggregate saving and investment, as proportion of GDP, from 1968 to 1988. It is difficult to determine simply by inspection of this and the data in Table 5.2, how well the pattern of Indonesian short-run adjustment has conformed to the pattern of optimal adjustment outlined above. To examine this issue more satisfactorily, some statistical analysis is required.

To study the response of saving to changes in petroleum revenues, the following regression, using annual data from 1968 to 1988, was run.[4]

$$S_t = -546394 + 18.8\ Y_t^N + 90.76\ Y_t^P + 347\ r_t - 1465\ E_t$$

$$\ (2.90)\quad\ (8.90)\quad\ \ (2144)\quad\ (2176)$$

$$\ \ \ 1\%\quad\ \ \ \ 1\%\quad\ \ \ \text{n.s.}\quad\ \ \text{n.s.}$$

$$\bar{R}^2 = 0.958\qquad DW = 0.924\qquad \rho_1 = 0.494$$

In this equation S_t denotes total saving in year t deflated by the GDP deflator, Y_t^N denotes real non-oil GDP, Y_t^P denotes the petroleum and

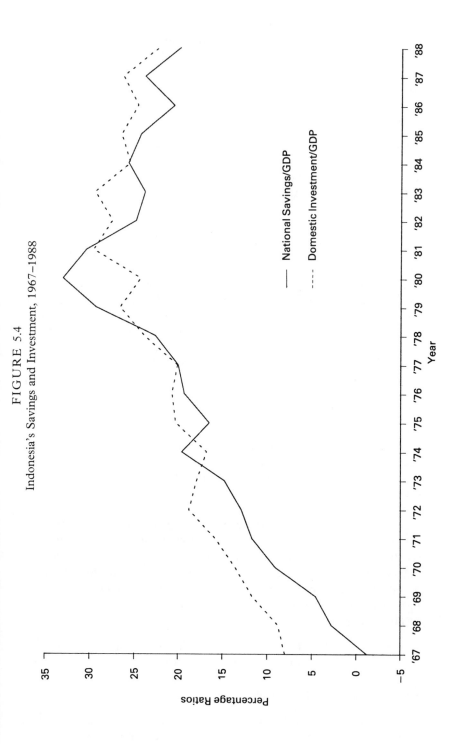

FIGURE 5.4
Indonesia's Savings and Investment, 1967–1988

gas real contribution to GDP, r_t is the real interest rate on banking deposits, and E_t is the proportional change in the nominal exchange rate relative to the previous year minus the rate of inflation. The numbers in parentheses are standard errors and the percentages below them are significance levels from standard two-tailed t-tests. Non-significant coefficients are marked n.s., $\bar{R}^2$ denotes the coefficient of determination adjusted for degrees of freedom, DW is the Durbin–Watson statistic and ρ_1 is the first-order autocorrelation coefficient.

Investment response was studied with the following regression:[5]

$$I_t = 1131902 - 62.2\ Y_t^N + 50.9\ Y_t^P + 41.7\ K_{t-1} - 1909\ r_t + 1047\ E_t$$
$$\qquad\qquad\ \ (19.16)\quad (10.17)\quad (6.52)\quad (2110)\quad (2113)$$
$$\qquad\qquad\ \ \ 1\%\qquad\ 1\%\qquad\ 1\%\qquad \text{n.s.}\qquad \text{n.s.}$$
$$\bar{R}^2 = 0.981 \qquad DW = 1.672 \qquad \rho_1 = 0.143$$

The variable I_t denotes real domestic investment in year t, K_{t-1} represents the aggregate real capital stock in year t–1 and is included to capture partial adjustment of the actual capital stock towards the desired level.

The regression results are highly significant and enable some strong conclusions to be drawn about the pattern of Indonesian adjustment. First, from the savings function one sees that saving responds positively to changes in petroleum revenue. Moreover, it responds more to fluctuations in the petroleum-based component of GDP than the non-petroleum component. Both coefficients were significant at the 1 per cent level and the difference between them was significant at the 5 per cent level. These results support the interpretation that fluctuations in petroleum revenues were seen within Indonesia as being more transitory than other sources of income fluctuations. Second, investment also responds positively to changes in petroleum revenues, but with a coefficient around half the corresponding coefficient for saving. Overall, the results suggest that fluctuations in petroleum revenues were perceived as being mainly but not exclusively temporary.

The results also suggest that the investment–savings gap—the current account deficit—is narrowed by increases in petroleum revenues and widened by declines. This conclusion follows from the fact that the coefficient on petroleum revenues in the savings function is approximately double that in the investment function. This conclusion may be tested more directly by regressing the investment–savings gap on the right-hand-side variables appearing in each.

The results are:

$$I_t - S_t = 41842 - 1.9\ Y_t^N - 14.5\ Y_t^P + 3.7\ K_{t-1} + 1370\ r_t + 3612\ E_t$$
$$\qquad\qquad\quad\ (17.1)\quad (9.5)\quad (5.8)\quad (1886)\quad (1890)$$
$$\qquad\qquad\quad\ \text{n.s.}\quad\ 20\%\quad \text{n.s.}\quad \text{n.s.}\quad\ 10\%$$
$$\bar{R}^2 = 0.504 \qquad DW = 1.688 \qquad \rho_1 = 0.149$$

The results suffer from lack of degrees of freedom but nevertheless support the conclusion that increases in petroleum revenues reduce the magnitude of an investment–savings gap. The results further suggest, though somewhat weakly, that the short-run effect of a devaluation is to increase rather than reduce the magnitude of a current account deficit.[6]

Long-run Adjustment to the Petroleum Boom

The above analysis concentrates on Indonesia's short-run responses to fluctuating petroleum revenues. Regressions such as these, based on annual data, are less suitable for analysis of long-run adjustments. Despite the very considerable fluctuations in petroleum prices that have occurred since the 1973–4 oil price shock, the real price received by Indonesia for its petroleum exports, and the real value of the revenue so derived, have been very much higher since the 1973–4 shock than previously. Suppose the actual revenue received from Indonesia's petroleum exports is compared with an estimate of what that revenue would have been if the real price had remained at its 1972 level. The difference in each year would be an estimate of the value to Indonesia of the increase in international oil prices since 1972. What has Indonesia done with that windfall gain?

To answer the question in detail would require looking at the division of Indonesia's increased absorption between consumption and investment, the distribution of the increased consumption across income groups, the types of investments that were undertaken, and the growth of the public versus private sector, among other things. Here only the most aggregate of these issues will be dealt with.

Suppose Indonesia had absorbed all of its additional petroleum revenues—no more and no less. Then the real value of Indonesia's debt, minus the level of its international reserves, would have remained the same. If total absorption had been less than the total increase in revenue, debt minus reserves would have fallen. It is obvious from Table 5.2 that the reverse actually occurred. Debt net of reserves clearly grew, implying that the increased absorption exceeded the increased revenues. But what were the relative magnitudes?

Table 5.3 presents calculations which attempt to answer this question. All calculations are presented in millions of US dollars. Actual petroleum revenues over time (row 1) are compared with the hypothetical value of these revenues assuming that the real price of petroleum remained the same in real terms as its 1972 level (row 2). The deflator in these calculations is the Export Unit Value index of the industrialized countries published by the International Monetary Fund. The annual difference between these amounts (row 3) is the estimated value of Indonesia's increased revenue from petroleum due to the post-1972 price increases. Over the 16-year period from 1973 to 1988, this amount was a total of US$103 billion.

The change in Indonesia's total external debt (row 4) minus the change in reserves (row 5) gives the net change in Indonesia's total indebtedness (row 6). When added to the increased revenue from petroleum (row 3), this gives an estimate of the total increase in absorption resulting from the petroleum price increase (row 7). Over the 16-year period, this amount reached a total of US$151 billion.

TABLE 5.3

Indonesia: Absorption of Increased Petroleum Revenues (US$ million)

	1972	1973	1974	1975	1976	1977	1978	1979
1. Actual petroleum revenue	913	1,609	5,211	5,311	6,004	7,298	7,439	8,871
2. Hypothetical revenue at 1972 real petroleum price	913	1,089	1,361	1,530	1,545	1,667	1,881	2,172
3. Increased revenue (1 − 2)	0	519	3,849	3,781	4,458	5,630	5,557	6,698
4. Actual change in debt	0	1,600	2,500	2,600	2,800	1,600	2,800	2,200
5. Actual change in reserves	0	233	−315	94	913	1,012	117	1,436
6. Net change in indebtedness (4 − 5)	0	1,367	2,815	2,506	1,887	588	2,683	764
7. Total increased absorption (3 + 6)	0	1,886	6,664	6,287	6,345	6,218	8,240	7,462
8. Ratio of increased absorption to increased revenue (7/3)	0	3.63	1.73	1.66	1.42	1.10	1.48	1.11

	1980	1981	1982	1983	1984	1985	1986	1987	1988
1. Actual petroleum revenue	12,850	14,390	14,861	13,478	12,097	7,670	5,157	5,919	7,681
2. Hypothetical revenue at 1972 real petroleum price	2,447	2,355	2,271	2,195	2,141	2,131	2,430	2,745	2,926
3. Increased revenue (1 − 2)	10,402	12,034	12,589	11,282	9,955	5,538	2,736	3,173	4,754
4. Actual change in debt	1,300	4,700	5,000	3,400	1,000	5,900	7,400	10,000	−1,900
5. Actual change in reserves	1,530	−578	−1,870	574	1,055	201	−923	1,541	−544
6. Net change in indebtedness (4 − 5)	−230	5,278	6,870	2,826	−55	5,699	8,323	8,459	−1,356
7. Total increased absorption (3 + 6)	10,172	17,312	19,459	14,108	9,900	11,237	11,059	11,632	3,398
8. Ratio of increased absorption to increased revenue (7/3)	0.98	1.44	1.55	1.25	0.99	2.03	4.04	3.67	0.71

Sources: As for Table 5.2.

Over the entire period the ratio of increased total absorption to the total increase in revenue was 1.47. For each dollar of increased petroleum revenue, Indonesia absorbed this amount *plus* roughly half as much again. This ratio was reasonably stable throughout the period following 1972. While there was year to year variation, in most of the years covered by the calculations (all but 4 of the 16), the ratio was between 1 and 2. There was no apparent long-term trend over the period, but one feature of the data does seem notable. Following each of the devaluations of 1978, 1973, and 1986, but especially the first two, a significant slow-down in the rate of aggregate absorption can be observed.

Exchange Rate Policy and Relative Prices

What role did exchange rate and demand management policy have in directing the macroeconomic adjustments Indonesia made through the 1970s and 1980s? This section examines the role of relative price movements within Indonesia in regulating the adjustment process. First, a simple theoretical model to illustrate the respective roles of external shocks, exchange rate policy, and domestic relative prices in balance of payments adjustment is presented. Next, the actual behaviour of key relative prices within Indonesia is examined, and the degree to which their movements improve one's understanding of the course of Indonesian macroeconomic adjustment is considered.

A Model of the Balance of Payments and External Shocks

A simple model of the balance of payments known as the 'Australian' model is first examined.[7] The fundamental distinction in this theory is between goods which are exchanged internationally—termed tradables—and those which are not—termed non-tradables. Most (but not all) primary commodities and manufactured goods are examples of tradables while most (but not all) services are examples of non-tradables. The relevance of distinguishing between them is that the nominal domestic prices of tradables are determined by their international prices, the exchange rate, and any subsidies, tariffs, or other taxes that may be applied to them. In contrast, the nominal prices of non-tradables are determined by domestic supply and demand conditions.

The role of the domestic prices of tradables relative to non-tradables in influencing the balance of payments is depicted in Figure 5.5. Value-weighted aggregated quantities of tradables are shown on the vertical axis and a similar aggregate of non-tradables is shown on the horizontal axis. The schedule PP shows production possibilities for these two categories of goods and social preferences regarding aggregate 'absorption' of them are shown by indifference curves such as U' and U". They are assumed to have the usual regularity properties. The distinction between investment and consumption is not important for this analysis and so for simplicity, both are treated as 'absorption'.

The crucial difference between tradables and non-tradables in this analysis is that the absorption of non-tradables must be matched by domestic production, but the same does not apply to tradables. If more of a particular tradable good is absorbed than is produced, then this good is a net import. The reverse is a net export. If in total more tradables (by value) are absorbed than are produced, this corresponds to a current account deficit, since the difference between absorption and production of tradables must correspond to an excess of net imports over net exports. A current account surplus is the reverse. By definition, non-tradables cannot be either imported or exported, so their domestic absorption cannot exceed their production.

Current account balance is indicated by point A in Figure 5.5. At this point consumption and production are equal for both tradables and non-tradables. The slope of the price line P_0 gives the prices of non-tradables relative to tradables. Now consider a current account imbalance. Assume production possibilities to remain at PP, disregarding the schedule QQ for the moment. Suppose the price of non-tradables relative to tradables rises above p_0, e.g., to p_1. The possible causes of this event will be discussed presently. Production of non-tradables now rises

FIGURE 5.5
Tradables, Non-tradables, and the Balance of Payments

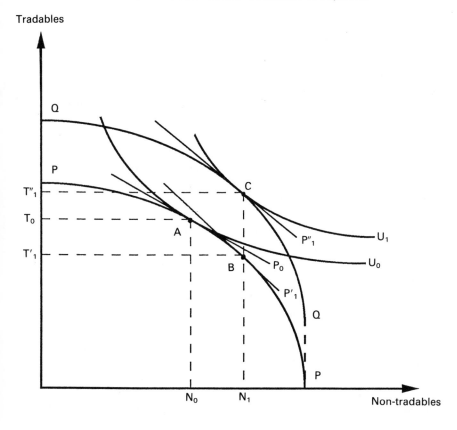

and that of tradables falls. Production will now occur at point B. At this higher price ratio, however, tradables will no longer be consumed in the same quantities in which they are produced. The lower price of tradables encourages their absorption relative to non-tradables, but has the reverse effect on production.

As seen above, a divergence between absorption and production can only occur in the tradables market; absorption and production of non-tradables cannot differ. The possible absorption outcomes which might occur under price p_1 thus lie along a vertical line drawn through the production point, B. These are the points at which production and absorption of non-tradables are equal. The actual solution will be that point along this line at which an indifference curve has a slope equal to that of p_1, e.g., point C. At point C, absorption of tradables exceeds their production. The difference is a current account deficit, equal to the vertical distance between point B and C.

How might a current account deficit like that occurring at point C arise? The key lies in the way tradable prices and non-tradable prices are determined. Suppose that domestic monetary expansion occurs with a fixed exchange rate.[8] The monetary expansion will raise domestic demand and thus increase domestic prices. But these price increases will be concentrated in non-tradables rather than tradables because the nominal prices of tradables are determined by international prices expressed in foreign exchange, the exchange rate, and any subsidies, tariffs, or other taxes which may be present. Thus the monetary expansion bids up the prices of non-tradables relative to tradables, producing a current account deficit.

Now consider an external shock such as an increase in petroleum prices. Because of the enclave nature of Indonesia's petroleum sector, this shock will be represented as a vertical shift in the production possibilities frontier, to QQ, i.e. as a quantum increase in the economy's capacity to produce traded goods. For convenience in the diagram, an external shock which has the same foreign exchange value as the current account deficit arising in the previous analysis is chosen. There will now be no current account deficit if production and absorption both occur at point C. Point C is now an equilibrium with zero current account deficit and a price ratio given by the slope of p_1.

Several conclusions can be drawn from this analysis. First, absorption of the effects of a positive external shock, such as an increase in petroleum prices, requires an increase in the ratio of non-tradables to tradables prices. Under a fixed exchange rate policy, this means that inflation at home must exceed inflation abroad, at least temporarily. Inflation abroad determines the rate of increase of tradable prices, so long as the exchange rate remains fixed. For non-tradable prices to rise relative to them, this means that the average price level at home must rise faster than the average level abroad.

Second, this higher than normal rate of inflation, consistent with absorption of the revenues from the boom, is temporary. Once the required domestic price ratio has been attained, further inflation above the world rate will further raise the non-tradable/tradable price ratio and induce a current account deficit, exactly analogous to the one analysed above in the pre-shock economy.

Third, the 'Dutch Disease' phenomenon, under which non-booming tradable production such as agriculture and manufacturing is harmed by absorption of booming sector revenues, has a monetary component as well.[9] The rate at which petroleum revenues are actually absorbed into the domestic economy depends on the rate at which the non-tradable/tradable price ratio rises, which in turn depends on domestic aggregate demand.

Fourth, a negative external shock, such as a reduction in petroleum revenues, requires a decline in the non-tradable/tradable price ratio, if the current account deficit is to be contained. Under a fixed exchange rate policy, this requires *lower* inflation domestically than the rate abroad, thus putting severe pressure on domestic monetary and fiscal policies.

Finally, the likely relative price effects of a devaluation can be inferred from Figure 5.5. A devaluation will raise the nominal prices of tradables and will do so relatively quickly. The subsequent behaviour of non-tradable prices will be strongly affected by monetary and fiscal policies. If the initial position was one of an unsustainable current account deficit, and the views of those government officials and advisers arguing for monetary and fiscal restraint then prevail, the initial increase in prices of tradables relative to non-tradables may be sustained for some time. But if domestic aggregate demand grows at a higher rate, leading to continued rapid inflation, the price ratio will steadily decline from its post-devaluation peak.[10]

Relative Prices within Indonesia

Indices of tradable prices relative to non-tradable prices have been constructed for several combinations of tradable and non-tradable goods. Three examples are shown in Figure 5.6. The proxy for non-tradable prices used in each of the three series is the housing component of the Jakarta Consumer Price Index. Three proxies for tradable prices are used—the wholesale prices of imported cement, transport equipment, and textiles. The three tradable/non-tradable relative price series are labelled 'Cem/Hsg', 'Tran/Hsg', and 'Tex/Hsg', respectively, in the diagram. There is considerable variation in the results depending on the particular commodity groups chosen for this exercise. Nevertheless, a consistent feature of the results is a surge of the relative price following a devaluation. The key dates are November 1978, March 1983, and October 1986. Following this surge, there is a steady decline in the price ratio until it roughly reaches its value before the devaluation.

To overcome the arbitrariness entailed in choosing particular tradable and non-tradable commodities groups, it is desirable to attempt to construct a broader, more representative index. Such an index of the tradable/non-tradable price ratio within Indonesia is reported in

FIGURE 5.6

Indonesia: Three Indices of Tradable/Non-tradable Price Ratios, 1977–1989[a]

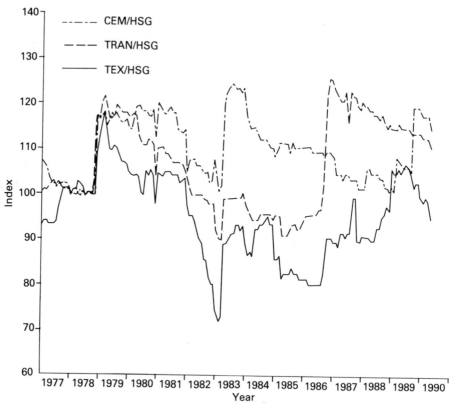

[a]October 1978 = 100.

Figure 5.7. The detailed construction of this index is described else-where (Warr, 1984 and 1986). Briefly, the index of tradable prices is the Indonesia-wide wholesale price index for imported commodities. Exports are excluded because, especially in the case of primary com-modity exports, their prices are more subject than import prices to inter-national price fluctuations not directly related to the issues central to this study. The index of non-tradable prices is formed from eight com-ponents of the Consumer Price Index which appear to satisfy well the economic definition of non-tradables.[11] In examining Figure 5.7, the dashed line marked 'competitiveness' should be disregarded for now.

Focusing on the relative price series, a number of features are notable. First, following the 1973–4 oil shock, the price ratio declined steadily until late 1978. The decline is consistent with the 'Dutch Disease' effects of absorbing the burgeoning petroleum revenues, but the very high inflation in Indonesia in the 1973–5 period suggests that the rela-tive price decline may well have gone beyond the amount required for absorption of the petroleum revenues. The calculations summarized above in Table 5.3 confirm this conjecture.

FIGURE 5.7

Indonesia: The Tradable/Non-tradable Price Ratio and 'Competitiveness',
1971–1989

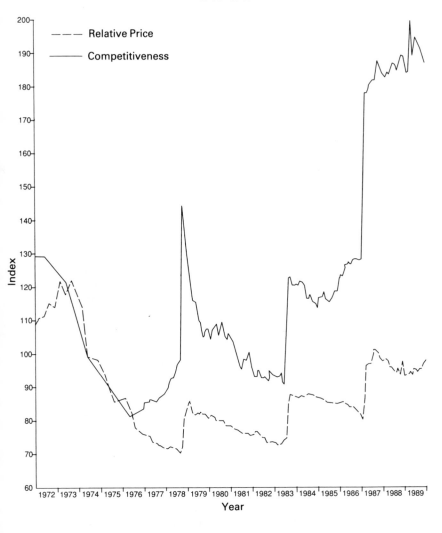

Following the 50 per cent devaluation of November 1978, the relative price series surged upwards, but only by around one-quarter of the massive decline seen over the previous five years. The 1978 devaluation partially reversed the decline in the profitability of the non-oil tradable industries that had occurred during the 1970s period. Statements by Indonesian officials at the time suggested that this was indeed a major objective of the devaluation. For example, a senior official of Bank Indonesia subsequently wrote that the 1978 devaluation 'was carried out with a view to improve Indonesia's international competitive position and thus to stimulate the development of export and import substitution industries which had been under increasing cost pressure due to a faster rate of inflation in Indonesia in the recent years than the rate abroad'.[12]

Corden (1981) has termed devaluations undertaken for the above reasons 'exchange rate protection'. This refers to devaluations aimed specifically at restoring the profitability of tradable industries relative to non-tradable industries. Such devaluations are to be distinguished from those aimed at eliminating balance of payments difficulties and in particular, those aimed at protecting the level of reserves in a fixed or pegged exchange rate regime. In practice, of course, deciphering the political motivation behind devaluations is very difficult.

While a serious balance of payments difficulty did not exist in Indonesia in 1978, as measured by the adequacy of reserves, for example, a speculative capital outflow did occur in the few months immediately preceding the November devaluation, possibly in anticipation of the devaluation itself. It is significant that in 1978, mainly due to the petroleum boom, Indonesia was a borrower in good standing in the international capital market, quite unlike the situation a decade before. The adequacy of reserves is therefore not the most appropriate indicator of whether external balance was or was not a problem. A more relevant indicator is whether the rate of absorption of the petroleum revenues, including changes to the level of indebtedness as well as changes in the level of reserves, was judged to be excessive, or in danger of becoming so. Whether the 1978 devaluation was motivated by concern about external balance, interpreted in this way, or by purely protectionist objectives, is unclear.

Indonesian policy debate at the time of the devaluation stressed the importance of retaining the productive capacity of the non-oil traded goods industries. The 'Dutch Disease' effects of absorption of petroleum revenues were well understood to include the movement of resources away from those industries. Because the known petroleum reserves were finite and the exportable surplus was expected to decline because of growing domestic consumption, it was considered essential not to allow the non-oil tradable sectors to run down excessively.

Clearly, the level of 'known' reserves reflects past exploration activity, which responds to economic forces in a similar way to any other form of risky investment. The level of known reserves is thus an economic concept rather than a purely geological one. Indonesia's known reserves have probably increased since 1978 in response to exploration activity. Nevertheless, it remains obvious that Indonesia's true petroleum reserves will not last indefinitely.[13] One of the reasons for maintaining the profitability of the non-oil traded goods industries reflected this perspective. It was expected that as the reserves dwindled, the non-oil traded goods industries would be increasingly required for Indonesia's export revenue earnings and for import replacement.

As events transpired, the non-oil traded goods industries were required for these purposes much sooner than expected. The main reasons were not diminution of known oil reserves or accelerated domestic demand but the collapse of international petroleum prices in the mid-1980s. The point is that the 1978 devaluation seems to have been motivated partly by these long-run considerations of external balance—

the perceived necessity of preventing the non-oil traded goods sectors from running down excessively in the short run, only to require revitalization a decade or two later—and partly by the purely protectionist motive of maintaining the return to investments already made in those sectors, most notably in manufacturing. The balance between these objectives is unknown, but both were apparently important. Finally, it must be said that if the magnitude of the 1979–80 international petroleum price increase had been anticipated, the November 1978 devaluation may have been deferred for several years.

Following the 1978 devaluation, the ratio of tradable to non-tradable prices declined gradually, but not at the rate observed prior to the 1978 devaluation. From Table 5.3, the rate of absorption of petroleum revenues slowed for about two years. By early 1983 this tradable/non-tradable price ratio had declined to roughly its value just prior to the 1978 devaluation and a further (37 per cent) devaluation followed. The subsequent decline of the price ratio was at first slower than during the 1978–83 period, but the rate of decline had accelerated by 1986. It is notable how closely these relative price movements correlate with the calculated rates of absorption presented in Table 5.3. Following devaluations, the tradable/non-tradable price ratio surges upwards and the rate of aggregate absorption slows markedly. Subsequently, as the tradable/non-tradable price ratio declines, the rate of aggregate absorption accelerates.

From inspection of the tradable/non-tradable relative price series shown in Figure 5.7, both the effects of devaluations and the underlying economic reasons for their occurrence are easily explained. When the price ratio declines to an unacceptable level, a devaluation is implemented to raise it. This hypothesis explains the 1978 and 1983 devaluations well. It also explains the 1986 devaluation if one notes that, in the two years prior to 1986, oil prices had fallen precipitously (Figure 5.1). The tradable/non-tradable price ratio that was deemed to be critical had thus risen. Short-run balance of payments concerns seem to have played a greater role in motivating the 1983 and 1986 devaluations than was the case in 1978. The significance of the tradable/non-tradable relative price series shown in Figure 5.7 in explaining the occurrence of devaluations is nevertheless very striking.

An index used much more frequently to analyse the causes and effects of devaluation is often called the 'real effective exchange rate' or just the 'real exchange rate', and sometimes an 'index of competitiveness'. This index of competitiveness—the term preferred in this chapter—is used especially frequently in reports from the World Bank and the International Monetary Fund. The index, C_t, is formed from the calculation

$$C_t = E_t \, p_t^*/p_t$$

where C_t is the index of competitiveness at time t, E_t is the nominal exchange rate (say in rupiah per US$), p_t^* denotes the 'foreign price level', a weighted index formed from trading partners' price levels, and

p_t is an index of the domestic price level. The reason that this index is thought to be a guide to competitiveness is that the numerator, Ep_t^*, is taken to indicate average prices received from traded goods production domestically and the denominator, p_t , is taken to indicate the domestic costs faced by these traded goods producers.

Calculations of 'competitiveness' or the 'real exchange rate' for Indonesia are shown in Figure 5.7. The computational details are explained in Warr (1984 and 1986). The figure is based on exchange rate and price level data for Indonesia and its seven major trading partners. The data show that, as a proxy for the domestic tradable/non-tradable relative price ratio, the index of the real exchange rate performs poorly. This is especially so when the relative price effects of a devaluation—one of the major purposes for which such an index is frequently computed—are considered. Both the magnitude of the relative price effects of a devaluation and the subsequent pattern of relative price adjustments are badly distorted by this type of index. The reasons for these distortions are discussed in greater detail in Warr (1984 and 1986). It is hazardous indeed to use so-called 'competitiveness' indices as proxies for domestic relative price movements and their use for this purpose should surely be discontinued.

Conclusions

Indonesia has on the whole pursued a cautious exchange rate policy aimed at regulating the rate of absorption of petroleum revenues into the domestic economy and restraining the growth of external debt. This analysis suggests that Indonesia responded in the short term to fluctuating petroleum revenues in a manner consistent with optimal macroeconomic adjustment. Over the longer term, while there have been exceptions, the petroleum revenues and other resources absorbed domestically seem to have been used in a manner which promoted economic growth, and the growth performance which resulted has been impressive. Despite this, Indonesia's total indebtedness has become a cause for concern. Calculations indicate that for each dollar of increased petroleum revenues Indonesia received from its exports as a result of the post-1972 price increases, the country absorbed that much and borrowed externally an additional half as much again. The cumulative effect of this policy must be to reduce the range of Indonesia's future options considerably if international petroleum prices remain low throughout the 1990s.

1. For background on the Indonesian petroleum sector, see Arndt (1983). For discussions of the Indonesian policy background to the issues discussed in this chapter, see McCawley (1980a and 1980b), Paauw (1978a and 1978b), Rosendale (1981), Warr (1984 and 1986), Glassburner (1988), and Woo and Nasution (1989).

2. There is some debate as to whether Indonesian growth was slightly negative in per capita terms in 1982. The GDP data in 1973 prices show a slight growth while those in 1983 prices show a decline.

3. This section has benefited greatly from the author's discussions with Soonthorn Chaiyindeepum. For further analytical background, see Corden (1977).

4. Quantity variables were not expressed as a proportion of GDP because the non-petroleum contribution to GDP divided by GDP and the petroleum contribution to GDP divided by GDP variables would then sum identically to unity.

5. The author wishes to acknowledge the kind assistance of Will Martin of the Australian National University in suggesting this methodology and in providing the capital stock series for Indonesia.

6. On this, see Connolly and Taylor (1976a and 1976b) and Cooper (1971a, 1971b, and 1973).

7. For further details, see Corden (1977 and 1984).

8. In this discussion, as elsewhere in this chapter, it is assumed that domestic monetary policy is capable of influencing the domestic money supply, and hence the price level, in spite of Indonesia's quasi-pegged exchange rate policy. That is, the control of domestic interest rates, together with the thinness of Indonesia's organized capital markets, are assumed to prevent the full operation of the Fleming-Mundell mechanism. See Kenen (1985: 346–64).

9. For further analytical discussion of the 'Dutch Disease', see Corden and Neary (1982), Corden (1984), and Cassing and Warr (1985).

10. For further discussion, see Corden and Warr (1981).

11. For further details, see Warr (1984: 74).

12. Ismael (1980: 103). See also the 1978/9 *Annual Report* of Bank Indonesia.

13. Lukman and McGlinchey (1986: 78) suggest that proven crude reserves may have declined between 1980 and 1985, although considerable exploration activity has continued in Indonesia through the 1980s, and optimism has been expressed about the potential of the Timor Gap fields. The most reliable estimates put Indonesia's proven reserves at slightly more than 10 billion barrels.

REFERENCES

Arndt, H. W. (1983), 'Oil and the Indonesian Economy', in *Southeast Asian Affairs 1983*, Singapore: Institute of Southeast Asian Studies, pp. 136–50.

Booth, Anne and McCawley, Peter (eds.) (1981), *The Indonesian Economy during the Soeharto Era*, Kuala Lumpur: Oxford University Press.

Cassing, J. H. and Warr, P. G. (1985), 'The Distributional Impact of a Resource Boom', *Journal of International Economics*, 18: 301–19.

Connolly, M. and Taylor, D. (1976a), 'Testing the Monetary Approach to Devaluation in Developing Countries', *Journal of Political Economy*, 84: 849–59.

_____ (1976b), 'Exchange Rate Changes and Neutralization: A Test of the Monetary Approach Applied to Developed and Developing Countries', *Economica*, 46: 281–94.

Cooper, R. N. (1971a), 'Currency Devaluation in Developing Countries', *Essays in International Finance*, No. 86 (June), New Jersey: Princeton University.

_____ (1971b), 'An Assessment of Currency Devaluation in Developing Countries', in G. Ranis (ed.), *Government and Economic Development*, New Haven, Conn.: Yale University Press, pp. 472–513.

_____ (1973), 'An Analysis of Currency Devaluation in Developing Countries', in M. B. Connolly and A. K. Swoboda (eds.), *International Trade and Money*, Toronto: University of Toronto Press, pp. 67–196.

Corden, W. M. (1977), *Inflation, Exchange Rates and the World Economy*, Oxford: Clarendon Press.

_____ (1981), 'Exchange Rate Protection', in R. N. Cooper et al. (eds.), *The*

International Monetary System under Flexible Exchange Rates: Global, Regional and National, Cambridge, Mass.: Ballinger, pp. 17–34.

_____ (1984), 'Booming Sector and Dutch Disease Economics: A Survey', *Oxford Economic Papers*, 36: 359–80.

Corden, W. M. and Neary, J. P. (1982), 'Booming Sector and De-industrialization in a Small Open Economy', *Economic Journal*, 92: 825–48.

Corden, W. M. and Warr, P. G. (1981), 'The Petroleum Boom and Exchange Rate Policy in Indonesia', *Ekonomi dan Keuangan Indonesia*, 29: 335–59.

Glassburner, Bruce (1988), 'Indonesia: Windfalls in a Poor Rural Economy', in Alan Gelb (ed.), *Oil Windfalls, Blessing or Curse*, New York: Oxford University Press, pp. 197–226.

Ismael, J. E. (1980), 'Money and Credit in Indonesia, 1966 to 1979', *Ekonomi dan Keuangan Indonesia*, 28: 97–101.

Kenen, Peter B. (1985), *The International Economy*, Englewood Cliffs: Prentice-Hall.

Lukman, Nasrun and McGlinchey, James M. (1986), 'The Indonesian Petroleum Industry: Current Problems and Future Prospects', *Bulletin of Indonesian Economic Studies*, 22(3): 70–92.

McCawley, P. T. (1978), 'Some Consequences of the Pertamina Crisis in Indonesia', *Journal of Southeast Asian Studies*, 9: 1–27.

_____ (1980a), 'Indonesia's New Balance of Payments Problem: A Surplus to Get Rid of', *Ekonomi dan Keuangan Indonesia*, 28: 39–58.

_____ (1980b), 'The Devaluation and Structural Change in Indonesia', in *Southeast Asian Affairs 1980*, Singapore: Institute of Southeast Asian Studies, pp. 145–57.

Paauw, D. S. (1978a), 'Exchange Rate Policy and Non-extractive Exports', *Ekonomi dan Keuangan Indonesia*, 26: 205–18.

_____ (1978b), 'The Labor-intensity of Indonesia's Exports', *Ekonomi dan Keuangan Indonesia*, 26: 447–56.

Rosendale, Phyllis (1981), 'The Balance of Payments', in Anne Booth and Peter McCawley (eds.), *The Indonesian Economy during the Soeharto Era*, Kuala Lumpur: Oxford University Press, pp. 162–80.

Warr, P. G. (1984), 'Exchange Rate Protection in Indonesia', *Bulletin of Indonesian Economic Studies*, 20: 53–89.

_____ (1986), 'Indonesia's Other Dutch Disease: Economic Effects of the Petroleum Boom', in J. P. Neary and S. van Wijnbergen (eds.), *Natural Resources and the Macroeconomy*, Oxford: Basil Blackwell, pp. 288–320.

Woo Wing Thye and Nasution, Anwar (1989), 'Indonesian Economic Policies and Their Relation to External Debt Management', in J. D. Sachs and S. M. Collins (eds.), *Developing Country Debt and Economic Performance*, Vol. 3, Chicago: University of Chicago Press, pp. 17–149.

PART II
SECTORAL GROWTH

6

Agriculture in Transition*

Steven R. Tabor

Introduction

THE agricultural sector in the 1980s experienced moderate and steady growth in an otherwise slowing economy. This suggests that Indonesia was wise to give agricultural growth priority during the oil boom era, rather than to emphasize exclusively domestic manufacturing and construction as many OPEC economies did. The agricultural sector has continued to be a primary source of income and employment for more than half the labour force. Agricultural growth has also been important in stimulating demand for domestically produced non-agricultural goods. Through import substitution, export expansion, and export diversification, agriculture has continued to contribute to the economy-wide imperative of foreign exchange generation. And by providing an adequate diet and generating employment for the rural poor, the sector has contributed to the alleviation of poverty and to improvement in economy-wide living standards. But there have been some disappointments. Certain regions and subsectors of agriculture have outperformed others and these disparities may widen in the future. As the 1990s begins, it is this legacy of past performance, together with a very different set of national goals and priorities, that will shape the future course of agricultural development.

This chapter discusses agricultural development in Indonesia in the 1980s. The first section examines the overall performance of the agricultural sector and its evolving role in the broader economy. The second section looks at developments in the food subsector, focusing primarily on rice. The third section discusses agricultural diversification, both in foodstuffs and in tree-crop commodities. The final section examines prospects for agricultural policy in the 1990s.

*The following individuals are to be thanked for their comments and suggestions on earlier drafts of this chapter: J. Edwin Faris, John Wilton, Klaus Altemeier, Wim van Veen, and Geert Overbosch. Responsibility for all errors and omissions rests with the author alone. The views and opinions expressed in this chapter are those of the author and do not represent the official views of the World Bank or any of its affiliates.

The Role of Agriculture in the Economy

The Role of Agriculture in GDP

After dropping precipitously in the 1970s, agriculture's share of GDP declined more slowly in the 1980s (Table 6.1). Within agriculture, food crops continued to dominate in terms of income and employment. Tree crops and livestock are a distant second and third, providing 16 per cent and 11 per cent of agricultural GDP respectively in 1988. Agricultural growth has been slower in the 1980s than in the 1970s due to a combination of depressed agricultural commodity markets, a slow-down in expansion of the land frontier, ecological limits on increases in cropping intensity, and the near-completion of green revolution advances for rice. Agricultural growth reached 6.1 per cent between 1978 and 1981, at the height of the green revolution technological transformation, and then slowed to a respectable 3.1 per cent between 1982 and 1988. During the 1980s, the agricultural sector has grown at about the same rate as the services sector, far faster than the declining mining sector, but at less than half the rate of the manufacturing sector.

Market Expansion

Agricultural growth in the 1980s contributed to the growth of the domestic market for non-agricultural goods. The share of rural incomes spent on non-food commodities increased from 26 per cent in 1980 to 33.1 per cent in 1987, according to the results of the National Socio-economic Surveys (*Survei Sosial Ekonomi Nasional* or *Susenas*).[1] About one-third of total rural income growth was used to expand the market for non-agricultural goods and services. Since agricultural incomes are lower and more evenly distributed than urban incomes, this increase in rural non-food expenditures had a greater impact on the market for domestically produced manufactured goods than an equivalent increase in urban incomes would have done. The high marginal propensity of agricultural households to consume domestically produced tradables has been of considerable importance in stimulating the rise of secondary and tertiary activities in the smaller cities and the rural areas (Boediono, 1987).

Foreign Exchange

Agricultural growth in the 1980s has contributed directly to the diversification of Indonesia's export base, through import substitution, new product development, and intensification of traditional export crops. Indonesia has saved foreign exchange directly from import substitution in rice, although because of the various capital and input subsidies used to stimulate rice production, the net foreign exchange savings are small. The traditional export crops contributed foreign exchange earnings of $1.8 billion annually. On average this amounted to 27 per cent of total non-petroleum export earnings. Earnings from timber exports rivalled

TABLE 6.1

Agricultural GDP[a] by Subsectoral Origin, 1978–1988 (Rp billion: 1983 constant prices)

Year	Food Crops[b]	Tree Crops[c]	Livestock	Fisheries	Forestry	Agriculture	Percentage of GDP
1978	8,400	1,880	1,248	983	1,871	14,381	25
1979	8,856	2,129	1,440	1,046	1,867	15,338	25
1980	9,661	2,335	1,586	1,116	1,701	16,399	25
1981	10,639	2,528	1,621	1,139	1,261	17,187	24
1982	10,736	2,626	1,696	1,167	1,146	17,371	24
1983	11,126	2,670	1,754	1,220	994	17,765	23
1984	11,680	2,795	1,890	1,253	894	18,513	22
1985	11,986	3,087	2,037	1,341	851	19,300	23
1986	12,287	3,142	2,064	1,418	889	19,799	22
1987	12,415	3,258	2,111	1,472	968	20,224	21
1988[d]	12,974	3,413	2,212	1,557	1,013	21,168	21

Annual Average Growth[e]

1978–81	8.2	10.4	9.1	5.0	−12.3	6.1	
1982–8	3.2	4.5	4.5	4.9	−2.0	3.3	
1978–88	4.4	6.1	5.9	4.7	−6.0	3.9	

Source: BPS.

[a] Data from 1978 to 1982 are taken from unpublished World Bank sources.
[b] Includes rice, corn, cassava, other root crops, pulses, fruits, and vegetables.
[c] Includes smallholder and estate production of rubber, coffee, coconuts, sugar-cane, tea, palm oil, spices, and coffee.
[d] Provisional data.
[e] Calculated from data for 1978, 1981, 1982, and 1988.

tree-crop exports at $1.5 billion annually, accounting for 23 per cent of total non-oil export earnings. In addition, a very strong performance was registered by relatively new agricultural exports such as shrimp and cocoa. Shrimp export earnings rose from $93 million in 1980 to $610 million in 1988, the fastest growth of any of the agricultural commodities. Combined exports from all agricultural activities averaged 61 per cent of total non-oil exports, in value terms, between the years 1981 and 1988 (BPS, 1985–8).

Offsetting the foreign exchange gains from rice import substitution and cash crop export growth has been an increase in the import requirements for other foodstuffs. Import demand for soy beans, soy bean meal, and wheat has climbed sharply. The combined value of food imports (including wheat) fell from $938 million in 1980 to $458 million in 1986 (Department of Agriculture, 1988). But this decline is the result of rice import substitution and a sharp drop in international commodity prices, and was offset to some extent by the increase in import demand for wheat and soy beans.

Employment

The agricultural sector has continued to exhibit an enormous capacity to absorb ever-growing quantities of labour. Agricultural employment increased from 29.1 million to 38.7 million persons between 1976 and 1987, growing at an estimated 2.6 per cent per annum. (Further discussion of the role of agriculture in the Indonesian labour force can be found in Chapter 11.) Expansion in agricultural employment occurred because of the growth in the number of farms and the increase in use of hired labour in agricultural operations. The number of agricultural households increased at an average rate of 1 per cent between 1973 and 1983, rising from 14.4 million to 15.9 million during this period (BPS, 1983: Table 2.1).

In the 1980s, the majority of farm households continue to be located on Java, although the share has been declining since the early 1960s (Booth, 1985; Hart, 1986).[2] The fastest growth in number of farm households, between 1973 and 1983, has been in Kalimantan (1.7 per cent per annum). The number of farm households in Sumatra and Sulawesi has tended to increase at about the same rate as in Java (0.8 per cent per annum) reflecting the more advanced degree of settlement in these large islands (BPS, 1983: Table 2.1).

Although agricultural growth increased labour demand, such growth was probably not sufficient to offset the existing high degree of rural underemployment (Rucker, 1987). Inspection of agricultural wage data suggests that real wages for agricultural hired labour have tended to rise, but continue to be very close to subsistence levels, with considerable regional and subsectoral variation in wage rates. Although the wage data do vary widely, there is evidence that real wages by task in the agriculture sector have risen moderately in the 1980s, after some stagnation between 1975 and 1980 (Korns, 1988). This suggests that, within an overall labour surplus environment, there may be periodic shortages of labour in local markets leading to upward pressure on wages (Kasryno, 1985).[3]

The expansion of agricultural employment opportunities has acted as a brake on the flow of the rural population to the urban areas. The share of the rural population in the total population fell from 82.7 per cent in 1971 to 77.6 per cent in 1981 and then to 73.7 per cent in 1985 (BPS, 1985–8). The fact that the agriculture sector has apparently been able to absorb more labour during a period of slowing growth with little evidence of downward pressure on living standards is nothing short of remarkable. Compared with other countries with similar per capita incomes, Indonesia's urbanization rate is quite low. Other developing nations which experienced similar natural resource booms in the late 1970s and early 1980s, such as Nigeria and Mexico, have fared far worse in terms of generating rural employment and braking the rural–urban drift (World Bank, 1989: 224–5).

Productivity

Agricultural productivity has continued to lag behind that of the more capital-intensive industrial sector. Average returns to labour, measured in terms of agricultural GDP per person employed in agriculture, rose from Rp 455,889 in 1978 to Rp 520,021 in 1987 (in constant 1983 rupiah terms). In US dollar terms, however, there has been a fall in output per worker; 1978 average earnings were $484 per capita compared with $456 in 1987. While labour productivity was growing very slowly in the agriculture sector, it was rising quickly in manufacturing. Returns to labour increased from Rp 1.7 million per capita in 1980 to Rp 2 million per capita in 1987. Hence, the gap between agricultural and industrial labour productivity has continued to widen, although differences in capital intensity make intersectoral, single factorial comparisons hazardous. Productivity comparisons are likewise difficult to make because of the increasing tendency for farm households, particularly in Java, to derive a significant share of household income from non-agricultural activities (Rietveld, 1986).

Growth in off-farm activities has reduced rigidities in the labour market and has helped to spread the benefits of urban growth to the rural areas (Rietveld, 1986; see also Chapter 10, Table 10.13, and relevant discussion there). Microfield surveys by Collier et al. (1982 and 1987), show flourishing rural cottage industries and services in villages that had been principally agricultural a decade ago. Collier refers to this tendency for agricultural growth to lead to rural manufacturing and service sector development as the 'urbanization' of rural Java.

Area Expansion and Distribution

The decade of the 1980s has witnessed a continued expansion of the land frontier, almost entirely outside Java and in the non-irrigated or

TABLE 6.2

Landholdings by Agricultural Households According to the Agricultural Census, 1963–1983

('000 hectares)

Island	1963		1973		1983		Growth Rate: 1973–83 (per cent per annum)	
	Wet Land	Dry Land	Wet Land	Dry Land	Wet Land	Dry Land	Wet Land	Dry Land
Java	2 558	3 119	2 631	2 874	2 946	3 448	1.1	1.8
Sumatra	779	3 130	1 038	2 764	1 294	3 993	2.2	3.8
Sulawesi	247	719	445	1 078	523	1 862	1.6	5.6
Nusa Tenggara	243	701	291	917	360	1 174	2.2	2.5
Kalimantan	278	1 140	434	1 434	615	2 250	3.6	4.6
Other	n.a.	n.a.	0	259	7	586	n.a.	n.a.
Indonesia	4 075	8 809	4 840	9 328	5 746	13 313	1.7	3.6

Sources: 1963, 1973, and 1983 Agricultural Census, BPS, as cited in Kasryno et al. (1986: 157).

n.a. = Not available.

dry-land regions of the country. Between 1973 and 1983, the total wet-land (*sawah*) area in Java is estimated to have increased by 1.1 per cent per annum. Irrigated areas increased at twice this rate in Sumatra and more than three times as fast in Kalimantan (Table 6.2). The largest increase, however, was in dry-land resources. Together, a total of 2.8 million hectares of new dry land was brought under cultivation in Sumatra, Sulawesi, and Kalimantan between 1973 and 1983.[4] Throughout Indonesia, a total of just under 4 million hectares of dry land was brought under cultivation, compared to an increase of just over 900 000 hectares of irrigated lands, between 1973 and 1983.

Growth in the agricultural resource base, particularly through dry-land expansion, has probably had an equalizing rather than a polarizing effect on rural asset holdings. This is because a large share of the Outer Island's dry-land expansion was used for transmigration and smallholder tree-crop programmes, both of which are schemes in which the landless or land-poor receive a small plot (normally 2 hectares) for new settle-ment. Although access to land is far from completely equal, landhold-ings remain far more evenly distributed in Indonesia than in many other developing countries. There is little evidence of massive labour displace-ment or of excessive concentration resulting from introduction of 'green revolution' technologies (Kasryno, 1981; Teken and Soewardi, 1982; Keuning, 1984; Hart, 1986; Booth, 1988: Chapter 5; Manning, 1988). According to the results of the 1983 Agricultural Census, only 4.4 per cent of Javanese and 1.2 per cent of non-Javanese agricultural house-holds are landless (Table 6.3). This, coupled with the relatively low rural to urban migration rates and the rise in agricultural employment levels, provides empirical support for the argument that green revolution advances have increased labour demand and improved returns in agri-culture without marginalizing the small farmers.

A large share of agricultural households operate holdings that are too small to generate adequate incomes. Taking 0.25 hectares in Java and

TABLE 6.3
Farm Households in 1983 by Operated Holding Size

	Java (per cent)	*Outer Islands* (per cent)	*Indonesia* (per cent)
Landless farmers[a]	4.4	1.2	3.1
Farmers with under 0.25 hectare	31.3	11.0	23.2
Farmers with 0.25 to 0.49 hectare	25.8	16.8	22.2
Farmers with 0.5 to 0.99 hectare	21.4	25.4	23.0
Farmers with 1.0 to 1.99 hectares	10.7	26.0	16.8
Farmers with 2.0 hectares or more	6.4	19.6	11.7
Total numbers of farmers (millions):	10.28	6.80	17.08

Source: BPS, 1983 Agricultural Census, Series B: Table 17.
[a] Defined as those operating less than 0.05 hectare.

TABLE 6.4

Average Landholding Size by Island, 1973 and 1983 (hectares)

Island	1973	1983
Java	0.64	0.66
Sumatra	1.33	1.44
Sulawesi	1.38	1.45
Kalimantan	2.71	2.78
Nusa Tenggara/Bali	1.27	1.22
Others	2.17	2.04
Indonesia	0.99	1.05

Source: BPS, 1983 Agricultural Census, Series B: Table 2.1.

0.5 hectares outside Java as cut-off points, nearly 44 per cent of all agricultural households operate landholdings that are, under present technology, too small to generate a significant surplus over and above subsistence requirements (Keuning, 1984). Another 30 per cent of the Javanese farm households and another 43 per cent of the non-Javanese households have holdings that are between the minimum cut-off points and 2 hectares. In total then, more than three-quarters of all rural households can be classified as either 'smallholder', 'land-poor', or 'landless'. In Java, holdings under 2 hectares account for 75 per cent of the total. Outside Java, where land fertility is poorer, slightly over half of all landholdings are in parcels greater than 2 hectares in size (Tjondronegoro, 1986).

While there are a great number of small or marginal rural households, there is no evidence that excessive land fragmentation has taken place. Indeed the average landholding size has increased slightly from 1973 to 1983 in all regions except Bali and the Eastern Islands (Table 6.4). This tendency for the average landholding size to stabilize suggests that, on Java, the majority of holdings have reached the minimum viable size, while, outside Java, landholding size has tended to stabilize at a level optimal for a single-family enterprise with limited access to capital and hired labour (Booth, 1985; Keuning, 1984).

Food and Welfare

Although the figures are sparse and often contradictory, there is little doubt that agricultural growth in Indonesia in the 1970s and 1980s has contributed to an improvement in food consumption standards and an increase in general levels of living. The greatest growth in food availability occurred between 1973 and 1980, coinciding with the most rapid period of green revolution gains and the growth in agricultural imports. Since 1980, average caloric availability, measured from the BPS Food Balance Sheets, has stagnated at about 2,500 calories per day. Average protein consumption levels have increased marginally, from 48.5 grams to 52.7 grams per day, reflecting also a slight improvement in the composition of the diet in favour of animal protein sources (BPS, 1985–8). The Indonesian diet has become increasingly dominated by rice (Mears, 1981; Monteverde, 1987; Tabor, 1989a). On average, 56 per cent of all calories come from rice. Rice is also the single largest source of protein in the diet. With increased affluence, Indonesian consumers have switched from corn and cassava to rice, as the superior staple food (Dixon, 1982; Tabor and Altemeier, 1989). While there is evidence of qualitative improvement amongst the starchy staples, the Indonesian diet remains largely grain- and vegetable-based. Meat provides only 11 per cent of total proteins, one of the lowest shares in the Asian region.

Although average caloric availability levels have stabilized, there is indirect evidence that agricultural growth has contributed to an improvement in nutrition levels (Johnson et al., 1988). Over the past decade, the infant mortality rate has declined, average life expectancy increased, and fertility rates declined (see Chapter 12 for further details). Such outcomes can best be explained as the combined effect of all factors which determine health status, including improved nutrition (Pitt and Rosenzweig, 1986).

The Role of the External Environment on Agriculture

The agricultural growth record of the 1980s is quite remarkable considering the adverse external environment in which agriculture has had to operate. External factors hindering agricultural performance have included unfavourable movements in world markets for the major traded commodities, a decline in government expenditures on agriculture, a high degree of trade protection for manufactured goods, and periodic and protracted drought. Each of these factors is examined in turn.

Prices

After rising rapidly in the late 1970s, international prices for a number of key agricultural commodities peaked in 1979 and 1980 and fell sharply thereafter. Rice, rubber, and coffee all suffered simultaneously from adverse movements in their international terms of trade. In 1980, the world rice price (Thai 15 per cent brokens) reached $446 per metric ton (MT). By 1985, the price has fallen to $215 per MT and hovered at about that level before recovering marginally in 1988 and 1989. Likewise, rubber prices (RSSI, C and F, New York) peaked at $1,624 per MT in 1980 before plummeting to $924 per MT in 1985. Coffee prices (Robusta average grade) averaged $1.70 per pound between 1977 and 1980, but fell to $1.33 per pound in 1981–8 (World Bank, various years).

The fall in agricultural commodity prices had a relatively limited effect on public investment since long-term project commitments in irrigation, land settlement, rural roads, agricultural input manufacturing, and the like were based on price projections prevailing during the late 1970s. Adverse world market developments were offset by moderately high rates of trade protection (largely quantity rationing under non-tariff barriers), a high degree of capital and other input subsidization, and export tax reduction (Glassburner, 1985). These measures acted to dampen the domestic effects of adverse commodity price movements by shifting part of the burden of low prices from producers to consumers and the government budget (Fane and Phillips, 1987).

Public Expenditures

The fall in primary commodity prices did, however, adversely affect the government's ability to finance agricultural public expenditures because of the reduction in export tax revenues and the burgeoning domestic subsidy bill. This higher fiscal burden from protecting agriculture was partly offset by higher tariffs on food imports. But since 1985 import tariffs on foodstuffs have been insufficient to offset the cost of domestic distribution of publicly stockpiled grains (Falcon et al., 1986). The net effect of government policy designed to insulate domestic from world markets has been an increase in the burden on the budget.

On balance, however, agricultural market developments had a rather minor impact on the overall capacity of the government to finance agricultural expenditures. The main macroeconomic shocks were the post-1983 fall in petroleum prices, the post-1985 depreciation of the dollar, and the rise in real international interest rates. These changes in the international economy contributed to severe pressure on the Indonesian balance of payments and resulted in the reduction of government expenditures economy-wide, which has been discussed in Chapter 2. It must be emphasized that the development budget for agriculture and irrigation grew more rapidly in nominal terms through *Repelita IV* than the budget for any other sector, except housing and science (see Table 2.7). But in real terms, public funding of agricultural development grew far less rapidly between 1984 and 1989 than it had over the previous decade.

The austere fiscal environment penalized agricultural growth in one sense and benefited agricultural growth in another. Government reacted to the macroeconomic shocks by reducing and deferring capital expenditures and subsidy transfers in agriculture. Non-fertilizer development expenditures on agriculture and irrigation were reduced from Rp 967 billion in 1984/5 to Rp 660 billion in 1985/6 and then to Rp 434 billion in 1986/7. In US dollar terms, this amounted to a cut-back of nearly two-thirds in a two-year period. Agricultural development expenditures were increased again in 1987/8 but because of inflation and devaluation, the real value of these expenditures was less than 75 per cent of those in 1985/6. To the extent that these investments were uneconomic under current conditions, deferral or cancellation was the appropriate policy. To the extent, however, that such investments remained economically viable, but could not be financed due to the adverse macroeconomic environment, then budgetary retrenchment will have reduced the medium- and long-term production capacity of the sector.

There was also a positive side to the impact of the fiscal crisis on agricultural performance. The government acted to overcome the adverse external environment by introducing policies designed to improve competitiveness. This included two large rupiah devaluations and a series of financial market reforms and trade liberalization measures which have been discussed in detail in previous chapters. The investment and expenditure switching effects of these reforms have been shown to be generally favourable to production of domestic tradables, of which agricultural commodities predominate. For the export commodities capitalized under fixed (and often below market) nominal interest rates, such as tree crops, currency devaluation provided a major short-term windfall gain.

Externally, agriculture has also been penalized, indirectly, by the relatively high degree of industrial protection. In the early phases of industrialization, special interest groups obtained a wide range of trade protection, domestic monopolization, and other forms of non-market assistance. Effective rates of protection, estimated for 1986, have been found to be considerably higher for industrial goods (42 per cent) than for agricultural goods (24 per cent) (Fane and Cutbush, 1988). Protection rates are higher for import substitutes than for export oriented commodities, reflecting a generally inward-oriented growth strategy. However, the actual indirect, intrasectoral resource allocation effects from industrial protection have been less severe than would be expected by examination of a comparative ranking of effective protection coefficients alone. Direct transfers to the agricultural sector, in terms of publicly financed capital investment, have acted to offset the bias induced by heavy rates of industrial trade protection (Fane and Phillips, 1987).

An examination of trends in net barter terms of trade indicate that agriculture has not been excessively penalized by public policy in order to finance industrialization or to offset balance of payments difficulties. The net barter terms of trade for farmers in Java, as measured by the Biro Pusat Statistik, has not shown any marked deterioration over a significant period since 1976. Between 1983 and 1988 the index in fact improved in each of the four provinces of Java, although there was some deterioration in 1989 as prices of farm inputs increased more rapidly than output prices.[5]

Climatic Shocks

Indonesian agriculture continues to be highly dependent on the natural environment. Although irrigated land accounts for more than 80 per cent of the harvested area of rice production, the irrigation systems serve to supplement rather than to replace rainfall. With near continuous rice cropping, the adequacy of rainfall can affect production at any point in the year. For most of the early 1980s, Indonesia was fortunate in that there was relatively good weather and an absence of severe pest outbreaks. In the mid-1980s, the vagaries of climate and pests added to the adverse external environment. Pest outbreaks and drought came on the tail of the collapse of world market prices for agricultural commodities and the sharp retrenchment in government agricultural expenditures. After reports that breeding and the breakup of continuous cultivation had eliminated the most serious rice pest problem, a major outbreak of brown planthopper was reported in 1986. This was followed by two years of unusually dry weather, bordering on drought in many regions (Damardjati et al., 1988). Good weather in 1989 ushered in an abundant rice harvest once again. But the main lesson of the years 1986 to 1988 was quite clear—that is, Indonesian agriculture is still highly vulnerable to the vagaries of pests and weather.

The Food Subsector

Rice

Rice self-sufficiency has been the most notable accomplishment of the agricultural sector in the 1980s. The campaign for rice self-sufficiency was not only the prestige project of the decade, but was also a highly productive, competitive, and equitable use of national resources (Timmer, Falcon, and Pearson, 1983; Manning, 1987; Pearson et al., 1988). In 1979, Indonesia was the world's largest importer of rice, with annual imports of 2.9 million metric tons (MMTs) costing about $600 million per year (Department of Agriculture, 1988). By 1985, the rice economy was in sharp excess supply, with end-year public stocks in excess of 2.3 MMTs (Ellis, 1988).

Rice production grew by 7.1 per cent between 1980 and 1985 thanks largely to good weather and the 'sinking in' of green revolution technology (Falcon et al., 1986). In 1986, owing largely to pest attacks, rice production grew by only 1.7 per cent. Actual production may not have increased at all according to econometric assessment (Altemeier, Tabor, and Adinugroho, 1988). In 1987 and the first half of 1988, a drought over most of Java contributed to a shortfall in production, rapid consumer price escalation, and a sharp run-down in public sector stocks (Ellis, 1988). At the end of 1988, the government took the difficult decision to import 450 000 MTs to rebuild domestic stocks and meet budget group ration requirements. In 1989, thanks largely to favourable rainfall, wet season rice production was well in excess of expectations and the government was able to rebuild domestic stocks and plan for possible end-year exports (Tabor, 1989b). While rice production has suffered from sharp, discrete environmental shocks, the rice economy has essentially stayed on a self-sufficiency course since 1984/5 (Table 6.5).

Many factors contributed to the rapid growth in rice production.

TABLE 6.5
Production and Trade in Rice and Wheat

Year	Rice Production/Imports[a]				Wheat Imports[b] ('000 MT)
	Area ('000 ha)	Yield (MT/ha)	Production (MMT)	Imports ('000 MT)	
1970	8 135	2.38	19.3	771	624
1975	8 495	2.67	22.3	670	834
1976	8 368	2.78	23.3	1 508	987
1977	8 360	2.79	23.3	2 308	1 002
1978	929	2.89	25.7	1 266	1 239
1979	8 850	2.97	26.3	2 579	1 356
1980	9 005	3.29	29.6	1 213	1 281
1981	9 382	3.49	32.7	437	1 418
1982	9 162	3.74	33.6	505	1 557
1983	9 169	3.85	35.3	1 109	1 704
1984	9 768	3.91	38.1	185	1 192
1985	9 905	3.94	39.0	0	1 511
1986	9 988	3.98	39.7	0	1 626
1987	9 923	4.04	40.1	0	1 603
1988	10 089	4.13	41.6	50	1 500
1989	10 167	4.23	43.0	400	1 500

Sources: BPS, Department of Agriculture, and Bulog.
[a] Rice area figures are gross area harvested. Production and yield are in rough rice terms. Imports are in milled rice. Figures for 1989 are preliminary Department of Agriculture, Bulog, and BPS first forecast (Ramalan I) estimates.
[b] Wheat imports in 1970 are in terms of wheat flour. Thereafter they are in terms of wheat grain.

Between 1975 and 1985, the share of farmers using new HYVs increased from 50 per cent to 85 per cent. The consumption of chemical fertilizers for food crops increased fourfold from 900 000 MTs in 1976 to 3.8 MMTs in 1986, assisted by a growing level of price support and market control.[6] Government investment in irrigation in the 1970s and early 1980s led to a net increase of the total irrigated area by approximately 500 000 hectares, and also resulted in the upgrading of 300 000 hectares of small-scale irrigation facilities to technical irrigation standards. Irrigation investment facilitated area expansion and rice intensification (Rosegrant and Kasryno, 1988). In addition to irrigation investment, significant infrastructural improvements were registered in roads, transport facilities, communication facilities, rice mills, grain storage facilities, and fertilizer factories (Mears, 1981; Squires and Tabor, 1987).

Investment in physical capital was complemented by development of public sector institutions charged with providing the rice economy with financial marketing and extension services. Institutional innovation served as an important link between expanding production possibilities and improved physical infrastructure by providing the financial and educational prerequisites for technological innovation. Growth in infrastructure, both physical and institutional, is summarized in Table 6.6.

During the past decade, the government has actively intervened to influence prices in the rice market. Provision of subsidized production credit, subsidized seeds, fertilizers, and pesticides, together with a guaranteed floor price, provided farmers with an incentives environment conducive to adoption of the new rice technology. Apart from declining somewhat in 1985 and 1986, real rice prices were held constant (through trade protection and stock subsidization) throughout the 1980s, a period in which productivity per unit area increased by 3.4 per cent per annum. This combination of relatively stable real output prices with rapid technological transformation contributed to a steady increase in the profitability of rice cultivation (Ellis, 1988).

Strong domestic investment in production capacity, together with Bulog buffer stocking and trade management enabled Indonesia, as a large-country rice trader, to transfer a portion of domestic supply instability to the world rice market. Indonesian rice prices have been held

TABLE 6.6
Agricultural Infrastructure Growth in Indonesia, 1969–1985

Category[a]	Capital Stock Level 1969	Capital Stock Level 1985	Growth Rate (per cent per annum)
Public irrigation (million ha)	2.45	3.23	2.2
Other irrigation (million ha)	1.11	0.86	− 1.9
Paved roads ('000 km)	84	204	5.7
Trucks ('000 units)	94	845	14.7
Boats (units)	89	398	10.5
Planes (units)	163	772	10.2
Telephones ('000 units)	184	829	9.9
Milling facilities ('000 units)	16.3	28.3	4.0
Rice storage capacity (MMT)	1.5	5.7	10.0
Fertilizer supply (MMT)	0.5	5.1	29.4
Fertilizer kiosks ('000 units)	1.9	20.3	19.8
Farmers' groups ('000 units)	40	225	11.6
Field extension agents ('000)	1.6	22.2	19.2
Rural banks ('000 units)	0.5	3.7	12.6
Co-operatives ('000 units)	0.1	6.9	32.6

Sources: BPS, Statistik Indonesia, various issues; Department of Agriculture, Mill Registration Records; Department of Public Works, Irrigation Records; PT Pusri, Annual Fertilizer Production Statistics; Bimas Secretariat, 'Pelestarian Swamsembada Pangan', 1987; Weitz-Hettelsater, Rice Storage: Handling and Marketing, 1972.
[a]Irrigation figures refer to a 1973 base and 1986 end year. Fertilizer kiosks figures refer to a 1973 base year, fertilizer supply refers to domestic production for a 1976 base year, and figures for mill units, storage capacity, and co-operatives to a 1971 base year. Rice storage capacity figures are for facilities owned or rented by the government.

moderately above (20 to 40 per cent nominal rates of protection) world market prices for most of the 1980s (Table 6.7). In addition, in terms of interannual fluctuations, Indonesian urban rice prices have been more stable than prices prevailing on the world market. Between 1980 and 1988, the detrended coefficient of variation in Jakarta medium-quality rice prices was 12.2 per cent compared to a coefficient of variation of 42 per cent in the price of Thai 15 per cent broken rice for export (Ellis, 1988). Prices were held stable in the early and mid-1980s. In 1987 and 1988, as Bulog lost its grip on the rice market, domestic prices rose sharply, as did prices on the world market (Timmer, 1988b). With the resumption of imports and the build-up of public stocks in 1989, domestic prices once again began to stabilize.

The government has also used a number of interventions in other food commodity markets to influence performance in the rice market. Although these interventions have been designed to achieve specific objectives in their own markets, their design and implementation have taken into account the spillover effects in the rice market. The most important are examined below.

TABLE 6.7
Implicit Tariffs for Rice and Sugar[a]

Year	CIF Rice Price ($/ton)	Domestic Price (Rp/kg)	Implicit Tariff (per cent)	CIF Sugar Price ($/ton)	Domestic Price (Rp/kg)	Implicit Tariff (per cent)
1975	336	118	−28	106	175	239
1976	259	145	16	124	189	216
1977	296	154	8	185	201	126
1978	359	157	−13	233	223	90
1979	357	196	−12	248	262	70
1980	446	221	−20	679	316	−25
1981	436	242	−11	399	488	96
1982	289	273	43	213	551	291
1983	271	328	33	213	562	190
1984	243	347	39	140	612	326
1985	215	360	51	115	604	373
1986	213	431	58	158	620	205
1987	220	490	35	174	656	129
1988	251	548	30	213	715	100
1989	276	510	4	298	790	50

Sources: World Bank, Quarterly Price Projections, various issues, and Bulog.
[a]Rice price comparisons are Thai 15 per cent brokens, CIF Jakarta compared to Jakarta wholesale price of Saigon–Bandung 1. Sugar prices are Jakarta wholesale market compared to the ISA–Caribbean price (sugar). Incidental costs are put at $25 per ton for sugar-cane and $20 per ton of rice to derive Jakarta CIF values. International prices are converted to rupiah values at the prevailing nominal exchange rate. Values for 1989 refer to the arithmetic average of January to May prices.

Wheat Imports

During the 1980s, under monopoly import and processing control, wheat imports have increased from 1.3 MMTs in 1980 to between 1.5 and 1.6 MMTs in the mid- and late 1980s (USDA, 1986–8). Domestic wheat flour prices were held at an average of 15 to 20 per cent (implicit tariff) above import parity prices due to a combination of restrictions on wheat flour imports, wheat flour price controls, and monopolization in wheat milling (Tabor, 1989b; World Bank, 1988). The rationing of wheat imports has had the effect of increasing rice demand (for higher-quality rice in particular) and limiting Indonesia's dependence on imported grains because of the high degree of substitution in urban demand between wheat and rice (Magiera, 1981).

Soy Bean Imports

During the 1980s, Indonesia emerged as one of the world's largest soy bean importers (Table 6.8). Soy bean imports increased from 193 000 MTs in 1980 to 628 000 MTs in 1988. Rapid growth in soy bean import demand is a reflection of the highly elastic demand for eggs and chicken, which rely on soy meal in their feed, and the moderately elastic demand for *tempe* and *tahu* (fried and fermented soy bean cake), the major non-rice sources of vegetable protein in the diet. To contain soy bean import demand, government followed a high-price domestic policy by restricting imports. Domestic soy bean prices were held at just

TABLE 6.8
Production and Trade of Soy Beans and Soy Bean Meal

Year	Area ('000 ha)	Yield (MT/ha)	Production ('000 MT)	Imports ('000 MT)	Meal Imports ('000 MT)
1970	695	0.72	498	0	0
1975	752	0.78	590	0	1
1976	646	0.81	522	0	8
1977	646	0.81	523	0	9
1978	733	0.84	617	130	21
1979	785	0.87	680	160	28
1980	732	0.89	653	193	27
1981	810	0.87	704	351	169
1982	608	0.86	521	354	72
1983	640	0.84	536	391	104
1984	859	0.89	769	400	206
1985	896	0.97	870	301	175
1986	1 252	0.98	1 227	359	313
1987	1 095	1.06	1 161	600	180
1988[a]	1 142	1.10	1 260	628	120

Sources: Department of Agriculture, Bulog, and BPS.
[a] 1988 values are Bulog estimates.

under twice the world market price level from 1983 to 1986 (Tabor and Gijsbers, 1987). Since 1986, protection levels have narrowed and, in early 1989, domestically produced soy beans enjoy a protection level (corrected for quality differences) of approximately 50 per cent (Tabor, 1989b). Since soy beans are a common break-crop in an irrigated rice rotation, high prices, combined with government exhortations to increase soy bean cultivation, had the effect of discouraging continuous rice cultivation and dampening dry-land rice production (Department of Agriculture, 1988). In 1986, soy bean area increased by more than 45 per cent in a single year, thanks largely to non-market exhortations to eliminate imports. This increase was largely in marginal areas and left the actual soy bean supply/demand balance practically unchanged.

Sugar-cane

Nearly three-quarters of domestic sugar-cane cultivation in Java competes directly with irrigated rice production (Pearson et al., 1988). Rapidly rising sweetener demand has been met through increased sugar imports and the rising use of imported cyclamates in place of sugar. Indonesian retail sugar prices have been four to six times higher than the artificially depressed world market sugar prices (Tabor, 1989b). The government controls the vast majority of sugar-cane milling capacity and has been slowly shifting production and processing capacity to the Outer Islands. From 1980 to 1985, sugar-cane production grew at 9.5 per cent per annum, from about 1.4 MMTs to 2.0 MMTs. Since 1985, output has fallen to around 1.9 MMTs. Since 1985, the area allocated to sugar-cane has fallen from 385 000 hectares to 328 000 hectares, reflecting government policy to release resources for rice cultivation (BPS, 1985–8).

While on much of the irrigated land, smallholder sugar-cane cultivation follows the long established pattern of forced-cultivation, the government's Smallholder Sugar Intensification Project, TRI (Tebu Rakyat Intensifikasi), acted to offset some of the adverse forced-cultivation effects (Brown, 1982). Most importantly, the artificial maintenance of the uneconomic sugar-cane programme has acted as a brake on rice production growth (Pearson et al., 1988). This has explicitly been recognized by Indonesian policy-makers and the priority of the rice objective over the sugar-cane objective has been stated as one means of maintaining the rice growth momentum (Affandi, 1986).

High-cost Subsidies: A Negative Externality Resulting from the Rice Success

It is well known and well documented that the Indonesian government has provided a wide range of agricultural input and credit subsidies in order to accelerate the adoption of green revolution technology. The record of the past two decades suggests that this was a wise policy. In the second half of the 1970s, factor subsidies were an effective means of lowering search costs and inducing early adoption of new agro-inputs

(Timmer, 1986). When few farmers were using HYVs, the subsidy bill was kept at a manageable level. As adoption of the HYV technology package became more widespread, the fiscal cost of maintaining subsidies grew faster than the government's ability to marshal domestic resources or to target benefits. Furthermore, the adverse institutional effects of chronic market distortion blunted the economic effectiveness and efficiency of subsidies as a food policy tool. Several examples of these subsidies are examined in order to illustrate the problems involved.

Bimas

The Mass Guidance Programme (Bimas) involved the provision of subsidized credit, partly in cash and partly in kind, to farmers adopting recommended rice technology packages. At its peak in 1980, this programme was lending $130 million annually. However, the programme was plagued by high default rates; a disproportionate share of programme credit accrued to the wealthier farmers and non-agriculturalists and there were high administrative costs (World Bank, 1988). Between 1981 and 1984, the programme was cut back sharply. A multipurpose rural credit programme was initiated and, partly as a means of spreading (and limiting) institutional risks, rural co-operatives (KUDs) were enlisted as village credit financial intermediaries (World Bank, 1987a). While dismantling the rice production credit programme, the government also removed interest rate ceilings and authorized the Bank Rakyat Indonesia to mobilize savings and lend at competitive market rates. Since that time, rural savings and non-programme lending have increased at a phenomenal rate. The combination of financial market reform, together with the shedding of non-market commodity loan programmes, has contributed to a deepening and formalization of the rural financial system (World Bank, 1987a).

Pesticides

Another subsidized input which lost its fiscal support in the 1980s was pesticides. The pesticide subsidy peaked in 1987 at Rp 175 billion. Prices were increased in 1988 and the annual realized subsidy fell to Rp 151 billion. Starting in 1989, pesticides were sold, without subsidy, at competitive prices. At its peak of fiscal support, price subsidies accounted for nearly two-thirds of retail agrochemical prices. This, combined with import controls, enabled the domestic agrochemical industry to expand total domestic sales from about 1,000 tons in 1970 to 17,000 tons in 1986. But pesticide overuse leading to increased pest resistance was cited as a primary cause of the brown planthopper outbreak in 1986. Growing recognition of the hazards of pesticide overuse led the government to outlaw selected pesticides in 1987 and then declare, in 1988, that Indonesia would universally adopt a programme of 'Integrated Pest Management' as the preferred means of pest control (Damardjati et al., 1988). The growing environmental ground swell against pesticide overuse, combined with the administrative difficulties of controlling prices and allocating industrial subsidies in a highly heterogeneous product market, led the government to abolish pesticide price controls and subsidies in 1989.

Irrigation O and M

One of the Indonesian government's long-standing practices has been to provide irrigation services at no charge to the immediate users of the improved land resource. In part, this was justified because of the limited capacity of smallholders to finance capital works, the high administrative costs associated with irrigation charge collection, and the benefits accruing to consumers from increased food availability. However, the provision of irrigation supplies at near-zero user cost has contributed to substandard management and inadequate system maintenance (Rosegrant et al., 1987).

The combined effect of more intensive use of irrigation facilities (due to the increased cropping intensities possible with the HYVs), the rapid expansion of irrigation systems in the 1970s and early 1980s, an underestimation of the recurrent cost of efficiently managing irrigation resources, and overall fiscal retrenchment led to a sharp reduction in irrigation operation and maintenance (or O and M) spending in the 1980s. In real 1983 terms, government spending on irrigation O and M, already low by international standards, fell from Rp 7,600 per hectare in 1982/3 to Rp 6,100 per hectare in 1988/9 (Table 6.9). Inadequate irrigation O and M, together with improper system design, were cited as major factors explaining the low efficiency with which irrigation waters

TABLE 6.9
Government Financing of Irrigation O and M[a]

Fiscal Year	Total Current Expenditures (Rp billion)	Average Expenditures/Hectare (Rp/ha)	Average Real Expenditures/Hectare (1983 Rp/ha)
1979/80	13.3	2,965	4,485
1980/1	19.9	4,398	5,763
1981/2	26.0	5,685	6,857
1982/3	31.2	6,920	7,663
1983/4	32.9	7,093	7,093
1984/5	44.2	8,625	7,721
1985/6	46.4	8,955	7,640
1986/7	39.9	8,268	6,688
1987/8	37.5	7,702	5,717
1988/9	43.5	8,936	6,120

Sources: Directorate-General of Water Resources Development and BPS.
[a]Total current costs of Irrigation O and M include Inpres–APBD and DIP APBN and PBB financing. Average costs refer to expenditures on the total command area serviced by the Directorate-General for Water Resources Development. Real costs are computed by deflating using the 17 cities CPI.

were used. In order to reduce the fiscal burden of maintaining irrigation systems, and to stimulate improved site management, the government broke with tradition and authorized collection of a water user fee for irrigation O and M starting in 1986 (World Bank, 1988). Implementation of this cost recovery device has proceeded very slowly.

Fertilizer Subsidies

The largest of the agricultural subsidies is that on fertilizer. The fertilizer subsidy has ballooned from Rp 32 billion in 1978 to just over Rp 1 trillion in 1988. This subsidy provided, on average, approximately 45 per cent of the total revenues of the domestic fertilizer industry (Hedley and Tabor, 1989). From 1970 to 1989, the government has followed a policy of pan-territorial, pan-product fertilizer pricing with prices set at an average of 40 to 50 per cent of equivalent world market border prices. Subsidies were much higher on phosphatic fertilizers, which Indonesia imported, than on urea, of which Indonesia has become an exporter (Hedley and Tabor, 1989; Sastrohoetomo, 1982). Low prices, together with improved availability, resulted in a phenomenal growth in fertilizer demand. To keep pace with the burgeoning domestic market, urea supply rose from 1.4 MMTs to 4.2 MMTs, a 12.4 per cent per annum growth rate, between 1978 and 1988. Thanks to trade protection and highly subsidized domestic consumption, Indonesia was able to substitute domestic production for imports of urea and TSP, emerging from 1985 onwards, as a major exporter of urea in the region (Table 6.10).

By the mid-1980s, the total cost of fertilizer subsidies had grown to rival the total development budget expended on agriculture and irrigation development (Table 6.11). A portion of the subsidy is provided indirectly by providing natural gas at below market prices to the industry and by providing capital subsidies for plant construction (Fane and Phillips, 1987). In addition, since 1986, a growing portion of the fertilizer subsidy has been financed by the state banks rather than through the budget (Tabor, 1989b). The maintenance of low, subsidized fertilizer prices was justified by referring to the need to maintain 'incentive parity', measured using the 'farmer's formula' (*rumus tani*), or the ratio of the administered fertilizer price to the rough rice floor price. It was argued that maintaining a favourable ratio of rice to fertilizer prices will ensure adequate producer incentives and that this is a key instrument for stimulating rice supply in the face of growing consumer demand (Timmer, 1986 and 1988b).

By the latter part of the 1980s, the logic underlying the use of fertilizer subsidies as a mechanism for influencing agricultural supply had come under increasing attack (World Bank, 1988; Fane and Cutbush, 1988). In a highly commercialized rice economy, the share of fertilizer in variable costs, compared to the cost of hired labour, had dropped precipitously. Fertilizer accounted for less than 15 per cent of the paid-out costs of rice production for the average farm household. For other commodities, the contribution of fertilizer to total costs was even less.

TABLE 6.10

Fertilizer Production: Imports and Exports, 1978–1987[a] ('000 metric tons)

Year	Production				Imports					Exports		
	Urea	Ammonium Sulphate	TSP	Total	Urea	TSP	Potash	Other	Total	Urea	Other	Total
1978	1 450	129	0	1 583	0	270	109	172	551	0	0	0
1979	1 828	152	114	2 099	0	30	122	195	347	0	0	0
1980	2 001	180	465	2 765	210	60	137	285	692	0	0	0
1981	2 012	195	559	2 780	150	125	248	382	905	0	0	0
1982	1 961	210	577	2 761	435	438	139	254	1 266	0	0	0
1983	2 241	208	783	3 259	0	0	325	287	612	316	30	346
1984	2 906	302	1 002	4 210	189	10	164	230	593	218	34	252
1985	3 585	476	1 007	5 068	85	0	278	150	513	685	0	685
1986	4 023	582	1 116	5 415	1	0	224	78	303	1 514	0	1 514
1987	4 046	561	1 205	5 812	0	0	206	0	206	907	0	907
1988	4 160	570	1 200	5 930	0	0	n.a.	n.a.	n.a.	1 040	n.a.	n.a.

Sources: PT Pusri and BPS.

[a]Total production also includes natural phosphates, DAP and blended fertilizers. Other exports refer to TSP and DAP. The growth rate for potash and other fertilizer imports refers to the period 1978 to 1987.

Other imports include ammonium sulphate, DAP, rock phosphate, and blended

n.a. = Not available.

TABLE 6.11

Fertilizer and Pesticide Subsidies Compared to the Agricultural Sector
Development Budget[a] (Rp billion)

Fiscal Year	Fertilizer and Pesticide Subsidy (actual)	Net Agriculture and Irrigation Sector Development Budget
1975/76	134.5	122.5
1976/77	107.3	248.7
1977/78	31.8	348.2
1978/79	82.6	367.4
1979/80	125.0	383.0
1980/81	283.6	645.4
1981/82	371.4	582.6
1982/83	420.1	510.9
1983/84	324.2	588.8
1984/85	731.6	967.5
1985/86	838.1	660.4
1986/87	842.5	434.0
1987/88	1014.9	977.2

Sources: *Nota Keuangan* and Department of Finance, Directorate of Food Affairs and Non-tax Revenue.

[a]Fertilizer and pesticide subsidy values are actuals. Pre-1984 figures refer to that paid out from the APBN budget. Post-1984 values also include accumulated subsidy arrears. Budget values for agriculture and irrigation are realized development expenditures reported in the President's Budget Speech. APBN fertilizer and subsidy expenditures are netted out from the agriculture and irrigation development expenditures to yield a net value.

Thanks largely to the continuing commercialization of the rural labour market, the fertilizer subsidy accounted for only a rather small portion of variable production costs (Hedley and Tabor, 1989).

As would be expected, the marginal productivity of fertilizer dropped in proportion to increasing consumption. Econometric estimates of the actual aggregate rice supply response to fertilizer prices vary widely, although all are in the range of inelastic to highly inelastic (Ellis, 1988; Rachman and Montgomery, 1980; Rosegrant et al., 1987; Klumper, 1986; Sastrohoetomo, 1982; Pitt, 1983; Altemeier, Tabor, and Adinugroho, 1988). In terms of affecting agricultural supply, fertilizer pricing policy has become a most ineffectual instrument. Econometric studies of the agricultural sector have suggested that removal of the subsidies will have few adverse effects on agricultural incomes or crop supply due partly to the asymmetric nature of fertilizer demand and partly to the flexibility of rural labour markets to adjust to changes in prices of complementary factors (Department of Agriculture, 1988; Rosegrant et al., 1987; Centre for World Food Studies, 1988; Fane and Phillips, 1987; World Bank, 1988).

A high degree of fertilizer subsidization has also reduced farmers' incentives to adopt land-conserving technologies. This has been an important contributor to upland erosion in the heavily populated high-land areas of Java. Increasing concern over the sustainability of a highly agrochemical-intensive rice development model has caused researchers to question the wisdom of sustained fertilizer subsidization (Dove, 1985; Damardjati et al., 1988). The use of uniform prices for all types of fertilizers has also contributed to uneconomic applications of phosphatic fertilizer in the non-phosphate deficient, alluvial soils of Java. The inability to fine-tune farmers' use of chemical fertilizers can be traced, in part, to uniform pricing. Improving the balance of fertilizers used in food-crop production has been cited as an important means of raising productivity (Affandi, 1986; Bappenas, 1989).

In the industrial sector, the perpetuation of fertilizer subsidies has entrenched what was designed to be an infant industry protection policy. This has led to the rise of cost-plus pressures by the manufacturers in favour of expanded capacity, high stocks, and high sales, in order to increase the subsidy pay-out to the industry. Although segments of the Indonesian fertilizer industry, principally urea, are competitive by world market standards, the severe distortions resulting from heavy domestic fertilizer subsidization have hindered rational industrial investment and market development practices (Hedley and Tabor, 1989). The government held nominal fertilizer prices constant at Rp 70/kg from 1976 to 1979, at Rp 90/kg from 1980 to 1982, and at Rp 100/kg from 1983 to 1986. From 1980 to 1986, administered fertilizer prices rose just 12 per cent while, over this same period, non-agricultural prices rose on average by 70 per cent (Ellis, 1988). Starting in 1986, the government has made a conscious effort to contain the fertilizer subsidy bill. Nominal fertilizer prices were increased by 25 per cent in 1986 and by a further 46 per cent in 1988. Due in part to devaluation and to an ageing capital stock, fertilizer production costs continued to climb, and the subsidy bill continued to rise. In 1989, the government also increased the price of TSP, the most heavily subsidized fertilizer, by Rp 5 per kilogram over that of the other fertilizers. This was considered a policy of 'testing the waters' for a fuller reintroduction of differential fertilizer product pricing (Tabor, 1989b). In 1989, an inter-ministerial committee reporting to the Economic Co-ordinating Minister was formed to recommend proposals for phasing out fertilizer subsidies by the end of *Repelita V*.

High-cost Rice Stocks and the Role of Bulog

The other side of the 'farmer's formula' has been rice price administration. In the 1980s, domestic rice prices have been held at, or somewhat above, world market price levels, for comparable quality grains. Bulog, the State Logistics Board, has become increasingly effective at insulating the domestic market from variations in world rice market prices. Bulog has been able to stabilize domestic market prices by building up large reserves of rice for meeting budget group subsidy requirements and for interseasonal and interannual 'iron' stock requirements (Ellis, 1988; Falcon et al., 1986; Timmer, 1988a and 1988b).

The switch in Indonesia's status from being a major importer to being self-sufficient in rice has led to major changes in the mechanics of price control. Bulog found itself shifting from the role of a monopoly trader selling low-cost imports at a profit in the domestic market to that of procuring rice domestically at a loss and providing it to civil servants. In mid-1985, when self-sufficiency was declared, Bulog found itself with over 3.5 MMTs worth of rapidly deteriorating rice stocks (Mitchell and Gray, 1985). Quality standards were then tightened to limit domestic procurements in 1986. In 1987 and 1988, the combination of poorer harvests and political restrictions on imports led to a run-down in Bulog stocks. With domestic prices (for comparable qualities) at 20 per cent above world market prices and rising, Bulog made repeated appeals for

TABLE 6.12
Bulog Rice Operations[a] ('000 metric tons)

Year	Procurements		Releases to Budget Groups	Market Operations	Other	Year-end Stocks
	Imports	Domestic				
Repelita I						
1969/70	805	244	873	204	55	236
1970/1	773	5 316	835	228	45	397
1971/2	527	562	767	202	106	387
1972/3	1 229	138	726	768	14	198
1973/4	1 230	268	752	418	30	418
Repelita II						
1974/5	1 130	536	758	343	176	778
1975/6	667	539	749	559	87	522
1976/7	1 506	410	755	979	88	572
1977/8	2 308	404	693	2 006	87	470
1978/9	1 266	881	696	1 032	130	708
Repelita III						
1979/80	2 580	431	756	2 053	42	806
1980/1	1 213	1 635	738	1 628	114	1 242
1982/3	437	1 952	901	1 033	80	1 591
1982/3	506	1 933	1 425	1 517	29	1 013
1983/4	1 115	1 189	1 462	399	11	1 417
Repelita IV						
1984/5	187	2 374	1 427	69	118	2 347
1985/6	0	1 947	1 490	272	465	2 040
1986/7	80	1 500	1 543	250	223	1 584
1987/8	0	1 368	1 497	642	12	765
1988/9	450	1 275	1 520	750	18	110

Source: Bulog, December 1988.

[a] 'Other' includes exports and rice distribution in disaster regions. Imports for 1986/7 were repayment of a rice loan. Imports for 1988/9 are part repayment, part concessionary assistance, and part commercial imports.

imports but was turned down. The political imperative of maintaining the appearance of rice self-sufficiency took priority over the goals of stabilizing prices, controlling inflation, and feeding the poor. In 1988, Bulog jettisoned its aim of domestic price stabilization, and in the face of rapidly rising prices, issued ambitious targets for domestic stock procurements of 2 million tons (Timmer, 1988a). In 1989, with the resumption of imports and an abundant harvest, Bulog was once more able to build stocks (Table 6.12).

Unlike those countries, such as India, where public grain stocks are used to feed the poor, Indonesia's public stocks are used primarily to feed civil servants and other special budget groups (army officials, plantation workers, and transmigrants). In the 1960s and 1970s, provision of part of the civil service wage in kind was used as an indexing mechanism to protect civil servant incomes when inflation was rampant and the rice markets were incomplete (Anderson, 1966; Bulog, 1970). But in the 1980s, with the vast improvement in market infrastructure, the commercialization of the rice trade, the absence of high rates of inflation, and the fall in the share of rice in the expenditure budgets of most public servants, the arguments in favour of maintaining such a transfer mechanism have lost much of their analytical force (Timmer, 1988a and 1988b).

In addition to rice, Bulog also has the monopoly for imports of wheat, corn, soy beans, soy bean meal, sugar, fish-meal, and a number of smaller products. For non-rice crops, there has not been sufficient technological progress, behind protected trade barriers, to justify the adverse costs of trade protection. For these commodities, the government has faced mounting pressure to liberalize as part of the overall trade liberalization movement (Department of Agriculture, 1988, Fane and Cutbush, 1988, World Bank, 1988).

Increased Dependence on Macroeconomic Performance

One of the consequences of a highly 'public capital-intensive' agricultural development regime is that the fortunes of the agricultural sector have become closely interwoven with the fortunes of the economy as a whole. During the period of fiscal expansion from the mid-1970s to 1985, Indonesia made extensive investments in the agricultural sector. During the period of sharp fiscal contraction, from 1985 onwards, Indonesia has found it difficult to maintain those investments that had only recently been undertaken. Agricultural planners and policy-makers, by and large, were unprepared to handle fiscal contraction, particularly coming so soon after the large-scale build-up of capital stock and agricultural support services.

In response to the economic downturn in the early 1980s, agricultural development spending dropped sharply. The sharpest cut-backs were registered in the larger, more capital-intensive projects. Due to funding cut-backs, the total area of new irrigation facilities completed fell from 436 000 hectares during the Third Plan period to only 197 000 hectares

TABLE 6.13

Physical Area Completed by Type of Irrigation Development, *Repelita I* to *Repelita IV* ('000 hectares)

Type of Development	Repelita I	Repelita II	Repelita III	Repelita IV[a]
Rehabilitation	953.5	527.8	394.7	151.7
New construction	191.2	325.9	436.2	197.9
Swamp/Tidal	178.7	179.2	454.5	120.3
Flood control and conservation	289.4	613.7	578.5	256.0

Sources: Department of Public Works and Directorate-General of Water Resources Development.

[a]Figures refer to actual completions in 1984/5 to 1985/6. Figures for the years 1986/7 to 1988/9 refer to physical target areas.

during the Fourth Plan period (Rosegrant and Kasryno, 1988). Other irrigation and flood control programmes were also severely reduced in the Fourth Plan period (Table 6.13).

The traditional agricultural support services were also forced to absorb financial cut-backs as a result of overall retrenchment in government spending. The extension corps, which at the farm level had swelled from less than 5,000 persons in 1980 to more than 36,000 persons in 1988, was operated on a recurrent budget of less than $150 per field officer per year. Officials in the Department of Agriculture estimated that this was less than half the amount required simply to run a motor cycle at the field level for a year.[7] The Agricultural Research Service, a major beneficiary of donor investment in the 1970s and early 1980s, was faced with a sharp contraction in public funding. Development spending on agricultural research fell from an average of Rp 25 billion per annum from 1980 to 1986 to only Rp 6 billion per annum in 1987 and 1988, of which 86 per cent was foreign donor financed. The operations budget for agricultural research, already low compared to research capacity and certainly low compared to the importance of agriculture in the economy, fell from US$9 million in 1986 to US$7 million in 1988. Special donor intervention was required to rescue the service from fiscal collapse.[8] As the 1980s drew to a close, the agricultural support services were 'on-hold', with expenditures barely sustaining the wage bill, because of the cumulative effects of budgetary retrenchment.

Agricultural Diversification

Diversification: Food Crops

One of the important rallying cries of the 1980s was agricultural diversification. The concentration of public investment on rice resulted in very little technical and administrative attention being given to development of other foodstuffs, or to off-farm activities. In the mid-1980s, with international rice prices at historic lows, with domestic rice production growth showing signs of levelling out and with evidence of sharp productivity gaps between farmer and research station practices for non-rice food commodities, the government began to turn its attention to food-crop diversification (Hedley, 1987; Tyers and Rachman, 1982). In 1986, the government declared its desire to achieve self-sufficiency for corn and soy beans, following on the rice self-sufficiency model (Affandi, 1986). However, due to the constrained fiscal environment, the government was unable to offer much more than trade protection and official exhortation to support these new self-sufficiency campaigns. As mentioned above, in the case of soy beans, this did not so much increase productivity as divert resources from less protected commodities and encourage intensification on marginal lands (Tabor and Gijsbers, 1987).

For corn, a self-sufficiency campaign was hardly necessary as the market was already in slight surplus in some years (Timmer, 1987). Of the major non-rice food crops, only corn experienced significant technical change during the 1980s. Corn yields increased from 1.5 tons per hectare to 2.1 tons per hectare between 1980 and 1988, reflecting the adoption of improved open-pollinated varieties in place of traditional corn varieties (Table 6.14). Corn production was also stimulated by growing domestic demand from the feed industry, but was adversely affected by the shift away from corn in the consumer diet, as increasing affluence enabled a rising share of consumers to switch to rice as the primary staple food (Dixon, 1982; Department of Agriculture, 1988).

Cassava, the other major starchy staple, experienced a great degree of instability, technological stagnation, and a trend decline in area. Cassava production has oscillated between 13.7 MMTs in 1980 and 15.2 MMTs in 1988 (Table 6.14). The domestic cassava market has experienced two major excess-supply periods, one in 1984 and the other in 1989, when market prices fell well below average costs of production (Tabor, 1989b). The market has become increasingly dependent on domestic starch demand and on the export of chips and pellets to the European community (Department of Agriculture, 1988; Falcon et al., 1984). The combination of growing demand instability due to substitution possibilities in the domestic starch industry, wide fluctuations in world markets for cheap feed grains, and periodic diversion of cassava lands to the Outer Islands' sugar-cane and the soy bean programme has contributed to a high degree of domestic market instability.

In many respects, food-crop diversification, or the lack thereof, stands in sharp contrast to the success of the rice sector. The lack of diversification, or more specifically the lack of productivity growth in a wide range of non-rice food crops, can be treated as one of the hidden costs of Indonesia's rice success story. Outside food crops, the government has made important efforts to diversify the agricultural base, particularly with regard to investments in livestock, fisheries, and

TABLE 6.14
Production and Trade of Corn and Cassava[a]

Year	Corn				Cassava			
	Area ('000 ha)	Yield (MT/ha)	Production (MMT)	Trade[b] ('000 MT)	Area ('000 ha)	Yield (MT/ha)	Production (MMT)	Export ('000 MT)
1970	2 930	1.0	2.8	282	1 398	7.5	10.5	n.a.
1975	2 445	1.2	2.9	51	1 410	8.9	12.5	299
1976	2 095	1.2	2.6	(30)	1 353	9.0	12.2	150
1977	2 567	1.2	3.1	(10)	1 364	9.2	12.5	183
1978	3 025	1.3	4.0	21	1 383	9.3	12.9	308
1979	2 594	1.4	3.6	(20)	1 439	9.6	13.8	709
1980	2 735	1.5	4.0	(5)	1 413	9.7	13.7	386
1981	2 955	1.5	4.5	13	1 388	9.6	13.3	407
1982	2 061	1.6	3.2	(243)	1 324	9.8	12.9	257
1983	3 002	1.7	5.1	16	1 220	9.9	12.1	358
1984	3 086	1.7	5.3	(47)	1 350	10.5	14.2	365
1985	2 440	1.8	4.3	(52)	1 292	10.9	14.1	543
1986	3 143	1.9	5.9	(60)	1 170	11.4	13.3	424
1987	2 620	2.0	5.2	220	1 222	11.7	14.4	825
1988	3 206	2.1	6.6	100	1 267	12.0	15.2	869

Sources: Department of Agriculture and BPS.
[a] Corn production is in dried grain form. Cassava production is in dried tuber (gaplek) form. Cassava exports are all chips and pellets.
[b] Figures in brackets refer to imports; others to exports.
n.a. = Not available.

smallholder tree crops. Because the scale of the diversification effort has been so very large, and because the subsector is economically very important, the diversification effort in tree crops merits special attention.

Diversification: The Tree-crop Subsector

During the 1970s and early 1980s, the government focused the bulk of its non-rice agricultural public investment on expanding production capacity in the tree-crop sector. The main objectives of public investment in this sector were to accelerate development in the more underdeveloped regions of the Outer Islands, raise smallholder incomes and technical production standards, increase and diversify export earnings, and provide raw materials for downstream industrialization. In addition to public investment, the government has influenced performance in the tree-crop sector through restrictions on trade and private investment in production and processing of numerous tree-crop commodities (World Bank, 1986).

The performance of the sector has been mixed. Total export earnings have stagnated at between $1.5 and $2 billion per annum between 1980 and 1988. In terms of export volumes and values, coffee and rubber are the most important crops, with palm oil exports important in some years. Smallholder productivity, for the more important tree crops, has stagnated, with very little evidence of broad-based technical change. The tree-crop sector has retained much of its enclave character, producing raw materials mainly for export. Downstream industrialization linked directly to tree-crop production has occurred only to a very limited extent and then primarily for commodities such as edible oils, tobacco, and cloves, which are domestically consumed (World Bank, 1986; Budiman, 1987; Godoy and Bennett, 1987a). Tree-crop schemes have provided a useful mechanism for advancing the land frontier, but the mixed quality of many of the schemes calls into question the economic rationale for this pattern of extensification.

The performance of the tree-crop sector is closely linked to the fortunes of the world market. In contrast to rice, Indonesia is unable to exercise much control over prices for its export commodities. Major multi-year public investment commitments were made to increase production of rubber, coconut, oil palm, and beverage crops in the late 1970s and early 1980s. This was at a period of cyclically high prices for nearly all of these commodities (Table 6.15). As the trees have begun to come into production in the mid- and late 1980s, world market prices have slumped to cyclical lows. This has adversely affected smallholder incentives to adopt improved cultivation techniques (World Bank, 1986). The downturn in primary commodity prices, international commodity agreements which have served to restrict Indonesia's exports (coffee and cocoa), and punitive tariffs and restrictions on processed imports by the Organization for Economic Co-operation and Development (OECD) nations (most obvious in edible oils and timber) have all combined to limit growth in the subsector (McStocker, 1987; Dillon and Tabor, 1988).

TABLE 6.15

Trends in World Market Prices for Estate Crop Exports[a]

Year	Rubber ($/ton) Nominal	Rubber ($/ton) Real	Coffee (cents/lb) Nominal	Coffee (cents/lb) Real	Tea (cents/kg) Nominal	Tea (cents/kg) Real	Cocoa (cents/kg) Nominal	Cocoa (cents/kg) Real	Crude Palm Oil ($/ton) Nominal	Crude Palm Oil ($/ton) Real	Crude Coconut Oil ($/ton) Nominal	Crude Coconut Oil ($/ton) Real	Tobacco ($/ton) Nominal	Tobacco ($/ton) Real	MUV Index[b] 1985 = 100
1970	463	1,275	41	114	109	303	–	–	260	712	307	1,088	988	2,744	36
1971	399	1,042	42	111	105	276	–	–	261	678	371	964	970	2,552	38
1972	401	962	45	107	105	250	–	–	217	518	234	558	962	2,290	42
1973	785	1,622	50	104	106	221	–	–	378	778	513	1,056	962	2,004	49
1974	869	1,475	59	100	140	237	–	–	669	1,130	998	1,686	1,280	2,169	59
1975	659	1,006	61	92	138	209	–	–	434	660	394	599	1,517	2,298	66
1976	873	1,315	128	194	154	233	–	–	407	610	418	627	1,411	2,138	66
1977	917	1,256	224	307	269	368	–	–	530	723	578	789	1,670	2,287	73
1978	1,107	1,319	147	175	219	261	–	–	600	712	683	810	1,690	2,011	84
1979	1,424	1,497	165	174	216	227	–	–	654	685	984	1,030	2,130	2,242	95
1980	1,624	1,557	147	141	223	214	260	250	584	558	674	644	2,300	2,212	104
1981	1,242	1,195	103	98	202	192	208	198	571	543	570	542	2,350	2,238	105
1982	1,002	970	111	108	193	187	174	169	445	429	464	447	2,410	2,340	103
1983	1,238	1,229	124	123	232	230	212	210	501	496	730	723	2,245	2,223	101
1984	1,096	1,107	138	139	346	349	240	242	729	734	1,155	1,163	1,990	2,010	99
1985	924	924	146	146	198	298	225	225	501	501	590	590	2,052	2,052	100
1986	920	778	195	165	193	166	207	175	257	217	297	251	2,027	1,718	118
1987	1,120	862	114	88	171	132	199	153	342	261	442	338	2,035	1,565	130
1988	1,444	1,026	136	96	175	124	160	113	464	330	580	412	2,053	1,456	141

Source: World Bank, Commodity Trade and Price Trends, various issues.
[a]Rubber is RSS1, C and F New York.
Coffee is ICCO indicator price for Robusta average grade, US, and Europe.
Tea is average price in London Auctions.
Cocoa is daily price in New York and London.

CPO is 5 per cent bulk CIF NW Europe.
CCO is CIF Rotterdam.
Tobacco is average export unit value for flue cured Indian.
[b]MUV refers to the index of the unit value of manufactured goods exported from developed nations.

Although the world economy in the 1980s was generally adverse to tree crops, this had relatively little influence on actual investment since a large share of public investment was undertaken as a means of recycling windfall gains from the petroleum price increase in the late 1970s and government entry restrictions acted to limit the flow of large-scale private investment into the sector (World Bank, 1986). For small-holders, low world prices together with a dearth of opportunities to adopt improved technology have served to reinforce the prevailing cycle of low-input, low-output, extensive cultivation. Although smallholders form the backbone of the Indonesian tree-crop sector, and account for 82 per cent of mature area allocated to rubber and coffee, 99 per cent of mature area allocated to coconuts, pepper, and cloves, and between 40 and 45 per cent of area allocated to oil palm and tea, the quality of smallholder produce is, by world market standards, generally low and irregular. This can be traced, in part, to the tenuous linkages between smallholder producers and the processing factories (Budiman, 1987; Soemardjan et al., 1988; Godoy and Bennett, 1987b). Between 1980 and 1987, approximately US$3.5 billion in public funds were invested in smallholder tree-crop schemes.[9] Roughly half of this was in foreign-financed projects with the balance financed from the export tax and from the government's development budget (Table 6.16). Since the bulk of these investments were in previously unsettled areas, actual project development costs, including all expenditures associated with trans-migration, preparation of sites, transport, and provision of social overheads, amounted to several times the amount invested in tree-crop production alone. Two main types of tree-crop projects were financed.

TABLE 6.16

Public Sector Tree-crop Investments, 1979–1987[a] (Rp billion: 1983 prices)

| | Smallholder | | Estates |
| | | | (PTPs) |
Year	Credit	Non-credit	
1979	29.1	11.3	n.a.
1980	101.9	61.9	n.a.
1981	180.9	59.8	n.a.
1982	239.4	44.5	216
1983	116.4	34.9	252
1984	58.8	84.1	294
1985	66.8	28.2	402
1986	133.8	31.0	321
1987	96.4	27.1	433

Sources: Department of Finance and Department of Agriculture.

[a] Investment values have been provided by the Department of Agriculture, Directorate-General of Estate Crops and BUMN bureau. Values deflated by the 17-city CPI reported by the BPS. Values include domestically and foreign financed capital investments.

n.a. = Not available.

These are the Project Management Unit (PMU) type and the Nucleus Estate Scheme/Perkebunan Inti Rakyat (NES/PIR) type. In both schemes, farmers were provided with small stands of tree crops, planted using full input packages and modern cultivation techniques. The PMU schemes were designed primarily for upgrading the quality of existing smallholder tree-crop operations. In the PMU model, project participants were selected from among already established tree-crop producers and other residents of affected regions. In these schemes, a project manager was provided with authority to finance planting and to organize the maintenance of a stand of trees.

In the NES/PIR model, a large-scale enterprise, either a government estate or a private firm was given responsibility for developing a factory, the 'nucleus' portion of an estate, which comprised 20 to 40 per cent of the total holdings, and the balance of the land which was to be converted to smallholder operation and ownership. The NES/PIR scheme was one of the important mechanisms used for resettlement of farmers from Java and the eastern islands to other parts of the country. Under these schemes, settlers were provided accommodation, access to 2 hectares of tree-crop stands and 0.5 hectares of food-crop land. In both the PMU and the NES/PIR type schemes, the smallholders were expected to apply high-quality management techniques and to repay a portion of the development costs of the tree-crop stand (World Bank, 1986; Hutabarat, 1988).

Both types of investment have had a mixed track record. The large rubber and coconut projects, in particular, have been plagued by grossly substandard plantings and by difficulties in converting estate lands to smallholder ownership (World Bank, 1987b; Soemardjan et al., 1988). Poor planning and project implementation resulted in a lack of co-ordination between planting trees and building processing factories. The projects have also been plagued by difficulties in screening candidates for resettlement and by a myriad of technical problems that result when farmers unfamiliar with tree crops are given access to a newly mature stand of trees (World Bank, 1986). In sharp contrast to the rice case, the smallholder tree-crop projects have been unsuccessful in stimulating widespread diffusion of improved technology. Approximately 10 per cent of tree-crop smallholders have had access to project-financed replanting or to new planting investment. This has proven to be something of a windfall to a fortunate few in that the various capital cost-recovery schemes have proven to be complete failures. The lack of viable cost-recovery mechanisms and the pattern of on-again, off-again government financing for the tree-crop projects have together limited the replicability and viability of these types of investments (World Bank, 1986).

The tree-crop projects have drawn criticism for devoting limited extension resources to project administration rather than to broad-based development work (Barlow and Muharminto, 1982). The projects have also been criticized for their attempt to cast smallholders into the mould of the large, well-capitalized estates, rather than to design interventions appropriate to the limited financial and economic capacity of the participants (Barlow, Shearing, and Dereinda, 1988; Godoy and Bennett, 1987b). Certainly the most successful of the smallholder public investment projects in terms of cultivating households involved have been the oil palm schemes (Table 6.17). These projects have the advantage of a strong, growing, but tightly controlled domestic market.[10] In addition, the technical nature of palm oil production is such that output is relatively invariant to smallholder cultivation practices. Put simply, the plant is very difficult to kill off (University of Indonesia, 1986). But in spite of the greater profitability of oil palm, smallholder investment was concentrated primarily on rubber (World Bank, 1986). This was, in retrospect, an unfortunate choice of commodity for public investment.

Although hundreds of millions of dollars have been spent on smallholder tree-crop development, productivity has still tended to stagnate. Smallholder rubber yields (in dry rubber content) remain at about 0.5 MT per hectare, smallholder coffee yields at 0.3 MT per hectare, and coconut yields (in copra equivalent) at 0.9 MT per hectare. In these commodities, Indonesia is a very competitive producer in world markets, but also a very low productivity producer (Landall Mills, 1986 and 1987; McStocker, 1987). Except in oil palm, government investment has accomplished very little in terms of breaking the cycle of low use of inputs leading to low productivity and land-extensive cultivation that characterizes the smallholder tree-crop sector. As the 1980s drew to a close, the government continued to search for an appropriate public investment model to reach smallholders.

Inevitably, comparisons must be made between the rice intensification programme and public investment in smallholder tree-crop projects. Why did the one perform so well and the other not? The record suggests that financial commitment alone cannot explain the differences in performance. Both programmes were reasonably well endowed. Nor can the difference be explained in terms of different technological possibilities. The technological shelf for smallholder tree-crop interventions was, and is, no less bountiful than the stock of interventions available, and successfully adopted, for rice. Factors which weighed heavily against success on the smallholder tree-crop front have included the subsuming of the tree-crop objective within a more broadly defined area development focus, the dependence of tree-crop projects on a high

TABLE 6.17
Tree-crop Smallholder Households, 1986 ('000 households)

Crop	Assisted	Per Cent	Unassisted	Per Cent	Total
Rubber	97	(14)	620	(86)	717
Oil palm	42	(100)	–	–	42
Coconut	80	(4)	1,749	(96)	1,829

Sources: Directorate-General of Estate Crops and BPS, unpublished tabulations.

degree of management intensity and effective interdepartmental co-ordination, clear conflicts of interest over asset control and product pricing between smallholders and nucleus estate companies, the government's inability to control effectively the external incentives environment, the haste with which the tree-crop projects were designed, the administrative difficulty of sustaining management and technical support for a multi-year investment venture, and, in sharp comparison to the Javanese rice case, the inability to use non-market forces to command technological change (Habir, 1984; *FEER*, 1985).

Larger Entities

The second part of the tree-crop investment programme has been that undertaken by large-scale public and private firms. Larger enterprises are important producers of palm oil, rubber, coffee, tea, and cocoa. These producers are dominated by the 17 tree-crop parastatal corporations (PTPs). Commodities for which public investment has been particularly important have included palm oil, rubber, and sugar-cane. Output of these firms has expanded rapidly in the 1980s, reflecting the effects of the rehabilitation of government estates in the 1970s, independent expansion financed from the strong commodity prices in the late 1970s, and involvement of the state firms in smallholder project implementation. Between 1977 and 1988, PTP holdings increased from about 600 000 hectares to just over 1 million hectares, of which 35 per cent is in oil palm, 26 per cent in sugar-cane, and 22 per cent in rubber. PTPs produce 12 per cent of total rubber production and about 70 per cent of palm oil and kernals. The turnover of the 17 tree-crop PTPs reached US$632 million in 1987, growing at a rate of 18 per cent per annum over the previous five years. Collectively, these tree-crop parastatals are a major force in the economy, with total assets valued, in 1987, at about Rp 3.4 trillion (Tabor, 1989b).

Government policy has been to pamper the PTPs with subsidized investment credits and low cost access to public lands. PTPs have been allowed to leverage their assets well beyond the limits of financial prudence and to incur debt which is, for all practical purposes, irretrievable. These benefits have then been offset by high rates of taxation and by assigning the PTPs the social responsibility for smallholder development. The combination of provision of special favours and imposition of development burdens has created endemic PTP mismanagement, marked by a cycle of rapid investment growth (in high price periods), liquidity crises as prices have fallen, and government bail-outs (World Bank, 1986).

After a decade of little growth, and of active discouragement by the government, large-scale private investment in the tree-crop sector began to flourish in the 1980s. A major turning-point has been the termination of the implicit policy of restricting access to large landholdings by Indonesian Chinese investors. However, the impact has not been uniform across crops. During most of the 1980s, large-scale private investment in the traditional tree crops such as rubber and coconuts has stagnated or declined. Private estate rubber area fell from 306 000 hectares in 1971/2 to 240 000 hectares in 1987. In contrast, investment in commodities for which there was relatively little previous private presence, such as cocoa and palm oil, has grown rapidly. Total private estate oil palm plantings have increased from 47 000 hectares in 1970 to 146 000 hectares in 1987, with output rising from 70 000 MTs to 385 000 MTs over the same period. Due largely to private investment, cocoa production increased from 1 100 MTs in 1975 to 51 000 MTs in 1987 (World Bank, 1986; Tabor, 1989b).

The government has moved cautiously, and with a very heavy regulatory hand, in allowing private investors to establish tree-crop plantations. The government has regulated access and operation of private investment by restricting access to entry permits, HGU (*hak guna usaha*) and HPH (*hak pengusahaan hutan*), providing subsidized credit for investment in priority crops, limiting rights to establish processing factories, restricting access of foreign investors to agricultural land, and, particularly in the edible oils case, controlling trade through marketing and export/import restrictions. In order to avoid the negative consequences of plantation economies, the government has also required large-scale investors in tree-crop ventures to share part of the smallholder development burden. It has done this by requiring that the private sector follow an investment pattern modelled on the publicly financed NES/PIR programmes (World Bank, 1986).

Future Diversification Prospects

The rapid and successful growth of private investors in certain tree crops and other cash crop commodities, the bleak outlook for large-scale public investment, and the mixed performance of non-rice public investments has led the government to call for the private sector to play the leading role in the commercialization and diversification of the agricultural sector in the 1990s. The technical and financial ability of the large-scale private investors to open up large blocks of land in the 1980s surpassed government expectations. The economics of the large-scale private investments, not only in tree crops but also in shrimp and horticultural commodities, look particularly good in comparison with the problem-plagued efforts of the government to reach non-rice smallholders. The government has indicated, in its Fifth Plan, that the private sector should become the lead agent for change in agriculture (Bappenas, 1989). However, the government has also indicated that, in return for 'access' to lucrative investment opportunities, the private sector will be expected to bear part of the smallholder development burden. Hence, the government has given the go-ahead to large-scale investment in agriculture while, at the same time, cautioning the private sector against a development strategy based solely on 'mining' abundant land and labour resources.

This proposed turnover in 'lead-agent status' implies that private investors will be granted entry permits, and various investment subsidies, in return for their commitment to develop holdings for smallholders, following the NES/PIR lines. This same philosophy of utilizing privately financed and managed nucleus estate schemes for smallholder development purposes has been extended to livestock and fisheries projects, with varying degrees of success. Early efforts at promoting privately financed PIR schemes suggest that investment opportunities tend to be limited to only the politically well-connected firms; that the turnover of assets from these firms to smallholders is difficult; that private firms have relatively little experience or interest in extending new technologies to smallholders; that investment becomes concentrated in a few key commodities; but, also, that the relaxation of regulatory restrictions on private investment does produce a ground swell of investment and output growth.

Policy Challenges for the 1990s

With the achievement of rice self-sufficiency, agriculture has been moved from the spotlight to the wings of the political arena, even though the challenges facing the sector promise to be far more formidable in the 1990s. The economic role of agriculture in the 1990s will be much as it was in the 1980s. Agriculture will be expected to create productive employment, feed the population, expand domestic markets for non-agricultural goods, and earn foreign exchange. However, agriculture will have to achieve these objectives with more limited public resources, without a unified sense of policy purpose, and with a capital stock and policy tool kit designed primarily to tackle the problems of a nation struggling to achieve rice self-sufficiency, rather than a nation bent on achieving broad-based agricultural growth and development.

The 1980s' experience has been a mix of policy success and failure. In a qualitative sense, Indonesia should receive top marks for its rice programme, mixed scores for the food-crop diversification effort, rather lower scores for the smallholder tree-crop programmes, lower scores still for efforts to contain the subsidy bill (and other costs of operating agricultural policy), and almost no marks for management of the public capital stock. Many agricultural policy objectives of the 1980s have yet to be fulfilled. The nation's performance in rice has contributed to the illusion that agricultural development has been a singular success. One of the main challenges for the government in the 1990s will be to improve performance in those areas where implementation of past policy has been ineffective, inefficient, or both.

As industrialization gathers pace, policy support for agriculture will tend to recede. The nature of strong central planning is such that support is progressively placed on the politically targeted leading sector which is now industry, and progressively withdrawn from the lagging sector, agriculture. The Fifth Plan explicitly flags the importance of the industrial sector as the engine of growth for the 'take-off' phase of Indonesia's development. Implicitly, the Fifth Plan flags agriculture as the sector in decline. Thus, in the 1990s, the agricultural sector's claim on new public investment resources will diminish, largely by default, as the inner circle of public planners and private financiers rally to place funds in the 'leading' industrial sector. In negotiations over trade protection, subsidy votes and investment restrictions, agricultural preferences will be accorded less weight, particularly in cases where there is strong opposition from a well-organized industrial lobby. Agricultural policy-makers may very well spend most of the 1990s on the political defensive, fending off attacks on past entitlements from rising special interest groups in the manufacturing industry and in financial services.

As the 1990s begins, agricultural policy-makers find themselves lacking the sort of development objective that can rally broad-based support across all parts of government. The quest for rice self-sufficiency provided such a clear, unifying objective in the 1970s and early 1980s. In the 1990s, agricultural policy-makers find themselves in a very different environment, one in which the evolving sectoral aims and objectives are replete with conflict, contradiction, and complexity. They must balance the competing objectives of maintaining rice output growth, diversification, sustaining environmental resources, expanding agricultural frontiers, and encouraging the development, in established agro-economic zones, of dynamically evolving comparative advantage. This balancing act will not produce a single policy goal. The emerging absence of focus in agricultural policy implies also that agriculture will lose much of its 'single-issue' basis of support in the political arena. For much of the past two decades, Indonesian policy-makers have concentrated on developing the capital stock and support services in order to increase rice production. In the 1990s, the primary challenge will be to consolidate past investments and improve operating efficiency of the capital stock. To do this in a fashion which will support a more diversified and technically efficient agricultural sector will also require shifting public resources out of rice and therefore away from Java. The adjustment costs involved in this change in policy will be very high in the short term, with the benefits coming only after a lag of several years, and perhaps decades.

Agricultural policy-makers in the 1990s find themselves saddled with an expensive and increasingly ineffectual agrochemicals subsidy policy, an institutionally ingrained, inward-oriented trade protection regime (replete with rent-seekers and rent-granters), a large number of parastatal companies which no longer have a valid reason for being in the public sector, a capital stock which is suited mainly to producing rice, and a huge number of poorly paid personnel trained and residing, for all practical purposes permanently, in Java. In short, the government in the 1990s will inherit the very high recurrent-cost burden of maintaining both capital stock and support services which were developed primarily to support the rice programme. Under the present policy regime, these costs will be high and will leave the government with little freedom to address evolving agricultural development concerns. The government faces the difficult task of restructuring the policy portfolio in order to tailor agricultural support to changing sectoral needs and priorities.

The 1990s promises to be a decade of agricultural transition. In line with past trends, agriculture will probably become increasingly commercialized, diversified, and better integrated with the growing service and industrial sectors. Prospects for the agriculture sector to continue absorbing labour are not good, with the slow-down in irrigation investment and with cropping intensities on irrigated lands near to their technological maximum. Maintaining the growth and employment momentum of the sector will require a continuing effort to diversify activities and raise non-rice crop productivity.

To maintain growth, the government will need to retool the agricultural policy kit, redefine objectives, and adjust to the realities of public policy in an economy for which agriculture is no longer the *top priority* sector. Indonesia has inherited a high-cost agricultural policy regime. Retooling the policy kit will be difficult and the adjustment costs associated with reform will be high. Declaring that the private sector should play a lead role in development is one thing, but asking the public sector to abdicate its previously dominant position is quite a different problem. Furthermore, with only a few hundred private business groups wealthy enough to gain access to special agricultural investment programmes, compared with more than 18 million agricultural households (in 1985), it is hard to imagine the private corporate sector effecting very widespread change. Given the important role that the public sector has played in the past, and the crucial role that the provision of public goods continues to play in agricultural development, the nature and scope of government policy in agriculture will continue to be a key determinant of the sector's performance in the decade to come.

1. By comparison, non-food budget shares of urban consumers increased from 40.2 per cent in 1980 to 47.3 per cent in 1987, reflecting the higher average incomes in the urban areas.

2. The 1985 Intercensal Survey (*Supas*, Seri 5: Table 58.3) reported that there were 21.4 million agricultural households in Indonesia, of which 12.6 million were on Java. The definition of an agricultural household was one where any part of the household income was derived from agriculture.

3. Trends in real wages are of course very sensitive to the deflator used. For a careful discussion of the available data, see Naylor (1990).

4. It should be stressed, however, that the 1973 data were probably understated, so these growth rates are rather too high.

5. The Farmers' Terms of Trade Index (*Indeks Nilai Tukar Petani*) is published by the Biro Pusat Statistik in the *Buletin Ringkas*. It was originally based on 1976. In 1987 a revised index based on 1983 was issued.

6. These figures refer to Bimas and PT Pusri estimates of urea, TSP, and AS offtake in food-crop producing areas. Approximately 90 per cent of this would be allocated to rice (Hedley and Tabor, 1989).

7. Budget estimates and extension costs were provided by Department of Agriculture Planning Agency officials in a personal communication, 1989.

8. Actual budget expenditures and sources of financing were provided by officials from the Department of Agriculture, Agency for Agricultural Research and Development, in a personal communication in 1989.

9. This includes actual expenditures for government-financed investments for smallholders and for the PTPs. The bulk of public smallholder investments were undertaken on

a subsidized credit basis. Since the credit-recovery mechanisms have not operated, these investments are best treated as a lump-sum transfer to the assisted smallholders. By comparison, the PTP investments are also made on a credit basis, but with a smaller (15 per cent) element of capital subsidy attached. A very large implicit subsidy was accorded to these investments because publicly held lands were provided to the projects at zero or little cost. Were this in-kind element to be accounted for, actual public investment costs would increase by a factor of approximately 50 per cent.

10. CPO market controls, for both domestic utilization and exports, have led to a high and unstable consumer price and producer prices well below import parity levels (Godoy, 1986). Cooking oil policy is one of the sources of large rents in the agricultural sector.

REFERENCES

Affandi, A. (1986), 'Agricultural Development in Indonesia', Jakarta: Department of Agriculture, mimeo.

Altemeier, K., Tabor, S., and Adinugroho, B. (1988), 'Supply Parameters for Indonesian Agricultural Policy Analysis', *Ekonomi dan Keuangan Indonesia*, 36 (1).

Anderson, B. (1966), 'The Problem of Rice' (Translated Stenographic Notes on the Fourth Session of the *Sanyo Kaigi*, 8 January 2605), *Indonesia*, 2(October): 77–124.

Bappenas (1989), *Repelita V*, Jakarta.

Barlow, C. and Muharminto (1982), 'Smallholder Rubber in South Sumatera: Towards Economic Improvement', Canberra: Australian National University, mimeo.

Barlow, C.; Shearing, C.; and Dereinda, R. (1988), 'An Alternative Approach to Smallholder Rubber Development', Jakarta: Center for Policy and Implementation Studies, mimeo.

Biro Pusat Statistik (BPS) (various issues), *Buku Saku Statistik Indonesia*, Jakarta.

____ (monthly), *Indikator Ekonomi*, Jakarta.

____ (various issues), *Neraca Bahan Makanan di Indonesia*, Jakarta.

____ (various years), *Survei Sosial Ekonomi Nasional (Susenas)*, Jakarta.

____ (1983), *Sensus Pertanian, 1983: Hasil Sensus Sampel, Seri B*, Jakarta.

____ (1985–8), *Statistical Yearbook*, Jakarta.

Boediono (1987), 'Indonesia: Past and Future Sources of Growth and the Role of Agriculture', Paper presented at the Roundtable on Indonesian Agricultural Development for *Repelita V*, Jakarta.

Booth, Anne (1985), 'Accommodating a Growing Population in Agriculture', *Bulletin of Indonesian Economic Studies*, 21(2): 115–45.

____ (1988), *Agricultural Development in Indonesia*, Sydney: Allen & Unwin for the Asian Studies Association of Australia.

Brown, C. (1982), 'The Intensified Smallholder Cane Programme: The First Five Years', *Bulletin of Indonesian Economic Studies*, 18(1): 19–60.

Budiman, S. (1987), 'Masalah Karet Indonesia: Tinjauan dari Aspek Pengolahannya', Paper presented at the Seminar on Strategic Factors Related to the Rubber Trade, Jakarta.

Bulog (1970), *Seperempat Abad Bergulat dengan Butir-butir Beras*, Jakarta: Bulog, Vols. I and II.

Centre for World Food Studies (1988), *Agriculture in Repelita V: A Review of Policy Issues*, Amsterdam: Free University.

Collier, W.; Soentoro; Wiradi, G.; Pasandaran, E.; Santoso, K.; and Stepanek, J.F. (1982), 'Acceleration of Rural Development in Java', *Bulletin of Indonesian Economic Studies*, 18(3): 84–101.

Collier, W. et al. (1987), 'The Economic and Social Transformation of Rural Java', Jakarta: USAID, mimeo.

Damardjati, D.; Tabor, S.; Oka, I.; and David, C. (1988), 'Emerging Problems Arising from the Indonesian Success in Rice Production', *IARD Journal* (Jakarta): 10(1).

Departemen Perdagangan (1989), *Statistik Perdagangan dalam Negeri, 1988*, Jakarta: Department of Trade.

Department of Agriculture (1988), 'Supply and Demand for Foodcrops in Indonesia', Jakarta: Department of Agriculture, Directorate of Food Crop Economics and Post-harvest Processing, mimeo.

Dillon, H.S. and Tabor, S. (1988), 'The Value of the International Rubber Agreement to Producers and Consumers of Natural Rubber', *Proceedings of the International Rubber Study Group*, Hamburg.

Dixon, J. (1982), *Food Consumption Patterns and Related Demand Parameters in Indonesia: A Review of Available Evidence*, Working Paper No. 6, Washington, DC: International Food Policy Research Institute.

Dove, M. (1985), 'The Agroecological Mythology of the Javanese and the Political Economy of Indonesia', *Indonesia*, 39 (April): 1–36.

Ellis, F. (1988), *Future Rice Strategy in Indonesia: Rice Self-sufficiency and Rice Price Stability*, IPU Technical Paper No. 7, Jakarta: Bulog Integrated Planning Unit.

Falcon, Walker P.; Jones, William O.; Pearson, Scott R. et al. (1984), *The Cassava Economy of Java*, Stanford: Stanford University Press.

Falcon, W. et al. (1986), *Rice Policy in Indonesia, 1985–1990: The Problems of Success*, Jakarta: Bulog.

Fane, G. and Cutbush, G. (1988), *Agricultural Policy in Indonesia: Existing Policies and the Scope for Reform*, Manila: Asian Development Bank.

Fane, G. and Phillips, C. (1987), *Effective Protection in Indonesia*, Jakarta: Department of Industry, mimeo.

Far Eastern Economic Review (*FEER*) (1985), 'The NES Takes Root—But Will It Flourish', 7 February, pp. 56–9.

Glassburner, B. (1985), 'Macroeconomics and the Agriculture Sector', *Bulletin of Indonesian Economic Studies*, 21(2): 51–73.

Godoy, R. (1986), 'Indonesia's Cooking Oil Policy and the Development of the Coconut Smallholder Sector', Jakarta: HIID, mimeo.

Godoy, R. and Bennett, C. (1987a), 'Monocropped and Intercropped Coconuts in Indonesia: Project Goals Which Conflict with Smallholder Interests', Jakarta: HIID, mimeo.

_____ (1987b), 'Coffee Quality among Smallholders in South Sumatera', Jakarta: Center for Policy and Implementation Studies, mimeo.

Habir, M. (1984), 'Seeds of Resurgence', *Far Eastern Economic Review*, 26 June, pp. 61–2.

Hart, Gillian (1986), *Power, Labor and Livelihood: Processes of Change in Rural Java*, Berkeley: University of California Press.

Hedley, Douglas (1987), 'Diversification: Concepts and Directions in Indonesian Agricultural Policy', in J.W.T. Bottema (ed.), *Soybean Research and Development in Indonesia*, Bogor: CGPRT Centre.

Hedley, D. and Tabor, S. (1989), 'Fertilizer in Indonesian Agriculture: The Subsidy Issue', *Agricultural Economics*, 3: 49–68.

Hutabarat, B. (1988), *Description of Food Crops Policies in Indonesia*, Working Paper No. 6, Bogor: Australia–CAER Project.

Johnson, S.; Myers, W.; Jenson, H.; Teklu, T.; and Wardhani, M. (1988), *Evaluating Food Policy in Indonesia Using Full Demand Systems*, Ames: Center for Agricultural and Rural Development, Iowa State University, mimeo.

Kasryno, Faisal (1981), 'Technological Progress and Its Effect on Income Distribution and Employment in Rural Areas: A Case Study of Three Villages in West Java, Indonesia', *Kajian Ekonomi Malaysia*, 18: 113–38.

____ (1985), 'Structural Change in Rural Employment and Agricultural Wages in Indonesia', Bogor: Center for Agro-economic Research.

Kasryno, Faisal; Saleh, Chaerul; and Utomo Hadi, Prayogo (1986), 'Pola Usaha Pertanian dan Pola Tanam', in *Sensus Pertanian 1983 Seri J4 Aplikasi Teknologi Pertanian, Intensifikasi Tanaman Pangan dan Pola Usaha Tani*, Jakarta: Biro Pusat Statistik.

Keuning, S. (1984), 'Farm Size, Land Use and Profitability of Food Crops in Indonesia', *Bulletin of Indonesian Economic Studies*, 20(3): 58–82.

Klumper, S. (1986), 'Towards an Approach to Food Policy Planning—The Case of Indonesia', in *Appropriate Techniques for Development Planning*, Heidelberg: University of Heidelberg.

Korns, A. (1988), *Wage Data at BPS*, Development Studies Project Paper No. 22, Jakarta: USAID.

Landall Mills (1986), *Natural Rubber: A Chronic Glut*, London: Landall Mills Ltd.

____ (1987), *Oils and Oilseeds: Costs of Production*, London: Landall Mills Ltd.

McStocker, R. (1987), 'The Indonesian Coffee Industry', *Bulletin of Indonesian Economic Studies*, 23(1): 40–69.

Magiera, S. (1981), 'The Role of Wheat in the Indonesian Food Sector', *Bulletin of Indonesian Economic Studies*, 17(3): 48–73.

Manning, C. (1987), 'Public Policy, Rice Production and Income Distribution: A Review of Indonesia's Rice Self-sufficiency Program', *Southeast Asian Journal of Social Science*, 15(1): 66–82.

____ (1988), 'Rural Employment Creation in Java', *Population and Development Review*, 14(1).

Mears, L. (1981), *The New Rice Economy of Indonesia*, Yogyakarta: Gadjah Mada University Press.

Mears, L. and Moelyono, S. (1981), 'Food Policy', in Anne Booth and Peter McCawley (eds.), *The Indonesian Economy during the Soeharto Era*, Kuala Lumpur: Oxford University Press.

Mitchell, M. and Gray, J. (1985), *Report on Phase II of a Study of Minimum Grain Stock Reserves*, London: Tropical Development and Research Institute.

Monteverde, R. (1987), 'Food Consumption in Indonesia', Ph.D. dissertation, Harvard University.

Naylor, Rosamond (1990), 'Wage Trends in Rice Production on Java: 1976–1988', *Bulletin of Indonesian Economic Studies*, 26(2).

Pearson, S. et al. (1988), *Rural Income and Employment Effects of Rice Policy in Indonesia*, Stanford: Food Research Institute, Stanford University, for USAID.

Pitt, M. (1983), 'Farm-level Fertilizer Demand in Java: A Meta-Production Function Approach', *American Journal of Agricultural Economics*, 61: 982–7.

Pitt, M. and Rosenzweig, M. (1986), 'Agricultural Price, Food Consumption and the Health and Productivity of Indonesian Farmers' in I. Singh, L. Squire, and J. Strauss (eds.), *Agricultural Household Models*, Baltimore: Johns Hopkins University Press.

Rachman, A. and Montgomery, R. (1980), 'Asian Fertilizer Demand Reconsidered: An Application to Java and Bali', *Ekonomi dan Keuangan Indonesia*, 28(3): 139–71.

Rietveld, P. (1986), 'Non-agricultural Activities and Income Distribution in Rural Java', *Bulletin of Indonesian Economic Studies*, 22(3): 106–17.

Rosegrant, M. et al. (1987), 'Price and Investment Policies in the Indonesian Food Crop Sector', Bogor: International Food Policy Research Institute and Center for Agro-economic Research for Asian Development Bank, mimeo.

Rosegrant, M. and Kasryno, F. (1988), 'Irrigation Investment in Indonesia: Trends and Prospects,' Bogor: International Food Policy Research Institute and Center for Agro-economic Research, mimeo.

Rucker, R. (1987), 'Indonesia's Employment Problem', Jakarta: USAID, mimeo.

Sastrohoetomo, M. (1982), 'Analisa Kebijaksana Subsidi Pupuk', *Ekonomi dan Keuangan Indonesia*, 30(4): 445–79.

Soemardjan, S. et al. (1988), *Petani Kelapa*, Jakarta: University of Indonesia and the Center for Coconut Research.

Squires, D. and Tabor, S. (1987), 'Integration of Staple Food Commodity Markets in Java', *Singapore Economic Review*, 32(2): 1–15.

Tabor, S. (1989a), *Price and Quality of Rice in Java: An Investigation into the Demand for Closely Related Goods*, Amsterdam: Free University Press.

_____ (1989b), 'Agricultural Policy in Indonesia: The 1980s' Experience and the Outlook for the 1990s', Paper presented at the Department of Agriculture Workshop on Agricultural Policy, Jakarta, June.

Tabor, S. and Altemeier, K. (1989), 'Foodcrop Demand in Indonesia: A System's Approach', *Bulletin of Indonesian Economic Studies*, 25(2): 31–52.

Tabor, S. and Gijsbers, G. (1987), 'Soybean Supply/Demand Prospects for Indonesia', in J. W. T. Bottema (ed.), *Soybean Research and Development in Indonesia*, Bogor: CGPRT Centre, pp. 51–63.

Teken, I. G. B. and Soewardi, H. (1982), 'Food Supply and Demand and Food Policies', in Mubyarto (ed.), *Growth and Equity in Indonesian Economic Development*, Jakarta: Yayasan Agro-ekonomi.

Timmer, C. (1986), *Getting Prices Right: The Scope and Limits of Price Policy*, Ithaca: Cornell University Press.

_____ (1988a), 'Regulation and Deregulation of Rice Markets in Indonesia: Reflections on Bulog's Changing Role and Mission', Cambridge: Harvard University, mimeo.

_____ (1988b), 'Agricultural Prices and Stabilization Policy', Cambridge: Harvard University, mimeo.

_____ (ed.) (1987), *The Corn Economy of Indonesia*, Ithaca: Cornell University Press.

Timmer, C.; Falcon, W.; and Pearson, S. (1983), *Food Policy Analysis*, Baltimore: Johns Hopkins University Press.

Tjondronegoro, Sediono (1986), 'Analisa Masalah Pertanahan dan Kedudukan Petani', in *Sensus Pertanian 1983, Seri J3, Penggunaan Tanah Pertanian Masalah Pertanahan dan Kedudukan Petani*, Jakarta: Biro Pusat Statistik.

Tyers, R. and Rachman, A. (1982), 'Food Security Consumption, Diversification and Foreign Balances in Indonesia: Results from a Multi-commodity Simulation', *Journal of Policy Modeling*, 4(3): 363–93.

University of Indonesia (1986), *Pengkajian Penelitian Potensi, Masalah dan Prospek Minyak Nabati di Indonesia 1969–2000*, Jakarta.

USDA Agricultural Attache Service (1986–8), *Annual Agricultural Situation Report*, Jakarta.

World Bank (1986), 'Indonesia: Tree Crops Sector Review', Washington, DC, mimeo.

_____ (1987a), 'Indonesia: Rural Credit Sector Review', Washington, DC, mimeo.

_____ (1987b), 'Upgrading of Substandard Smallholder Plantings on Indonesian Tree Crop Projects', Jakarta, mimeo.

_____ (1988), 'Indonesia: Agricultural Policy: Issues and Options', Washington, DC, mimeo.

_____ (1989), *World Development Report*, Washington, DC.

_____ (annually), *Commodity Trade and Price Trends*, Washington, DC.

7

Manufacturing Industry*

Hal Hill

Introduction

INDONESIA emerged as a significant industrial power among developing countries in the 1980s, for the first time in the nation's history. Although its manufacturing sector is not comparable in size to that of Brazil, China, and India, nor as sophisticated as any of the four Asian newly industrializing economies (NIEs), its record of industrialization since 1966 is none the less creditable. Economic historians will undoubtedly judge this industrial growth and transformation as one of the achievements of Indonesia's 'New Order', along with prudent macroeconomic management of the oil boom and bust, the green revolution in agriculture, and the dramatic changes in transport and infrastructure.

In the mid-1960s, Indonesia was perhaps the least industrialized of the world's large developing countries (McCawley, 1981; Soehoed, 1967). Economic stagnation and political turbulence had disrupted business for almost a decade, resulting in very limited industrial investment apart from a few showcase (and generally incomplete) public projects. Manufacturing in the main consisted of small and medium enterprises engaged in simple, resource-based processing activities, such as rice milling and rubber, and a few footloose industries, of which weaving was the most important. There was no foreign equity capital in the sector, while the Soviet Union and other East European countries constituted the principal source for the trickle of imported industrial technologies. A modern capital goods sector barely existed, and much of the factory sector had progressed little, if at all, since the country's first episode of industrialization, in the 1930s.

The economic stabilization and liberalization of the late 1960s ushered in an era of unprecedented industrial growth, comprising four broad phases of development. Initially the major stimulants to growth were the backlog in consumer demand, rapid economic growth, and new investment opportunities for foreign and domestic firms alike. For the first time in over a decade, investors were able to obtain virtually

*For helpful comments on an earlier draft, the author is indebted to H. W. Arndt, Howard Dick, Helen Hughes, Adam Schwarz, Thee Kian Wie, and Louis T. Wells, Jr.

unrestricted access to inputs and finance, and they found a ready market for their products.[1] The second phase corresponds broadly to the oil-boom era, 1973–81, a period characterized by accelerating yet inefficient industrial growth. The oil boom had four major effects on the path of industrial growth: it generated rapid economic growth, which spilled over into rising domestic demand for manufactures; it emboldened the government to force the pace of industrialization through extensive investments in many large capital-intensive, resource-based activities such as oil refining, LNG, fertilizer, petrochemicals, and cement; it engendered a 'lazy' policy regime in which vested producer interests were able to exploit nationalist sentiment opposed to a liberal economic order (especially after the *malari* protests of January 1974) to in effect 'capture' the government's trade and protection policy; and it resulted in the familiar intersectoral effects of a booming sector, namely the squeeze on non-oil tradable goods activities.

That the first three, favourable, factors outweighed the last negative influence is evidenced clearly by the rapid industrial growth. Yet the second and third factors were to lay the foundations for serious structural inefficiencies when oil revenue began to decline after 1981. This third phase, lasting approximately from 1981 to 1985, saw the beginnings of a major reassessment of industrial policy. Many of the large industrial projects which had their origins in the late 1970s came on stream, producing quite high growth rates in certain years. And the government's fourth Five-Year Plan, formulated in the early 1980s and unveiled in 1984, envisaged a headlong rush into heavy engineering and resource processing activities. Yet the Plan and the ideology underlying it were overturned by mounting balance of payments difficulties. The resulting major policy reappraisal ushered in a series of increasingly bold and effective reform packages in the fourth phase, from 1985 onwards. In this latest phase, 'state investments', 'government guidance', and 'import substitution' have all given way to an export-oriented strategy dominated by the private sector responding to market signals.

Although frequently grouped with the dynamic East Asian industrial economies, owing to its rapid growth and increasing outward orientation, Indonesia's path to industrialization has been different. Until very recently, it has been quite unlike its neighbours which, apart from the Philippines, have successfully engineered fast labour-intensive, export-oriented growth. Indonesia's large natural resource endowment has dictated a different industrial sector and, even during the recent export-oriented phase, a distinct export composition. Moreover, the boom and decline in oil price have produced the very opposite 'Dutch Disease' effects in Indonesia compared to the resource-poor Asian NIEs. Neither, however, has Indonesia much in common with Asia's other two developing giants, India and China. It possesses neither their longer industrial experience nor their stronger capital goods sector. It also appears to have managed the transition to outward-looking industrial growth more successfully, although China's manufactured exports remain significantly larger. Perhaps the appropriate parallels are with resource-rich countries such as Brazil and Mexico, although both these countries have much higher per capita incomes, larger industrial sectors, and now more serious problems of external indebtedness and macro-economic management.

Indonesia's industrialization since 1966 is of interest not just for the patterns of growth and structural change but also because the sector has been the focus of many of the economic policy debates during the New Order. Contending ideologies debate manufacturing much more commonly than, for example, food crops, mining, and transport. How much foreign participation should be permitted? What is the appropriate balance between Java and the rest of the country? How should cottage industry and the *golongan ekonomi lemah* (weaker economic groups) be protected and promoted? How should the interface with the international economy be managed? What is the most effective means of employment creation? Who really owns Indonesia's modern corporate economy? An analysis of these and other prominent issues of the past quarter century obviously goes to the heart of the New Order's leading economic policy debates and controversies.

This chapter comprises two main sections. The first, essentially factual, looks at what happened to the industrial sector, mainly from the mid-1970s onwards.[2] The second section examines some of the key industrial policy issues, including the trade regime, ownership, regional patterns, the size distribution of industry, and employment growth.

Two general observations should be stressed at the outset. First, Indonesian industry is extraordinarily diverse, ranging from the huge resource-based installations in the Outer Islands to the thousands of tiny cottage industries scattered throughout the country: the former foreign-controlled with investments of millions of dollars, operating throughout the year, selling to (and perhaps possessing stronger commercial links with) the world's major industrial centres; the other locally owned, some with a total capitalization of as little as $100, organized on a household basis, operating seasonally, employing simple technologies and selling to a very localized clientele. To speak of the 'industrial sector' as a homogeneous entity is clearly misleading. In particular, it is useful to view Indonesia's industrial sector as consisting of two entities: an 'oil and gas' sector comprising a handful of petroleum refineries and LNG installations (which are not recorded in the industrial statistics), and the 'non-oil' sector. The latter of course is still extremely diverse. Secondly, the industrial data base has improved immeasurably since the mid-1960s. Indonesia's first industrial census was undertaken in 1964, but in a period of hyperinflation and political turmoil little credence can be given to its results. For the period before 1966, even basic information such as output and employment is unreliable. Thereafter, the quality and range of industrial statistics developed markedly. Annual production and trade statistics are regarded as reasonably reliable, and two industrial censuses have been conducted, in 1974/5 and 1986. A number of general studies of industry are available,[3] and the Jakarta economic press is lively and informative.

However, a number of important lacunae remain. First, very few *detailed* industry case studies are available, although the secondary data base is good and the business community in Indonesia generally accessible. Secondly, the industrial statistical base, while now very good in key respects following the generation of a new annual series commencing in 1975, still has some gaps; the most important of these is capital stock estimates, the absence of which precludes examination of total factor productivity and capacity utilization, for example. Finally, and perhaps understandably, very little is known about cottage industry, defined in Indonesia as establishments with less than five 'workers'. Both industrial censuses were unable to obtain accurate information on this sector, and it is not possible to determine whether it is expanding or contracting. Perhaps these lacunae are the result of the relatively underdeveloped state of industrial economics and organization in Indonesian universities. Most of the major studies of Indonesian industrialization have been written by foreigners, in contrast to the much stronger domestic research base in agricultural economics.[4]

Industrial Structure and Trends

Two Decades of High Growth

Indonesia's extraordinarily rapid industrial growth since 1970 is illustrated by the fact that all but five years registered a double-digit expansion in real industrial output (Figure 7.1).[5] As a result, the manufacturing sector has been transformed, with real output increasing ninefold in less than two decades. Nor has this high growth been merely a 'small initial base' phenomenon: average growth over the half decade 1984–8, for example, exceeded that of the period 1974–8. This industrial expansion has hardly been a smooth process, reflecting both the large exogenous shocks experienced by the Indonesian economy since 1970 and the 'lumpy' nature of several huge investment projects. Growth was very fast at the peak of the two oil booms, 1973–4 and 1979–80, before tapering off on both occasions, the recession of 1982–3 being particularly severe.

Since 1978 the Biro Pusat Statistik (BPS) has released a breakdown of manufacturing output into its three components—oil, gas, and other—thereby facilitating the construction of a 'non-oil' manufacturing series separate from the uneven expansion in oil refining and LNG capacity. The data reveal, for example, that oil and gas led the rapid though erratic growth from 1979 to 1984, whereas the 'non-oil' sector grew more rapidly after 1984. It is also evident that there was quite a strong recovery from the virtual standstill of 1982 and 1983, but that the very high growth rate for 1984 was primarily the result of new oil- and gas-processing capacity. Given the long lead times in such investments, capacity was being brought on stream just as world prices were about to collapse.

In spite of this rapid growth, the share of manufacturing in GDP did

208

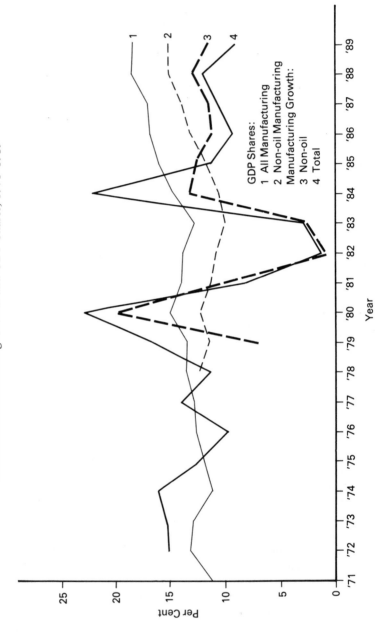

FIGURE 7.1
Indonesian Manufacturing Growth and GDP Shares, 1971–1989

not rise appreciably until the mid-1980s; in fact, through a juggling of end-point years, it is possible to demonstrate a slight *decline* in manufacturing (compare, for example, 1972 and 1983) over this period (Figure 7.1). Since the data are at current prices, the explanation, of course, was the boom in the oil sector, which squeezed not only the competitiveness of other tradables but also their shares of GDP. The relative constancy of the share of manufacturing until the mid-1980s was the cause of considerable consternation in some senior industrial policy circles in Indonesia, and was used as an argument for the ambitious but ultimately aborted heavy industry programmes outlined in *Repelita IV*. Hastened by falling oil prices and an increasingly buoyant non-oil sector, the share of manufacturing has risen sharply since 1984, by almost 50 per cent in the case of the non-oil component.

Rapid Structural Change

Rapid industrial growth has generated equally far-reaching structural change in Indonesian manufacturing, although not always in the direction posited by economic theory. The 'typical' pattern of industrialization involves an evolution from simple, labour-intensive activities towards more skill and technology-intensive industries, propelled by rising real wages, an increasing stock of human capital, and a more sophisticated industrial infrastructure. Indonesia was in this first phase until around 1970, when the modern factory sector was so small, but then departed from the 'East Asian' model characterized by rapid export-oriented, labour-intensive growth. One reason for this departure was the country's much stronger natural resource endowment—the exploitation of which required large complementary inputs of capital—as compared to the Asian NIEs and Japan. Another was the effects of the oil boom and the policy regime through to 1985. In consequence, Indonesia began to exploit its strong potential comparative advantage in labour-intensive manufactures only in the late 1980s, a decade after its Association of South-East Asian Nations (ASEAN) neighbours and two decades after the NIEs.

These developments explain the otherwise puzzling picture of structural change revealed in Figures 7.2a and 7.2b.[6] Including oil and LNG, which are classified as heavy processing industries, the latter's share of manufacturing output almost doubled from 1975 to 1984, before declining somewhat. The share of both light industry and engineering fell for the period as a whole, substantially in the case of the latter. These changes are more discernible in the non-oil case: the share of processing industries rose, though not as sharply, and (contrary to the case where oil is included) they have held their relative position since 1984, owing to the continued growth of industries such as fertilizer; the share of engineering industries rose around 1980 in response to very heavy protection and other investment opportunities created by the government's promotional policies, but then subsided. In contrast, the relative importance of light industries fell almost continuously through to 1985, but

210

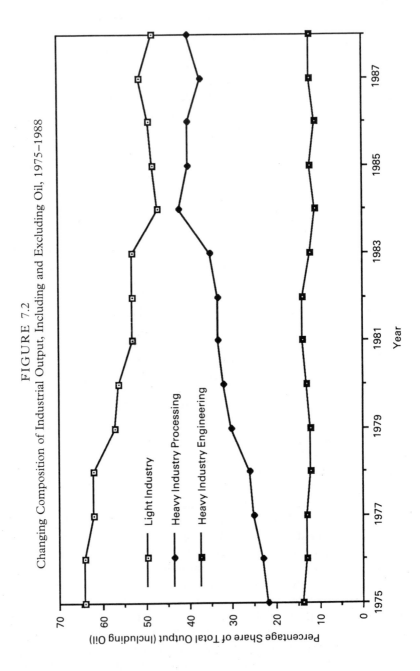

FIGURE 7.2

Changing Composition of Industrial Output, Including and Excluding Oil, 1975–1988

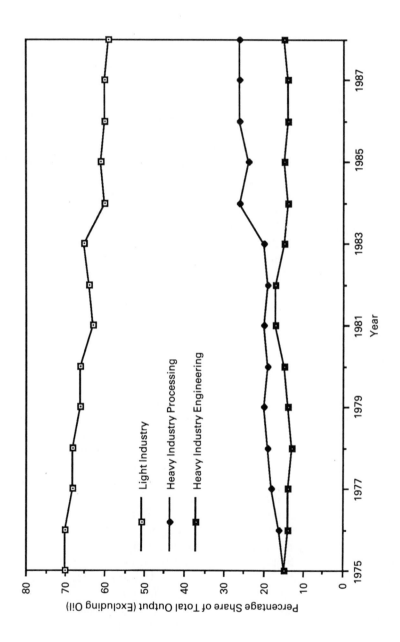

their share then stabilized and rose slightly in the late 1980s as these activities grew under the impetus of the export drive.

In spite of these major structural changes, most sectors of industry have grown rapidly since the mid-1970s: output in all of the principal industry groups rose by at least 7 per cent per annum, while employment grew by at least 5 per cent in all but the large food, beverages, and tobacco group (Table 7.1). Indonesia has yet to cope with the problems of declining industries, although many firms have experienced difficulty, particularly during the recession of the mid-1980s.

The transformation is evident from the fact that in 1975 food and textiles generated some 45 per cent of output, chemicals (including oil) 33 per cent, and engineering about 13 per cent; no other industry groups were of much significance. By 1988 the structure was much more diversified, with most of the major industries having a share of at least 10 per cent.[7] The large increases for wood products and basic metals, to which we return shortly, are especially pronounced. That the rapid changes in technology and the flood of new investments have had their impact primarily on output rather than employment is also illustrated in Table 7.1. Apart from the declining share of food and related products and the approximately equal increase in the share of wood products, the employment structure of the factory sector at this aggregated level has changed remarkably little.

Even within the factory sector, Indonesian industry is characterized by diversity in scale and technology, as revealed by a comparison of output and employment shares in Table 7.1. In the most capital-intensive industry, basic metals, labour productivity is about 20 times that of the least capital-intensive, textiles, leather products, and footwear. The next most capital-intensive, chemicals, has a ratio some four times that of the second most labour-intensive, the food group. Disaggregating into finer industrial classifications and various size groups of course produces immeasurably greater variations. A comparison of output and employment growth rates also identifies the primary source of output expansion in each of the major industry groups. For industry as a whole over the period 1975–88, employment growth contributed about 33 per cent of the increase, a high share in view of the still very labour-intensive nature of much of manufacturing in 1975 and the rapid infusion of modern technologies thereafter. The cases where the employment contribution was higher—and the pace of technological change thereby lower—are unsurprising: the highly protected and inefficient engineering industries and the traditionally labour-intensive wood products and miscellaneous groups. The two cases where productivity increases were the major source of growth were paper products and basic metals, both of which were completely transformed by the introduction of new products and production processes (see Hill, 1990b, for further discussion of productivity levels and changes across industries).

TABLE 7.1
The Structure of Industrial Output and Employment, 1975 and 1988

Industry	Output (Rp billion)		Employment ('000)		Distribution (percentage of total)							
					Output				Employment		Annual Growth, 1975–88	
					1975		1988					
	1975	1988	1975	1988	Incl. Oil/LNG	Excl. Oil/LNG	Incl. Oil/LNG	Excl. Oil/LNG	1975	1988	Output	Employment
31 Food, etc.	326	4,522	386	636	34	40	21	27	39	28	9.5	3.9
32 Textiles, etc.	108	2,010	237	533	11	13	9	12	24	23	15.3	6.4
33 Wood products	24	2,116	42	328	2	3	10	13	4	14	27.6	17.1
34 Paper products	27	760	31	75	3	3	4	5	3	3	28.1	7.0
35 Chemicals	318	7,696	}156	356	33	–	36	–	}16	15	13.5	}6.6
excl. Oil/LNG	175	2,722			(18)	21	(13)	16			7.2	
36 Non-metallic mins.	31	632	38	107	3	4	3	4	4	5	16.9	8.3
37 Basic metals	3	1,326	2	22	n	n	6	8	n	1	57.9	20.3
38 Metal goods	130	2,394	91	223	13	15	11	14	9	10	8.9	7.1
39 Other	2	78	5	22	n	n	n	n	n	1	19.2	20.3
Total	963	21,534	}988	2,302	}100	}100	}100	}100	}100	}100	13.9	}6.7
excl./Oil/LNG	820	16,560									13.2	

Source and Notes: The data are based on the revised and as yet unpublished 'back-casted' series of BPS, *Statistik Industri*, which show significantly higher output and employment levels than the published series. Data refer to firms employing at least 20 workers; 'output' refers to value added; 'output growth' is value added growth deflated by the relevant wholesale price index. Figures in brackets are not included in the totals. 'n' indicates less than $1 million, and growth rates rendered irrelevant by very small initial base. 'n.a.' indicates comparison not applicable. In calculating the growth of export values, data have been deflated by the relevant US producer prices series, as reported in various issues of the *Monthly Labor Review*, US Department of Labour, Washington.

Trends in Major Sectors

It is not possible to examine developments among the major sectors in any detail, but it will be useful to summarize a few highlights since the data in Table 7.1 and Figure 7.2 provide a highly aggregated picture of Indonesia's industrial transformation. Many major industries simply did not exist in the late 1960s; these 'latecomers' generally have grown extremely rapidly, compared to the more subdued performance of traditional industries (Table 7.2).[8] In fact, a very crude indication of the far-reaching structural changes over the two decades 1969–89 is the number of new products flooding on to the market. The annual *Nota Keuangan*, for example, now records some 102 industrial products (excluding oil and gas), barely one-third of which were produced in 1969 and about two-thirds in 1979.[9]

Particularly notable was the expansion in the range of engineering products, compared to miscellaneous manufactures which includes the traditional food and textile groups. These figures vastly understate the magnitude of the changes, since they do not incorporate the great improvements in quality and variety within each product group. But the data provide an approximate overview.

The output of food and related products has grown quite slowly (Table 7.1), in part because an efficient export-oriented agribusiness industry capitalizing on Indonesia's strong comparative advantage in cash crops is only just emerging. In the 1960s, the food-processing industry was dominated by sugar refining and rice milling. The latter industry modernized rapidly (Timmer, 1973), while the former has had a particularly unhappy history, being technologically backward, inefficiently managed by state enterprises, and processing a highly protected agricultural activity. The old established tea industry has also grown slowly. By contrast, other products have performed better, including the rapidly growing palm oil industry, new dairy products (under the impetus of very high protection), and the fruit and vegetable canning industry, much of it located in southern Sumatra and further north. In cigarettes, the ubiquitous *kretek* (clove) has pushed aside the foreign-owned international brand name 'white' cigarette competitors. Annual output has grown at 10 per cent since 1969, much to the consternation of the health community. The *kretek* industry, centred around the East Java towns of Kediri and Malang, and Kudus in Central Java, has shed its extremely labour-intensive character (on which see Castles, 1967, and Manning, 1979), following the government's partial removal of a ban on mechanization. But it continues to employ thousands of mostly unskilled female workers in several enormous factories.

The transformation of the textile, garments, and footwear industries has been especially rapid. Dominated until the mid-1960s by a large hand-loom sector located around Bandung–Majalaya (Palmer, 1972), these traditional producers were unable to withstand the competition from power looms in the new liberalized environment after 1966, and have retreated to peripheral production of a few specialist product lines

Output of Selected Industrial Products, 1969–1989[a]

Product	Unit	Year				Annual Growth (per cent)	
		1969	1979	1984	1989[b]	1979–89	1969–89
Consumer Goods							
Cooking oil	'000 ton	263	452	267	486	0.7	3.1
Margarine	'000 ton	7.5	18.5	34.1	37.6	7.3	8.4
Kretek cigarettes	bn. sticks	19.0	41.5	79.7	129	12.0	10.1
White cigarettes	bn. sticks	11.0	28.6	26.9	17.4	-4.8	2.3
Yarn	'000 bales	182	998	1,782	3,438	13.2	15.8
Textiles	m. metres	450	1,910	2,402	4,494	8.9	12.2
Garments	m. dozen	n.a.	n.a.	26	49	n.a.	n.a.
Intermediate Goods							
Plywood	'000 cu.m.	n.a.	n.a.	4,249	7,692	n.a.	n.a.
Paper	'000 ton	17	214	543	1,133	18.1	23.4
Fertilizer(all types)	'000 ton	85	2,089	4,427	6,446	11.9	24.1
Soap	'000 ton	133	203	160	178	-1.3	1.5
Auto tyres	'000	366	2,898	3,944	7,377	9.8	16.2
Cement	'000 ton	542	4,705	8,854	15,738	12.8	18.3
Glass sheets	'000 ton	n.a.	67.3	152.1	325	17.1	n.a.
Steel ingots	'000 ton	n.a.	122	901	1,736	30.4	n.a.
Aluminium sheets	'000 ton	n.a.	9.5	24.5	41	15.6	n.a.
Engineering Goods							
Dry batteries	million	54.0	462.0	771.8	1,077	8.8	16.1
Motor vehicles	'000	5.0	102.5	153.7	177	5.6	19.5
Motor cycles	'000	21.4	221.6	272.2	281	2.4	13.8
TV	'000	4.5	659.8	772.8	797	1.9	29.5

Sources: Department of Finance, *Nota Kenangan*, 1990; Department of Information, *Lampiran Pidato Kenegaraan, 1990.*
[a]Data refer to fiscal years, that is, 1969 to 1969/70, etc.
[b]Estimates.
n.a. = Not available.

(Hill, 1983). At the same time, the few state-owned spinning mills of the early 1960s have given way to a rapidly expanding yarn sector—often fully integrated with the downstream stages—and synthetic fibre producers. Garment manufacture has long been a feature of Indonesia, in the form of many small tailor shops, but large-scale commercial manufacture for export and for Indonesia's rapidly expanding middle classes emerged only in the late 1970s. Similarly, the dormant footwear industry, long dominated by one huge foreign firm (Bata) (Rice, 1986), suddenly became a major source of exports following the policy reforms of the late 1980s and the infusion of foreign technology and skills, mainly from Asia's NIEs.

The wood and paper products industries, in which Indonesia has a strong potential comparative advantage, emerged only on a commercial scale in the 1970s. Traditionally comprising sawmills and a few other processing activities, plywood developed as a 'boom' industry in the early 1980s following the phased introduction of a log export ban. This contentious measure, designed to promote increased local value added and to secure forest conservation, ushered in a tremendous expansion in processing capacity, primarily in the heartland of Indonesia's tropical forest reserves, East Kalimantan (Pangestu, 1989). But the cost was considerable. The ban has been a blunt instrument, in which forest concessionaires have often recklessly established uneconomic processing capacity, thus dissipating resource rents which could have been extracted through a more efficient fiscal regime.[10] Rattan, of which Indonesia is the world's largest producer, has been handled in a similarly unfortunate fashion. Furniture making, long a cottage industry activity in centres such as Bali and Jepara (Central Java), has evolved as a commercial export business only in the late 1980s.

The chemicals and non-metallic metals industries are dominated by three huge processing activities, all featuring extensive government participation. The oil-refining industry dates back to the colonial era establishments in Balikpapan (East Kalimantan) and North Sumatra (Lindblad, 1989), but most of the rapid expansion occurred after the first oil boom, and the major plants—all government-owned—are located at Cilacap (Central Java), Musi (South Sumatra), Dumai and Sungai Pakning (Riau), and Balikpapan. Several huge LNG trains have been established in Aceh and East Kalimantan, as joint ventures between Pertamina and foreign firms. Little is known about the efficiency of the industry, apart from the teething problems associated with the start-up phase of the batch of new oil refineries in 1983–5.[11] Fertilizer has been one of the most heavily promoted industries since 1966, regarded by the government as a strategic industry for its backward linkages to the energy sector (which explains the location of major plants in Aceh, South Sumatra, and East Kalimantan), and its forward linkages to the food-crop sector. Initially controlled almost entirely by the state, foreign and domestic investors entered the industry in the 1980s. Cement is another strategic industry in the government's view. It has assumed something of a 'boom and bust' character, growing extremely rapidly through to the early 1980s under the impetus of the construction boom, before experiencing a major crisis in the mid-1980s, which led to a government bail-out in 1985 of the huge Indocement concern owned by Indonesia's largest business conglomerate, the Liem Sioe Liong group. The industry recovered in the late 1980s through a marginal-cost export strategy and stronger domestic demand.

The basic metals and engineering goods industries have perhaps been the most contentious of all during the New Order's rapid industrialization. Basic metals are dominated by two giant industrial complexes, steel at Cilegon (West Java) and aluminium ingots at Asahan, North Sumatra, the latter being the largest investment project undertaken since 1966. Both projects have been dogged by controversy, both are shrouded in mystery, and both feature extensive government equity with foreign participation. The steel industry had its origins in an ambitious Russian plan developed in the late 1950s, partially implemented, then deferred, in the late 1960s, and reactivated following the oil boom (Arndt, 1975). Enjoying 'made-to-measure' protection since its inception, it has now become a quite significant exporter, but there are doubts regarding its technology (particularly the direct-reduction process which came on stream in the mid-1980s) and its financial viability. Government subsidies, both in the form of concessional fuel prices and a recent bank bail-out (again of a Liem concern), have been a continuous feature of the industry. The huge Asahan project has received extensive publicity, on environmental and financial grounds, and more recently for the dispute with its Japanese partners, but the future of the smelter component seems assured as long as world aluminium prices hold up.[12]

The diverse engineering goods industries displayed a patchy record in the 1980s, some industries recording very slow growth during this decade (Table 7.2). Intense protection and regulation facilitated very rapid growth in automotive production through to the early 1980s, but the subsequent collapse in domestic demand exposed the extreme fragmentation and inefficiency of the industry, particularly passenger cars and consumer electronic appliances. Several 'high tech' components of the engineering industry have flourished under the patronage of the powerful Minister for Research and Technology, Dr Habibie. The most prominent of these has been the aircraft industry in Bandung (PT Nusantara), in joint production with several European and North American firms (Hill and Pang, 1988). Economic data on Nusantara are not published, but it is unlikely to be viable, and in any case the government has resorted to justification of the large public investments on the grounds of 'technology acquisition and development' and a range of non-economic considerations. At the other end of the spectrum, Indonesia has yet to develop a labour-intensive electronics industry which has been such an important feature of neighbouring Singapore and of Malaysia's Free Trade Zones. Two large multinationals ceased operations in 1985/6, just prior to the implementation of the country's highly effective export liberalization measures, claiming the trade and regulatory regime rendered their operations unprofitable. This may be about to change, however, owing to several large investments planned for Batam Island, to attract the spillover from Singapore's booming industry.

The Export Boom, Post-1985

The dramatic expansion in developing East Asia's manufactured exports has been one of the dominant features of the global economy during the past quarter century. Yet until the mid-1980s Indonesia was out of step with its neighbours, even the Philippines (Riedel, 1989). During the 1970s Indonesia's manufactured exports were negligible, never exceeding $500 million and always less than 3 per cent of total merchandise exports. Indeed, a pervasive export pessimism prevailed in much policy and intellectual thought over this period. It was widely held that Indonesia could never match the NIEs' record, whether because of the 'Dutch Disease' effects of the oil boom, or because it had left its entry into now increasingly protectionist world markets too late, or because of domestic supply-side factors (a stifling bureaucratic framework, poor business efficiency and productivity). McCawley's comments are symptomatic of influential thinking at the time:

It does seem true that for quite a while to come Indonesian manufacturers will find it difficult to compete in international markets.... One wonders whether, under present circumstances, [export promotion] is a suitable policy for Indonesia because it might be more fruitful to tackle some of the basic causes of Indonesia's protectionism more directly. (McCawley, 1980: 236, 238.)

Initial efforts at export promotion seemed to reinforce these pessimistic sentiments. There was a short-lived boom in garment exports following the November 1978 devaluation, but these exports stagnated until 1982, partly because the effects of the devaluation were eroded by subsequent inflation. In the early 1980s plywood dominated the picture, generating over half of manufactured exports in some years; yet this was a case of clumsy and costly export promotion as indicated above. However, as the export momentum continued, it was clear that a major transformation was under way. Manufactured exports more than doubled in nominal value between 1980 and 1983, and doubled again between 1983–6 and 1986–8 (Table 7.3). For the period 1980–9, real annual average export growth was 30 per cent; that the growth has not been a 'small initial base' phenomenon is illustrated by the fact that real growth over the reform period 1985–9 (33.1 per cent) was marginally higher than that of 1980–5 (28.2 per cent). The share of manufactures in total merchandise exports soared from 2 to 32 per cent, an increase of course accelerated by declining oil prices.[13]

Several features of the export boom should be emphasized. First, consistent with the early outward experience of most countries, there was an initial strong reliance on a small number of commodities, in particular plywood, clothing, and textiles. These three accounted for as much as three-quarters of the total in some years, and plywood nearly one-half. As the growth gathered pace, however, and the demonstration effects and commercial experience of the 'big three' spread, many new exports emerged, some at astonishing speed. Footwear exports, for example, a significant component of the NIEs' sales but barely evident in Indonesia before 1986, suddenly expanded by about threefold each year from 1986 to 1989. A range of other resource-based products—cement, fertilizer, paper, steel—became significant, as did furniture, jewellery, and glass products. The only disappointing aspect, noted above, has been the demise of electronics exports, although there are signs of a recent recovery.

A second feature of these exports is that their pattern is strongly consistent with Indonesia's comparative advantage in natural resource and labour-intensive activities. Some 40–50 per cent of the total have been resource-based manufactures, dominated by plywood (Table 7.3), and a further 35–45 per cent have been in the labour-intensive group. Even capital-intensive exports, about 17 per cent of the total, have a large natural resource component and possibly could be included in this group. Indonesia's specialization in 'comparative advantage' goods is illustrated by the indices of revealed comparative advantage for each factor intensity grouping and for the three major exports (Table 7.4). The indices, which assume a value of unity when a product's share of Indonesian exports equals that of world exports, have risen for all manufactures, but remain well below unity. They are still very low for the capital-intensive group, but extremely high for resource-intensive manufactures and rising progressively for labour-intensive products. The index for plywood is extraordinarily high, indicating the magnitude of Indonesia's export specialization in that product, and reflecting its significant supplies of tropical timber and the effects of the log export ban. The specialization in garments is also considerable, while that for the more capital-intensive textiles group somewhat less.

Thirdly, Indonesia appears to have been more successful at market diversification than product diversification in its export drive (Hill, 1990a). As would be expected, Japan and the United States are the major markets, the former especially for plywood and the latter for clothing and textiles. Nevertheless, other markets have been penetrated with some success: Europe and Singapore for garments and textiles, especially as quota ceilings have been reached for these products in the US market; and China and neighbouring East (and even South) Asian markets for fertilizer, steel and paper products, and plywood.

At the heart of this export success story has been a major reorientation in policies, commencing in a hesitant manner in the early 1980s, but implemented in an increasingly bold and effective fashion after 1985. Two crucial ingredients have been successful exchange rate management—in particular the sharp depreciation in the real effective exchange rate—and the trade policy liberalization, especially the drawback facility for exporters. While it is difficult to model the effects of these two measures with any precision, it is likely that the former has been more powerful for products comprising a higher 'domestic value added' component (mainly the resource-based group), while the latter has been of great importance for the footloose, labour-intensive group.

TABLE 7.3
Major Manufactured Exports of Indonesia, 1980–1989 ($ million)

	1980	1982	1984	1985	1986	1987	1988	1989	Average Annual Growth, 1980–9	
									Real Value	Volume
Resource-intensive										
Total	119	354	832	992	1,209	2,036	2,575	2,838	39.2	n.a.
Percentage of all manufactures	24	44	45	49	46	52	47	40		
Major items										
Plywood	68	316	791	941	1,127	1,901	2,368	2,414	45.5	34.6
Cement	26	8	13	22	41	57	80	133	16.6	26.5
Leather	6	7	7	8	15	45	68	69	26.8	21.9
Labour-intensive										
Total	287	323	826	785	1,054	1,303	2,061	3,017	26.3	n.a.
Percentage of all manufactures	57	40	45	38	40	33	38	43		
Major items										
Clothing	98	116	296	339	522	596	797	1,170	28.4	28.9
Woven fabrics	43	43	183	227	287	385	571	727	33.6	40.6
Yarn	3	1	17	13	20	84	109	112	45.8	48.1
Oils and perfumes	21	17	29	23	27	34	34	32	1.1	0.6
Glass and glassware	3	3	10	8	13	31	75	77	39.5	42.1
Electronics	94	117	214	77	29	15	41	67	-6.6	n.a.
Musical instruments	7	11	26	39	43	28	33	41	18.4	19.8
Furniture	3	2	5	7	9	27	70	167	52.9	62.3
Footwear	1	3	5	8	8	22	82	220	n	54.8
Jewellery	n	1	8	8	37	5	78	98	n	n

Capital-intensive

Total	97	131	181	266	377	556	839	1,163	28.1	n.a.
Percentage of all manufactures	19	16	10	13	14	14	15	17		
Major items										
Fertilizer	35	10	37	80	127	86	134	164	14.5	23.0
Paper products	5	2	20	21	33	96	128	138	37.3	44.7
Steel products	8	8	7	28	58	188	269	343	47.4	47.5
Inorganic chemicals	n	2	33	35	27	25	32	35	n	n
Rubber tyres	n	n	2	7	11	23	45	65	n	n
Total, all manufactures	501	809	1,839	2,044	2,639	3,895	5,476	7,018	30.3	n.a.
Three largest as percentage of total	52	68	71	74	73	74	68	61		
Manufactures as percentage of total exports	2	4	8	11	18	23	28	32		

Sources: BPS, *Ekspor* [Exports], Jakarta, various issues.

Notes: 1. The following definitions are used:

Resource intensive—SITC items 61, 63, 66 (excluding 664–666), 671.

Labour intensive—SITC items 54, 55, 65, 664–666, 695–697, 749, 776, 778, 793, 81–85, 89.

Capital intensive—SITC items 5 (excluding 54 and 55), 62, 64, 67 (excluding 671), 69 (excluding 695–697), 7 (excluding 749, 776, 778, 793), 86–88. This classification was developed by Krause (1982), and subsequently modified by Ariff and Hill (1985) for ASEAN, and by the author for Indonesia.

2. The following SITC codes are used for the major exports (corresponding ISIC codes in parentheses): plywood 634 (33113); cement 661 (3631); leather 611 (323); clothing 84 (322); woven fabrics 652–9 (32112); yarn 651 (32111); oils and perfumes 551 (35233); glass and glassware 664–5 (362); electronics 749, 776, 778 (3833); musical instruments 898 (3902); furniture 821 (332); footwear 851 (324); jewellery 897 (3901); fertilizer 562 (3512); paper products 641 (341); steel products 672–9 (371); inorganic chemicals 522 (3511); rubber tyres 625 (3551).

3. 'n' indicates less than $1 million, and growth rates rendered irrelevant by very small initial base. 'n.a.' indicates comparison not applicable. In calculating the growth of export values, data have been deflated by the relevant US producer price series, as reported in various issues of the *Monthly Labor Review*, US Department of Labor, Washington.

TABLE 7.4

RCA Indices for Indonesian Manufactured Exports, 1970–1988[a]

	All Manufactures	Major Categories[b]			Major Products[b]		
		Labour-intensive	Resource-intensive	Capital-intensive	Plywood (634)	Clothing (84)	Textiles (652–9)
1970	0.02	0.03	0.02	0.02	n.a.	n.a.	0.06
1975	0.02	0.02	0.01	0.02	0.02	0.02	0.01
1980	0.04	0.10	0.20	0.01	1.05	0.23	0.09
1985	0.21	0.26	2.26	0.09	18.00	0.71	0.57
1986	0.27	0.38	3.11	0.10	24.77	1.14	0.80
1987	0.35	0.41	4.46	0.11	31.93	1.05	0.91
1988[c]	0.28	0.41	3.83	0.07	25.46	1.23	0.76

Source: International Economic Data Bank, Research School of Pacific Studies, Australian National University.

[a]The RCA (revealed comparative advantage) index is defined as:

$$\frac{X_{ij}}{X_i} \Big/ \frac{X_{wj}}{X_w}$$

where
X_{ij} = country i's exports of commodity j
X_i = country i's total exports
X_{wj} = world exports of commodity j
X_w = world exports.

[b]Categories as defined in notes to Table 7.3; figures in parentheses below products are the SITC codes.

[c]1988 data are estimates and may be understated.

An assessment of the remarkable growth of manufactured exports would be incomplete without a few qualifications. First, as noted, the net economic benefits of the log export ban (and other similar regulations) remain controversial, and there is increasing evidence to suggest that this renewable natural resource is being managed poorly. Secondly, the net economic benefits of the export drive have to be carefully assessed where subsidized state enterprises are involved, especially in the case of steel, but also fertilizer, cement, and paper products. There is little doubt that Indonesia has a comparative advantage in the export of many of these products, but the plethora of state subsidies received by such firms is probably lowering the effective returns from export sales. Thirdly, the trade reforms have so far been incomplete: they have placed exporters on a free trade footing but many domestic-market-oriented activities continue to receive very high protection; the result has been something of a 'dualistic' industrial structure in which the transition to exporting status has not always been easy. These issues will be discussed in the next section.

Indonesian Industrialization in International Perspective

That Indonesia's industrialization is still some way behind its neighbours is evident from Table 7.5. Despite two decades of rapid growth, its manufacturing sector is appreciably smaller than that of South Korea and India (and Mexico), and little larger than Thailand's. In per capita terms, manufacturing output is only about 40 per cent larger than India and Nigeria, and half that of the Philippines. Its engineering goods industries are relatively smaller than in most of these countries, in part because of Indonesia's larger heavy processing subsector. Similarly, although the very recent export surge is not captured fully in the comparative picture presented in Table 7.5, Indonesia's manufactured exports are still small by any yardstick, and in per capita terms were less than half those of the Philippines in 1988 and about one-fifth those of Thailand. Indonesia's limited export specialization in labour-intensive manufactures—a key element in the export explosion of resource-poor Asian developing countries—is revealed both by the modest share of manufactures in total merchandise exports and by the small share of textiles and clothing in the total. Thus Indonesia's pattern of industrialization is an unusual one, sharing common features with its East Asian neighbours in the recent export drive, with Mexico and Nigeria as a 'petroleum economy', and with India in its large domestic market. But it closely resembles none of these.

Issues in Indonesia's Industrialization

Ideology and Policy-making Processes

An understanding of the ideological backdrop and bureaucratic processes is crucial in any examination of industrial policy-making in Indonesia.

TABLE 7.5
Indonesian Industrialization in Comparative Perspective[a]

	GNP per Capita, 1988 ($)	Manufacturing Growth, Real Annual Average, Percentage		Manufacturing Output, 1988 as Percentage of		Manufacturing Output, 1987			Manufactured Exports, 1988		
		1965–80	1980–88	GDP	Agriculture	($m.)	Per Capita ($)	Engineering Goods as Percentage of Total	As Percentage of Merchandise Exports	Per Capita ($)	Textiles and Clothing as Percentage of Total
Indonesia	440	12.0	13.1	19	79	12,876	73.7	8	29	32.6	8
Other ASEAN											
Malaysia	1,940	n.a.	7.3	n.a.	n.a.	n.a.	n.a.	22	45	555.1	4
Philippines	630	7.5	–0.3	25	109	8,424	140.6	8	62	73.2	7
Thailand	1,000	11.2	6.8	24	141	11,543	211.8	13	52	150.8	17
Other Asia											
India	340	4.5	8.3	19	59	43,331	53.1	26	73	13.1	25
Korea	3,600	18.7	13.5	32	291	42,286	1,006.8	28	93	1,344.0	22
Other Oil Exporters											
Mexico	1,760	7.4	0.2	26	289	36,381	434.7	14	55	135.7	2
Nigeria	290	14.6	–2.9	18	53	5,196	47.2	n.a.	2	1.3	0
Lower middle-income countries	1,380	7.9	2.4	25	179	225,539	304.1	n.a.	46	107.1	7

Source: World Bank, *World Development Report 1990*, Washington, DC.
[a]In some cases data refer to one year earlier than that indicated.

The country has experienced apparently wild swings in policy orientation, from the nationalist xenophobia of the early 1960s to a very open
and liberal regime at the end of that decade. Similarly the grandiose
plans of the early 1980s were quickly replaced by a successful return to
liberalism a few years later. Nevertheless, it is important not to lose sight
of continuities throughout this period: the policy framework has always
contained powerful elements of both pragmatism and *dirigisme* (not to
say autarchy), and which of these is in the ascendancy is often determined by exogenous factors, particularly the price of petroleum.

The political economy of industrial policy-making in the New Order
has yet to be written, although political scientists are now providing
valuable insights.[14] Certainly the *Repelita* provide little guidance, other
than to general policy thrusts which are in any case obvious to observers
of the Jakarta scene.[15] Industrial policy priorities tend to be couched in
vague and all-embracing terms, encompassing the usual range of objectives from regional dispersal to small enterprise development. But the
explicit weighting of goals and trade-offs is rarely explored, and production targets are at best indicative. Several of the plans have been overtaken by external events. *Repelita II* was substantially formulated before
the massive oil price increases of 1973 widened the government's
options, while the grand plans of *Repelita IV* were aborted by the sharp
decline in the terms of trade in 1983–6.

At the risk of great oversimplification, industrial policy-making interest groups in Indonesia may be represented schematically as a triangle,
with contending groups each vying for the support of the ultimate
arbiter, the president. First, there is one often labelled the 'technocrats',
comprising a group of officials in the Department of Finance and
Bappenas, many affiliated with the University of Indonesia who, while
often mistakenly labelled libertarians, tend to favour a market-oriented
regime. Secondly, there are those who might be termed the 'nationalists',
located in key ministries (such as Industry and Trade) and the powerful
State Secretariat, together with vocal components of the press, who
favour regulation, protection, and more import substitution. A crude
view of the thinking of this group might be that it has been captured by
vested producer interests. While this may be accurate in certain circumstances, it fails to recognize the deep mistrust of a *laissez-faire* philosophy in many influential quarters of Indonesia, borne out of the colonial
experience, the vestiges of pre-1966 ideology, and misgivings at the
extent of non-*pribumi* (mainly Chinese) domination of much of the
modern sector of the economy.[16] The third, somewhat amorphous,
group features elements of the first two but is distinguished by its ad-
vocacy of a bold and adventurous strategy emphasizing government
support for large technology-intensive projects designed to overcome
Indonesia's perceived 'backwardness'. This group has come to be
defined in terms of its key personalities rather than its institutional bases:
the awe-inspiring but ultimately flawed vision of Pertamina's Ibnu
Sutowo in the mid-1970s (McCawley, 1978); the ambitious plans of
A.R. Soehoed, a Minister and key industrial policy-maker for much of

the New Order (see Soehoed, 1988, for a reflection on his policy experiences); and most recently the key role of the brilliant Minister for Research and Technology, Dr Habibie, in promoting his 'high tech' vision. All three individuals derived their authority from strong presidential connections (particularly Sutowo and Habibie)[17] which facilitated generous financial support for their projects; all shared an impatience with the cautious ways of the technocrats; and all three have had a grand vision of an Indonesian industrial super-state transcending the more modest goals of the nationalists.

The shape of this industrial policy-making triangle has altered radically in the last 25 years. A nationalist and 'think big' ascendancy during the two oil booms has given way to a stronger role for the technocrats both during the Pertamina debacle of 1976 and in the liberal era since 1985. It is possible that the very success of the export drive of the late 1980s in engineering Indonesia's integration into the international economy has altered the political economy triangle irrevocably. For the first time in Indonesia's history, a powerful export lobby has emerged, from which the major demand on government—apart from rent-seeking activity associated with controls over the export of unprocessed primary products—is a commercial environment designed to enhance international competitiveness. Whereas trade and business regulations were the key to commercial success in the 1970s, the new concerns are the exchange rate, import and export procedures, and social and physical infrastructure. The policy levers—licences, controls, protection—under the jurisdiction of the Department of Industry are now much less relevant. The rapidly changing circumstances brought about by the technocrats are forcing the hand of the Department, from a posture of paternalism and protection to one of promotion. In the late 1980s there was an evident change of heart at very senior levels within the Department, although such a reorientation was far less obvious among the middle-level echelons and within the Department of Trade.

Trade and Regulatory Policies

Indonesia's trade and regulatory policy regimes have long been the *béte noire* of liberal economists, and many detailed studies—often under foreign sponsorship—have been undertaken, of the trade regime in particular.[18] The intensity of these interventions reached their peak in the early 1980s and, although there have been major reforms since, the system still impedes the development of an efficient and outward-looking manufacturing sector.

Once Indonesia's parlous economic circumstances became evident in the mid-1980s and the technocrats reasserted their supremacy, the government has moved, in an increasingly decisive fashion, to reform the chaotic system of incentives and regulations through the series of packages described in previous chapters.

In addition, the government has introduced a number of other reforms to the trade and regulatory environment. The annual licensing list issued by the Capital Investment Co-ordinating Board (Badan Koordinasi Penanaman Modal, BKPM) has been progressively simplified, and now takes the form of a *Daftar Negatif* (Negative List) specifying areas closed to foreign firms, and domestic enterprises licensed with the Board. All sectors not listed are automatically open, in contrast to the previous annual *Daftar Skala Prioritas* (Investment Priority List), which listed only those fields open to foreign firms. Foreign investment regulations have also been liberalized, in terms of the minimum investment requirements, the pace of localization, the areas of permitted entry, and domestic distribution arrangements; 100 per cent foreign ownership remains prohibited, however, except for the special case of Batam Island. Beginning gradually in 1987 the government has begun to tackle the problems of the huge and largely inefficient state enterprise sector, through a range of privatization and other reform measures, the impact of which remain, however, quite limited. Accompanying these changes has been an effectively managed exchange rate regime. The large devaluations of April 1983 and September 1986 have not been eroded by inflation, and the managed downward float since then has consolidated these gains. Consequently, however the real effective exchange rate is measured, there is no doubt that it fell significantly during the decade.[19] Above all else, the exchange rate and the drawback facility have been the two principal factors underlying the dramatic growth in footloose manufactured exports.[20] With these initiatives, exporters were able to capitalize on a propitious external environment, including the loss of comparative advantage in labour-intensive activities among the Asian NIEs, emerging infrastructure constraints in Thailand, and political instability in the Philippines (and more recently in China).

Nevertheless, these important developments need to be seen in proper perspective. In spite of the reforms to the trade regime, many of its undesirable features persist. Half of the non-oil manufacturing sector is still covered by NTBs, as is 55 per cent of tradable goods output, according to the most recent estimates prepared by Wymenga (1990) (Table 7.6). Average effective protection rates for non-oil manufacturing remain very high. However, it is not so much the high average effective protection which is the problem—a uniform protective rate is, after all, equivalent in its effects to a 'one-sided' devaluation—but the extreme dispersion in rates and the continuing lack of transparency in the regime. Manufacturing as a whole is protected at the expense of agriculture, and export-competing sectors are penalized as compared to import-competing activities. Within manufacturing, even at the highly aggregated 2-digit ISIC classification, average effective rates vary from negative to 150 per cent. Disaggregating further, an alarming number of industries receive very high protection (an effective protection rate or EPR in excess of 100 per cent in 38 out of the 87 activities identified as manufacturing in the input–output table); many of these receive extraordinary protection, in excess of 300 per cent (Table 7.6).

The effects of the system of protection are obvious enough.

TABLE 7.6
Estimates of Effective Protection, 1989[a]

	(1) Sectoral Averages	
	Effective Rates (per cent)	Coverage of Non-tariff Barriers (per cent)
Agriculture	13.9	58.2
Mining (incl. oil)	− 0.7	74.9
Non-oil manufacturing	63.6	50.8
All tradables	15.0	55.1
Import-competing sectors	44.4	
Export-competing sectors	− 6.4	

	(2) Major Industrial Sectors EPR (per cent)
Food, beverages, tobacco	149.5
Textiles, clothing, footwear	66.6
Wood products	− 4.5
Paper products	20.2
Chemicals	33.9
Oil and gas	− 1.2
Non-metallic products	89.7
Basic metals	10.7
Engineering	147.1
Other manufacturing	77.4

(3) Extremely high protection (EPR > 300%): processed meat, processed fish, wheat flours, other flours, bread, chocolate and confectionary, non-alcoholic beverages, cigarettes, footwear, wooden building materials, furniture, cleansers and cosmetics, tyres, plastic wares, ceramics, electrical machinery, household electricals, batteries, motor vehicle and assembly, and motor-cycle assembly.

(4) Negative protection (EPR < 0): vegetable and animal oil, other milled cereals, processed tea, leather, sawn and processed wood, printing and publishing, oil refining, LNG, rubber processing, and shipbuilding.

Source: Wymenga, 1990: Tables 1, 3, 4, and A.1.
[a]Sectoral averages weighted by 1987 value added at unassisted prices.

Dispersions in effective rates of this order distort the allocation of productive resources within and between sectors. Many of the industries which receive high protection are activities in which Indonesia does not possess a comparative advantage (for example, some engineering and capital goods industries), while other industries in which Indonesia has the capacity to be internationally competitive, especially the resource-based activities, receive negative protection. Import-competing activities are greatly assisted at the expense of exports. That the dispersion in effective rates has no economic rationale is illustrated by significant differences in closely related activities—for example, rubber processing 'receives' 2.9 per cent, whereas tyres and tubes have a rate of 600 per cent. Moreover, the resort to non-tariff barriers (NTBs) and the wide variations in protection have created a highly politicized, rent-seeking entrepreneurial environment, in which access to bureaucratic facilities rather than entrepreneurial talent is a major determinant of commercial success.

But while much remains to be done, the above assessment may be excessively gloomy. Exporting sectors, as noted, have been placed on a free trade footing, a measure not fully captured in the estimates of Table 7.6. The incidence and intensity of NTBs have fallen quite sharply. And, although Indonesia does not yet have a mechanism for public exposure of protection policies, such as an independent Industries Commission, countervailing pressures to the rampant and chaotic system of incentives which developed in the early 1980s are now more powerful: the weight of influential intellectual opinion in favour of reform is now considerable, buttressed by the careful documentation referred to in footnote 16, and the new export industries have developed quickly into a vocal lobby against excessive protectionism.

Progress in the general area of business licensing and regulation during the 1980s has been substantial but uneven. The controversial and still unpublished report by McCawley (1983) remains the most comprehensive scrutiny of the issues and, although now rather dated, many of the principal findings remain valid. The licensing regime has three main undesirable features. First, it is costly—procedures are time-consuming and unclear, and many trivial approvals and signatures are required. This imposes a direct burden on firms, who frequently engage staff simply to expedite the processing of these licensing requirements. Secondly, the effects of the regulatory regime are sometimes unpredictable. Implementation varies across different tiers of government and between key officials; different departments or agencies may issue conflicting edicts. Thirdly, the effects of regulations often bear little relationship to the initial objectives, and the rationale for many requirements is unclear. Capacity constraints may be imposed, for example, to prevent 'excessive competition', while safety and environmental concerns are largely neglected. The regulatory apparatus of course impinges mainly on the factory sector, and cottage industry activities remain essentially unregulated.

Two major improvements in the licensing regime occurred after 1984. First, as noted, NTBs have been gradually replaced by tariffs, and the restrictiveness of existing barriers diluted. This constituted a major step towards a simplified, less politicized regulatory system. Secondly, the BKPM's procedures have become simpler, faster, and more transparent. Foreign investment projects which previously might have taken 18 months to get off the ground can now be operating in about half that time—still slow compared to Singapore or even Thailand, but a considerable improvement. Since the 1984 tax reform, BKPM incentives are minimal and many domestic firms, for which Board licensing is not essential, now just obtain a licence from the Department of Industry, a much simpler procedure.

However, the government has yet to undertake a sweeping reform of the licensing regime, and an assessment of the system during the 1980s needs to balance these improvements against regression or inactivity elsewhere. The backtracking has occurred principally in the area of export regulation, where measures introduced ostensibly for economic or environmental reasons (enhanced domestic processing or conservation of resources) have often been captured by business groups who view the future commercial potential as lying in the export sector rather than the import-competing industries which were the focus of their activities before 1985. Examples of these regulations include timber, rattan, certain grades of rubber, some fish products, raw skins and hides, and some coconut products. There can be little doubt that appropriate fiscal measures and vigorous supervision would be a more effective means of securing economic and environmental objectives. Government regulation of export industries subject to international quotas has also been a contentious issue, particularly in the case of textiles and clothing, where quota allocation mechanisms have been slow, opaque, and (it is widely alleged) corrupt. There are many additional instances where little progress has been achieved. One recent and topical issue is landownership titles, which has become important as industrial estates have moved out of the traditional city and fringe-urban locations in Java and a few centres in the Outer Islands in search of cheaper land prices. Problems have arisen not only in the co-ordination of industrial infrastructure services associated with this expansion, but in establishing clear tenure rights. The BKPM has often been powerless to assist investors in this regard and a number of acrimonious land disputes have broken out, particularly in West Java.[21] Nevertheless, the rapid growth of industrial estates since the mid-1980s may ameliorate some of these obstacles in time.

Ownership: Who Owns What?

Ownership has been an ever-present issue in Indonesia's industrialization policies since 1966, perhaps less prominent than in Malaysia under its New Economic Policy but certainly more important than in neighbouring Thailand or the Philippines. In the mid-1960s, the state owned or controlled the 'commanding heights' of what little manufacturing there was. The liberal policies of the early New Order years, reinforced by investment incentives and laws introduced in 1967 and 1968 for foreign and domestic enterprise respectively, overturned this strategy, although many of the foreign firms nationalized between 1957 and 1964 remained in state hands. This private sector dominance was profoundly affected by the oil booms of the 1970s which resulted in a resurgence of nationalist sentiment and had two important effects on ownership patterns: rapidly rising government revenues provided the funds for ambitious government investment projects, and the early imperative to attract foreign capital quickly gave way to a quite restrictive foreign investment code. The recession of the early to mid-1980s witnessed another significant change in the policy environment, which by the late 1980s again resembled the liberal code that had prevailed 20 years earlier. The very success of the reforms after 1985 produced what appears in 1990 to be yet another change in direction. Concern that *pribumi* business groups, apart from the well-connected, are not sharing in the new commercial opportunities prompted the president to urge owners—almost entirely Chinese—of the large business conglomerates to ensure adequate participation in and ownership of their firms by co-operatives.

The policy environment has resulted in a larger state enterprise sector and a smaller foreign ownership share than in many neighbouring countries (Table 7.7), but ownership patterns can be explained quite accurately by the interplay of 'policy' and 'industrial economic' factors. In 1988 firms which were partially or wholly state-owned generated an extraordinary 44 per cent of manufacturing value added among firms in the factory sector (that is, firms employing 20 or more workers).[22] Much of this derives from their involvement in oil refining and gas processing (the latter with foreign partners), but even for non-oil manufacturing their share is nearly 25 per cent. Although represented in most major industry groupings, they are especially prominent in activities considered to be 'strategic' by the government—basic metals (steel and alumina), basic chemicals (fertilizer), cement, paper products, and machine goods. The high share for food products (ISIC 311) is explained by sugar processing, an industry bequeathed to the New Order government from the nationalizations of 1957/8. Other instances of a large government presence include slaughtering, tea processing, miscellaneous tobacco products, repair of electrical equipment, shipbuilding, and 'other transport equipment' (mainly aircraft)—all comparatively small industries. The industrial location of these state enterprises illustrates the accuracy of Thee and Yoshihara's (1987: 343) characterization of manufacturing ownership patterns as one of 'upstream socialism, downstream capitalism'.

Foreign firms occupy a modest position in Indonesian manufacturing, although their importance is understated in Table 7.7. In some instances, for example automobile assembly after 1974, foreign equity participation is prohibited but foreign partners play a key role through technology licensing and other arrangements. Indeed, there is hardly a large firm which has not had some type of contractual relationship with a foreign party since 1966, such has been Indonesian businesses' weak technological capacity and limited commercial experience. The links ranged from intense equity and technological ties with prominent Japanese multinationals to occasional marketing assistance from a cousin in Hong Kong. Abstracting from the investment regulatory regime, foreign investors' shares are broadly consistent with the postulates of the industrial economics theory of foreign investment, especially at the finer levels of industrial classification. In particular, the interplay of technology advantages, ownership of brand names, and superior international marketing expertise generally explains above-average foreign

TABLE 7.7
Ownership by Major Industry Group, 1985[a]
(percentage of each industry's output)

	Industry	Private	Government[b]	Foreign
311 }	Food products	53.9	36.7	9.4
312		53.8	18.6	27.6
313	Beverages	39.2	34.2	26.6
314	Tobacco	95.9	0.8	3.3
321	Textiles	68.1	7.1	24.8
322	Garments	98.0	0.2	1.8
323	Leather products	99.1	0.9	0
324	Footwear	86.9	0.2	12.9
331	Wood products	83.3	3.7	13.0
332	Furniture	91.8	1.8	6.4
341	Paper products	50.2	10.1	39.7
342	Printing and publishing	64.4	24.3	11.3
351	Basic chemicals	14.6	72.6	12.8
352	Other chemicals	54.6	7.8	38.6
353/4	Oil and gas processing	0	100	0
355	Rubber products	47.5	34.9	17.6
356	Plastics	91.2	0.3	8.5
361	Pottery and china	76.3	0.5	23.2
362	Glass products	88.5	3.6	7.9
363	Cement	24.8	61.5	13.7
364	Structural clay products	91.4	1.5	7.1
369	Other non-metallic minerals	95.9	4.1	0
37	Basic metals	6.0	89.1	4.9
381	Metal products	50.8	22.4	26.8
382	Non-electric machinery	31.9	31.0	37.1
383	Electrical equipment	59.9	13.8	26.3
384	Transport equipment	59.0	13.8	27.2
385	Prof. equipment	77.0	0	23.0
39	Miscellaneous	88.3	0.2	11.5
Total				
	excl. oil and gas	59.1	24.2	16.7
	incl. oil and gas	43.8	43.8	12.4

Source: BPS, unpublished data.
[a] Refers to firms with a workforce of at least 20 employees.
[b] Includes all firms with a government equity.

ownership. The former is significant in industries such as 'spinning' (mostly synthetic fibres), certain chemicals, sheet glass, agricultural equipment, batteries, electrical equipment, and motor cycles, while brand names are of relevance for 'white' cigarettes, breweries, pharmaceuticals, and musical instruments. In the recent export drive, foreign firms have played an important facilitating role in industries such as footwear, where industries have been transplanted from the high-wage NIEs, transferring with them knowledge of international marketing channels.

Private firms, mostly Chinese-owned among the larger enterprises, have generally prospered under the New Order. They have always been the major source of employment, even during the socialist 'Guided Economy' period, and in the 1980s they provided about three-quarters of employment in the factory sector. These firms are, on average, considerably smaller than other firms, and generally less capital-intensive, but the differentials are narrowing, indicative of Indonesia's more 'even' industrial structure. As would be expected, they are relatively more important in labour-intensive, low-skill activities where scale economies are less important. Examples include food processing (apart from sugar and dairy products), garments, leather products, furniture, wood products, printing and publishing, rubber products (apart from tyres and tubes), ceramics, bricks and tiles, and miscellaneous manufactures.

Normative dimensions of the ownership and control of Indonesian industry are much more controversial. Contentious aspects of ownership in Indonesian manufacturing include high levels of concentration and the dominant role of newly emerging business conglomerates, debate over the benefits and costs of foreign investment, and the role and performance of state enterprises. Each of these aspects requires brief elaboration.

That Indonesian manufacturing industry is highly concentrated is beyond dispute (Hill, 1990b: Table 6; Hill, 1987: Tables 1–5). According to the 1986 Census, in 19 per cent of industries, generating 28 per cent of non-oil manufacturing output, the four largest plants produced at least 70 per cent of industry output; the inclusion of the oil and gas industry almost doubles the share of highly concentrated industries, to 54 per cent of total output. Moreover, these figures understate the true extent of concentration for at least two reasons. First, the measures are taken at *plant* level, and so multi-plant operations are generally enumerated separately. Secondly, Indonesia's modern corporate economy is increasingly dominated by a number of large conglomerates with widely dispersed activities in industry and commerce. Estimates of the size of these conglomerates are subject to a wide margin of error, but the Jakarta business press has produced some broad orders of magnitude (see, for example, *Warta Ekonomi*, 31 July 1989). Notwithstanding the data limitations, the picture is most illuminating. These groups are very large: the two biggest, Salim (Liem) and Astra, rank with the major corporations of East Asia and control several hundred firms; the Salim group has sales comparable to those of the giant Pertamina complex. They are also very diversified, the larger ones in particular having interests in many branches of manufacturing, together with plantations, finance, trading, and real estate. Most also have substantial offshore investments in the Asia–Pacific region, especially Singapore and Hong Kong. A third important feature is ownership. All the really big concerns are non-*pribumi* (Chinese) owned, a fact of considerable political significance in light of frequent and vocal exhortations that the government should be seen to be doing more to assist *pribumi* entrepreneurship. The owners of most of these huge conglomerates have close personal ties with the President and senior figures in the New

Order, in many cases dating back to the pre-1966 era. It is therefore no exaggeration to state that a dozen or so of these groups, in combination with a few large state and foreign enterprises, dominate much of Indonesia's 'modern sector' economy.

It is virtually impossible to detect trends in the significance of these conglomerates in Indonesian business. The very large firms have been expanding aggressively since the economic reforms began in 1985. Equally, however, new enterprises are emerging, some of which are *pribumi*. Although generally not in the big league, 10 of the top 40 domestic private groups identified by *Warta Ekonomi* are *pribumi*, all but three in the bottom half of the ranking. Many have impeccable New Order political credentials, such as Bimantara, Nugra Santana (owned by the Ibnu Sutowo family), and Hanurata (based around the well-known foundation, *Yayasan Harapan Kita*).

Does the rise of mega-corporations matter? The answer is probably 'no' in economic terms but possibly 'yes' politically. To compete in international markets, larger corporate structures are generally desirable—there are economies of scale in finance, marketing know-how, and technology which these conglomerates are able to internalize, and they may be able to negotiate with foreign partners more effectively from a position of strength. Moreover, apart from the very big entities—such as Liem and Astra—most of these conglomerates are not large by international standards, certainly not when compared to the Korean *chaebol* or the huge Japanese groups. Finally, the nascent stock market might have an ameliorating influence on this trend towards concentration, although its capitalization is still small and its holdings not widely diffused. Against these positive features must be counted two concerns. First, the most effective competition policy in the face of highly concentrated ownership is an open, transparent trade regime. As we have seen, the Indonesian regime possesses neither of these attributes, and many of the highly concentrated industries also receive high protection. Secondly, the prominence of so many huge corporations, almost all owned and controlled by the Chinese, poses a political problem for the government. Asset redistribution is generally a clumsy, arbitrary, and ineffective means of achieving equity goals, but the political imperative to demonstrate the government's 'pro-*pribumi*' credentials is forcing the government's hand in 1990, just as in 1974.

Foreign firms occupy a surprisingly modest position in Indonesian manufacturing, at least in terms of equity investments, for a number of reasons: the regulatory regime and the prominence of state enterprises; the reluctance of foreign firms to invest in Indonesia in the aftermath of the Sukarno era and during the period of restrictive policies from 1974 to 1986; and perhaps even cultural and historical factors which have enabled local firms to compete effectively with foreign corporations in industries of traditional MNC dominance such as cigarettes and cosmetics.[23]

Nevertheless, foreign (and domestic) investment approvals began to rise steeply in the late 1980s, and something of a boom mentality developed, hastened by the range of deregulation measures, by the strong performance of non-oil exports, by the spectacular growth of the stock market, and by diminished investment opportunities elsewhere in the region. For example, foreign investment approvals rose more than three-fold between 1986 and 1989, from 93 to 294 projects, and the total for the first half of 1990 was some 70 per cent of the 1989 figure. In value terms, the increase was much faster still, with that for the first half of 1990 nearly equal to the 1989 value. (Equally sharp rises were recorded for domestic investments.) Even though these BKPM data are at best approximate, they demonstrate strong investor interest. Moreover, the rise in export-oriented projects among both groups of investors is unmistakable. Some 75 per cent of foreign investment projects (and 71 per cent of domestic investments) approved from 1988 to mid-1990 intended to export at least 70 per cent of their output, up from about 25 per cent in 1986–7. That this trend is closely related to the relocation of industrial activity from the high-wage Asian NIEs is revealed by the fact that these four states constituted 70 per cent of approvals in the sensitive textile, garment, and footwear category in 1989.

Among foreign investors, Japanese firms have been of paramount importance, accounting for over 70 per cent of the total (Table 7.8[24]— this excludes the large 'multi-country' group), so that one is tempted to conclude that the history of foreign investment in Indonesia's industrialization since 1966 is synonymous with the extraordinary growth of the Japanese presence. Japanese firms are prominent in virtually all sectors which have received major foreign investments. They led the foreign entry into the textile industry from the late 1960s, and have played a key role in the establishment of basic metals and engineering industries. Strong economic complementarities and a web of political, aid, and strategic ties have underpinned this key position.

None of the other investors is of much significance. Investments from the United States and Germany, two leading global investors, are quite insignificant (although the former has a large stake in the oil and gas industries); the large Belgium share is explained by this country's involvement in the Krakatau steel complex; Hong Kong is the leading 'developing country' investor, figuring prominently in food, textiles, and paper and wood products, followed by Korea. The data do not capture the recent surge in Taiwanese investment in export-oriented light manufactures, although in any case country nationalities for the three 'Chinese' NIEs are not always accurate (Wells, 1983, and Wells and Warren, 1979). There has yet to be a systematic study of the substantial 'multi-country' group, some of which are thought to be Hong Kong–British joint ventures domiciled in the city-state, and some to be motivated by a desire to preserve corporate flexibility if country discrimination reappears as a feature of Indonesia's foreign investment regulatory environment.

This is not the place to examine the benefits and costs of foreign

TABLE 7.8

Major Foreign Investors in Manufacturing, 1967–1989[a]

Sector	Total		Major Investors[b] (and percentage of total)		
	$ million	Per Cent	I	II	III
Food products	179.3	(4.1)	Hong Kong (28.3)	Japan (23.9)	Switzerland (14.4)
Textiles	618.9	(14.3)	Japan (64.0)	Multi-country (19.8)	Hong Kong (12.0)
Wood products	57.1	(1.3)	Hong Kong (36.4)	Korea (32.6)	Japan (20.1)
Paper products	57.2	(1.3)	Hong Kong (41.6)	Taiwan (17.8)	Multi-country (17.3)
Chemicals	669.9	(15.4)	Multi-country (35.5)	Japan (16.3)	USA (15.3)
Non-metallic minerals	510.7	(11.8)	Multi-country (48.0)	Japan (46.1)	USA (3.2)
Basic metals	1,838.7	(42.3)	Japan (84.5)	Belgium (13.6)	Multi-country (1.0)
Metal goods	404.6	(9.3)	Japan (58.7)	USA (10.9)	Germany (7.8)
Other	6.5	(0.1)	UK (33.8)	Japan (27.7)	Germany (18.5)
Total	4,342.7	(100)	Japan (60.1)	Multi-country (15.7)	Belgium (6.2)

Source: Bank Indonesia.

[a] Data refer to realized foreign investment through to June 1989, and include equity and loan capital. Oil processing and LNG are excluded.

[b] Major foreign investors, excluding the 'multi-country' group which comprises 15.7 per cent of the total, include Japan (70.5 per cent of the 'non multi-country' group), Belgium (7.3 per cent), USA (6.1 per cent), Hong Kong (6.0 per cent), Germany (2.3 per cent), Holland (2.2 per cent), Korea (1.5 per cent), Switzerland (1.1 per cent), United Kingdom (1.1 per cent), and Australia (0.9 per cent).

investment in Indonesian manufacturing in any detail. Clearly, Indonesia's rapid industrialization would have been impossible without the infusion of new technologies, products and processes, and marketing and managerial expertise. Since the country's technological base was so underdeveloped in 1965, a strategy of 'technological self-reliance' would have been very costly and in any case incompatible with moves towards a more liberal economy. Whether Indonesia has adopted the 'right' channels for importing these skills (Thee, 1990), and how substantial are the costs of foreign ownership, are more complex issues. Critics of foreign investment in Indonesia maintain that foreign firms have exacerbated employment problems, owing to their introduction of capital-intensive technologies, and that they have promoted uneven spatial development by locating in the two major industrial centres of Java (Jakarta and Surabaya and their surrounds) and a few resource-based 'enclaves' in the Outer Islands. Some also point to the alleged 'closed management' styles of foreign, particularly Japanese, firms, to the high cost of royalties and other exactions of foreign partners, and to the limited extent of technology transfer. Many of these assertions remain untested empirically, however, and in any case nationalist critiques of foreign investment in Indonesia and elsewhere often attach more importance to non-economic considerations. Perhaps the most significant economic criticism of foreign investment in Indonesia should be directed towards the commercial policy regime which, through high and uneven protection, has induced foreign capital to enter inefficient industries and to appropriate the rents created by a lack of competition from abroad (and domestically also in some instances). Prior to the major tax reform of 1984, a similar criticism could be directed at the costly but ineffective range of incentives offered to foreign investors. Tax incentives are now minimal, apart from special arrangements for Batam and eastern Indonesia.

An evaluation of the state enterprise sector also raises issues too complex for consideration in this paper (see Pangestu and Habir, 1989, for a recent overview of major issues). The two dominant and inter-related features of these firms are their generally poor performance and the wide range of objectives to which they are assigned by the government. The evidence on performance is patchy but consistent. Unpublished data from the Department of Finance indicate that the rate of return on capital for all state enterprises was a low 3 per cent in the mid-1980s. That for firms controlled by the Department of Industry was somewhat lower (in most years over this period in the range 2.5–2.8 per cent), while the 'Non-Department' group—principally those under Dr Habibie's control—returned less than 0.5 per cent in 1985 and 1986. Even these figures are almost certainly an overstatement of the real return, in view of the plethora of open and hidden subsidies these firms receive. Micro, firm-level studies, generally dated, strongly reinforce this conclusion.[25]

But this outcome needs to be assessed in light of the range of non-economic objectives under which these firms must labour, including prestige, technological mastery (aircraft), state control of 'strategic' industries (oil and gas processing), regional development (certain cement plants), price restraint, assistance for small-scale producers (for example, the *bapak angkat* (foster parent) scheme in textiles), and, over-riding all of these, the encouragement of *pribumi* participation in the modern economy. Moreover, these firms are saddled with formidable operating restrictions, regarding labour recruitment, salary structures, capital investments, location, and product mix. Many operate as 'pro-duction units' attached to a central bureaucratic apparatus, lacking the autonomy and flexibility of their private sector competitors. In view of these constraints, their poor performance is hardly surprising.

By the late 1980s it was obvious that these firms were on the govern-ment's reform agenda. But thoroughgoing reform is and will be a difficult process: the country can ill afford to have such a large portion of its manufacturing sector performing so badly, yet the government is mindful of the potential political backlash of extending foreign and non-*pribumi* control of the corporate sector. Management contracts or partial divestment, which improve efficiency through greater commercial autonomy while preserving the 'façade' of state control, may be the most promising solution.

Spatial Patterns of Industrialization

Indonesia is an extraordinarily diverse country, in its demography, eco-logy, and economy, and this is nowhere better illustrated than in its industrial development. Much of the nation's large industrial base is located in Java, complemented by several enormous resource-based developments in Sumatra and Kalimantan. Equally, however, large parts of the Outer Islands, including much of Kalimantan and virtually all of the eastern provinces, could aptly be described as a non-industrial eco-nomy. Three important questions need to be addressed in examining these spatial patterns of industrialization. Which are the major regional industrial centres, and how has their role changed since 1966? What factors—policy, comparative advantage, or other—explain the structure of industry in these major centres? And, related to the second, what have been the principal policies affecting spatial industrialization?[26]

Java dominates Indonesia's non-oil manufacturing economy, gen-erating almost three-quarters of value added among large and medium firms according to the 1986 Census (Table 7.9). The major province, West Java, contributes over one-third of this total, and its industrial out-put exceeds that of the entire Outer Islands. Moreover, the combined Jakarta–West Java figure is over 45 per cent of the national total, in-dicative of the very high level of spatial concentration in Indonesia. What might be termed 'Greater Jakarta'—the city itself plus the sur-rounding *kabupaten*, the city of Bogor and the Cilegon complex to the west—produced about 36 per cent of the nation's non-oil industrial out-put in 1985.[27] These two provinces and the other major industrial region, East Java, account for two-thirds of the total; Java's three big cities, Jakarta, Surabaya, and Bandung and their surrounds generate some 54 per cent of the total. No other province is of much significance. Central Java/Yogyakarta is surprisingly small—only about one-sixth of the Jakarta–West Java total and not much larger than the most industrialized province outside Java, North Sumatra. Indeed, Java's industrialization appears to be evolving towards a bipolar pattern of development centred around Jakarta and Surabaya. Apart from North Sumatra, the provinces of some note outside Java are East Kalimantan with its huge fertilizer installation and its plywood industry, South Sumatra (fertilizer and rubber processing), and Riau, a substantial part of which is in the much-vaunted rival to Singapore, Batam Island.

The inclusion of oil alters these figures dramatically (Table 7.9). East Kalimantan, with its LNG and oil-refining facilities, actually produces more manufacturing value added than any other province, followed by West Java, East Java, and Aceh, the other LNG producer. While it is appropriate to include these oil and LNG installations in each province's regional output, their impact on and links to the local economy are very limited, apart from some downstream linkages (fertilizer plants in each province), the spin-offs to the construction industry in the establishment phase, and minor contributions to the local government revenue base. These investments are immensely capital-intensive, which explains why the employment shares of the two provinces (and Riau and South Sumatra also) are much smaller than their share of national output. The converse is the case for the other 'oil province', Central Java, the site of the Cilacap complex, because this region has long been the heartland of small industry in Indonesia.

Notwithstanding the Jakarta–Surabaya concentrations, a frequently overlooked feature of industrialization in the New Order is that a measure of industrial dispersal has been achieved. Java's share of non-oil manufacturing output (among large and medium firms) has been declining, from approximately 83 per cent in 1963 to 81 and 74 per cent respectively in 1974 and 1985. If time series data for the oil and gas sector were available, the recorded decline would have been sharper still. A decline of a similar order of magnitude has been recorded in employment shares also. Most of the increase in the Outer Islands' share is attributable to the rise of Kalimantan, due to the enormous fertilizer plant and the timber boom. Sumatra, also, has experienced a modest increase. In many cases, of course, these provinces lack industrial 'depth', in the sense that a small number of firms dominate provincial industrial output.[28]

Spatial variations in industrial composition largely reflect differences in relative factor endowments. In particular, resource-based activities predominate in the Outer Islands, while Java is the repository of most of the nation's footloose industry (Table 7.9, columns 4 and 5). Indeed, such activities are insignificant outside Java: Kalimantan has its oil, gas, and fertilizer plants, and little else besides timber and rubber processing;

TABLE 7.9
Spatial Patterns of Industrialization, 1985

Region/Province	Percentage of National Total[a]			Major Industries[b] (Percentage of Regional/Provincial Output)	
	Output		Employment, L+M+S	I	II
	L+M excl. Oil/LNG	L+M+S incl. Oil/LNG			
SUMATRA	14.4			311 : 22	355 : 16
incl. oil/LNG		24.4	12.0	353/4 : 52	311 : 11
Aceh	1.8			351 : 46	352 : 29
incl. LNG		11.1	1.0	353/4 : 84	351 : 17
North Sumatra	5.1			311 : 32	371 : 17
incl. oil		3.4	4.9	311 : 31	371 : 17
Riau	2.0			381 : 28	331 : 27
incl. oil		4.3	1.2	353/4 : 65	381 : 10
South Sumatra	2.4			351 : 46	355 : 17
incl. oil		3.5	2.0	353/4 : 50	351 : 23
Lampung	1.6	1.0	1.3	311 : 49	355 : 26
JAVA	74.4			321 : 14	314 : 12
incl. oil		53.5	78.2	321 : 9	353/4 : 8
Jakarta	18.7	12.1	12.2	384 : 17	352 : 14
West Java	26.9	16.8	21.0	371 : 21	321 : 20
Central Java/Yogyakarta	7.6			321 : 32	311 : 15
incl. oil		11.1	21.63	353/4 : 46	321 : 17
East Java	21.1	13.5	23.4	314 : 37	311 : 17

KALIMANTAN	7.5				
incl. oil/LNG		19.5	4.9	331 : 59	351 : 21
West Kalimantan	1.8	1.1	1.0	353/4 : 68	331 : 19
South Kalimantan	1.9	1.1	1.2	331 : 71	355 : 27
East Kalimantan	3.1			331 : 52	355 : 43
incl. oil/LNG		16.8	1.9	351 : 49	331 : 47
SULAWESI	2.5	1.8	2.5	353/4 : 84	351 : 8
EASTERN INDONESIA[c]	1.2	0.9	2.4	384 : 51	311 : 23
INDONESIA	100	100	100	331 : 66	311 : 11
incl. oil/LNG				353/4 : 28	314 : 12
excl. oil/LNG				314 : 17	321 : 12

Source: BPS, unpublished data.

[a]'Output' refers to value added; 'L+M' to large and medium firms (those employing at least 20 workers); 'L+M+S' to large, medium, and small firms (those employing at least five workers).

[b]Data refer to percentage of regional/provincial value added among large and medium firms. Industries are as defined in Table 7.7. For example, '384 : 17' for Jakarta in column I indicates that transport equipment is the largest industry, generating 17 per cent of value among large and medium firms.

[c]Includes Bali, West and East Nusa Tenggara, East Timor, Maluku, and Irian Jaya.

in Sumatra, the dominant activities are oil refining, gas, fertilizer, cement, aluminium, rubber processing, a few metal workshops catering to the estates, and some timber and food processing (much of the latter in Lampung, based on coffee and tropical fruits, and in North Sumatra, centred around its estates); timber and coconut processing (and a cement factory) now dominate in Sulawesi, while timber is the major activity in Maluku and Irian Jaya. The few exceptions to this pattern of resource-based industries are some small-scale activities which by necessity locate near markets (such as printing and ice manufacture), and special cases: Batam Island, Riau, which is tied increasingly to the Singapore economy, and Bali—whose relative factor endowments are more akin to Java's—with its thriving garment and handicraft activities centred around tourism. Java, too, has its resource-based industries, if they may be termed as such, including steel, located on the mistaken assumption that good-quality iron ore deposits were available in nearby southern Sumatra, and cement factories situated adjacent to the major sources of demand in Jakarta and Surabaya.[29] But footloose industries are more important, including the major textile centres found mainly in the west, the booming *kretek* factories located principally in the east, the 'modern sector' consumer goods industries of Jakarta, and the nascent engineering goods industries around the two large cities.

Regional dispersal of industry has always featured in the government's planning, but implementation of this objective has rarely been a high priority. It is difficult to identify—much less quantify—the impacts of myriad government interventions on spatial patterns of industrialization, but the following appear to be the most important. First, there has been a dramatic improvement in the quantity and quality of physical infrastructure throughout Indonesia since 1966, encompassing land transport, air and sea networks, and public utilities (discussed in Chapter 8). As a result, the business environment has improved markedly and Indonesia's scattered population settlements have become economically integrated as never before. Whether this has exerted a positive effect on the *shares* of industrial output across the nation is more problematic, however. To the extent that the Outer Islands have 'caught up' with Java's hitherto superior amenities, these infrastructure investments would have provided a spur to the former; nevertheless, local industries now receive less 'natural protection' in the form of transport costs, and the reach of Java's factories now extends throughout the archipelago, *dari Sabang ke Merauke.*

Indonesia's complex trade and regulatory regime has also had a mixed but probably centralizing effect on spatial patterns of industrialization. The cascading structure of protection has conferred primary benefit on the footloose consumer durables industries located mainly on Java. The ubiquitous licensing regime, and the consequent need to be near the nation's powerful regulators, has biased industrial location decisions towards Java, and particularly Jakarta. The government's rigid nationwide electricity pricing policies have had a similar effect, since they discriminate against (the mainly Outer Islands) energy-rich provinces.[30] Against these factors, it might be argued that the government's policy of prohibiting the export of unprocessed timber has promoted Outer Islands industrial development, albeit in a perverse, sub-optimal fashion. The optimal fiscal strategy for rent appropriation in these circumstances would be the imposition of tax and lease provisions which maximize government revenues from these resources, consistent with conservation and other objectives. Since almost all of such revenue would accrue to Jakarta, the timber provinces, principally East Kalimantan, have been the unwitting beneficiaries of the current regime, at the cost of reduced national welfare. Another aspect of the government's regulatory regime—BKPM incentives and directives—has had a minimal impact on spatial patterns, although in the past the priority accorded to the goal of regional development was in principle quite considerable.

A third mechanism through which the government has affected spatial patterns is by its own investments. According to the 1986 Census, state enterprises dominate manufacturing in Sumatra and Kalimantan, generating 74 and 82 per cent of these islands' manufacturing output respectively, compared to 30 per cent on Java and much lower shares elsewhere. Excluding oil and gas, Sumatra still has the highest government (and related joint-venture) share, at 32 per cent, although that of Kalimantan falls to slightly below the figure for Java. In the Old Order regime, in particular, state investments were used as a means of diffusing regional discontent with Jakarta's rule. But since 1966 these investments have been undertaken more with a view to fulfilling the government's strategic industrial objectives—the promotion and control of key industries—rather than regional development. Sumatra and Kalimantan, which are fortunate enough to contain the major energy reserves, have been the principal beneficiaries of these investments. That the government has not sought to promote the regions outside Java through direct investments is illustrated by the absence of any significant plants in the poor, 'non-industrial' economies of Sulawesi, Nusa Tenggara, Maluku, and Irian Jaya, apart from two small and poorly performing cement factories near Ujung Pandang and Kupang, and a few other minor investments.

Finally, the government's population redistribution programmes and its centralized structures of finance and authority have had some impact on spatial industrial patterns. The former, through transmigration and through faster implementation of family planning on Java–Bali, have contributed to the growing proportion of the population residing outside Java. Such a redistribution would have had its effects on industry shares, to the extent that the faster growing Outer Island centres are not served entirely by Java's footloose manufacturing industries. The heavily centralized system of government in Indonesia, extending also to the regional finance regime and the management of state enterprises, has probably operated to the benefit of poorer and more remote provinces by guaranteeing them access to central government support. But the cost has been a stifling of regional initiative, and local government, however development-oriented, has very little opportunity to exert a major influence over the course of its region's development.

The net effect of all these interventions has obviously been positive, as revealed by the growing share of the Outer Islands in national manufacturing. But there has been no concerted or consistent strategy of spatial industrial development, and growth patterns outside Java inevitably have been very uneven, clustering around a few large mainly coastal centres, and bypassing the interiors and virtually the entire eastern region.

The Size Distribution of Industry and Employment Growth

Scale is an important issue in Indonesian manufacturing for a number of reasons. First, consistent with Indonesia's past status as an industrial laggard, manufacturing plants are on average quite small, though rising, from just 92 employees for large and medium firms in 1974 to 131 persons in 1985. To the extent that scale economies are important, this small average size constitutes a handicap to efficiency and growth. Secondly, there is some correlation between size and ownership, in the sense that foreign and government joint-venture operations are on average significantly larger than private firms. Consequently, the debate over ownership inevitably spills over into that concerning size. Finally, the promotion of small and cottage industry is a recurrent theme in government plans and strategies. These operations are regarded as important for a variety of economic and non-economic reasons. However, the absence of reliable data, particularly on the vast cottage industry sector, hampers informed analysis and discussion.

The size distribution of Indonesian manufacturing resembles the typical developing country pattern in that larger firms generate most of the output while smaller ones provide most of the employment (Table 7.10). The share of large firms is particularly high if oil and gas are included, but even without this subsector, large firms produced 60 per cent of the output in 1986; large and medium firms together produced almost 80 per cent. By contrast, small and cottage industry absorbed over 60 per cent of the manufacturing workforce, assuming the estimates of 'full-time' equivalent employment in cottage industry are reliable. These employment shares appear to have remained approximately unchanged between industrial censuses. Such employment estimates need to be treated with considerable caution, especially in drawing conclusions regarding trends over time (Table 7.11). It is likely that employment in large and medium firms grew at about 5.6 per cent annually between the two censuses, and perhaps slightly faster among small firms. These rates are very similar to the estimates for total manufacturing employment growth derived from the Intercensal Population Surveys (Supas) conducted in 1976 and 1985.

The Pandora's box is of course cottage sector employment. In Table 7.10 the figures are calculated as a residual, as explained in the notes. It is possible to calculate alternative estimates of employment in cottage industry, by simply including the number of 'workers' in these enterprises, or some notional 'full-time equivalent' on the (probably realistic) assumption that employees in small, medium, and large firms have such an employment status. However, neither approach is particularly satisfactory. According to the former, cottage industry employment

TABLE 7.10

Size Distribution of Industry, 1986

Size Group[a]	Percentage of Total — Output Incl. Oil/LNG	Percentage of Total — Output Excl. Oil/LNG	Percentage of Total — Employment	Industrial Composition[b] (percentage of total) — Output 31	32+39	33+34	35+36	37+38	Total	Industrial Composition[b] — Employment 31	32+39	33+34	35+36	37+38	Total
Large															
Incl.															
Oil/LNG	68.6	–	}26.2	16.9	9.2	9.0	48.7	16.1	100	}31.8	23.0	13.5	20.6	11.1	100
Excl.															
Oil/LNG	–	59.5		25.5	13.9	13.6	22.7	24.3	100						
Medium	15.2	19.6	12.3	18.9	11.7	12.2	38.1	19.1	100	27.5	23.0	15.0	22.4	12.1	100
Small	5.7	7.3	17.3	37.1	19.7	20.6	16.0	6.7	100	41.4	19.9	16.6	17.0	5.1	100
Cottage	10.5	13.6	44.2[c]	40.5	11.5	25.3	17.5	5.1	100	43.9	11.4	30.5	12.8	1.4	100
	100	100	100												

Sources: BPS, Statistik Industri, Industri Kecil, Industri Rumah Tangga, and unpublished data.

[a] The following definitions apply for workforce size (n): Large n > 200; Medium 20 < n < 200; Small 5 < n < 20; Cottage n < 5.

[b] The industry groups are as defined in Table 7.7. The cottage industry composition data refer to 1982.

[c] Cottage industry employment has been adjusted to estimate 'full-time equivalents'.

TABLE 7.11

Estimates of Manufacturing Employment by Size Group, 1975 and 1986

Size Group (Persons employed)	1975		1986		Annual Growth (per cent)
	('000)	(percentage of total)	('000)	(percentage of total)	
> 20	1,025.7	(30.4)	1,869.0	(30.6)	5.6
5–19	442.8	(13.1)	840.5	(13.8)	6.0
< 5	1,904.4	(56.6)	3,400.8	(55.7)	5.4
Total	3,372.9	100	6,110.3	(100)	5.6

Sources and Notes: The total employment estimates have been derived from *Supas*, 1976 and 1985, adjusted to 1975 and 1986 by the average annual growth rate 1976–85 in the original figures (which were 3.56 and 5.789 million persons respectively). The estimates for large and medium firms (employing at least 20 persons) are from the revised BPS, *Statistik Industri* series. The figures for small industry (5–19 persons) employment are from the *Industri Kecil* components of the *Sensus Industri*, 1974/5 and 1986 (which refer respectively to 1975 and 1986) adjusted up by the 'understatement ratio' in the original large and medium figures for the two censuses. (These ratios are 1.29 and 1.09 respectively; see Hill, 1990b: Table A.1.) Cottage industry estimates are obtained as a residual. According to the censuses, cottage industry employment was 3.9 million in 1974/5 and 2.85 million in 1986.

actually fell by about 1 million persons between 1974/5 and 1986. Yet this suggests, implausibly, a *decline* in total manufacturing employment, and contradicts all other estimates. The alternative approach of full-time equivalents is also fraught with difficulty. On various assumptions regarding working days and months recorded in the 1986 Census, for example, the relevant figure for cottage employment in 1986 might be about 2.15 million persons,[31] a good deal lower than the implied residual in Table 7.11, for which no adjustment is made. But since the 1974/5 Census provides less information from which such estimates can be derived, and the data were in any case regarded as very approximate, an attempt to calculate trends in full-time equivalent cottage employment is almost certainly a fruitless exercise. For all their weaknesses, then, the data in Table 7.11 are probably the best available. They suggest quite strong and even employment growth across all sectors, casting doubt on some of the gloomy prognostications of the late 1970s regarding the demise of small and cottage industry.[32] Undoubtedly there have been some backwash and displacement effects associated with the rapid factory sector growth. But smaller production units appear to have adapted to this environment with some success.

There is considerable industrial specialization by firm size (Table 7.10, third and fourth panels). As would be expected, small and cottage enterprises are located disproportionately in food-processing industries, where scale economies are less significant, and where perishability and the need for on-site processing may confer advantages on smaller operations, and such activities blend more easily into the income-earning opportunities of rural households. Wood and paper products—mainly rudimentary timber processing—figure prominently, for a similar set of reasons, as does brick and tile manufacture, a feature obscured by the aggregated data in Table 7.10.[33] Perhaps surprisingly, the labour-intensive 'textile, leather, footwear, and other' group (ISIC 32 and 39) is not especially small-scale intensive as it once was, either with respect to employment or output. This underlines the transformation of the textiles industry noted above, and reflects also the fact that the new export-oriented garment industry, though very labour-intensive, is not especially small-scale. Other industries of relative specialization among large and medium firms include chemicals and non-metallic minerals, and basic metal and machine goods. The dominance of oil and gas of course explains the prominence of chemicals among large firms; a general explanation is that these industries are large-scale and capital-intensive activities better suited to larger enterprises.

Our understanding of small-scale and cottage industry in Indonesia and elsewhere is all too limited, which is especially regrettable since these firms employ over half the industrial labour force. There is a widespread view that these sectors have been one of the casualties of rapid modernization and industrialization after 1966, and that new technologies and a more liberal commercial environment have led to their rapid demise. For small firms at least, according to the two industrial censuses, this view is incorrect. Although annual output of small firms over the period 1975–86 grew more slowly than that of large and medium firms (9.4 per cent compared to 15.1 per cent), their employment growth was similar; in any case, annual output growth of 9.4 per cent is hardly sluggish. No such positive assertions can be made for the cottage industry sector, however, and as noted above, any estimate of employment growth must be precarious.

If the census data are correct, popular perceptions are mistaken, and small firms have prospered during the New Order, what explains their success? At least four hypotheses can be advanced, the most appealing intuitively being that rapid economic growth has provided enough 'niches' which these firms have been able to exploit.

One explanation is government promotion. All five *Repelita* have accorded a strong priority to small industry, which is regarded as desirable on the grounds of employment promotion, as a breeding ground for future entrepreneurs, and for social reasons—the encouragement of *pribumi* business and the so-called *golongan ekonomi lemah*. To this end, industrial training and demonstration programmes have been established, such as the large Textile Technology Institute (Institut Teknologi Tekstil or ITT) in Bandung, and various small industry centres (*lingkungan industri kecil* or LIK). Costly and elaborate credit schemes were instituted at the height of the oil boom, notably the KIK (*kredit investasi kecil*, small investment credit) and KMKP (*kredit modal kerja permanen*, permanent working capital credit), although these have been gradually eliminated in the series of banking reforms after 1983. State enterprises and other large firms have been exhorted to assist small firms through the *bapak angkat* (foster parent) scheme. Reservation schemes along the lines of those employed in India have been mooted, but never formally introduced. A mandatory deletion programme designed to encourage subcontracting to generally smaller firms in the automotive and appliance industries was introduced in the late 1970s. And other measures have been in force periodically, such as a stipulation that state textile mills should set aside a certain proportion of their yarn, at specified prices, to small-scale weavers.

Several features of these promotional measures deserve comment. One is that assistance, such as it is, has often been nullified by the effects of other government policies which discriminate against small firms. There are pecuniary economies of scale in dealing with a complex licensing apparatus, and for a variety of commercial and political reasons large firms are generally more effective at extracting government largesse, including protection.[34] There can be no presumption, there-fore, that the deregulation measures of the late 1980s, accompanied by the reduction in subsidies to small firms, will harm small industry, as is often asserted. Another feature of these schemes is that there has been no co-ordinated and consistent approach to small industry development. Policies have been introduced, sometimes with external assistance, before being overturned by new measures; different arms of the govern-ment have emphasized a variety of approaches. Finally, there is no per-suasive evidence to suggest these policies have been particularly effective. Subsidized credit is just as likely to produce rent-seeking behaviour and bureaucratic irregularities as it is to spur entrepreneurial endeavour.[35] The argument that government policies have been res-ponsible for the growth of small industry therefore remains at best unproven.

A second possible explanation for the success of small industry may be market segmentation, either in factor markets or spatially in the prod-uct markets. While such a factor may partially explain the existence of small industry—small firms may procure labour more cheaply (although not necessarily if adjusted for 'quality') or be protected by remoteness—it cannot explain *trends*. Indeed, since 1970 both product and factor markets have become far more integrated. Wage differentials nationally and within manufacturing have narrowed (Chapter 11) and the correlation across provinces between small industry shares and dis-tance from Jakarta (or 'remoteness' by some other measure) is weak (Hill, 1990b).

Thirdly, there is the issue of subcontracting and vertical linkages between large and small enterprises. These links were an important fea-ture of Japanese industrialization (Odaka, Ono, and Adachi, 1988), and they are present in Indonesian industry: garment factories, for example, find it profitable to engage outworkers to cope with fluctuations in demand or for specialized functions such as elaborate embroidery. But subcontracting is unlikely to have been the key to small industry progress since the 1970s, and in some quarters there is an excessively 'romantic' view of its role, akin to the ideals of the *koperasi* movement. (The historical reality in Japan was of course the reverse, of low wage, 'sweatshop', semi-feudal relationships in some instances.) From the late 1970s until the industrial downturn of the mid-1980s, the government sought to impose subcontracting requirements in the form of mandatory deletion programmes on large electronic, automotive, and machine goods firms, but with limited success (Thee, 1985). Several factors contributed to this indifferent outcome—heavy-handed and ambitious programmes, underlying technological and managerial weaknesses among the small firms, the structure of protection, and perhaps also ethnic divisions in the business community.[36]

Since small firms are generally unable to compete directly with large firms, in the presence of scale economies and given the latter's superior productivity and marketing reach, and better quality control, the most likely explanation for the success of small enterprises is their ability to exploit market niches, to concentrate on activities not characterized by scale economies as noted above, to serve particular markets not of commercial interest to larger firms, and to produce goods not easily adapted to mass production technologies. The limited amount of detailed research on small industry, such as the study of Majalaya textile mills by Hardjono (1990) and of the tile industry in Central Java by Sandee and Weijland (1989), seems to support this conclusion, although more research is required.

Conclusion

In just a quarter of a century there has been a major transformation in Indonesia's manufacturing industry. In 1965 the sector was small, its range of activities was limited, and its technology backward; firms were forced to operate in an increasingly chaotic and unpredictable commercial environment. By the late 1980s, the sector was much larger and more diversified, and employed more sophisticated technology. Aided by a politically stable regime with a creditable record of macroeconomic management, industrial enterprises were becoming internationally competitive on a significant scale for the first time in Indonesia's history.

The challenge for the 1990s will be to consolidate the hard-won gains of the late 1980s. In long-term historical perspective, Indonesian industry is still in its infancy. As a latecomer, the country can learn from the costly mistakes of countries in Latin America and South Asia which embarked on comprehensive and disastrous programmes of import substitution. While Indonesia's record since 1965 is impressive, much more remains to be done. To sustain the momentum, there needs to be a maintenance of the cautious and flexible macroeconomic management regime, a continuing commitment by the government to the efficient provision of public sector goods and services, and a renewed zeal towards reform. By 1990, some danger signals were emerging, however: the very success of the late 1980s appeared to be breeding a sense of complacency in certain circles; there was some backtracking on the general thrust towards deregulation, particularly in the area of export regulation and licensing; cronyism and political patronage had become hotly discussed issues; and the debate on ownership—especially co-operatives and conglomerates—created uncertainty in the business community. Finally, the sharp, if temporary, rise in international oil prices raised once again the spectre of 'Dutch Disease' and a return to *dirigisme*. If exchange rate management were to slip, if the customs and export promotion reforms were to be undone, or if the trade controls were to be reinstated, the gains recorded over the period 1985–9 would quickly disappear and Indonesia could follow the same unfortunate path to industrialization evident in many other developing countries. How Indonesian policy-makers respond to these challenges will have a crucial bearing on industrial and economic growth in the 1990s and beyond.

1. There are very few detailed studies of industrialization in Indonesia before 1965. One exception is Palmer (1972) on the textile industry. Based on fieldwork just prior to the change in regime, her study provides useful insights into business conditions. The textile industry, for example, was crucially dependent on supplies of imported yarn. On the frequent occasions when these supplies were exhausted, the industry virtually ground to a halt.

2. The mid-1970s is chosen as a starting point partly because it resumes the story of the first decade of the New Order's industrial growth contained in McCawley (1981) (see also Donges, Stecher, and Wolter, 1974 and 1980), and partly for convenience as the period for which the first comprehensive industrial census results are available.

3. General studies of Indonesian industrialization since 1966, in addition to the three in footnote 2, include: Anwar (1980), Beals (1987), Hill (1987, 1990a, 1990b), Kuyvenhoven and Poot (1986), Poot (1981), Poot, Kuyvenhoven, and Jansen (1990), Roepstorff (1985), and Thee (1988). The 'Survey of Recent Developments' in each *Bulletin of Indonesian Economic Studies* provides a running commentary on industrial trends, and several major unpublished World Bank reports have been prepared.

4. As an illustration, in the late 1980s it was not uncommon to find university students still using Professor Sadli's excellent 30-year-old industrial economics text. An industrial economics textbook is being prepared by Dr Nurimansjah Hasibuan of Universitas Sriwijaya, Palembang.

5. The data in Figure 7.1 are constructed on the basis of a spliced set from the constant price series for 1973 and 1983. They contain the revised estimates of industrial output released with the President's speech of 17 August 1989. However, BPS has yet to publish a consolidated set of national accounts for the entire period, and it is possible that the very low industrial growth rates of, for example, 1982 and 1983 would be revised upwards if the complete series were prepared.

6. It needs to be emphasized that data in Figure 7.2 and Table 7.1 refer only to firms employing at least 20 persons.

7. This transformation is more pronounced still if the (admittedly somewhat shaky) 1964 Census is included: excluding oil and gas, for example, the share of food, beverages, tobacco, and rubber products fell from a dominant 70 per cent in 1963 to 53 per cent in 1975 and just 33 per cent in 1986 (Hill, 1990b).

8. The *Nota Keuangan/Lampiran* data are used here in preference to the BPS quarterly manufacturing production index for two reasons: the former are more comprehensive and they appear to be more accurate. The index is based only on a limited sample of firms and should be used primarily as an early indicator of trends rather than as a complete statistical picture. There are considerable discrepancies between the two series (Hill, 1990b:

Table A2), although hopefully these will become smaller with the release of a new index series from 1988.

9. The following tabular summary illustrates this point:

Number of Industrial Products Recorded in the 1990 *Nota Keuangan*

	1969	1979	1989
Metal and machine goods	6	25	40
Chemicals	9	20	22
Miscellaneous manufactures	20	27	40
Total	35	72	102

10. There is now a substantial literature examining the economics of the log export ban, including the argument that the net economic benefits have been negative. For an illuminating analysis of the fiscal regime in the 1970s, see Ruzicka (1979). Contending views on the economics of the ban are found in Fitzgerald (1987) and Lindsay (1989).

11. By far the most informative account of developments in the industry is that provided in the annual *Petroleum Sector Report* published by the United States Embassy in Jakarta.

12. Perhaps it will be assured in any case, given the symbolic importance of the project as the largest Indonesian–Japanese joint venture. Barlow and Thee (1989) provide a brief account of the project. Personal reminiscences of the project by the key officials in its implementation are contained in Siahaan (1986) and Soehoed (1983).

13. The data in Tables 7.3 and 7.4 are based on the conventional definition of manufactures, SITC groups 5–8 less 68. These categories include mainly footloose manufactures, and constitute a much narrower definition than that of the national accounts (i.e. ISIC 3). In the Indonesian case, the difference is significant, since some major resource-based activities (e.g. refined petroleum) are not included in the narrow definition, the total for which is only one-third to one-half of the broader concept (see Hill, 1986, for further discussion). The narrow definition is used here, consistent with the general empirical trade literature and as dictated by data availability.

14. See, for example, Chalmers (1988), McIntyre (1988), and Wibisono (1989); see also the important contribution of Glassburner (1978).

15. For example, *Repelita I* contained a strong emphasis on rehabilitation and recovery; *Repelita II* shifted the focus somewhat to equity goals; *Repelita IV* outlined the government's ambitious upgrading proposals; and *Repelita V* foreshadowed the key role of the private sector in industrial growth.

16. For some fascinating insights into the diversity of influential opinion on a wide range of economic and ideological issues, see the survey of Kuntjoro-Jakti et al. (1983: 54).

17. The nature of these strong personal links was revealed in one candid press interview provided by Minister Habibie, who recalled after a meeting with the President that he [Soeharto] '... spoke of his long-range vision for Indonesia's economy, focusing on his goal of achieving a "take-off" into industry by the mid 1990s. Mr Soeharto said he needed someone to advise him on getting and applying modern technology. "I've decided you are the man to do that." When Mr Habibie suggested he start by using his expertise to build planes, ... Mr Soeharto said "You know how to do it. You just do it."'(*Asian Wall Street Journal*, 2 September 1985.)

18. Detailed empirical studies of Indonesian trade policies include Fane and Phillips (1987), Pangestu and Boediono (1986), Parker (1985), Pitt (1981), Wymenga (1990), and a large but unpublished study under World Bank auspices in 1980. The World Bank has been involved in three of these six studies.

19. For further discussion of this point, see Chapter 5. See also Arndt and Sundrum (1984), Warr (1984), and Hill (1990a).

20. The drawback and exemption scheme announced in May 1986 replaced the clumsy

and inefficient Export Certificate (Sertifikat Ekspor, SE) scheme, which was abolished in 1985 following Indonesia's accession to the General Agreement on Tariffs and Trade (GATT) code. Known initially as P4BM (Pusat Pengolahan Pembebasan dan Pengembalian Bea Masuk, Centre for the Processing of Import Duty Exemptions and Drawbacks), its responsibilities (and acronym) were later extended under its current title, Bapeksta (Badan Pelayanan Kemudahan Ekspor dan Pengolahan Data Keuangan, the Board for the Facilitation of Exports and Processing of Financial Data). A key feature of both the P4BM and Bapeksta has been their exceptionally capable leadership.

21. The issue is sometimes a good deal more complex than simply establishing clear ownership titles for the purposes of industrial expansion. For example, one simmering dispute in 1989/90 involved allegations of wholesale dispossessions to make way for a large golf course and resort complex near the Puncak region south of Jakarta.

22. The three ownership groups in Table 7.7 represent a summary of the seven enumerated in the Census, with the four joint-venture combinations being assigned to the generally dominant partner—foreign firms in the case of private–foreign operations, and government enterprises in all other cases.

23. Thee and Yoshihara (1987) examine these factors in some detail. General studies of foreign investment in Indonesia include Dickie and Layman (1988), Hill (1988), Kinoshita (1986), Kuntjoro-Jakti et al. (1983), Kuntjoro-Jakti (1985), Robison (1986), Thee (1984a and 1984b), and Wells and Warren (1979).

24. A note of caution is appropriate in interpreting Table 7.8, since the totals represent aggregates of current-price realized investments, which thus overstate the importance of industries which have been more recent recipients of foreign investment such as basic metals (and the sources of such investment, notably Belgium) as compared to the early wave investments, especially textiles. However, Japan's dominant position is unaffected by these measurement problems, as its firms have been investing on a large scale throughout the New Order.

25. See, for example, Dick (1987) on the state shipping company Pelni, Funkhouser and MacAvoy (1979) on a sample of 150 firms, Gillis (1982) on mining, Hill (1982) on weaving, and McCawley (1971) on the State Electricity Company, PLN.

26. For general overviews of provincial economic development, see the surveys in Hill, ed. (1989). See also Hill (1991), McAndrews, ed. (1986), and the writings of Indonesia's foremost regional economist, Iwan Azis (for example, Azis, 1989).

27. Some of the data in this and the following sections are from Hill (1990b: Part 2, Tables 9–13, and Figures 2–4).

28. A few examples illustrate this proposition, in the case of large and medium firms in the non-oil manufacturing sector in 1985: three large petrochemical and fertilizer plants produced 69 per cent of Aceh's output; the fertilizer plant in East Kalimantan generated 47 per cent of that province's output; the Pusri complex near Palembang accounted for 42 per cent of South Sumatra's output; a motor vehicle plant (since closed) constituted 70 per cent of the North Sulawesi total; and a large sawmill in Irian Jaya produced 84 per cent of that province's total. Nor is the phenomenon of single-plant dominance restricted to the Outer Islands: Krakatau accounted for 20 per cent of the West Java total, while one huge *kretek* plant generated a staggering 28 per cent of East Java's output.

29. That Java has an increasing comparative disadvantage in resource-based activities is attested by mounting concern over associated pollution problems. A notable example is the huge Cibinong cement plant south of Jakarta, which emits large quantities of dust and contributes to the national capital's already grave air quality problems.

30. This effect is ameliorated partially by the special tariffs offered to the huge processing complexes adjacent to the major oil and gas centres. But this is not a general facility, and provinces such as West Sumatra which have electricity sources other than oil and gas are not able to offer such concessions.

31. Briefly, this figure is calculated as follows: the recorded employment figure of 2.727 million persons is adjusted upwards by the same understatement ratio as for large and medium firms (1.09), giving 2.973 million. The data on months worked per year and days worked per week suggest a full-time equivalent ratio of about 0.72, giving a figure of 2.147 million persons. The crude assumptions employed underline the extremely approximate nature of this estimate.

32. See the exchange between McCawley and Tait (1979) and Dapice and Snodgrass (1979). See also Hugo et al. (1987: Chapter 8) and Chapter 11 of this volume.

33. See Hill (1990b) for a more disaggregated analysis of the size distribution data, excluding cottage industry for which such information is not available.

34. For general discussion of these issues in an Asian context, see Anderson (1982), Bruch and Hiemenz (1984), Chee (1986), and Little (1987).

35. Several studies of small-scale credit underline this point. In a large project contrasting small firms with and without access to subsidized credit, Bolnick and Nelson (1990) pointed to the mixed record of business success of the two groups. McLeod (1984) provides a more sceptical view of the value of such schemes.

36. It should be noted here that the BPS definition of small industry (5–19 employees) is a somewhat restrictive one. Firms of this size are hardly able to manage the often sophisticated requirements of large electronic and automotive firms. The Department of Industry definition of 'small' is rather more comprehensive, however.

REFERENCES

Anderson, D. (1982), 'Small Industry in Developing Countries: A Discussion of Issues', *World Development*, 10(11): 913–48.

Anwar, M. A. (1980), 'Trade Strategies and Industrial Development in Indonesia', in R. Garnaut (ed.), *ASEAN in a Changing Pacific and World Economy*, Canberra: Australian National University Press, pp. 207–31.

Ariff, M. and Hill, H. (1985), *Export Oriented Industrialisation: The ASEAN Experience*, Sydney: Allen & Unwin.

Arndt, H. W. (1975), 'PT Krakatau Steel', *Bulletin of Indonesian Economic Studies*, 11(2): 120–6.

Arndt, H. W. and Sundrum, R. M. (1984), 'Devaluation and Inflation: The 1978 Experience', *Bulletin of Indonesian Economic Studies*, 20(1): 83–97.

Azis, I. J. (1989), 'Key Issues in Indonesian Regional Development', in H. Hill (ed.), *Unity and Diversity: Regional Economic Development in Indonesia since 1970*, Singapore: Oxford University Press, pp. 55–74.

Barlow, C. and Thee Kian Wie (1989), 'North Sumatra: Growth with Unbalanced Development', in H. Hill (ed.), *Unity and Diversity: Regional Economic Development in Indonesia since 1970*, Singapore: Oxford University Press, pp. 409–36.

Beals, R. E. (1987), 'Trade Patterns and Trends of Indonesia', in C. I. Bradford, Jr., and W. H. Branson (eds.), *Trade and Structural Change in Pacific Asia*, Chicago: University of Chicago Press, pp. 515–45.

Bolnick, B. R. and Nelson, E. R. (1990), 'Evaluating the Economic Impact of a Special Credit Program: KIK/KMKP in Indonesia', *Journal of Development Studies*, 26(2): 299–312.

Bruch, M. and Hiemenz, U. (1984), *Small- and Medium-scale Industries in the ASEAN Countries: Agents or Victims of Economic Development?*, Boulder: Westview Press.

Castles, L. (1967), *Religion, Politics and Economic Behaviour in Java: The Kudus Cigarette Industry*, Cultural Report Series No. 15, Southeast Asia Studies, New Haven: Yale University.

Chalmers, I. M. (1988), 'Economic Nationalism and the Third World State: The Political Economy of the Indonesian Automotive Industry, 1950–1984', Ph.D. dissertation, Australian National University.

Chee P. L. (1986), *Small Industry in Malaysia*, Kuala Lumpur: Berita Publishing.

Dapice, D. and Snodgrass, D. (1979), 'Employment in Manufacturing 1970–77: A Comment', *Bulletin of Indonesian Economic Studies*, 15(3): 127–31.

Dick, H. W. (1987), *The Indonesian Interisland Shipping Industry: An Analysis of Competition and Regulation*, Singapore: Institute of Southeast Asian Studies.

Dickie, R. B. and Layman, T. A. (1988), *Foreign Investment and Government Policy in the Third World: Forging Common Interests in Indonesia and Beyond*, London: Macmillan.

Donges, J. B., Stecher, B., and Wolter, F. (1974), *Industrial Development Policies for Indonesia*, Kieler Studien 126, Tubingen: J. C. B. Mohr.

_____ (1980), 'Industrialization in Indonesia', in G. F. Papanek (ed.), *The Indonesian Economy*, New York: Praeger, pp. 357–405.

Fane, G. and Phillips, C. (1987), 'Effective Protection in Indonesia', Report submitted to the Department of Industry, Jakarta.

Fitzgerald, B. D. (1987), 'Export Bans for Industrial Development: The Costs of Indonesian Plywood', Unpublished paper, Country Policy Department, Washington, DC: World Bank.

Funkhouser, R. and MacAvoy, P. W. (1979), 'A Sample of Observations on Comparative Prices in Public and Private Enterprises', *Journal of Public Economics*, 11: 353–68.

Gillis, M. (1982), 'Allocative and X-Efficiency in State-owned Mining Enterprises: Comparisons between Bolivia and Indonesia', *Journal of Comparative Economics*, 6: 1–23.

Glassburner, B. (1978), 'Political Economy and the Soeharto Regime', *Bulletin of Indonesian Economic Studies*, 14(3): 24–51.

Hardjono, J. (1990), *Developments in the Majalaya Textile Industry*, West Java Rural Nonfarm Sector Research Project, Project Working Paper Series No. B-3, The Hague and Bandung.

Hill, H. (1982), 'State Enterprises in a Competitive Industry: An Indonesian Case Study', *World Development*, 10(11): 1015–23.

_____ (1983), 'Choice of Technique in the Indonesian Weaving Industry', *Economic Development and Cultural Change*, 31(2): 337–53.

_____ (1986), 'LDC Manufactured Exports: Do Definitions Matter? Some Examples from ASEAN', *ASEAN Economic Bulletin*, 3(2): 269–74.

_____ (1987), 'Concentration in Indonesian Manufacturing', *Bulletin of Indonesian Economic Studies*, 23(2): 71–100.

_____ (1988), *Foreign Investment and Industrialization in Indonesia*, Singapore: Oxford University Press.

_____ (1990a), 'Indonesia: Export Promotion in the Post-OPEC Era', in C. Milner (ed.), *Export Promotion Strategies: Theory and Evidence from Developing Countries*, London: Harvester Wheatsheaf Press, pp. 184–212.

_____ (1990b), 'Indonesia's Industrial Transformation, Parts I and II', *Bulletin of Indonesian Economic Studies*, 26(2): 79–120; 26(3): 75–109.

_____ (1991), 'Regional Development in a "Boom and Bust Petroleum Economy": Indonesia since 1970', *Economic Development and Cultural Change*, 40(1).

_____ (ed.) (1989), *Unity and Diversity: Regional Economic Development in Indonesia since 1970*, Singapore: Oxford University Press.

Hill, H. and Pang E. F. (1988), 'The State and Industrial Restructuring: A Comparison of the Aerospace Industry in Indonesia and Singapore', *ASEAN Economic Bulletin*, 5(2): 152–68.

Hugo, G. J.; Hull, T. H.; Hull, V. J.; and Jones, G. W. (1987), *The Demographic Dimension in Indonesian Development*, Singapore: Oxford University Press.

Jansen, J. C. and Kuyvenhoven, A. (1987), 'Capital Utilisation in Indonesian Medium and Large Scale Manufacturing', *Bulletin of Indonesian Economic Studies*, 23(1): 70–103.

Khong C. O. (1986), *The Politics of Oil in Indonesia: Foreign Company–Host Government Relations*, London School of Economics Monographs in International Studies, Cambridge: Cambridge University Press.

Kinoshita, T. (1986), 'Japanese Investment in Indonesia: Problems and Prospects', *Bulletin of Indonesian Economic Studies*, 22(1): 34–56.

Krause, L. B. (1982), *US Economic Policy towards the Association of Southeast Asian Nations: Meeting the Japanese Challenge*, Washington, DC: Brookings.

Kuntjoro-Jakti, D. (1985), 'Indonesia', in *Patterns and Impact of Foreign Investment in the ESCAP Region*, Bangkok: United Nations Economic and Social Commission for Asia and the Pacific, pp. 69–95.

Kuntjoro-Jakti, D. et al. (1983), 'Japanese Investment in Indonesia', in S. Sekiguchi (ed.), *ASEAN–Japan Relations: Investment*, Singapore: Institute of Southeast Asian Studies, pp. 27–59.

Kuyvenhoven, A. and Poot, H. (1986), 'The Structure of Indonesian Manufacturing Industry: An Input–Output Approach', *Bulletin of Indonesian Economic Studies*, 22(2): 54–79.

Langhammer, R. J. (1988), 'Investment and Trade Flows: The Case of Indonesia', *Bulletin of Indonesian Economic Studies*, 24(1): 97–114.

Lindblad, J. T. (1989), 'The Petroleum Industry in Indonesia before the Second World War', *Bulletin of Indonesian Economic Studies*, 25(2): 53–77.

Lindsay, H. (1989), 'The Indonesian Log Export Ban: An Estimation of Foregone Export Earnings', *Bulletin of Indonesian Economic Studies*, 25(2): 111–23.

Little, I. M. D. (1987), 'Small Manufacturing Enterprises in Developing Countries', *World Bank Economic Review*, 1(2): 203–35.

McAndrews, C. (ed.) (1986), *Central Government and Local Development in Indonesia*, Singapore: Oxford University Press.

McCawley, P. (1971), 'The Indonesian Electric Supply Industry', Ph.D. dissertation, Australian National University.

_____ (1978), 'Some Consequences of the Pertamina Crisis in Indonesia', *Journal of Southeast Asian Studies*, 9(1): 1–27.

_____ (1980), 'Comment', on Anwar (1980), in R. Garnaut (ed.), *ASEAN in a Changing Pacific and World Economy*, Canberra: Australian National University Press, pp. 233–8.

_____ (1981), 'The Growth of the Industrial Sector', in A. Booth and P. McCawley (eds.), *The Indonesian Economy during the Soeharto Era*, Kuala Lumpur: Oxford University Press, pp. 62–101.

_____ (1983), 'Industrial Licensing in Indonesia', Unpublished paper, Australian National University.

_____ (1984), 'A Slowdown in Industrial Growth?' *Bulletin of Indonesian Economic Studies*, 20(3): 158–74.

McCawley, P. and Tait, M. (1979), 'New Data on Employment in Manufacturing, 1970–76', *Bulletin of Indonesian Economic Studies*, 15(1): 125–36.

McIntyre, A. (1988), *Politics, Policy and Participation: Business–Government Relations in Indonesia*, Ph.D. dissertation, Australian National University.

McLeod, R. H. (1984), 'Financial Institutions and Markets in Indonesia', in M. T. Skully (ed.), *Financial Institutions and Markets in Southeast Asia*, London: Macmillan, pp. 49–109.

Manning, C. G. (1979), *Wage Differentials and Labour Market Segmentation in Indonesian Manufacturing*, Ph.D. dissertation, Australian National University.

Odaka, K., Ono, K., and Adachi, F. (1988), *The Automobile Industry in Japan: A Study of Ancillary Firm Development*, Kinokuniya Coy Ltd., Oxford University Press, for the Institute of Economic Research, Hitotsubashi University, Tokyo.

Palmer, I. (1972), *Textiles in Indonesia: Problems of Import Substitution*, New York: Praeger.

Pangestu, M. (1989), 'East Kalimantan: Beyond the Timber and Oil Boom', in H. Hill (ed.), *Unity and Diversity: Regional Economic Development in Indonesia since 1970*, Singapore: Oxford University Press, pp. 151–75.

Pangestu, M. and Boediono (1986), 'Indonesia: The Structure and Causes of Manufacturing Sector Protection', in C. Findlay and R. Garnaut (eds.), *The Political Economy of Manufacturing Protection: Experiences of ASEAN and Australia*, Sydney: Allen and Unwin, pp. 1–47.

Pangestu, M. and Habir, A. D. (1989), 'Trends and Prospects in Privatization and Deregulation in Indonesia', *ASEAN Economic Bulletin*, 5(3): 224–41.

Parker, S. (1985), 'A Study of Indonesian Trade Policy Between 1980 and 1984', Unpublished paper, Washington, DC.

Pitt, M. M. (1981), 'Alternative Trade Strategies and Employment in Indonesia', in A. O. Krueger et al. (eds.), *Trade and Employment in Developing Countries*, Vol. 1, Chicago: University of Chicago Press, pp. 181–237.

Pitt, M. M. and Lee L-F (1981), 'The Measurement and Sources of Technical Inefficiency in the Indonesian Weaving Industry', *Journal of Development Economics*, 9: 43–64.

Poot, H. (1981), 'The Development of Labour Intensive Industries in Indonesia', in R. Amjad (ed.), *The Development of Labour Intensive Industry in ASEAN Countries*, Asian Employment Programme, Bangkok: ILO-ARTEP, pp. 77–140.

Poot, H.; Kuyvenhoven, A.; and Jansen, J. (1990), *Industrialization and Trade in Indonesia*, Yogyakarta: Gadjah Mada University Press.

Rice, R. C. (1986), 'Export Promotion of Labor-intensive Footwear Products in Indonesia', Employment Creation Strategy Project, Jakarta: United Nations.

Riedel, J. (1989), 'Economic Development in East Asia: Doing What Comes Naturally?' in H. Hughes (ed.), *Achieving Industrialization in East Asia*, Cambridge: Cambridge University Press, pp. 1–38.

Robison, R. (1986), *Indonesia: The Rise of Capital*, Sydney: Allen and Unwin.

Roepstorff, T. M. (1985), 'Industrial Development in Indonesia: Performance and Prospects', *Bulletin of Indonesian Economic Studies*, 21(1): 32–61.

Ruzicka, I. (1979), 'Rent Appropriation in Indonesian Logging: East Kalimantan, 1972/3–1976/7', *Bulletin of Indonesian Economic Studies*, 15(2): 45–74.

Sandee, H. and Weijland, H. (1989), 'Rural Cottage Industry in Transition: The Roof Tile Industry in Kabupaten Boyolali, Central Java', *Bulletin of Indonesian Economic Studies*, 25(2): 79–98.

Siahaan, B. (1986), *Kenangan Membangun Proyek Raksasa Asahan* [An Account of the Development of the Giant Asahan Project], Jakarta: Penerbit Sinar Harapan.

Sitsen, P. H. W. (1942), *Industrial Development of the Netherlands Indies*, New York: Institute of Pacific Relations.

Soehoed, A. R. (1967), 'Manufacturing in Indonesia', *Bulletin of Indonesian Economic Studies*, 8: 65–84.

____ (1983), *Asahan, Impian Yang Menjadi Kenyataan* [Asahan, A Dream Which Became a Reality], Jakarta (privately published).

____ (1988), 'Reflections on Industrialisation and Industrial Policy in Indonesia', *Bulletin of Indonesian Economic Studies*, 24(2): 43–57.

Thee Kian Wie (1984a), 'Japanese Direct Investment in Indonesian Manufacturing', *Bulletin of Indonesian Economic Studies*, 20(2): 90–106.

____ (1984b), 'Japanese and American Direct Investment in Indonesian Manufacturing Compared', *Ekonomi dan Keuangan Indonesia*, 32(1): 89–105.

____ (1988), *Industrialisasi Indonesia: Analisis dan Catatan Kritis* [Industrialisation in Indonesia: Analysis and Critical Notes], Jakarta: Pustaka Sinar Harapan.

____ (1990), 'Indonesia: Technology Transfer in the Manufacturing Industry', in H. Soesastro and M. Pangestu (eds.), *Technological Challenge in the Pacific*, Sydney: Allen & Unwin, pp. 200–32.

____ (ed.) (1985), *Kaitan-Kaitan Vertikal Antarperusahaan dan Pengembangan Sistem Subkontraktor di Indonesia: Beberapa Studi Kasus* [Vertical Interfirm Linkages and the Development of the Subcontracting System in Indonesia: Several Case Studies], *Masyarakat Indonesia*, 12(3).

Thee Kian Wie and Yoshihara, K. (1987), 'Foreign and Domestic Capital in Indonesian Industrialization', *Southeast Asian Studies*, 24(4): 327–49.

Timmer, C. P. (1973), 'Choice of Technique in Rice Milling in Java', *Bulletin of Indonesian Economic Studies*, 9(2): 57–76.

United States Embassy (annual), *Indonesia's Petroleum Sector*, Jakarta.

Warr, P. G. (1983), 'The Jakarta Export Processing Zone: Benefits and Costs', *Bulletin of Indonesian Economic Studies*, 19(3): 28–49.

____ (1984), 'Exchange Rate Protection in Indonesia', *Bulletin of Indonesian Economic Studies*, 20(2): 53–89.

Wells, L. T., Jr (1983), *Third World Multinationals*, Cambridge: MIT Press,

Wells, L. T., Jr. and V'E. Warren (1979), 'Developing Country Investors in Indonesia', *Bulletin of Indonesian Economic Studies*, 15(1): 69–84.

Wibisono, M. (1989), 'The Politics of Indonesian Textile Policy: The Interests of Government Agencies and the Private Sector', *Bulletin of Indonesian Economic Studies*, 25(1): 31–52.

Witoelar, W. (1983), 'Ancillary Firm Development in the Motor Vehicle Industry in Indonesia', in K. Odaka (ed.), *The Motor Vehicle Industry in Asia*, Singapore: Singapore University Press, pp. 17–84.

Wymenga, P. (1990), 'The Structure of Protection in 1989 in Indonesia', Unpublished paper, Jakarta.

Yoshihara, K. (1988), *The Rise of Ersatz Capitalism in South-East Asia*, Singapore: Oxford University Press.

8

Transport and Communications: A Quiet Revolution*

Howard Dick and Dean Forbes

Introduction

ECONOMIC historians have long recognized the role of transport as a catalyst for economic growth. Lower transport costs reduce the costs of production and widen the market, while facilitating personal mobility. Turnpikes and canals paved the way for the Industrial Revolution in Britain. As a product of that revolution, railways, steamships and, later, motor vehicles and aeroplanes, transformed the economy and way of life of almost the entire world. Yet in the late twentieth century, preoccupied with production and figures on agriculture, industry and GDP, we risk becoming blasé about transport, sometimes perceiving it as an 'obstacle', but seldom as a dynamic element in economic development.

Especially in the case of such a large, island nation as Indonesia, to disregard the role of transport is to study development out of context. Yet the transport sector is not particularly large in its own right, accounting for about 5 per cent of GDP and 3 per cent of the workforce in the mid-1980s (Forbes and Adisasmita, 1989: 17). None the less, all other sectors depend upon it. To state the obvious, the present level of economic activity could not have been accommodated by the transport system of 1966. Transport improvements have been, at the very least, a 'permissive' factor in development by reducing bottlenecks in the movement of goods and people. Yet improved mobility and accessibility, especially in rural areas, has also been a catalyst for development. Within a mere two decades, a fairly self-sufficient mode of production has given way to an integrated economy.

Given its importance to the economy, it is notable how little published analysis is available on Indonesian transport and its contribution to development.[1] Pond's (1968) study considers transport in early New

*The authors would like to thank Christine Tabart, Barbara Banks, and Carol McKenzie for their assistance in the preparation of this chapter. Hal Hill and Heinz Arndt kindly read earlier drafts of the chapter and made helpful comments.

Order Indonesia, while Rogers (1983) reviews developments to the early 1980s. A recent survey by Leinbach (1986) provides a useful overview of the sector as a whole, but with a strong emphasis on road transport. Leinbach and Chia (1989) have reviewed recent overall transport development in the ASEAN region, whereas the ESCAP Secretariat (1987) has covered the Asian region as a whole.

Of a more specialized nature, Dick (1985a and 1987) has compiled detailed studies of the inter-island shipping industry, while the Brooks (1989) edited collection looks at seafarers throughout ASEAN. Urban public transport issues have been examined by Dick (1981), whereas Pendakur (1984) and Rimmer (1986) survey the whole of South-East Asia, including Indonesia. The informal transport sector has been extensively researched (Forbes, 1981; Kartodirdjo, 1981; Soegijoko, 1984). Leinbach (1981, 1983a, and 1983b) and Hugo (1981) have reviewed the impact of improved land transport on social organization and population mobility in rural Indonesia.

One problem which hinders analysis of transport and development is lack of data. For example, while information is issued on the length and condition of roads and the numbers of registered vehicles, none is available on inter-*kabupaten* goods movements. The abolition of highway weigh-stations has meant that even incomplete primary data are no longer collected. The most recent survey, carried out in 1982 as part of the National Urban Development Strategy (NUDS) project, revealed that 85 per cent of inter-*kabupaten* cargo movement and 97 per cent of inter-*kabupaten* passenger trips were by road (Table 8.1). In neither case was rail important. Shipping was significant only for goods movement. Sea and air transport would, however, assume greater prominence on a ton-kilometre and passenger-kilometre basis.

This chapter provides a 'then' and 'now' comparison of the transport sector at the beginning of the New Order with that in the late 1980s. Urban public transport, inter-city transport, rural/urban transport, and inter-island transport are looked at in turn. First the appalling state of transport in the mid-1960s is described. Then the situation in the mid-1980s is summarized, highlighting the changes that occurred during the

TABLE 8.1
Inter-*kabupaten* Passenger and Cargo Traffic, 1982

Mode	Passenger Trips (per cent)	Cargo Tonnage (per cent)
Road	97	85
Rail	3	2
Sea	0	12
Air	1	–
Total	100	100

Source: NUDS (1985: 46).

New Order government and identifying the main problems and bottle-necks which remain in Indonesia's transport system. Finally the policy reforms of the second half of the 1980s are detailed. These have been aimed at making the transport sector more responsive to market forces by deregulation and the development of state enterprises. The chapter concludes with a brief overview of the plans set down in *Repelita V*, and comments on the scope for further deregulation.

The New Order Inheritance

At the beginning of the New Order, the transport system of Indonesia was in a sorry state, rather similar to that of contemporary Myanmar/Burma or Vietnam. The root cause was neglect. The colonial Dutch, sharing the nineteenth-century preoccupation with modern transport, had invested heavily in ships, ports, railways, tramways, roads, and, in the last years, airfields. Much of this extensive transport infrastructure was badly damaged during the Second World War and the subsequent revolution and was never properly rehabilitated. The Dutch could not regain control of the countryside and, after independence, the new Indonesian government lacked the funds. Roads were vulnerable to rapid deterioration from monsoon rains and use. The Outer Islands were badly neglected and the situation worsened after the regional rebellions of the late 1950s. Bridges were not rebuilt and roads were reclaimed by the jungle. Railway track received little maintenance. Tramways, especially the systems associated with the sugar mills on Java, became overgrown. Ports remained cluttered with wartime wrecks and silted up for want of dredging. Few airfields and terminals were upgraded to accommodate the larger aircraft of the post-war period. All these problems became acute after the seizure of Dutch-owned transport enterprises at the end of 1957 and the inauguration by President Sukarno of Guided Democracy. A good proportion of scarce foreign exchange was still allocated to buy transport equipment (motor vehicles, rolling stock, ships, and aircraft) but little was spent on infrastructure. In the absence of foreign pressure to maintain technical and safety standards, infrastructure had a low priority.

Roads

The condition of roads was outlined in the First Five-Year Plan (1969–74) on the basis of 1967 figures (Table 8.2). Less than a fifth of the length of national roads and only a tenth of the length of provincial roads was assessed as in 'good' condition (the term itself being undefined). Of the *kabupaten* roads which constituted 60 per cent of the total length, none were reckoned to be in good condition. This meant that wheeled communications between village and market town ranged from difficult to impossible, especially in the wet season. Many villagers reverted to walking to market and carrying heavy loads on their backs. That this was not more of an obstacle was attributable to the low yields

TABLE 8.2
Condition of Roads, 1967

Category	Length (km)	Percentage of Total	Percentage in 'Good Condition'
National	10 150	12	17
Provincial	22 700	27	10
Kabupaten	51 000	61	–
Total	83 850	100	5

Source: Department of Information (1969: 92).

of cash crops and consequent low purchasing power for goods from outside the village. While many villages had not altogether disengaged themselves from the cash economy, their participation was marginal. Communications between market towns and provincial capitals were also hampered. On Java, buses made occasional round trips with passengers and small loads, while ox-carts carried large loads such as bricks and rice. Journeys were slow because of the need to weave between potholes, cross temporary bridges, and, in the wet season, plough through mud.

Railways

For inter-city travel, railways were the fastest and most reliable means of land transport. On Java, by 1965, railways carried one and a half times the pre-war number of passengers according to official figures (Table 8.3), though given the prevalence of fare evasion, actual numbers were probably much greater. Average distance travelled had increased by some two-thirds. However, lack of maintenance over many years reduced railway tracks to 70 per cent of their nominal capacity, and 60 per cent in the case of feeder lines (Department of Information,

TABLE 8.3
Railway Passengers and Cargo: Java and Sumatra

Item	Unit	Java				Sumatra			
		1939	1965	1975	1985	1939	1965	1975	1985
Passengers	million	46	113	20	44	12	12	25	3
Passenger-kilometres	billion	1.4	6.6	3.1	6.3	0.3	0.7	0.3	0.5
Cargo	m. tons	6.9	2.7	2.7	3.2	2.8	1.7	1.4	3.5
Ton-kilometres	billion	0.9	0.7	0.7	0.8	0.3	0.2	0.2	0.5

Source: BPS (1989b).

1969: 105). This necessitated slower running speeds and reduced frequencies. In practice, schedules had little meaning. One went to the station and waited. Arriving trains were already overcrowded. A mêlée would ensue, in which the prize was not a seat but standing room. Air-conditioning rarely worked and ventilation was minimal. Matters would have been far worse had the propensity to travel not been so low. Personal mobility was still sufficiently unusual that anyone from village or *kampung* going on even an overnight trip required an official permit (*surat jalan*) from the local headman. This colonial hangover—which was also a useful source of income to the headman—was still in force in the early 1970s, though increasingly ignored.

Freight movements by rail were subsidiary to passengers. In the late colonial period, the state railways had turned to regulation to control competition from trucks. After independence the battle was lost: pilferage of rail freight was so bad that few traders were any longer prepared to take the risk for small consignments. Railway freight carriage was more and more confined to bulk commodities. Whereas on Java, in 1939, ton-kilometres had been about two-thirds of passenger-kilometres, by 1965 the proportion had fallen to barely 10 per cent (Table 8.3).

Domestic Shipping

Until the end of 1957 an extensive and efficient network of inter-island shipping routes had been maintained by the large fleet of the Dutch-owned KPM (Koninklijke Paketvaart Mij). While the state-owned Pelni (Pelayaran Nasional Indonesia) and a large number of small private firms had made substantial inroads into what, pre-war, had been a virtual monopoly (Dick, 1987: 18–23), the KPM had continued to set the standard of service. Seizure by the trade unions of KPM assets in December 1957 resulted in the withdrawal of all its ships.[2] Although the loss of capacity was quickly made good by chartered tonnage, regular services were never restored. As more ships had to be withdrawn from commission for want of imported spare parts, and port conditions slowed turn-around time, capacity became less adequate. Ships could pick and choose the most profitable cargoes. The so-called 'thin' routes to the eastern part of the archipelago were ignored. Many islands in Nusa Tenggara and Maluku were left totally dependent upon *prahu* (sailing ships). When trade with Singapore was suspended during Confrontation (1963–6), the trade of the western part of the archipelago was reoriented towards Java. However, the commercial attractions of Singapore, plus the inefficiency of Indonesian-flag shipping, ensured a quick reversion to the former *status quo* after trade with Singapore officially resumed in mid-1966.

Shipping lines remained hard pressed to provide sufficient space for the great majority of people who still travelled by sea as deck passengers. On the main trunk routes from Java to Sumatra and to Sulawesi, however, the government did provide funds to Pelni to buy and charter large passenger liners to provide a fairly regular express service.

Air

One of the features of the 1950s was the rapid growth of domestic air travel, monopolized by Garuda Indonesian Airways, the company formed in 1950 as a joint venture between the government and the Dutch company KLM (Koninklijke Luchtvaart Mij). The demand for cabin class accommodation by sea collapsed as those who could afford to fly (mainly officials and businessmen) naturally preferred the faster air travel. Garuda's passenger numbers grew from 270,000 in 1952 to a peak of 437,000 in 1957, and then fluctuated around an average of about 350,000, according to military demands upon the aircraft (Table 8.4). As a monopolist, Garuda had no incentive to improve the quality of service and, especially in the period of Guided Democracy, schedules were erratic. Nevertheless, air transport probably suffered least from the chaos of the Old Order, perhaps because those who could afford the fares were mainly government officials, businessmen, and foreigners.

Urban Public Transport

Within the main cities, the formal and state-owned urban public transport system had almost collapsed by the beginning of the New Order. In Jakarta, the PPD (Perusahaan Pengangkutan Djakarta or Jakarta Transport Corporation) had, in 1954, taken over the formerly Dutch-owned tramway system. After 1962 it ran only buses, few of which were actually in service at any one time. In Surabaya, the tramways operated after a fashion until the beginning of 1968, when they were replaced on a token basis by a handful of East German minibuses. In both cities the backbone of the fixed route public transport system became privately owned jitneys (*jeepneys*), known as *opelet* (Jakarta) or *bemo* (Surabaya), and an untold number of human-powered trishaws (*becak*).[3] Taxis were still unknown except for a few, old American sedans which waited outside the main hotels for hire by foreign tourists. Yet because of the vitality of the informal sector, urban public transport was probably the only sector able to cope with the needs of users. Most government departments and larger private companies, however, provided their own buses,

TABLE 8.4
Domestic Airline Passengers (million departures)

Year	Total
1952–4 (average)	0.3
1957–65 (average)	0.4
1975	2.5
1982	6.4
1985	6.3

Source: BPS (1989b).

which was also a way of ensuring that employees did in fact report for work. Those who could afford to bought private cars—perhaps the ultimate status symbol. Many cars and jeeps under private control, however, were official civilian or military vehicles.

Transport Improvements under the New Order

Between 1971 and 1985 the transport contribution to Indonesia's GDP increased from Rp 1,400 billion to Rp 4,032 billion (at constant 1983 prices), slightly increasing its share of GDP from 4.4 per cent to 5.0 per cent (Table 8.5). This is comparable with other large Asian developing countries. Indonesia's transport sector made a marginally greater contribution to GDP than China, but a little less than in India (ESCAP Secretariat, 1987: 2). Employment in transport, storage, and communications in Indonesia more than doubled from 951,000 in 1971 to 1,958,000 in 1985, increasing its share of the total workforce from 2.3 per cent to 3.1 per cent, at the same time achieving an increase in labour productivity (Table 8.5). However, transport has close links with growth in the main centres of production in the economy, and this is inadequately conveyed in data on either GDP or employment.

Transport Planning in Repelita I–IV

Principal government responsibility for transport in Indonesia rests with the Department of Communications and, specifically, its three directorates-general: Sea, Land, and Air Transport. The Directorate-General of Roads (Bina Marga) is located within the Department of

TABLE 8.5
Transport Component of GDP and Labour Force
(1983 constant prices)

	1971	1978	1980	1985
Transport contribution to GDP (Rp billion)	1,400	2,470	2,756	4,032
Transport share of GDP (per cent)	4.4	4.5	4.3	5.0
Transport, storage, and communications labour force ('000)	951	1,289	1,468	1,958
Transport, storage, and communications (TSC) share of total labour force (per cent)	2.3	2.5	2.8	3.1
Transport GDP (Rp million)				
Labour Force in TSC	1.47	1.92	1.88	2.06

Sources: Based on data in BPS (1989b and 1978).

Public Works, and has responsibility for road construction and maintenance. Postal and telecommunications services are managed by a separate ministry. Finally, the Bureau of Communications and Tourism in Bappenas has an overall strategic planning and monitoring role. Central government directorates-general are also generally represented at the provincial level (and below), where they share responsibilities with provincial government agencies.

Transport planning in New Order Indonesia focused initially on the rehabilitation of the transport system (*Repelita I*, 1969/70–1973/4), a goal shared with the Eight-Year Plan (1961 to 1969). The latter, however, had only been partially implemented, leaving the New Order government to begin the rehabilitation of transport, particularly of the road system, which it undertook with the support of a series of World Bank projects. *Repelita II* (1974/5–1978/9) saw the programme of rehabilitation continue, supplemented by an emphasis on the upgrading and expansion of the transport system, an orientation which extended through to *Repelita III* (1979/80–1983/4) (Leinbach, 1986). With the slow-down in the collection of government revenues, priorities in *Repelita IV* (1984/5–1988/9) highlighted the need to impose greater scrutiny over transport investment criteria, raised concerns over public subsidies for transport enterprises, drew attention to the maintenance of the transport infrastructure, and questioned the role of government in the sector (Maspaitella, 1987: 84–5).

The proportion of public investment allocated to transport and tourism from the development budget declined from 15.8 per cent in *Repelita II* to 15.5 per cent in *Repelita III*, reaching its lowest at 12.3 per cent of investment in *Repelita IV*. Judged by these measures, support for transport has been steadily declining, although it remains one of the most significant sectors of public investment. In *Repelita II*, for instance, transport and tourism ranked third in development spending (after agriculture and irrigation, and regional development), second in *Repelita III* (after industry, mining and energy), and fourth in *Repelita IV* (following industry, mining and energy, education and youth affairs, and agriculture) (Booth, 1989: 12). *Repelita V* has placed transport and tourism at the top of the sectoral list, with an overall increase in share to 19.1 per cent.

Land transport has been Indonesia's main priority, particularly spending on infrastructure. About 55 per cent of expenditure in transport has been allocated for the development and maintenance of the road system, 20 per cent for maritime transport, 15 per cent for railways, with the remaining 10 per cent shared between air and river transport (Leinbach, 1986: 196; Tas'an, 1987: 95–6).

Vehicles and Roads

Between 1968 and 1986 the total number of registered (civilian) motor vehicles increased twelvefold, a compound growth rate of about 14 per cent per annum (Table 8.6). The trend was dominated by motor cycles,

TABLE 8.6
Number of Registered Motor Vehicles,[a] 1968 and 1986 ('000)

Year	Cars	Per Cent	Buses[b]	Per Cent	Trucks	Per Cent	Motor Cycles	Per Cent	Total
1968	202	32	20	3	93	15	308	50	623
1986	1,064	14.5	257	3.5	882	12	5,119	70	7,322
Growth rate, 1968–86 (per cent)	427		1,185		843		1,562		1,075

Source: BPS (1989b).
[a]Excluding armed forces and diplomatic corps vehicles.
[b]Including 'pick-ups'.

whose share of the total rose from 50 per cent to 70 per cent. Automobile numbers, by contrast, grew much more slowly than any other category; their share of the total declined from almost a third in 1968 to less than half that in 1986. This was due to the high price of cars brought about by heavy protection. The number of trucks and buses (including minibuses and pick-ups) increased about two to three times as fast.

The regional distribution of vehicles in 1968 and 1986 has been fairly stable (Table 8.7). In the case of automobiles, the share of Jakarta alone and of all Java remained at a little over one-third and three-quarters respectively. A marked bias against the Outer Islands is, therefore, not just a New Order phenomenon. The distribution was also fairly stable in the case of trucks, though here the share of Jakarta alone was under a fifth and the split between Java and the Outer Islands around 60 : 40. In the case of buses and pick-ups, growth was strongly biased towards Java, while for motor cycles, the bias ran the other way.

TABLE 8.7
Regional Distribution of Registered Motor Vehicles, 1968 and 1986
(percentage)

Region	Cars 1968	Cars 1986	Buses 1968	Buses 1986	Trucks 1968	Trucks 1986	Motor Cycles 1968	Motor Cycles 1986	Total 1968	Total 1986
Jakarta	36	34	21	43	19	17	27	14	28	18
Java	77	76	44	65	58	62	79	62	74	64
Outer Islands	23	24	56	35	42	38	21	38	26	36
Indonesia	100	100	100	100	100	100	100	100	100	100

Source: Calculated from BPS (1989b).

TABLE 8.8
Growth in Length of Roads by Level of Government (kilometres)

Year	Central	Per Cent	Province	Per Cent	Kabupaten	Per Cent	Total
1967	10 150	12	22 700	27	51 000	61	83 850
1972	10 980	12	25 966	27	58 517	61	95 463
1985	12 486	6	38 939	19	155 812	75	207 237
Growth, 1967–85 (per cent)	23		50		206		117

Sources: Department of Information (1969: 92); BPS (1989b).

Some of the rapid growth in vehicle numbers is, of course, due to road improvements.[4] The length of roads increased between 1967 and 1985 some 2.5 times: reflecting the contribution of Inpres funds, about 85 per cent of this was represented by local (i.e. kabupaten) roads (Table 8.8). In the late 1970s, though, Indonesia was still well behind comparable countries such as India, which had three times the road length per capita, and almost eight times as much road per unit of area (ESCAP Secretariat, 1987: 2). Probably more important has been the improvement in the condition of roads. The proportion of roads under asphalt purportedly rose from 24 per cent in 1970 to 40 per cent in 1985 (Table 8.9). This statistic is somewhat misleading, however, because in the late 1960s much of the road nominally under asphalt was badly pot-holed and not necessarily superior to gravel. More qualitative data on the condition of roads suggest that in 1967 only some 5 per cent of all roads were in 'good' condition, but by 1985 this had increased to 31 per cent (in the case of national roads, the corresponding figures were 17 per cent and 59 per cent) (Table 8.10).

By 1985, a third of the total road length was still judged to be more or less badly 'damaged'. Not surprisingly, local roads (44 per cent) were much more affected than national roads (7 per cent), suggesting a protracted lack of investment in the former. It should, however, be borne in mind that one of the reasons local roads are still in such bad condition is their increasingly heavy use. The funds provided under Inpres schemes did not permit the construction of surfaces able to withstand the weight

TABLE 8.9
Length of Roads by Surface, 1970 and 1985 (kilometres)

Year	Asphalt	Per Cent	Non-asphalt	Other	Total
1970	20 444	24	43 320	20 533	84 297
1985	83 566	40	111 622	12 049	207 237

Source: BPS (1989b).

TABLE 8.10

Length of Roads by Surface Condition and Level of Government,[a] 1985
(kilometres)

Level	Good	Per Cent	Moderate	Per Cent	Damaged	Per Cent	Total
Central	7 432	59 (17)[b]	4 191	34	863	7	12 486
Provincial	11 985	31 (10)	20 079	51	6 875	18	38 939
Municipal	4 806	43 (n.a.)	3 825	35	2 499	22	11 083
Kabupaten	39 722	27 (–)	41 687	29	63 323	44	144 732
Total	63 945	31 (5)	69 782	100	73 510	35	207 237

Source: BPS (1989b).
[a]Excluding Jakarta.
[b]Figures in brackets denote 1967 percentages.
n.a. = Not available.

of trucks in the wet season, so that heavy annual maintenance is
necessary.

Though it might be expected that the condition of roads would be
much worse in the Outer Islands than in Java, official figures do not
uniformly bear this out. Looking at the condition of local roads on each
island (Table 8.11) suggests that in Sumatra and Kalimantan road conditions are proportionally only marginally worse than Java, though the
east of the archipelago is clearly disadvantaged.

Urban Transport

At the beginning of the New Order, Jakarta was the city in which urban
transport was perceived to be least adequate. In many ways, it remains
so. Compounded by the great area and population of the capital, the
problem is one of too many vehicles for the road system. Whereas at the
beginning of the New Order the *becak* was blamed for traffic congestion

TABLE 8.11

Condition of *Kabupaten* Roads by Island, 1985 (kilometres)

Island	Good	Per Cent	Moderate	Per Cent	Damaged	Per Cent	Total
Java[a]	13 151	31	13 016	31	15 701	38	41 868
Sumatra	10 821	27	12 242	30	17 681	43	40 744
Kalimantan	4 114	31	3 532	27	5 556	42	13 202
Sulawesi	6 825	28	6 169	25	11 811	48	24 805
Other[b]	4 811	20	6 728	28	12 574	52	24 113
Total	39 722	27	41 687	29	63 323	44	144 732

Source: BPS (1989b).
[a]Excluding Jakarta.
[b]Bali, Nusa Tenggara, Maluku, and Irian Jaya.

and soon banished to the side streets, twenty years later peak-hour congestion remains acute, though Jakarta has not yet strangled itself like Bangkok. All the expedients, such as one-way streets, traffic lights, and investment in arterial roads, have done no more than keep pace with the rapid growth of motor-vehicle traffic. Moreover, better roads have permitted the city to sprawl, which has both lengthened the distance between residence and workplace and boosted the amount of awkward cross-city traffic.

In Jakarta, as in other cities, it would seem that the benefits of road widening have flowed disproportionately to the vehicle-owning middle class. Those who must walk, cycle, or use urban public transport have tended to suffer a loss of accessibility. This is especially so for pedestrians, whose footpaths have been sacrificed to road widening and for whom far too few overhead bridges are provided to cross dangerous multi-lane roads.

Urban public transport is the preserve of the less well-off. Especially in Jakarta, the upper middle class—almost by definition—travel by car and, mindful of pickpockets and knife-carrying robbers lurking on public transport, have their children driven to and from school. Except for taxis, they no longer have the experience of crowding on to public transport.[5] Despite rapid growth of the bus and minibus fleet, now supplemented by rail transport, overcrowding remains typical of the peak hour. Although the flat-rate fare structure subsidizes commuting over long distances, for those who must change vehicles the cost is a significant proportion of income.

In Jakarta, as in most other large cities, the central government has underwritten what Dick and Rimmer (1980) referred to as a strategy of 'modernisation and incorporation'. City buses operated by the government-owned land transport enterprise have been introduced to replace *bemo* on main fixed routes. Small motorized vehicles such as *bajaj*—an Indian-designed two passenger vehicle driven by a motorcycle engine—have been brought in to replace *becak* in main streets.[6] To what extent these investments have actually benefited users is unclear. Insufficient buses has meant that passengers have to stand, which has led to buses becoming a haunt of pickpockets. Enclosed, noisy and polluting *bajaj* are not necessarily a more comfortable means of travel than the *becak*. The main beneficiary of these changes has probably been the private vehicle owner, who enjoys a faster flow of traffic, though, as suggested above, any gains tend to be swamped by growth in vehicle numbers.

Inter-city Transport

The high priority given by the New Order government to the repair of roads had an immediate impact. Although at first little more could be done than filling in pot-holes, even this raised speeds and markedly reduced transit times. Relaxation of foreign exchange controls allowed entrepreneurs to import buses to meet the excess demand for inter-city travel. Being modern (some had air-conditioning), as well as enabling passengers to get a seat, these buses quickly gained patronage. One very popular service was a night bus (*bis malam*) between Jakarta, Central Java, and Surabaya, and on to Bali. Municipal governments soon organized terminals to handle the booming traffic.

For short inter-city runs such as Jakarta/Bogor and Surabaya/Malang, a competing form of transport appeared in the form of Colts (Mitsubishi vans fitted to carry about a dozen passengers but, in practice, able to squeeze in about eighteen), which took over the role of shared taxis, formerly large, American-built sedans. Faster than buses—but willing to pick up and put down on demand—these Colts gained a reputation for being dangerous, yet they still attracted many passengers. In time they became ubiquitous, operating on rural routes as well as on the principal inter-city links.

With railways continuing to face capacity constraints, buses and Colts accommodated the growth in passenger demand. Whereas at the outset of the New Order most inter-city passengers travelled on the train, by the 1980s this had shrunk to a small minority. Indeed, in 1985, the number of passengers carried by rail in Java was marginally below the pre-war (1939) figure and in Sumatra only a quarter of that level (Table 8.3).

A similar trend was apparent in the case of inter-city freight. Before the Second World War, the state railways had, through regulation, heavily constrained the growth of road freight. After independence, these regulations ceased to be effective and, as mentioned above, general freight shifted to road transport. By the mid-1960s, railway ton-kilometres were already well below pre-war levels. In Sumatra the carriage of rail freight stagnated and in Java declined until the late 1970s. In other words, the entire growth in land transport was met by road transport. That railways continued to play some role in freight carriage was attributable to bulk items, most notably petroleum products, fertilizer, cement, and, in Sumatra, coal. In the 1980s, railways have redefined their task, downgrading unprofitable passenger operations and concentrating upon profitable bulk cargo. With the volume of goods growing by around 15 per cent per annum, the ratio of passengers to freight fell from 7 : 3 in 1981/2 to 5 : 3 in 1988/9 and is projected to reach 1 : 1 in 1993/4 (*Business News*, 3 February 1989). While this will relieve some of the pressure on the road system, the role of railways will remain marginal.

Rural–Urban Transport

Perhaps the most dramatic improvement in land transport has been between village and market town. At the outset of the New Order, walking was still the normal means out of the village, at least as far as the main road, if not all the way to the market town. For the wealthier, the most reliable mechanical assistance was provided by a bicycle, even if it did have to be wheeled through the worst stretches. During the 1970s this began to change. First, central government development funds, swelled by oil tax revenues, were channelled through various programmes—most notably the Inpres (Instruksi Presiden) *kabupaten* and village schemes—into local feeder roads (Leinbach, 1986: 204). Fairly reliable access to towns was thereby provided, if road maintenance was kept up. Secondly, the Green Revolution meant that much larger quantities of rice, *palawija*, and other cash crops required transport out of the village, while loads of fertilizer and cement, plus a growing variety of consumer goods, had to be brought in. Thirdly, rising purchasing power meant that households could now afford to buy vehicles. Bicycles and motor cycles were not just consumption items but, with panniers, a means of carrying small quantities of goods. Young motor-cycle owners enjoyed unprecedented freedom and also could earn an income by ferrying passengers to and from the highway to catch passing inter-city buses, the usual form of travel for millions of circular migrants with temporary employment in town or city. Entrepreneurs in villages and market towns had the funds to invest in pick-ups and small trucks.

The pick-up (included in traffic figures as buses or trucks) turned out to be an ideal multi-purpose vehicle. When first used in cities such as Surabaya, it resembled a jitney, being somewhat larger than a *bemo*, but with similar parallel rows of seats in a small rear cabin. A larger version able to carry 14 to 16 passengers began to find favour in the mid-1970s as a means of ferrying villagers to and from the market towns with small bundles of produce. Their numbers soared and by the late 1970s in Java they had almost displaced the once common market bus. This, being larger, offered a much lower frequency of service and could not detour from the main roads into the villages. Yet, just by raising the benches along either side of the cabin, these pick-ups could also, within a moment, be converted to a small truck for carrying bags of rice, fertilizer, or cement. Owners would willingly accept such charters. In this role, by the late 1970s, the pick-ups and trucks had taken over the work of the ox-cart (*cikar*), which could carry more but only at a walking pace. Ox-carts were left to carry low-value bricks and tiles from village to town.

By the 1980s, at least in most parts of Java, Bali, and Lombok, transport between village and market town and between market town and city was quick, frequent, and cheap. Indeed, there was now often a choice of means. From the village, people could travel by foot, bicycle, motor cycle (*ojek*), or pick-up, and from the market town by bus or Colt (and sometimes train). There was no need to book and, during busy periods, little waiting time. Travel no longer held any terrors, except perhaps for the elderly. Most villagers have seen something of the wider world and many have worked in the city, a considerable literature attesting to the prevalence of circular migration. Even in the colonial period, when transport infrastructure was relatively well developed, there was no such revolution in personal mobility. In the Outer Islands, where population density is lower and distances greater, the level of accessibility and mobility has been rather less but the trend is in the same direction. The Trans-Sumatra, Trans-Kalimantan, and Trans-Sulawesi highways are beginning to provide a backbone for improved local roads.

Inter-island Transport: Shipping and Air

Although few data are published on inter-island trade, it appears that its growth, which was very rapid during the 1970s, has since slowed down.[7] Between 1983 and 1988 dry cargo tonnage grew at an average of only 4 per cent per annum, though growth of liquid cargo (mainly crude oil and oil products) was about three times greater. During the New Order, the mix of cargo has changed with raw materials (such as crude oil, vegetable oils, and timber) and industrial inputs (such as oil products, fertilizer, and cement) assuming a more prominent role. This reflects growth and structural change in the economy, as well as a tendency to shift general cargo to road transport when it becomes feasible. For large tonnages of bulk cargoes, shipping remains much cheaper, though until recently regulation has discriminated against the provision of specialist ships.

At the same time, vehicular ferries have enabled road transport to erode what formerly was the preserve of sea freight. The first such craft were introduced to run across Bali Strait between Ketapang (East Java) and Gilimanuk (Bali): by the early 1970s most general cargo to and from Bali already moved almost entirely by truck. In 1978 vehicular ferries were also placed in service across Sunda Strait from Merak to Bakahuni using second-hand vessels imported from Japan. General freight quickly shifted to road between Java and the provinces of Lampung and South Sumatra. Simultaneous improvement of the Trans-Sumatra Highway allowed trucks to load direct from Jakarta to Jambi, Padang, and Medan. Despite the muddy conditions, many traders preferred to use road. Door-to-door consignment not only eliminated double-handling at both ends but also minimized pilferage. Shipowners serving the line between Jakarta and Belawan (Medan), once the busiest route for general cargo, have been hard hit. Buses have also taken advantage of the vehicular ferries to run from Java to Sumatra, with regular services carrying labour between the poor Gunung Kidul district of Central Java via Jakarta to the coffee districts of South Sumatra. Road transport is feasible from Aceh as far east as Bima (Sumbawa), beyond which roads and shipping services are still primitive.

Despite the switch since the 1950s of first- and second-class cabin passengers to air travel, inter-island shipping has remained important for the carriage of large numbers of low-income passengers. Between main ports, this trade remains a virtual monopoly of the state-owned inter-island shipping enterprise, Pelni. Until the mid-1980s passengers slept on woven mats under canvas or in the 'tweendecks' of small combination passenger/cargo ships under much more crowded and primitive conditions than had been allowed by the KPM in the 1950s. Since 1983 Pelni has taken delivery from Germany of a series of large, fast, and quite luxurious passenger liners, which have greatly upgraded the comfort, speed, and frequency of service, though fares are not cheap. The improvement in ferry services across Sunda Strait, however, has meant that many who used to travel by ship on the two main passenger routes to and from Medan and Padang now travel by bus. This trend away from relatively expensive shipping parallels that for general cargo.

A long-standing problem which seems to have been brought under control since the mid-1970s is that of providing for regular calls at remote ports in the archipelago. In the days of the KPM, visits at minor ports were cross-subsidized by those at main ports; very remote places were served by the 'white ships' (*kapal putih*) of the Department of Shipping, in the course of maintaining navigational aids. By the 1960s both services had lapsed. Attempts to oblige private firms to call at outports as a condition of their licences had little success. In 1974, at the start of the Second Five-Year Plan, the Directorate-General of Sea Communications re-introduced ships of the navigation service as 'pioneer ships' (*kapal perintis*) to call at remote outports on a regular monthly schedule (Dick, 1987: 130–5). Remote provinces such as Nusa Tenggara (East and West), Maluku, and Irian Jaya—all heavily dependent upon shipping for local communications—thereby benefited, especially by facilitating the flow of passengers to and from market and government centres. While in the past cargo has been carried mainly by the ubiquitous motor *prahu*, economic development has now been felt even in remote districts, with the greater flow of cargo making the provision of regular visits commercially viable.

Air services now fall into three categories. First, Garuda (which has a fleet of 73 jets), and, very recently, Merpati (a subsidiary of Garuda), provide jet services between main cities. Secondly, Merpati and private airlines (such as Bouraq and Mandala) provide some cheaper and slower non-jet services between main cities as well as feeder services to outlying centres. Merpati operates 60 propeller-driven and prop-jet aircraft and concentrates more on short-haul routes. Its passenger load of 600,000 in 1978 increased to over a million in 1986 and has remained at that level in subsequent years (*Indonesia Development News*, 12(4): 7). Sempati has recently been licensed to import jets for domestic routes. Thirdly, the system of 'pioneer ships' has its parallel in pioneer air services. These are services provided to airports which would not justify a connection on a commercial basis. About half of Merpati's 120 routes serve remote areas. No province benefits more from such services than Irian Jaya, which still lacks road links between the coast and the highlands, but other Outer Island provinces are also served. Government officials and businessmen are thereby saved the time and discomfort of conventional sea or land transport.

Telecommunications

Under the Old Order, telecommunications deteriorated more than any other subsector of transport and communications. This was most apparent in the case of telephones. By the mid-1960s, the automatic exchanges installed in the main cities since independence had ceased to function effectively. Systems were so overloaded and in such poor repair that connections could not be made. Rather than waste time in trying to telephone, people developed the habit of calling on one another at home in the evening. While a pleasant social custom, it was an inefficient way of doing business, particularly in busy Jakarta. Not until the late 1970s were new exchanges installed so that, in Jakarta, one could at last use the telephone as in any other modern city. Improvements followed in provincial cities.

Indonesia established an international direct-dialling facility in 1974. The first of the Palapa telecommunications satellites was launched in 1976, creating an integrated telephone system covering the entire archipelago, and linking this with the International Subscriber Dialling (ISD) system. Replacement satellites were launched in 1983 and 1985, but the latter failed to reach its planned orbit and had to be replaced in 1987. The launching of the Palapa satellite system transformed telecommunications in Indonesia by creating an effective national network, although Indonesia's telephone density remains among the lowest in South-East Asia. Initially derided as a wasteful prestige project, the satellite has not only achieved efficient interlocal and international telecommunications but also has made television signals available to every village in the country (Setiawan and Effendi, 1989: 24–6).

While foreigners are inclined to criticize the quality of programmes and the political content of the national television network (TVRI), Indonesians of all classes in both cities and villages have demonstrated their appreciation of this new form of communication. In the main cities, television sets are now a typical household consumer durable, while even in the *kampung* those who cannot yet afford sets watch those of their neighbours; in villages, communal sets attract large audiences. The pattern of social activities, especially in the evening, has markedly changed.

Transport Policies and Future Plans

Transport Problems in the 1980s

Despite the dramatic improvement in transport infrastructure since the mid-1960s, the rapid growth in passengers and cargoes continues to place strain on the transport system. Inadequacies in transport and communications are still identified as contributing to the high costs of production and distribution (Economist Intelligence Unit, 1988: 49). Indonesia is not alone in this regard. In recognition of the significant need for transport and communications improvements in the continued social and economic development of the region, ESCAP has declared the period 1985–94 the 'Transport and Communications Decade for Asia and the Pacific' (Anwar, Gunawardana, and de Silva, 1989: 58).

Despite considerable investments, the road system, for instance, is still a bottleneck for freight movements. Indonesia's total road length is well below comparable Asian countries and the Outer Islands have been somewhat neglected in road-building programmes compared to Java. Primitive road construction methods, combined with inadequate maintenance programmes, mean that more than two-thirds of the network is in poor condition (Table 8.10). This limits the size of trucks and the maximum loads to well below the allowable levels typical in Europe and North America, though exceptions have been made for the carriage of marine containers. Urban transport also remains a serious problem in the large cities, particularly Jakarta. Despite extensive freeway and overpass development, the city's traffic is congested and the public transport under stress.

Inter-island trade is still hampered by irregular and high-cost shipping services. Inefficiency has been underpinned by regulations which maintained barriers to entry, subsidized inefficient firms while discouraging the growth of better-organized ones, imposed a rigid pattern of routes, and impeded the introduction of new technology such as vehicle deck and cellular container ships (Dick, 1987). Whereas container ships were introduced to inter-island trade in the Philippines over a decade ago, their use in Indonesia has remained largely confined to feeder lines with Singapore, while inter-island (as opposed to export/import) cargo is only just beginning to be containerized. In the absence of containerization and the discipline which it imposes, ship turn-around is slow and the movement of cargo through ports is often impeded.

The problem for air transport is overcapacity, even though air fares are government-controlled and set artificially low. Garuda, for instance, filled an estimated average of 50 per cent of international seats and 42 per cent of domestic seats in 1985, and as a result, had been operating until 1988 at a financial loss (Economist Intelligence Unit, 1988: 52). The company responded to this late in 1989 by announcing that in future it would concentrate on what it perceived to be the more lucrative overseas routes, leaving the less profitable domestic routes to Merpati and private airlines (Schwarz, 1989a: 71–2).

In terms of telecommunications the main problem is the need to expand the network through the provision of more telephones, to bring it up to the level in other Asian developing countries, while improving the quality of the available services.

Transport safety issues are still a major problem, particularly road transport and inter-island shipping. Indonesia recorded 10,809 deaths and 20,987 serious injuries as a result of road traffic accidents during 1987 (BPS, 1989a: 33–7). Large numbers of passengers are carried between minor ports, on vessels no larger than fishing trawlers, in dangerous conditions in clear breach of international regulations for the protection of life at sea. One notorious example is the busy emigration route across Makassar Strait, from Pare Pare in South Sulawesi to Balikpapan in East Kalimantan.

Institutional deficiencies have been a significant factor in the failure to overcome problems in the transport network. Despite the funds poured into transport infrastructure during the decade of the oil boom, there was little institutional reform. Transport planning remained highly centralized in the directorates-general in Jakarta with little sensitivity to local needs. Moreover, each directorate-general has been used to behaving like an autonomous fiefdom. For example, there was little co-ordination between the Directorate-General of Roads in the Department of Public Works and the Directorate-General of Land Transport in the Department of Communications, even though they have overlapping responsibilities in road construction and traffic management (Tas'an, 1987: 98). The Directorate-General of Land Transport (Inland Waterways and Ferries) and the Directorate-General of Sea Communications could not agree which was to have authority over inter-island vehicular ferries. Intermodal co-ordination was still in its infancy.

The root of many transport problems has been that the bureaucracy has tried to undertake too many tasks, by not only providing the essential infrastructure, but also running transport enterprises and regulating commercial operators. Although this propensity was inherited from the Old Order, it was perhaps reinforced under the New Order. The technocratic approach which encouraged freer play for market forces did not penetrate to the transport and communications sector. Thus, directorates-general continued to license entry, allocate routes, specify fares and freight rates, and restrict capacity. As problems emerged, they tended to increase regulatory controls rather than to identify and eliminate the original distortion. This was accompanied by a wilful lack of curiosity as to what conditions really were like, as opposed to what they were laid down to be. None the less, bureaucrats could earn steady unofficial incomes from allowing businessmen to find their way through the maze of regulations.

Transport Policy Reform

In Indonesia's Fifth Development Plan, *Repelita V* (1989/90 to 1993/4), transport investment has increased to 19.1 per cent of the development budget, up from 12.3 per cent in *Repelita III*. As with previous plans, the road development programme is provided with the lion's share, totalling 60 per cent of investment, while the rest is spread between rail, air, sea, and river transport (Department of Information, 1989a and 1989b). Institutional problems have also been tackled in parallel with *Repelita V*, but the origins of these moves occurred earlier in the decade.

Because of declining oil revenues, since the mid-1980s Indonesia has pushed to boost non-oil exports. As a result, the transport and communications sector has become a major target in the government's programme of micro-economic reform, the aim of which is to reduce the high cost of production in Indonesia. This has led to new trends towards deregulation and, more tentatively, to privatization. Institutional barriers to more efficient functioning of transport subsectors were identified, beginning with domestic shipping. For the first time the transport sector was identified as a service sector where the needs of shippers and passengers should be paramount. Shippers and operators were emboldened by the campaign against the 'high cost economy' to complain about bureaucratic rigidities, which became a common item in the press.

The first serious moves towards deregulation of transport occurred in 1985 in relation to sea transport and ports with the promulgation of Inpres No. 4, 1985. The most controversial and strikingly effective measure was the reform of the notoriously corrupt Directorate-General of Customs. The investigation and clearance of import consignments worth more than US$5,000 was transferred to the Swiss firm, Société Générale de Surveillance (SGS) and customs controls over exports and inter-island trade were abolished altogether. The other major reform was the opening of well over a hundred ports to foreign-flag shipping and the abolition of general agency permits, which had been the basis for restriction of access by foreign-flag ships. Hitherto, policy had been to constrain Indonesia's trade to direct shipment through the 'gateway ports' of Jakarta, Surabaya, Belawan, and Ujung Pandang and to restrict transhipment via Singapore. Containerization was thereby inhibited. Once operators were free to provide feeder services to link up in Singapore with large container vessels, containerization suddenly took off in Indonesia's foreign trade, with marked savings in transport costs.

The emergency and rather *ad hoc* measures contained in Inpres No. 4 of 1985 did not constitute a reform of inter-island shipping. Far from tackling the underlying causes of inefficiency, they allowed exporters and importers to bypass inter-island shipping by facilitating direct access to Singapore. The protection enjoyed by inter-island shipping was removed but nothing was done to improve its efficiency. Economic integration was still inhibited. Inpres No. 4 of 1985 nevertheless helped to expose the problem. On 21 November 1988 the government introduced a follow-up package of reforms (Paket November 21 or Paknov) which substantially deregulated inter-island shipping: licences were to be provided virtually as of right, operators were free to determine the routing of their ships, foreign-flag ships could be chartered subject only to notification, and permits were abolished for docking overseas. While the response to this deregulation has so far been very uneven, the release of dynamism and innovation is unmistakable and bodes well for the future. The main problem is now to eliminate institutional rigidities, especially in pricing and labour markets, that sustain low utilization of ships and port facilities.

In addition to investment plans, another series of transport sector reforms was released in 1989 coinciding with *Repelita V* (Department of Information, 1989a and 1989b). These commenced with deregulatory measures for land transport, including an attempt to redefine the role of government in land transport, improved procedures for investment planning, and a freer role for the market to determine the supply of land transport. Restrictions on firms entering the transport sector are being reduced, while the private sector is to be encouraged to invest in public transport, the development of transport terminals, and other facilities and infrastructure. New vehicle weight and dimension limits are being introduced and it is intended to improve road safety and environmental protection by better driver-training programmes and vehicle-inspection procedures. It is too early to assess the effect of the reform measures on land transport, which have hardly had time to make much of an impact.

The airlines have also been examined with the purpose of improving efficiency and increasing their exposure to market demand. The first moves were made in October 1989 when air fares were increased by 20 per cent, as a means of testing the strength of demand. Meanwhile, domestic flight routes previously operated by Garuda in the eastern part of the country have been transferred to Merpati and private airlines, with routes in the western half of the country scheduled for 1990 (*Business News*, 15 December 1989, p. 4). The transfer of airport management from the Directorate-General of Air Transport to several state enterprises (Perusahaan Umum Angkasa Pura) is planned to continue.

The deteriorating railway system has been the focus of increased investment, particularly in new rolling stock, over the past decade, while current plans promote rail as a carrier of bulk goods. In institutional terms, railways have been brought under the control of a state enterprise titled Perusahaan Umum Kereta Api, which reports to the Directorate-General of Land Communications.

The problems and solutions in urban traffic and transport management are common across the larger cities of the archipelago, but reach their apotheosis in the case of Jakarta. Chronic traffic congestion and poor standards of service continue to plague Jakarta's planners. However, urban transport is the one major transport subsector in which market reforms have received limited acceptance. The Jakarta 2005 Plan moots the possibility of introducing area controls on vehicle access to the central city in the near future. In the meantime, emphasis is being put on public transport, particularly in the form of large buses and minibuses, the elevation of Jakarta's suburban railway, and taxis. Some of the city's most popular forms of transport—the *becak, bajaj* (or 'fourth class' vehicles) and *mikrolet*—are to be either phased out or severely limited in their operations. The *becak*, for instance, were due to be eliminated from the city by 1990. City planners seem particularly anxious to replace all these effective community-based modes of transport, despite the fact that there is a demonstrable demand for them, and substitute large buses which hitherto have not proved economical to operate.

Less expensive planning solutions are surely required for Indonesia's medium and smaller cities. *Mikrolet* and *becak* are able adequately to provide the basic requirements for urban transport. Local government's role would seem best restricted to the provision of basic infrastructure (roads and transport stations), whilst making sure that the transport operators are able to operate with as few restrictions as possible, beyond the kinds of standard regulations necessary to ensure adequate traffic control and safety.

Indonesia's transport-reform measures since 1985 have both targeted specific subsectors, and included measures for broader institutional reorganization and corporatization. In general, the Department of Communications is gradually withdrawing from the direct provision of transport services and facilities, and is building its role around the supervision of state transport enterprises and the regulation, monitoring, and administration of the sector as a whole. At the provincial level, all the activities of the Department of Communications are being brought under a single regional office (the *kantor wilayah* or *kanwil*) in an attempt to streamline local functions. New state-owned enterprises have been created to manage transport operations, while existing state enterprises are being encouraged to become more efficient and competitive. The government's concern with public finance has meant it has looked closely at the level of subsidies for state-owned transport companies. In the case of Jakarta's major bus company, PPD, this has meant scrutiny of the efficiency of operations, together with allegations of graft and corruption (*Jakarta Post*, 29 September 1989). There has also been a trend towards the construction of toll-roads as a means of offsetting the high costs of transport infrastructure. These are operated by the state enterprise, PT Jasa Marga, which has raised capital by issuing bonds on the Jakarta Stock Exchange.

Finally, the government is supporting a degree of privatization in transport and communications. Apart from the role of the private customs firm, SGS (whose contract ends in 1991, when, according to Schwarz, 1989b, responsibility will return to the government), this has not meant the government is transferring state responsibilities to the private sector, in the fashion of Malaysia or Britain. However, it is strongly encouraging expanded private sector involvement and competition in several parts of the transport sector by reducing entry requirements.

Conclusion

There is nothing unique about the transport revolution in New Order Indonesia. In Asia, the revolution in rural–urban transport occurred first in Japan during the 1950s, with the agent of change being the tiny three-wheeled (later four-wheeled) vehicle known in Indonesia as a *bemo*. In the 1960s similar changes could be observed in Thailand, induced by similar vehicles imported cheaply from Japan. The *bemo* were also imported into Indonesia from the early 1960s but, due to balance of payments constraints, only in small numbers and for use as urban public transport. This reinforces the point that its introduction to rural areas required not just the vehicle but also some measure of prosperity.

What is unusual in Indonesia is its archipelagic geography and, hence, a reliance upon sea transport matched in Asia only by the Philippines.

This imposes more constraints upon land transport than in a country such as Thailand. Nevertheless, the improvement of highways and introduction of inter-island vehicular ferries has started a trend which is, unmistakably, the same as that observed in Japan, and before that, in Western countries. General cargo is moving from sea to road, leaving to the shipping industry the carriage of bulk cargoes. The development of aviation and telecommunications are other means whereby the long-sought integration of the archipelago is at last being achieved.

Because most of these changes are introducing what is familiar in the West, it is easy to forget how much things have changed in Indonesia over the past twenty-five years and to miss their historical significance. In the late nineteenth century the Industrial Revolution technologies of steamships, railways, and tramways were applied to Indonesia by a colonial power seeking to develop a production structure of benefit to the motherland. The outcome was a process of what has been referred to as 'dependent development'. Under the New Order, the twentieth-century technologies of the internal combustion engine and telecommunications have been applied by Indonesians in the service of national development and integration. During the oil boom, from the mid-1970s to the early 1980s, the transport system was transformed by government investment programmes. Now it is being transformed by institutional reforms, most notably deregulation. While autonomy is being enhanced, Indonesia is also being tied ever more closely into dynamic international systems from which, at the outset of the New Order, it had been isolated.

1. This excludes, of course, a mass of internal reports by various international agencies and their consultants.

2. Those ships seized in Indonesian ports were released after negotiations with the insurers; only the assets on shore were nationalized and transferred to Pelni.

3. *Opelet* had appeared in the 1930s; *bemo* (derived from *becak* motor) came on to the scene in 1962, when first imported from Japan and intended, as the name suggests, to replace the *becak*—instead they found their niche as small jitneys (Dick, 1981).

4. Leinbach (1986: 194–206) gives a good overview of New Order road-improvement programmes.

5. See Dick (1985b: 74–5).

6. Dick (1981) has described this process for Surabaya.

7. The last published set of Origin–Destination (OD) data is for 1983. Since the abolition of customs controls over inter-island trade with Inpres No. 4, 1985, the documents upon which data were based can no longer be obtained. Total inter-island tonnages are available for individual ports but these figures are not processed on an Origin–Destination basis.

REFERENCES

Anwar, M., Gunawardana, K. K., and de Silva, A. J. S. (1989), 'Asia–Pacific Telecommunity: A Focal Point for Regional Telecommunication Planning', *APT Journal of the Asia Pacific Telecommunity*, 1(1): 58–68.

Biro Pusat Statistik (BPS) (1978), *Keadaan Angkatan Kerja di Indonesia*, Jakarta.

_____ (1989a), *Statistik Kendaraan Bermotor dan Panjang Jalan 1987*, Jakarta.

_____ (1989b), *Statistik Indonesia, 1988*, Jakarta.

Booth, A. (1989), 'Repelita V and Indonesia's Medium Term Economic Strategy', *Bulletin of Indonesian Economic Studies*, 25(2): 3–30.

Brooks, M. (ed.) (1989), *Seafarers in the ASEAN Region*, Singapore: Institute of Southeast Asian Studies.

Department of Information (1969), *The First Five-Year Development Plan 1969/70–1973/74*, Volume IIB, Jakarta.

_____ (1989a), *Rancangan Rencana Pembangunan Lima Tahun Kelima 1989/90–1993/94*, Jakarta.

_____ (1989b), *Pidato Kenegaraan Presiden Republik Indonesia Soeharto di Depan Dewan Perwakilan Rakyat, 16 Agustus 1989*, Jakarta.

Dick, H.W. (1981), 'Urban Public Transport: Jakarta, Surabaya and Malang', *Bulletin of Indonesian Economic Studies*, 17(1): 66–82 and 17(2): 72–88.

_____ (1985a), 'Inter-island Shipping: Progress, Problems and Prospects', *Bulletin of Indonesian Economic Studies*, 21(2): 95–114.

_____ (1985b), 'The Rise of a Middle Class and the Changing Concept of Equity in Indonesia: An Interpretation', *Indonesia*, 39: 71–92.

_____ (1987), *The Indonesian Interisland Shipping Industry: An Analysis of Competition and Regulation*, Singapore: Institute of Southeast Asian Studies.

Dick, H.W. and Rimmer, P.J. (1980), 'Beyond the Formal/Informal Sector Dichotomy', *Pacific Viewpoint*, 21: 26–41.

Economist Intelligence Unit (1988), *Country Profile: Indonesia 1987/88*, London: Economist Publications Limited.

ESCAP Secretariat (1987), 'Review of the Transport and Communications Development of the ESCAP Region', *Transport and Communications Bulletin for Asia and the Pacific*, 59: 1–14.

Forbes, D.K. (1981), 'Production, Reproduction and Underdevelopment: Petty Commodity Producers in Ujung Pandang', *Environment and Planning A*, 13(7): 841–56.

Forbes, D.K. and Adisasmita, R. (1989), *Enhancing Employment and Productivity in the Land Transport Sector in Indonesia*, Department of Manpower/ILO Employment Creation Strategy Project, Jakarta.

Hugo, G. (1981), 'Road Transport, Population Mobility and Development in Indonesia', in G.W. Jones and H.V. Richter (eds.), *Population Mobility and Development: Southeast Asia and the Pacific*, Canberra: Australian National University, pp. 355–81.

Kartodirdjo, Sartono (1981), *The Pedicab in Yogyakarta: A Study of Low Cost Transportation and Poverty Problems*, Yogyakarta: Gadjah Mada University Press.

Leinbach, T. R. (1981), 'Travel Characteristics and Mobility Behaviour: Aspects of Rural Transport Impact in Indonesia', *Geografiska Annaler Series B*, 63: 119–29.

_____ (1983a), 'Rural Transport and Population Mobility in Indonesia', *Journal of Developing Areas*, 17(3): 349–64.

_____ (1983b), 'Transport Evaluation in Rural Development: An Indonesian Case Study', *Third World Planning Review*, 5: 23–35.

_____ (1986), 'Transport Development in Indonesia: Problems, Progress and Policies under the New Order', in C. MacAndrews (ed.), *Central Government and Local Development in Indonesia*, Singapore: Oxford University Press, pp. 190–220.

Leinbach, T.R. and Chia Lin Sien (1989), *South-East Asian Transport: Issues in Development*, Singapore: Oxford University Press.

Maspaitella, P. F. L. (1987), 'Indonesia: Regional Transport', in P. J. Rimmer (ed.), *The ASEAN–Australian Transport Interchange*, Canberra: National Centre for Development Studies, pp. 81–93.

NUDS (National Urban Development Strategy) (1985), *NUDS Final Report*, Jakarta: Directorate-General of Human Settlements.

Pendakur, V. S. (1984), *Urban Transport in ASEAN*, Research Notes and Discussion Paper No. 43, Singapore: Institute of Southeast Asian Studies.

Pond, D. (1968), 'Indonesian Surface Transport Facilities and Investment', in R. van Niel (ed.), *Economic Factors in Southeast Asian Social Change*, Asian Studies Program, Honolulu: University of Hawaii, 53–70.

Rimmer, P. J. (1986), *Rikisha to Rapid Transit: Urban Public Transport Systems and Policy in Southeast Asia*, Sydney: Pergamon Press.

Rogers, L.H. (1983), 'Resources Optimization in a City of Twenty Million', *Proceedings of Fourth Conference of the Road Engineering Association of Asia and Australia, August 22–26, Jakarta, Vol. 1*, Kuala Lumpur: Director-General of Public Works, pp. 395–410.

Schwarz, A. (1989a), 'Uncharted Skies', *Far Eastern Economic Review*, 21 September, pp. 71–2.

_____ (1989b), 'Local Customs Revival', *Far Eastern Economic Review*, 21 December, p. 57.

Setiawan, S. and Effendi (1989), 'Telecommunication Industry in Indonesia, Facing the Challenge of a Developing Nation', *APT Journal of the Asia Pacific Telecommunity*, 1(1): 24–6.

Soegijoko, B. T. S. (1984), 'Becaks as a Component of Urban Public Transportation in Indonesia', *Prisma*, 32: 64–77.

Tas'an, Darmawan (1987), 'Indonesia: Land Transport', in P. J. Rimmer (ed.), *The ASEAN–Australian Transport Interchange*, Canberra: National Centre for Development Studies, pp. 95–102.

9

The Service Sector

Jennifer Alexander and Anne Booth

Introduction

IN Indonesia, as in most other developing countries, the service sector plays an important role in the economy both in terms of contribution to GDP and in terms of employment. In 1987, the service sector, defined to include wholesale and retail trade, hotels and restaurants, transport and communications, financial and professional services, and public, domestic, and community services accounted for almost 38 per cent of GDP, and for 37 per cent of the labour force. The wholesale and retail trade sector alone (including hotels and restaurants) accounted for 17 per cent of GDP in 1987, and 15 per cent of the labour force. This sector of the economy was also unique in employing more women than men in 1987. Almost half of all women employed in non-agricultural occupations in 1987 were employed in the trade sector. The male service sector labour force by contrast was more concentrated in the 'other services' category which included both public servants, and people employed in a range of personal, social, and domestic services.

Because of the highly disparate nature of the service sector, there has been much debate over its role in the process of economic development and structural change. In the early literature, following what is often called the 'Fisher-Clark' hypothesis, there was a tendency to assume that as countries developed, the role of the agricultural sector declined relative to that of industry in terms of both GDP and labour force shares. Then as they matured into what Rostow termed 'high mass consumption' economies, the share of the service sector in both employment and GDP would grow relative to that of industry. However, the time series evidence from the now-developed countries examined by Kuznets did not entirely confirm this hypothesis. According to Kuznets (1966: 96–7), reviewing the data from thirteen developed countries over the years from 1800 to 1960: 'While the downward trend in the share of the agricultural sector and the upward trend in that of the industry sector are prominent and affect all countries except Australia, the movements in the share of the service sector are neither marked nor consistent among countries or among long sub-periods.' This statement appeared

correct for both the share of GDP and the share of employment. While
the proportion of the labour force in agriculture fell with rising per
capita incomes in such a consistent way that it could in fact be used as a
convenient proxy for per capita income, there was a wide variation in
the distribution of the non-agricultural labour force between industry
and services for any given percentage share of the labour force in agriculture. This point was also emphasized by Berry (1978: 215), who
plotted data for a range of countries at various stages of development on
the agricultural share of the labour force and the services share of the
non-agricultural labour force. An updated version of the Berry diagram
is given in Figure 9.1. It is at once obvious that for any given share of
the labour force in agriculture there has been a wide variation in the role
of services in absorbing non-agricultural labour. Broadly speaking, the
now-developed countries shown in the figure (France, United Kingdom,
Japan) form one cluster, where the service sector share in non-
agricultural employment (S/NA) never rose much above 50 per cent.[1]

FIGURE 9.1

Trends in the Agricultural Share of the Labour Force and the Service Share of
the Non-agricultural Labour Force in Selected Countries, 1800–1985

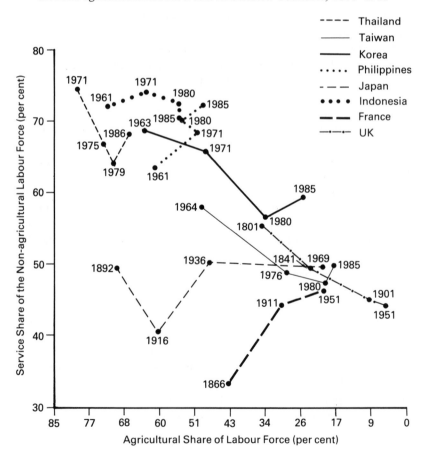

By contrast a group of developing countries in South-East Asia, including Indonesia, the Philippines, and Thailand, forms another cluster where for any given agricultural share, the S/NA ratio has been much higher than in the historical experience of the developed countries. Although data for African and Latin American countries are not shown in the diagram, Berry's figures indicate that they would also form part of this second cluster. Taiwan and Korea are interesting intermediate cases; in 1964 the S/NA ratio in Taiwan was higher than for the developed country cluster, but in more recent years it has conformed quite closely to their experience. In 1963 the S/NA ratio in Korea was similar to that in many parts of South-East Asia, but over the next two decades it fell as the share of agriculture in the labour force also declined.

The experience of Indonesia and the Philippines also contrasts with that of the now-developed economies in another important way. Historically, service sector productivity has grown more slowly than that in the rest of the economy, but in the early stages of development in most European countries and in Japan, labour in the service sector was much more productive than in the economy as a whole, because the economy was still dominated by the low productivity agricultural sector. Thus there has been a tendency for the ratio of service sector labour productivity to economy-wide productivity to fall gradually until it approaches unity. This has also happened in Korea, Taiwan, the Philippines, and Indonesia but at a much more rapid rate, so that in 1985 this ratio was about where it was in the United Kingdom, Germany, and Italy in the 1960s and Taiwan in 1985 (Table 9.1), although obviously per capita income in Indonesia and the Philippines in 1985 was still far below that of the other countries. An even more dramatic contrast emerges if one examines the ratio of service sector labour productivity to that in industry. In 1985 service sector labour productivity in Indonesia was only 75 per cent of that in industry. This was much lower than in the United Kingdom, Italy, Japan, or Taiwan at comparable stages of development. It was slightly higher than in Thailand in 1971 and the Philippines in 1985, although the ratio has been increasing in Thailand (Table 9.1). On the other hand, both Korea in 1963 and Japan in 1910 had a similar ratio to that in Indonesia in 1985; it should also be noted that, according to Minami's calculations, the Japanese ratio of service sector to industrial productivity fell sharply between 1910 and 1938 (when it was only 0.56), and then rose again after the war (Minami, 1986: 279). In Korea the evidence indicates that the ratio has been quite stable over the period of rapid growth from the early 1960s to the mid-1980s.

These data thus suggest that the service sector accounts for a much greater share of the non-agricultural labour force in contemporary Indonesia than was the case in countries such as France, Italy, Japan, or Taiwan at a comparable stage of development. Partly as a result of this, relative service sector labour productivity is rather low compared with at least some of the now-developed countries at comparable stages in their development, as well with countries such as Taiwan and Thailand

TABLE 9.1
Long-term Trends in Relative Product per Worker
(current price data)

	Labour Productivity in Services[a] as Ratio of	
	Total Labour Productivity	Industrial[b] Labour Productivity
United Kingdom		
1801–11	1.28	2.03
1963–7	0.98	0.96
Germany		
1913	2.20	3.10
1965	0.83	0.69
Italy		
1861–70	1.89	2.33
1963–7	1.17	1.04
Japan		
1910	1.51	0.88
1980	1.01	0.87
Korea		
1963	1.40	0.87
1985	0.90	0.73
Taiwan		
1964	1.48	0.93
1985	1.14	1.12
Philippines		
1961	1.88	1.14
1985	1.11	0.50
Thailand		
1971	2.98	0.67
1985	2.53	1.02
Indonesia		
1961	1.81	1.11
1985	1.28	0.75

Sources: UK, Germany and Italy: Kuznets (1971: 290–1).

       Japan: Minami (1986: 279).

       Indonesia: BPS, *Statistical Pocketbook of Indonesia*, 1972/3.

       Statistik Indonesia, 1982, 1986.

       Thailand: National Statistical Office, *Statistical Yearbook of Thailand*, Nos. 31 and 35.

       Taiwan: Directorate-General of Budget, Accounting and Statistics, *Statistical Yearbook of the Republic of China*.

       Korea: National Bureau of Statistics, *Korea Statistical Yearbook*.

       Philippines: National Economic and Development Authority, *Philippine Statistical Yearbook*.

[a] Includes transport, trade and financial, government, and community services.

[b] Manufacturing and construction.

(although not Japan and Korea). Of course these conclusions might have to be modified in the light of objections of a technical and statistical nature.[2] But it seems clear that the evolution of the Indonesian service sector is following a pattern established in many developing countries in Latin America, Africa, and some other countries in South-East Asia such as the Philippines, rather than that established in the now developed countries of West Europe and North-east Asia. It is thus useful to examine some of the explanations put forward in the literature for the divergence of so many contemporary developing countries from the historical trend.

The Growth of the Public Sector

One explanation for the rapid growth of tertiary sector employment in many contemporary developing countries is that it is due in large part to governments assuming a much more dominant role in the economy than was the case in the now-developed countries at a similar stage in their development. As Katouzian (1970: 381) has argued, 'existing international and ideological standards, being superimposed on these countries, compel their governments to act, especially in the provision of services'. Many developing countries have set themselves ambitious targets for achieving universal education, and typically young people with post-primary education want to work in the 'modern' sector of the economy. If the private sector cannot provide enough employment of the kind which suits the aspirations of educated youth, they and their parents exert pressure on the government to expand public sector employment. In many countries, government wage and salary structures are often inflated in comparison with the private sector because public sector unions wield considerable political power. Young people are then encouraged to invest in liberal arts or legal education because these qualifications are seen as a passport to well-paid public sector employment (Gemmell, 1986: 183–4).

These arguments clearly have considerable support in the context of many developing countries, although some caveats are in order. In particular, the extent to which the growth of tertiary sector employment is due to growth in public sector (or 'non-market') employment is often not clear in the labour force statistics. Typically, service sector employment is divided into trade and commerce, transport and communications, and 'other services' which embrace not just labour in public sector activities but also that in private and religious educational and health facilities, and personal and domestic services. To assume as some writers seem to do (see, for example, Gemmell, 1986: 112) that the 'other services' category is mainly non-marketed may not be correct. Certainly, recent studies have argued that the numbers of public officials per head of population is quite low in many parts of the developing world compared with most OECD countries. In fact, in the early 1980s, India and Indonesia—two countries which are often considered to have 'bloated bureaucracies'—had fewer than two public employees per hundred people. The American figure was 7.8 and the Swedish 14.7 (Edgren, 1987: 7).

Rapid Population Growth, Disguised Unemployment, and the Informal Sector

A second reason for the rapid growth in tertiary sector employment in many parts of the developing world is that there has been a rapid growth in what is frequently termed the 'urban informal sector', which typically consists of a range of small-scale, family-based enterprises producing both goods and services. This growth is due to a number of factors, including rapid overall rates of population growth and slow growth in the rural sector (often at least partially induced by government policies which discriminate against agriculture) which together produce high rates of urban in-migration. Such migration is further encouraged by expectations of highly paid formal sector employment which in turn are encouraged by high levels of remuneration in the public sector. Since the early 1970s, numerous studies of the urban informal sector have been carried out, many of them under the auspices of the International Labour Office.[3] It has become clear that the informal sector, defined to include small, owner-operated enterprises in sectors such as trade, transport, and the manufacturing industry is not simply a sponge, soaking up labour which cannot find employment elsewhere. Many so-called informal enterprises are in fact efficiently operated and producing goods and services for which there is a large and growing demand, often on the part of middle-class consumers.

Patterns of Technological Change

A further reason for the rapid growth in service sector employment in the developing world is that, over time, there has been more rapid technological change in agriculture and in industry than in services. In today's developed countries, labour-saving agricultural and industrial technologies have been developed that are so efficient that they are profitable to adopt for virtually any positive price of labour. They are therefore widely used in many developing countries as well despite the fact that the price of labour relative to capital is much lower in these economies. This appears to be especially true in the manufacturing industry, where there can be little doubt that production technologies are more capital-intensive than was the case fifty or one hundred years ago. In addition many new industrial products are in demand in the developing countries which did not exist when the now-developed countries were at a similar stage of development, and which can only be produced by capital-intensive means.

While there can be little doubt of the validity of this argument, it does not entirely explain the patterns shown in Figure 9.1. In particular it does not explain the different performance of Taiwan and (to a lesser extent) Korea from countries in South-East Asia, Latin America, and Africa. Why has Taiwan been so successful in absorbing a large proportion of its rapidly growing non-agricultural labour force in industry rather than in services? To answer this question, one needs to examine the industrialization and trade policies which have been pursued in different countries and their impact on employment generation.

Protection and Foreign Investment

Several radical critics of contemporary development strategy have attributed the 'hypertrophy' of the tertiary sector in countries in Latin America and Africa to the capital-intensive production techniques used by foreign investors in both the agricultural and the industrial sectors (Amin, 1976: 239 ff.; Evans and Timberlake, 1980). According to this argument, integration of many developing economies into the world economy leads to a process of capital accumulation which is 'strongly exclusionary and inegalitarian' (Evans and Timberlake, 1980: 547). Foreign investors are induced to invest in capital-intensive ventures in resource-based and manufacturing industries by a variety of protective devices and the profits are either remitted abroad or shared among a very small élite within the country itself. This results in a high proportion of the labour force being driven into 'informal' employment in small-scale industry and services and a highly skewed distribution of income and wealth. The process is aggravated when national governments themselves invest heavily in capital-intensive state enterprises, many of them of a prestige nature.

Income Inequalities

A number of writers who would not necessarily subscribe to the views cited above would none the less concede that the growth in the tertiary sector in contemporary developing countries may be related to their increasingly skewed distribution of income (see Berry, 1978: 221). It is argued that the rich spend a greater share of their disposable income on services and in countries where the richest 10 per cent of households account for around 50 per cent of total expenditure, as is the case in contemporary Brazil, the total demand for services will be greater than in countries where the richest decile account for only 27.5 per cent of expenditure as in Korea.[4] While this argument may be at least a partial explanation for the very different share of services in non-agricultural employment in Brazil or the Philippines compared with Korea or Taiwan, it is less plausible as an explanation of the difference between today's developing countries and France or Britain a century ago. Certainly there is little persuasive evidence that these countries had a more egalitarian distribution of income than Thailand, the Philippines, or Indonesia today.

Changing Patterns of Comparative Advantage

Yet another reason for the rapid growth in the service sector in some economies has been that, given their resource endowments on the one hand and patterns of international demand on the other, these economies have a strong comparative advantage in the export of services rather than goods. The most obvious example concerns the role of tourism in many small economies in the Caribbean, the Pacific, and elsewhere. But even in larger economies, including the ASEAN nations, tourism has been one of the fastest growing export industries over the past two decades, and has had a significant impact on employment not just in the accommodation industry, but also in a range of ancillary service activities.

Private and Public Service Sector Development in Indonesia

It will be argued in this chapter that each of these arguments has some validity in the Indonesian case. However, it is not enough simply to catalogue reasons for the rapid growth in tertiary sector output and employment in Indonesia over the past two decades. One must also explore the consequences of this growth for labour productivity and the distribution of income. To a considerable extent, these consequences will depend on the relative productivity of service sector labour, which in turn depends on the extent to which both large and small enterprises in the service sector are demand, rather than supply, driven. If labour is pushed into informal service sector employment because there are no other employment opportunities, it is likely that productivity and remuneration will be low. Similarly if the public sector is forced to act as a sponge, soaking up secondary and tertiary graduates who cannot find employment elsewhere, productivity must, over time, decline. Productivity in the public sector is notoriously difficult to measure, and in Indonesia the problem has been aggravated by the oil boom and the post-oil boom restructuring process. Civil service salary increases in the 1970s and declines in the 1980s reflected changing budgetary conditions rather than trends in public sector productivity *per se*.

In spite of these problems, enough data are now available from various sources to compare productivity in the different components of the service sector in Indonesia with other parts of the economy. The national income statistics provide a useful starting point, and they can be supplemented by data collected in the 1986 Economic Census (see, for example, BPS, 1987a and 1988). These latter data are particularly useful for the light they throw on the small-scale trade sector, usually considered to be the most 'porous' part of the service sector, with the fewest barriers to entry, and thus the most likely to soak up labour unable to find work elsewhere. But before these are studied in detail, the most recent labour force data are used to examine the structure of service sector employment in Indonesia, and the extent to which it is dominated by government or private sector activities.

Structure of Service Sector Employment

If the sectoral breakdown of the labour force in Indonesia is compared with that of Thailand and the Philippines, one point that emerges clearly is that by 1985 employment in the wholesale and retail trade sector in Indonesia accounted for a larger proportion of the labour force than in the other countries. The only exception was for women workers in the Philippines where the percentage in trade was only slightly higher than for Indonesia, in spite of the very low proportion of women workers in agriculture (Table 9.2). By contrast 'other services' which included government employees, workers in private health and educational facilities, and domestic servants absorbed a much larger proportion of the female labour force in the Philippines than in Indonesia, although the proportions for males were quite similar. Also striking is the sharp increase in the proportion of the female labour force employed in trade in Indonesia since 1971, and the slight decline in the proportion absorbed in 'other services'. Indeed it is arguable that trading is the most important source of cash income for rural women in Indonesia, and that most will be employed in the trading sector at some time in their lives, although many small traders often switch from trading to other activities such as harvesting when wages in these other activities are at a seasonal high (Mai and Buchholt, 1987; Stoler, 1975 and 1977; White, 1976).

Of the almost 20 million people enumerated as employed in services in the 1985 Intercensal Survey, over one-third were self-employed workers in the trade sector (Table 9.3). The trade sector also accounted for most of the family workers in the service sector. By contrast it contained relatively few employees (people working for wages or salaries);

TABLE 9.2

Distribution of the Labour Force by Sector, 1971 and 1985 (percentage)

				Services		
		Agriculture	Industry[a]	Trade/ Commerce	Transport	Other[b]
Male						
Indonesia	1971	64.1	9.0	8.9	3.4	14.6
	1985	55.3	14.1	11.5	4.8	14.3
Philippines	1971	59.4	15.7	8.0	6.0	10.9
	1985	58.3	14.5	6.7	7.1	13.4
Thailand	1971	76.7	6.2	6.5	2.3	8.3
	1985	67.2	12.6	8.1	3.5	8.6
Female						
Indonesia	1971	60.4	10.9	13.7	0.1	14.9
	1985	53.6	12.2	21.2	0.1	12.9
Philippines	1971	31.7	15.5	21.6	0.5	30.5
	1985	35.0	12.8	23.6	0.6	27.9
Thailand	1971	82.0	4.3	7.8	0.1	5.8
	1985	69.8	8.9	10.5	0.4	10.4

Sources: As for Table 9.1.
[a] Includes mining, manufacturing, construction, and utilities.
[b] Includes activities not elsewhere included.

TABLE 9.3

Percentage Breakdown of the Service Sector Labour Force
by Job Status, 1985

	Sex	Trade	Transport and Communications	Financial Services	Community and Social Services	Total
Self-employed	M	12.4	3.7	–	4.1	20.2
	F	12.6	–	–	2.1	14.7
Self-employed	M	4.4	0.5	–	0.9	5.8
and family	F	4.2	–	–	0.3	4.5
workers						
Employers	M	0.4	0.3	–	0.5	1.2
	F	0.1	–	–	0.2	0.3
Employees	M	3.7	5.2	0.9	21.8	31.6
	F	1.4	0.1	0.2	10.3	12.0
Family workers	M	2.0	0.1	–	0.4	2.5
	F	5.6	–	–	1.2	6.8
Other	M	–	–	–	0.2	0.2
	F	–	–	–	0.2	0.2
Total	M	22.9	9.8	0.9	27.9	61.5
	F	23.9	0.1	0.2	14.3	38.5

Source: BPS, Supas No.5 (1985).

most of these were located in either transport or other services. There were relatively few own-account (self-employed) workers in the other services category; such workers accounted for only about 7.5 per cent of all those employed in the service sector. Transport and communications accounted for slightly under 10 per cent of all service sector workers; about half of these were employees and most of the rest self-employed.

A picture thus emerges of the Indonesian service sector divided almost equally into two distinct groups: the trade sector dominated by self-employed and family workers, and transport and 'other services', which are dominated by employees. As by definition civil servants and the military must be classified as employees, it is clear that most workers in the trade sector are employed in private enterprises, many of them owner-operated, with assistance from other family members. But it cannot be assumed that all employees in 'other services' are necessarily in the public sector; most domestic servants, for example, would probably fall under this classification, as would teachers and health workers employed in non-government facilities. Estimating the public (or 'non-market') share of the 6.4 million people classified as employees in the other services sector in 1985 is thus a difficult task. There were 2.96 million people classified as 'civilian state servants' (pegawai negeri sipil) in Indonesia in 1985, but this figure does not include a large number of temporary government employees taken on as schoolteachers, health workers, agricultural extension officers, drivers, and so on. Neither does it include the military, whose establishment is estimated to be around 300,000.[5] It seems probable that at least 4 million people were employed as civilian and military state servants in the mid-1980s. The actual figure could well have been higher, although it is unlikely to have been much beyond 5 million.[6]

Growth of Public Sector Employment

Whatever the true share of the public sector in total service sector employment in 1985, there seems to be little doubt that public sector employment has been growing rather more rapidly than other components of the service sector since the late 1970s. Between 1971 and 1985, the total labour force grew at around 3.3 per cent per annum and employment in services at 4.4 per cent per annum, while the number of civilian state servants grew at 5.9 per cent per annum between 1975 and 1988.[7] By 1980 civil service numbers had reached 2 million, and the growth continued through the 1980s so that by 1988 civil service numbers had reached 3.53 million. As has already been noted, these figures do not give a complete picture of the size of the government establishment as they exclude temporary employees and the military. It is indeed probable that the continued growth in numbers through the 1980s is largely due to the fact that many who were taken on as temporary or 'honorary' government employees in the 1970s were given permanent appointments after 1980, when they had already served for a number of years.

The reasons for the growth of public sector employment through the 1970s are not hard to find. As oil revenues grew and budgetary expenditures accelerated, the government embarked on an ambitious programme of economic and social infrastructure development which necessitated the recruitment not just of administrative and clerical staff but also of a wide range of skilled workers, including teachers, health workers, engineers, economists, statisticians, and financial managers. Although the published data do not give information on changes in the composition of the civil service by professional training, they do show a marked change in the composition by rank and educational status. Whereas in 1975 almost 60 per cent of all permanent government employees had at most lower secondary education, by 1988 this had fallen to under 30 per cent. Almost 15 per cent had some tertiary qualifications (Table 9.4). Accompanying this change was a marked fall in the proportion of employees in the lowest grade and an increase in the higher grades. In 1988, 2 million of the 3.53 million civil servants had been employed for less than ten years and 1.51 million were in the teaching service. There seems to be no doubt that the recruitment of teachers for the Inpres schools was a major reason for the growth in the Indonesian civil service since the mid-1970s, a point which is also brought out in the high proportion of civil servants in 1988 who were graduates of vocational secondary schools.[8]

Throughout the oil boom period, and indeed afterwards, it is probably

TABLE 9.4

Changes in the Composition of the Indonesian Civil Service
by Class and Educational Attainment

Class	Breakdown (per cent)		Educational Attainment[a]	Breakdown (per cent)	
	1975	1988		1975	1988
I	52.7	19.1	Less than PS	38.7	17.0
II	40.7	66.8	LSS	21.9	11.5
III	4.2	13.3	HSS	32.1	56.9[b]
IV	0.4	0.8	Academy	4.7	9.1
Other	2.0	0.0	Graduate	2.5	5.5
Total	100.0	100.0	Total	100.0	100.0

Sources: 1975: *Lampiran Pidato Kenegaraan 1975*, pp. 798–9.
           1988: *Repelita V*, 1989/90–1993/4, Vol. III, p. 534.
[a] PS = Primary school.
   LSS = Lower secondary school.
   HSS = Higher secondary school.
   Academy includes bachelor degrees (*sarjana muda*).
[b] In 1988 46 per cent of civil servants were graduates from vocational upper secondary schools and only 11 per cent from general upper secondary schools. Most of the former would be primary school teachers who graduated from the SPG. These teacher training high schools will be phased out over *Repelita V* and primary teachers will be trained at the tertiary level.

more accurate to see the growth in numbers of civil servants as 'demand-induced' rather than 'supply-induced' in the sense that new recruits were taken on in order to implement new government programmes rather than simply to provide employment to a growing number of secondary and tertiary graduates. The Indonesian situation was thus rather different from that in a country such as Egypt where the education system was expanded much earlier and where the government was legally obliged to provide employment for graduates who could not find employment elsewhere (Gemmell, 1986: 153). However, there can be little doubt that through the 1970s and the early 1980s, the government service did absorb a substantial proportion of new entrants to the labour force with upper secondary and tertiary qualifications. An estimate based on a comparison of the 1976 National Labour Force Survey (*Sakernas*) and the 1985 Intercensal Survey (*Supas*) indicates that over 75 per cent of the increment in the labour force with tertiary qualifications were absorbed in 'other services'. A large share of these would have been in the public sector (Booth and Sundrum, 1988: Table 3.13).

     The available evidence from other parts of Asia indicates that the growth in numbers of civil servants in Indonesia in recent years has not been unusually fast. Neither is the number of civil servants relative to population very high. There was faster growth in both Thailand and

TABLE 9.5
Growth in Numbers of Government Employees[a]

Country	Annual Average Growth Rate[a] (%)	Government Employees per 100 Population[b]
Indonesia (1975–88)	5.8	2.0
Bangladesh (1972–83)	3.7	0.7
India (1961–85)	3.8	1.5
Malaysia (1971–85)	6.4	4.5
Philippines (1963–83)	5.5	3.2
Thailand (1971–86)	6.5	2.9

Sources: Indonesia: As for Table 9.4.
  Other countries: Edgren (1987: 7); Desai and Desai (1987: 71); Ali (1987: 134); Canlas (1987: 151); Chira et al. (1987: 206).
[a] Growth rate between years indicated.
[b] Indian data refer to 1985, Thai data to 1980, and Malaysian data to 1986. Data for other countries refer to final year shown in the country column. All data exclude public servants employed in state enterprises.

Malaysia (Table 9.5). In Thailand, a significant part of the growth was attributed to expansion in teaching services, as was the case in Indonesia (Chira et al., 1987: 175). In India and Bangladesh, civil service growth was slower, which probably reflects the fact that educational services grew more slowly than in South-East Asia. The tendency for the public sector to employ a high proportion of the labour force with vocational and tertiary education seems universal throughout the region. In Thailand, Chira et al. (1987: 182) report that 67 per cent of those who have graduated from vocational schools and teacher colleges and 57 per cent of university graduates work in the public sector. In India, Desai and Desai (1987: 84–5) have estimated that over 70 per cent of all graduates are in the public sector; the proportion is much higher for engineers and doctors.

Labour Productivity in the Service Sector

An important indicator of the extent to which the various components of the service sector are being used as residual absorbers of labour which cannot find employment elsewhere is their productivity relative to that of the economy as a whole. In Indonesia it is striking that labour in each part of the service sector is more productive than the national average, and much more productive than labour in agriculture. Although the trade sector absorbs a high proportion of the non-agricultural labour force in Indonesia, labour productivity in that sector in 1985 was 12 per cent above the national average, and well over twice that in agriculture. It was also slightly higher than that in 'other services', which strengthens the point made above, that this sector is not completely

TABLE 9.6

Relative Labour Productivities:[a] Indonesia, the Philippines,
Taiwan, and Thailand, 1985

	Indonesia	Philippines	Taiwan	Thailand
Agriculture	0.43	0.54	0.33	0.25
Mining	20.84	2.91	1.25	10.49
Manufacturing	1.83	2.53	1.11	2.51
Utilities	5.37	4.86	9.04	2.32
Construction	1.46	1.30	0.61	5.89
Trade	1.12	1.47	0.76	0.99
Transport	1.90	1.33	1.16	8.86
Other services	1.09	0.80	1.52	2.52
Total	1.00	1.00	1.00	1.00

Sources: As for Table 9.1.

[a]Output per unit of labour as a ratio of the national average. Output (value added) in current prices.

dominated by relatively well-remunerated public sector employees. The situation in the Philippines was similar to Indonesia, although there labour productivity in 'other services' was markedly less than the national average, again suggesting it is not dominated by public sector employment. In Thailand and Taiwan, by contrast, labour productivity in trade was below the national average, but that in other services was well above it.

Employment and Productivity in the Trade Sector

The Structure of the Trade Sector

The 1985 Intercensal Survey reported that about 14 per cent of the labour force was absorbed in the trade sector; the percentage was rather higher for women than for men (Table 9.2; see also Table 11.12). The trade sector was the most important single component of service sector employment accounting for almost half of the total. But in spite of its obvious importance, surprisingly little economic research has been carried out on the trade sector in Indonesia, and much of what is known is due to the work of anthropologists, sociologists, and geographers.[9] Part of this neglect has been due to lack of data; whereas the Biro Pusat Statistik and other government agencies have regularly collected and published data on the agricultural, manufacturing, mining, and transport sectors since the early 1970s, very little enterprise-level data have been available on the trade sector. This deficiency was remedied only in 1986 with the Economic Census of that year which carried out a census of all 'incorporated' trading enterprises, including hotels and restaurants, and an extensive sample survey of unincorporated trading enterprises, including both those with fixed premises and those with no fixed premises.[10] The latter in turn were divided into traders in food and drinks, agricultural products, manufactured products, and 'other' trading enterprises.

The Economic Census (EC) reported that there were slightly over 5 million unincorporated trading enterprises in Indonesia in 1986, about half with fixed premises, and half without fixed premises. Almost 74 per cent were in Java (Table 9.7). About two-thirds of all enterprises with fixed premises were in rural areas and 70 per cent of those without fixed premises. In total, these enterprises employed 8.7 million people, the great majority as 'unpaid workers', which means they were either self-employed or unpaid family workers. As the 1986 *Sakernas* reported 9.8 million workers in the trade sector as a whole, it is clear that the great majority must be in unincorporated enterprises. Female workers dominated in fixed-premise enterprises in Java, although they were less important than male workers in enterprises without fixed premises. Almost 40 per cent of enterprises without fixed premises were trading agricultural products, almost 30 per cent were trading processed food and drinks, and the rest were trading manufactured and miscellaneous goods. Over 80 per cent were in Java. Traders in agricultural products in rural Java alone comprised almost one-quarter of all such enterprises (Table 9.8).

The great majority of unincorporated trading enterprises (65 per cent of those with fixed premises and 72 per cent of those without fixed premises) had been in business for three years or more at the time of the EC enumeration (October 1986). Of those without fixed premises, and not involved in activities of a seasonal nature, the great majority operated more than 21 days per month (Table 9.9). On average, workers in

TABLE 9.7

Percentage Breakdown of Establishments and Labour Force
in Unincorporated Enterprises in the Trade Sector, 1986

	Number of Establishments	Paid Workers		Unpaid Workers[a]		
		Male	Female	Male	Female	Total
Fixed Premises						
Java	33.3	2.9	2.1	12.9	20.2	38.1
Outer Islands	16.5	1.7	0.5	8.5	9.7	20.4
Mobile						
Java	40.3	1.7	0.5	18.0	12.8	33.0
Outer Islands	9.9	0.6	0.1	4.5	3.2	8.4
Total	100	6.9	3.2	43.9	45.9	100
Numbers (million)	5.05	0.61	0.28	3.80	3.98	8.67

Source: BPS, *Sensus Ekonomi 1986*, Seri C62, C63.
[a]Workers not receiving salary or wage.

TABLE 9.8

Percentage Breakdown of Unincorporated Trading Enterprises
without Fixed Premises by Location and Nature of Business

	Nature of Business				
	Food/ Drinks	Agricultural Products	Manufactured Products	Other	Total
Urban					
Java	9.9	5.3	4.9	2.7	22.8
Outer Islands	2.3	2.0	2.0	0.8	7.1
Rural					
Java	14.3	24.5	12.9	5.7	57.4
Outer Islands	2.3	5.3	3.5	1.5	12.6
Total	28.8	37.1	23.3	10.7	100

Source: BPS, Sensus Ekonomi 1986 (Seri C63): Statistik Usaha Rumahtangga Perdagangan dengan Tempat Tidak Tetap, 1986.

TABLE 9.9

Percentage Breakdown of Trading Enterprises
by Days Worked per Month

	Days Worked Per Month			
	1–10	11–20	21+	Total[a]
1986 Economic Census				
Seasonal enterprises				
without fixed premises	17.9	38.2	43.9	100 (7)
Non-seasonal enterprises				
without fixed premises				
Food/Drinks	2.7	14.6	82.6	100 (8)
Agricultural products	9.1	23.2	67.7	100 (7)
Industrial products	8.6	22.9	68.5	100 (8)
Others	7.8	19.4	72.8	100 (8)
Total	6.9	20.1	72.9	100 (7)
1985 Susenas[b]				
fixed premises	9.6	19.9	70.6	100
without fixed premises	15.9	32.7	51.4	100

Sources: As for Table 9.8. Data from 1985 Susenas as reported in BPS, Statistik Usaha Jasa Rumahtangga.
[a] Figures in brackets refer to average numbers of hours worked.
[b] Includes trading enterprises and household service enterprises.

these enterprises worked 7 hours a day. The picture of the small-scale trade sector that emerges from the EC is thus one of owner-operated enterprises where the operator is working around 150 hours or more a month in an activity in which he or she has been engaged for several years. Certainly there is little support for the view that many workers in trading enterprises, whether with or without fixed premises, are 'under-employed' in the sense that they are working short hours in an activity in which they only expect to be engaged for a brief period of time. On the contrary, most small traders are working normal hours in enterprises which have been operating for several years.

The EC also provides valuable data on incomes of trading enterprises, especially for those without fixed premises. On average the monthly income of households running trading enterprises without fixed premises was Rp 118,000 which was rather higher than the average household expenditure reported in the 1987 *Susenas* survey (Table 9.10). Allowing for the fact that the *Susenas* data were collected six months later than the EC data, it appears that trading households were earning incomes which were slightly above the national average, although there was considerable variation by location and by type of enterprise. Urban trading households were earning incomes which were 64 per cent higher than those in rural areas; traders in agricultural products were earning the largest incomes in both urban and rural areas, and traders in prepared food and drinks the lowest. There was substantial variation across provinces; in the case of rural households trading in agricultural produce, incomes in Java were much lower than in most parts of the Outer Islands. However, in almost all provinces, rural trading households were earning more than agricultural households (Table 9.11). On

TABLE 9.10

Average Monthly Income of Households Engaged in Trading[a] Activities, 1986 (Rp '000)

Type of Trade	Urban	Rural	Total
Food/Drinks	115	85	97
Agricultural products	175	122	133
Industrial products	152	102	118
Others	157	96	117
Total	n.a.	n.a.	118
Susenas 1987[b]	156	82	101

Source: BPS, *Sensus Ekonomi 1986 (Seri C63): Statistik Usaha Rumahtangga Perdagangan dengan Tempat Tidak Tetap, 1986.*

[a] 'Trading' refers to traders with non-fixed premises only. The survey was held in October 1986, and the income data refer to the previous month.

[b] Data refer to household expenditures in January 1987. The 1987 *Susenas* data were given in per capita terms; they have been adjusted to a household basis using the data on average household size for urban and rural areas contained in the 1985 Intercensal Survey.

n.a. = Not available.

TABLE 9.11

Household Incomes of Rural Trading Households without Fixed Premises
and Agricultural Households, 1986 (Rp '000)

	Agricultural Traders	Traders in Industrial Products	Traders in Food and Drinks	Other	Agricultural Households[a]
Lampung	344	124	105	90	57
West Kalimantan	281	130	148	162	63
Central Kalimantan	225	133	65	164	82
North Sulawesi	198	130	92	134	87
Irian Jaya	197	n.a.	161	196	74
North Sumatra	192	110	92	148	71
West Sumatra	185	120	102	149	71
East Nusa Tenggara	182	88	52	41	65
Jambi	171	124	92	173	70
Maluku	161	167	127	77	87
Aceh	155	272	103	103	76
South Kalimantan	155	150	79	88	55
Bengkulu	153	54	83	81	79
Riau	147	140	177	159	104
East Kalimantan	146	208	113	156	67
South Sumatra	141	136	99	184	84
South-east Sulawesi	140	160	98	199	63
South Sulawesi	139	182	103	121	61
Bali	129	121	104	139	81
West Java	128	90	85	81	66
Jakarta	123	312	179	148	n.a.
Yogyakarta	117	103	86	127	78
East Java	108	80	80	95	62
Central Java	102	96	77	90	63
West Nusa Tenggara	99	85	69	101	50
East Timor	55	181	89	99	65
Indonesia	122	102	85	96	66
	(42.6)	(23.5)	(23.7)	(10.3)	

Sources: As for Table 9.10. Data on incomes of agricultural households taken from BPS,
   Sensus Pertanian 1983 Sensus Sampel Pendapatan Petani (Seri I), Table 9.
[a] Data refer to 1984 and were adjusted to October 1985 prices using the rural nine-
commodity index for Java and the Outer Islands respectively.

average households trading in agricultural produce had monthly
incomes almost twice those of agricultural households, although the gap
was less marked for other types of trading households. The EC data also
make it clear that, especially for trading households at the lower end of
the income scale, income from the trading enterprise contributed less
than half of the total household income (Table 9.12).

TABLE 9.12
Breakdown of Households Operating Trading Enterprises
without Fixed Premises by Income Sources

Household Income Derived from Trading Enterprises (Rp '000)	Percentage of Enterprises	Total Household Income per Month (Rp '000)		
		From Trading Enterprises	Other	Total
Under 25	24.9	13	37	50
25–49	26.3	37	30	67
50–74	17.2	61	32	93
75–99	9.9	86	27	113
100–49	10.5	121	31	152
150–99	4.3	171	32	203
200–99	3.6	241	48	289
300–99	1.9	376	44	420
Over 500	1.3	1,250	64	1,314
Total	100.0	84	34	118

Source: BPS, *Sensus Ekonomi 1986 (Seri C63): Statistik Usaha Rumahtangga Perdagangan dengan Tempat Tidak Tetap, 1986*, p. 487.

The Operation of the Pasar Economy

Most unincorporated trading enterprises in Indonesia can be said to belong to the '*pasar* economy', which, although a cultural construct (in the sense that markets in Java are not identical to those in Kalimantan or Sulawesi), should also be viewed as an adaptation to a specific set of economic conditions. The *pasar* economy in Indonesia has much in common with what has often been called the bazaar economy in other parts of Asia and Africa.[11] In Indonesia, as in many other parts of the developing world, the typical trading business is run by a single person, (in Java often a woman), although unpaid family workers are frequently used and occasionally wage workers are hired. Enterprises deal mainly in locally produced, non-standardized commodities which are often subject to seasonal fluctuations. At each step in the market hierarchy, commodities are sold in larger quantities and are drawn from a wider area, with the extent of bulking at each step being determined by the characteristics of transport and economies of scale. In reverse fashion, commodities intended for retail markets are progressively broken down into smaller packages for eventual sale to individual consumers. Different businesses in the *pasar* economy are linked by trading relationships often formed over a number of years, which serve to channel supplies and credit. Many traders do not make a 'subsistence' income from their own efforts, but in most cases they are making a significant contribution to the household income, although in at least 25 per cent of households operating as traders without fixed premises, income from the trading enterprise is only about one-quarter of total household income.

The dichotomy used in the EC enumeration between trading enterprises with fixed premises and those without fixed premises is also useful in examining the structure of the *pasar* economy in Indonesia. Typically, Indonesians distinguish between several types of trading operations with fixed premises (*pasar*, depot, *toko*, *warung*) and several types of itinerant traders (*agen*, *bakul*, *penebas*, *kaki lima*, *pedagang keliling*) who, while usually operating without fixed premises of their own, are nevertheless crucially dependent on one or more of the first type of trader. While there is often overlap between these groups, each has its own economic function, deals with a particular clientele, and has its own set of norms governing transactions.

The *pasar* in the strict sense includes both the official market-places and premises nearby where similar transactions take place. Townspeople buy commodities for daily use in the *pasar*, but villagers who visit *pasar* regularly are mainly buying goods for resale. Other villagers make infrequent trips to the *pasar* to buy expensive household items. Prices are not marked or fixed and bargaining is normal for most purchases. Supplies to the *pasar* are provided by wholesalers 'breaking down' packages of manufactured goods; by agents purchasing agricultural produce in the villages; and by wholesalers with ties to agricultural buyers in other regions. Vendors also purchase stock from other traders within the *pasar*, from visiting farmers, or from travelling sellers. *Pasar* enterprises vary considerably in scale, from a trader selling 5 kilograms of home-produced sweetmeats to cloth traders with scores of pieces of *batik* in stock. Vendors operating from large lockable stalls within the *pasar* may appear to have more in common with operators of shops (*toko*), than with their fellow traders in the *pasar* if only the structure and size of their operation is considered, but in fact their business is based on rather different principles.

Depot operators buy agricultural produce for bulking or transport outside the region. They bargain when buying from producers or small-scale traders, but often sell larger quantities at relatively fixed prices or on consignment. Depending on local transport needs, depot are situated either inside the *pasar* or on the periphery of a market town. Although *toko* are usually larger and occupy more substantial buildings, it is not easy to distinguish *toko* from *kios* or *warung* on appearance alone. But there is a clear difference in their economic function. *Toko* retail expensive manufactured goods usually produced outside the locality, ranging from furniture to motor bikes, or wholesale manufactured commodities such as canned foods and cigarettes. Goods are typically standardized, prices are calculated by adding percentage mark-ups, and prices are supposedly fixed for all customers, although in fact discounts are frequently negotiated by regular buyers, or buyers in large bulk. Sales staff are more likely to be wage employees. By contrast, *warung* and *kios* retail commodities of all types, and wholesale locally produced manufactured goods and non-perishable agricultural products such as rice, dried fish, or peanuts to smaller traders. Some may also sell cooked foods and snacks. *Kios* situated within a *pasar* are often involved in 'breaking-down' activities. Labour is almost always supplied by the operator and his or her close relatives.

With the exception of *toko*, which in some important respects lie outside the *pasar* economy, some general points can be made about all these trading enterprises. An obvious common feature is the large number of traders, many of whom are selling identical goods and services. Equally obvious are the considerable differences in scale among enterprises. Almost anyone can become a small trader retailing a few cigarettes or some vegetables but the finance required to establish a viable enterprise with returns even approaching a subsistence income is almost impossible to acquire for most villagers. While traders do expand their businesses and increase their wealth, those who began with very little finance are unlikely to be among them. More commonly, it is traders who began their enterprises with capital running into hundreds of thousands of rupiah and substantial experience who expand quite rapidly and become prosperous entrepreneurs (Alexander, 1986: 91 ff.).

Several trading practices differentiate enterprises in a *pasar* economy from those in a mature industrial economy. Advertising, even in the most basic sense of marking prices on goods or on the stall, is almost unknown. Commodities are often not of standard quality and are subject to marked fluctuations in supply. Production or overhead costs are seldom calculated and most traders do not keep written records after a transaction is completed. As bargaining is the usual means of setting prices, prices within the *pasar* economy are always conceptualized within a range. The range for cheap, frequently purchased products is narrow, but for more expensive consumer items, which are not often bought, it may approach 40 per cent. Nor is there any real distinction between wholesale and retail prices, for while purchases intended for resale will usually be in the bottom half of the range, clever consumers can obtain the same price.

Because of these conditions, accurate price information is both differentially allocated and difficult to acquire. Whereas in an industrial economy the main locus of competition is between sellers—the buyer searches for the seller with the lowest price, in the *pasar* economy the competition is between a specific buyer and a specific seller. This competition is by no means equal. Sellers may be said to have perfect information, in the sense that they have a very good knowledge of the long- and the short-term price ranges for the commodities in which they deal. The extent to which the buyer has also acquired this information is the main determinant of the sale price within the ruling price range. It is for this reason of superior knowledge, rather than because of any special treatment, that traders normally buy at lower prices than others.

Although *pasar* traders attempt to obtain the highest possible price in any particular transaction, and do expand their businesses, the main goal of their trading activity is neither to increase their capital stock nor to maximize their profits. Rather, their aim through a series of transactions is to maintain their *modal* (capital) at about the same level while extracting sufficient cash each day for household expenses. This is a rational approach in the economic context in which they operate. Trading, which as we have noted is often not the main source of household income, provides a more stable cash flow over the year than agricultural income, and is thus available to meet daily expenditure needs. But as a consequence, there are unlikely to be sufficient savings available to finance expansion of the enterprise, unless they have been accumulated through an *arisan* (see pp. 308–9).

The second crucial component of the *pasar* economy are the itinerant traders without fixed premises. As we have seen, the 1986 EC reported that about 70 per cent of them were trading agricultural, industrial, and miscellaneous products and the rest prepared food and drinks. The role of agricultural traders has been described by Alexander (1986: 97) using the case of chilli production; this marketing chain is probably similar to that for most agricultural goods. Broadly speaking producers of both agricultural and non-agricultural output have three outlets for their goods which can be described in terms of a particular type of trader: *bakul, agen,* and *juragan.* Agricultural producers can also sell to a *penebas. Bakul* are small traders, usually women, dealing in a wide range of both agricultural and manufactured commodities. Though some *bakul* obtain most of their supplies in the *pasar,* many make their purchases in the village in which they live, or buy from producer–vendors at other sites. They purchase in amounts which can be carried on a bike, or at most in a minibus or taxi, often in conjunction with other *bakul* (Peluso, 1981; Chandler, 1984; Alexander, 1989). *Bakul* of this type sell their purchases either to traders further up the marketing chain or to village *warung,* but seldom retail themselves. Bargaining is fierce for all purchases. Strangers are paid in cash but local villagers might be paid the next day after the *bakul* has resold the goods.

The defining characteristic of an *agen,* who are mainly but not exclusively men, is that he operates with finance provided by another person. *Agen* buying agricultural produce are normally provided with a sum of money by a *juragan* and have to return it when the season is finished. They normally buy on a larger scale than do *bakul,* often in truckloads, and usually pay in cash. They resell to the *juragan* who provided the finance, but attempt to do so at a profit because they are not paid wages or a commission. They will normally be told the buying price of the *juragan* a day in advance and will bargain accordingly with producers. *Agen* selling locally manufactured goods are often closely associated with the producers, who may be their spouses or other close relatives. They transport the goods around the regional markets, selling to the larger traders on short-term credit. Outside Java, the meaning of the term *agen* is further extended to encompass the traders who are referred to below as *juragan* wholesaling from depot.

The defining feature of *penebas* is that they purchase crops before harvest.[12] In theory, the farmer is paid an agreed price for the standing crop and the *penebas* then takes responsibility for the harvest, bearing any risk and taking any profit. It has been argued that this system leads to producer exploitation, especially with low-risk crops such as rice, but in practice the arrangement appears to suit both sides. The *penebas*, who is often a fellow villager, relieves the farmer of the trouble of finding harvest labour, and his superior knowledge of market conditions allows him to strike a better bargain than the farmer could, especially in the case of fruit and vegetable crops. He may negotiate a price for the entire crop and pay before the harvest, but more commonly he negotiates a unit price and pays only after the crop is sold.

As rural roads and transport networks improve, and the farmers grow more non-rice crops which are wholly marketed, the numbers of *agen* and *penebas* will tend to increase at the expense of *bakul*. *Agen* already appear to dominate the sale of agricultural produce in South Kalimantan and West Java (Anderson, 1980), but in Central Java the units of production are so small that scope remains for the bulking activities of *bakul*.

The cusps of the *pasar* marketing structure are the *juragan*, located either in depot or in large permanent stalls in the *pasar*. A reasonably successful *juragan* will have three or four *agen* and perhaps a dozen *bakul* as regular suppliers but will buy from a large number of producer–vendors as well. Regular suppliers receive relatively fixed prices which they are aware of before they make their own purchases, but other sellers must bargain strongly. *Juragan* keep track of transactions through a simple system of bills, but they seldom keep formal books. Although wage labour is used for menial tasks, buying and selling is always done by the *juragan* themselves.

Juragan have numerous avenues for the disposal of their purchases, but the bulk is shipped by truck to *juragan* in other regions of the province, or indeed in other provinces. Often such *juragan* will visit to make their purchases, and to check on local supply conditions, but it is common for goods to be sent first and prices negotiated later. This is possible because trading relations between *juragan* in different regions are established over a long period of time to the mutual benefit of both partners and there is thus little incentive to cheat on a single transaction. In addition to their sales to other *juragan*, they will also sell to *bakul* reselling in the local *pasar*, or to groups of *bakul*, who will then arrange transport of the goods by minibus to markets perhaps hundreds of kilometres away. *Juragan* thus serve a bulk-breaking function, especially for processed foodstuffs such as dried chillies and cassava chips, or for agricultural produce shipped in from outside the region. But manufactured goods are normally sold through *toko*, or by manufacturers' employees.

The marketing path from the *juragan* or wholesaling level to the consumer is less complex in the sense that it involves fewer types of trader, but it may involve as many levels. Relatively expensive items such as fruit may pass through the hands of four *bakul*, each of them selling in smaller quantities, before reaching the consumer. Similarly something as standardized as cigarettes may be sold in cartons by the *toko*; in packets at a *warung* and in single sticks by a street trader. But the number of levels is diminishing as communications improve and large manufacturers adjust their marketing strategies to meet the requirements of rural users. Commodities such as washing powders, cooking oil, and spices are now being packaged in smaller quantities, which reduces the opportunities for *warung* owners, or *bakul*, to buy in bulk and repackage the goods themselves. These trends will doubtless accelerate, and further reduce the chances of *bakul* and *warung* operators making a living from specialized market information or bulk-breaking.

The Role of Credit in the Small-scale Trade Sector

The dynamo of the *pasar* economy is the provision of credit by one partner in a trading relationship. In the case of non-agricultural commodities, credit normally flows from the producer to the trader. With agricultural produce, the direction of the flow is reversed, at least below the level of the depot. But while all traders within the *pasar* obtain credit, they do not all do so on the same terms. Because it determines the size of a trader's capital stock (*modal*), the form in which credit is acquired is the major determinant of a trader's marketing strategy and hence of her income.

In both Java and Kalimantan, as well as in other Indonesian cultures, supplier credit is channelled through one of two types of relationships termed *langganan tetap* and *utang-piutang* (Siegel, 1969; Forbes, 1978 and 1979; Mai and Buchholt, 1987; Alexander, 1987). For the more substantial traders the main source of capital stock is through their *langganan tetap* which can be literally translated as 'regular customer' but among traders the term refers to a particular kind of debt relationship. Stripped to its essentials, such a relationship connotes a set line of credit; the creditor advances goods up to the fixed limit, and the debt must be paid in full at Lebaran. In most cases the line of credit will then be extended for a further year. The trader normally pays cash for her fortnightly or monthly purchases (although often a fortnight in arrears), so that the total debt does not exceed the fixed limit, but short-term credit outside this limit may occasionally be granted.

An important feature of the *langganan tetap* relationship is that despite the fact that a line of credit is extended for up to one year, and that considerable amounts of capital are involved, there are no overt interest charges. In fact stocks can often be replenished at a discount rate if payment is made in full for the regular purchases. It is more difficult to determine if there are hidden interest charges on the fixed debt (*utang pandemen*). While it is impossible to be certain that an inflated price has not been charged for the original goods, it is doubtful that this is the case, for prices are usually set by bargaining and both parties are aware of current prices. More to the point, it is doubtful that charging interest, either overtly or covertly, would be in the supplier's long-term advantage. Traders, recognizing that the relationship has advantages for both parties and probably mindful of the Islamic prohibition against interest, would not accept such charges and as there are more wholesalers willing to extend credit than established traders willing to accept it, would seek other suppliers (Mai and Buchholt, 1987).

A variant of the *langganan tetap* relationship which is found in Java but is more prevalent in the Outer Islands is the *bon* (bill) system. This is particularly common in the case of goods manufactured by large firms such as cigarettes and cosmetics, which are transported directly to the *pasar* traders or to the larger *warung* by the manufacturer's own vans. In this case there is no agreed *utang pandemen*, but the trader always makes payments one trip in arrears. Traders who do not pay the full amount may be permitted to procure stock up to the amount of their payment.

Langganan tetap are advantageous to suppliers because they ensure a regular cash flow and a reliable outlet for goods, but against this must be weighed the risks of default. Traders who have debts with their *langganan tetap* above Rp 100,000 tend to be younger, better educated, have more rapid turnovers and work at least some of the time in the larger markets. By contrast, *langganan tetap* relationships within the smaller regional markets involve much smaller debts, and personal characteristics play a larger role in their establishment.

While successful traders acquire much of their stock from one or two *langganan tetap*, they also buy from the dozens of wholesalers or producer–vendors who visit the market. Less successful traders buy almost all of their stock from this source. Commodities distributed by these traders are usually sold on the *utang-piutang* ('take possession of, then repay the debt') system. In a strict sense, *utang-piutang* is the provision of very short-term credit; goods are distributed in the morning and paid for at noon.[13] In periods of slow sales, all or some of the goods may be returned in lieu of payment. *Utang-piutang* differs from commission selling in that a price is agreed between supplier and trader and the *bakul* then sells for whatever she can obtain.

In practice credit arrangements which *bakul* describe as *utang-piutang* only approximate to the above description, as they often involve longer periods of credit. In particular, clothing and textile traders who are seldom able to sell all their newly purchased goods on the same day make a token payment from the proceeds of other sales, and delay final payment until the cloth is sold perhaps two to three weeks later. Traders in goods with a more rapid turnover, especially fruit and vegetables, are more likely to pay at the end of the day, although paying for supplies one market day in arrears is also common. The extension of credit from one market day to the next has advantages for the suppliers; not only can they visit the several regional markets which are open on any one day, but they can sometimes send goods on consignment. As with *langganan tetap*, *bakul* attempt to repay all debts at Lebaran, when the high volume of sales ensures that they have sufficient cash in hand.

It would appear that many *bakul* and other small traders without fixed premises do not regard these advances of goods as 'credit', as the EC reports that over 90 per cent of traders without fixed premises reported that they had no access to credit at all (Table 9.13). In addition, 87 per cent reported that they were relying entirely on their own capital (*modal sendiri*). Certainly there are several formal credit sources available in the *pasar*, both government and private, although it is the larger traders with fixed premises and other assets which can be used as collateral who are most likely to use them. Loans, when they are contracted, are usually short-term, at most three months, and seldom exceed Rp 150,000 in size. A wide variation in interest rates is apparent; the *bank pasar* charge 56 per cent per annum, and the savings co-operatives (*koperasi simpang pinjam* or Kosipa) 167 per cent. Traders also have access to credit through the *koperasi unit desa* (KUDs) and the village banks, although these sources do not appear to be frequently used to expand the scale of the enterprise because while loans are relatively quick and easy to obtain, the repayment criteria are strict and relatively few traders could meet the repayment schedule on even a small loan.[14] Most loans, in fact, are used for consumption purposes, especially school fees and medical expenses. The major informal supplier of credit is the *tukang kredit ngider* who supply credit on similar terms to the *bank pasar*. Many traders prefer to borrow from them for if they are short of cash they can, with a little pressure, delay repayments. Another major reason given by female traders for using informal credit sources is that they can deal with other women.

The major exception to the use of supplier credit to finance stock is the *arisan* or rotating credit association (Geertz, 1962; Alexander,

TABLE 9.13

Percentage of Trading Enterprises without Fixed Premises, without Access to Credit, and Using Own Capital in Urban and Rural Areas

	Type of Percentage of Enterprises without Fixed Premises					
	Not Using Credit		*Relying Entirely on 'Own Capital'*		*Reporting 'Capital Shortage' as a Problem*	
Enterprise	*Urban*	*Rural*	*Urban*	*Rural*	*Urban*	*Rural*
Food/Drinks	94.4	93.2	90.1	87.8	41.0	40.6
Agricultural products	92.7	90.5	85.0	89.9	48.0	49.8
Industrial products	94.1	89.1	82.7	82.0	47.6	43.1
Others	95.6	91.6	81.2	87.7	47.6	50.8
Total	91.8		87.0		45.8	

Source: BPS, *Sensus Ekonomi 1986 (Seri C63): Statistik Usaha Rumahtangga Perdagangan dengan Tempat Tidak Tetap 1986*, Tables 12, 13, and 19.

1987). Most traders belong to the market or village *arisan*. Small contributions are made on a regular basis and a periodic draw ensures each contributor receives a lump sum once each cycle. Traders use *arisan* as a savings device to ensure their *modal* is not fragmented by daily household expenses. Typically they use the pool to purchase stock or perhaps an expensive household item. If the EC results are broadly correct, then it is obvious that most people would not regard membership of an *arisan* as at all the same as obtaining credit from a formal financial institution, which indeed it is not.

But in spite of the increasing number of credit institutions making their services available to traders in both urban and rural areas, almost half of enterprises reported in the EC claimed that 'capital shortage' (*kekurangan modal*) was the major difficulty which they encountered in operating their business (Table 9.13). In addition 20 per cent complained of marketing problems and about 6 per cent of difficulties in ensuring merchandise supply. It is of course difficult to know how to interpret complaints of capital shortage; in many cases they probably boil down to the fact that the trader concerned was not generating sufficient income to be able to service the interest charges on a loan from any type of formal credit institution, even if such an institution were prepared to lend. This does not in itself mean that credit markets are 'imperfect', although it is true that, until very recently, few banks, state or private, were either able or willing to operate in rural areas or even in smaller urban centres. As more banks take advantage of the 1988–9 liberalization measures, and begin to operate in rural areas, it is probable that more traders will gain access to formal credit at competitive rates of interest to expand their enterprises.

The Future of Small Trading Enterprises

Much of the work carried out on the small-scale trading economy in Indonesia over the past decade or so throws doubt on at least some of the conclusions reached by writers such as Dewey (1962) and Geertz (1963) in their classic studies of Javanese markets. Geertz (1963: 28 ff.) found that the traders he studied in the town of Pare in East Java were not impeded by lack of capital, or by a disdain for the supposed 'Protestant' values of thrift, frugality, and hard work, which in fact their Islamic upbringing had endowed them with 'in almost excessive abundance'. Their main lack was 'the power to mobilise their capital and channel their drive in such a way as to exploit the existing market possibilities. They lack the capacity to form efficient economic institutions; they are entrepreneurs without enterprises' (Geertz, 1963: 28).

This conclusion has been challenged by Alexander (1986) who argues that over the past two decades, Javanese traders have been willing and able to expand their enterprises by ploughing back profits and taking advantage of new opportunities as they arise. Doubtless they have been assisted by the buoyant economic conditions of much of the period, and by the great improvements in rural infrastructure. The disappearance of

Chinese traders in rural areas has also assisted the emergence of medium-scale and even large-scale indigenous traders, although Chinese and state enterprises still dominate the large-scale, formal wholesaling and retailing businesses. The available evidence also indicates that it is those traders who begin with some capital and experience who are best able to take advantage of opportunities for expansion. But even at the bottom end of the income scale, the evidence indicates that petty trade is a valuable source of extra income for rural households with few assets except their labour, and in many cases serves to push the total household income above the poverty threshold.

There are, however, signs that the capacity of the trade sector to continue to generate productive employment opportunities may be constrained by a number of changes which are taking place in the wider economy. One of the most important of these changes is the replacement of locally produced goods by the products of urban factories. Ten years ago, the most profitable commodities for many market traders were copperware and *batik*. Both these commodities are now disappearing from the *pasar*. Copperware cannot compete with cheaper factory-produced goods made of aluminium, stainless steel, and plastic, and the skilled artisans who made copper products are ageing and not being replaced. The cheaper types of *batik* are being replaced, initially by machine-printed textiles with *batik* motifs, and now by factory-made clothes. Even in Java, *batik* in the *pasar* is increasingly concentrated in the middle and higher price ranges, and is produced in large factories in Solo and Yogyakarta.

Indeed the displacement of locally made goods by urban manufactures is occurring throughout the *pasar*. Local cigarettes and soft drinks disappeared a decade ago; palm oil is replacing coconut oil for cooking; locally made lamps and cooking utensils are difficult to sell and cheap wooden furniture faces increasing competition from plastic and Formica. In almost all cases, the factory-made product is not only cheaper but is of better quality and appears to be more 'modern', so the demise of the local product is inevitable. In addition urban manufacturers are becoming better attuned to the marketing needs of lower-income, rural customers, and are packing their goods in smaller quantities. In many cases, they are bypassing the *pasar* altogether, and selling their products in *toko*, which in turn are becoming more specialized in the sale and service of a particular line of goods. In the larger towns and cities, factories do not even use *agen* to distribute their goods to retailers, but use their own employees, selling from factory-owned vans.

In the case of agricultural products, better transport and better roads are rapidly eliminating small traders in favour of the depot operator, who can, with motorized transport, purchase in truckloads at the farm gate, thus eliminating one or two levels of bulking traders. In addition the government-supported KUDs are eliminating private traders in rice and other cash crops. Although all the available evidence indicates that farmers prefer to deal with private traders, the continued support, and in many cases subsidies, provided by the government to the co-operatives must, over time, promote their growth and further aggravate the decline of the rural trader.

As factory goods become more widely distributed, the role of the *pasar* is undergoing substantial changes, and a striking dichotomy is emerging between large and small *pasar*. As products become more standardized, there is less reason to buy everyday small household items at a small *pasar*, rather than at a *toko* or *warung*. The number of traders in the smaller *pasar* has gradually diminished until, as is now the case in West Java, South Kalimantan, or North Sulawesi, only small traders remain and the quality and range of goods is no better than at a *warung* (Anderson, 1978; Alexander, 1989; Mai and Buchholt, 1987). At the same time, small traders are eliminated from the larger *pasar* because they can no longer pay the fees, nor compete with larger traders having more extensive and more attractively displayed stocks. Such larger *pasar* are open every day, and increasingly the stallholders are selling direct to consumers, rather than to wholesalers. For these larger *pasar*, the most effective competition comes from more modern shops (*toko*), which often provide a wider range of goods, better displayed, and at much the same price. The *pasar* traders must compete by offering credit, which the *toko* are still reluctant to do.

Many of these changes are the inevitable consequence of rapid economic growth and industrialization, together with changing social attitudes towards the sale and purchase of goods. They can hardly be reversed. But their implications for the *pasar* economy are profound. For many employed in it, old skills are rapidly becoming worthless and new ones must be learnt if they are to survive. Bargaining becomes less central to trading success, because most traders have much the same goods purchased at much the same price. Incomes become more closely related to turnover, which in turn is a function of the level of finance. Traders must learn to calculate mark-ups, and keep at least rudimentary accounts, as well as pay complicated taxes such as the value added tax. Those *pasar* traders who have already made the transition from dealing in locally produced goods to dealing in factory products are, as a rule, among the youngest and best-educated, and often come from the richer rural families. Many of the rest, whether *pasar* traders, operators of *kios* and *warung*, or *bakul*, *agen*, or *penebas*, face gradual extinction. Their children will not follow them in these occupations but instead will seek employment as wage workers in factories, shops, or large-scale trading enterprises.

International Demand for Service Sector Output

Indonesia has traditionally been, and remains, a net importer of many services, including transport and a wide range of professional and consulting services. As in most other developing countries, by far the most important service sector exports are those associated with foreign tourism. Even here, Indonesia has been a relative latecomer compared with many other parts of the developing world. During the 1970s, the growth of the Indonesian tourist industry was hampered by the same constraints as those affecting most of the other non-oil export and import-competing industries. The real appreciation of the rupiah induced by the oil boom made Indonesia a high-cost destination compared to many other Asian and Pacific countries, while the growth of government regulation of foreign and domestic investment and aviation, together with time-consuming visa requirements, combined to restrict the development of international standard tourist facilities. Although there was some development on the island of Bali, much of the tourist potential of the archipelago remained untapped, and in 1979 the number of foreign visitors amounted to just half a million, the lowest figure in the ASEAN (Association of South-East Asian Nations), region and less than 10 per cent of the ASEAN total.

In the 1980s by contrast, the tourist sector has benefited from many of the measures designed to simplify government regulatory procedures and boost non-oil exports. Measures designed specifically to benefit the tourist sector have included the abolition of visa requirements for OECD and ASEAN nationals, the granting of additional landing rights to foreign airlines in Jakarta, Medan, and Bali, and a reduction in the number of licences required to build hotels and other tourist facilities. As a result of these initiatives, there has been a rapid increase in foreign arrivals over the *Repelita IV* period from 701,000 in 1984 to an estimated 1.62 million in 1989. This implies an annual growth of over 18 per cent per annum, which is among the fastest in the region. Although the total number of foreign arrivals is still quite small compared with Thailand and Singapore (where arrivals in 1989 were each in the vicinity of 4 million), foreign tourists do tend to stay rather longer in Indonesia than in most Asian destinations, and thus spend more. A survey carried out in 1988 found that the average foreign tourist in Indonesia spent $790 (exclusive of international airfares) and stayed 11.6 days.[15] In Thailand by contrast the average length of stay is 7 days, and it is less again in Singapore.[16]

Over half of all expenditures by foreign tourists within Indonesia are for accommodation, food and drinks. Eighteen per cent are for souvenirs and the rest for recreational and transport services, including sightseeing trips. Thus in terms of the national accounts, the trade, transport, and other services sectors are the main beneficiaries of tourist expenditures. However, their total contribution to value added in these sectors is rather small. In 1984, it was estimated that foreign tourist expenditures accounted for only about 1.6 per cent of value added in the trade and other services sectors, 1 per cent in the transport services, and about 0.2 per cent in the manufacturing sector (Kodhyat, 1987: 32). In total these expenditures amount to 0.4 per cent of GDP. By 1988 this share had increased to 0.7 per cent of GDP, and it is probable that it will continue to increase over the next decade. But even so, the contribution of foreign tourist expenditures to GDP is unlikely to exceed 3 per cent by the end of the century.[17]

Even to achieve this, value added from foreign tourist expenditures will have to increase by 20 per cent per annum in real terms. This will mean either that numbers of arrivals will have to increase by this amount, assuming real expenditure per arrival stays constant, or that expenditure per arrival will have to increase. In the latter case, each arrival will have to stay longer, or spend more per day. Even given the current optimistic projections about growth in world demand for tourism, the Indonesian industry will have to capture a much greater share of the market than it currently holds. To do this, there will have to be a sustained increase and improvement in international class tourist facilities. Much of the current debate about how this can be done centres around whether facilities in current tourist destinations (especially Bali) should be increased, or whether new resorts should be developed in other parts of the archipelago. If more and more facilities are developed in existing locations, there is a real danger of congestion and pollution spoiling the attractions which the tourists have come to enjoy. On the other hand, development of new facilities in other parts of the country involves substantial investment in infrastructure such as airports, roads, electricity, and sewerage. That it is possible to develop new resorts profitably if their location is carefully chosen is demonstrated by the successful growth of Batam as a weekend resort for Singaporeans. The challenge will be to find and develop other sites with similar potential over the next decade.

Future Service Sector Developments

The various reasons discussed at the outset for the higher share of the service sector in non-agricultural employment in Indonesia compared with the historical trend in the now-developed countries can now be assessed more thoroughly. Certainly it is true that employment in the public service has been growing rapidly in Indonesia since independence and that this is a factor contributing to the high percentage of the non-agricultural labour force in services. But it is by no means the only explanation. At the very most, only about 30 per cent of the service sector labour force in Indonesia are employees in government, community, domestic, and social services, and not all of these would be in the public sector. Although there can be little doubt that the government sector absorbs a high percentage of workers with post-secondary qualifications in Indonesia, it is not true that civil service employment has been expanding simply to accommodate the supply of post-secondary graduates. Rather the rapid growth in professional and technical employment opportunities engendered by the expansion of education, health, and other services in the 1970s and 1980s has created demand for the services of people with post-secondary qualifications, while at the same time there were relatively few openings for them in industry or in sectors such as private banking, or consulting services. This may well change over the coming decades. On the one hand, the government is clearly not prepared to be the 'employer of last resort' for all secondary and tertiary graduates wanting clerical or administrative jobs. And on the other hand, as manufacturing output and complementary services grow in the 1990s, more and more secondary and tertiary graduates should be absorbed in the private sector in industry, banking, and finance.

There can be little doubt that the industrialization which has occurred in Indonesia since the late 1960s has been more capital-intensive than Indonesia's basic resource endowments would warrant, and that this is an important reason for the low share of the non-agricultural labour force which has been absorbed into industrial employment. As has already been argued in Chapter 7, during the 1970s, much of the industrialization which took place was import-substituting, protection being granted through high tariffs and quantitative import controls. Production technologies were imported from the developed countries, and were highly capital-intensive. The 1980s have seen a number of government initiatives designed to ameliorate the anti-export bias in the trade regime, and encourage export-oriented industrialization (described in Chapter 7). However, it is probable that the employment effects of these policies will not be very substantial in the short run. Many of Indonesia's non-oil exports are either exported in unprocessed form, or where the processing takes place, as with wood products, the direct employment impact is small. Certainly, the growth of export industries such as garments, footwear, and furniture can be expected to generate an increasing number of new employment opportunities, but even so the proportion of the non-agricultural labour force which is employed in services is likely to fall only slowly over the next decade.

Rather than entering employment in manufacturing industry, many Indonesian workers, especially women, have found employment in small-scale trading enterprises. Women in particular take up this occupation because little capital is required and the necessary skills can be acquired even if their educational level is low. There are few regulatory barriers to entry, except for some types of hawking in urban areas. Trading activities fit in with domestic responsibilities, and at least in Java there appear to be few social constraints on a woman doing this type of work even when it involves considerable travel outside the home. All the available evidence indicates that the employment generated by trading enterprises is not casual or part-time, but typically occupies people for a normal working day; the majority of traders have been active for a number of years. The remuneration, while lower than that in more 'formal' occupations in urban areas, is greater than that which a worker could expect to get in agriculture, and indeed many rural people enter trading activities as a way of supplementing inadequate incomes from agriculture.

To a considerable extent, the growth in trading and transport activities in Indonesia over the past two decades can be seen as a complement to the growth which has occurred in other parts of the economy. Broadly based economic growth has led to increased real purchasing power on the part of both urban and rural populations, and increased demand for a range of trading, transport, and financial services. This demand will continue to grow, and will receive extra impetus from the projected growth in international tourism. However, it is probable that the employment opportunities created by the growing demand for what Katouzian (1970) has called complementary and new services will be very different from those created by traditional service occupations such as petty trade. The small self-employed trader operating with very limited capital in a restricted market is already being displaced by large-scale wholesaling and retailing operations using paid labour, and this process will certainly continue. In urban areas, the displacement process is likely to be accelerated by government regulations which seek to restrict the operations of small traders, both with and without fixed premises, and remove them altogether from the new, modern, shopping complexes and their surroundings. The impact of these developments on the incomes and living standards of low-income households with restricted asset bases will depend on their access to alternative employment as wage labourers.

1. According to the most recent OECD data, the S/NA ratio has risen in the high-income countries since the 1960s as the process of 'de-industrialisation' gathered pace. In France, for example, the share of services in total employment has increased from 40 per cent in 1960 to almost 60 per cent in 1984. In Belgium, Denmark, Canada, Australia, Norway, Sweden, the UK, and the USA, the service sector now accounts for more than 65 per cent of total employment. As the share of agriculture in the total labour force is under 10 per cent in almost all these countries, this means that the S/NA ratio would be close to 70 per cent. But this is a very recent development.

2. Two such objections deserve mention. Kuznets and others have pointed to the fact that prices of service sector output rise much faster as the economy matures than other prices. Thus the fall in relative service sector productivity in the now-developed countries shown in Table 9.1 is probably understated because the data are all in current prices, and thus do not allow for the relative price changes that have occurred over long periods. If the relative productivity calculations are made in constant price terms, they tend to show steeper falls (Kuznets, 1971: 289–92). Another problem involves the data for Thailand. The very high ratio of service sector labour productivity to that in the economy as a whole reflects the fact that the Thai labour force figures apparently use a very generous definition of economically active in agriculture which captures large numbers of women as family workers. Labour productivity in agriculture in Thailand is thus very low by international standards.

3. The literature on the informal sector in Indonesia is now quite large. Recent contributions include Sethuraman (1985), Forbes (1985), Institute for Development Studies (1987), Sasono and Rofi'ie (1987), and Sigit (1987). Sigit estimates that the non-agricultural informal sector accounted for 36.7 per cent of urban employment in 1985 and 18.2 per cent of rural sector employment.

4. These figures are taken from World Bank (1989), especially Table 30.

` 5. This figure comes from the 1989/90 issue of the annual publication, *The Military Balance*, published by the International Institute for Strategic Studies in London. Their estimate of the size of the Indonesian armed forces in 1987/8 was 285,000, although this does not include paramilitary forces and police. Data for the civilian civil service are published annually in the *Statistical Yearbook of Indonesia*. The study by Edgren cited above appears to have used only the data on permanent civil servants, and may thus understate the true size of the public sector.

6. The 1986 Economic Census (Seri AA: Results of Establishment Listings) reported that 2.12 million people were employed in non-government enterprises producing social, community, and personal services. Many of these would have been self-employed, but 500,000 were employed as private sector teachers and health workers, and many of these would probably be salaried. Around 1.26 million people were employed as home cleaners, laundry workers, etc., and it is likely that some of these would also be salaried.

7. This growth rate is based on figures from the *Lampiran Pidato Kenegaraan, 1975*, p. 798, and from the *Statistical Yearbook of Indonesia, 1988*, p. 89. It should be noted that the 1974 edition of the *Lampiran* gave a much lower figure for civil service establishment in 1974 (621,000 compared with 1.7 million in 1975). As an increase of over 1 million in one year is improbable, it appears that from 1975 onwards a broader definition of civil servant was used, embracing those in non-departmental government institutions and in regional governments. The figure can be compared with the 1.03 million employed by central and regional governments and state enterprises in 1961 (*Statistical Pocketbook of Indonesia*, 1964–67, pp. 28–31), although it is not clear that the 1961 and the post-1975 figures are fully comparable. To the extent that they are, we can use them together with data from the 1961 Population Census (BPS, 1963) and the 1985 Intercensal Survey (BPS, 1987b) to estimate the change in the proportion of total service sector employment accounted for by permanent civil servants. In 1961 the figure was 15.6 per cent; in 1985 it had declined slightly to 14.8 per cent. In 1961, there were 1.1 permanent civil servants per 100 population; by 1985 this had increased to 1.8. In this context it is worth noting that different authors have come up with very different estimates of the growth of the Indonesian civil service since independence. Evers (1987: 674) claims that there were only about 400,000 civil servants in 1960, expanding to more than 1.8 million by 1980. He does not cite precise sources for these figures, and the figure for 1960 would appear to be too low.

8. A breakdown of the civil service in 1988 by position, location, and period of service is given in the *Repelita V* document, Vol. 3, Table 30.1.

9. See in particular studies by Alexander (1986, 1987, and 1989); Alexander and Alexander (1987); Anderson (1978 and 1980); Chandler (1984); Forbes (1978 and 1979); Jellinek (1978); Mai and Buchholt (1987); and Peluso (1981). Economists have tended to focus their attention on marketing channels for agricultural produce; see in particular Kawagoe and Hayami (1989) and the literature cited therein.

10. The distinction between 'incorporated' (*berbadan hukum*) and 'unincorporated' (*tidak berbadan hukum*) revolves around whether or not the enterprise was formed with a legal title (*akte notaris*) such as PT (*perseroan terbatas*, meaning limited liability company), CV (*commanditaire vennootschap*, meaning partnership), Firma, etc. Those with no such legal title, which of course comprise the vast majority, were considered 'unincorporated' for the purposes of the census.

11. For a discussion of the anthropological literature on the bazaar economy and its links with recent developments in economic theory which are concerned with the role of information, communication and knowledge in exchange processes, see in particular Geertz (1978 and 1979).

12. The literature on the use of *tebasan* in Indonesian food-crop agriculture is now quite extensive. Koentjaraningrat (1985: 171–3) points out that it is not a new phenomenon, but its incidence has increased in the 1970s and 1980s. Collier, Wiradi, and Soentoro (1973), Wiradi (1978), and Hayami and Hafid (1979) discuss its use in rice agriculture; Bottema and Altemeier (1990) examine the factors determining the incidence of *tebasan* in maize, soy bean and groundnut cultivation.

13. For further discussion, see Geertz (1963: 37–8) and Dewey (1962: 106–7).

14. According to the Economic Census, only about 73,000 trading enterprises without fixed premises are members of co-operatives and of these 13,000 have never actually used any service offered by co-operatives. More than 2.4 million enterprises have never availed themselves of any service offered by a co-operative.

15. These figures are from BPS (1989).

16. These figures refer to 1986, and are taken from *Statistical Yearbook of Thailand*, Vol. 36 (1989): 95.

17. The estimate of 0.7 per cent of GDP for 1988 is given in Booth (1990: Table 7). If we assume that the value added from tourist expenditures grows at 20 per cent per annum in real terms between 1988 and 2000, while GDP grows at 6 per cent per annum, then by 2000 foreign tourism should be contributing about 3 per cent of GDP.

REFERENCES

Alexander, J. (1986), 'Information and Price Setting in a Rural Javanese Market', *Bulletin of Indonesian Economic Studies*, 22(1): 88–112.

_____ (1987), *Trade, Traders and Trading in Rural Java*, Singapore: Oxford University Press.

_____ (1989), *Enhancing Productivity and Employment in the Rural Trade Sector*, Jakarta: UNDP/ILO.

Alexander, J. and Alexander, P. (1987), 'Striking a Bargain in Javanese Markets', *Man* (New Series), 22: 42–68.

Ali, Supian Haji (1987), 'Malaysia', in Gus Edgren (ed.), *The Growing Sector: Studies of Public Sector Employment in Asia*, New Delhi: International Labour Organization, Asian Regional Team for Employment Promotion.

Amin, Samir (1976), *Unequal Development: An Essay on the Social Formations of Peripheral Capitalism*, New Delhi: Oxford University Press.

Anderson, A.G. (1978), *The Structure and Organisation of Rural Marketing in the Cimanuk River Basin, West Java*, Rural Dynamics Series No. 3, Bogor: Agro-economic Survey.

_____ (1980), 'The Rural Market in West Java', *Economic Development and Cultural Change*, 28: 757–77.

Berry, Albert (1978), 'A Positive Interpretation of the Expansion of Urban Services in Latin America, with Some Colombian Evidence', *Journal of Development Studies*, 14(2): 210–31.

Biro Pusat Statistik (BPS) (annually), *Statistik Indonesia* [Statistical Yearbook of Indonesia], Jakarta.

_____ (annually), *Buku Saku Statistik Indonesia* [Statistical Pocketbook of Indonesia], Jakarta.

_____ (1963), *Sensus Penduduk 1961* [1961 Population Census], Serie S.P. II, Jakarta.

_____ (1987a), *Sensus Ekonomi 1986: Hasil Pendaftaran Perusahaan Usaha* [1986 Economic Census: Results of Establishments Listing], Jakarta.

_____ (1987b), *Penduduk Indonesia: Supas No. 5* [Indonesian Population: Results of 1985 Intercensal Survey No. 5], Jakarta.

_____ (1988), *Sensus Ekonomi 1986 (Seri C63): Statistik Usaha Rumahtangga Perdagangan dengan Tempat Tidak Tetap, 1986* [1986 Economic Census: Statistics on Trading Household Without Fixed Premises], Jakarta.

_____ (1989), *Penelitian Pengeluaran dan Pandangan Wisatawan Manca Negara, 1988*, Jakarta.

Booth, Anne (1990), 'The Tourism Boom in Indonesia', *Bulletin of Indonesian Economic Studies*, 26(3): 45–73.

Booth, Anne and Sundrum, R.M. (1988), *Employment Trends and Policy Issues for Repelita V*, Jakarta: UNDP/ILO.

Bottema, Taco and Altemeier, Klaus (1990), 'Market Channels, Quality Incentives and Contract Harvesting: The Case of Maize, Soybean and Groundnut', *Bulletin of Indonesian Economic Studies*, 26(1): 91–116.

Canlas, Dante B. (1987), 'Philippines', in Gus Edgren (ed.), *The Growing*

Sector: Studies of Public Sector Employment in Asia, New Delhi: International Labour Organization.

Chandler, G. (1984), *Market Trade in Rural Java*, Monash University Papers on Southeast Asia, No. 11, Clayton: Monash University, Centre of Southeast Asian Studies.

Chira Hongladarom; Isarankura, Watana; Raksasap, Somrux; and Panipat-Greer, Saowanee (1987), 'Thailand', in Gus Edgren (ed.), *The Growing Sector: Studies of Public Sector Employment in Asia*, New Delhi: International Labour Organization.

Collier, William L.; Wiradi, Gunawan; and Soentoro (1973), 'Recent Changes in Rice Harvesting Methods', *Bulletin of Indonesian Economic Studies*, 9(2): 35–45.

Department of Information (annually), *Lampiran Pidato Kenegaraan* [Appendix to the State Speech], Jakarta.

Desai, Ashok and Desai, Ena (1987), 'India', in Gus Edgren (ed.), *The Growing Sector: Studies of Public Sector Employment in Asia*, New Delhi: International Labour Organization.

Dewey, Alice (1962), *Peasant Marketing in Java*, Glencoe: The Free Press.

Edgren, Gus (1987), 'The Growth of Public Sector Employment in Asia', in Gus Edgren (ed.), *The Growing Sector: Studies of Public Sector Employment in Asia*, New Delhi: International Labour Organization.

_____ (ed.) (1987), *The Growing Sector: Studies of Public Sector Employment in Asia*, New Delhi: International Labour Organization, Asian Regional Team for Employment Promotion.

Evans, Peter B. and Timberlake, Michael (1980), 'Dependence, Inequality and the Growth of the Tertiary: A Comparative Analysis of Less Developed Countries', *American Sociological Review*, 45: 531–52.

Evers, Hans-Dieter (1987), 'The Bureaucratization of Southeast Asia', *Comparative Studies in Society and History*, 29: 666–85.

Forbes, Dean (1978), 'Urban–Rural Interdependence: The Trishaw Riders of Ujung Pandang', in P. J. Rimmer et al. (eds.), *Food, Shelter and Transport in Southeast Asia and the Pacific*, Canberra: Australian National University Press.

_____ (1979), *The Pedlars of Ujung Pandang*, Working Paper No. 17, Clayton: Monash University, Centre of Southeast Asian Studies.

_____ (1985), 'Urban Development Strategies and Policies for the Informal Sector in Indonesia', *Australian Urban Studies*, 13(3): 17–19.

Geertz, Clifford (1962), 'The Rotating Credit Association: "A Middle Rung" in Development', *Economic Development and Cultural Change*, 10: 241–63.

_____ (1963), *Peddlers and Princes: Social Change and Economic Modernization in Two Indonesian Towns*, Chicago: University of Chicago Press.

_____ (1978), 'The Bazaar Economy: Information and Search in Peasant Marketing', *American Economic Review*, 68(2): 28–32.

_____ (1979), 'Suq: The Bazaar Economy of Sefrou', in C. Geertz, H. Geertz, and L. Rosen, *Meaning and Order in Moroccan Society: Three Essays in Cultural Analysis*, Cambridge: Cambridge University Press.

Gemmell, Norman (1986), *Structural Change and Economic Development: The Role of the Service Sector*, New York: St Martin's Press.

Hayami, Y. and Hafid, Anwar (1979), 'Rice Harvesting and Welfare in Rural Java', *Bulletin of Indonesian Economic Studies*, 15(2): 94–112.

Institute for Development Studies (1987), *The Informal Sector: Economic Analysis*, Informal Sector Policy Studies Project, Jakarta.

Jellinek, L. (1978), 'The Rise and Development of a Vegetable Trading Enterprise', *Indonesia Circle*, 15: 29–38.

Katouzian, M. A. (1970), 'The Development of the Service Sector: A New Approach', *Oxford Economic Papers*, 22: 362–82.

Kawagoe, Toshihiko and Hayami, Yujiro (1989), 'Farmers and Middlemen in a Transmigration Area in Indonesia', *Bulletin of Indonesian Economic Studies*, 25(3): 73–98.

Kodhyat, H. (1987), *Analisa Statistik Pariwisata dan Perhotelan*, Jakarta: Biro Pusat Statistik.

Koentjaraningrat (1985), *Javanese Culture*, Singapore: Oxford University Press.

Kuznets, Simon (1966), *Modern Economic Growth: Rate, Structure, and Spread*, New Haven: Yale University Press.

____ (1971), *Economic Growth of Nations: Total Output and Production Structure*, Cambridge: The Belknap Press of Harvard University Press.

Mai, U. and Buchholt, H. (1987), *Peasant Pedlars and Professional Traders: Subsistence Trade in Rural Markets of Minahasa*, Indonesia, Singapore: Institute of Southeast Asian Studies.

Minami, Ryoshin (1986), *The Economic Development of Japan: A Quantitative Study*, London: Macmillan.

Peluso, Nancy L. (1981), *Survival Strategies of Rural Women Traders or a Woman's Place Is in the Market*, World Employment Programme Research Working Paper, Geneva: International Labour Organization.

Sasono, Adi and Rofi'ie, Achmad (1987), *People's Economy*, Jakarta: Southeast Asian Forum for Development Alternatives.

Sethuraman, S. V. (1985), 'The Informal Sector in Indonesia: Policies and Prospects', *International Labour Review*, 124(6): 719–35.

Siegel, J. (1969), *The Rope of God*, Los Angeles: University of California Press.

Sigit, Hananto (1987), 'Memperkirakan Besarnya Sektor Informal', *Forum Statistik*, 6(1): 54–60.

Stoler, Ann (1975), 'Some Socio-economic Aspects of Rice Harvesting in a Javanese Village', *Masyarakat Indonesia*, 2: 51–87.

____ (1977), 'Class Structure and Female Autonomy in Rural Java', *Signs*, 3: 74–89.

Thailand, National Statistical Office (various years), *Statistical Yearbook of Thailand*, Bangkok.

White, Ben (1976), 'Population, Employment and Involution in Rural Java', *Development and Change*, 7: 267–90.

Wiradi, G. (1978), *Rural Development and Rural Institutions: A Study of Institutional Changes in West Java*, Rural Dynamics Series No. 6, Bogor: Agro-economic Survey.

World Bank (1989), *World Development Report*, Washington, DC.

PART III
HUMAN RESOURCE
DEVELOPMENT

10
Income Distribution and Poverty
Anne Booth

Introduction

VERY early in the life of the New Order government, disquiet began to be expressed about the distributional consequences of accelerated economic growth, and as the issue of 'redistribution with growth' attracted increasing attention worldwide in the 1970s it was inevitable that both domestic and foreign students of the Indonesian economy became concerned about distributional questions. It was also inevitable, given the paucity of reliable evidence and the political overtones of much of the international debate, that many contributions reflected the ideological convictions of the authors rather more than analysis of the available data. The situation changed somewhat in the latter part of the 1970s, as more information became available and more scholars turned their attention to Indonesia as an important case-study of the effects of oil-induced income growth on living standards and the distribution of income and wealth. But even so, the chapter on income distribution in *The Indonesian Economy during the Soeharto Era* found the picture 'a blurred and confused one', although the hope was expressed that as more information became available, a clearer picture would emerge, which in turn would facilitate policy formulation (Booth and Sundrum, 1981: 214).

Certainly the data situation has improved considerably in the ten years since these words were written. There are now ten rounds of the consumer expenditure survey component of the National Socio-economic Survey (usually referred to as the *Susenas*), spanning the years from 1963/4 to 1987, as well as data from the National Labour Force Surveys (*Sakernas*), carried out in 1976–8 and again in 1986–8, the three Agricultural Censuses, and the two sets of urban Cost of Living Surveys.[1] In addition the Biro Pusat Statistik (BPS) has begun work on the construction of social accounting matrices.[2] Taken together, these data sets represent as rich a source of information on the distributional consequences of economic growth as is available in most developing countries. One is therefore in a much better position to analyse the distributional implications of economic development in Indonesia than ever before.

As was pointed out in Chapter 1, an investigation of recent trends in income distribution and poverty in Indonesia is particularly timely because Indonesia offers a fascinating case-study of the impact of both an oil boom and post-boom restructuring on living standards and income distribution. A considerable international literature has grown up in the past two decades on these issues, and it will be useful to review it briefly, before examining the Indonesian evidence.

The Impact of Commodity Booms and Post-boom Reconstruction on Income Distribution

Studies of the distributional consequences of petroleum-led growth tend to fall into two broad categories. One influential body of literature has studied the impact of a 'booming sector' on the rest of the economy using analytical tools derived mainly from the neoclassical theory of international trade. This literature grew rapidly in the 1970s and early 1980s, and was applied to a number of countries experiencing resource booms, including those with rapidly growing mineral exports, such as Australia, the coffee-producing economies of East Africa, and petroleum economies in both the developed and the developing world (Corden, 1984). It stressed the movement of resources away from sectors producing 'traditional' traded goods, and towards both the 'booming sector' and non-traded goods and services. In the OPEC economies, the distributional consequences of these movements depended on a number of assumptions about the rate of domestic absorption of the petroleum revenues, factor mobility, and the working of both product and factor markets, but broadly the models suggested that the real income of factors used intensively in the production of traditional tradables would fall in terms of all commodities, both relative to real incomes of factors used in the production of non-traded goods and services, and even in absolute terms (Cassing and Warr, 1985). In the context of an economy such as Indonesia, incomes of farmers producing crops such as rubber, coffee, and vegetable oils could be expected to fall relative to incomes of people in sectors such as construction, transport, and trade.

These shifts in relative producer incomes would in turn have important implications for the distribution of incomes by sector and region. Urban incomes would almost certainly increase relative to rural incomes, given that most traditional export staples were agricultural, and many non-traded goods and services, including public administration, were produced mainly in urban areas. Output and incomes in regions specialized in producing traditional export and import-substituting staples would decline relative to those producing non-traded goods and services, and could decline in absolute terms. At the household level, those households producing traded goods would experience a loss in incomes relative to those producing non-traded goods. Furthermore, households with members who are mobile between occupations and regions would be likely to gain relative to those whose members are less mobile, especially if the latter were specialized in producing export- or import-substituting staples.

These predictions depend crucially on the role of government. The 'Dutch Disease' literature is concerned not just with positive economic analysis of the consequences of resource booms but also addresses policy issues, and especially the degree of protection which governments should provide to the traditional traded goods industries. Resource booms usually mean increased government revenues through increased royalty payments (in the case of the OPEC economies), or through increased export or income taxes. Inevitably the government will come under pressure to use these resources to provide some form of assistance to those sectors producing traditional traded goods. Such protection could be justified on purely distributional grounds, although relocation and retraining subsidies could be a more efficient way of providing transitional assistance. But producers of traded goods can also argue that the resource boom is likely to be short-lived, and that if the traditional export- and import-substituting sectors are squeezed of their resources too drastically, the economy will be in deep trouble when the boom collapses and these sectors are once again needed to earn, or save, foreign exchange. In many developing countries, it is also probable that a massive movement of resources away from traded goods production would lead to rapid rural depopulation and urbanization, given that traditional traded goods are usually agricultural, while non-traded goods and services are often produced in urban areas. Both these trends lead to negative externalities, and may be difficult to reverse if the boom collapses.

Governments may not, however, be exclusively motivated by considerations of economic rationality. A second very influential strand in the literature on the distributional consequences of resources booms, which may be termed the 'political economy' approach, emphasizes the crucial role of the government in spending the greatly increased resources which the boom puts at its disposal. Because of the sheer magnitude of these resources relative to gross domestic product in many petroleum economies, the pattern of government expenditures can have profound social and political as well as economic consequences. Traditional power élites, especially those whose wealth is derived from agriculture, are likely to undergo a sudden and severe decline in their power relative to new social groups whose position in the military or civilian bureaucracies means that they have preferential access to the oil revenues. An Iranian study posed the issue in the following terms:

... the state has become the exclusive fountain of economic and social power; a power, moreover, which is independent of the productive effort of the community. Thus, it tends to accumulate all rights and obligations, and through this process it affects the form and substance of the class structure. The formal traditional class structure may remain intact, but it loses a large part of its explanatory power in determining social relations, social mobility and income distribution. For in this case, the most clear line of demarcation between different social categories is not so much their common relations with the means of *production*, but their common relations with the chief supplier of the means of *consumption*—i.e. the state. Social stratification then becomes a function of economic dependency on the state. (Katouzian, 1978: 349.)

In a later study of Iran, Katouzian (1981: 246) has stressed that

in a larger, agricultural oil country—where the oil revenues per head of population are not large enough to ensure a reasonable living standard for literally everyone—this type of relationship gives rise to a new, petrolic system of social stratification: the state has to be selective in affording even the minimum standard of comfort to individuals, and those who benefit constitute only a small percentage of the urban population. (Katouzian, 1981: 246.)

According to Katouzian, the bulk of the oil revenues will be spent in ways which benefit the military–bureaucratic complex, professional, and other educated groups, and some business groups. The rest of the urban society will benefit only incidentally, while in rural areas the bulk of the population will benefit hardly at all from budgetary expenditures, while at the same time they suffer indirectly from the resource shifts predicted in the neoclassical models.

Studies of the political economy of other petroleum economies in the 1970s have also stressed the importance of existing power relationships in determining the allocation of government expenditures, and predict changes in resource flows in the economy as a result of the oil boom on the basis of these relationships rather than simply on the basis of shifts in relative prices of traded and non-traded goods. In a country such as Venezuela, where a private capitalist class was already well-entrenched politically before the oil boom, the government

sought to regulate foreign capital operations in order to create 'economic space' for accelerated indigenous private capital accumulation and growth.... The state increasingly performed as a redistributive organ of this rising entrepreneurial bourgeoisie who preferred to recycle the wealth into 'services', imports, commerce, real estate, and liquid bank deposits, rather than undertake investments in long-term, large-scale productive enterprise. In addition to financing a capitalist class that lacked a commitment to dynamic industrial growth, state petroleum income funded an ever-expanding and unproductive state sector which rapidly became the focal point of widespread corruption in society. In large part, corruption resulted from the close ties between the national bourgeoisie and the state, a relationship that led to the massive allocation of resources toward private capital accumulation and profitmaking. (Petras and Morley, 1983: 7.)

In Nigeria, where the oil boom followed soon after the conclusion of a bitter and divisive civil war, the new government of General Gowon 'tried to build support by investing rapidly and by handing out wage increases to public sector employees. The large new oil revenues were therefore funneled disproportionately to the urban sector where political pressures were strongest and where government could give money out quickly.' (Bienen, 1983: 23.) It is striking that, in spite of their very different approaches, the predictions of the neoclassical model are very close to those of the political economy studies. Both suggest that the rural sector is likely to be penalized by a resource boom, either because this sector is relatively specialized in the production of traded goods (the neoclassical model), or because the rural population is politically marginalized. Both suggest that the urban middle class is likely to emerge as the main beneficiary, either because they are more specialized in the production of non-traded goods and services, or simply because they can influence the government to spend the revenues from the resource boom in ways which would benefit them. But while the political economy approach might appear to have greater realism, it suffers from an important flaw, in that it tends to regard government policy as wholly determined by the vested interests of the state's clientele, whoever they may be, and therefore quite impervious to any external pressures for change. In particular it ignores the possibility that the clientele of the state are not a homogeneous group, but have different interests, some of which may be harmed by the oil boom, and the resulting growth in government expenditures. To the extent that this is true, the oil boom might trigger dissension and even open conflict within the ruling group. It may also cause that part of the ruling group whose interests have been hurt by the oil boom to forge new alliances with the 'voiceless masses' whose interests the government has ignored. Indeed such shifting alliances within the ruling group, and between parts of the ruling group and outsiders, appear to be the reason for the chronic political instability in the 1970s in a country such as Nigeria.

If one concedes that some governments are not wholly subservient to a closed circle of clients, but reasonably independent actors with a genuine perception of, and concern for, longer-run considerations of the national interest, then the neoclassical model of resource booms can perform a salutary role. In particular it forces the analyst to entertain the possibility that government policy can make a significant difference to the distributional outcomes of resource booms in ways that are not allowed for in much of the political economy literature. Thus in seeking to determine the distributional consequences of the oil boom and its aftermath in the Indonesian economy one must confront the data with an open mind, and allow for the possibility that what has been found to occur in Iran or Nigeria or Venezuela did not happen in Indonesia because of the rather different behaviour of the government.

If the neoclassical and political economy literature makes much the same kind of predictions regarding the distributional consequences of a resource boom, they appear to offer very different predictions on what will happen when the boom ends. The neoclassical model would predict that the factor movements which occurred during the boom would simply be reversed, as a result of the post-boom adjustment in the real exchange rate. It is implicit in the political economy model, however, that clients of the state who were rapidly enriched during the boom would resist any policy change which affected their incomes relative to other economic groups. Thus government employees, both civilian and military, would press for the maintenance of their real wages, even if government revenues are much reduced as a result of the fall in commodity prices. Similarly those in the private sector who benefited from the boom would do everything in their power to prevent a decline in their real incomes, both by seeking more direct government assistance, and by opposing policies, such as a currency devaluation, designed to assist domestic producers of traded goods.

Trends in Indicators of Income Distribution

Urban–Rural Disparities

Several scholars have pointed out the 'Dutch Disease' literature's predictions on intersectoral resource movements receive considerable support from the Indonesian data after 1973, although allowance had to be made for government protection of sectors producing traded goods, especially agriculture and manufacturing. Certainly there was an acceleration in the growth of sectors producing non-traded goods and services; especially striking was the large increase in the growth of public administration after 1973 (Sundrum, 1986: Table 13). This acceleration is explained in the neoclassical model in terms of changing relative prices of traded and non-traded goods resulting from the oil boom-induced real appreciation. The increase in the relative price of non-traded goods induces a shift of factors away from traditional export- and import-substituting activities into sectors producing non-traded goods. There can be little doubt that relative prices in Indonesia in the 1970s did move in the way which the neoclassical model predicted (Warr, 1986; see also Chapter 5 of this volume). From 1971 to 1973, non-oil export and import prices rose relative to the housing component of the Jakarta cost of living index, which is widely used as an index of non-traded goods prices. After 1974 the ratios fell sharply, and in the case of non-oil exports only began to recover after 1979.

A decline in the relative price of traded goods of this magnitude can be expected to have a considerable impact on the distribution of income by sector, region, and household. The neoclassical model predicts widening urban–rural disparities because urban areas produce most of the non-traded goods; in addition the political economy argument would suggest that this would be particularly pronounced in Java where incomes of the 'military–bureaucratic élite', who are concentrated in Jakarta and the other large conurbations, would increase relative to the rest of society. There is also likely to be an increase in regional inequalities, while at the household level we would expect households with incomes derived mainly from service occupations to increase relative to the rest. This would be especially true of households in public sector employment. By contrast, when the resource boom ends and a real depreciation occurs (i.e. prices of traded goods rise relative to others) the neoclassical model would predict some narrowing of the intersectoral and interregional disparities which opened up in the 1970s. The political economy model would suggest that this will occur only slowly and painfully as those groups who benefited from the boom seek to maintain their privileged status.

Certainly there can be little doubt that urban–rural disparities in consumption expenditures did widen markedly in Indonesia in the 1970s. For Indonesia as a whole, the ratio of urban consumer expenditures to those in rural areas increased by almost 35 per cent between 1969 and 1978; the increase was much greater for non-food expenditures (Table 10.1). The increase in the expenditure disparity was greater for Java than for the Outer Islands (Sundrum and Booth, 1980: Table 4). It could be argued that the increase in these ratios was mainly due to faster inflation in urban areas, which in turn could be attributed to the higher weight given non-traded goods such as housing in the urban cost of living indexes. But in fact the Jakarta cost of living index rose at almost exactly the same rate in the 1970s as the rural Java index of nine basic commodities, although the difference between urban and rural inflation was rather greater outside Java. If the increases in per capita consumption expenditures are adjusted by appropriate price deflators for urban and rural areas in Java and elsewhere, it is clear that

TABLE 10.1

Urban Per Capita Expenditures in Indonesia as a Percentage
of Rural Expenditures, 1969–1987

	Expenditures			
	Cereals	*All Food*	*Non-food*	*Total*[a]
1964/5[b]	101	130	164	137
1969[c]	106	131	194	145
1970[d]	107	129	198	143
1976[e]	101	143	280	173 (250)[f]
1978[e]	102	151	314	195
1980[g]	95	137	261	169 (207)
1981[e]	101	143	248	179 (234)
1984[g]	95	149	275	189 (250)
1987[h]	94	144	269	185 (271)

Sources: BPS, *Survei Sosial Ekonomi Nasional, Pengeluaran untuk Konsumsi Penduduk*, various rounds.
[a] Figures in brackets refer to Jakarta expenditures as a percentage of rural expenditures.
[b] Data exclude Jakarta.
[c] October–December. Data exclude several provinces outside Java.
[d] January–April.
[e] Annual data.
[f] Preliminary data for January–April only.
[g] February.
[h] January.

in the first part of the 1970s, real expenditure growth in urban Java was much higher than anywhere else (Table 10.2). In the latter part of the 1970s, real expenditure growth in rural Java caught up with that in urban areas, implying that disparities stayed constant in real terms. Consumption expenditures in both urban and rural areas of Java grew faster than in the Outer Islands.

A serious criticism of the consumer expenditure survey data is that they consistently show a lower real growth in the 1970s for Indonesia as a whole than the household consumption component of the national income accounts (Table 10.2). This is widely considered to be due to progressively greater understatement of non-food expenditures by wealthier households, especially in urban areas. Thus the disparities between urban and rural expenditures shown in Tables 10.1 and 10.2 are, if anything, understated, especially as they relate to non-food expenditures. In the 1980s by contrast the growth of consumer expenditures shown by the *Susenas* data has been rather faster than that shown by the household consumption component of the national income account. This could be due to the fact that societal norms about 'appropriate' consumption standards had by the early 1980s caught up with actual consumption standards, especially in urban areas, so the extent of expenditure understatement declined.[3]

A striking feature of the post-1981 household expenditure figures is that they show little narrowing of the nominal urban–rural differentials. Particularly important is the widening gap between Jakarta expenditures

TABLE 10.2
Average Annual Growth in Real Per Capita Monthly Expenditures[a]

	1969/70–76[b]	1976–81[c]	1981–7[d]
Java			
Urban	4.2	4.1	4.5
Rural	−0.8	5.9	0.6
Outer Islands			
Urban	2.5	3.3	4.0
Rural	0.8	−0.3	0.3
Indonesia			
Urban	3.8	3.4	4.3
Rural	−0.4	3.6	0.5
Whole Country	0.8	4.1	2.0
Private Consumption Expenditure[e]	4.8	8.7	1.4

Sources: As for Table 10.1; 17 city price index as reported in *Indikator Ekonomi*.
[a]For 1969/70 to 1981, deflators used were those reported in Asra (1989: Table 3). For the period 1981–7, the 17 city index was used to deflate urban expenditures, and the rural 9 commodity index was used to deflate rural expenditures.
[b]1969/70 data refer to the months October through to April.
[c]Annual data.
[d]1987 data refer to the month of January.
[e]From the national accounts data. Revised data were used from 1983 onwards.

TABLE 10.3
Percentage Average Annual Growth in Real Per Capita Consumption
Expenditures: Java and Indonesia, 1980–1987[a]

	Urban	Rural
Jakarta	9.3	n.a.
West Java	4.5	2.2
Central Java	5.0	2.7
DIY	1.7	5.1
East Java	6.9	3.1
Indonesia	5.6	1.4

Sources: As for Table 10.2.
[a]The consumer price index for each capital city was used to deflate the urban consumer
  expenditure data, and the rural Java 9 commodity index was used to deflate the rural
  data. 1980 data refer to the month of February and 1987 to the month of January.
n.a. = Not available.

and the average for rural areas since 1980 (Table 10.1). Indeed the differentials were much the same in 1987 as they had been in the mid-
1970s. As the available price indexes suggest that rural inflation, in both
Java and the Outer Islands, was rather faster than inflation in Jakarta
over the decade 1976–86, and faster than the growth in the household
expenditure component of the GDP deflator, it is probable that in real
terms the urban–rural, and especially the Jakarta–rural, differential could
have widened in the decade from the mid-1970s to the mid-1980s. This
is confirmed by the figures on real expenditure growth by province in
Java between 1980 and 1987 (Table 10.3). These show that Jakarta consumption expenditures have been growing not just much more rapidly
than in rural areas, but also more rapidly than in other urban areas in
Java, and in urban Indonesia as a whole. While these results could be
influenced by declining understatement in urban expenditures through
the 1980s, it still seems probable the consumption standards in the
national capital, already higher than elsewhere in 1980, have been
increasing more rapidly since then.

Regional Disparities

The evidence that real per capita expenditure growth was faster in Java
than elsewhere in the 1970s raises the issue of regional disparities. These
have usually been studied in Indonesia using the provincial gross domestic product data prepared by the BPS. Following Esmara (1975),
who in turn used a technique put forward by Williamson (1965), most
analysts have used the regional GDP data to calculate a coefficient of
variation weighted by the population of different provinces. Using the
nominal provincial GDP data, and including mining output in the GDP
of the oil-producing provinces, it is clear that the coefficient of variation
increased considerably during the 1970s, and declined between 1980
and 1986 (Table 10.4). But if the mining sector is excluded, the

TABLE 10.4

Population Weighted Coefficients of Variation of Per Capita RGDP

	Current Prices		Current Jakarta Prices[a]	
	With Oil	*Excluding Oil*	*With Oil*	*Excluding Oil*
1971	0.76	0.43	0.65	0.49
1975	1.29	0.41	1.18	0.37
1980	1.34	0.54	1.16	0.47
1984	0.99	0.47	0.83	0.50
1987	0.87	0.43	0.74	0.45

Sources: BPS, *Pendapatan Regional Provinsi-provinsi di Indonesia* [Provincial Income in Indonesia] 1971–7 (LYR 80-04), 1976–80(VN. NK.0774.8301), 1983–7 (04400 8902); BPS, *Nilai Rata-rata Indeks Kebutuhan Fisik Minimum Pekerja dan Keluarga Selama Sebulan di Setiap Provinsi*, 1979–87.

[a]Converted using an index of regional price disparities (RPI). For 1971 and 1975 the RPI was based on that estimated by Arndt and Sundrum (1975). For 1980 the RPI was based on the KFM data, published by the BPS. An RPI for 1984 and 1987 was derived by adjusting the 1980 RPI upwards by the rate of inflation shown by the consumer price index for each capital city.

coefficient drops, and the increase is less marked. This shows the importance of the oil and mining sectors in causing disparities in regional GDP in Indonesia.

Another factor promoting regional disparities is the very considerable difference in the price level in different parts of Indonesia, reflecting high transport costs, and also differences in the speed with which inflationary shocks are transmitted to different parts of the archipelago (Arndt and Sundrum, 1975). This regional price disparity can be partially corrected if the Williamson coefficient is calculated using the RGDP data in constant prices, but this procedure still does not take account of price disparities between provinces in the base year. The most satisfactory way of overcoming the problem is to calculate provincial GDP for a given year in Jakarta prices, using a regional price deflator. Such a deflator was calculated by Arndt and Sundrum for the years 1966–74; for 1980 onwards a regional price deflator can conveniently be calculated from the KFM (*Kebutuhan Fisik Minimum* or Minimum Physical Needs Index) data collected by the Department of Labour.[4] If these indexes are used to convert the nominal RGDP data to Jakarta prices, and then calculate a Williamson coefficient, one finds that it increased considerably between 1971 and 1975, stayed fairly constant between 1975 and 1980, and dropped again between 1980 and 1986, so that by 1986, regional income disparities were much what they had been in 1971. Removing the direct and indirect effect of mining sector incomes from the RGDP data in Jakarta prices, one finds that there was actually some decline in the Williamson coefficient between 1971 and 1975, an increase between 1975 and 1980, and some decline thereafter (Table 10.4).

If one is interested primarily in estimating disparities in living standards, rather than in regional gross domestic product, it is not enough just
to remove the effect of enclave sectors such as mining, output from
which does not greatly affect the rest of the regional economy. One must
also allow for different rates of saving and investment between
provinces, for the impact of government tax and expenditure policies
and for private transfers between individuals and corporate bodies in
different parts of the country.[5] The net effect of all these resource movements is reflected in the figures on household consumption expenditures
which are collected in the *Susenas* surveys. If the provincial *Susenas* data
on per capita consumption expenditure are converted to Jakarta prices
and Williamson coefficients are calculated, it is at once clear that the
degree of regional disparity in per capita consumption is lower than the
disparity in regional incomes, even without the mining sector. But in
contrast to the RGDP data, there does appear to have been an increase
in regional disparities in consumption expenditures in the 1980s. This
increase has in turn been due to growing disparities within urban areas,
and between urban and rural areas; within rural areas there appears to
have been some decline in the weighted coefficient of variation between
1980 and 1987 (Table 10.5).

The *Susenas* data also show that, between 1980 and 1987, there was a
considerable 'catching up' process, in the sense that those provinces

TABLE 10.5

Population Weighted Coefficients of Variation of Per Capita
Consumption Expenditures[a]

	Urban	Rural	Urban and Rural[b]
1976	n.a.	n.a.	0.22
1980	0.18	0.18	0.22
1984	0.20	0.15	0.29 (0.33)
1987	0.25	0.13	0.32 (0.33)
Correlation Coefficient 1980 expenditures correlated with growth for 1980 to 1987	−0.45[c]	−0.63[c]	

Sources: 1976: Islam and Khan (1986: 84).
    1980–7: BPS, *Pengeluaran untuk Konsumsi Penduduk Indonesia per Propinsi*, 1984,
    1987.
    1984–7: BPS, *Pendapatan Regional Provinsi-provinsi di Indonesia menurut
    Pendapatan*, 1983–7 (04440.9001).

[a]PCE data for each province were adjusted to Jakarta prices using a regional price index
based on the 1980 KFM data. For 1984 and 1987 this index was adjusted upwards to
allow for inflation using the consumer price index for each capital city. The 1976 data (in
Jakarta prices) were taken from Islam and Khan (1986: 84).

[b]Figures in brackets are calculated from the household expenditure data in the regional
income accounts.

[c]Significant at 5 per cent.

TABLE 10.6
Average Annual Growth in Nominal Per Capita Expenditures
in Jakarta Prices, 1980–1987[a]

Province	Urban and Rural	Urban	Rural
Jakarta	18.7	18.7	n.a.
East Java	15.5	16.2	14.5
Central Java	15.4	14.1	15.1
DI Yogyakarta	14.8	10.5	16.6
Bali	14.8	14.8	14.3
West Java	14.1	13.5	13.7
West Nusa Tenggara	13.6	12.0	17.5
East Nusa Tenggara	13.5	16.5	12.8
West Sumatra	13.5	13.3	13.4
North Sumatra	12.6	14.2	9.5
South Sulawesi	12.5	13.9	11.9
North Sulawesi	12.3	12.6	12.0
Maluku	11.8	17.1	10.5
South Kalimantan	11.3	11.0	11.3
Lampung	11.3	13.1	10.7
South Sumatra	10.7	14.3	8.9
Riau	10.3	12.2	9.1
South-east Sulawesi	10.3	14.0	9.5
Jambi	10.1	11.0	9.7
Central Sulawesi	10.0	12.0	9.6
Bengkulu	9.5	8.5	9.5
West Kalimantan	7.9	12.8	6.1
East Kalimantan	7.8	9.8	5.7
Aceh	7.1	10.5	7.3
Central Kalimantan	5.1	4.3	7.0
Irian Jaya	4.7	12.7	2.1
Jakarta CPI	8.7		

Sources: As for Table 10.5.
[a]See footnote(a) to Table 10.5 for details of the regional price index.

with relatively low per capita expenditures in 1980 (in Jakarta prices) experienced more rapid growth than those with relatively high expenditures. This is reflected in the significant degree of negative correlation between expenditure in 1980 and growth in expenditure in 1980–7 in both urban and rural areas (Table 10.5). The provinces of Java, Bali, and West and East Nusa Tenggara experienced the most rapid growth in expenditure in nominal Jakarta prices, while relatively resource-rich provinces such as Aceh, Irian Jaya, and East Kalimantan experienced the slowest growth (Table 10.6). This was also broadly true in urban and rural areas considered separately, although in most of the provinces where total expenditures grew slowly, expenditures in urban areas grew more rapidly than those in rural areas.

Interpersonal Disparities

The successive rounds of the *Susenas* from 1964/5 to 1987 are useful in examining trends in interpersonal as well as interregional and intersectoral disparities. The BPS has used the data on per capita consumption expenditures to estimate Gini coefficients for both urban and rural areas of Indonesia. In rural Indonesia, the Gini coefficient showed very little change in the years from 1964/5 to 1978, but between 1978 and 1984 there appears to have been a downward trend (Table 10.7). In urban areas, the Gini coefficient increased considerably up to 1978, but declined after that.[6] But given the understatement in these data, especially in non-food expenditures, they may not be an entirely reliable guide to trends in inequality.[7] A check is provided by the figures on household income collected in successive rounds of the *Sakernas* between 1976 and 1978, and in the 1982 *Susenas*. The Gini coefficients calculated from these data are consistently higher than those calculated from the consumer expenditure survey data, which could indicate either understatement of consumption expenditures or higher savings in the higher-expenditure groups. The trend towards declining inequality after 1978 in both urban and rural areas shown in the expenditure data is confirmed in the income figures. But they show that rural income inequalities were higher than urban inequalities in all years, in contrast to expenditure inequalities which were higher in urban areas (Table 10.7). Again this could reflect either understatement of consumption expenditures or higher savings in rural areas.

TABLE 10.7
Trends in the Gini Coefficient in Indonesia

Year	Whole Country	Urban	Rural
Household Per Capita			
Consumption Expenditure			
1964/5	0.35	0.34	0.35
1969/70	0.35	0.33	0.34
1976	0.34	0.35	0.31
1978	0.38	0.39	0.34
1980	0.34	0.36	0.31
1981	0.33	0.33	0.29
1984	0.33	0.32	0.28
1987	0.32	0.32	0.26
Household Per Capita Income			
1976	0.47	0.42	0.46
1977	0.50	0.44	0.50
1978	0.47	0.41	0.48
1982	0.44	0.38	0.44

Sources: BPS, *Statistik Indonesia*, various issues; BPS, *Tingkat dan Perkembangan Distribusi Pendapatan Rumahtangga*, 1976–8, 1978–82.

The data on per capita consumption expenditures can be obtained in a regionally disaggregated form and have been used by some scholars to examine regional differences in expenditure inequalities in Indonesia. Hughes and Islam (1981: 52–3) showed that there was a substantially greater increase in urban inequalities in Java than elsewhere between 1970 and 1976; the increase was particularly marked for inequality measures which are sensitive to changes at the top end of the income distribution. This was interpreted as implying that the rich were quite clearly becoming richer. In rural Java there was a fall in inequality, which was largest for those inequality measures emphasizing changes in the bottom end of the income distribution. The poor were thus not becoming poorer; in fact their relative position improved rather than declined. Outside Java, the increase in inequality was quite modest compared to Java, and the decline in rural inequality much greater. Even within urban Java, where the most pronounced increases in inequality occurred in the 1970s, there has been considerable differences in trends in inequality over time. The largest percentage increase in personal inequality, as measured by the Gini coefficient, occurred not in Jakarta but in West and Central Java and in Yogyakarta (Table 10.8). Similarly after 1980, when inequality fell in urban Indonesia as a whole, the fall was most pronounced in Jakarta, and in East Java. In urban West Java, inequality actually increased between 1980 and 1984, while it declined only slightly in Central Java and Yogyakarta.

Because of the problems of understatement, and other possible inaccuracies in the consumer expenditure data, it is useful to check the trends shown by them wherever possible with the results of other surveys. In urban areas, the two Cost of Living (COL) surveys carried out in 1968/9 and 1977/8 can be used. These give estimates of income as well as expenditure; if the Gini coefficients calculated from the household income data for the two periods are compared, it is seen that there has been an increase in each of the main cities of Java, although that for

TABLE 10.8

Trends in Gini Coefficient of Per Capita Expenditure in Urban Areas

	1967	*1980*	*1984*	*1987*
Jakarta	0.29	0.35	0.29	0.29
West Java	0.26	0.34	0.35	0.31
Central Java	0.26	0.35	0.31	0.28
Yogyakarta	0.31	0.40	0.37	0.31
East Java	0.29	0.36	0.29	0.32
Java	0.31	0.37	n.a.	n.a.
Indonesia	n.a.	0.36	0.32	0.32

Sources: As for Tables 10.1 and 10.5.
n.a. = Not available.

TABLE 10.9
Gini Coefficients of Household Income by City

City[a]	1968/9	1977/8
Jakarta	0.41	0.41
Surabaya	0.35	0.42
Bandung	0.40	0.44
Semarang	n.a.	0.40
Medan	0.38	0.36
Palembang	0.39	0.33
Ujung Pandang	0.40	0.44
Padang	n.a.	0.32
Yogyakarta	0.39	0.45
Banjarmasin	0.34	0.36
Pontianak	0.38	0.37
Menado	0.34	0.39

Sources: BPS, Cost of Living Surveys, 1968–71, 1977–8.
[a]Cities ranked by population in 1971.
n.a. = Not available.

Jakarta was negligible (Table 10.9). But outside Java, the Gini coefficient actually fell in Medan, Palembang, and Pontianak, while it increased in Ujung Pandang and Menado. These trends seem to confirm the trends shown in the expenditure surveys, although the COL surveys throw doubt on the large increase in inequality in Jakarta in the 1970s shown by the *Susenas*.

An important problem with the various estimates of the Gini coefficient (and of other inequality indicators) which have been made on the basis of the *Susenas* and other Indonesian data is that they do not allow for different rates of price increases in different expenditure groups. Asra (1989) has argued that such differences were quite significant in Indonesia in the 1970s, because the various inflationary shocks to which the economy was subjected affected different income groups differently. In the early 1970s, when the price of rice increased rapidly, the poor were hurt more than the rich because rice and other basic food staples accounted for a higher percentage of their expenditures. Thus especially in rural areas, the poorest two quintiles experienced a faster rate of inflation than the top quintile. But the reverse was true between 1976 and 1981 when housing and other prices of non-traded goods rose rapidly, and the the cost of living rose faster for the rich. Asra concludes that for the 1970s as a whole, adjustments for inflation tend to moderate the fall of the Gini coefficient in rural areas and accelerate its rise in urban areas. Asra did not extend his analysis beyond 1981, but given the fact that inflation has on average been rather lower in the 1980s than in the 1970s, its impact on different income groups and thus on indicators of inequality is likely to have been less marked.

Disparities between Socio-economic Groups

Another important set of questions relates to trends in inequality between socio-economic classes in Indonesia since the late 1960s. What has happened to incomes of professionals, managers, and government workers compared to the average? What has happened to incomes of highly educated workers relative to those of the less well-educated? It is known that in Indonesia, as in most other societies, educational attainment is an important determinant of earnings, because access to high-paying jobs in both the public and the private sectors is determined mainly by qualifications. In the late 1960s, the monthly earnings of a worker with a university qualification in Jakarta was over five times that of a worker with incomplete primary education (Booth and Sundrum, 1981: 199). Although comparable data are not available from later surveys, it is widely believed that during the 1970s the incomes of highly qualified workers rose relative to the national average because demand exceeded supply. Many of these workers were employed in the public sector, and it is possible to use data collected from the urban COL

TABLE 10.10

Ratio of Family Income[a] Where Family Head Is in Government Service to Average Household Income

City[b]	1968/9	1977/8
Jakarta	1.24	1.34
Surabaya	1.16	1.35
Bandung	1.30	1.52
Semarang	n.a.	1.42
Medan	1.22	1.46
Palembang	1.15	1.41
Ujung Pandang	1.10	1.58
Padang	n.a.	1.24
Yogyakarta	1.29	1.54
Banjarmasin	1.41[c]	1.57
Pontianak	1.27[c]	1.48
Menado	1.22[c]	1.24
Ambon	n.a.	1.19
Denpasar	1.17	1.40
Mataram	n.a.	1.43
Kupang	n.a.	1.05
Jayapura	n.a.	1.10

Sources: BPS, Cost of Living Surveys, 1968–71, 1977–8.
[a]Includes money income, income paid in kind, and income earned by family members in occupations other than that of the family head.
[b]Cities ranked in order of population size in 1971.
[c]Data refer to 1970–1.
n.a. = Not available.

TABLE 10.11

Growth in Monthly Household Income by Status of Household Head,
1976–1982

Status of Head	Monthly Household Income (Rp '000)		Gini Coefficient[a]	
	1976	1982	1976	1982
Managerial	109.8	203.9	0.46	0.38
Administrative	40.5	85.3	0.42	0.35
Professional, etc.	37.3	84.2	0.35	0.34
Sales workers	21.3	49.2	0.44	0.41
Production workers	20.8	44.7	0.38	0.36
Service workers	18.7	44.3	0.41	0.39
Agricultural	12.3	27.9	0.48	0.44
Other	44.9	39.1	0.35	0.36
Average	17.6	41.2	0.49	0.45

Sources: BPS, Tingkat dan Perkembangan Distribusi Pendapatan Rumahtangga, 1976–8,
1978–82.
[a]Refers to household income.

TABLE 10.12

Average Monthly Earnings of Employees by Educational Attainment,
1976–1986 (Rp '000)

	1976	1978	1982	1986
Incomplete Primary School	7.5	8.7	23.4	35.4
Primary School	12.7	16.9	36.0	51.3
Junior High School				
General	22.4	29.3	58.7	77.7
Vocational	21.4	30.0	57.1	76.4
Senior High School				
General	31.3	44.1	78.4	99.0
Vocational	24.9	34.2	67.6	93.6
Diploma[a]	n.a.	n.a.	n.a.	105.7
Academy/University	57.6	78.5	117.9	152.4
Average[b]	12.4	15.0	38.8	63.3
Ratio of Academy/University to Average	4.6	5.2	3.4	2.4

Sources: BPS, Indikator Tingkat Hidup Pekerja, 1986.
[a]Refers to one- and two-year diploma courses only. Others are included in academy/university.
[b]Excluding those not responding.
n.a. = Not available.

surveys carried out in the late 1960s and late 1970s to estimate the disparity between incomes of households where the household head was in government service relative to the average. This disparity widened in the 1970s in almost all cities (Table 10.10).

But in the latter part of the 1970s and the early 1980s it seems that differentials between well-educated professional and technical workers and others began to narrow. Between 1976 and 1982, the evidence from the *Sakernas* and *Susenas* suggests that the household income of managerial, professional, and administrative households declined relative to the average, and relative to that of farm workers, the poorest category. The degree of income disparity within each of these classes, as measured by the Gini coefficient, also declined over these years (Table 10.11). There was also evidence of a decline in earnings differentials by educational attainment (Table 10.12). By 1986, the *Sakernas* showed that an employee with a tertiary qualification earned about four times one with incomplete primary schooling, compared with more than seven times a decade earlier. The rapid decline in differentials by educational status was no doubt due to the growth in supply of educated workers, and the decline in demand due to slower growth after 1981.

Have Rural Disparities in Income and Wealth Narrowed?

While few observers of economic and social change in Indonesia over the last two decades would be surprised by evidence of large and growing urban–rural income differentials, especially in Java, the apparent decline in inequalities within rural areas since the late 1960s is more controversial. Asra (1989) has argued that once allowance is made for differential rates of inflation in different expenditure groups, the decline in the Gini coefficient in the 1970s could well have been less than that shown in Table 10.7, although he still finds evidence of a decline. But many scholars have argued that, in rural Java in particular, disparities in income and wealth have widened since the late 1960s, even if in absolute terms most people have experienced some improvement in living standards. Much of the evidence for these arguments comes from village studies, rather than from analysis of data collected by the BPS, but it is frequently argued that data collected by the BPS are inaccurate in that they underestimate income and expenditure on the part of the richest people in rural areas. Therefore inequality indicators calculated from them are unreliable, and probably misleading.

Such criticisms may well be valid, although they are very difficult to test. It is easier to evaluate some more specific arguments which have been made concerning the causes of increasing income disparities in rural areas of Indonesia. One of these arguments relates to the role of off-farm, or non-agricultural earnings of rural households. There is an abundance of evidence to suggest that most rural households in Indonesia today are deriving their incomes from a variety of sources, both agricultural and non-agricultural. The sample survey of farm household incomes that was carried out as part of the 1983 Agricultural

Census found that the average agricultural household in Indonesia earned only 55 per cent of its total income from its own agricultural holding, and that the rest of the household income was derived from a variety of sources including wage labour and from activities such as trade and transport (BPS, 1987a: 18). There also appears to be little doubt that, in absolute terms, incomes from non-agricultural activities are a positive function of agricultural incomes which in turn are closely related to the quality and quantity of land controlled. This point has been argued by several scholars on the basis of village data collected in the Agro-economic Survey (White, 1986: 36–7; Rietveld, 1986: 106–17) as well as from several surveys carried out by the BPS. Some authors, especially White (1986), have tended to use this evidence as support for the argument that the growth in non-agricultural earnings has aggravated income differentials in rural areas.

But in fact the reverse appears to be the case. Rietveld (1986: 114) has argued that the Agro-economic Survey data show that 'non-agricultural activities have a mitigating effect on income differentials resulting from differences in land endowment'. The data Rietveld analyses from fourteen villages show a significant degree of negative correlation between the absolute size of the income derived from agriculture and the percentage increment derived from other sources; such a negative correlation is also found in several of the larger data sets published by the BPS (Table 10.13). This implies that by the early 1980s, agricultural households with a very restricted resource base were able to earn substantial increments in their incomes from other activities, thus offsetting their small income derived from their own farm. There can be

TABLE 10.13

Relationship between Average Household Income from Farming and the
Percentage Increment Derived from Non-farm Activities
by Province, 1983–1984

Source of Data	Number of Provinces	Correlation Coefficient
1983 Agricultural Census[a]		
Rubber Households	13	−0.485
Coffee Households	20	−0.492
Coconut Households	26	−0.394
Cloves Households	20	−0.620
All Farm Households	26	−0.645
BPS 1984 *Susenas* Survey[b]	13	−0.797
SAE Village Sample[c]	14	−0.609

Sources: BPS, Agricultural Census 1983, Series F5, Series I; BPS and Department of Transmigration, *Survey Pendapatan Rumahtangga di Daerah Transmigrasi 1984*; Rietveld (1986: Table 1).
[a] Data collected through 1983 and 1984.
[b] Data refer to six transmigration source provinces in Java, Bali, and West Nusa Tenggara and seven receiving provinces in southern Sumatra, Kalimantan, and Sulawesi.
[c] Data refer to fourteen villages in Java and South Sulawesi.

little doubt that it was the rapid growth in such off-farm employment opportunities which was a major reason for the decline in rural poverty which occurred in many parts of Indonesia in the latter part of the 1970s and the early 1980s. In the next section this poverty decline is examined in more detail.

Trends in Indicators of Poverty: 1969–1987

Since the early 1970s, there has been much discussion in Indonesia about trends in poverty. As in most other countries, attempts have been made to compute poverty lines, and to estimate the proportion of the population who fall below that line, and how it has changed over time, for the country as a whole, and for different regions. Individual scholars, the BPS, and the World Bank have all published estimates of trends in poverty, each using rather different poverty line concepts, and thus reaching rather different results. In recent years, however, the poverty line estimates put forward by the BPS have gained prominence as the 'official' figures, and it is these data which are referred to by the President and cabinet ministers. It is therefore useful to begin with a discussion of the BPS estimates, before examining the results of other poverty studies which have been carried out over the last few years.

The BPS Poverty Line

According to the BPS, there has been a steady decline in the percentage of the population living below the poverty line in both urban and rural areas of Indonesia since 1976 (Table 10.14). The decline has been particularly marked in rural areas; whereas 40.4 per cent of the rural population were below the poverty line in 1976, by 1987 this percentage had fallen to 16.4. The decline in urban areas was less dramatic, although the percentage was almost halved over the eleven-year period. However, the urban population has been growing more rapidly than the rural population over these years, so the decline in the absolute numbers in poverty has been much slower in urban areas, and the urban poor accounted for almost one-third of the total poor by 1987 (Table 10.15).

The very rapid decline in the incidence of rural poverty over these years, sustained at an even rate over both the oil boom era and the post-1981 years of adjustment, might appear surprising. As has been seen, the growth in real per capita consumer expenditures in rural areas decelerated sharply after 1981 (Table 10.2), and this should in turn have led to a slower decline in rural poverty incidence than in fact occurred. There are two main reasons why the actual decline continued to be quite rapid. One is that inequality in rural areas declined between 1981 and 1987 (Table 10.7). Another is that the rural poverty line set by the BPS in fact increased rather less rapidly between 1981 and 1987 than the rural price indexes used in Table 10.2. This in turn reflects the fact that prices of basic foodstuffs, particularly rice, have increased less rapidly since 1981 than other prices. As rice prices have a higher weight in

TABLE 10.14

Decline in Percentage of Population under the Poverty Line According
to Three Measures

	Urban			Rural		
	BPS[a]	Sajogyo[b]	Esmara	BPS[a]	Sajogyo[b]	Esmara
1964/65[c]	n.a.	65.1	44.0	n.a.	49.3	51.6
1970	n.a.	45.4	38.1	n.a.	31.3	49.1
1976	38.8	31.2	39.9	40.4	28.1	46.4
1978	30.8	27.2	41.6	33.9	29.7	46.6
1980	29.0	24.4	37.3	28.4	17.1	43.2
1981	28.1	13.2	32.3	26.5	8.0	40.0
1984	23.1	31.3	31.3	21.2	7.4	39.3
1987	20.1	30.4	30.4	16.4	3.2	36.0

Sources: BPS (1987b); BPS (1989); Esmara (1986: Chapter 9).
[a]Not calculated for 1964/5 or 1970.
[b]Implicit cereal price derived from *Susenas* publications. The poverty line was set in terms
   of 20 kg of cereal in rural areas and 30 kg in urban areas.
[c]Excludes Jakarta, NTB, Maluku, and Irian Jaya.
n.a. = Not available.

establishing the BPS poverty line than they do in the various price
indexes used in Table 10.1, the poverty incidence estimates based on it
fall more rapidly than the data in Table 10.1 might have led one to
assume.

Another important point regarding the BPS poverty line concerns the
trends in the incidence of urban and rural poverty. One reason for the
increasing share of the urban poor in total poverty in Indonesia is that
the urban population has been increasing more rapidly. Another reason

TABLE 10.15

Percentage of the Poor Population Living in Urban Areas According
to Different Poverty Measures

	BPS		Sajogyo	Esmara
	Actual	Adjusted[a]		
1976	19.3	17.8	13.2	17.7
1978	20.8	17.3	15.2	19.3
1980	22.8	21.6	16.4	19.9
1981	24.2	19.9	21.5	19.5
1984	27.1	19.7	22.5	21.4
1987	32.2	25.4	37.3	24.6

Sources: As for Table 10.14.
[a]To derive these percentages, the BPS poverty line for 1976 for both urban and rural areas
   was increased by the household consumption component of the GDP deflator.

is the urban poverty line put forward by the BPS has in fact increased more rapidly than the rural poverty line since 1976, so that by 1987 the urban poverty line was almost 70 per cent higher than in rural areas. It has been argued that a differential of this magnitude is much higher than the actual differences in the cost of a given basket of basic needs in urban and rural areas of Indonesia (Ravallion and Huppi, 1989). The differential can only be justified if the actual basket of basic needs comprising the poverty line has to be more diversified in urban than rural areas, because certain goods and services, such as transport, are judged to be 'basic needs' in urban areas, but not in rural areas. Whether both the cost and the composition of the urban basket of basic needs has in fact been changing relative to the rural basket in such a way as to justify the rising urban–rural disparity in the BPS poverty line is far from clear. It is possible that part of the reason for the growing urban share in total poverty in Indonesia is that the disparity in the poverty line has been exaggerated. Certainly, when the BPS poverty line is adjusted to allow for a constant urban–rural differential, the increase in the urban share of total poverty is moderated (Table 10.15).

Other Poverty Lines

Although in recent years the BPS poverty line has assumed the status of an official poverty line, there are several other poverty lines which have been put forward by Indonesian scholars, and which have had wide currency in the literature. The best known of these is that of Professor Sajogyo, who in a number of studies over the years has used a poverty line based on the price of rice.[8] Applying this poverty line to the *Susenas* household expenditure data for the years from 1976 to 1987, one gets the results shown in Table 10.14. Because the rice-based poverty line is lower in absolute terms than the BPS poverty line, the percentage below the poverty line is correspondingly lower in each year, although, unlike the BPS poverty line, the Sajogyo measure does not indicate the same smooth decline in poverty incidence in each year. There was in fact an increase between 1976 and 1978 in both urban and rural areas, and a slight increase again in rural areas between 1981 and 1984. However, over the entire eleven-year period, the Sajogyo measure does show a substantial decline in poverty incidence in both urban and rural areas. As with the BPS measure, the Sajogyo measure also shows a rapid growth in the urban share of poverty through the 1980s.

The Sajogyo measure can be criticized on the grounds that it is based entirely on one price, and while rice continues to be an important staple for most Indonesians, its share in the budgets of even the poorer sections of society has been falling rapidly.[9] In addition rice prices during the 1980s have not been increasing as rapidly as the various price indexes published by the BPS, so that the Sajogyo poverty line has been increasing less rapidly than these indexes, and less rapidly than the BPS poverty line. Thus the very rapid decline in both rural and urban poverty shown by the Sajogyo measure after 1980 is in part due to the modest increase in rice prices.

In view of these problems, other Indonesian economists have put forward other poverty line concepts. For example, Professor Hendra Esmara has set an urban and rural poverty line in terms of the actual expenditure on a basket of 'essential' goods and services, as revealed in successive rounds of the *Susenas* (Esmara, 1986: 320 ff.). Because it captures both the effects of inflation and the impact of higher real incomes on the quantity of essential goods consumed, this poverty measure increases rather more rapidly than either the BPS or the Sajogyo measure. But in spite of this, there has been a steady decline in the incidence of poverty as measured by the Esmara poverty line since 1978, in both urban and rural areas, although the rate of decline is somewhat slower than that shown by either of the other two measures (Table 10.14). The Esmara measure also confirms the trend towards an increasing urban share of the total number of poor, although the rate of increase is rather slower than with the other two measures (Table 10.15).

In discussing inequality measures, the point was made that different expenditure classes have experienced different rates of inflation since the late 1960s. This problem also affects poverty line calculations, and in fact several attempts have been made to estimate rates of inflation by expenditure class, based on the *Susenas* data. These have been summarized by Asra (1989: Table 3), and have been used to construct a further set of poverty lines, and poverty incidence estimates, this time for Java and the Outer Islands separately.[10] They again show a steady decline in the incidence of poverty in all parts of the country since 1969/70, with the exception of rural Java where poverty incidence increased up till 1976, and then began to decline (Table 10.16). However, it should be noted that, according to this set of poverty lines, the proportion of the poor population living in urban areas actually declined between 1976 and 1987, in contrast to the estimates shown in Table 10.15. This point is discussed below.

Regional Distribution of Poverty

A further important issue concerns trends in the regional distribution of poverty in Indonesia. Estimates made by the World Bank (1980: 84) using the 1976 *Susenas* showed that over 70 per cent of the poor were located in Java. This appeared to confirm the opinion, widely held in Indonesia since 1900, that poverty in Indonesia was overwhelmingly a Javanese problem. The World Bank calculations for 1976 are confirmed by those in Table 10.17. But by 1987 the regional distribution of poverty appeared to have altered quite dramatically. Only 43 per cent of the total poor population in Indonesia were to be found in rural Java, compared to 46 per cent in the rural areas of the Outer Islands. There has been a steady decline in the proportion of the poor population located in both urban and rural Java, and little change in the proportion located in the urban areas outside Java; the decline in Java has been almost entirely balanced by an increase in rural areas outside Java. Indeed there has been a slight increase in the absolute numbers of poor outside Java

TABLE 10.16
Incidence of Poverty and Affluence[a] in Java and the Outer Islands

	Java		Outer Islands	
	Urban	Rural	Urban	Rural
Percentage of the Population under the Poverty Line				
1969/70	41.7	43.7	39.4	29.3
1976	28.3	51.1	32.6	27.9
1981	13.1	21.3	17.7	23.9
1987	4.5	15.3	9.1	21.5
Percentage of the Decline in Poverty due to Expenditure Growth[b]				
1969/70–76	126	–[c]	164	209
1976–81	69	75	69	–[c]
1981–7	90	38	114	47
Percentage of the Population above the Affluence Line				
1969/70	7.8	2.3	8.5	7.2
1976	15.3	2.6	10.1	11.5
1981	24.1	5.2	15.2	9.7
1987	39.8	9.8	22.6	9.0
Percentage of Growth in Affluence due to Expenditure Growth[b]				
1969/70–76	90	–[c]	228	31
1976–81	77	130	100	–[cd]
1981–7	86	55	102	53[d]

Sources: As for Table 10.1.

[a] See Appendix for details of construction of the poverty and affluence lines.

[b] See Appendix for details of decomposition method.

[c] In these periods there was a decline in real per capita expenditures (see Table 10.2). In rural Java between 1969/70 and 1976 there was also an increase in the proportion of the population below the poverty line, which was entirely due to the fall in real expenditures. The distributional effect alone would have led to a slight decline in poverty. In the rural Outer Islands between 1976 and 1981 a marked improvement in distribution offset the effect of falling real expenditures, so that the incidence of poverty declined. The small increase in the proportion of the population in rural Java over the affluence line between 1969/70 and 1976 was due to distributional factors.

[d] Over this period the percentage of the population in the affluent class declined in rural areas outside Java. Between 1976 and 1981 about one-third of this decline was due to growth factors and two-thirds to distribution. Between 1981 and 1987 the decline was entirely due to distributional factors; growth in income alone would have raised the percentage over the affluence line.

TABLE 10.17

Numbers in Poverty[a] and Distribution of Poor and Total Populations,
1969/70–1987

	Java			Outer Islands		
	Numbers in Poverty (million)	Distribution (%)		Numbers in Poverty (million)	Distribution (%)	
		Poor	Total		Poor	Total
Urban						
1969/70	5.4	12.1	11.3	2.5	5.6	5.6
1976	5.1	9.7	13.7	2.7	5.2	6.3
1981	3.2	10.3	16.2	1.8	6.0	7.0
1987	1.5	6.1	19.7	1.3	5.1	8.2
Rural						
1969/70	26.6	59.6	53.0	10.1	22.7	30.1
1976	33.5	63.5	49.3	11.4	21.6	30.7
1981	14.6	47.4	45.7	11.2	36.3	31.2
1987	10.7	42.6	40.7	11.6	46.2	31.4

Sources: As for Table 10.1.

[a] Poverty line in 1969/70 Rp 1,260 in urban Java, Rp 1,540 in urban Outer Islands, Rp 850 in rural Java, and Rp 1,030 in rural Outer Islands. The poverty line was increased to 1976, 1981, and 1987 prices by the price indexes given in the Appendix.

between 1969/70 and 1987, compared with a 60 per cent decline in Java (Table 10.17).

There are two distinct reasons for the marked shift in the regional distribution of the rural poor in Indonesia within the short space of just one decade. One is the shifting distribution of the rural population as a whole from Java to the Outer Islands, as a result of falling fertility in Java and of migration.[11] The other is that poverty incidence has in fact been falling more sharply in Java than elsewhere. It is clear that population shifts alone explain only a small part of the dramatic rise in the proportion of the poor located in rural areas outside Java. These areas have not in fact greatly increased their share of total population over the past two decades; high rates of in-migration and high fertility in some regions have been offset by out-migration and falling fertility in others. It is the much slower decline in poverty incidence which explains their growing share of the nation's poor. Conversely, although the share of total population located in urban Java has been growing rapidly since the late 1960s, its share of the poor population has been falling, because of the very rapid decline in poverty incidence.

The more rapid decline in the proportion of the population below the poverty line in Java compared with the rest of the country is further illustrated in Table 10.18. In 1980 there were ten provinces where 40 per cent or more of the rural population was below the poverty line; of these three were in Java (Central Java, Yogyakarta, and East Java). By

TABLE 10.18

Proportion of Urban and Rural Population below the Poverty Line[a]
by Province, 1980 and 1987

Province[b]	Urban		Rural	
	1980	1987	1980	1987
Irian Jaya[c]	53.8	33.0	37.0	67.0
South-east Sulawesi	37.9	19.2	50.2	40.7
East Nusa Tenggara	53.9	24.2	63.1	37.6
Maluku	51.7	10.2	52.4	36.3
East Kalimantan	42.0	34.4	25.6	34.8
Lampung	48.7	27.3	47.8	34.6
Bali	58.0	32.7	57.0	34.2
Central Kalimantan	19.6	20.1	13.0	28.6
South Sulawesi	48.0	22.3	47.1	25.2
Central Sulawesi	28.5	13.0	29.2	21.4
West Nusa Tenggara	51.8	31.6	44.7	18.9
East Java	45.4	13.6	50.0	17.8
West Kalimantan	24.2	11.5	13.8	15.4
Central Java	49.4	17.9	49.4	15.1
West Java	45.4	21.0	36.6	13.0
South Kalimantan	24.7	8.6	20.2	11.5
North Sulawesi	36.7	14.4	29.3	11.4
Bengkulu	20.8	15.0	15.5	9.9
South Sumatra	33.4	12.3	9.8	9.8
North Sumatra	31.8	8.6	15.1	9.2
Aceh	11.7	9.0	11.2	8.9
Riau	23.1	9.5	13.5	8.9
Yogyakarta	37.3	16.5	45.7	8.2
Jambi	27.7	8.6	7.0	6.4
West Sumatra	14.9	2.1	14.8	1.9
Jakarta	22.9	1.4	n.a.	n.a.
Indonesia[d]	38.8	14.7	39.0	17.2

Sources: 1980 provincial data taken from Susenas printouts prepared for the World Bank;
1987 data from BPS, Pengeluaran untuk Konsumsi Penduduk Indonesia per Propinsi,
1987.

[a]A poverty line for rural and urban areas in each province in 1980 was estimated by taking
the 1976 BPS national poverty lines, inflating them to 1980 prices using the GDP
deflator, and converting them to provincial poverty lines using a regional price index
based on the 1980 KFM data. The 1987 poverty lines were derived by inflating the 1980
poverty line by the increase in the CPI for each provincial capital.

[b]Ranked in terms of the incidence of rural poverty in 1987.

[c]The marked increase in the incidence of rural poverty in 1987 could be due to the extension of the Susenas survey to more remote, and poorer, areas compared with the coverage
in 1980.

[d]Calculated by summing the provincial totals of numbers in poverty and dividing by the
population for all Indonesia (excluding East Timor).

n.a. = Not available.

1987 the incidence of rural poverty in these three provinces had declined to under 20 per cent. Of the ten provinces where the incidence of rural poverty exceeded 20 per cent of the population in 1987, none was in Java. Of the eight provinces where urban poverty incidence exceeded 20 per cent, only one was in Java (West Java). The relatively high incidence of urban poverty in West Java, combined with its virtual absence in Jakarta, probably reflect an increasing tendency for the poor of the nation's capital to live in the surrounding towns rather than inside the metropolitan boundary.

Variations in poverty incidence between regions and over time must be due either to variations in per capita expenditures or to variations in inequality. In 1980, variations in per capita consumption expenditure alone explained almost 70 per cent of the observed interprovincial variations in poverty levels; in 1987 this had increased to 84 per cent (Table 10.19).[12] Inequality (as proxied by the Gini coefficient) explained much less of the interprovincial variation in poverty levels. But if the changes in poverty over time are decomposed into that part due to expenditure growth and that part due to inequality reduction, a rather mixed result is obtained (Table 10.16). In urban areas most of the observed fall in poverty incidence in all parts of the country has been due to growth in real expenditures; indeed between 1969/70 and 1976 the contribution of inequality alone would have increased poverty incidence. In rural areas the picture is less clear. Between 1976 and 1981, both the increase in real expenditures and the decline in inequality contributed to the rapid decline in the proportion under the poverty line in rural Java. But in the 1980s it has been improving distribution which has accounted for most of the poverty decline, especially in Java where real expenditures in rural areas have hardly grown at all.[13] In rural areas outside Java, real expenditure growth was negative between 1976 and 1981, and only slightly positive thereafter. Most of the rather modest decline in poverty incidence in rural areas outside Java since 1976 has been due to improving distribution.

If per capita consumption expenditures explain most of the observed

TABLE 10.19

Regression of Provincial Poverty Incidence on Per Capita Expenditures[a]

	log PCE	R^2
1980	-2.125 $(7.533)^{b}$	0.69
1987	-2.988 $(11.416)^{b}$	0.838

Sources: As for Table 10.18.

[a]In Jakarta prices.

[b]Figures in brackets refer to 't' ratios.

variation in poverty levels between provinces in the 1980s, what then explains variations in these expenditures? Not surprisingly, there was a very high correlation between per capita consumption expenditures in January 1987, as recorded in the *Susenas* survey, and per capita non-oil RGDP in 1986 (r = 0.93). Thus, although there can be a very wide gap between absolute RGDP and consumption expenditures, especially in the resource-exporting provinces, differences in income per capita between provinces are directly reflected in per capita consumption and in living standards.[14] Inequality in consumption standards by contrast appears to reflect inequality in the distribution of assets; there is a significant degree of positive correlation between the Gini coefficient of land distribution by province as shown in the 1983 Agricultural Census and the Gini coefficient of consumption expenditures in 1987 (r = 0.455).

Trends in Affluence

Inevitably, the issue of trends in poverty has received more attention in most developing countries than that of trends in affluence, although in a country such as Indonesia where the proportion of the population below the poverty line has been falling steadily over more than a decade it is of some interest to examine whether this fall has been accompanied by an increasing share of the population above a stipulated affluence line. Such a line is defined as that level of expenditure which was enjoyed by about 4 per cent of the population in 1969/70, and it has been increased, using a set of inflators explained in the Appendix. It is then possible to derive estimates of the population above the affluence line for Java and the Outer Islands for 1969/70, 1976, 1981, and 1987 (Table 10.16). As expected, given the rates of growth of average per capita consumption expenditures shown in Table 10.2, the most rapid growth in the proportion of the population over the affluence line has occurred in urban Java, so that by 1987 almost 40 per cent of the population could be classified as affluent. In rural areas of Java, and in urban areas outside Java, there has also been a considerable growth in the incidence of affluence, but in rural areas outside Java the increase has been far less obvious; indeed between 1976 and 1987 there has been a steady decline in the percentage of the population above the affluence line. As a result of these trends in the incidence of affluence, there has been a marked shift in the regional distribution of the affluent population away from rural areas outside Java, and towards urban areas on Java (Table 10.20). Whereas in 1976 almost half the affluent population of Indonesia was located in rural areas outside Java, by 1987 almost half was to be found in urban Java, compared with only 20 per cent of the total population. The proportion of the affluent located in rural Java and urban areas outside Java has not greatly altered.

Given these changes in the incidence of poverty and affluence, and its regional distribution, it is of interest to examine the probabilities of inter-class movement by region (Table 10.21).[15] The first point to note is that

TABLE 10.20
Distribution of the Affluent Population, 1969/70–1987[a]

	Java			Outer Islands		
	Numbers of Affluent (million)	Distribution (%)		Numbers of Affluent (million)	Distribution (%)	
		Affluent	Total		Affluent	Total
Urban						
1969/70	1.0	18.7	11.3	0.5	9.9	5.6
1976	2.8	27.7	13.7	0.8	8.4	6.3
1981	5.8	37.6	16.2	1.6	10.2	7.0
1987	13.5	47.6	19.7	3.2	11.2	8.2
Rural						
1969/70	1.4	25.7	53.0	2.5	45.7	30.1
1976	1.7	17.1	49.3	4.7	46.8	30.7
1981	3.6	23.0	45.7	4.5	29.2	31.2
1987	6.8	24.1	40.7	4.9	17.1	31.4

Sources: As for Table 10.1.
[a] Affluence line in 1969/70 Rp 3,600 for urban Java, Rp 3,000 for rural Java, Rp 4,320 for urban areas outside Java and Rp 3,600 for rural areas outside Java. The affluence lines were increased by the price indexes described in the Appendix.

TABLE 10.21
Probabilities of Inter-class Movement[a]

	1969/70–76	1976–81	1981–7
Urban Java			
Poor to medium	32.1	53.7	65.3
Medium to affluent	14.8	15.6	25.1
Rural Java			
Poor to medium	−16.9	58.3	28.2
Medium to affluent	0.6	5.6	6.3
Urban Outer Islands			
Poor to medium	17.2	45.9	48.5
Medium to Affluent	3.1	8.9	11.1
Rural Outer Islands			
Poor to medium	4.8	14.5	9.7
Medium to affluent	6.7	−3.0	−1.0

Sources: As for Table 10.19.
[a] The probability of moving from the poor to the medium group is defined as the percentage of the population below the poverty line in the initial year less that in the terminal year divided by the percentage in the initial year. The probability of moving from the medium to the affluent group is the percentage of the population classified as affluent in the terminal year less that in the initial year divided by the percentage of the population in the medium category in the initial year.

TABLE 10.22
Growth in Average Expenditures in Real Terms by Class of Population

	1969/70–81	*1981–7*
Urban Java		
Poor	15.2	22.1
Medium	9.0	14.4
Affluent	2.1	6.5
Total	5.8	9.3
Grand total[a]	59.5	35.0
Rural Java		
Poor	2.8	9.5
Medium	3.7	9.7
Affluent	2.6	− 57.4
Total	3.5	− 8.1
Grand total[a]	27.1	3.5
Urban Outer Islands		
Poor	17.9	2.7
Medium	14.3	6.6
Affluent	66.2	3.5
Total	27.6	5.1
Grand total[a]	38.4	19.1
Rural Outer Islands		
Poor	23.5	8.1
Medium	− 1.7	0.7
Affluent	− 19.6	0.4
Total	− 4.2	1.4
Grand total[a]	3.8	1.6

Sources: As for Table 10.2.
[a] Growth in total expenditures, reflecting both within class growth and the effect of movement between classes.

there has been a steady increase in the probabilities of social mobility both from the poor to the medium groups and from the medium to the affluent groups, with the exception of the rural Outer Islands after 1981. In all cases, except the rural Outer Islands in the years from 1969/70 to 1976, the probability of moving from the poor to the medium category has been much greater than that of moving from the medium to the affluent category. The probabilities for both types of movement have consistently been much higher in urban Java than elsewhere, which reflects the faster rate of decline in poverty incidence there, and the faster growth in the incidence of affluence.

   There is certainly very little evidence from successive *Susenas* of the 'rich getting richer' in the sense that the expenditures of those classified as affluent in successive surveys have experienced faster real expenditure growth than those classified as poor or as medium. Between 1969/70 and 1981, real expenditures of the poor in fact grew more rapidly than those of the affluent, with the exception of urban areas outside Java. From 1981 to 1987, the picture was more mixed, although only in urban areas outside Java did the expenditures of the poor grow more slowly than those of the medium and affluent groups. In rural Java over these years, the expenditure of the affluent decreased by more than 50 per cent (Table 10.22).The decline may reflect the expenditure understatement already referred to; it might also indicate a trend on the part of the rural rich to move to urban areas.

Trends in Inequality and Poverty: A Summing Up

The trends in inequality and poverty in Indonesia since the late 1960s can be summed up in the following propositions:

1. Urban–rural disparities increased between 1969 and 1978, and have declined only slightly in nominal terms since then. Much of this increasing disparity is due to non-food consumption expenditures. The gap between consumption expenditures in Jakarta, and those for the country as a whole has declined only slightly between 1976 and 1987 in nominal terms; in real terms it could have widened slightly.

2. Real consumer expenditure growth, as shown by successive rounds of the *Susenas*, grew much more rapidly in urban Java than elsewhere between 1970 and 1976, although expenditures rose as rapidly in rural Java after 1976 as in urban areas. Between 1980 and 1987 real consumer expenditure growth was faster in Jakarta than elsewhere in Java, faster in urban Java than in urban areas outside Java, and faster in urban than in rural areas.

3. Regional income disparities increased through the 1970s, but this was very largely due to the impact of oil on regional GDP, and to regional price disparities. The population-weighted coefficient of variation of regional income (excluding oil) in Jakarta prices showed very little change between 1971 and 1986.

4. But regional disparities in per capita consumption expenditures, corrected for regional price disparities, widened between 1980 and 1987. In nominal Jakarta prices, per capita consumption has grown far more quickly in Java than elsewhere since 1980, in both urban and rural areas. Some provinces outside Java actually experienced negative real growth in consumption expenditures over these years, although this could be due to sampling problems in some cases.

5. The evidence from both the *Susenas* and the COL surveys indicates that inequality deteriorated in urban Java in the 1970s, although less so in Jakarta than elsewhere. Both the *Susenas* and the *Sakernas* data indicate declining inequalities in per capita income in rural and urban areas between the late 1970s and the early 1980s.

6. The COL surveys indicated an increase in incomes of households headed by government employees relative to the average between

1968/9 and 1977/8 in most cities. But according to the *Sakernas*, 1976–82 saw an erosion of professional and managerial incomes relative to others. The decade from 1976 to 1986 also saw a very pronounced erosion of salary differentials according to educational attainment, although tertiary graduates still received over twice the average monthly earnings in 1986. To the extent that tertiary graduates are concentrated in the government sector, this indicates a decline in the relative remuneration of public sector employees.

7. The proportion of the population living below the poverty line has fallen quite sharply in both urban and rural areas since the late 1970s. This trend is shown in the semi-official BPS poverty line, and also can be derived from the poverty line estimates made by several independent scholars. However, different poverty lines give rather different results regarding the urban–rural distribution of the poor with some showing an increase in the urban share, and others showing a decline.

8. There has also been a sharp increase in the percentage of the poor living outside Java, especially in rural areas. This indeed follows from the fact that real per capita consumption has been growing more rapidly in Java than in many parts of the Outer Islands over most of the New Order period, and distributional changes have not been sufficient to offset these differences. In 1987 less than half the poor were located in Java, compared with over 70 per cent in 1976.

9. Not only has the proportion of the poor located in Java fallen, but the proportion of the affluent located there has risen sharply. The total number of Indonesians living above the affluence line has risen from around 5.4 million in 1969/70 to 28.4 million in 1987. More than half this increase has taken place in urban Java, and by 1987 almost half the affluent population was located there.

10. Because of the much faster decline in the incidence of poverty and the faster increase in the incidence of affluence in urban Java compared with the rest of the country, the probabilities of mobility from poor to medium and from medium to affluent there have consistently been higher than elsewhere in the country. After 1976 they have consistently been lowest in the rural areas outside Java.

How can these findings be reconciled with the predictions of the resource boom literature discussed in the first section? Certainly the evidence from the first part of the 1970s does confirm the predictions both of the booming sector models and of the political economy discussion. The faster growth of incomes in urban Java and the widening gap between urban Java and the rest of the country would have been predicted by both, as would the widening gap between government employees and the rest of the economy. The slow growth of expenditures in rural areas in these years could in part have been a reflection of the impact of the real appreciation of the rupiah on the incomes of producers of traded goods. But in the latter part of the 1970s, government programmes to increase food-crop production, and especially rice production, through a programme of lavish input subsidies, clearly had a favourable effect on rural incomes in Java. This effect was further strengthened by government expenditures on improving rural infrastructure. After 1976, there was a dramatic reduction in the incidence of poverty and in the absolute number of poor.

In addition, the latter part of the 1970s saw a substantial 'trickle-down' effect, particularly in Java, in which the benefits of faster growth in the urban sector spread out to many rural areas. One mechanism was the process of circular migration to which many scholars have drawn attention. In addition, the rapid growth in education and skill acquisition meant that some of the rents which accrued to skilled labour in the early 1970s were eroded; this seems to be the most plausible explanation for the declining inequality of incomes within the administrative and managerial classes shown by the *Sakernas* data (Table 10.11). But outside Java, real per capita consumption in both the urban and rural sectors grew less rapidly than in Java between 1976 and 1981; this reflects the concentration of producers of export crops in the Outer Islands, who received little, if any, direct assistance from government, and who thus bore the full brunt of the real rupiah appreciation.

It is perhaps surprising that the rural areas outside Java appear to have continued to fare relatively badly since 1980, in spite of the adjustment policies, including two devaluations, implemented after world oil prices began to decline in the early 1980s. This is in part due to falling world prices for commodities such as rubber and coffee, and the failure of government attempts to disseminate yield-raising technologies to non-food agricultural producers, most of whom are outside Java. It also reflects the rather slow dissemination of seed-fertilizer food-crop technologies outside Java, which is in turn due to inadequate irrigation facilities.[16] In addition the Outer Islands have probably been more affected by the decline in the government development budget compared with Java. This not only reduced opportunities for non-agricultural employment in rural areas, but also delayed the provision of infrastructure which would in turn have attracted more directly productive investment in both agriculture and industry. The continued rapid growth of real expenditures in urban Java (and especially in Jakarta) is also perhaps surprising, given the decline in real levels of remuneration in the civil service through much of the 1980s. A major reason for the strong performance of urban Java in the 1980s is that the various deregulation policies designed to promote non-oil exports, develop the financial sector, and give the private sector a larger role in the economy have so far had their main impact there.

Without doubt, the most impressive achievement of the past decade has been the remarkable decline in inequality and in the incidence of poverty in rural Java. There appear to be three distinct reasons for this. To begin with, population growth in rural areas in most parts of Java has been very slow, and this in turn has led to slow, or even negative, growth in the agricultural labour force. In addition agricultural output and the marketed surplus has been expanding rapidly in Java and this has created jobs not just in agricultural production but also in agricultural processing, trade, and transport. And lastly, while the end of the oil boom led to a much slower growth in output and employment in sectors such as construction, industry has grown rapidly in the 1980s, and provided new employment opportunities for both the urban and the rural labour force, both in manufacturing and in ancillary services. By 1984, many farm households in Java were deriving more than 50 per cent of their income from employment off the farm. Outside Java by contrast, there is much less off-farm employment available, and this, combined with faster population growth, poorer quality land, and inadequate infrastructure, has meant that the incidence of rural poverty has fallen less rapidly. In some provinces, numbers in poverty have actually been increasing in the 1980s, although this could reflect some understatement in the earlier data.

Both during the oil boom and during the process of post-boom restructuring, there has been little evidence of what may be termed the 'Katouzian' effect, in which the already rich succeed in appropriating all the benefits of the boom, and continue to enrich themselves even after the boom is over. Although the urban areas in Java have consistently experienced faster growth in real expenditures than elsewhere, within these areas real expenditures of the poor have grown more rapidly than those of other groups. This may of course reflect higher savings propensities on the part of the non-poor, or understatement of their expenditures. But there appears to be little doubt that, even if there has been a pronounced 'urban bias' and 'Java bias' in Indonesian economic growth over the past two decades, there has been no obvious bias against the urban poor in Java. In spite of rapid rates of in-migration to urban areas and a rapid growth in the urban labour force, the urban poor have apparently managed to maintain a surprisingly rapid rate of real expenditure growth. This suggests considerable flexibility in the functioning of urban labour markets, so that many of the poor have been able to secure sufficient employment to improve their living standards, even if they have not been able to rise above the poverty line.

This also appears to have been true of the rural poor outside Java. It has been stressed in this chapter that the incidence of poverty has declined more slowly in the rural areas outside Java than elsewhere in the country, with the result that a steadily increasing proportion of the poor population is located there. But it does appear that there has been considerable growth of real consumption expenditures *within* the poor population outside Java; indeed their consumption expenditures have consistently grown faster than those of other social classes. This would suggest that, to the extent that the poverty problem in many rural areas outside Java is connected with high rates of in-migration of poor people from Java, these new migrants have been able to improve their living standards, and will eventually be able to get above the poverty line.[17]

The evidence of the last two decades might suggest that Indonesia has been quite successful in exploiting what Hirschman (1973) in a well-known essay has termed the 'tunnel effect'. This is the tolerance for some degree of economic inequality, by region, class, and ethnic group, in the early stages of the development process. Hirschman has pointed out that for the tunnel effect to be strong, or even for it to exist at all, there must be a widespread feeling throughout society that the barriers to social and economic progress are not impassable.

One might conclude that the tunnel effect will always come into being as, within each social class, those who are not advancing empathize initially with those who are. But this need not happen if each class is composed of ethnic or religious groups that are differentially involved in the growth process. Hence, the contrast between fairly unitary and highly segmented societies is particularly relevant. . . . If, in segmented societies, economic advance becomes identified with one particular ethnic or language group or with members of one particular religion or region, then those who are left out or behind are unlikely to experience the tunnel effect: they will be convinced almost from the start of the process that the advancing group is achieving an unfair exploitative advantage over them. (Hirschman, 1973: 49.)

There is a clear warning for Indonesia here. Certainly the inequalities which have emerged over the past twenty years do not appear to have caused any grave social tensions, at least partly because the growth which has occurred has led to a considerable reduction in poverty among the group which was most deprived in the 1960s, the rural Javanese. But the evidence reviewed in this chapter suggests that new and more intractable regional divisions are opening up in Indonesian society which will require very different policy remedies from those adopted over the past two decades. To the extent that people living in rural areas outside Java feel that they have little chance of socio-economic mobility, except through migration, they are unlikely to view with tolerance signs of growing affluence in urban Java. This will be the case particularly in those regions which are well endowed with natural resources but where a significant proportion of the income accruing from the exploitation of these resources does not stay in the province. The challenge for government policy will be to devise new ways of sharing the nation's wealth, and thereby to enhance the confidence of local populations throughout the country that they too can share in the process of national development.

1. A third series of Cost of Living surveys was carried out in 1989 in order to reweight the Consumer Price Index. A further round of the *Susenas* was carried out in 1990.

2. See Sutomo (1989) for a discussion of progress.

3. For further discussion of this point, see Ravallion (1989). It is argued in that paper that, to the extent that the actual consumption of the rich exceeds their idea of 'normal' consumption standards, they will tend to understate their consumption expenditures in household expenditure surveys. Conversely the poor may tend to overstate their consumption. It could plausibly be argued that, because the rapid growth in consumer expenditures in the 1970s followed a long period of stagnating, or even declining, consumption in most parts of Indonesia, it took some time for society's norms to adjust to actual expenditure patterns. Thus the degree of understatement in the *Susenas* has tended to diminish over time.

4. The KFM data are collected as follows. The Department of Labour compiles a basket of goods and services considered 'basic needs' for a single worker and for a family of three, and prices it in a number of towns and cities in each province of Indonesia. The resulting figures are published on a semester basis by the Central Bureau of Statistics. The index of regional price disparities derived from the KFM in 1980 correlates well with the earlier index calculated by Arndt and Sundrum (1975).

5. The difference between per capita RGDP and per capita consumption is enormous in those resource-rich provinces where the export 'drain' is very large, but far less for those provinces where imports exceed exports. For example, in 1983 RGDP was 11 times household consumption expenditures in East Kalimantan, but only 1.4 times household consumption expenditures in Central Java. For further data on the size of the export surplus relative to RGDP, see Table 1.6 and the source document cited there.

6. Sundrum (1990: 126) has pointed out that inequality in consumption expenditures in Indonesia varies considerably by category of expenditure. The concentration ratios of per capita food expenditures were much lower than for non-food expenditures, especially in urban areas.

7. Given the tendency, referred to in footnote 1, for the degree of understatement on the part of the better-off to decline over time, it is possible that the inequality indicators based on the *Susenas* would have been more biased downwards in the 1970s than in the 1980s. Thus the actual decline observed during the 1980s may in fact understate the true decline in inequality.

8. Originally the 'poor' in Indonesia were defined by Sajogyo as those with annual incomes less than the monetary equivalent of 240 kilograms of rice in rural areas and 360 kilograms of rice in urban areas. Subsequently, this definition has been used to define the 'very poor' while the 'poor' are those with annual incomes, in rice equivalents, of less than 360 kilograms in rural areas and 480 kilograms in urban areas. See Sajogyo and Wiradi (1985).

9. In 1969/70, expenditures on cereals accounted for 31 per cent of total expenditures; by 1987, they had fallen to 17.5 per cent.

10. For details on the construction of these poverty lines, see the Appendix.

11. In addition East Timor and rural Irian Jaya were fully incorporated in the 1987 data, whereas they were excluded from the 1976 data.

12. As the equation in Table 10.18 is estimated in double log form, the coefficients can be interpreted as elasticities. In 1987, a 1 per cent increase in per capita income would lead to an almost 3 per cent decline in poverty.

13. Broadly, these findings coincide with the trends in the Gini coefficient shown in Table 10.7, although the Gini coefficient does not appear to have increased in rural areas between 1976 and 1981. Certainly, the calculations in Table 10.16 confirm the other evidence that rural inequalities in expenditure declined in the 1980s, especially in Java.

14. It is often argued in Indonesia that per capita RGDP, and consumption expenditures by province, correlate poorly with indicators of the 'quality of life', such as life expectancy, literacy, and infant mortality rates. This is because some provinces which are relatively poor by income criteria are well endowed with schools and hospitals and thus score better on these social indicators. But in fact the most recent estimate of a composite quality of life index made by the BPS for 1985, which includes the infant mortality rate, the adult literacy rate, and the expectation of life at one year, correlates quite well with per capita consumption expenditures in Jakarta prices ($r = 0.52$).

15. The author is most grateful to R.M. Sundrum for advice on the estimation of the probabilities shown in Table 10.21.

16. For further discussion of these points, see the discussion in Chapter 6 and in Booth (1989).

17. In the report published in 1988, the World Bank found that 67 per cent of official transmigrants reported that they are 'better off' as a result of their move, and only 16 per cent said that they were worse off. Adjusted transmigrant incomes were about the same as the average in the sending areas; to the extent that transmigrant families would be less well off than the average, they must have experienced some improvement in living standards even if they are still below the poverty line. See World Bank (1988: 17–40).

APPENDIX

Poverty and Affluence Lines Used in Table 10.16

The urban poverty line for Indonesia as a whole was taken as Rp 1,400 per capita per month in 1969/70. Following Sajogyo, it was assumed that the rural poverty line should be two-thirds of the urban one. Thus the rural poverty line for the country as a whole was set at Rp 940 in rural areas. The poverty line in urban Java was set at 90 per cent of the national one and that in urban Outer Islands was set at 110 per cent of the national one. Rural poverty lines were set at two-thirds of the urban one in each case. The poverty lines for 1969/70 were adjusted to 1976 and 1981 prices using the indexes given in Asra (1989: Table 3) for the bottom 40 per cent of the respective populations in 1976 and the bottom 20 per cent in 1981. Between 1981 and 1987 the poverty lines were adjusted upwards for inflation using the rural 9 commodity index for rural Java and rural Outer Islands and the 17 city index for all urban areas. The actual poverty lines (rupiah per capita per month) were as follows:

	Urban Java	Rural Java	Urban Outer Islands	Rural Outer Islands
1969/70	1,260	850	1,540	1,030
1976	3,800	2,941	4,178	2,905
1981	7,019	5,100	9,034	6,448
1987	11,048	9,893	14,220	11,491

The affluence line was set at Rp 3,600 per capita per month in urban Java in 1969/70; only 7.8 per cent of the population were above this line. The rural Java affluence line was set at 80 per cent of the urban one. For both urban and rural areas, the Outer Islands affluence lines were set at 20 per cent more than the Java ones, which roughly reflects the regional price disparities as estimated by Arndt and Sundrum (1975). The 1969/70 affluence lines were adjusted upwards to 1976 and 1981 prices using the indexes estimated by Asra (1989: Table 3) for the top 40 per cent of the population. Between 1981 and 1987 the affluence lines everywhere in the country except rural areas outside Java were adjusted upwards by the 17 city index. In the rural areas outside Java the rural 9 commodity index was used. These procedures produced the following set of affluence lines:

	Urban Java	Rural Java	Urban Outer Islands	Rural Outer Islands
1969/70	3,600	3,000	4,320	3,600
1976	10,857	9,210	11,719	7,848
1981	20,052	18,632	25,358	17,697
1987	31,562	29,327	39,913	31,536

Decomposition of Changes in Poverty and Affluence in Table 10.16

In order to determine how much of the observed change in the proportion of the population below the poverty line between 1969/70 and 1976 was due to growth in per capita income, the following calculations were carried out:

1. An estimate was made of the proportion of the population below the poverty line in 1976 assuming that all incomes (as proxied by expenditures) increased by the real rate of growth of average per capita expenditures between 1969/70 and 1976, as calculated in Table 10.2. A short-cut way of doing this is to adjust downwards the 1969/70 poverty line by the growth in real average expenditures, and apply this adjusted poverty line to the 1969/70 distribution of the population by per capita expenditure group. The difference between the actual proportion in poverty in 1969/70, and the (lower) proportion using the adjusted poverty line can be called the proportion of the actual decline in poverty which is due to real growth in expenditure. The balance (which could be positive or negative) is the part which is due to the improvement (or deterioration) in the distribution of expenditures.

2. An alternative method would be to take the 1976 poverty line, adjust it upwards to allow for the increase in real per capita expenditures between the two years, and apply this to the 1976 expenditure distribution. The difference between this (higher) proportion in poverty in 1976 and the actual proportion can be called the share of the actual decline due to real expenditure growth, while the balance is the share due to distributional changes between the two years.

3. As both these methods are equally valid, it is best to calculate the share of the total poverty decline due to expenditure growth both ways, and then take an average. Similarly the residual due to distributional changes can be calculated both ways and the average taken.

4. The following example refers to urban Java between 1969/70 and 1976. As is shown in Table 10.16, the proportion in poverty fell from 41.7 per cent to 28.3 per cent between these two years. The growth in real per capita expenditures was 30.45 per cent (shown on an annualized basis in Table 10.2). The 1969/70 poverty line can be adjusted downwards by this amount, from Rp 1,260 to Rp 966; when this is applied to the 1969/70 expenditure distribution, a percentage in poverty of 25.04 is derived. The alternative procedure of adjusting the 1976 poverty line upwards from Rp 3,800 to Rp 4,957 yielded a proportion in poverty of 45.34 per cent. Thus the decline in poverty due to expenditure growth was either 41.7 minus 25.04 (equals 16.7) or 45.34 minus 28.28 (equals 17.06). The average of these two numbers is 16.85. As the actual decline in poverty between these two years was only 13.4 per cent, it is clear that the distribution of expenditures actually deteriorated between these two years, and had a negative impact on the decline in poverty. Expenditure growth alone would have led to a faster decline.

5. The same procedure can be used to decompose the increase in affluence between expenditure growth and changes in distribution.

REFERENCES

Arndt, H. W. and Sundrum, R. M. (1975), 'Regional Price Disparities', *Bulletin of Indonesian Economic Studies*, 11(2): 30–68.

Asra, Abuzar (1989), 'Inequality Trends in Indonesia, A Re-examination', *Bulletin of Indonesian Economic Studies*, 25(2): 100–10.

Bienen, Henry (1983), 'Oil Revenues and Policy Choice in Nigeria', *World Bank Staff Working Papers*, No. 592, Washington, DC: World Bank.

Booth, Anne (1989), 'Regional Aspects of Indonesian Agricultural Growth', Paper presented at the Conference on Indonesia's New Order, Canberra, 4–8 December. A revised version of this paper is published in Joan Hardjono (ed.), *Indonesia: Resources, Ecology, and Environment*, Singapore: Oxford University Press, 1991.

Booth, Anne and Sundrum, R.M. (1981), 'Income Distribution', in Anne Booth and Peter McCawley (eds.), *The Indonesian Economy during the Soeharto Era*, Kuala Lumpur: Oxford University Press.

BPS (Biro Pusat Statistik) (1987a), *Sensus Pertanian 1983: Sampel Pendapatan Petani, Seri I*, Jakarta.

____ (1987b), *Indikator Pemerataan Pendapatan; Jumlah dan Persentase Penduduk Miskin di Indonesia*, Jakarta.

____ (1989), *Kemiskinan, Distribusi Pendapatan dan Kebutuhan Pokok*, Jakarta.

Cassing, J.H. and Warr, Peter G. (1985), 'The Distributional Impact of a Resource Boom', *Journal of International Economics*, 18: 301–20.

Corden, W.M. (1984), 'Booming Sectors and Dutch Disease Economics: A Survey', *Oxford Economic Papers*, 36: 359–80.

Esmara, Hendra (1975), 'Regional Income Disparities', *Bulletin of Indonesian Economic Studies*, 11(1): 41–57.

____ (1986), *Perencanaan dan Pembangunan di Indonesia*, Jakarta: Penerbit PT Gramedia.

Hirschman, Albert O. (1973), 'The Changing Tolerance for Income Inequality in the Course of Economic Development', *Quarterly Journal of Economics*, 87: 544–65; reprinted in Albert O. Hirschman, *Essays in Trespassing: Economics to Politics and Beyond*, Cambridge: Cambridge University Press, 1981.

Hughes, G.A. and Islam, I. (1981), 'Inequality in Indonesia: A Decomposition Analysis', *Bulletin of Indonesian Economic Studies*, 17(2): 42–71.

Islam, I. and Khan, H. (1986), 'Spatial Patterns of Inequality and Poverty in Indonesia', *Bulletin of Indonesian Economic Studies*, 22(2): 80–102.

Katouzian, M.A. (1978), 'Oil Revenues and Policy Choice: A Case of Dual Resource Depletion in Iran', *Journal of Peasant Studies*, 8(3): 347–69.

Katouzian, Homa (1981), *The Political Economy of Modern Iran: 1926–79*, London: Macmillan.

Petras, James and Morley, Morris H. (1983), 'Petrodollars and the State: The Failure of State Capitalist Development in Venezuela', *Third World Quarterly*, 5(1): 7–27.

Ravallion, Martin (1989), 'Consumption Norms and Measurement Errors in Household Surveys', Washington, DC: World Bank, mimeo.

Ravallion, Martin and Huppi, Monika (1989), 'Poverty and Undernutrition in Indonesia during the 1980s', Washington, DC: World Bank, mimeo. A revised version of this paper is published as 'Measuring Change in Poverty: A Methodological Case Study of Indonesia during an Adjustment Period', *World Bank Economic Review*, 5(1): 57–82.

Rietveld, Piet (1986), 'Non-agricultural Activities and Income Distribution in Rural Java', *Bulletin of Indonesian Economic Studies*, 23(3): 106–17.

Sajogyo and Wiradi, Gunawan (1985), *Rural Poverty and Efforts for its Alleviation in Indonesia: A Sociological Review*, Paper prepared for the WCARRD Follow-up Programme, Rome: FAO.

Sundrum, R.M. (1986), 'Indonesia's Rapid Growth: 1968–81', *Bulletin of Indonesian Economic Studies*, 22(3): 40–69.

_____ (1990), *Income Distribution in Less Developed Countries*, London: Routledge.

Sundrum, R.M. and Booth, Anne (1980), 'Income Distribution in Indonesia: Trends and Derterminants', in R.G. Garnaut and P.T. McCawley (eds.), *Indonesia: Dualism, Growth and Poverty*, Canberra: Research School of Pacific Studies, Australian National University.

Sutomo, Slamet (1989), 'Income, Food Consumption and Estimation of Energy and Protein Intake of Households: A Study Based on the 1975 and 1980 Indonesian Social Accounting Matrices', *Bulletin of Indonesian Economic Studies*, 25(3): 57–72.

Warr, Peter G. (1986), 'Indonesia's Other Dutch Disease: Economic Effects of the Petroleum Boom', in P. Neary and S. van Wijnbergen (eds.), *Natural Resources and the Macroeconomy*, Oxford: Basil Blackwell.

White, Ben (1986), *Rural Non-farm Employment in Java: Recent Developments, Policy Issues and Research Needs*, Jakarta: UNDP/ILO.

Williamson, Jeffery G. (1965), 'Regional Inequality and the Process of National Development', *Economic Development and Cultural Change*, 13: 3–45.

World Bank (1980), *Employment and Income Distribution in Indonesia: A World Bank Country Study*, Washington, DC.

_____ (1988), *Indonesia: The Transmigration Program in Perspective*, Washington, DC.

11
Labour Force and Employment during the 1980s

Gavin W. Jones and Chris Manning

Introduction

Two earlier overviews of the labour force and employment situation in Indonesia during the Soeharto era concentrated on the period up to 1971 (Jones, 1981) and on the period up to 1980 (Hugo et al., 1987: Chapter 8). In both cases, the main data sources used were the population censuses. In this chapter the emphasis will be on the 1980s, and a variety of sources will be used. Because data from the 1990 Population Census are not yet available, non-census sources will also be utilized. One of these is the National Labour Force Surveys (*Sakernas*) with comparisons being made over the ten-year period between 1976/7 and 1986/7. The National Socio-economic Survey (*Susenas*) and Intercensal Survey (*Supas*) data for 1982 and 1985 respectively will also be used.

It is clear that the population censuses tend to record lower proportions of the working-age population in the labour force than do the other sources of labour force data. This leads to difficulties in attempting to measure time trends in the labour force by comparing censuses with other sources (Jones, 1987; Hugo et al., 1987: Chapter 8; Bakir and Manning, 1983; Korns, 1987). The emphasis on *Sakernas* will help to overcome this problem, as well as provide richer detail on the labour force based on the availability of quarterly rounds and more detailed questions than were used in the census. The main disadvantage in the use of *Sakernas* is its smaller sampling fraction, and the consequently higher degree of sampling variability. The 1987 *Sakernas* also combined some sectors, thus reducing its value for studies of sectoral employment change.[1]

During the New Order period, the Indonesian labour force has doubled in size and become less Java-centric, less concentrated in primary industries, and much better educated. It has remained a very youthful workforce, and although youth unemployment has been a worry, the main problem has been low productivity and low earnings rather than overt unemployment. The 1990s are expected to see even faster changes in labour supply and demand than have characterized the New Order period to date.

The Demographic Underpinnings of Labour Force Growth

The 1980s was the last decade in which the numbers entering the labour force were largely unaffected by the fertility decline which began in the early 1970s. Resulting as they did from the high birth rates and falling infant and child mortality rates of the late 1960s and early 1970s, the cohorts entering the labour force in the 1980s were very large, and contributed to an average annual growth rate of 2.8 per cent in the labour force age groups during the 1980s. This equalled the 1970s as the fastest decade of growth ever recorded, or indeed ever likely to be recorded, in Indonesia. By the mid-1990s the youngest segment of the labour force will have almost ceased to grow at all, and the numbers in the labour force age groups as a whole will grow by 'only' 23 per cent during the 1990s, compared with 33 per cent during the 1980s (Gardiner, 1989). During the decade to 1987, Java's share of the workforce fell quite substantially (Table 11.1) and the share of Java excluding Jakarta and West Java fell particularly rapidly—from 46 per cent to 41 per cent.[2] More than half of this fall was offset by a rise in Sumatra's share, due both to higher natural increase and net migration.

One of the most dramatic changes in recent decades has been in the educational attainment of the labour force. As recently as 1971, 70 per cent of the population of working age still had no education at all or incomplete primary school. By 1987, this proportion had fallen to 41 per cent. Table 11.2 shows that the improvement has been particularly striking for females. The still low educational attainment of the labour force as a whole (4.6 years of education, compared with more than 7 years in both Malaysia and the Philippines: Jones, 1989) is due to the slow movement of older, poorly educated cohorts out of the labour force. The educational gradient from the younger to the older ages is

TABLE 11.1
Changing Regional Distribution of the Workforce (percentage)

Total Workforce	1977[a]	1980[b]	1985
Jakarta–West Java	19.4	20.1	20.6
Rest of Jakarta	46.0	43.6	41.8
Total Java	65.5	63.8	62.4
Sumatra	16.1	18.4	18.8
Kalimantan	4.8	4.7	4.8
Sulawesi	7.5	7.4	7.9
Rest of Indonesia	7.5	7.4	7.9
Total Outside Java	34.5	36.2	37.6

Sources: BPS, National Labour Force Survey (*Sakernas*), 1977; Population Census, 1980, Series S2; and Intercensal Population Survey (*Supas*), 1985, Series 5.
[a] 1977 'Rest of Indonesia' data adjusted.
[b] 1980 East Timor data adjusted.

TABLE 11.2

Indonesia: Population Aged 15 Years and Over, by Educational Attainment, 1961–1985

Sex	Year	No Schooling	Incomplete Primary Schooling	Completed Primary Schooling	Completed Lower or Upper Secondary Schooling	Academy or University Education	Total Percentage
Males	1961	55.7	22.6	16.7	4.8	0.2	100
	1971	32.4	29.4	27.1	10.4	0.7	100
	1976[a]	26.0	38.9	22.6	10.7	1.8	100
	1980	21.8	35.9	25.5	15.9	0.9	100
	1985	14.4	30.1	30.8	23.3	1.4	100
Females	1961	79.6	11.2	7.3	1.9	0.0	100
	1971	57.0	21.2	16.5	5.1	0.2	100
	1976[a]	47.5	31.3	14.8	5.8	0.7	100
	1980	41.4	30.4	18.8	9.1	0.3	100
	1985	30.6	29.3	25.0	14.6	0.5	100
Both sexes	1961	68.1	16.7	11.8	3.3	0.1	100
	1971	45.2	25.1	21.6	7.7	0.4	100
	1976[a]	37.2	34.9	18.6	8.1	1.2	100
	1980	31.9	33.1	22.1	12.4	0.6	100
	1985	22.7	29.7	27.8	18.9	0.9	100

Percentage of Population with

Sources: BPS, Population Census, 1961; Population Census, 1971 (Series D); 1976; Intercensal Population Survey (*Supas*), 1985, Series S5. Population Census, 1980 (Series S2); Intercensal Population Survey (*Supas*), [a] 1976 *Supas* figures are not adjusted for the regions not covered.

very steep indeed (Figure 11.1). Among the population aged 15–29 in 1987, only 25 per cent had less than completed primary school education. This is testimony to the success of the compulsory education policies instituted in the 1970s.

Growth rates of the labour force can change not only because of changes in the growth of the labour force age groups, but also because of changes in proportions of those who are economically active. Such changes have occurred in Indonesia in recent decades; however, it has been extremely difficult to distinguish real changes from apparent changes resulting solely from changes in definitions or procedures in collecting labour force data in censuses and surveys (Hugo et al., 1987: Appendix 2).

Comparison of participation rates between the *Sakernas* of 1977 and 1987 should give a fairly reliable picture of trends in participation rates because definitions and procedures were similar[3] and figures from both are the result of an averaging of four rounds, thus avoiding the problems of comparing data collected at different times of the year. The participation rates measured for females in urban and rural areas in the two years are shown in Figure 11.2. For comparison, rates measured in the 1982 *Susenas* and the 1980 Population Census are also shown. The female rates were substantially higher in both urban and rural areas in 1987 than in 1977. But for this rise in participation rates, the female workforce in 1987 would have been almost 6 million smaller than that actually recorded.

The rise in female participation rates between the two *Sakernas* is also consistent with rates measured in the 1982 *Susenas* and the 1985 *Supas*, which in both urban and rural areas are intermediate between the two *Sakernas* figures. *Sakernas*, *Susenas*, and *Supas* rates are well above those measured in the 1980 Population Census, thus following an established pattern in Indonesia of lower participation rates measured by censuses than by other sources. The lower rates in the 1980 Population Census, generally judged to have resulted primarily from differential recording of female workers, especially unpaid family workers (Jones, 1987; Manning, 1989), may result from the employment of a one-off group of teachers and other government employees as enumerators in the census instead of the well-trained *mantri statistik* (statistical officers) employed in the other surveys. Improved data collection procedures and more intensive training of interviewers have also almost certainly increased the coverage of the labour force in more recent *Sakernas* (Korns, 1987). However, the steady increase in *Sakernas*, *Susenas*, and *Supas* rates between 1977 and 1987 suggests that part of the rise between the 1980 Population Census rates and those in the more recent sources was real. The substantial rise in the urban rates is particularly important in this context, because by and large there is less uncertainty in determining whether urban women are in the labour force or not. Employment data for rural women are much more affected by problems of maintaining a consistent treatment of unpaid family workers. Part of the very substantial increase in rural participation rates across almost all age categories in

FIGURE 11.1
Working Population by Age and Educational Attainment, 1987

PERCENTAGE

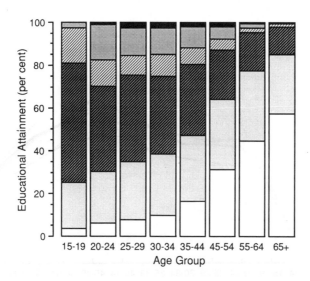

ABSOLUTE NUMBERS

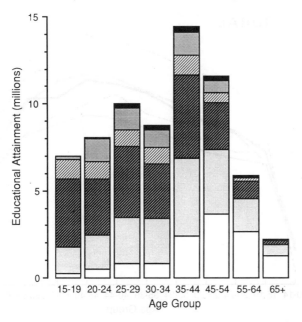

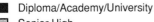

■ Diploma/Academy/University   ▨ Completed Primary
▦ Senior High   □ Incomplete Primary
▨ Junior High   □ No Schooling

FIGURE 11.2
Female Activity Rates by Age and Rural–Urban Residence,
1977–1987

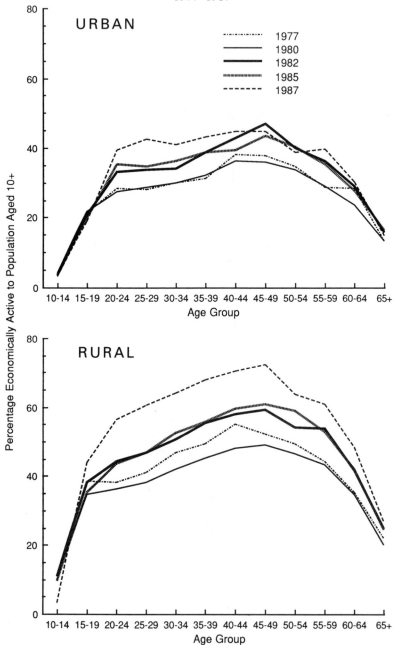

the period 1982–7 must be attributed to greater coverage of family workers in 1987 (see Appendix).

The important point to make about the rise in female participation rates in the present context is that this rise complemented underlying demographic trends in pushing labour force growth rates to record levels in the 1980s. For planning purposes, it is important to know whether the rates will continue to rise in future; a forecast requires some understanding of why they rose from the late 1970s onwards.

Changes in female participation rates are likely to be determined by interactions between a number of factors, including trends in marital status, fertility, and education (all of which are basically supply-side factors) and economic conditions influencing the demand for workers in occupations where female employment is important, along with changing perceptions about what is suitable female work (which are basically demand-side factors). Supply and demand cannot be so neatly separated, however. For example, for many women, decisions about marriage, childbearing, and education may not be divorced from labour market considerations.

Rising ages at marriage and falling fertility undoubtedly have contributed to the growth of female employment, because participation rates have always tended to be higher for single than for married women and for women who do not have children of preschool age. Between 1977 and 1987, there may also have been a slight shift in the occupational structure towards occupations in which women are normally strongly represented. However, the most intriguing questions concern the effect on female employment of the changing education of both males and females as well as the effect of changing economic conditions.

Participation rates for Indonesian women have always differed markedly depending on the level of education (Widarti, 1984; Jones, 1986). A U-shaped pattern has prevailed, with the lowest rates for those with junior secondary school education and the highest rates for those with no education or tertiary education. This pattern has been maintained in the 1987 *Sakernas* figures (Figure 11.3). On balance, the changing educational composition of the female working-age population between 1977 and 1987 (a fall in the share of the uneducated and a rise in the share of those with completed primary school education and above) should have led, other things being equal, to a slight fall in the female participation rate, because the share of those with completed primary school and junior high school education, whose participation rates are low, increased the most.

Participation rates for women within different educational groups, however, are not static, but are influenced by economic trends affecting their job opportunities and felt need to work, as well as by changes in perceptions about appropriate activities for women. Equally important, when education expands rapidly, as it has in Indonesia, the composition of educational attainment by economic class tends to change. Thus girls from lower socio-economic groups start to enter lower secondary education, and the motivations influencing work decisions of this group are

FIGURE 11.3
Female Activity Rates by Age and Educational Attainment,
1977 and 1987

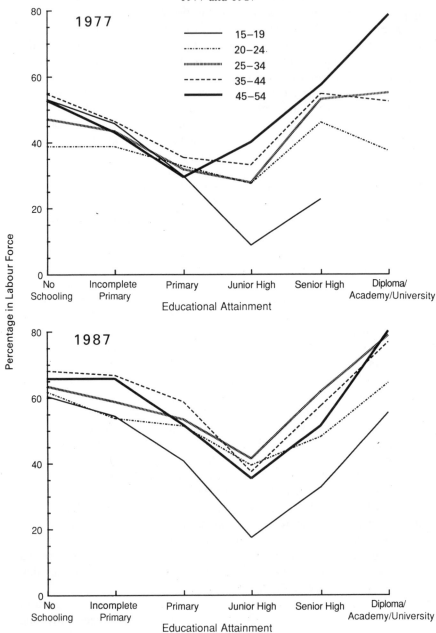

FIGURE 11.4
Female Activity Rates by Age for Each Educational Attainment
Level, 1977 and 1987

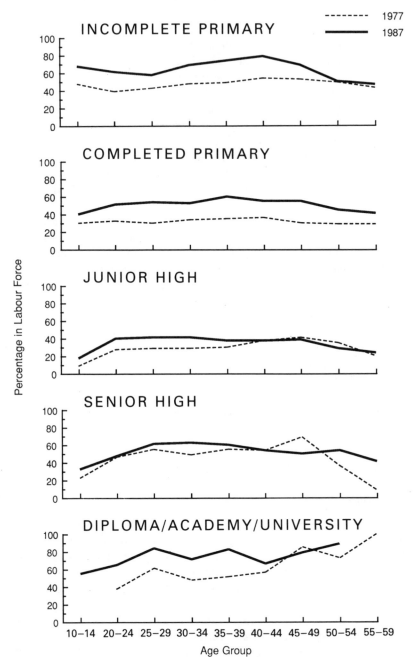

likely to differ from motivations of earlier cohorts drawn more exclusively from the higher socio-economic groups.

Figure 11.4 shows that between 1977 and 1987, labour force participation rates for women from each educational group have changed.
To some extent the marked increases at primary and less than primary
levels can be attributed to better coverage of unpaid family workers in
1987. At the younger ages, they rose in each case, but at the older ages,
they rose only in the case of the uneducated and those with primary
school education. It might be hypothesized that the rise across the board
at the younger ages reflects primarily a greater community acceptance of
economic activity as appropriate for women, whereas at the older ages
the rise among the less well-educated may reflect perceived economic
pressures, particularly during the 1982–7 period.

One issue related to trends in participation rates is the high and somewhat unstable share of the residual 'other' category outside the labour
force that has been identified in Indonesian labour force surveys and
censuses as particularly important among young people (Jones, 1974;
Bukit and Bakir, 1984; Cremer, 1990). It appears that this proportion
has risen steeply in recent years particularly among persons aged 15–24
(and especially females in this age category): according to *Sakernas* data,
the share of 'other' rose from less than 10 per cent in 1976–8 to closer
to 20 per cent in 1986–7 among both males and females in this age category (Cremer, 1990: 72–4). One possible interpretation of this development is that a higher proportion of young people are involved
in waiting periods during the transition from school to work and
many may comprise a growing number of 'discouraged' workers. While
this may be true, more careful analysis of the socio-economic characteristics of young people outside the labour force (those classified as
'other', at school, and performing housework) is required to draw clear
conclusions.

An Overview of Employment and Wage Trends by Sector

Employment Trends by Region and Sector

There are some very real difficulties in deriving plausible and consistent
estimates of employment change by sector in Indonesia over the past
20 years. First, one must deal with the problem of sharp discontinuities
in total labour force growth suggested by the various data sources (see
above) which is crucial to an assessment of the rate of change in
employment by sector. Second, industry shares have tended to vary considerably, and sometimes implausibly, in data reported in the various
censuses and surveys, *Sakernas*, *Supas*, and *Susenas*.[4] After some experimentation, the approach here has been to accept trends suggested by the
1971 and 1980 censuses and to compare these with data which give the
most believable and consistent set of time trends for the subsequent
period 1980–5.[5] Separate tables have been prepared for males and
females since the former have shown a much more stable trend over
time than the latter.

Despite these data problems, however, several broad trends can be stated with some certainty for the entire period 1971–85. First, non-agricultural sector employment growth rates have been much more rapid (around 4–5 per cent) than those in agriculture (1–2 per cent) and the share of the latter in total employment has fallen quite dramatically: from slightly under 70 per cent in 1971 to closer to 55 per cent in 1985. Second, non-agricultural employment growth has been relatively broad-based, covering all major service industries, manufacturing, and construction. It has also occurred at a similar rate in Java (where such activities traditionally have been concentrated) and in the Outer Islands. Third, agricultural sector employment growth rates have been very much higher in the Outer Islands (2–2.5 per cent) than in Java (0.5–1 per cent), a trend which is projected increasingly to dominate employment dynamics in the coming decade.

Taking the three-way division of the labour force into A, M, and S sectors as a basis for comparison,[6] the rate of decline in agriculture's share of employment in Indonesia over the period 1971–85 (−1.4 per cent per annum) appears to have been about average when compared with neighbouring countries. Even if one accepts the reportedly high share of agricultural employment in 1985, the decline was considerably more rapid than that recorded for the Philippines or India (around −0.5 per cent per annum) but it was significantly slower than in Malaysia and rapidly industrializing Taiwan and South Korea (Table 11.3). Despite the quite rapid growth in M sector employment in Indonesia, the decline in the agricultural share was primarily offset by a rise in the S sector's share whereas in Malaysia, and more demonstrably in Taiwan and South Korea, the M sector was much more prominent.

It is clear that there have been some important differences in the pattern of Indonesian employment growth in the 1970s compared with in the first half of the 1980s. Trends for the 1970s implied by the 1971 and 1980 census results are well known and will not be discussed in detail here.[7] Non-agricultural employment grew rapidly, especially in the oil boom supported service and construction industries, and to a lesser extent in manufacturing (particularly among males) (Tables 11.4–11.6). Agricultural employment growth was sluggish, accounting for around 20 per cent of total employment growth. New agricultural jobs were heavily concentrated in the Outer Islands, although the agricultural labour force still continued to grow on Java, primarily due to expansion of employment among males.

Slower overall economic growth rates in the period 1980–5 appear to have been associated with much less rapid growth in non-agricultural employment. This was counterbalanced by higher rates of labour absorption in agriculture in Java and the Outer Islands than in the previous decade. Even after adjusting for the implausibly high recorded rates of growth in female employment in agriculture in Java for the period 1980–5 (over 4 per cent per annum), the data suggest that total agricultural employment grew at around 1 per cent per annum in Java compared with around 0.6 per cent in the previous decade. Among males, agriculture was reported to have accounted for close to 30 per cent of

TABLE 11.3

Shift[a] in Employment Share by Major Industry Sectors in Indonesia, the Philippines, India, Republic of Korea,
Peninsular Malaysia, and Taiwan, over Several Periods (percentage)

Country/Indicator

Broad Industry Group[b]	Indonesia[c]			Philippines		
	1971	1985	1971–85 (shift p.a.)	1970	1980	1970–80 (shift p.a.)
A	67.5	55.4	−1.4	55.1	52.7	−0.4
M	11.0	15.9	2.6	20.8	20.4	−0.2
S	21.5	28.7	2.1	24.1	26.9	0.3
Total	100.0	100.0		100.0	100.0	
n (m.)	41.3	62.5		11.8	14.2	

Broad Industry Group[b]	India			Republic of Korea		
	1961	1981	1961–81 (shift p.a.)	1960	1980	1960–80 (shift p.a.)
A	76.6	69.4	−0.5	67.2	26.0	−4.7
M	12.7	15.7	1.1	10.9	34.4	5.7
S	10.7	14.9	1.7	21.9	39.6	3.0
Total	100.0	100.0		100.0	100.0	
n (m.)	188.2	222.6		7.0	15.0	

	Peninsular Malaysia			Taiwan		
	1957	1985	1957–85 (shift p.a.)	1957	1985	1957–85 (shift p.a.)
A	61.8	27.3	-2.9	60.5	25.2	-3.1
M	13.8	29.4	2.7	12.0	37.1	4.0
S	24.4	43.3	2.0	27.5	37.7	1.1
Total	100.0	100.0		100.0	100.0	
n (m.)	2.1	4.6		6.1	9.0	

[a] Shift means rate of change in percentage points in employment share per annum since the previous period. Persons with activities not adequately defined have been allocated to industry groups pro rata.

[b] A means agriculture, hunting, forestry, fishing, mining, and quarrying.
M means manufacturing, electricity, gas, water, construction, transport, storage, and communication.
S means trade, restaurants, hotels, financing, insurance, real estate, business services, community, social, and personal services.

[c] Unadjusted data.

Sources: 1. Indonesia: Population Census, 1971, Series C and Intercensal Population Survey (Supas), 1985, Series 5.
2. Peninsular Malaysia: 1957 and 1970 Population Censuses and 1985 Labour Force Survey.
3. Korea: 1960—Population and Housing Census of Korea, Vol. 2, Table 14, p. 168; 1971 and 1985—United Nations, Statistical Yearbook for Asia and the Pacific, 1979 and 1988.
4. Taiwan: 1975 and 1985, Statistical Yearbook of the Republic of China.
5. Philippines: 1970, 1975, and 1980 Population Censuses.
6. India: 1961, 1971, and 1981 Censuses of India, Subsidiary Table B-I.6(i): 3; Table B-I, Part A: 16; and Table B.3: 238, in that order.

TABLE 11.4
Growth of Male Employment in Indonesia, 1971–1987[a]

Sector	Share of Employment (%)		Growth Rates (% p.a.)			Percentage of Increment	
	1971	1985	1971–80	1980–5	1985–7[c]	1971–80	1980–5
Agriculture	66	55	1.4	2.0	(2.4)	29	42
Manufacturing	6	8	5.6	4.0	(0.2)	12	11
Construction	3	5	8.5	4.6	n.a.	10	8
Trade	9	12	4.2	5.4	(4.2)	13	20
Transport	3	5	5.0	5.7 }	(3.6)	6	9
Services	12	14	5.9	1.7 }		26	9
Other[b]	1	1	12.9	1.5		4	–
Total	100	100	3.0	2.9	(3.1)	100	99
n ('000)	26,184	42,480					

Sources: BPS Population Census, 1971, Series C; Population Census, 1980, Series S1; Intercensal Population Survey (Supas), 1985, Series 5; and National Labour Force Survey (Sakernas), 1987.
[a]Excludes employment in Irian Jaya and East Timor for comparability over time. Not stated/unclear redistributed on a pro rata basis.
[b]Mining and public utilities.
[c]In 1987 data for services and transport included in the same category. No breakdown for construction.
n.a. = Not available.

	Share of Employment		Growth Rates (% p.a.)		Share of Employment Growth (%)	
Region/Sector	1971	1985	1971–80	1980–5	1971–80	1980–5
Java						
Agriculture	63	50	1.0	1.1	19	27
Manufacturing	7	10	5.2	4.3	15	16
Construction	3	6	9.3	4.5	13	10
Trade	11	13	3.8	5.3	14	26
Transport	4	6	5.1	6.5	7	13
Services	12	15	6.0	1.3	29	8
Other	*	1	14.1	1.3	3	*
Total	100	100	2.9	2.5	100	100
n ('000)	17,010	24,975	n.a.	n.a.	5,006	2,959
Outer Islands						
Agriculture	74	64	2.0	2.9	42	59
Manufacturing	3	5	7.0	2.8	9	4
Construction	2	4	8.0	4.8	7	6
Trade	7	9	5.5	5.6	12	15
Transport	3	4	5.0	3.9	5	4
Services	10	13	6.4	2.6	22	11
Other	1	1	11.3	1.6	3	1
Total[a]	100	99	3.3	3.2	100	100
n ('000)	9,174	14,478	n.a.	n.a.	3,184	2,119

Sources: As for Table 11.4.
[a] Includes mining and utilities
*Less than 0.5 per cent.
n.a. = Not available.

TABLE 11.6

Recorded and Estimated Female Employment in Indonesia and Java, 1971–1985[a]

Region/Sector	Share of Employment			Growth in Employment (% p.a.)			Share of Employment Growth (%)		
		1985			1980–5			1980–5	
	1971	Recorded	Estimated	1971–80	Recorded	Estimated	1971–80	Recorded	Estimated
Indonesia[b]									
Agriculture	65	54	48	0.8	5.3	1.1	17	51	17
Manufacturing	11	12	13	3.4	4.3	3.9	16	9	14
Trade	15	21	23	6.0	7.8	7.3	35	29	45
Services	9	12	15	7.9	4.5	5.6	30	11	23
Other	*	1	1	(13.9)	(3.3)	(3.3)	2	*	*
All sectors	100	100	100	2.9	5.6	3.3	100	100	99
n ('000)	13,026	22,472	19,986				3,792	5,384	3,168
Java									
Agriculture	58	45	42	0.1	4.3	0.9	2	41	14
Manufacturing	13	14	14	3.7	3.6	2.7	21	11	13
Trade	18	26	27	5.2	6.9	6.1	41	35	51
Services	10	14	16	7.1	4.0	4.1	34	12	21
Other	1	1	1	(12.6)	(4.7)	(3.5)	2	1	1
All sectors	100	100	100	2.6	4.8	3.0	100	100	100
n ('000)	8,747	13,981	12,776				2,263	2,971	1,766

Sources: As for Table 11.4.

[a]Estimate for 1985 derived by applying growth rates for family workers and earnings workers (separately) for 1977–85 to base population in each category in 1980 to obtain total employment in 1985. Sectoral share of family and earnings workers in 1985 applied to total estimated employment in each category to derive employment by sector. See Appendix.

[b] Excludes data for Irian Jaya and East Timor.

*Less than 0.5 per cent.

all employment growth in the early 1980s while outside Java close to 60 per cent of the increment in employment was absorbed in this sector (Table 11.4).[8] As discussed below, the underlying factors contributing to the more rapid rate of employment growth in Java are not altogether clear. In part this appears to have been associated with a decline in average hours worked, which in turn was related to greater participation of secondary workers in agriculture, and in part it may be due to expansion of labour demand which accompanied rapid rice sector growth and diversification in agricultural production in the early 1980s. The greatly expanded transmigration programme, support for agricultural growth through the Nucleus Estate Scheme (PIR) and the expansion of small-holder agriculture all help to explain the quite rapid growth of employment in agriculture in the Outer Islands (Booth, 1989).

Lower recorded growth rates in non-agricultural employment compared with the 1970s were mainly the result of a marked slow-down in employment expansion in services and construction. Primarily, this consisted of a slower rate of increase in wage employment among males, a trend heavily influenced by cut-backs in the growth of public spending from the early 1980s.[9] Despite slower economic growth in the early to mid-1980s, manufacturing employment continued to grow at around 4 per cent, although there appears to have been a sharp fall in employment growth rates among males in manufacturing in the Outer Islands.

One important development in the 1980s, consistent by gender and region, has been the increased importance of trade and transport in overall employment growth. As will be seen from data on hours worked, it seems likely that this development (as with expansion of labour absorption in agriculture) reflects labour supply pressures—growth in informal sector and low-income work in response to difficulties in obtaining wage employment from the early 1980s (Hasibuan, 1987).

Wage Trends

Assessment of the labour market and welfare implications of these employment trends depends considerably on how earnings have fared over time in various sectors. Here again the available data need to be interpreted with caution, as various series—both the data collected by the Biro Pusat Statistik (BPS) and that obtained from field research—often show contrasting patterns of change (Table 11.7). Nevertheless, the following broad patterns would seem to hold.[10] Unskilled wage rates, particularly in rice and construction, stagnated for much of the 1970s but began to rise—quite sharply in some sectors such as manufacturing and estate agriculture—towards the end of the decade and in the early 1980s. They appear to have levelled off again, and in some cases declined from around the mid-1980s.

Thus, although there appears to have been a brief period in the past 20 years when the economy faced a general shortage of unskilled labour—albeit at extremely low absolute wage rates even when compared with neighbouring countries—rapid change in employment structure has occurred for the most part under conditions of a relatively

TABLE 11.7

Real Wage Trends in Various Sectors: Java and Indonesia, 1966–1988

Sector/ Subsector	Region	Data Resource	Sample	Deflator	Years	Activity/ Gender	Change in Real Wages (% p.a.)
Agriculture							
Rice	West Java	Agro-economic Survey[a]	6 villages	Rice price	1966/7–76/7	Hoeing (male)	0.5
						Weeding (female)	1.0
	West Java	Agro-economic Survey[b]	6 villages	Local 9 commodity index	1977–83	Hoeing (male)	2.6
						Planting (female)	2.7
	Java	BPS[c]	Approx. 550 kecamatan (1 farmer)	Java rural 9 commodity index	1976–80	Hoeing	0
						Planting	0.5
					1980–5	Hoeing	6.0
						Planting	5.6
					1985–8	Hoeing	−4.8
						Planting	−4.8
Estates	Indonesia	BPS[d]	All state-owned estates	Java/Outer Is. rural 9 commodity index	1976/7–79/80	All activities	8.0
					1979/80–85/6		3.7
							−7.7

Manufacturing							
Medium and large firms	Indonesia	BPS[e]	Annual survey all firms	Jakarta CPI	1975/6–79/80	Av. wage cost/worker	4.8
					1979/80–85/6		5.4
	Indonesia	BPS[f]	Census 1974 and 1985	?	1974–85	Av. wage cost/ worker	5.6
	Java	BPS[f]	Census 1974 and 1985	?	1974–85	Av. wage cost/ worker	5.0
Construction							
Bricklayers	Large Outer Islands	BPS[g]	Small panel of workers	City CPI	1979/80–85/6	Male	1.5
	Resource-rich cities						7.1
	Java cities						4.5

Sources: [a] Makali and Sri Hartoyo (1978: Table 15); unweighted village average.
[b] Mazumdar and Sawit (1986: Table 4).
[c] Jayasuriya and Manning (1990: Table 2); data for planting to June 1988.
[d] BPS, *Average Wages of Estate Workers*, various years (two-year averages).
[e] BPS, *Survey of Medium and Large Manufacturing Establishments*, various years (two-year averages).
[f] Hill (1989: Table 25); data for all Java unweighted average of Jakarta and West, Central, and East Java.
[g] Jayasuriya and Manning (1988: 34). 'Large Outer Islands', includes Medan, Padang, Ujung Pandang; 'Resource-rich cities' includes Pekanbaru and Samarinda; 'Java cities' includes Bandung, Semarang, and Surabaya. All unweighted averages.

elastic labour supply. In the Lewisian sense, despite rapid rates of economic growth and structural change, Indonesia for the most part has remained a surplus labour economy. Real wages for the same work (efficiency wages) appear to be higher than they were in the early 1970s in most activities—perhaps by a margin of around 10–50 per cent on average—but there is no indication of sustained growth such as has occurred in Malaysia, Taiwan, or Korea in the past two decades.

This does not mean, however, that average wages have not risen or that a significant proportion of the workforce has not experienced higher earnings as a consequence of the changing composition of total employment. Constant wage rates within particular subsectors, especially at the lower end of the skill range and 'earnings ladder', are not necessarily inconsistent with improved living standards or indeed with the declining levels of poverty discussed in Chapter 10. Average earnings have clearly increased as labour has entered more productive and higher-paying jobs both across and within broad sectors. Despite constant wage rates in rice agriculture in Java for most of the 1970s, the transfer of labour from very low-productivity agricultural employment to more productive non-agricultural work, much of it in the urban informal sector, is one important example (Hugo, 1978; Jayasuriya and Manning, 1990). Hill (1989a) finds that average manufacturing wage costs have risen quite steeply across industry and region in manufacturing over the period 1975–86 with few major exceptions. Part of the increase is due to the movement of workers into relatively high-wage, capital-intensive, large firms in rapidly growing industries. The increase can also be attributed to the impact of new, higher-wage activities on average wages within industries, especially if these displace extremely low-wage workers in traditional sectors. On Java two good examples of this process are the replacement of much of the rural-based mat-weaving and handloom cloth-weaving industries by much more urban-centred, mechanized production of plastic mats and cloth.

Before turning to a more detailed discussion of changing employment conditions in individual sectors, it is important to stress the significance of short-term variations in economic activity for labour market conditions. It is most likely that quite marked short-term (1–3 years) variations in economic activity around the longer-term trend line of rapid economic growth over the past 20 years have been associated with significant changes in key labour market variables—sectoral rates of labour absorption, participation of secondary workers (especially females) in the workforce, unemployment rates, hours worked, and wage rates especially in specific regions or industries. It will become easier to discern these variations through a closer monitoring of standard labour market indicators (adapted to suit local conditions) as the wage-worker share of total employment rises and employment becomes increasingly concentrated in non-agricultural activities in urban areas.[11]

The need to monitor short-term variations in labour market conditions is an issue which is beginning to receive some attention from policy-makers and there has been considerable discussion within government circles of several 'early warning' indicators which may be appropriate to Indonesian conditions. Although the choice of one or even a small number of indicators is not easy in such a fragmented and geographically dispersed labour market, the close monitoring of labour market changes through data from early· warning indicators would appear to be an urgent priority both for policy formulation in the short term and also to enable researchers to separate shorter-term fluctuations from changes occurring over a longer time span.

Rural and Agricultural Employment

The crux of Indonesia's employment and, indeed, development problem has long appeared to be the need to increase the production, and incomes, of the rural Javanese. Central to this issue is the prospect of raising employment and income in agriculture, to be dealt with below. Before turning to that discussion, however, it is necessary to deal first with a popular misconception: the tendency to assume that almost everybody in rural areas is employed in agriculture.

The employment structure of rural areas, especially in Java, has long been complex. Primary industry (agriculture, forestry, hunting, and fishing) is dominant but less so than is commonly believed. Moreover, international experience leads us to expect that over time, the share of primary industries in rural employment will tend to decline (Anderson and Leiserson, 1980) and this expectation is being fulfilled. Table 11.8 shows that the share of non-agricultural activities in rural employment has increased steadily, the main gains being registered in trade, construction, and services. The actual situation is undoubtedly even more complex than the table suggests, because of the prevalence of multiple activities for individuals and households.

The rural–urban distinction itself is becoming much more questionable in Java, not only because of the increasingly diversified employment structure in rural areas, but also owing to the blurring of many rural–urban distinctions. This in turn is due to developments in transportation and communications, the spread of schooling, health, and other facilities previously rarely available in rural areas, and the spread of a much more diverse range of consumer goods over large areas. This is of particular importance in relation to employment, because it means that options facing millions of workers in areas defined as rural include working in local factories, transport, or service industries, commuting daily to work in the city or engaging in 'circular migration' between city and countryside (McGee, 1990).

The macro data problems discussed above have made it especially difficult to interpret trends in employment in the agricultural sector where the large majority of family workers are concentrated. It seems clear that employment in this sector grew quite rapidly in the Outer Islands during the 1970s and especially the 1980s. There is some doubt, however, about trends in Java particularly in the latter period. The judgement that employment growth probably increased on Java in the

TABLE 11.8

Percentage Distribution of Rural Employment by Industry: Indonesia and Java, 1971–1985[a]

Major Industry Group	Rural Indonesia				Rural Java			
	1971	1980	1985	1987	1971	1980	1985	1987
Agriculture, hunting, forestry, and fishing	75.4	71.4	67.4	67.6	71.0	66.7	61.8	61.4
Manufacturing	7.1	6.6	7.8	6.7	8.5	7.9	9.4	8.3
Construction	1.4	2.0	2.7	*	1.4	2.4	3.3	*
Trade, restaurants, and hotels	8.3	9.2	11.1	10.9	10.7	11.5	13.7	13.6
Transport, storage, and communication	1.3	1.6	2.1	*	1.3	1.7	2.5	*
Community, social, and personal services	6.4	8.4	8.0	10.1	7.0	9.1	8.5	11.8
Other	0.1	0.6	0.7	4.7	0.1	0.5	0.6	4.9
Total	100.0	100.0	100.0	100.0	100.0	100.0	100.0	100.0
n ('000)	33,414	41,531	48,975	55,336	21,775	25,540	29,035	31,804

Sources: BPS, Population Census, 1971 and 1980; Intercensal Population Survey (Supas), 1985, Series 5, Table 7: 59 and Table 7.1: 62; Series C (1971), Table 58.6: 32 (1980) and Table 45.6: 248 (1985); National Labour Force Survey (Sakernas), 1987, Tables 12 and 24.

[a] Persons with activities not adequately defined have been allocated to industry groups pro rata.

*Less than 0.5 per cent.

early 1980s is at odds with many of the predictions (mainly based on micro studies conducted in the 1970s)[12] that both limited land availability and technical change in agriculture had already begun to act as a severe constraint to further labour absorption in this sector from around the mid-1970s.

A careful examination of the data from the National Labour Force Surveys and Censuses conducted from 1971 to 1987 nevertheless supports this conclusion. The share of agricultural employment among males and females remained relatively constant for the first half of the 1970s, then dipped quite markedly towards the end of the decade before levelling out at just under 50 per cent in the 1980s (Figure 11.5).[13] These trends are interpreted as follows. Despite the introduction of labour-replacing technology (especially the sickle) in rice agriculture, rapid growth in agricultural output contributed to continued growth in employment in the early 1970s (although it is possible that average hours worked may have declined). This was followed by the economic boom period (whose effects were especially important in 1979–81) in which labour was drawn out of agriculture owing to the growth in employment opportunities in other sectors, and also presumably as a consequence of the expanded transmigration programme in 1979. As shown in Table 11.7, after a long period of stagnation, real agricultural wage rates began to increase in Java over this period.

The boom period was short-lived, however, and it appears that many workers may have responded to the economic slow-down in the early

FIGURE 11.5

Agricultural Employment as a Share of Total Employment in Java,
1977–1987

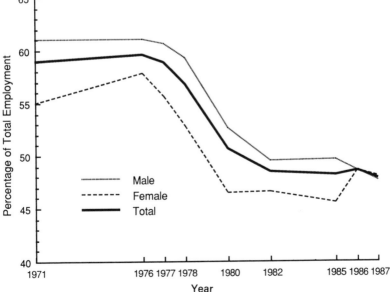

Note: Missing years indicate non-availability of data.

1980s by returning to agriculture as their principal source of employment, especially given the maintenance of relatively rapid growth rates in this sector (and particularly in rice production) through to the middle of the decade. Data on hours worked in agriculture in West and Central Java for 1980 and 1985 (Table 11.9) suggest that this increase in employment was accompanied by a rise in the proportion of underemployed workers (a return to the 'involutionary' patterns of the past?), although these data need to be interpreted with some care given the concentration of those working less than 35 hours among female family workers.[14] Taken at face value, the data imply that one response to more difficult economic circumstances in the early to mid-1980s was an increase in the secondary worker component of the workforce in agriculture on Java (Hasibuan, 1987). Thus the increase in the rural labour force was particularly marked among women and children who worked relatively short hours. Although the data on hours worked by work status are not broken down separately for Java, data from *Sakernas* suggest a sharp increase in the proportion of both male and female family workers working less than 35 hours in 1986 compared with a decade earlier for Indonesia as a whole (Booth and Sundrum, 1989: 88). Their observation that these data reflect 'generally less favourable labour market conditions' in the mid-1980s would seem to apply to Java as well as many Outer Island areas.

Surprisingly, despite slower economic growth from the early 1980s, real agricultural wage rates appear to have continued to increase in Java to the mid-1980s. It has been argued that continued real wage growth in rice agriculture might be explained by strong labour demand in response to continued production growth in this sector to 1985, maintenance of high levels of government spending in rural Java (primarily through the Inpres programmes) through the middle of the decade and a temporary lessening of labour supply pressures in rural Java as a result of the expanded transmigration programme in *Repelita III* (Jayasuriya and Manning, 1990). But the increase in real wages was also clearly related to the sharp decline in the rate of increase in rice prices in 1984–5 associated with the achievement of self-sufficiency.[15]

Because of the data problems it is difficult to draw conclusions on employment trends in Java after 1985. Nevertheless, consistent with some of the other indicators of rural economic activity mentioned above, wage data suggest that rural employment conditions remained relatively depressed. The BPS series suggest that real wage rates declined in both rice and estate agriculture from 1985 to 1988 (Table 11.7). Possible explanations for the timing of this decline are slower output growth in the rice sector from the mid-1980s and the more general impact of tight fiscal and monetary policy on rural labour markets, especially after the slump in oil prices in early 1986 and the subsequent devaluation in September of that year.[16]

What about trends in agricultural employment in the Outer Islands? As noted, there is much less controversy over general trends in agricultural employment outside Java, with most observers agreeing that there

TABLE 11.9

Percentage of Workforce Employed Less than 35 Hours a Week in Main Job by Sector of Activity:
West and Central Java, 1980–1985[a]

| | West Java | | | | Central Java | | | |
| | Agriculture | | Non-agriculture | | Agriculture | | Non-agriculture | |
Gender/ Hours Worked	1980	1985	1980	1985	1980	1985	1980	1985
Male								
1–9	3.9	1.9	2.7	1.3	2.2	2.8	1.3	1.6
10–24	20.1	17.6	9.4	7.1	15.7	20.2	7.6	8.2
25–34	19.7	25.0	8.7	10.7	14.8	21.1	8.6	10.7
Subtotal	43.7	44.5	20.8	19.1	32.7	44.1	17.5	20.5
n ('000)	1,209	1,449	650	739	1,118	1,665	431	621
Female								
1–9	9.9	7.8	5.7	3.8	6.2	8.8	3.0	3.3
10–24	40.8	38.3	20.6	20.8	35.8	42.8	19.9	20.9
25–34	20.2	27.0	12.2	15.3	19.9	21.3	14.0	16.7
Subtotal	70.9	73.1	38.5	39.9	61.9	72.9	36.9	40.9
n ('000)	773	1,098	390	631	984	1,368	695	1,000

Sources: BPS, Unpublished data from Population Census, 1980, Intercensal
Population Survey (Supas), 1985, Series 5.
[a] Excludes all those temporarily not working (recorded as 0 hours).

was probably a marked increase in the rate of labour absorption during the 1980s (Booth, 1989; Booth and Sundrum, 1989). However, the wide range of factors which have contributed to agricultural employment growth in the Outer Islands make it much less easy to generalize about the impact on economic welfare. On the negative side, one would include increased labour supply pressures in agriculture arising from slower non-agricultural sector growth, especially the cut-back in public spending and civil service employment growth which was clearly the most dynamic influence on income generation in many Outer Island areas in the 1970s and early 1980s (Hill, 1989b). Poorer regions (such as West Nusa Tenggara and East Nusa Tenggara) which depend heavily on agriculture for employment—58 and 82 per cent of the workforce in 1985 compared with 55 per cent for Indonesia as a whole—and with limited prospects for productive labour absorption in agriculture have probably been particularly hard hit by such developments.

Transmigration clearly contributed to agricultural labour absorption outside Java (albeit mainly of Javanese) especially during the peak years of the programme in the early 1980s. Income growth has been generally low and quite uneven in many transmigration areas, even after several years of settlement (World Bank, 1988). High levels of poverty and environmental stress in Lampung where agriculture continues to dominate employment (75 per cent of the total in 1985) appears to be the most severe example of 'second stage' problems arising from overcrowding in agriculture primarily as a consequence of transmigration. Also uncertain is the fate of many new settlers moved throughout the archipelago to PIR (Perkebunan Inti Rakyat) schemes which were a central thrust of agricultural development policy in the 1980s but which appear to offer little prospect for significant income generation for the majority of smallholder participants (Barlow and Tomich, 1989).

Much neglected in the discussion of employment—and receiving little assistance from government—but probably of much greater quantitative significance than all the above for employment and income generation has been the growth in smallholder cash cropping in the Outer Islands—in rubber, coffee, cocoa, cloves, tobacco, and other cash crops. Booth (1989: 27–8) estimates that around 19 million new jobs for family workers were created in agriculture in these activities in Indonesia over the period 1971–86, primarily on small farms in the Outer Islands (although many would have been only part-time). She suggests that one major challenge in employment policy is the provision of extension to these millions of 'forgotten farmers' who hold the key to productive labour absorption in agriculture in Indonesia in the coming decades.

Manufacturing Employment

Five important points should be made, by way of introduction, about manufacturing employment in Indonesia. First, although the proportion is gradually increasing, manufacturing employs a much smaller proportion of the labour force in Indonesia than in most of its Asian neighbours (such as Malaysia, Thailand, and Korea). The share is very similar to that in India. Second, manufacturing has been relatively un-important in providing additional employment; it provided 14 per cent of the increase in total employment during the 1970s and less than this during the first half of the 1980s.[17] Third, manufacturing output and employment are disproportionately concentrated in Java. Fourth, the structure of manufacturing employment is quite different from that of the more industrially advanced countries, including some neighbouring countries such as Thailand and Malaysia, with a high proportion of employment in cottage and small-scale industries and only a third in large and medium firms employing 20 or more workers (Hill, 1989a: 6).

Fifth, and related to the previous point, there is an enormous differ-ence in labour productivity between L and M (large and medium) industry and S and C (small and cottage) industry: in the mid-1970s, value added per worker in the former exceeded that in the latter by a factor of more than 20 (Hugo et al., 1987: Table 8.16). The concentra-tion of low-productivity small-scale and cottage industries in Java is reminiscent of the pattern in heavily populated South Asian countries.[18] Considering only medium and large firms, productivity differences are also large between different sectors of manufacturing: for example, value added per employee in basic metals industries is more than five times as high as in electrical equipment or transport equipment and more than ten times as high as in food products or textiles (Hill, 1989a: Table 4). Labour productivity in major Indonesian industries, excluding the cot-tage sector, compares unfavourably with Malaysia and Korea, though it is somewhat ahead of that in India (Hill, 1989a: Table 8).

The high proportion of manufacturing employment in cottage and small-scale industries is an important barrier to rapid rates of growth of manufacturing employment. Even if high rates of growth of employ-ment in larger-scale, modern industry are achieved, the impact will be diluted by the slower growth in the small and cottage sector which still employs the bulk of the manufacturing workforce. Just how slowly small-scale and cottage industry will increase is hard to predict: this sec-tor will do better under an export-oriented strategy, but there is consid-erable potential for labour displacement in small and cottage industries that are in competition with the new firms, e.g. in textiles and clothing (McCawley, 1979).

In discussing trends in manufacturing employment over the 1980s, it is important to distinguish between those in medium- and large-scale industry and those in small-scale and cottage industry. New data from the 1986 Economic Census (Hill, 1989a) provide a firmer base for estimating employment trends in the large, medium, and small industry sectors, which together provide about half of total employment in manu-facturing. Unfortunately, however, there are great difficulties in ana-lysing time trends in employment in cottage industries, largely because they are characterized by a great deal of part-time employment and probably by shifts in reporting of employment between this sector and others such as agriculture.

Total employment in manufacturing almost doubled from 3 million in 1971 to just under 6 million in 1987. As shown in Table 11.10, both in

TABLE 11.10

Indonesia: Employment in Manufacturing Industry, 1971, 1980, 1985, and 1987

	Numbers				Percentage Change		
	1971 (Series C)	1980 (Series S)	1985 (Supas)	1987 (Sakernas)	1971–80	1980–7	1971–87
Total	2,931	4,680	5,796	5,916	60	24	99
Males	1,515	2,584	3,170	3,184	71	23	110
Females	1,416	2,096	2,626	2,634	48	26	86
Urban	661	1,362	1,960	2,092	106	54	217
Rural	2,270	3,318	3,836	3,726	46	12	64
Jakarta	118	285	348	500	142	75	324
Remainder of Java	2,168	3,289	3,723	3,885	52	18	79
Outer Islands	646	1,109	1,725	1,483	72	29	122

Sources: Hugo et al. (1987: Table 6.14); BPS, Intercensal Population Survey (Supas), 1985, Series 5; National Labour Force Survey (Sakernas), 1987.

the 1970s and in the 1980s, manufacturing is increasingly urban, with a decreasing share in Java outside Jakarta. The male share of employment increased during the 1970s, but in the 1980s the female share appears to have grown slightly faster. The traditional, female-dominated cottage industries of Central Java and Yogyakarta are an example of a sector of manufacturing that is not holding its own from an employment point of view.

There has been controversy about trends in large- and medium-scale manufacturing compared with small-scale and cottage industry (Hugo et al., 1987: 275–6). During the 1970s, employment in manufacturing appeared to grow by about 5 per cent per annum, enough to raise manufacturing's share but not dramatically. During the 1980s, manufacturing production has certainly grown rapidly in the L, M, and S sectors, though with an employment–output elasticity of about 0.4 (Hill, 1989a: 11), the effect of this on employment has been more modest, leading to an employment growth rate of above 5 per cent per annum between 1975 and 1986 according to the Industrial Census data. Growth in total manufacturing employment, including the cottage industry sector, has been far from dramatic if the evidence for the period 1980–7 shown in Table 11.10 is to be relied on.

Geographically, growth of factory employment has been reasonably broadly based, though there has been an increasing concentration in Jakarta and surrounding areas of West Java (accounting for a third of total factory output but less of employment) and a declining share elsewhere in Java, offset by an increased share in some Outer Island areas, notably Kalimantan, mainly in wood-based industries. In Java, manufacturing provides a relatively substantial share of total employment (more than 10 per cent) throughout much of Central Java–Yogyakarta. In West and East Java, areas exceeding 10 per cent are mainly found in and near the big cities of Jakarta, Bandung, Cirebon, Surabaya, and Kediri. Outside Java, manufacturing provides a very low share of total employment at the *kabupaten* level throughout most of Sumatra and Kalimantan, whereas it is more important in parts of North and South Sulawesi, Bali, and Nusa Tenggara. In North Sulawesi and Nusa Tenggara, the protection provided by isolation and high transport costs no doubt provides part of the explanation, whereas in Bali textiles and garments have been largely responsible for the growth (Chomitz and Wheeler, 1987).

In interpreting employment trends in manufacturing, the distinction needs to be made between large and medium industries and small and cottage industries. The proportion of manufacturing in large and medium firms tended to be higher in the cities than in the *kabupaten* in Java in 1980, though *kabupaten* located close to some of the large cities (e.g. Jakarta, Bandung, and the Surabaya–Mojokerto–Pasuruan–Probolinggo region) had quite a high share of employment in medium and large industries (Jones, 1984: Figure 10).

Table 11.11 shows the distribution of employment in medium- and large-scale industries (those employing over 20 workers) in Java in 1980.

TABLE 11.11

Distribution of Employment in Large and Medium Manufacturing
by Location: Java, 1980

Province	Kotamadya	Kabupaten Surrounding Kotamadya	Other Kabupaten	Per Cent	Total n ('000)
Jakarta and West Java	59.1	33.1	7.8	100.0	362
Central Java	28.8	8.5	62.8	101.1	197
East Java	44.6	26.2	29.2	100.0	276
All Java	47.1	25.0	27.8	99.9	835

Source: Survey of Large and Medium Industry, 1980, taken from Jones (1984: 114).

Overall, almost half of this employment was in the cities, and one-quarter in the *kabupaten* surrounding the large cities, leaving only just over one-quarter in the remainder of Java. The patterns differ substantially by region. In West Java, only 7 per cent of such employment is found in *kabupaten* located further from the big cities, whereas in Central Java–Yogyakarta almost two-thirds of employment in large and medium firms are found in such *kabupaten*. This appears to reflect the larger number and more even spread of smaller cities in Central Java, and the very high population densities prevailing in most areas, thus ensuring an adequate labour force for firms setting up in 'rural' areas.[19] East Java is intermediate between these two extremes.

The planners in Bappenas (Badan Perencanaan Pembangunan Nasional) have targeted a growth rate of employment in the manufacturing sector of 6.7 per cent per annum over the 1988–93 period, the fastest of any sector and certainly faster than that recorded in the previous two decades. The need for rapid growth in manufacturing is clear and changes in policies and regulations favourable to the growth of manufacturing exports suggest that fairly rapid rates of employment growth in large- and medium-scale manufacturing will be achieved. What is much less certain is whether this will be enough to maintain high rates of employment growth in the sector as a whole, because of the much larger share of employment in rural cottage and small-scale industries.[20] The strong export orientation, which has been accompanied by deflationary policies to ensure international competitiveness in recent years, is likely to hold back domestic demand for industrial products in the short to medium term, which may adversely affect employment in small industries.

The *Repelita* target would therefore seem to be unrealistically high. In any case, as Hill (1989a: 6) appropriately stresses, with little over a 4 per cent share of total Indonesian employment, the factory sector is simply too small to provide more than modest—though increasing—incremental employment absorption in the near future. Even with a 10 per cent growth per annum, it would absorb about 16 per cent of the labour force increment in the 1990–5 period, rising to 26 per cent in the 1995–2000 period.

Trade and Services Employment

Over the past two decades, the service (S) sector (trade, finance, and public services) has played a major role in employment growth. In the 1960s, if the figures are to be trusted, these industries provided three-quarters of all additional employment for males and one-quarter for females. In the 1970s, trade and services provided almost twice as many new jobs as agriculture even in rural areas; in the country as a whole, they provided more than three times as many new jobs as manufacturing. The dominance of trade and services in providing new jobs in the 1970s was especially marked in Java and among females; among females in Java, trade and services provided three-quarters of all new jobs (Hugo et al., 1987: 277).

In the first half of the 1980s, the share of the employment increment absorbed by these sectors fell substantially among males and remained constant among females, the fall being particularly striking in the case of males in services, which accounted for only 9 per cent of the total increase in employment (Table 11.4). This decline is consistent with the slower growth of government expenditure and the limited expansion of the public service. The recorded rise in trade's contribution to 20 per cent of the increment among males and 45 per cent among females was probably exaggerated by the tendency for the 1985 *Supas* to overrecord unpaid family workers (who are strongly represented in trade) in comparison with the 1980 Population Census. An additional difficulty in measuring trends in trade and services employment is that because of overlapping activities of many workers, designation of a person as working in a particular sector is somewhat arbitrary and could lead to comparability problems between data sources. But the prior problem of more or less liberal recording of unpaid family workers is more important; there is no reason to expect major shifts in classifying such workers by industry once they are included in the workforce.

Assuming that these problems of measuring trends in trade and services employment leave a remnant of reality in the figures finally obtained, a more basic problem in interpreting trends in S sector employment still remains. This stems from the extraordinarily wide range of activities, from the lowliest of 'informal sector' activities to banking and finance, that are included within the S sector. Although it is clear that the bulk of employment in trade is towards the low-productivity and non-formal end of the scale, the difference between this and the public services sector, where well-educated workers employed on a formal basis in stable work situations are the norm, is seldom recognized in discussions of 'informal sector' services which stress admittedly colourful activities such as roadside barbering, car 'minding', or prostitution.

It is important to discover whether a move towards greater formality is

TABLE 11.12
Some Characteristics of Workers in Trade and Services, 1971, 1980, 1985, and 1987[a] (percentage)

	Trade				Services[b]		
	1971	1980	1985	1987	1971	1980	1985
Female	44	48	51	52	27	30	33
Completed lower secondary education	8	21	17	22	34	44	56
Employees	15	8	11	9	83	66	77
In professional, managerial, and clerical occupations	2	1	1	n.a.	45	38	48
Working 35–59 hours a week	n.a.	44	46	51	n.a.	57	59

Sources: BPS, 1971 and 1980 Population Censuses; Intercensal Population Survey (Supas), 1985, Series 5; National Labour Force Survey (Sakernas), 1987.

[a]Services include 'finance, real estate, insurance, and business services'.

[b]Details on public services not available for 1987, as they were combined with transportation.

n.a. = Not available.

tending to occur in the trade sector as well—a move hinted at, especially in the urban areas, by the mushrooming of shopping complexes and supermarkets. Despite their visibility, one would not expect a massive shift of employment in trade away from its informal sector and low-productivity roots, given the traditional role of petty trade in absorbing surplus labour and the continuing rapid growth of the labour force. To what extent did the increases in employment in this sector over the 1970s and 1980s merely replicate the pre-existing pattern and to what extent was there a shift in new employment towards modern sector and higher-productivity activities? In considering this question, one needs to keep trade and public services separate.

Employment in public services grew more rapidly than in trade over the 1970s, whereas the reverse was true over the early 1980s. Table 11.12 compares characteristics of workers in trade and services in 1971, 1980, and 1985. Some basic differences are clearly highlighted: workers in trade are more likely to be female, much less likely to be well educated, or to work as employees, or to work in white-collar positions, than those in public services. They are also more likely to work very long hours. There is some untidiness in apparent trends, partly due to the problems of data comparability already referred to. However, a rise is evident since the early 1970s in the average educational levels, as well as in the female proportion, of workers in trade (Manning, 1989).

In public services, a rise in the female share and in the educational level is also apparent. S sector jobs in rural areas provided a large proportion of the additional employment generated in rural areas during the 1970s. In 1980, of all workers in rural areas with a lower secondary school education and above, 46 per cent were in public and community services alone, and 56 per cent were in the S sector as a whole. Nearly 40 per cent of the workforce in services in rural areas were professional, managerial, or clerical workers, most of them presumably government employees, reflecting the large investments in education and rural health facilities. By 1985, public services, which provided only 8 per cent of total employment in rural areas, were providing 65 per cent of all rural employment of those with a senior high school or tertiary education.

The important point to stress about employment in public services is that its rapid growth during the 1970s represented an important aspect of expansion of higher-productivity employment over that decade (see Hugo et al., 1987: 277–81), and its failure to grow much during the 1980s reflects the difficulty the Indonesian economy has faced in providing suitable employment for an increasingly well-educated labour force. The greater role apparently played by trade than by services in employment growth during the 1980s signifies a failure of the S sector as a whole to play the more dynamic role in providing employment for the better-educated that it performed during the 1970s.

Unemployment and Underemployment

It might be expected that open unemployment rates would have risen significantly in the 1980s, given the low rate of labour absorption in non-agriculture and services in particular, the remarkable growth of enrolments at secondary and tertiary levels, and the increasing prominence of urban wage employment and associated 'formal sector' labour market structures. Surprisingly, the data show no general upward trend in open unemployment rates although certain groups in the work-force—educated females in particular—registered significantly higher rates in the mid-1980s than a decade earlier. In part, in the context of labour-surplus, agrarian economies like Indonesia, this can be attributed to major shortcomings in the concept and definition of work (especially the 'labour force' approach to defining the workforce) that have been applied in national censuses and labour force surveys.[21] Thus, for example, these sources show rural unemployment rates as fluctuating around 1 to 2 per cent with no clear time trend over the past 20 years.

Even in urban areas, however, there has not been a major change in the overall structure of unemployment nor any marked upward movement in unemployment rates—crude rates for males actually declined slightly from 6.8 per cent in 1976–8 to 6.3 per cent in 1985–7 (Manning, 1989: Table 2). Thus as Table 11.13 suggests, open unemployment rates in urban areas were highest among young secondary school-leavers aged 15–24; they fell very sharply among those aged 25–29 (but were quite high at the tertiary level in this age group). Among those aged 30 and above, unemployment rates were very low for all educational levels in 1976, 1982, and 1986 (not shown in the table). The urban unemployed were dominated by first job seekers (over 75 per cent in the mid-1980s) and a high proportion of those actively looking for work reported durations of job search of less than 6 months (close to 60 per cent in 1986).

Nevertheless, urban unemployment data lend support to other indicators which suggest that the employment situation had worsened especially among females and young, upper secondary-educated in the mid-1980s compared with ten years earlier. Unemployment rates among senior high graduates aged 20–24 from academic (non-vocational) schools had risen to 42 and 50 per cent for males and females respectively (see Table 11.13) and this group accounted for over 25 per cent of all urban job seekers in 1986. Unemployment rose quite substantially among young, educated females and total female unemployment rates were reported to have risen from around 5 per cent in 1976 to 8 per cent in 1986. Unemployment rates appear to have also risen quite steeply (to close to 30 per cent among those aged 25–29 in 1986) among young tertiary graduates in the 1980s. The latter undoubtedly reflects the substantial increase in supply relative to demand for tertiary-educated manpower especially in government jobs. It is probably also an indication of the variable quality of graduates associated with the proliferation of private universities and academies over the past ten years.

TABLE 11.13
Unemployment Rates by Age and Education: Urban Indonesia,
1976, 1982, and 1986

Age/Educational Category	Males			Females		
	1976	1982	1986[a]	1976	1982	1986[a]
15–19						
< Primary	22.3	11.4	10.2	6.5	7.1	5.0
Primary	26.2	20.3	16.1	7.5	10.2	11.4
Lower Secondary	32.3	24.2	20.3	25.9	19.9	21.6
All 15–19	26.3	20.4	21.2	9.9	12.9	16.6
20–24						
< Primary	11.5	9.9	8.1	3.0	4.1	4.3
Primary	13.9	9.3	12.2	8.3	10.0	6.1
Lower Secondary	19.5	16.7	20.3	20.7	22.5	24.9
Upper Secondary:						
Academic	32.2	37.1	41.5	33.4	38.0	50.2
Vocational	27.6	25.1	35.1	21.9	32.9	25.5
All 20–24	18.2	17.6	26.1	14.4	18.8	24.4
25–29						
< Primary	3.0	3.2	5.5	2.0	3.3	2.0
Primary	4.7	3.4	3.6	3.4	5.9	2.0
Lower Secondary	7.8	4.6	5.2	10.9	4.2	11.9
Upper Secondary:						
Academic	8.4	7.2	8.7	5.9	11.8	13.9
Vocational	5.8	7.2	11.3	9.1	6.7	8.5
Tertiary	7.4	9.4	19.6	13.6	30.5(?)	15.6
All 25–29	5.8	4.9	7.1	5.5	6.9	7.0
All Ages 15–64						
< Primary	5.1	3.1	2.5	1.7	2.2	1.8
Primary	7.1	4.5	4.2	5.5	5.9	4.5
Lower Secondary	8.0	5.9	6.4	11.3	9.2	11.2
Upper Secondary:						
Academic	9.7	9.3	14.8	18.6	22.5	31.0
Vocational	10.6	10.3	11.8	12.1	6.1	11.7
Tertiary	1.9	3.9	6.9	9.3	11.5	14.4
Total	6.9	5.5	6.9	5.1	6.5	8.1

Sources: BPS, National Labour Force Survey (*Sakernas*), 1976; National Socio-economic
Survey (*Susenas*), 1982; National Labour Force Survey (*Sakernas*), 1986. See Manning
(1989: Table 3).
[a] Diploma I and II graduates included in the upper secondary vocational school group.

The duration of unemployment also seems to have lengthened, with close to 20 per cent of all job seekers reporting a period of job search of over one year in 1986 compared with 12 per cent in 1978 (Booth and Sundrum, 1989: 77). Finally, as noted above, the discouraged worker component of the young-aged population—many of whom were persons classified as 'other' outside the workforce—may have risen quite substantially, especially among females in the decade 1977–87 (Manning, 1989: Table 4).

The government has anticipated these problems—indeed fear of the politically destabilizing effects of unemployed, educated youth has been a major preoccupation for a number of years—and has initiated several programmes to assist unemployed persons. Provision of job opportunity information through provincial labour exchanges and substantial investment in vocational training centres (including mobile units) have been two programmes given increasing emphasis since the early 1980s (World Bank, 1985). Quite a high proportion of young people seeking work in urban areas reported registration in labour exchanges (around 35 per cent of all male and female job seekers and a slightly higher proportion of younger people) as one of their major job-search activities in 1987. Nevertheless the low ratio of vacancies to job seekers registered (below 5 per cent in the mid-1980s) and the continued importance of family and other contacts (koneksi) in successful job-search activities in the modern sector suggest that labour exchanges will continue to play a relatively minor role in assisting job placement of unemployed youth in the future.

As noted in the discussion of agricultural employment, overall levels of underemployment also appear to have risen during the 1980s. It is difficult to give much credence to these figures, however, especially given the much better coverage of unpaid family workers (who tend to work much shorter hours than other employment status groups) in more recent National Labour Force Surveys. Given the large discrepancy in hours worked recorded by village studies and national surveys—the former reporting relatively low levels of underemployment especially among the poor—and the seasonal nature of much agricultural work, a clearer picture of overall levels of underemployment and their impact on welfare can be obtained only through careful micro-level research on earnings, labour inputs, and productivity in specific sectors and regions.

Educational Developments and Occupational Change

Although a great deal remains to be done, the 1970s and 1980s have seen remarkable progress in Indonesian education. Figure 11.6 shows a range of indicators of educational progress, including literacy rates, current school enrolment rates, and educational attainment. Basically, universal primary school education has been achieved, although problems of early drop-out still remain. The Fifth Five-Year Development Plan aims for a rise in the lower secondary school enrolment rate from 53 per cent in 1988 to 67 per cent in 1993.

FIGURE 11.6
Indicators of Educational Progress, 1971–1985

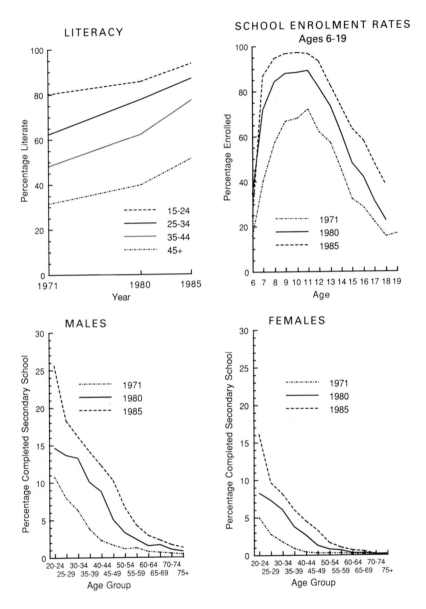

These trends have led to rapid improvement in the educational attainment of the labour force, as Table 11.2 showed. Younger cohorts in the
labour force have much higher educational attainment than older
cohorts (see Figure 11.1). But the better-educated workers have
continued to be heavily concentrated in certain occupational groups—
notably in professional, managerial, and clerical occupations. In 1985,
these three occupational groups provided 48 per cent of all employment

for workers with upper secondary education, 54 per cent for those with vocational high school education and 89 per cent for those with tertiary education. Moreover, the high school and college-educated constituted 87 per cent of all persons employed in these occupations. By contrast, only 5 per cent of farmers had secondary school education or better, although the proportion of farmers with completed primary school education was 31 per cent in 1985, up from 21 per cent in 1971.

The rapid growth in the number of better-educated labour force entrants has led to concern about rising levels of educated unemployment as the economy has not grown rapidly enough to provide enough suitable job opportunities to absorb them all.

The 1990s and Beyond

During the 1990s, many of the trends apparent in the 1980s are expected to continue: for example, a continuing rapid growth in the labour force, and a fall in agriculture's share and in Java's share of total employment. The Fifth Plan period will see considerable strain in the labour market, and uncertainty as to whether modern sector employment opportunities will increase rapidly enough to absorb the growing labour force, especially the younger, better-educated workers.

It would be quite incorrect, however, to think of the 1990s as merely bringing 'more of the same'. There will be some sharp discontinuities which will call for fresh policy initiatives. One fundamental change will be the slackening of labour force growth, especially after the Fifth Plan period, due to the fertility declines in the 1970s and 1980s. Young labour force entrants will cease to grow at all by the mid-1990s. The slackening, but still quite rapid, labour force growth thereafter will result from continued growth in the middle- and older-age groups of the labour force. This also means that the labour force will age markedly. Between 1995 and 2010, the number of young potential workers (aged 15–29) will grow by less than 10 per cent, compared with a 56 per cent growth in numbers aged 40–64. The share of the working-age population aged 40 and over will rise from 31 per cent in 1995 to 36 per cent in the year 2010, and the share of those aged 55 and over will rise from 10 per cent to 13 per cent over the same period. The actual extent of ageing of the workforce may be much influenced by retirement policies and developments in pension and superannuation schemes.

The growth of the young segments of the workforce could be further slowed by young people staying on longer in educational institutions, though this could be offset by a rising participation rate for young females. Other things being equal, the falling share of the poorly educated, and the rising share expected in the junior high school-educated section of the working-age female population would make for a fall in female participation rates, because of the differential labour force participation of these groups already discussed.[22] Other things, however, are seldom equal, and the trend towards mass education at the secondary level will no doubt mean that the motivations of those receiving school-ing at this level in future will differ from those of the select group who previously attended secondary school (Jones, 1986).

Indonesia is approaching the point at which only half of all employ-ment is in the agricultural sector. When this point was reached in some countries (e.g. Korea, Taiwan, and Malaysia), further sharp declines in agriculture's share, and indeed a decline in the absolute size of the agri-cultural workforce, took place. Comparable trends in Indonesia would lower agriculture's share of employment to 30 per cent as early as the year 2000 or 2005. Whether declines even approaching this magnitude can be reached will depend on many factors, not least the advantage taken of the considerable opportunities to increase labour productivity and employment in agriculture. But the shift in employment's 'centre of gravity' towards non-agriculture will certainly be facilitated by the decel-eration in the rate of growth in the labour force beginning in the 1990s.

A continued trend towards greater diversification of the rural employ-ment structure can be expected, with a further 'blurring' of urban–rural distinctions, particularly in regions surrounding the larger cities. This trend will be fostered by rising levels of education of young people in these areas, which will provide a labour force more attractive to potential investors.

Not all regions will grow at the same pace. The growth of natural resource-based export industries will boost development in some areas outside Java, and the growth of substantial markets in some areas (e.g. Sumatra's climb towards a population of 50 million by the year 2000) will encourage consumer goods industries. But Java's advantages of market and infrastructure will remain. Within Java, there are signs that the higher wages and diseconomies of agglomeration in the Jakarta region may be beginning to push industrial development in the Surabaya direction.

The educational developments of the 1970s and 1980s, together with those expected in the Fifth Plan period and beyond, will result in very sharp increases in the well-educated groups within the labour force (Keyfitz, 1989; Jones, 1989). In one set of projections, the rate of growth of the number of 'potential workers' (aged 20–64) with senior high school education will be 7.5 per cent per annum over the 1985–95 period and 6.5 per cent per annum over the 1995–2000 period. The rate of increase of the tertiary educated would be even faster—13.6 per cent and 10.5 per cent, respectively (Jones, 1989: Table 6).

The growth of job opportunities in occupations traditionally filled by the better-educated, in particular those in professional, administrative, managerial, and clerical fields, is likely to be more rapid than employ-ment growth as a whole, for two reasons: first, a shift in the industrial structure towards industries tending to employ a higher proportion of workers in these occupations; and second, a shift towards a higher pro-portion of professional, managerial, and clerical workers within indus-tries (Jones, 1989). Moreover, the increased supply of better-educated workers will no doubt in itself, through adjustments in wage differentials, encourage structural changes in favour of sectors which utilize such manpower. Nevertheless, in the short to medium term the rapid growth in the number of better-educated is certain to outstrip the growth of professional, managerial, and clerical jobs, many of which are in the now-slowly-growing public sector. Drastic changes in expectations will therefore be required as the 'scarcity rent' enjoyed until recently by the better-educated disappears, and many are forced to take jobs previously considered inappropriate for the better-educated, or to adjust to narrowed earnings differentials.

1. The 1977 *Sakernas* also failed to cover the whole country: in NTT it covered only *kabupaten* Kupang, in Maluku only Kotamadya Ambon, and in Irian Jaya only urban areas of *kabupaten* Jayapura. The omitted regions amounted to about 3.3 per cent of the total population, so their omission should not greatly distort comparisons with other data sources. However, it should be borne in mind that they would contain a disproportionate rural and agricultural population.

2. This paralleled a fall in the share of Central and East Java in Indonesia's total population, to a level even lower than that of the labour force (37 per cent in 1985). The reason for the higher share of Central and East Java in Indonesia's labour force than in its population is its higher female labour force participation rates.

3. In the 1977 *Sakernas*, the working population was defined as those who worked at least one hour a day during the reference week. In 1987, the *Sakernas* report at one point gives the same definition (p. xi); in two other places, however (pp. x and xviii), one hour of work during the reference week is stated to be the cut-off. If there was indeed a difference, it does not appear to have had much effect on the measurement of the labour force; the proportion of those working who worked between one and nine hours varied only between 2.5 per cent in 1977 and 3.2 per cent in 1987. These figures are much closer than those for the proportion of the workforce who worked zero hours because they were temporarily not working: 5.8 per cent in 1977 and 1.5 per cent in 1987.

4. These problems are discussed in the Appendix. See especially Jones (1981); Bakir and Manning (1983); Nagib and Jones (1987); Hugo et al. (1987); Korns (1987); and Booth and Sundrum (1989) for an examination of some of the methodological issues. Of primary importance is the problem of a widely fluctuating share of family workers (who are heavily concentrated in agriculture) and a marked tendency for this share to rise more recently. Korns' proposal that analysis of trends over time should be restricted to earning workers (total employment minus family workers) is helpful but does not entirely solve the problem. Besides higher or lower recording of the share of family workers in different surveys, it is clear that there is a tendency for enumeration of individuals in various work status groups to differ between surveys either due to subtle definitional changes, or to different interpretation of definitions in the field.

5. Initially it was hoped that it may be possible to compare trends for three periods (1971–7, 1977–82, and 1982–7) which would facilitate relating employment trends to general economic developments. But the data suggest quite implausible trends—even if the analysis is restricted to 'earnings' workers, and especially if one disaggregates by sex and island group (Java/Outer Islands).

6. The A sector includes agriculture, forestry, hunting and fishing, and mining and quarrying; the M sector, manufacturing, construction, utilities, and transport; and the S sector, trade, finance, and services.

7. See especially Hugo et al. (1987).

8. More extensive coverage of the family worker group among males as well as females in 1985 has probably contributed to a slight overstatement of the trend in male employment in agriculture in the period 1980–5 (Nagib and Jones, 1987).

9. Our estimates of female employment growth suggest, on the other hand, that service sector employment growth remained strong in the 1980s, a development which may be explained by the important role which females have played in the expanding areas of teaching and health care which suffered major shortages of skilled labour in the early 1980s. The 1985 *Supas* data record the service sector as accounting for almost 40 per cent of total wage employment in Indonesia.

10. See especially Makali and Sri Hartoyo (1978); Lluch and Mazumdar (1985); Mazumdar and Sawit (1986); Manning (1988a); Jayasuriya and Manning (1988 and 1990); Hill (1989a); and Naylor (1990).

11. Hitherto attention in Indonesia has been focused on longer-term labour market changes mainly through point-to-point comparisons. Given data problems which are inevitably associated with particular national surveys and short-term fluctuations in labour market conditions which are likely to be reflected in the results of individual surveys, it seems clear that analysis of longer terms trends should increasingly depend on a careful analysis of time trends revealed by all comparable sources, e.g. National Labour Force Surveys (see Sigit, 1988).

12. See especially, village surveys conducted by the Rural Dynamics Study of the Agro-economic Survey, Bogor, discussed in Manning (1988b); see also White (1979) and Collier (1981) for surveys of village studies.

13. Given some of the data problems discussed in the Appendix, one cannot draw firm conclusions based on trends in the female share, especially the apparent increase from 1985.

14. The increase in the proportion of the agricultural labour force on Java working short hours in 1985 compared with 1980 is primarily related to the much higher share of female family workers recorded in agriculture in 1985 (i.e. it is partly the result of much more intensive enumeration of this category of worker in 1985). Also it should be noted that not all those working less than 35 hours are underemployed in the sense of having their work restricted involuntarily; according to *Sakernas* 1976 and *Susenas* 1982, a high proportion (over 80 per cent) of females working short hours were part-time workers who did not want additional work.

15. Nominal wage growth appears to have been relatively constant throughout the period and the sharpest rise in real wages occurred in 1985 when the rural 9 commodity price index actually declined slightly in Java.

16. These findings of a wage slow-down are also supported by the Bogor Center for Agricultural Research *Patanas* study of wages in East Java (Swenson and Rasahan, 1986). The sharp decline in estate wages was probably partly influenced by the freeze on public sector wages in 1985–8 since only state-owned estates are covered by the BPS data and they refer to permanent (rather than casual) labourers in harvesting, sorting, and processing.

17. According to *Sakernas* data, manufacturing provided only 7.5 per cent of the increase in total employment during the 1977–87 period. Comparison of the 1980 Census with the 1985 *Supas* indicates a 10 per cent share of the increase over that period, although this increase may be somewhat understated by the tendency for the increase in agricultural employment to be exaggerated.

18. This point is reinforced by the data on hours worked. Among the large rural female component of the manufacturing workforce in 1980, 34 per cent worked less than 25 hours a week.

19. One partial explanation for the Central Java pattern is the location of a number of cities in the 100,000 to 150,000 range in this region, falling below the cut-off size for large cities used in the table. But even when one recalculates the table, lowering the 'threshold' size of large cities to 100,000, the share of large and medium manufacturing employment in the *kabupaten* of Central Java/Yogyakarta that are not close to large cities only falls from 62 per cent to 54 per cent (Jones et al., 1984: 95).

20. The Asian NIEs are the only countries to have ever achieved sustained rates of growth in manufacturing employment similar to those projected in *Repelita V*, and all these countries differed from Indonesia at the time they started their take-off in having a much smaller proportion of labour in low-productivity manufacturing jobs.

21. See Godfrey (1987) for a discussion of these issues in the Indonesian context.

22. The rising proportion in the group with tertiary education, whose participation rates match or equal those of the uneducated, will not be large enough to offset the overall tendency towards falling participation rates.

APPENDIX

Data Sources and Problems of Estimating
Recent Labour Force and Employment Growth
in Indonesia

Given quite large differences in estimated growth rates depending on data sources used, it is necessary to provide a brief clarification of some of the difficulties encountered in attempting to calculate recent trends in labour force and employment. Hugo et al. (1987: Appendix 2) discuss some of the problems which emerge from comparisons of the 1961, 1971, and 1980 Censuses, 1976 *Supas*, and 1976–8 *Sakernas* data. This section will concentrate on the data collected in the 1980s and implied changes in the growth and structure of the labour force compared with the previous decade.[1]

Two key problems are encountered in attempting to derive a set of estimates of labour force and employment growth rates in the 1980s. The first is the increasing share of unpaid family workers and associated higher labour force participation rates and implied growth rates, primarily among females, recorded in the 1986 and 1987 *Sakernas* surveys. The second is the very low share of this same group of workers, and consequently very much lower female labour force participation rates, reported in the 1980 Census compared with the 1985 *Supas* and all other data sources for the 1970s and 1980s except the 1971 Census (Table 11.A1). The data show markedly lower female labour force participation rates in 1980 (33 per cent) compared with those recorded in 1976–85 (36–40 per cent) and the much higher rates of 44–45 per cent recorded in 1986 and 1987. Female activity rates appear to be closely correlated with the recorded share of unpaid family workers, especially in the agricultural sector, and the share of total female employment in the agricultural sector.[2]

Two solutions have been proposed to overcome these difficulties. The first is to compute the growth of the labour force and employment for 'earning' workers only: these cover all employment status groups except family workers (Korns, 1987). The second is to bypass the 1980 Census data and estimate trends in the 1970s and 1980s based on the *Sakernas* data. Both approaches have their difficulties, however. Reliance on earning workers as a basis for estimating labour force growth encounters the problem that the fluctuating share of female family workers is not merely a consequence of better coverage of the employed population in some surveys than others. It also appears to be related to different treatment of status groups in various surveys. Thus, for example, a comparison of the 1980 Census and 1985 *Supas* data indicates that the higher share of family workers in 1985 was almost entirely compensated by a declining share of self-employed workers (Manning, 1989); both categories combined, as well as employees, were recorded as growing much more rapidly (implausibly so) in the period 1980–5 compared with 1971–80.[3]

Some authors (e.g. Booth and Sundrum, 1989) have used earning workers to estimate employment growth 1971–85. Overall employment growth rates produced by this approach for the periods 1971–80 and 1980–5 are quite unstable, however, especially among females (Table 11.A2). Whereas the data show very

TABLE 11.A1

Female Labour Force, Unpaid Family Workers, and Agricultural Employment: Indonesia, 1971–1987

Year	Source	Population Aged 10+ (m.)	Labour Force (m.)	Labour Force Participation Rate	UPFW[a] as Percentage of Employment			Agriculture as Percentage of Employment	
					Total	Agriculture	Non-agriculture	Total	Java
1971	Census (C)[b]	41.4	13.3	32.1	39.2	50.7	18.2	64.7	54.7
	(D)[b]	41.3	13.7	33.1	38.9	52.1	16.9	65.4	58.8
1976	Sakernas	45.0	16.6	36.8	43.5	n.a.	n.a.	59.6	57.5
1977	Sakernas	46.8	16.6	35.5	41.5	58.1	17.5	59.2	55.5
1978	Sakernas	48.3	19.2	39.8	32.9	47.4	13.2	57.7	52.8
1980	Census	53.0	17.3	32.7	29.6	41.5	15.7	53.8	46.1
1982	Susenas	56.2	21.5	38.3	41.4	60.0	19.7	53.8	46.6
1985	Supas	61.1	23.0	37.6	42.5	62.3	19.4	53.6	45.4
1986	Sakernas	62.2	27.6	44.5	49.9	70.0	24.5	55.7	48.4
1987	Sakernas	63.8	28.6	44.8	50.5	71.8	23.8	55.7	48.0

Sources: BPS, Population Census, 1971 and 1980; *Sakernas*, 1976–8 and 1986–7; *Susenas*,
1982; *Supas*, 1985.
[a]UPFW = Unpaid Family Workers.
[b] Series C and Series D.
n.a. = Not available.

TABLE 11.A2
Reported Employment Growth Rates by Work Status Groups:
Indonesia, 1971–1985[a]

	Males		Females	
	1971–80	1980–5	1971–80	1980–5
Earnings workers	4.2	2.8	5.7	1.8
Family workers	− 1.3	2.7	− 0.2	12.8
All workers	3.0	2.9	2.9	5.6

Sources: BPS, 1971 and 1980 Population Census, 1971 and 1980 (Series C and S2); *Supas*, 1985.
[a]'Not Stated' redistributed on a pro rata basis.

much higher growth rates (5.6 per cent per annum) for 1980–5 compared with the 1970s for all female workers, growth in earning workers shows the opposite trend: very much higher growth rates in 1971–80 than in the subsequent five years (5.7 compared with 1.8 per cent per annum). One major implication from growth rates of all workers 1971–80 and 1980–5 is the marked increase in labour absorption in agriculture in the latter period (again especially among females). The opposite conclusion holds for apparent trends indicated by the data on earning workers; these suggest that agricultural labour absorption was quite rapid in 1971–80 even in Java but much slower (and indeed negative among females in Java) in the period 1980–5. Clearly, quite different policy implications emerge from these contrasting patterns of employment growth.

The authors have some sympathy with the view that the 1980 Census must be treated as an outlier; the apparent underreporting of family workers poses a problem for comparison with *Supas* and *Sakernas* data. But the 1980 and 1971 Census data on participation rates and employment appear to be broadly comparable whereas both of them differ in some important ways from the national survey data (Bakir and Manning, 1983; Hugo et al., 1987). Because the censuses and *Supas* alone provide cross-tabulations of data broken down by province, the strategy in this chapter has been therefore to adjust the 1985 *Supas* data to reflect rates of labour force growth for the period 1980–5 which might be considered broadly consistent with those observed from the intercensal comparison of the 1970s.

There is an additional reason for not basing the estimates here on the *Sakernas* data. Owing to the small sampling fraction, reported growth rates by sex, industry, and major island group may be quite unstable from survey to survey. Table 11.A3 provides an example. Data on employment growth rates for males by sector in Java for the ten-year period 1977–87 are compared with the census and *Supas* data reported in Table 11.5. The two series show contrasting trends and the 1977–87 *Sakernas* data some surprising, rather implausible, turnabouts.

Thus the authors have opted for the 1971–80 and 1980–5 comparison. For males the recorded growth rates seem quite plausible, although there may be some overstatement of agricultural sector employment growth because of the more careful enumeration of family workers in 1985. As noted in Table 11.6, the 1985 data by sector for females are obtained by applying observed growth rates for total employment 1977–85 to recorded employment in 1980 for earnings workers and family workers separately to derive total employment in 1985.[4]

TABLE 11.A3
Recorded Growth Rates in Male Employment by Sector: Java,
1971–1985 and 1977–1987

Sector of Activity	1971–80	1980–5	1977–82	1982–7
Agriculture	1.0	1.1	− 1.9	1.1
Manufacturing	5.2	4.3	8.2	1.4
Construction	9.3	4.5	17.6	n.a.[a]
Trade	3.8	5.3	4.9	2.5
Transport	5.1	6.5	6.0 }	3.9
Services	6.0	1.3	4.7 }	
All sectors[b]	2.9	2.5	2.1	1.9

Sources: BPS, Population Census, 1971 (Series C) and 1980; *Susenas*, 1982; *Sakernas*, 1977 and 1987.
[a]No separate breakdown in 1987.
[b]Includes mining and public utilities (and construction in 1982–7).

Each group was then distributed according to shares in employment by sector and region recorded in 1985 to obtain an estimate of the absolute numbers of females in each sector in that year.

1. In doing this the authors wish to emphasize that the Biro Pusat Statistik has provided a rich collection of data on labour force which, if used with care, throws light on many important dimensions of the employment problem in Indonesia. As in many developing countries, labour force and employment data are notoriously difficult to collect and interpret at a national level. Inevitable shortcomings in definitions, undercoverage of certain groups of workers, and the play of seasonal factors and short-term shifts in labour demand all make it extremely difficult to derive a consistent set of data on medium- and longer-term trends from national censuses and labour force surveys.

2. The one exception is 1978 when female activity rates rose but the share of family workers was quite low.

3. This is not the case in the 1986 and 1987 *Sakernas*, however, where a considerable part of total employment growth appears to be due to the much better coverage of female family workers.

4. Separate estimation of family workers and earnings workers by sector is essential since a high proportion of the former were concentrated in agriculture in 1985; reliance on an estimated growth rate for all workers as a basis for calculating employment in 1985 results in continuing implausibly high rates of employment growth in agriculture compared with other sectors.

REFERENCES

Anderson, D. and Leiserson, M. W. (1980), 'Rural Non-farm Employment in Developing Countries', *Economic Development and Cultural Change*, 28(2), 227–48.

Bakir, Zainab and Manning, Chris (eds.) (1983), *Partisipasi Angkatan Kerja, Kesempatan Kerja dan Pengangguran di Indonesia*, Yogyakarta: Pusat Penelitian dan Studi Kependudukan, Universitas Gadjah Mada.

Barlow, Colin and Tomich, T. (1989), 'Developments in Plantation Agriculture and Small Holder Cash Crop Production', Paper presented at the Conference on Indonesia's New Order, Australian National University, Canberra, 4–9 December.

Booth, Anne (1989), 'Angkatan Kerja Pertanian', *Prisma*, 18(5), 15–28.

Booth, Anne and Sundrum, R.M. (1989), *Employment Trends and Policy Issues for Repelita V*, Jakarta: ILO.

Bukit, Dollar and Bakir, Zainab (1984), 'Partisipasi Angkatan Kerja Indonesia: Hasil Sensus 1971 dan 1980', in Zainab Bakir and Chris Manning (eds.), *Partisipasi Angkatan Kerja, Kesempatan Kerja dan Pengangguran di Indonesia*, Jakarta: Rajawali, pp. 29–78.

Chomitz, Kenneth and Wheeler, David (1987), *The Boom on Bali: Implications for Research and Policy*, Development Studies Programme Research Memo No. 6, Jakarta.

Collier, William L. (1981), 'Agricultural Evolution in Java', in Gary E. Hansen (ed.), *Agricultural and Rural Development in Indonesia*, Boulder: Westview Press, pp. 147–78.

Cremer, Georg (1990), 'Who Are Those Misclassified as Others? A Note on Indonesian Labour Force Statistics', *Bulletin of Indonesian Economic Studies*, 26(1), 69–90.

Gardiner, Peter (1989), 'Population Prospects in Indonesia: Size, Structure and Distribution', Paper presented at the Conference on Indonesia's New Order, Australian National University, Canberra, 4–9 December.

Godfrey, Martin (1987), *Planning for Education Training and Employment Summary Report*, Jakarta: Department of Manpower–ILO, March.

Hasibuan, Sayuti (1987), 'Labour Force Growth, Structural Change and Labour Absorption in the Indonesian Economy', Unpublished paper, Jakarta.

Hill, Hal (1989a), 'Indonesia's Industrial Transformation', Paper presented at the Conference on Indonesia's New Order, Australian National University, Canberra, 4–9 December.

_____ (1989b), 'Regional Development in Indonesia: Patterns and Issues', in Hal Hill (ed.), *Unity and Diversity: Regional Economic Development in Indonesia since 1970*, Singapore: Oxford University Press, pp. 3–54.

Hugo, Graeme (1978), *Population Mobility in West Java*, Yogyakarta: Gadjah Mada University Press.

Hugo, Graeme; Hull, Terence H.; Hull, Valerie J.; and Jones, Gavin W. (1987), *The Demographic Dimension in Indonesian Development*, Singapore: Oxford University Press.

Jayasuriya, Sisira and Manning, Chris (1988), 'Survey of Recent Economic Developments', *Bulletin of Indonesian Economic Studies*, 24(2): 3–42.

_____ (1990), 'Agricultural Wage Growth and Rural Labour Market Adjustment: The Case of Java, 1970–1989', Unpublished paper, Flinders University.

Jones, Gavin (1974), 'What Do We Know about the Labour Force in Indonesia?', *Majalah Demografi Indonesia*, 2(Tahun ke-I): 7–36.

____ (1981), 'Labour Force Developments since 1961', in Anne Booth and Peter McCawley (eds.), *The Indonesian Economy during the Soeharto Era*, Kuala Lumpur: Oxford University Press, pp. 218–61.

____ (1984), 'Links between Urbanization and Sectoral Shifts in Employment in Java', *Bulletin of Economic Studies*, 20(3): 120–57.

____ (1986), 'Differentials in Female Labour Force Participation Rates in Indonesia: Reflection of Economic Needs and Opportunities, Culture or Bad Data?' *Majalah Demografi Indonesia*, 26 (Tahun ke-XIII): 1–28.

____ (1987), *The 1985 Intercensal Survey of Indonesia: 5. The Labour Force*, International Population Dynamics Project, Research Note No. 78, Canberra: Department of Demography, Australian National University.

____ (1989), 'Dilemmas in Expanding Education for Faster Economic Growth: Indonesia, Malaysia and Thailand', Paper presented at the Nihon University International Symposium on the Sources of Economic Dynamism in the Asian and Pacific Region: A Human Resource Approach, Nihon University, Tokyo.

Jones, Gavin; Nurhidayati; Simandjuntak, Fritz; and Prakosa, Djaka (1984), *Urbanization and Structural Change in Employment in Indonesia: Evidence from Province and Kabupaten Level Analysis of 1971–1980 Census Data*, Report T 1.4/C2, National Urban Development Strategy Project Directorate of City and Regional Planning, Jakarta: Department of Public Works.

Keyfitz, Nathan (1989), 'Putting Trained Labour Power to Work: The Dilemma of Education and Employment', *Bulletin of Indonesian Economic Studies*, 25(3): 35–55.

Korns, Alex (1987), *Distinguishing Signal from Noise in Labour Force Data for Indonesia*, Development Studies Programme Research Paper No. 1, Jakarta.

Lluch, Constantino and Mazumdar, Dipak (1985), *Wages and Employment in Indonesia*, Washington, DC: World Bank.

Makali and Sri Hartoyo (1978), 'Perkembangan Tingkat Upah adan Kesempatan Kerja Buruh Tani di Pedesaan Jawa', *PRISMA*, 7(3): 33–45.

McCawley, Peter (1979), *Industrialization in Indonesia: Developments and Prospects*, Development Studies Centre, Occasional Paper No. 13, Canberra: Australian National University.

McGee, T. G. (1990), 'The Emergence of *Desakota* Regions in Asia: Expanding a Hypothesis', in Norton Ginsberg, Bruce Koppell, and T. G. McGee (eds.), *The Extended Metropolis in Asia*, Honolulu: University of Hawaii Press.

Manning, Chris (1988a), 'Rural Employment Creation in Java: Lessons from the Green Revolution and Oil Boom', *Population and Development Review*, 14(1): 47–80.

____ (1988b), *The Green Revolution, Employment and Economic Change: A Reassessment of Trends Under the New Order*, Occasional Paper No. 84, Singapore: Institute of Southeast Asian Studies.

____ (1989), 'Employment Trends in Indonesia in the 1970s and 1980s', Paper presented at the Conference on Indonesia's New Order, Australian National University, Canberra, 4–9 December.

Mazumdar, Dipak and Sawit, M. Husein (1986), 'Trends in Rural Wages Java 1977–83', *Bulletin of Indonesian Economic Studies*, 22(3): 93–105.

Nagib, Laila and Jones, Gavin (1987), *The Intercensal Survey of Indonesia: Employment by Industry and Occupation*, International Population Dynamics Project, Research Note No. 83, Canberra: Department of Demography, Australian National University.

Naylor, Rosamond (1990), 'Wage Trends in Rice Production in Java:

1976–1988', *Bulletin of Indonesian Economic Studies*, 26(2): 133–56.

Sigit, Hananto (1988), *Perkembangan Angkatan Kerja dan Kesempatan Kerja*, Paper presented at the National Conference of Population Institutes, Jakarta, January.

Swenson, C. G. and Rasahan, C. A. (1986), 'Wage Rates for Agricultural Labour', in Faisal Kasryno (ed.), *Profil Pendapatan dan Konsumsi Pedesaan Jawa Timur*, Bogor: Centre for Agro-economic Research, pp. 130–41.

White, Benjamin (1979), 'Political Aspects of Poverty, Income Distribution and Their Measurement: Some Examples from Rural Java', *Development and Change*, 10(1): 91–114.

Widarti, Diah (1984), 'Analisa Ketenagakerjaan di Indonesia Berdasarkan Data Sensus Penduduk Tahun 1971 dan 1980', in Chris Manning and Michael Papayungan (eds.), *Analisa Ketenagakerjaan di Indonesia Berdasarkan Data Sensus Penduduk 1971 dan 1980*, Jakarta: Biro Pusat Statistik.

World Bank (1985), *Indonesia: Policies for Growth and Employment*, Washington, DC.

_____ (1988), *Indonesia: The Transmigration Program in Perspective*, Washington, DC.

12

Population and Health Policies

Terence H. Hull and Valerie J. Hull

Introduction

AT the beginning of the 1980s, family planning and health policies of the New Order government were shown to have been very successful. Fertility, which had been at very high levels in 1965, had fallen by upwards of 20 per cent, and infant mortality was down by a third. Both the energetic family planning programme and the rapid spread of health centres contributed to these changes, but as later data have indicated, the demographic transition has in part been caused, and certainly reinforced, by substantial improvements in the income, nutrition, and education enjoyed by the population. Commentators reviewing the period hailed the demographic results as key successes for the government, and noted that these changes were among the most cogent evidence of the beneficial, and fairly egalitarian impact of the 1970s' oil boom in Indonesia. In sum, the results seemed to vindicate both the strategy and the implementation of government policy since the late 1960s.

Since 1980 the economic picture has been less rosy, the social agenda more complicated, and policy directions more diffuse. Falling oil prices reduced the availability of funds for development purposes, but at the same time the government has promoted economic restructuring, deregulation, and the expansion of the private sector. The changing policy environment has had important implications for social welfare activities including health care and family planning. As these sectors have come under economic pressure, many observers are concerned that there may be reversals in previous accomplishments, or at least a slowing of the pace of improvements.

None the less, the data available up to the mid-1980s indicate that fertility and mortality continued to fall, with both reaching moderate levels by 1985. In some ways, the 1980s present demographic analysts with more puzzles than was the case for the 1970s, and some of these raise issues which are particularly vexing for a government attempting to integrate discussions of population policy into broader development strategy. For instance, once basic health and family planning services are available to the population, should the next step be the provision of new government services (perhaps stressing quality of care or more advanced technologies) or the replacement of government activities by growing private sector involvement? Further, irrespective of the strategy chosen, what measures of demographic change are relevant to monitor the impact of policies and programmes? Should general demographic targets still be set, or should policy stress operational targets, while relying on the assumption that demographic rates will naturally decline if services expand? Finally, are there demographic imperatives that override other economic and social goals, which should be pursued irrespective of short-term economic indicators, or should demographic goals be constantly redefined and redirected in the planning process, much as the various elements of macroeconomic policy are subject to constant review?

The Place of Population in National Planning and Policies

Demographic policies and programmes are incorporated in the national planning framework in combination with economic, social, and political development policies.[1] At the most general level, fertility and mortality control goals are codified in the Broad Guidelines for State Policy (*Garis-garis Besar Haluan Negara* or GBHN) which are formulated by Council of People's Representatives (Majelis Perwakilan Rakyat or MPR) every five years (1973, 1978, 1983, and 1988). The opening sections of the GBHN set out general goals, and include a call for 'voluntary family planning' in line with religious principles in order to assist in the rapid economic and social welfare of the Indonesian people (GBHN, 1983: B 8). There is no general goal for the reduction of morbidity or mortality, but in a number of contexts stress is placed on the need to increase the people's welfare in an equitable manner.

The general guidelines for policy are accompanied by more specific statements designed to serve as the framework for the development plans. In 1983 these included specific calls for the improvement of health services, in the context of developing human resources, and support for the intensification of the family planning programme as a means of reducing the population growth rate and establishing the norms of a small, healthy, happy family (paragraphs 18 and 28). These statements were further elaborated through calls for the development of the National Health System (Sistem Kesehatan Nasional or SKN), including the establishment of health facilities closer to the people, and the assurance of an equitable distribution of services and medicines (Section 5), and the extension of family planning messages through a wide variety of social organizations, in particular those which will reach the younger generation (Section 6). Similar principles were laid down in the 1988 GBHN. Following the publication of the GBHN each government department has the responsibility to formulate projects and programmes to achieve these goals. Departmental submissions to the National Development Planning Board (Badan Perencanaan Pembangunan Nasional or Bappenas) are reviewed, modified, costed, and combined into the national Five-Year Development Plan (*Repelita*), of which there have now been five in the life of the New Order government. Health has always been a core welfare element of the plans, while family planning was mentioned only briefly in the first plan, and developed an increasingly prominent role in successive plans as the family planning programme grew and gained legitimacy.

Observers attempting to evaluate population policy initiatives are often baffled by a comparison of statements in the GBHN and *Repelita* with the actual activities of departments. In some ways the policy documents follow departmental initiatives and statements of goals rather than setting wholly innovative policies. This is because the policy-making process, from the formulation of GBHN through the setting of the plans, and on to the review of experience by the various Commissions of the House of People's Representatives (Dewan Perwakilan Rakyat or DPR) is heavily influenced by the submissions, debates, and suggestions of departmental bureaucrats who essentially promote their own formulations of policy. Thus the catchwords, slogans, and projects heard around a department one year are quite likely to turn up in the GBHN or *Repelita* in the next round. Official policy statements tend to lag by a few years the material found in newspaper accounts of seminars, workshops, or testimony to the DPR. This helps to explain why the privatization issue, which is the major policy for both health and family planning in the late 1980s was not a major element in either the GBHN or the *Repelita V*, which in theory should provide the framework for government initiatives of the period.

In the remainder of this chapter the experience of the New Order government in formulating and implementing population policy in the 1980s and into the 1990s will be reviewed. In line with the process outlined above there is a substantial temporal gap between the formal statements of policy, and the nature of contemporary programmes, and sometimes a more important substantive gap between the rhetoric of policy and demographic realities. Despite these gaps, though, Indonesia has been remarkably successful in reducing fertility and mortality in the past two decades. This experience raises the question of whether observers should concentrate on formal statements of policy, or the more complex and often obscure political processes of population policy formation.

Shaping Population Growth to the National Purpose: Fertility Control

Trends in Marriage

The Indonesian family has long been the focus of attempts to reform Indonesian society. From the early days of nationalism, women's organizations expressed concern over patterns of marriage and childbearing which they found to be deleterious to the health and welfare of women and children. They campaigned strongly to reform the Marriage Law, with the aim of reducing or eliminating polygamy, child marriage, and unequal regulations concerning divorce. While it took decades to convert these aims into law (in 1973), one impact of the campaign was to promote new patterns of marriage, and a more companionate form of marital relationship among younger generations of Indonesians. The impact of the campaigns and the consequent legal changes is reflected in the steady change of marital status patterns found in censuses and surveys over the years, and the implied steady rise in the average age at marriage.

The various statistics in Table 12.1 are measures of changing marriage patterns which have had a significant impact on the level and pattern of fertility. On the top line, the singulate mean age at marriage (SMAM) roughly reflects the rising age of the onset of family building, though changes in marriage customs have modified this generalization. Traditionally, Indonesian girls married at very young ages (sometimes well before menarche) but did not cohabit with their spouses until they were regarded as being mature enough to begin childbearing. Over time, as the age at marriage has risen, the age of cohabitation has risen more slowly, leading to a convergence of the two events. Today, as increasing numbers of couples are initiating sex and sometimes cohabiting before marriage, it might even be said that the pattern has changed from one of delayed cohabitation to one of delayed marriage, although this remains a socially unacceptable practice.

To put the rising age at marriage into perspective relative to fertility, it is useful to look at the marital status indexes at the bottom of Table 12.1. There the index of the proportion single shows the portion of presumably fecund women (based on the Hutterite Natural Fertility

TABLE 12.1

Trends in the Marital Status Indexes[a] of Women in Indonesia, 1971–1987

Marital Status Index	Year of Estimate			
	1971	1980	1985	1987
SMAM[b]	19.3	20.0	21.1	n.a.
I_s (Single)	0.157	0.205	0.241	0.259
I_w (Widowed)	0.058	0.062	0.021	0.018
I_d (Divorced)	0.046	0.046	0.038	0.030
I_m (Currently married)	0.739	0.723	0.701	0.694

Sources: Calculated from the Population Census (1971, 1980), Intercensal Survey (1985), and Contraceptive Prevalence Survey (1987) data published by the BPS.
[a]Weighted (or standardized) according to the Hutterite 'Natural Fertility Pattern', thus giving greatest emphasis to the experience of women in the peak fecundity ages, 20–39.
[b]SMAM = Singulate mean age at marriage. Approximately equal to the average age at marriage of a cohort living through the marriage patterns reflected in current marital status reports of women.
n.a. = Not available.

Pattern) who have yet to marry. This rose from around a seventh to a quarter in less than two decades. This increase can be regarded as having a dampening effect on fertility since it delayed the age at which childbearing begins, and lengthened the average length of generations. At the same time the indexes of the proportions widowed and divorced both fell substantially, which would have acted to increase fertility. The index of the proportion currently married reflects the net effect of these changes in non-married status, with a moderate decline from 74 to 69 per cent.

While the changes in marital status and marriage customs have been going on for decades, it is important to note that they continued, and to some degree intensified, during the 1980s. While it is common for Indonesian commentators to urge the retention of various family values related to marriage, the trends imply that these values are in a state of turmoil, and that further change is inevitable. To the extent that these changes push the average age at marriage higher, and perhaps accelerate the growth of a group of people who will remain unmarried and childless throughout their lives, then the impact of marital status changes will be to further reduce fertility levels.

Official and Unofficial Approaches to Fertility Control

While marriage trends and the use of traditional forms of contraception and abortion were important components of the initiation of fertility decline in Indonesia, just as they were in nineteenth-century Europe, the 1970s and 1980s saw the development of government policies and programmes which were far more important in effecting reductions in family size through the promotion of voluntary use of modern contraception.

The most important motivation for the promotion of family planning in Indonesia in the 1960s was concern for the safety and welfare of young women and children. The use of traditional contraceptives and abortion was a major threat to the health of women, and doctors in particular were angry over the large numbers of patients suffering from sepsis due to excessive childbearing or unsafe abortions. They were well aware of the international availability of safe methods of birth control, and resented government intransigence over the domestic use of these life-saving materials. In coalition with strong women's leaders, medical practitioners established an Indonesian Family Planning Association (Perkumpulan Keluarga Berencana Indonesia or PKBI), set up private clinics to provide services, and strongly lobbied politicians and bureaucrats to support their cause.

With the change of government in 1966 came a change in attitude towards birth control. Not only were the welfare concerns of the PKBI more widely recognized, but the new group of technocrats in Bappenas voiced a concern then common in the international literature that rapid population growth constituted a major challenge to economic development. Backed by successive teams of World Bank, USAID, and Ford Foundation consultants, the technocrats were able to persuade the nation's leaders that unless they agreed to a programme of fertility control, the task of rebuilding an impoverished economy would be virtually impossible. Thus it was that a cautious and tentative approval was given to establish a national family planning programme. In recognition of what was perceived to be the sensitivity of the issue, this programme was declared to be in the interests of the welfare of mothers and children, and limited to activities which were not in conflict with religion.

The National Family Planning Co-ordinating Board (Badan Koordinasi Keluarga Berencana Nasional or BKKBN), formed in 1970, rapidly developed a strategy which was to set the basic framework for fertility control efforts. The programme offers a wide range of contraceptives free of charge, or at a heavily subsidized rate. While some of the methods require medical intervention in hospitals or clinics (e.g. sterilization), the overriding intention is to establish distribution points as close as possible to people's place of residence, through a network of village family planning service posts (*pos pelayanan keluarga berencana desa* or PPKBD), subclinics, fieldworker visits, and from the mid-1980s, integrated health service posts (*pos pelayanan terpadu* or *posyandu*) which combine contraceptive service with immunization and antenatal care. Family planning was first actively promoted in rural areas of Java and Bali, and then spread by stages to urban areas, and to the other islands of the archipelago. Since *Repelita III* the programme has been national in scope as well as name. Finally, while the BKKBN was responsible for the broad design of the programme, and recruited thousands of family planning fieldworkers, other departments (like Health, Education, and Information) and social groups (like the Muslim organizations, private clinics, and youth and women's groups) maintained responsibility for direct contact with clients in the provision of information, motivation, and services, funded either from their own budgets or from contracts with the BKKBN. It has been estimated that the BKKBN budget covers about 50 per cent of the cost of delivering family planning services in Indonesia, the Department of Health pays for 40 per cent, and the local community covers the remaining 10 per cent (Chernichovsky et al., 1989: ii).

Since 1987 this basic strategy has been elaborated with the addition of an initiative to increase the proportion of family planning services provided through the private sector. Known as the 'Blue Circle' (*Lingkaran Biru*) campaign, the major purpose is to promote the provision of contraceptives through pharmacies, private clinics, commercial outlets, and doctors' surgeries on a full cost or partially subsidized basis. This would both reduce the financial burden on the government and institutionalize contraceptive services firmly in the community. In 1990 the government provided about 80 per cent of the contraceptives distributed in Indonesia, and approximately 80 per cent of these were distributed free of charge (BPS, 1989: 40, 45). The private sector, including private doctors, private midwives, pharmacies, and other outlets, served just under 20 per cent of the couples using contraceptives in that year.

Under the Blue Circle campaign, the long-term target is to raise the proportion of services provided by the private sector to 80 per cent, with an
intermediate goal of raising the share of the private sector to around
50 per cent by the year 2000. The USAID project supporting this campaign targets a private sector share of 40 per cent by 1995 (USAID,
1989: 87).

While the family planning programme was initiated out of a concern
for the welfare of mothers and children, and though it continues to be
justified to some degree in these terms, the programme targets have
always centred on two key concepts: contraceptive use and reduction of
fertility rates. The impact on maternal and child mortality, or on morbidity and health measures, has not been taken up as a key monitoring
measure by the BKKBN, partly because these are notoriously difficult to
measure, and also because they are so clearly influenced by a wide range
of other health and nutritional inputs outside the direct responsibility of
the BKKBN. As a result, an impression has been created that the family
planning programme is simply interested in quantitative fertility targets,
but this is belied by the strong support given by the organization to
various activities 'beyond family planning' such as Family
Planning–Nutrition, Income Generation, Growth Monitoring, and
Antenatal Care projects. Despite these involvements, the BKKBN is
firmly tied in the minds of policy-makers and the public, with the goal of
fertility reduction, and for this reason is the focus of attention with the
release of each new estimate of fertility levels and trends. (See Sahala,
1986, for a BKKBN evaluation of programme impact reflecting this
concentration on the fertility rate.)

Constraints and Challenges

In contrast to the serious budget reduction experienced by the health
sector (see below), BKKBN's financial situation has been relatively
strong, even during the post-oil boom period. The fact that family
planning services operate through the existing health infrastructure,
however, means that developments in the health sector will have an
impact on contraceptive delivery. This is particularly important in the
context of the current international concern about *quality* of services.
Indonesia has not been immune to criticisms of emphasis on fertility
reduction leading to a target mentality, to the detriment of high-quality
services which include full information, free method choice, and good
clinical care, including follow-up services, set in a broader context of
reproductive health. Even programmes emphasizing community participation in family planning have been criticized for exploiting local
women's groups, rather than being responsive to the local situation and
individual client demand.

The issue of community participation will be an important one to follow over *Repelita V*. If decentralized planning and community involvement can be achieved on more than a rhetorical level, Indonesia has the

opportunity to reinforce its position at the forefront of family planning efforts in the Asian region.

Levels and Trends in Fertility

The fact of fertility decline had been established by the end of the 1970s, but the 1980s saw a continuing debate over the pace of the decline and the degree to which falling fertility could be attributed to the actions of the National Family Planning Programme. In part, the debate was fuelled by uncertainties over the reliability and validity of statistics on fertility and contraceptive use.

Lacking a universal system for registering births and deaths, analysts have been forced to rely on estimates of fertility derived from periodic surveys and censuses. These so-called 'indirect estimates' use information of children ever-born to women, births in the last year, and ratios of children aged 0–4 to women aged 15–49 to derive measures of fertility relevant to periods from one to five years prior to the enumeration. Because these procedures rely on a variety of assumptions concerning the stability of recent trends, the veracity of women's responses to census questions, and the statistical relation between the reported data and standard demographic measures, there is wide scope for debate over the accuracy of the estimates. Added to this is the problem that some analysts apply the indirect techniques without due regard to basic methodological requirements, and thus produce spurious results which tend to mislead unwary readers (Hull, 1988).

The debate over fertility trends was not limited to, or primarily concerned with, technical issues of demographic measurement. Instead it reflected the growing prominence of family planning in incidents of bureaucratic infighting and as the focus of criticism of government policy by disgruntled elements both in Indonesia and overseas (Hull, 1990). Tensions between the Biro Pusat Statistik (BPS) and the BKKBN over fertility trends, disagreements between the Ministry of Population and Environment and the BKKBN concerning programme strategies, and the complaints of Islamic leaders over secular tendencies in government policy have all involved some reference to the ethics and implementation of the Family Planning Programme.

The trend in national fertility, shown in Figure 12.1, indicates a decline from over 5 children, on average, to just over 3 in 1985. More recent data from the 1987 Contraceptive Prevalence Survey confirms the strength of this trend, and the best guess of fertility levels in 1990 is just on or under 3 children per woman. Confirmation of this guess will have to await the results of the 1990 Census, which will collect information on the date of the last birth. This in turn can be used to estimate fertility levels for the period from January to October 1990, up to the official enumeration date of the Census. These new data will also provide an indication of provincial variations, something we have not been able to monitor adequately since the Intercensal Survey of 1985.

FIGURE 12.1
Trends in the Total Fertility Rate at the National Level, 1968–1985

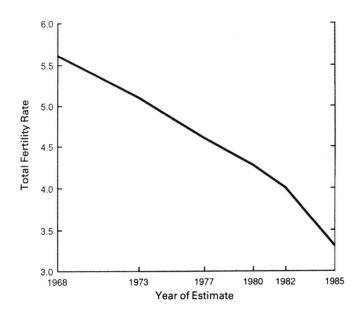

Provincial differentials are shown in Figure 12.2. Java had begun the transition to lower fertility before the onset of the Family Planning Programme in 1968, due in part to the widespread use of traditional forms of contraception and abortion, and in part to a substantial rise in the age at marriage in Javanese society. Though the other islands had much higher fertility in the late 1960s, they quickly joined in the national fertility decline, and by 1980 only the province of Maluku registered fertility above 6 children per women, and a number of important regions in Sumatra, Kalimantan, and Sulawesi had dropped below the 5 children per woman mark. The relatively well-educated province of North Sulawesi had gone from family sizes of over 6 to a total fertility rate of 3.6.

Strong confirmation of the national trends came in 1985 with the collection of data showing only two provinces (West Nusa Tenggara and South-east Sulawesi) with fertility over 5, and the island of Java attaining an overall fertility of 2.9, while Jakarta had achieved, and Yogyakarta was approaching, replacement levels of fertility (2.2 children per woman) which, if sustained over a long period of time, would be consistent with zero population growth.

Accepting the fact of widespread and substantial fertility decline in Indonesia gives rise to the question of what difference this has made to population growth, and the degree to which this is attributable to the Family Planning Programme. In some ways this is an unanswerable question, since it is obvious that signs of nascent fertility decline were

FIGURE 12.2
Provincial Variations in the Total Fertility Rate, 1967–70 and 1985

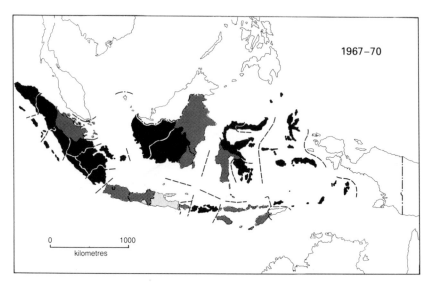

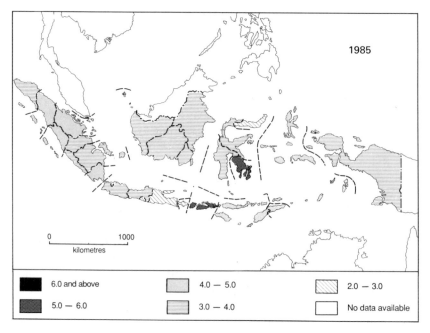

■ 6.0 and above	▢ 4.0 — 5.0	▨ 2.0 — 3.0
▩ 5.0 — 6.0	▤ 3.0 — 4.0	□ No data available

already evident in the years before the development of the National
Family Planning Programme. It would be pure speculation to ask exactly what fertility levels would have been in the absence of the programme. But the question does have an answer if one asks what
difference there would have been if fertility had been constant at 1961
levels, and mortality had continued its downward trend. This is the
scenario depicted in Iskandar's 'high' variant projection (1970).

FIGURE 12.3
Trends in Projected and Actual Population, 1960–2000

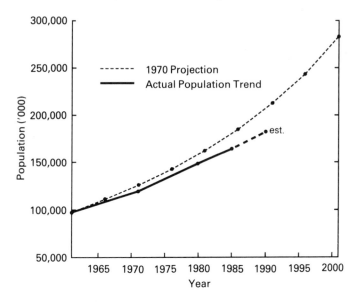

Comparing this with the actual trajectory of population shows a major gap opening up in the early 1970s and widening through the 1980s (Figure 12.3). By 1990 the difference is nearly 30 million, with Iskandar's figures showing a population approaching 210 million, and the actual estimate being just over 180 million. Looking even further into the future, Iskandar's projection shows a population of over 280 million in the year 2001. By contrast, current BPS projections put the population for the year 2000 at 216 million, and some analysts think the level will be held below that (BPS, 1987: 39). Future trends will depend on whether fertility continues to fall, and this in turn will be determined by trends in the demand for children and the accessibility to effective methods of fertility control.

The Falling Demand for Children

In the early years of the Family Planning Programme, surveys routinely reported that the women of the childbearing ages of 15–49 years regarded relatively large family sizes—four, five, or even six children on average—as 'ideal' but that generally they were actually producing slightly larger family sizes by the time they reached 50. On the other hand, younger women who had only one or two children said that they did not want to add many more because of the cost of raising children, and their desire that their offspring should have the advantage of good schooling, clothing, and nutrition. On average they wanted four or fewer children in their eventual completed families. These were small but important indicators of a latent demand for fertility control. Table 12.2 shows the ideal family size reported in the National Fertility Mortality

TABLE 12.2

Trends in the Reported Demand for Children, 1973–1987

Year of Survey	1973	1976	1987
Type of measure used	'Ideal'	'Desired'	'Ideal'
Marital status of women	Currently married	Currently married	Ever-married
Mean number of children	4.4[a]	4.2	3.2

Number of Children	Percentage Distribution of Responses		
0	n.a.	0.1	0.0
1	n.a.	3.0	1.9
2	n.a.	13.6	31.1
3	n.a.	20.9	23.1
4	n.a.	22.1	18.9
5	n.a.	15.2	6.6
6 or more	n.a.	19.9	5.4
Non-numeric response	n.a.	5.1	13.0

Sources: 1973: Demographic Institute (1974–5).
1976: BPS (1976: Table 4.3.1, 239).
1987: BPS (1989: 64).
[a] Average weighted according to numbers of women in each province in 1971.
n.a. = Not available.

Survey conducted by the Demographic Institute of the University of Indonesia in 1973 as 4.4, at a time when the Family Planning Programme was only beginning to promote smaller family sizes in Java.

Surveys in the mid-1970s asked women a somewhat different question: given the family sizes they had already achieved, how many more children would they like to add to produce a 'desirable' family size. While this measure would be expected to be larger than the prevailing 'ideal' (because women might have already exceeded the family size they might think 'ideal') it was in fact smaller than the sizes reported in the 1973 survey. None the less, relatively few women claimed to find a two-child family desirable, and over a third claimed to 'desire' a family size of 5 or more children.

By the late 1980s the 'ideal' family sizes reported by Indonesian women in surveys had fallen substantially. The proportion claiming four or more children as the ideal family size had nearly halved, while the proportion claiming that two children would be ideal rose to nearly a third, with an additional quarter saying three is ideal. This result is fully in line with the attempts of the BKKBN to propagate a two-child norm, and shows a pattern of 'ideal' evaluations which would presumably support further declines of fertility from the 1985 levels.

Towards a Healthy Population: Policy Approaches
and Health Indicators

Policy Parameters

Indonesia, like most developing countries, has adopted primary health care as the underlying philosophy of its public health policy since the 1970s. The basic features of primary health care, as articulated by world leaders at the 1978 WHO–UNICEF conference at Alma Ata, include an emphasis on preventive measures, integration of services, and community participation (WHO, 1978). In common with other developing countries which have put these concepts into practice, Indonesia has met with some success in specific areas, such as childhood immunization, but has encountered major problems in service integration and community mobilization.

Long-range policy guidance in health was articulated for the first time in 1982 with the development of a National Health System, elaborated in a Long-range Plan for Health. The Plan places emphasis on five tasks (*Panca Karya Husada*): community health; training of health personnel; supply, distribution, and quality control of drugs; nutrition and environmental health; and law and management, including decentralization. *Repelita V* priorities in health, although consistent with the Long-range Plan, give particular emphasis to operational efficiency. In presenting its fourteen health programmes *Repelita V* makes several references to community and private sector involvement, to user fees where consistent with ability to pay, and to health insurance. Local resource mobilization, consistent on an ideological level with emphasis on community self-reliance in primary health care, is also a pragmatic response to financial stringencies. Health financing is the focus of the World Bank's Third Health Project in Indonesia, and includes user fees, retention of local health revenues by health facilities for operation and maintenance, extension of health insurance schemes, and redistribution of central spending to poor provinces. Two provinces have been chosen for accelerated implementation of these strategies: West Nusa Tenggara representing a densely populated province with low potential for local resource mobilization and a low Physical Quality of Life Index (PQLI),[2] and East Kalimantan with contrasting characteristics.

Mirroring government policy in other sectors, decentralization has been a key policy of the Department of Health (DOH) over the 1980s. Early efforts were directed at developing *kecamatan* (subdistrict)-level facilities, followed by village-level programmes (see below), and during *Repelita III* and *Repelita IV*, resources were devoted to capacity building at the provincial level. Attention is now focused on the *kabupaten* level, to ensure integration and co-ordination of health activities (USAID, 1989: 66–7).

Policy Implementation Model

Indonesia's early attempts at expanding health care coverage to its population relied on public health campaigns such as the malaria, yaws, and smallpox programmes of the 1950s and 1960s, and a system of maternal and child health clinics. Under *Repelita I–III*, emphasis was on increasing human resources and facilities. *Repelita I* saw the development of the community health centres (*pusat kesehatan masyarakat* or *puskesmas*) as the core of an outreach system which was linked, over the next two development plans, with a succession of other programmes of nutrition improvement and village-level basic health care, in addition to the nationwide Family Planning Programme (Hugo et al., 1987: 112–13). The *puskesmas*, one for each subdistrict, functions as the clinical 'home base', and as the source of supplies and technical support from which a variety of health and family planning workers operate and to which they refer clients requiring specific, especially curative, services. There is also a network of *puskesmas pembantu* or *puskemas* subcentres, staffed on a periodic basis by paramedical personnel from the *puskesmas*, as well as mobile health clinics.

This basic model has persisted, but as part of *Repelita IV*'s efforts to extend and integrate health and family planning services, the new vanguard of village-level health care is the *posyandu*, which consists of monthly clinics held in borrowed premises. Staffed and managed by volunteers who work with visiting *puskesmas* staff, their main function is to integrate delivery of five primary health care services: child weighing (growth monitoring), immunization, diarrhoeal disease control through oral rehydration therapy, family planning, and maternal care.

The tertiary or hospital subsector remains a crucial part of the overall health referral system, though it has always received a disproportionate share of financial resources. Under *Repelita V*, emphasis is on operation and maintenance of hospitals, particularly the smaller peripheral hospitals.

Health Expenditure

Government expenditure on health in Indonesia is extremely low in international terms, and there have been marked declines in expenditure since the early 1980s. Allocation among functions and target populations is very unequal. Inadequate financial management has resulted in gross underspending, of the order of 40–50 per cent of the allocated budget. The complex and fragmented system of administration which characterizes health budget planning and monitoring both reduces efficiency and makes analysis of spending levels and trends extremely difficult.[3]

Available estimates indicate that the Indonesian government, from both central and regional sources, spends the equivalent of just over US$3 per capita annually on health. This represents seven-tenths of 1 per cent of total GNP, a level which compares poorly with other countries in the region (Table 12.3). Although public spending is estimated

TABLE 12.3
Health Expenditure in ASEAN Countries, *c*.1985

	Health Expenditure as a Percentage of		
Country	*Central Government Expenditure*[a] *(1988)*	*GNP*[b] *(1986)*	*US$ Per Capita*[c] *(1985)*
Indonesia	1.8	0.7	3.37
Malaysia	4.4[d]	1.8	23.40
Philippines	4.6	0.7	3.75
Thailand	6.2	1.3	8.98
Singapore	3.6	1.2	122.29

Sources: a. World Bank (1990: 198–9).
b. UNDP (1990: 148–9).
c. World Bank (1989: 13).
d. Data for Malaysia refer to 1981 and are from World Bank (1989: 13).

to be less than one-third of total health outlays, even aggregate public and private health spending in Indonesia is lower than in neighbouring countries, and is declining over time, from an estimated 2.7 per cent of GNP in 1982/3 to 2.2 per cent in 1986/7 (Government of Indonesia–UNICEF, 1989: 29). The WHO-recommended level is 5 per cent of GNP.

World Bank analysis of the main sources of central government expenditure in health—central DOH routine and development budgets, expenditure grant for regional hospitals, and Presidential Instruction (Instruksi Presiden or Inpres)—indicates that by 1987/8 real spending levels had declined by 45 per cent compared to the peak year of 1982/3, and were lower than the level achieved at the beginning of *Repelita III* in 1979/80 (World Bank, 1989: 14). Figure 12.4 illustrates these trends, and also shows differences among particular functional allocations since 1984/5. These latter figures indicate a particularly severe decline in support for communicable disease control, which was already disproportionately low compared to curative services support. As a result, funding was largely withdrawn from all but the three largest communicable disease programmes (immunization, malaria, and diarrhoeal disease).

Although these central government health expenditure figures are augmented by regional sources, the latter account for only about 15 per cent of total public spending, and in some cases they have also experienced declines. In the low income province of West Nusa Tenggara, for example, regional expenditure declines of nearly 10 per cent between 1982/3 and 1987/8 combined with declines in central spending to the province to produce an overall 23 per cent decline over that period (World Bank, 1989: 17). Further, central government allocations tend to reinforce existing disparities in local budgetary capacity: West Nusa Tenggara, with only 20 per cent of the local revenues of Jakarta, receives only half as much in central health subsidies.

FIGURE 12.4

Trends in Real Expenditures by the Central Government on Health,
1979/80–1987/8

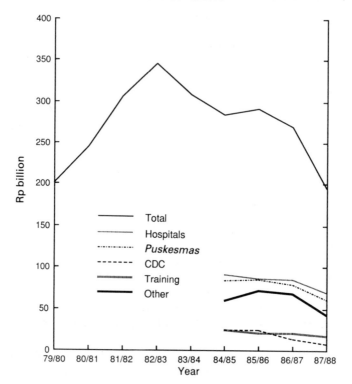

Despite rhetoric about primary and preventive health care, government expenditure tends disproportionately to support curative over preventive services. Private health expenditure accentuates this imbalance. Retail drug sales alone account for about 40 per cent of private health expenditure, added to over one-third going to hospitals (USAID, 1989: 55). Overall, about two-thirds of health expenditure in Indonesia is on curative services. In the absence of major budgetary increases for health, increased support for preventive and promotive programmes will involve difficult allocation decisions under *Repelita V*, bolstering motivation to implement cost-recovery measures for curative services.

Infrastructure and Personnel

The growth pattern of public health facilities, shown in Table 12.4, illustrates the dramatic increase in village integrated health service posts in *Repelita IV*, at a time when expansion of the core health centres stalled. Only a little over half of health centre and subcentre construction targets were achieved during *Repelita IV*, and many centres which have been built, particularly in remote areas, have yet to be adequately staffed. In contrast, the establishment of the village posts has been slightly ahead of projected targets. The goal is to have one *posyandu* per 100 children,

TABLE 12.4
Total Public Health Facilities, 1979/80–1989/90

Year	Health Centres	Health Subcentres	Mobile Health Centres	Village Health Posts
1979/80	4,553	7,342	729	–
1980/1	4,753	8,342	929	–
1981/2	4,953	10,342	1,479	–
1982/3	5,153	12,342	1,979	–
1983/4	5,353	13,636	2,479	–
1984/5	5,453	15,136	2,979	25,000
1985/6	5,553	16,636	3,479	39,000
1986/7	5,639	17,302	3,516	133,786
1987/8	5,642	17,372	3,516	199,614
1988/9	5,642	17,413	3,521	216,073
1989/90[a]	5,742	18,389	3,728	n.a.

Source: Republik Indonesia (1990: 480).
[a] Provisional figures.
n.a. = Not available.

and currently it is estimated that over 80 per cent of all young children have access to a *posyandu* (Government of Indonesia–UNICEF, 1989: 65). A large proportion of both the child-weighing and immunization programmes is being delivered through health posts; immunization coverage has increased from 10 per cent in 1984/5 to 65 per cent in 1987/8.

Although the statistics appear dramatic, it should be noted that not all *posyandu* offer all the five intended services; indeed, a post has only to offer two services to be classified as an 'integrated services' post. The extremely rapid growth of *posyandu* can also create management difficulties: in some parts of Indonesia there are 40–45 posts per *puskesmas*, raising the question of whether post volunteers can be given necessary training and supervision. Despite the growth of available facilities, ratios to population remain low compared with other developing countries, and there are consistently low utilization rates of all levels of facilities, particularly among poorer households. Overall, although total numbers have increased, services remain unequally distributed, less accessible to the poor, and of low quality resulting from inadequate recurrent funding and poor management.

Health services personnel have also increased in quantity over recent years, but ironically Indonesia is now faced with an apparent excess supply of health workers unable to be absorbed into the system. As part of the planned expansion of services during *Repelita IV*, large numbers of both doctors and paramedical personnel were trained, but budgetary constraints on hiring have meant the government could not provide placements for thousands of doctors and paramedical graduates in the government medical service. There have been improvements over the 1980s in provincial distribution of health personnel, though increased attention is being focused on intraprovincial distribution, particularly in light of reports of informal reallocation away from rural health centres to hospital or urban posts. It is reported that in eleven provinces, more than 25 per cent of health centres lack doctors (World Bank, 1989: Section IV). Other personnel issues include inappropriate basic training and inadequate in-service training, and relatively low worker productivity—factors which are being addressed as the Department of Health puts greater emphasis on training, and moves towards a more performance-based promotion system.

Health Indicators

Indicators of health status reflect both the impact of health services as well as wider changes in population welfare. There is little systematic research which has attempted to link health inputs directly with outputs, and those studies which have been done have not been conclusive (Berman, 1989: 21–2). Nevertheless, it is true that along with the expansion of health services in Indonesia, basic health indicators have shown marked improvement over the last two decades. Since the late 1960s, estimated infant mortality has fallen by nearly 50 per cent, and the average annual rate of decline has in fact accelerated over that period. Indonesian infant mortality is still considerably higher than the rates among its ASEAN neighbours, which range from 9 in Singapore to 48 in the Philippines. Within Indonesia, provincial differences range from 29 in Yogyakarta to 112 in West Nusa Tenggara. Further, the gap between provinces appears to be widening, as low mortality areas have experienced the greatest decline (see Table 12.5).

Infant and child mortality together account for nearly half of total deaths, and most of these are caused by infectious diseases, particularly acute respiratory infections, diarrhoeal diseases, and tetanus. It is estimated that immunizable diseases, particularly tetanus and measles, cause about 20 per cent of infant and child deaths in Indonesia (USAID, 1989: 29), despite the country's active immunization programme.

Poor nutrition is a contributory cause of death, especially among young children, and poor maternal nutritional status also has a bearing on perinatal deaths. National-level data is available for children under five years of age, showing that on average just under half of Indonesia's young children are adequately nourished, with lower nutritional status among female children and in rural areas (Table 12.6). Among those not adequately nourished, most suffer from a mild degree of malnutrition, but it is estimated that 11 per cent of children in Indonesia are moderately or severely undernourished, representing nearly 3 million children under five. Although strictly comparable time-trend data are not available, the 1987 *Susenas* estimate of 11 per cent compares with a 1978 large scale survey which found a 16 per cent level of moderate and severe malnutrition. In both surveys, West Nusa Tenggara and West Kalimantan showed the highest proportions malnourished, with Bali and

TABLE 12.5
Infant Mortality Rates by Province, 1971, 1980, and 1985[a]

Province	1971 Census	1980 Census	1985 Intercensal Survey	Percentage Reduction (1971–85)
DI Aceh	140	94	56	60
North Sumatra	116	89	58	50
West Sumatra	157	126	78	50
Riau	139	113	67	52
Jambi	157	118	70	55
South Sumatra	147	100	75	49
Bengkulu	167	105	61	63
Lampung	148	98	58	61
DKI Jakarta	122	81	33	73
West Java	164	129	91	45
Central Java	137	91	73	47
DI Yogyakarta	93	55	29	69
East Java	117	98	75	36
Bali	121	88	48	60
West Nusa Tenggara	219	190	112	49
East Nusa Tenggara	147	126	74	50
East Timor	–	–	93	–
West Kalimantan	141	120	71	50
Central Kalimantan	123	104	61	50
South Kalimantan	168	126	85	49
East Kalimantan	100	98	50	50
North Sulawesi	111	96	57	49
Central Sulawesi	142	134	105	26
South Sulawesi	160	107	73	54
South-east Sulawesi	164	107	82	50
Maluku	150	125	85	43
Irian Jaya	111	107	74	33
Indonesia	132	112	71	46
Urban	104	88	57	45
Rural	137	112	74	46

Source: BPS (1988: 51).
[a]Reference periods for the three data sources are 1968/9, 1977/8, and 1982/3, respectively.

Yogyakarta exhibiting the lowest levels (Government of Indonesia–UNICEF, 1989: 56).

Along with nutrition, high fertility is another contributory cause of both the high number of infant deaths (through producing more infants at risk of dying) as well as the high mortality rate, because probability of death is greater among higher-order births, when births are more closely spaced, or when the mother is in a very young or relatively old age group. The spread of family planning documented above has been an important factor in the decreased incidence of these higher-risk births, helping to lower infant death rates.

TABLE 12.6

Percentage of Adequately Nourished Children under 5 Years by Age Group
and Sex, Rural and Urban Areas of Indonesia, 1987[a]

Age Group/Sex	Urban	Rural	Total
Age <1			
Males	76.8	65.4	68.8
Females	71.6	59.1	63.1
Age 1–<2			
Males	60.5	46.8	51.2
Females	53.1	40.3	44.3
Age 2–<3			
Males	60.5	43.3	47.1
Females	53.8	38.2	42.4
Age 3–<4			
Males	58.2	43.5	47.5
Females	52.6	39.7	42.6
Age 4–<5			
Males	53.6	41.7	43.7
Females	51.6	38.0	40.4
Ages 0–5			
Males	62.0	47.7	51.2
Females	56.6	42.5	46.0

Source: Based on Departemen Kesehatan dengan Biro Pusat Statistik (1987: Tables II.1.1
and II.1.2).
[a] Equal to or greater than 80 per cent of the Harvard Standard index of weight for age.

Challenges and Constraints

Objectives in health for *Repelita V* and for the Long-range Plan for
Health are shown in Table 12.7. A targeted infant mortality rate of 45
by the year 2000 is fairly modest, being the rate reached by Malaysia
during the 1970s, and would seem well within reach in light of the rapid
progress made in Indonesia in the past two decades. There are several
factors which need to be taken into consideration, however, in achieving
mortality reduction and other objectives specified in the Long-range
Plan.

First, the indicators of mortality and health currently available are
both imperfect and out of date. Both health information and demographic systems provide estimates only; even basic measures such as
infant mortality are indirectly estimated. In addition, virtually all figures
cited above refer to the early to mid-1980s. The declining levels of
health expenditure and recent implementation problems noted above
may have led to stagnation or even deterioration in health status, which
has yet to be reflected in available statistics, and which may continue
into the next decade.

More importantly, the precise factors behind Indonesia's mortality
decline are not well understood, making it difficult to project which

TABLE 12.7
Selected Objectives in Health by the End of *Repelita V* and the Year 2000

	Estimated Achievement (1988/9)	*Planned Achievement (1994)*	*Target Achievement (2000)*
Infant mortality rate			
(per thousand live births)	70	49.8	45
Crude death rate	7.9	7.5	n.a.
Life expectancy at birth			
(per thousand population)	63	65	68
Child mortality rate			
(per thousand children 1–4)	10.6	6.5	n.a.
Maternal mortality rate			
(per thousand live births)	4.5	3.4	n.a.
Antenatal care (per cent)	n.a.	70	n.a.
Qualified birth attendants			
(per cent)	45	65	80
Nutritional anaemia			
during pregnancy (per cent)	55	40	35
Low birth weight(<2.5 kg)			
(per cent)	8.2	7.4	7
Neonatal tetanus prevalence			
(per thousand live births)	5	3	1
Tetanus toxoid coverage			
(per cent)	30	80	n.a.
EPI coverage of children			
< 14 (per cent)	65	80	80
Protein calorie malnutrition			
among children aged 0–4			
(per cent)	10.8	9.5	n.a.
Xerophthalmia among children			
aged 0–4 (per cent)	0.7	0.5	n.a.
Endemic goitre	5	4	Down 80
Diarrhoeal disease incidence			
(per thousand population)	350	300	200
Malaria prevalence:			
in Java and Bali (per cent)	1	1	n.a.
outside Java and Bali (per cent)	4	4	2
Clean water supply:			
rural population (per cent)	30.5	60	n.a.
urban population (per cent)	65.0	80	100
Population using latrines (per cent)	37.5	60	n.a.

Source: USAID (1989), based on *Repelita V* (1989) and SKN (1984).
n.a. = Not available.

approaches will bring about further declines. It is accepted, however, that in the earlier stages of mortality reduction, the prominence of infectious diseases implies that technological interventions such as immunization can have major impacts. To reduce mortality levels further, environmental health and nutrition require increased attention. As infant deaths become increasingly concentrated in the perinatal period, effective interventions must include good antenatal and childbirth care. And as mortality levels move further towards modern levels, the main causes of death are the so-called diseases of development, including cardiovascular disease and cancer, which require health promotion approaches to prevention and high-cost treatment. Already there are signs that cardiovascular diseases are becoming a significant cause of death, and high-risk health behaviour such as the high proportion smoking (around 70 per cent of males over the age of 24 (Budiarso et al., 1987: 69)) imply high levels of cancer. These evolving disease profiles imply a health system which must continually develop and expand to meet the new challenges if mortality reduction is to continue apace. It has been estimated that in the year 2000, expenditure of 5 per cent of GDP will be required in order to meet health needs (USAID, 1989: 5).

Although funding levels over the next decade will be of prime importance, improved efficiency should and will undoubtedly receive unprecedented emphasis in the current economic climate. In light of the factors noted above, advances in operational efficiency will involve not only increased productivity and better financial management, but also improved information systems and applied research to assist in planning and monitoring the most cost-effective programmes possible. Decentralization will continue to pose great challenges, but potential returns are great in the health sector, where resource allocation needs to be more responsive to local health needs. The rhetoric urging bottom up planning will need to be matched with increased commitment to devolution of real power and budgets if objectives are to be reached.

Community participation also has strong rhetorical support, related to decentralization aims, primary health care ideology, and the desire to mobilize community resources. *Posyandu*, family planning groups, and PKK (Pembinaan Kesejahteraan Keluarga or Family Welfare Education Movement) involvement in health activities are being touted as examples of community participation, yet in practice they have little autonomy in setting priorities, planning or monitoring, being instead instruments for implementing government policy. *Posyandu kader* are not necessarily genuine volunteers, and there is a high discontinuation rate. Cadre training is only of one week's duration, and services offered, such as child-growth monitoring, are sometimes characterized more by form than by substance. Achieving genuine community participation will require fundamental attitude change on the part of health administrators and clinical staff alike, and skills training in methods of community organization.

An expanded role for the private sector in health, supported more generally by government policy and by major foreign donors, will present challenges in terms of quality control and equity aims in areas such as private hospitals. Specific roles for private enterprise, such as in the social marketing of health messages, can be an effective way of complementing government initiatives.

Population Projections to the Year 2125

Just as the comparison of earlier population projections with the actual path of population growth reveals the implications of changing fertility trends, so projections into the future show what might be expected from the continuation of current trends of fertility and mortality, and the alternative scenarios which would be faced if current trends and policies are not realized.

Table 12.8 summarizes a variety of recent population projections to depict some of the potential demographic futures for Indonesia embedded in reasonable assumptions about fertility and mortality trends. At the more conservative end is the latest projection of the Central Bureau of Statistics (BPS, 1987: 39) which contains the assumption that all recent estimates of fertility were too low, and that fertility will not fall as rapidly as indicated by apparent recent trends or in line with BKKBN policy goals. The BPS projection of 231 million for the year 2005 is the highest among recent assessments.[4]

The second set of projections are those presented by the United Nations Population Division in the 1988 Assessment of World Population Trends (United Nations, 1989: 406–7). The medium projection for Indonesia shows a population of 263 million for the year 2025, while the high and low variants are 305 million and 228 million respectively.

One of the most detailed evaluations of recent demographic trends is that of Gardiner (1989). Five future scenarios are presented, each projecting the population over a century into the future. The first three contain variations in fertility corresponding to low, medium, and high variants depending on when the population is assumed to reach a replacement level of fertility (an average number of around 2.2 births per woman), after which time fertility is assumed to continue indefinitely at that level. The low, medium, and high variants reach replacement fertility levels in 2000, 2010, and 2020 respectively. The final two variations explore the paths by which the Indonesian population might be expected to reach a stationary level of 250 million, as called for in 1989 by President Soeharto. These projections are unusual in that they require some very uncommon—and virtually unthinkable—assumptions concerning fertility trends, and only attain the 250 million mark when fertility is raised and lowered dramatically (the fast variant), or when the population is allowed to grow dramatically beyond 250 million before dropping back to this arbitrary target (the slow variant).

The substantial gap between these variants is indicative of the wide

TABLE 12.8
Population Projections

Projection Year	BPS[a]	Variant		
		UN[b]		
		Low	Medium	High
1990	182.7	178.0	180.5	183.1
1995	199.6	189.8	194.8	200.9
2000	216.1	200.9	208.3	219.3
2005	231.4	210.1	220.6	236.8
2010	–	216.0	232.0	252.6
2015	–	221.0	253.6	269.2
2020	–	225.0	253.6	286.8
2025	–	227.8	263.3	305.0

Gardiner's Projections[c]
(Path to 250 million)

	Low	Medium	High	Fast	Slow
1990	180.1	180.6	180.6	180.1	180.6
1995	194.6	196.5	196.8	194.6	196.5
2000	208.4	211.9	213.0	208.4	211.9
2005	221.8	226.9	229.4	221.8	226.9
2010	235.4	241.1	245.3	230.2	241.1
2015	248.5	254.7	260.4	233.0	254.7
2020	260.9	267.9	274.5	235.1	266.8
2025	271.7	279.8	287.1	240.8	276.6
2030	280.9	290.3	298.6	248.8	283.9
2035	288.6	299.0	308.5	257.0	288.3
2040	294.6	305.8	316.7	260.4	290.7
2045	299.0	311.0	323.0	260.9	290.9
2050	301.7	314.5	327.4	257.6	289.9
2055	303.0	316.6	330.4	255.0	287.6
2060	303.4	317.7	332.4	253.2	284.5
2125	304.0	318.9	335.7	251.1	253.2

Sources: a. BPS (1987: 39).
          b. United Nations (1989: 406–7).
          c. Gardiner (1989: Table 1).

range of assumptions which must be entertained when considering Indonesia's demographic future. Fertility may very well continue its downward trend to levels below those of contemporary developed nations. On the other hand, the nation might experience reverses in its fertility policies if government policy became less supportive, or if serious economic difficulties beset the National Family Planning Programme. As the New Order government completes nearly a quarter of a century in power, the best that can be said is that Indonesia appears to be following the path traced by the lower variants of Gardiner's population projections, but that even these trends will take the country well beyond the 300 million mark before attaining a stationary population. Thus even great success in overcoming the classic demographic problems of high fertility and rapid population growth will leave the country with some formidable social and economic challenges in the decades to come.

1. See Hugo et al. (1987: Chapter 9), for a full description of the policy and planning process.

2. The Physical Quality of Life Index is a composite measure based on three factors: infant mortality, expectation of life, and literacy.

3. As part of the policy to increase efficiency, a detailed study of health expenditure and revenues was taken in 1986 by the Ministry of Health's Bureau of Planning with World Bank assistance. Much of the information in this section draws on this study as reported in the World Bank's (1989) study, *Issues in Health Planning and Budgeting*, though inherent limitations in the original data mean that caution in using the data is still advised.

4. Very similar levels are produced by the Scenario 1 projections of Ananta and Adioetomo, which assume a fertility decline of 2 per cent per year over the long term, the lowest assumption by these authors (1990: 50 ff.).

REFERENCES

Ananta, Aris and Adioetomo, Sri Moertiningsih (1990), *Perkembangan Penduduk Indonesia Menuju Tahun 2005*, Jakarta: Demographic Institute, Faculty of Economics, University of Indonesia.

Berman, Peter (1989), 'Community-based Health Programs in Indonesia: The Challenge of Supporting a National Expansion', in Tarimo and Frankel (eds.), *Community Health Worker Programs*, Oxford: Oxford University Press.

BPS (1976), *Indonesian Fertility Survey, 1976, Principal Report, Volume II*, Jakarta.

_____ (1987), *Proyeksi Penduduk Indonesia 1985–2005 Berdasarkan Hasil Survei Penduduk Antar Sensus 1985* [Indonesian Population Projections 1985–2005 Based on the Results of the 1985 Intercensal Population Survey], Jakarta.

_____ (1988), *Perkiraan Angka Kelahiran dan Kematian: Hasil Survei Penduduk Antar Sensus, 1985*, Jakarta.

_____ (1989), *National Indonesia Contraceptive Prevalence Survey 1987*, Jakarta, Central Bureau of Statistics, National Family Planning Co-ordinating Board, and Institute for Resource Development/Westinghouse.

Budiarso, L. Ratna; Soesanto, S.; Bakri, Z.; Kristanti, C.; Santoso, S.; Zalbawi, S.; Djaja, S.; Iskandar, J.; and Lubis A. (1987), *Prosiding Seminar Survai Kesehatan Rumah Tangga 1986*, Jakarta: Badan Penelitian dan Pengembangan Kesehatan, Pusat Penelitian Ekologi Kesehatan.

Chernichovsky, Dov; Pardoko, Henry; De Leeuw, David; Rahardjo, Poedjo; Lerman, Charles; and Mallinoux, John (1989), *The Indonesian Family Planning Program: An Economic Perspective*, Draft Report to the World Bank, BKKBN, and Government of the Netherlands, Jakarta: BKKBN.

Demographic Institute (1974–5), *1973 Fertility Mortality Survey*. Provincial Reports, Jakarta, Demographic Institute, Faculty of Economics, University of Indonesia.

Departemen Kesehatan Republik Indonesia dengan Biro Pusat Statistik (1987), *Status Gizi Balita 1987: Hasil Integrasi Antropometri dalam Susenas*, Jakarta: Biro Pusat Statistik.

Gardiner, Peter (1989), 'Population Prospects in Indonesia: Size, Structure and Distribution', Paper prepared for the Conference on the New Order in Indonesia, Canberra, Australia, 4–9 December.

GBHN (1983), *Tap MPR No. II/MPR/1983 tentang Garis-garis Besar Haluan Negara*, Jakarta: Penerbit Retu Agung.

____ (1988), *Ketetapan-ketetapan MPR, 1988*, Jakarta: Ghalia Indonesia.

Government of Indonesia–UNICEF (1989), *Situation Analysis of Children and Women in Indonesia*, Jakarta.

Hugo, G. J.; Hull, T. H.; Hull, V. J.; and Jones, G. W. (1987), *The Demographic Dimension of Indonesian Development*, Singapore: Oxford University Press.

Hull, T. H. (1988), 'Note on the Application of Brass P/F Adjustments in Estimates of Fertility Levels and Trends in Indonesia', *Population Today*, 16(7/8): 6–7.

____ (1990), 'The Politics of Family Planning in Asia', Paper presented at the Workshop on the Politics of Family Planning, Bellagio, 19–23 February.

Iskandar, N. (1970), *Some Monographic Studies on the Population in Indonesia*, Jakarta: Lembaga Demografi, Fakultas Ekonomi, Universitas Indonesia.

Republik Indonesia (1989), *Rencana Pembangunan Lima Tahun Kelima 1989/90–1993/94, Jilid III*, Jakarta: Percetakan Negara R.I.

____ (1990), *Nota Keuangan dan Rancangan Anggaran Pendapatan dan Belanja Negara Tahun 1990/1991*, Jakarta: Percetakan Negara R.I.

Sahala Pandjaitan (1986), *National Family Planning Program and Fertility Decline in Indonesia*, Technical Report Series, Monograph No. 48, Jakarta: National Family Planning Co-ordinating Board.

United Nations (1989), *World Population Prospects, 1988*, New York.

United Nations Development Programme (UNDP) (1990), *Human Development Report, 1990*, Oxford: Oxford University Press.

USAID (United States Agency for International Development) (1989), *USAID/Indonesia, Office of Population and Health: Strategic Plan, 1989–1994*, Jakarta.

World Bank (1989), *Issues in Health Planning and Budgeting*, Washington, DC.

____ (1990), *World Bank Development Report, 1990*, Oxford: Oxford University Press.

WHO (World Health Organization) (1978), *Primary Health Care: Report of the International Conference on Primary Health Care, Alma Ata, USSR*, Geneva.

Author Index

Adachi, F., 248
Adinugroho, B., 172, 182
Adioetomo, Sri Moertiningsih, 435
Adisasmita, R., 258
Affandi, A., 177, 183, 187
Alexander, Jennifer, 97, 303, 304, 306, 308, 309, 311, 316
Alexander, Paul, 97, 316
Ali, Supian, 295
Altemeier, Klaus, 169, 172, 182, 316
Amin, Samir, 289
Amsden, Alice H., 36
Ananta, Aris, 435
Anderson, A. G., 305, 311, 316
Anderson, B., 185
Anderson, D., 253, 383
Anwar, M., 275
Anwar, M. A., 250
Arndt, H. W., 26, 102, 130, 156, 217, 251, 332, 358, 359
Asher, Mukul G., 73
Asian Development Bank, 36
Asra, Abuzar, 330, 337, 340, 345, 359
Azis, I. J., 252

Bakir Zainab, 363, 372, 402, 406
Balino, Tomas J. T., 102, 103, 105, 130
Bank Indonesia, 48, 58, 62, 80, 89, 92, 125, 130, 157
Bappenas, 183, 195
Barlow, C., 192, 193, 251, 388
Bawazier, Fuad, 70, 71, 74, 75
Beals, R. E., 250
Bennett, C., 189, 191, 193
Berman, Peter, 428
Berry, Albert, 284, 285, 289
Bienen, Henry, 327
Bimas, 174
Binhadi, 78, 97, 109, 111, 115, 130
Boediono, 25, 162, 251
Bolnick, B. R., 253
Booth, Anne, 17, 24, 27, 31, 36, 43, 49, 54, 70, 71, 72, 73, 74, 164, 167, 168, 265, 294, 317, 323, 329, 338, 358, 379, 386, 388, 398, 402, 404
Bottema, Taco, 316
BPS (Biro Pusat Statistik), 2, 12, 24, 29, 80, 85, 139, 164, 165, 168, 169, 174, 177, 189, 193, 198, 213, 221, 246, 261, 263, 264, 266, 267, 268, 275, 286, 290, 292, 297, 298, 299, 301, 302, 308, 316, 329, 332, 333, 335, 337, 338, 339, 341, 343, 348, 364, 365, 376, 381, 384, 387, 390, 394, 397, 405, 407, 414, 416, 421, 422, 429, 430, 433, 434
Brooks, M., 259
Brown, C., 177
Bruch, M., 253
Bruton, Henry, 7
Buchholt, H., 291, 306, 307, 311, 316
Budiarso, L., 432
Budiman, S., 189, 191
Bukit, Dollar, 372
Bulog, 175, 185

Canlas, Dante B., 295
Cassing, J. H., 157, 324
Castles, L., 214
Centre for World Food Studies, 182
Chalmers, I. M., 251
Chandler, G., 304, 316
Chee, P. L., 252
Chernichovsky, Dov, 416
Chia Lin Sien, 259
Chira, Hongladarom, 295
Chomitz, Kenneth, 391
Clark, C., 283
Collier, W., 165, 316, 403
Connolly, M., 157
Conrad, Robert, 73
Conroy, J. D., 36, 130
Cooper, R. N., 157
Corden, W. M., 15, 35, 154, 157, 324
Cornwall, John, 35
Cremer, Georg, 372
Cutbush, G., 171, 180, 185

DAMARDJATI, D., 172, 178, 183
Dapice, D., 253
Davey, Kenneth, 71
De Silva, A. J. S., 275
Demographic Institute, 422
Department of Agriculture, 164, 172, 174, 177, 182, 185, 187, 189, 198
Department of Finance, 68, 215
Department of Information, 7, 60, 66, 69, 215, 261, 267, 276, 277
Department of Public Works, 174
Dereinda, R., 193
Desai, Ashok, 295
Desai, Ena, 295
Devas, N., 75
Dewey, Alice, 309, 316
Dick, H. W., 26, 252, 259, 262, 269, 273, 275, 280
Dickie, Robert B., 87, 130, 252
Dillon, H. S., 189
Directorate-General of Taxation, 51
Directorate-General of Water Resources Development, 179
Dixon, J., 169, 187
Donges, J. B., 250
Dornbusch, R., 65
Dove, M., 183
Drake, P. J., 36, 130

ECONOMIST INTELLIGENCE UNIT, 274, 275
Edgren, Gus, 288, 295
Effendi, 274
Ellis, F., 172, 174, 182, 183
ESCAP, 259, 264, 267
Esmara, Hendra, 331, 343, 345
Evans, Peter B., 289
Evers, Hans-Dieter, 316

FALCON, W., 170, 172, 183, 187
Fane, G., 170, 171, 180, 182, 185, 251
Fischer, S., 65
Fisher, A., 283
Fitzgerald, B. D., 251
Forbes, D. K., 258, 259, 306, 315, 316
Funkhouser, R., 252

GARDINER, PETER, 364, 433, 434, 435
Geertz, Clifford, 308, 309, 316
Gemmell, Norman, 287, 294
Gijsbers, G., 177, 187
Gillis, Malcolm, 45, 55, 56, 73, 252
Glassburner, Bruce, 22, 64, 156, 170, 251
Godfrey, Martin, 403
Godoy, R., 189, 191, 193, 199
Gray, J., 184
Gunawardana, K. K., 275

HABIR, MANGGI, 20, 34, 98, 194, 237
Hafid, Anwar, 316
Hanson, John R., 24
Hardjono, J., 249
Hart, Gillian, 164, 167
Hasibuan, Sayuti, 379, 386
Hayami, Yujiro, 316
Hedley, Douglas, 180, 182, 183, 187, 198
Hiemenz, U., 253
Hill, H., 212, 216, 217, 219, 233, 248, 250, 251, 252, 253, 381, 382, 388, 389, 391, 392, 403
Hirschman, Albert O., 356, 357
Hobohm, Sarwar O. H., 21
Hughes, G. A., 336
Hugo, G. J., 253, 259, 363, 364, 382, 389, 390, 391, 393, 395, 402, 404, 406, 424, 435
Hull, Terence H., 418
Huppi, Monika, 344
Hutabarat, B., 192

IMF (INTERNATIONAL MONETARY FUND), 54, 62, 74, 136, 139
Institute for Development Studies, 315
Iskandar, N., 420, 421
Islam, I., 333, 336
Ismael, J. E., 157

JANSEN, J., 250
Jayasuriya, Sisira, 381, 382, 386, 403
Jellinek, L., 316
Johnson, S., 169
Jones, Gavin, 363, 364, 366, 369, 372, 391, 392, 401, 402, 403

KARTODIRDJO, SARTONO, 259
Kasryno, Faisal, 165, 166, 167, 173, 186
Katouzian, Homa, 326
Katouzian, M. A., 287, 315, 326
Kawagoe, Toshihiko, 316
Kenen, Peter B., 157
Keuning, S., 167, 168
Keyfitz, Nathan, 31, 401
Khan, H., 333
Kinoshita, T., 252
Klumper, S., 182
Kodhyat, H., 312
Koentjaraningrat, 316
Korns, Alex, 164, 363, 366, 402, 404
Kuntjoro-Jakti, D., 225, 252
Kuyvenhoven, A., 250
Kuznets, Simon, 283, 286, 315

LANDALL MILLS, 193
Layman, Thomas A., 130, 252
Leff, Nathaniel H., 32

Leinbach, T. R., 259, 265, 271, 280
Leiserson, M. W., 383
Lerche, D., 54, 73
Lindblad, J. Thomas, 29, 216
Lindsay, H., 251
Little, I. M. D., 253
Lluch, Constantino, 403
Lukman, Nasrun, 157

McANDREWS, C., 252
Macavoy, P. W., 252
McCawley, P. T., 35, 54, 72, 73, 74, 156, 204, 218, 225, 229, 250, 252, 253, 389
McGee, T. G., 383
McGlinchey, James M., 157
McIntyre, A., 251
Mackie, J. A. C., 27, 36, 98, 104
McLeod, Ross H., 105, 253
McStocker, R., 189, 193
Magiera, S., 176
Mai, U., 291, 306, 307, 311, 316
Makali, 381
Mangkoesoebroto, Guritno, 57
Manning, C., 167, 172, 214, 363, 366, 381, 382, 386, 395, 396, 397, 398, 402, 403, 404, 406
Mansury, R., 73
Maspaitella, P. F. L., 265
Mazumdar, Dipak, 381, 403
Mears, L., 169, 173
Meek, Paul, 78, 97, 107, 110, 111
Minami, Ryoshin, 285, 286
Mitchell, M., 184
Molho, Lazaros, 107, 109, 130
Monteverde, R., 169
Montgomery, R., 182
Morgan, Frank B., 73
Morley, Morris H., 326
Muharminto, 192
Muir, Ross, 27

NAGIB, LAILA, 402
Nasution, Anwar, 104, 105, 111, 156
Naylor, Rosamond, 198, 403
Neary, J. P., 157
Nelson, E. R., 253

ODAKA, K., 248
Odano, Sumimaru, 73
Ono, K., 248

PAAUW, D. S., 156
Palmer, I., 214, 250
Pang, E. F., 217
Pangestu, Mari, 20, 25, 26, 34, 35, 98, 216, 237, 251
Parker, S., 251

Patten, Richard, 97
Pearson, S., 172, 177
Peluso, Nancy L., 304, 316
Pendakur, V. S., 259
Petras, James, 326
Phillips, C., 170, 171, 180, 182, 251
Pitt, Mark M., 25, 169, 182, 251
Pond, D., 258
Poot, H., 250
PT Pusri, 174

RACHMAN, A., 182, 187
Rasahan, A., 403
Ravallion, Martin, 70, 330, 344, 357
Rice, R. C., 216
Riedel, J., 218
Rietveld, P., 165, 341
Rimmer, P. J., 259, 269
Robison, R., 252
Roepstorff, T. M., 250
Rofi'ie, Achmad, 315
Rogers, L. H., 259
Rosegrant, M., 173, 179, 182, 186
Rosendale, Phyllis, 24, 156
Rosengard, Jay, 97
Rosenzweig, M., 169
Rucker, R., 164
Ruzicka, I., 251

SAHALA PANDJAITAN, 417
Sajogyo, 344, 358, 359
Sandee, H., 249
Sasono, Adi, 315
Sastrohoetomo, M., 180, 182
Sawit, M. Husein, 381, 403
Schwarz, A., 275, 279
Sethuraman, S. V., 315
Setiawan, S., 274
Shah, Anwar, 74
Shearing, C., 193
Siahaan, B., 251
Siegel, J., 306
Sigit, Hananto, 315, 403
Siregar, Arifin, 109
Sjahrir, 27, 36, 98, 104
Snodgrass, D., 253
Soegijoko, B. T. S., 259
Soehoed, A. R., 204, 226, 251
Soemardjan, S., 191, 192
Soemitro, Rachmat, 46
Soentoro, 316
Soesastro, M. Hadi, 36
Soewardi, H., 167
Squires, D., 173
Sri Hartoyo, 381, 403
Stecher, B., 250
Stoler, Ann, 291

Sundararajan, V., 102, 103, 105, 107, 109, 130

Sundrum, R. M., 2, 7, 12, 17, 18, 20, 21, 23, 251, 294, 323, 328, 329, 332, 338, 358, 359, 386, 388, 398, 402, 404

Sutomo, Slamet, 357

Suwidjana, Nyoman, 130

Swenson, C. G., 403

Tabor, S., 169, 172, 173, 176, 177, 180, 182, 183, 187, 189, 194, 195, 198

Tait, M., 253

Tas'an, Darmawan, 265, 276

Taylor, D., 157

Teken, I. G. B., 167

Thee Kian Wie, 231, 237, 249, 250, 251, 252

Timberlake, Michael, 289

Timmer, C., 172, 175, 178, 180, 183, 185, 187, 214

Tjondronegoro, Sediono, 168

Tomich, T., 388

Tyers, R., 187

UNDP (United Nations Development Programme), 425

UNICEF, 425, 427, 429

United Nations, 433, 434

United Nations Economic Commission for Asia and the Far East, 35

University of Indonesia, 193

USAID (United States Agency for International Development), 417, 423, 426, 428, 431, 432

USDA, 176

Van Hien, Leonard, 74

Wakui, Yoshiko, 74

Warr, Peter G., 15, 25, 35, 152, 156, 157, 251, 324, 328

Warren, V. E., 235, 252

Weijland, H., 249

Weitz-Hettelsater, 174

Wells, L. T., 235, 252

Whalley, John, 74

Wheeler, David, 391

White, Benjamin, 291, 341, 403

WHO, 423

Wibisono, M., 251

Widarti, Diah, 369

Williamson, Jeffery G., 331, 332, 333

Wiradi, Gunawan, 316, 358

Wolter, F., 250

Woo Wing Thye, 156

World Bank, 1, 2, 28, 30, 65, 66, 71, 74, 97, 136, 139, 163, 165, 175, 176, 178, 180, 182, 185, 189, 190, 191, 192, 193, 194, 195, 224, 251, 315, 345, 358, 388, 398, 425, 428, 435

Wymenga, P., 227, 228, 251

Yoshihara, Kunio, 36, 231, 252

Subject Index

ACEH, 29, 216, 239, 252
Affluence, 350–3; lines, 359
Africa, 285, 287–9, 324
Agricultural Research Service, 186
Agricultural sector: area expansion, 17, 165–8; contribution to GDP, 162–3, 165; development funds, 59, 170–1; diversification, 186–96; employment, 164–5, 167, 373, 383–8, 401; estate subsector, 17; exports, 164; extension, 186; food subsector, 16–17, 21, 25, 172–7, 186–9; growth, 13–14, 17, 20–2, 66, 161; households and access to off-farm employment, 340–2; infrastructure rehabilitation, 17; landholdings, 167–8; livestock sector, 21; non-food subsector, 25; policy challenges, 196–8; price movements, 169–70, 190; productivity, 165; research, 186; role in economy, 162–7; role of external environment on, 169–72; smallholders, 17, 189, 191; subsidies, 177–86; technical change, 16–17; tree-crop subsector, 189–96; wages, 164–5, 386, 403
Agrochemical industry, 178
Aircraft industry, 217, 231
Air travel, 263, 273, 275, 278
Aluminium industry, 217, 231
Arisan, 308–9
Asahan, 217
ASEAN, 1, 20, 209, 290, 312, 428
Astra conglomerate, 233–4
Australia, 283, 315, 324
Automobile assembly, 231

BADAN KOORDINASI KELUARGA BERENCANA NASIONAL (BKKBN), 416–18, 422, 433
Badan Koordinasi Penanaman Modal (BKPM), see Capital Investment Co-ordinating Board

Badan Pelayanan Kemudahan Ekspot dan Pengolahan Data Keuangan (Bapeksta), 252
Badan Pengembangan Pasar Modal (Bapepam), 87
Badan Perencanaan Pembangunan Nasional (Bappenas), see National Development Planning Board
Badan Urusan Logistik (Bulog), 21, 25, 130, 174–5, 183–5
Bakrie, Aburizal, 32
Bakrie, Achmad, 32
Balance of payments: deficits, 20–1, 25, 66, 136, 139; forecast, 107; model, 148–9; surpluses, 85 Bali: industry, 216, 242, 391; landholdings, 168; poverty, 29; tourism, 312
Balikpapan, 216
Bambang Trihatmodjo, 32
Bandung, 214, 239, 391
Bangladesh, 295
Bank Indonesia, 7, 34–5, 63, 79–81, 84–93, 102–29
Bank Pembangunan Indonesia (Bapindo), 98, 119
Bank Rakyat Indonesia, 178
Bank Tabungan Negara (BTN), 84
Banks, 13, 27, 78–9, 86–9, 93, 102–15
Bapak angkat scheme, 248
Bappenas, see National Development Planning Board
Basic metals industry, 212, 217, 231, 235, 247
Bata, 216
Batam Island, 218, 227, 237, 239, 242, 313
Belgium, 235, 315
Bimantara, 234
Bimas, 178
Biro Pusat Statistik (BPS), 7, 13, 168, 207, 296, 323, 335, 340–4, 379, 386, 407, 418, 421, 433

BKKBN, 416–18, 422, 433
BKPM, *see* Capital Investment Co-ordinating Board
'Blue Circle' campaign, 416–17
Board for the Facilitation of Exports and Processing of Financial Data, 252
Bogor, 238
BPS, *see* Biro Pusat Statistik
Brazil, 33, 64, 204, 206, 289
Brick and tile manufacture, 247
Broad Guidelines for State Policy, 412–13
Budget: deficits, 61–4; domestic, 77
Bulog, *see* Badan Urusan Logistik
Bureau of Communications and Tourism, 265

CANADA, 315
Capital: flight, 67, 97, 154; goods import, 19; growth, 16; markets, 87, 94–6
Capital Investment Co-ordinating Board (BKPM), 95, 227, 229–30, 235, 243
Caribbean, 290
Cassava, 187–8
Cement industry, 216–17, 219, 231, 252
Census: agricultural, 167, 323, 340–1, 350; economic, 233, 243, 246, 290, 296–300, 304, 308–9, 316, 389; industrial, 391; population, 366, 393, 404–7, 418
Central Bank, *see* Bank Indonesia
Central government expenditures, 57–60
Centre for the Processing of Import Duty Exemptions and Drawbacks, 252
Chemicals industry, 212, 216, 247
China, 204–5, 227, 264; exports to, 219
Chinese businesses, 32–3, 49, 55, 194, 225, 231, 233–4, 310
Cibinong cement plant, 252
Cilacap, 216, 239
Cilegon, 217, 238
Cirebon, 391
Cloves, 26, 189, 191, 388
Cocoa, 164, 195, 388
Coconut, 189, 191, 193
Coffee, 24–5, 169, 189, 191, 193, 388
Commodity: booms, 324–8; export earnings, 6; indexes, 57; international agreements, 189; prices, 189–90; terms of trade, 6, 169–70
Confrontation, 262
Conglomerates, 32–6, 233–4
Consumer goods imports, 10, 13, 16, 19, 21
Consumer price index, 56
Construction sector, 13–15, 18, 20–1
Consumption expenditures, 329–37, 342, 350, 353, 356–8

Co-operatives, 28, 34, 36, 231, 316; *see also Koperasi simpang pinjam*; *Koperasi unit desa*
Co-ordinating Minister for Economic, Financial and Industrial Affairs, 106, 183
Corn, 187–8
Cost of living: index, 328–9; surveys, 323, 336–40, 353, 357
Cottage industries, *see* Small-scale enterprises
Cotton, 26
Council of People's Representatives, 412
Credit, 306–9
Customs procedures, 26

DAIRY PRODUCTS, 26, 214
Danareksa, 87, 94, 98
Debt servicing, 42, 58, 67
Denmark, 315
Department of Agriculture, 186
Department of Communications, 264, 276, 279, 416
Department of Finance, 27, 103, 107, 122, 225, 237
Department of Health, 416, 423, 425, 428
Department of Industry, 230, 237
Department of Labour, 332, 358
Department of Public Works, 265, 276
Department of Shipping, 273
Department of Trade, 27, 226
Deposit money banks (DMB), 81, 84, 86, 104
Deregulation: financial, 84–96, 98–101, 105–7, 119–21; industry and trade policy, 226–30; transport, 276–9
Devaluation, *see* Rupiah devaluations
Development: assistance, 30; budget, 60–1; finance companies, 104
Dewan Perwakilan Rakyat (DPR), 413
Directorate-General of Air Transport, 278
Directorate-General of Customs, 26, 277
Directorate-General of Land Communications, 278
Directorate-General of Land Transport, 276
Directorate-General of Roads (Bina Marga), 264, 276
Directorate-General of Sea Communications, 273, 276
Directorate-General of Taxation, 55, 73
Domestic: borrowing, 61; deficit, 16, 62–3, 74; production of goods and services, 7, 10, 21; share market, 27
Dumai, 216
'Dutch Disease', 14, 24–5, 96, 151–4, 157, 205, 218, 250, 325, 328

EAST ASIA, 219
Eastern Europe, 204
Eastern Islands, 168
Economic: liberalization, 24–8; reforms, 2, 4, 26–8
Edible oils, 189
Education: development funds, 59; developments and occupational change, 398–400; expansion of, 16, 30–1, 34, 66, 364–6; impact on income, 339–40; private sector, 31; progress indicators, 399
Egypt, 133, 137, 294
Eight-Year Plan (1961–69), 265
Electricity pricing policies, 242, 252
Electronics industry, 217
Employment: agricultural, 164–5, 383–8; creation, 70; industrial, 212, 244–6, 252, 356, 388–93; informal sector, 315; oil industry, 239; public services, 293–5; service sector, 283–5, 291–2, 393–5; transport and communications, 264; trends, 372–8
Engineering goods industry, 214, 217, 223, 235
Entrepreneurial culture, 33–6
Environment sector funds, 59
ESCAP, 275
Esmara, Hendra, 345
Europe: exports to, 219
Exchange rate policy, 148–56, 219
'Exchange rate protection', 154
Expatriate presence, 33
Exports: bans, 28, 30, 216, 223, 243; commodity, 24; earnings, 33; growth, 21–2, 27; manufactured, 218–23; non-oil, 122, 137; surplus, 29; and world economy, 19
Extension services, 16, 186
External debt, 64–7

FAMILY PLANNING, 243, 411–18, 429, 432
Family Welfare Education Movement, 432
Farmers' Terms of Trade Index (Indeks Nilai Tukar Petani), 198
Fertility rates, 169, 345, 364, 400, 411, 417–21, 429
Fertilizer: consumption, 17, 173, 180; industry, 216, 219, 231, 239; price, 183; production, 180–1; subsidies, 16, 25, 180–3
Ficor, 110–19
Finance sector, 14, 27
Financial: assets as percentage of GDP, 82–3, 87; development, 77–84; reforms, 78–9, 84–97
Fiscal policy, 41–73

Five-Year Plan, see Repelita
Food: consumption standards, 168–9; domestic supply, 16; imports, 164, 168; industry, 212–14, 231–3, 235; monopolies, 25, 185; tariffs, 170
Footwear industry, 34, 212–16, 218, 235, 247
Ford Foundation, 415
Foreign aid, 30, 42, 59, 86
Foreign borrowing, 20, 41–2, 59, 61, 65–7, 78, 86
Foreign exchange: earnings, 6–7, 162–4; and imports, 19; limits, 94; market, 105; rate, 90, 97, 227; receipts, 20; reserves 7, 10; shortage of, 13, 78; system, 77, 84, 107–9, 132–3
Foreign investment: growth, 74; in manufacturing, 18, 231–7; incentives, 27, 237; joint ventures, 87, 93; regulations, 227; technical progress, 18; and world economy, 19
Forestry, 23
France, 284, 315
Fruit and vegetable canning industry, 214
Furniture industry, 216, 219, 233

GARIS-GARIS BESAR HALUAN NEGARA (GBHN), 412–13
Garment industry, 34, 214–16, 218, 230, 233, 235, 248, 391
Garuda Indonesian Airways, 263, 273, 275, 278
GBHN, 412–13
GDP, see Gross Domestic Product
GDY, see Gross Domestic Income
General Agreement on Tariffs and Trade (GATT), 252
German Technical Assistance Agency (GTZ), 55
Germany, 235, 285
Gini coefficient, 335–40, 349–50, 358
Glass products, 219
Government: consumption expenditure (GCE), 8–9, 20, 22; expenditure cutbacks, 19–20, 23; revenues, 4, 6–7, 24
Green revolution, 167–8, 271
Gross domestic capital formation, see Investment
Gross Domestic Income (GDY), 3, 7–10, 18, 22
Gross Domestic Product (GDP): agricultural, 162–3, 165; and budget deficit, 61–3; and central government expenditures, 57–9; and external debt, 64–5; and foreign exchange earnings, 6; and GDY, 8; and import duties, 54; and income tax, 50; and land and building

tax, 54; manufacturing, 207–9; and NOTR, 43–4, 47–54, 73; rate of growth, 1–4, 6, 8–10, 13–24, 35, 137, 156; regional, 332, 350, 358; tourism, 312; transport, 258, 264; and VAT, 50

HABIBIE, J., 217, 226, 237, 251
Hanurata, 234
Harvard Institute of International Development (HIID), 42
Hasan, Bob, 36
Hasibuan, Nurimansjah, 250
Health policy, 411–13, 423–33
High-cost economy, debate, 26
Hirschman, Albert O., 356–7
Hong Kong, 78, 86, 235
Horticulture, 195
House of People's Representatives, 413
Housing sector, 13–14, 59

IBNU SUTOWO, 32, 225, 226, 234
ICOR, 10–11, 22, 35
IMF, see International Monetary Fund
Imports, 8–13, 19, 21, 25–7, 35, 54
Income: distribution, 323–42, 353–5; growth, 16–17; inequalities, 289; per capita, 1; regional disparities, 331–4; tax, 44–6, 49–51, 87; in trading sector, 299–302
Incremental capital–output ratio (ICOR), 10–11, 22, 35
India: employment, 373–4, 389; industry sector, 204–5, 223; productivity, 389; public sector, 287, 295; transport sector, 264, 267
Indonesia Development News, 273
Indonesian Family Planning Association, 415
Industrial: concentration, 32–3; protection and agriculture, 171
Industrialization, 204–7, 223–49
Industry sector: employment, 388–93, 403; exports, 218–23; funds, 59; growth, 13–14, 18–23, 35; high-cost structure, 27; investment in, 18, 23; market concentration in, 33; output, 210–15; ownership, 230–8; protection of, 25; structure and trends, 207–23; technology, 212
Infant mortality, 169, 411, 417, 428–32
Inflation, 27, 84–6, 102, 136, 331, 337
Informal sector, 288–9, 315
Infrastructure, 10, 15, 17, 19, 72
Inpres, 30, 68–71, 267, 271, 277, 293, 386, 425
Institut Teknologi Tekstil (ITT), 247
Insurance companies, 84, 104

Interbank: market, 105; rates, 90–2, 108, 110, 113–15
Intercensal Survey, see Survei Penduduk antar Sensus
Interest rates, 84–90, 93, 103, 109, 113–17, 128
Intermediate goods, 19, 25
International Labour Office, 288
International Monetary Fund (IMF), 55, 61, 155
Investment (INV), 8–10, 15–16, 18, 20, 22–3; finance companies, 104–5; funds, 95, 98
Iran, 325–6
Irian Jaya, 29, 72, 242–3, 273
Iron and steel products: restriction on imports, 26
IRRI, 16
Irrigation, 16–17, 25, 67, 70, 171, 173, 179–80, 185–6
Italy, 285

JAKARTA: cost of living index, 328–9; fertility rate, 419; industry, 237–9, 391, 401; motor vehicles, 266; transport, 263, 268–9, 278; 2005 Plan, 278
Jakarta Stock Exchange, 94–5, 279
Jakarta Transport Corporation, 263, 279
Japan, 209, 219, 235, 248, 284–5
Java: affluence, 350–4; consumption expenditure, 329–31; élite, 33; employment trends, 373, 376–9, 383–6, 389–93, 403; farm households, 164; favouritism towards, 30; fertility rate, 419; industry, 214, 216–17, 237–43; landholdings, 168; oil, 216, 239; motor vehicles, 266; pasar economy, 305–7, 311; poverty, 28, 345–9, 354–5; sawah area, 167; share of labour force, 364, 402; trading enterprises, 297; unemployment, 31
Jepara, 216
Jewellery exports, 219

KALIMANTAN: agricultural land expansion, 167; export surplus, 29; farm households, 164; fertility rate, 419; health, 423, 428; industry, 216, 238–9, 243, 252, 391; oil, 164, 216, 239; pasar economy, 305–6, 311; poverty, 29, 72; roads, 268; wood industry, 216
Kediri, 214, 391
KFM (Kebutuhan Fisik Minimum), 332, 358
Koninklijke Paketvaart Mij (KPM), 262, 273
Koperasi simpang pinjam, (Kosipa), 308

Koperasi unit desa, (KUD), 36, 178, 308, 310
Krakatau steel complex, 235, 252
Kredit investasi kecil (KIK), 247
Kredit modal kerja permanen (KMKP), 247
Kretek industry, 214, 252
KUD, *see Koperasi unit desa*
Kudus, 214

LABOUR FORCE, 15–18, 363–72, 400–2; data sources, 404–7
Lampung, 388
Land and building tax (PBB), 46–7, 54–5, 73
Landholdings, 166–8
Landless, 167–8
Landownership, 230, 252
Latin America, 67, 77, 285, 287–9
Leasing companies, 84, 104
Liem Sioe Liong group, 217
Life expectancy, 169
Lingkungan industri kecil (LIK), 247
Living standards increase, 168
Long-range Plan for Health, 423

MACROECONOMIC PERFORMANCE, 133–7, 185–6
Majelis Perwakilan Rakyat (MPR), 412
Malang, 214
Malaysia: education, 364; electronics industry, 217; employment, 373–5, 388–9, 401; import duty/GDP ratio, 54; infant mortality, 430; NEP, 230; productivity, 389; public sector, 294; wages, 382
Maluku, 242–3, 262, 273, 419
Manufacturing sector, *see* Industry sector
Market programme, 69
Marriage trends, 413–15
Martin, Will, 157
Mass Guidance Programme, 178
Merpati airline, 273, 275, 278
Mexico, 33, 64, 133, 136–7, 165, 206, 223
Migration: circular, 355, 383; rural–urban, 165, 167, 288, 347; transmigration, 59, 167, 192, 243, 347, 356, 358, 379, 386, 388
Minimum Physical Needs Index, 332, 358
Mining and quarrying sector, 13–14, 17–18, 20–3, 59
Minister of Finance, 106, 115
Minister for the Promotion of Use of Domestic Products, 25
Minister of Research and Technology, 28, 217, 226
Minister of Trade, 106
Ministry of Finance, 35

Ministry of Health, 435
Ministry of Population and Environment, 418
Ministry of Trade, 95, 225
Monetary: authorities, 61, 63; deficit, 63–4; policies, 102–29; ratios, 79–81
Monetary Council, 106
Money market, 105, 109–12
Mortality, 428–9
Motor vehicles, 265–7
Musi, 216

NATIONAL ACCOUNTS STATISTICS (NAS), 7–10
National Development Planning Board, 35, 106, 225, 265, 392, 412, 415
National Family Planning Co-ordinating Board, 416–18, 422, 433
National Fertility Mortality Survey, 421–2
National Health System, 412, 423
National income statistics, 22–3
National Labour Force Survey, *see Survei Angkatan Kerja Nasional*
National Socio-economic Survey, *see Survei Sosial Ekonomi Nasional*
National Urban Development Strategy (NUDS) project, 259
Natural resources, 205
NBFI, *see* Non-bank financial institutions
NES/PIR, *see* Nucleus Estate Scheme
Netherlands Indies, 24
NIEs, 204–5, 209, 216, 218, 227, 232, 235, 403
Nigeria, 1, 133, 136–7, 165, 223, 326–7
Non-bank financial institutions (NBFI), 84, 93, 98, 104–5, 108–11, 119–20
Non-metallic metals industry, 216, 247
Non-rice food crops, 186–9
Norway, 315
Nota keuangan, 214, 250–1
NOTR/GDP ratio, 43–4, 47–55, 73
Nucleus Estate Scheme (NES/PIR), 192, 195–6, 388
Nugra Santana, 234
Nusa Tenggara: employment, 388, 391; fertility rate, 419; health, 423, 425, 428; industrial sector, 243; poverty, 29, 72; shipping, 262, 273
Nutrition, 169, 428–30, 432

OECD, 189, 287, 315
Off-farm activities, 165, 340–2, 356
Oil and gas refining, 14, 21, 209–13, 216
Oil boom: distributional impact of, 324–8; impact on relative prices, 151–6; legacy of, 24
Oil exports, 6, 16, 24, 133–7

Oil price changes: macroeconomic adjustment to, 137–48
Oil revenue, 41, 47–9, 60–3, 78, 86, 135, 145–7
OPEC, see Organization of Petroleum Exporting Countries
Organization for Economic Co-operation and Development (OECD), 189, 287, 315
Organization of Petroleum Exporting Countries (OPEC): 1, 6, 19–21, 324–5
Outer Islands: affluence, 350–3; agriculture, 177, 187, 189, 388; consumption expenditure, 329–31; credit system, 307; employment trends, 373, 376–9, 383, 386–8, 391; fertility rate, 419; industry, 206, 237–43; poverty, 345, 354–6; transport, 266–8, 273, 275

PAJAK BUMI DAN BANGUNAN (PBB), 46–7, 54–5, 73
Pajak Penghasilan (PPH), see Income: tax
Pakdes, 94, 97, 100
Pakistan, 33
Pakmar, 100–1
Paknov, 277
Pakto 27, 94, 98–100, 119
Palawija, 186–9
Palm oil, 24, 189–95, 214
Paper products industry, 212, 216, 219, 231–3, 235, 247
Pasar economy, 301–6, 310–11
PBB, 46–7, 54–5, 73
PCE, 8–10, 20, 22
Pelayaran Nasional Indonesia (Pelni), 262, 272, 280
Pembinaan Kesejahteraan Keluarga (PKK), 432
Pension funds, 84
Pepper, 191
Perkebunan Inti Rakyat (PIR), see Nucleus Estate Scheme
Perkumpulan Keluarga Berencana Indonesia (PKBI), 415
Pertamina, 78, 216, 225–6
Perusahaan Pengangkutan Djakarta (PPD), 263, 279
Perusahaan Umum Angkasa Pura, 278
Perusahaan Umum Kereta Api, 278
Pesticide subsidies, 25, 178–9
Philippines: agricultural employment, 373–4; education, 364; foreign debt, 64; GDP, 1; industry sector, 205, 218, 223; infant mortality, 428; political instability, 227; service sector, 285–7, 289–91, 296; shipping, 275, 279

PIR, see Nucleus Estate Scheme
Pollution, 252
Population: growth, 18; projections, 433–5; redistribution, 243; rural, 165
Posyandu, 426–8, 432
Poverty, 15, 28–9, 72, 353–5; lines, 342–5, 359; regional distribution of, 345–50
Pribumi businesses, 32, 49, 55, 231, 234, 247
Price: controls, 56; disparities, 332; ratios, 151–6
Primary school building programmes, 69
Private consumption expenditure (PCE), 8–10, 20, 22
Productivity, 15–19, 23, 285–6, 315, 389
P T Jasa Marga, 279
P T Nusantara, 217
Public expenditures: agricultural, 170–1; changing patterns in the 1980s, 57–60; on health, 424–5
Public sector: employment, 292–5, 316; growth, 13, 17–18, 20–1, 23, 287, 313–14, 328; industrial projects, 26; labour, 18; salaries, 18, 20, 23, 58–9, 185, 287, 290; spending, 19; unions, 287
Public utilities sector, 14
Purchasing power, 20
Pusat Pengolahan Pembebasan dan Pengembalian Bea Masuk (P4BM), 252

RAILWAYS, 261–2, 270, 278
Raw materials import, 13, 19, 25, 27
Reafforestation programme, 69
Real: appreciation effect, 15, 35; effective exchange rate, 27, 36; money supply, 21; per capita consumption expenditure, 28
Regional: finance, 68–73; rebellions, 30
Repelita: agriculture, 170, 183, 185–6, 195–6; and Bappenas, 107, 413; education, 30–1, 398; fiscal policy, 42–3, 47–9, 55, 57, 59–60, 66–70, 74; health, 413, 417, 423–4, 426–7, 430; industry, 10, 205, 209, 225, 247, 251, 403; transmigration, 386; transport, 260, 265, 276–7
Riau, 30, 216, 239, 242
Rice: and Bulog, 21, 25, 174–5, 183–5; crisis, 102; import, 172, 175; infrastructural improvements, 173–4; irrigation, 171, 173; milling, 214; pests, 172; price, 21, 169, 174–5, 183–5, 386; production, 17, 21, 172–3; role in diet, 169, 176, 187; self-sufficiency, 172, 184; and soy bean

growing, 177; subsidies, 25, 174, 178; and sugar-cane production, 177
Roads, 69–70, 260–1, 265–8, 271–2, 275, 279
Rotan: export ban, 28, 30
Rubber: cultivation, 189–95, 388; export, 6, 24, 187; products industry, 233; world price, 25, 169
Rupiah devaluations, 22, 25–7, 36, 41, 66–7, 79, 86–7, 97, 108, 113, 133, 153–5, 227
Rural credit programme, 178

SADLI, M., 250
Sajogyo, Pr ofessor, 344, 358
Sakernas, see Survei Angkatan Kerja Nasional
Salim (Liem) conglomerate, 233–4
Savings, 142–4; co-operatives, see Kosipa
SBI, *see* Sertificat Bank Indonesia
SBPU, *see* Surat Berharga Pasar Uang
Sempati, 273
Sertificat Bank Indonesia (SBI), 90–3, 108–22, 126–9
Service sector, 283–90; development, 290–6, 313–15; employment, 283–5, 290–5, 393–5; international demand, 211–13; percentage of GDP, 283; productivity, 285–6, 295–6, 315; trade subsector, 311
Shipbuilding, 231
Shipping, inter-island, 27, 262, 272–3, 275, 277
Shrimp, 164, 195
Singapore: electronics industry, 217; exports to, 219; financial centre, 77; infant mortality, 428; loans through, 78, 86; shipping with, 277; tourism, 312; trade with, 262
Sistem Kesehatan Nasional (SKN), 412, 423
SITC, 13
Smallholder Sugar Intensification Project, 177
Small-scale enterprises: and co-operatives, 28; discrimination against, 34; industrial, 206–7, 244–9, 389–92; service sector, 288, 301–11, 314–15
Société Générale de Surveillance (SGS), 47, 277, 279
Soedarpo Sastrosatomo, 32
Soeharto, President, 32, 42, 49, 87, 233, 251, 433
Soehoed, A. R., 225
Soonthorn Chaiyindeepum, 157
South Asia, 219
South-East Asia, 285, 287–8, 295

South Korea: conglomerates, 36; employment, 373–4, 388, 401; growth performance, 6; import duty/GDP ratio, 54; industrial sector, 223, 235; oil importer, 4; productivity, 389; service sector, 285, 288–9; wages, 382
Soviet Union, 204, 217
Soy beans, 26, 164, 176–7, 187
Stamp duty, 47
Standard International Trade Classification, 13
State enterprises, 26–8, 33, 227, 231, 237, 243, 247, 279
State Logistics Board, *see* Badan Urusan Logistik
State Savings Bank, 84
State Secretariat, 225
Steel industry, 217, 219, 231, 235
Stock market, 87, 94–6
Subcontracting, 248–9
Sugar, 24, 26, 175–7, 194, 214
Sukarno, President, 260
Sulawesi: agricultural land expansion, 167; export surplus, 29; farm households, 164; fertility rate, 419; industry, 242–3, 252, 391; *pasar* economy, 311
Sumarlin, Dr, 115
'Sumarlin Shock', 97
Sumatra: agricultural land expansion, 167; export surplus, 29; farm households, 164; fertility rate, 419; industry, 214, 216–7, 238–43, 252, 391; oil, 216; population, 401; roads, 268; share of labour force, 364
Sumitro Djojohadikusumo, 32
Sungai Pakning, 216
Supas, *see Survei Penduduk antar Sensus*
Surabaya: industry, 237, 239, 391, 401; public transport, 263
Surakarta Stock Exchange, 94, 98
Surat Berharga Pasar Uang, 90–2, 110–121, 125–6, 129
Survei Angkatan Kerja Nasional (Sakernas), 31, 74, 294, 297, 323, 340, 353–5, 363–6, 369, 372, 385–6, 398, 402–7
Survei Penduduk antar Sensus (Supas), 198, 291, 294, 296, 316, 363, 366, 372, 393, 403, 404–7, 418
Survei Sosial Ekonomi Nasional (Susenas), 162, 299, 323, 330, 333, 335, 337, 340, 344–5, 352–3, 357, 363, 366, 372, 428
Sweden, 288, 315

TAHIJA, JULIUS, 32
Taiwan: employment, 373–5, 401; growth performance, 6; investment in industry,

235; oil importer, 4; service sector, 285, 288–9, 296; wages, 382
Tariff and non-tariff barriers, 26, 28, 47, 54, 227–9
Tax: amnesty, 73; bank, 122; export, 4; income, 44–6, 49–51, 87; oil company, 61; reform, 26, 41–57, 87; revenues, 41, 52–3; trade, 24
Tea, 191, 214, 231
Tebu Rakyat Intensifikasi (TRI), 177
Technological progress, 16–18, 288–9
Technology: import of, 237
Telecommunications, 274–5
Tempo, 74
Textile industry, 212–16, 218, 230, 235, 247–8, 250, 389, 391
Textile Technology Institute (ITT), 247
Thailand: growth, 6; import duties, 54; industry, 223, 227; service sector, 285, 289–91, 294–6, 312, 315, 388–9
Timber: exports, 6, 162–4, 218; industry, 212, 216, 233, 235, 247; tariffs, 189
Timor, East, 72
Tobacco, 189, 231, 388
Tourism sector, 23, 27, 290, 311–13
Trade: inter-island, 26; liberalization, 185; terms, 4, 6–10, 19–22, 133–4, 169, 171
Trade sector: employment, 296–311, 393–5; growth, 8–9, 14, 18, 21; labour, 15, 18, 291–2; policies, 226–30; productivity, 296–311; structure, 27, 296–300
Trade unions, 262, 287
Transport and communications, 258–80; air, 263, 273, 275, 278; development funds, 59; growth, 13–18, 21, 66; inter-city, 269–70; inter-island, 27, 262, 272–3, 275, 277; labour, 15, 292;

policies, 274–9; railway, 261–2, 270, 278; safety, 275–6, 278; rural–urban, 270–2; urban, 263–4, 268–9, 275, 278–9
Tree crops, 164, 167, 186–96

UNDEREMPLOYMENT, 386, 398
Unemployment, 31, 396–8, 400
UNICEF, 423
United Kingdom, 284–5, 315
United Nations Population Division, 433
United States, 219, 235, 288, 315
United States Agency for International Development (USAID), 415, 417
United States Internal Revenue Service, 55
University of Indonesia, 225, 422

VAT PACKAGE, 43–4, 46–57, 87
Venezuela, 1, 326
Village co-operatives, see Koperasi unit desa

WAGES: agricultural, 164–5, 386, 403; industrial, 248; trends, 378–83
Warta Ekonomi, 36, 74, 233–4
Wealth redistribution, 34
Wheat imports, 26, 164, 176
Women: demand for children, 421–2; education, 364–5; in labour force, 15, 283, 291, 297, 301, 314, 366–72, 387, 391, 395, 403; unemployment, 396
World Bank, 1, 64, 155, 265, 342, 345, 415, 423, 425, 435
World economy, 19
World Health Organization, 423, 425

YAYASAN HARAPAN KITA, 234
Yogyakarta, 419, 428–9